African-American Writers

African–American Writers

A Dictionary

Shari Dorantes Hatch and Michael R. Strickland, Editors
Foreword by Dorothy Strickland

ABC-CLIO

Santa Barbara, California
Denver, Colorado
Oxford, England

All entries were written by Shari Dorantes Hatch except as otherwise signed.

Copyright © 2000 by Shari Dorantes Hatch

Library of Congress Cataloging-in-Publication Data

African-American writers : a dictionary / Shari Dorantes Hatch and Michael R.
Strickland, editors ; foreword by Dorothy Strickland.
   p. cm.
  Includes bibliographical references and index.
  ISBN 0-87436-959-2 (alk. paper)
  1. American literature—Afro-American authors—Dictionaries. 2. Afro-American
authors—Biography—Dictionaries. 3. Afro-Americans in literature—Dictionaries. I.
Hatch, Shari Dorantes. II. Strickland, Michael R.
PS153.N5 A3444 2000
810.9'896073'03—dc21
[B]   00-024422

06 05 04 03 02 01 00   10 9 8 7 6 5 4 3 2 1

ABC-CLIO, Inc.
130 Cremona Drive, P.O. Box 1911
Santa Barbara, California 93116–1911

This book is printed on acid-free paper ∞.

Manufactured in the United States of America

To Grace, who fostered my love of reading and writing; Page, whose lust for learning inspires me; Roxanne, whose strength and determination motivate me; Sarah and Bernie, who cheer me on; and Harrison, who now reads and writes superbly
—*Shari*

To Patrick and Brooke Tevlin, for all the love and support
—*Michael*

CONTENTS

Foreword by Dorothy Strickland, xi
Preface, xiii
Acknowledgments, xv

African-American Writers

Contents

FOREWORD

Many of my earliest memories center around my passionate love of reading. As a little girl, I was lucky enough to be able to walk to the little storefront branch library in my neighborhood. There, Mrs. Luex would greet me with a smile and a wink and would reach behind the counter to pull out a special book she had set aside just for me. I'd add to this special book a few other books I'd choose for myself, then I'd skip on home, heavily laden with books but light of heart. Between visits, I'd spend many an hour poring over my treasures.

Years later, in the mid-1950s, I started teaching schoolchildren, and among my favorite classroom activities was to read aloud to them and to find other ways to foster in them a love of reading. Two of my students flummoxed me, however. Everything I tried seemed destined to failure, so in the middle of the school year, I enrolled in a master's program in reading, to gain more insight into how to help them. What I learned in my studies helped my students—and helped me gain a deeper interest in finding out how to teach students to read. After a couple of years, I asked to teach first graders, so that I could be the first to teach young children how to read. This was a joyous task, watching my students' faces light up as they fig-

ured out the link between the printed symbols and meaningful words. Over time, my studies led me to become a reading specialist, a reading consultant, a professor of reading, and eventually the State of New Jersey Professor of Reading at Rutgers, my current position.

Throughout my own early experience with reading, I rarely came into contact with books involving children of color—certainly not during my experiences as a young reader—and even as a young schoolteacher, I rarely encountered such books. By the time my youngest son Michael was born, however, I was able to find numerous children's books to read to him that involved children and adults of color. In recent decades, young—and old—readers have available a wealth of literature centered in the life experience of African Americans and other persons of color. It gives me great pleasure to see the long, long list of entries in *African-American Writers,* which my son Michael and his colleague Shari Hatch have edited. I sincerely hope that you will use this volume to enhance your enjoyment of the riches of African-American literature.

Dorothy Strickland

PREFACE

We thoroughly enjoyed creating *African-American Writers: A Dictionary* for your reading pleasure. What a delight to see the tremendous wealth of literary works we now have available to us! At every turn, we came upon new riches, new discoveries, new treasures of literary achievement. The descendants of Africa have only been on the American continent for a few short centuries—and have only been completely free from enslavement for a little over a century—and yet we already have available this tremendous abundance of literary works.

We have made every effort to include as many authors as possible in this encyclopedic volume, but we readily acknowledge that we may have omitted some noteworthy authors who have not yet come into the full light of literary luminescence, and we joyously recognize that as this volume goes to press, significant contributors to this body of literature are continuing to emerge, whose achievements will have to wait for an updated edition. When we wrote this volume, we intended for it to be used as a reference tool for finding out about particular authors or particular works of literature. Nonetheless, we hope that you will also use it as a springboard for further investigation or even as a source of ideas for your own creative writing. You can open this volume at any page and find out what inspired various African-American writers to create poems, plays, short stories, novels, essays, opinion pieces, and numerous other works.

You can also use our encyclopedia to find out some of the intriguing connections among authors. For instance, what are some of the common characteristics and distinctive aspects of the narratives of former slaves? Which African-American writers were helped by the 1930s-era Federal Writers Project? Which writers were influenced by a distinctive region such as rural Mississippi or urban Detroit? Which writers were orphaned at a tender age? Which writers had to overcome tremendous economic and social hardships in order to put pen to paper? How did it affect writers to have particularly light skin and European facial features—or particularly dark skin and African facial features? Which writers mentored a series of contemporary writers? Which writers put their careers on hold while they stopped to raise children—their own or those of others—and which writers started writing as a means of supporting their children? Which writers fled to Paris to escape racism in the United States? Which writers returned to their rural Southern roots after trying to make it in the urban North? Which writers earned the Spingarn medal from the NAACP, or other prestigious awards? What were some of the firsts in African-American literature? In editing this volume, we had great fun discovering these and many other fascinating aspects of African-American literature. We hope that you will relish making your own discoveries as a reader of this work.

Shari Dorantes Hatch
and Michael R. Strickland

ACKNOWLEDGMENTS

Dorothy Strickland, Michael's mother, was instrumental in supporting the development of this book, and without her, it probably would not exist. Todd Hallman took a chance on having us write this book, and for that, we are most grateful. Melanie Stafford shepherded every step of producing this book: She kindly encouraged us, gracefully reminded us, and scrupulously attended to every detail that makes this book the best it can be, including its elegant design. We're also delighted that those who judge a book by its cover will surely have very high hopes indeed for its contents. We're deeply indebted to Silverander Communications for creating the enchanting cover design. We must also thank Alexandra Truitt, Jerry Marshall, and Liz Kincaid, the resourceful photo researchers who found the lovely photo that graces our cover, as well as the many others sprinkled throughout our book. We also thank Ingrid Becher, who created the thorough index that enables our readers to find information quickly and easily. Lyn Chaffee attentively typeset and laid out the pages of our book, with a careful eye for aesthetics, as well as accuracy. Beth Partin copyedited the manuscript and Merrill Gilfillan proofed the pages, catching many mistakes and offering many specific suggestions for improvement. In addition, many people were involved in the typographical composition and printing processes; in making the ink, the paper, and the bindings; and in doing all the other invisible tasks that make it possible for us to behold the miracle that is a book. We appreciate all their selfless efforts on our readers' behalf. We also thank Patience Melnik, Alexis Brown, and the numerous others who have helped to entice readers to choose our book from among many other worthy choices.

We particularly want to thank our contributors: Tonya Bolden, whose generous contributions aided us greatly; Lisa Bahlinger, who graciously filled in wherever there was a need; Diane Masiello, who took on some of the heavyweights with grace and skill; Randall Lindsay, who conducted thorough and detailed research and offered intriguing analysis of his findings; and Brenda Pilson, who thoughtfully prepared her entry. We also offer thanks to Mixay Phonh, Robert Ravago, Matt Romero, and numerous other students in Sarah Hatch's class at Rancho del Campo High School, for their excellent research assistance.

Finally, Shari wishes to thank her husband, Bernie Gately; her father, Page Hatch; and her daughter, Sarah Hatch, without whose loving support Shari's contribution to this book truly would not have been possible.

S.D.H. and M.R.S.

Abbott, Robert S. (Sengstacke)
(11/24/1868–2/29/1940)

Editorials

On May 6, 1905, Abbott founded the *Chicago Defender,* a four-page weekly newspaper. The *Defender* was not Abbott's first contact with the newspaper business, however. While he was studying printing at the Hampton Institute in Virginia, he worked with his stepfather, John Sengstacke (whom his mother had married in 1874), to produce Sengstacke's *Woodville Times* (in Georgia). Later, Abbott worked as a printer in Chicago to pay for his studies at Kent Law School (now Chicago–Kent College of Law). (The son of former slaves Thomas and Flora Abbott, he knew about and believed in the value of hard work.)

Although Abbott graduated from law school (1899) and started practicing law, within a few years, he realized that his race would continually limit his ability to earn a living with the law, and his true calling was to serve African Americans by publishing his own newspaper. Reportedly, at first, he operated the paper out of his kitchen, with only about 20–25 cents in cash and about $25 in borrowed resources to start his paper. He peddled it himself at African-American shops and churches, pubs and pool halls, as well as through door-to-door sales. During the paper's first several years of operation, Abbott's landlady, Henrietta Plumer Lee, almost single-handedly saved the paper from folding quite a few times. Among other things, Lee allowed Abbott to use the dining room of her apartment as the office for the paper, took care of him during a bout of double pneumonia, and accepted only nominal payments for the rent and food she provided him during those early years of the paper.

When Abbott started his paper, there were already three African-American newspapers in Chicago, and none of them were faring too well financially. At that time, most newspaper publishers (e.g., Hearst and Pulitzer) used sensational stories, dramatic writing styles, and high-profile techniques to beef up their circulation. By 1910, Abbott's paper was doing likewise. That year, Abbott had hired J. Hockley Smiley, who encouraged Abbott to use banner headlines (often in red print); to include sections on theater, sports, and society; to highlight sensational news (e.g., editorials railing against prostitution in the African-American community)—and even to make up a few stories if the real news wasn't juicy enough. In addition, Smiley encouraged Abbott's natural inclinations to write aggressively outspoken editorials lambasting lynchings and other post-Reconstruction horrors, which helped boost the fledgling newspaper's circulation, particularly in the Southern states. Pullman porters also played an important role for the *Defender* at this time, both distributing the paper to railroad passengers and gathering news from various printed materials the passengers left behind. By the time Smiley died (in 1915), Abbott's *Defender* was an eight-page, eight-column, full-size paper, and throughout the 1920s, nearly one quarter of a million readers were buying it each week.

Abbott's editorials also influenced his readers' opinions. For instance, he urged many Southern blacks to flee from the rural South to find work, better living conditions, and greater opportunities in the industrial North. The great migration to the North, when about one and one quarter million African Americans fled North between World War I (the late 1910s) and the Great Depression (the early 1930s), was at least partly attributable to Abbott's editorials. Another issue Abbott addressed was the segregation and unequal treatment of African-American soldiers during World War I.

Despite some financial ups and downs, the paper flourished in the 1920s and even survived the Great Depression. Abbott had more difficulty, however, with the magazine he started a month before the 1929 stock-market crash. His *Abbott's Monthly* survived until 1933, but widespread unemployment among African Americans eventually led to the magazine's demise.

In the mid-1930s, Abbott brought his nephew, John H. Sengstacke, into the operation of the paper. After Abbott's death, Sengstacke took over the paper, and he adopted many of Abbott's editorial stances, opposing the segregation and mistreatment of African-American soldiers during World War II. (The U.S. military wasn't integrated until after World War II had ended.) When Sengstacke and other African-American newspaper publishers urged African Americans to reevaluate their military service in light of this mistreatment, the U.S. Justice Department threatened charges of sedition against them. Fortunately, Sengstacke was able to thwart those charges and to negotiate for African-American journalists to have greater access to federal government officials in exchange for tempering their remarks about the military.

Under Sengstacke's leadership, the paper attracted numerous outstanding authors, including poet and columnist (his "Simple Says" stories) **Langston Hughes**, poet **Gwendolyn Brooks**, and novelist **Willard Motley**. In 1956, Sengstacke successfully moved the *Defender* to daily publication and added other newspapers to create a chain of African-American papers. In its heyday, the *Defender* could reasonably have been called the most widely circulated and most influential African-American newspaper in the country, but by 1995, its circulation had dropped below 30,000, and its ability to shape opinion declined concomitantly.

NOTE: There is some question about Abbott's birth and death dates, as one source (*EA-99*) cites his birth date as 11/28 and his death date as 2/22, and another source (*PGAA*) cites his birth year as 1870.

REFERENCES: *EA-99. EB-99. PGAA.* Johns, Robert L., in *BH2C.* Toppin, Edgar Allan, in *WB-99.*

Abu-Jamal, Mumia (né Wesley Cook) (4/24/1954–)
Essays

Because of his political activism (in association with the Black Panther Party) and his outspoken views, Abu-Jamal was forced to resign from hosting his own radio talk show. Following an incident with Philadelphia police and a highly questionable trial, he was convicted of first-degree murder and sentenced to death. Since then, Abu-Jamal has written various articles for *Yale Law Review* and other periodicals, and he has published two books of essays (*Live from Death Row,* 1995; and *Death Blossoms,* 1996). In 1994, National Public Radio canceled a series of radio commentaries it had commissioned

from Abu-Jamal as a result of pressure from Senator Bob Dole and the Philadelphia police.

REFERENCES: Taylor, April, in *EA-99.*

African American Review
See Black American Literature Forum

Ai Ogawa, Florence (née Florence Anthony) (10/21/1947–)
Poems

Known as "Ai," her self-chosen name means "love" in Japanese. Ai's books of poetry and other creative writing include *Cruelty* (1973), *Killing Floor* (1979), *Sin* (1985), *Fate: New Poems* (1991), and *Greed* (1993). Her own multiethnic heritage (African American; Native American; and Irish, Dutch, and Japanese American) influences her work, which offers a distinctively egalitarian perspective on diverse people. Her 1999 poetry collection, *Vice,* won the National Book Award for her stunning insights into the psyches of the famous and the infamous, giving voices to their vices.

REFERENCES: Lee, A. Robert, in *OCAAL.* Willis, André, in *EA-99.*

Allen, Richard (2/14/1760–3/26/1831)
Sermons, devotional pieces, addresses, autobiography, hymnal

Born into bondage, Richard's mind and spirit were freed before he was able to purchase his physical freedom. In 1777, he experienced both a spiritual awakening, converting to Methodism, and an intellectual awakening, teaching himself to read and write. In the early 1780s, Allen started serving as a lay preacher and was nominated for ministry of the newly denominated Methodist Episcopal (ME) Church.

By 1786, Allen had earned enough money to buy his freedom. Soon after, he met Absalom Jones and joined St. George's ME Church in Philadelphia. Although the church held segregated services and prayer meetings, the African-American congregants still supported the church with labor and donations. To provide aid to them, Allen and Jones organized the Free African Society in 1787. Allen's activism was guided by his religious conviction that Christianity and divine inspiration were intended to serve the needs of the oppressed, not the interests of the oppressors.

As the church authorities increasingly segregated blacks from whites, resentment built to the point where Allen and Jones led a walkout of the black congregants. Stories of the specific incident that triggered the walkout vary, but somehow, prayerful worship was interrupted by an affront to one or more black congregants. When they were asked to tolerate further segregation, enough was enough, and they left the sanctuary of St. George's to forge their own spiritual fellowship.

By 1794, the two leaders of the Free African Society had formed two new churches: Most worshipers followed Jones, the elder spiritual leader, to form the first black Protestant Episcopal church. Those blacks who wished to remain Methodists followed Allen to form the Bethel Church. In 1799, Allen became the first black officially ordained as a minister in the ME Church. Two years later, he compiled the first black hymnal—*Collection of Spiritual Songs and Hymns, Selected from Various Authors*—which included lyrics only, as the hymns were sung to the melodies of various traditional songs.

In 1816, Allen's Bethel Church hosted representatives from five Methodist congregations dissatisfied with how the ME Church was treating African Americans. Primed for action, they organized the African Methodist Episcopal (AME) Church, chose Allen as their first bishop, and named his Bethel Church the mother AME Church.

Allen also contributed to his community in various other ways: organizing schools for African-American children, preaching execution sermons for condemned African Americans, helping the **Freedom's Journal,** and denouncing slavery from any podium on which he could address a listening audience. Allen was also one of the first African Americans to author an autobiography (other than a **slave narrative**), titled *The Life, Experience and Gospel Labors of the Right Reverend Richard Allen* (published posthumously in 1833).

REFERENCES: *1TESK. AA:PoP. AWAW. BAL-1-P. BF:2000. E-97. EB-98. G-95. SMKC.* Saillant, John, in *OCAAL.*

Allen, Samuel W. (Washington)
(12/9/1917–)
Poems, criticism, anthologies, translations

Allen graduated magna cum laude from Fisk University in 1938. At Fisk, he had studied creative writing with **James Weldon Johnson**. After Fisk,

he earned his J.D. from Harvard Law School in 1941. Following a brief stint as a military officer, he spent the next two decades balancing a law career with his writing. For a time, he used his GI (veteran) benefits in Paris, where he learned French and studied at the world-famous Sorbonne university. There, he met **Richard Wright**.

In 1949, Wright helped Allen get his verse published in *Présence Africaine,* a journal highlighting Negritude poets (African Europeans and West Indians who wrote in French and who proudly embraced their African heritage). When Wright left Paris for a while, he asked Allen to take over editing the journal's English materials. While in this role, Allen unsuccessfully tried to interest U.S. editors in the Negritude poets' work, styles, and ideas.

During the 1950s and early 1960s, Allen focused on his law practice and worked in various governmental positions around the world. In Germany in 1956, he published his first volume of poetry (with all 20 poems in German and in English). When he returned to the United States, his poetry was virtually unknown until the 1960s, when **Arna Bontemps** (1963) and **Langston Hughes** (1964) first included his work in their anthologies.

In 1968, Allen stopped practicing law for profit, although he has still occasionally done pro bono (free of charge) work since then. That same year, his second volume of poetry was published in the United States. To support his poetry habit, he taught college from 1968 until 1981 and volunteered to teach writers' workshops for prison inmates for two years.

In 1973, Allen compiled the anthology *Poems from Africa,* including several poems he translated for it. Two years later, his third original poetry collection was published: *Paul Vesey's Ledger,* which traces the long history of oppression against African Americans. Other Allen poems address key African-American heroes, martyrs, and resisters, such as **Nat Turner**, **Harriet Tubman**, **Martin Luther King, Jr.**, and **Malcolm X**. His collection *Every Round and Other Poems* (1987) includes most of his previously published poems, some reworkings of old ones, and some outstanding new poems. He has also published essays on themes similar to those of his poetry. Throughout his writing, he interweaves African traditions and African-American culture.

Among the awards Allen has received are a National Endowment for the Arts Creative Writing Fellowship in Poetry and various residence grants.

In 1981, Allen retired from teaching, but he continues to write, give poetry readings, and conduct workshops across this country and abroad.

REFERENCES: *BAL-1-P.* Brookhart, Mary Hughes, in *OCAAL. BWA. EBLG. TtW.* (See also *BDAA.*)

Amini, Johari (née Jewel Christine McLawler) (1/13/1935–)

Poems, essays, movie reviews, short stories, nonfiction—monographs on health

Johari (Swahili: "Jewel") Amini (Swahili: "honesty and fidelity"), an editor for **Third World Press** and *Black Books Bulletin,* has authored numerous poetry collections, including *Images in Black* (1967), *Black Essence* (1968), *A Folk Fable* (1969), *Let's Go Somewhere* (1970), and *A Hip Tale in Earth Style* (1962). Her essays have been collected in *An African Frame of Reference* (1972), and many of her poems and short stories have been published in journals and in anthologies. Also, in association with her chiropractic practice, she wrote *A Commonsense Approach to Eating* (1975).

REFERENCES: Reid, Margaret Ann, in *OCAAL.*

Anderson (married name: Andrews), Regina M. (pen name: Ursala/Ursula Trelling) (5/21/1901–)

Plays

A librarian for the New York Public Library, Anderson and her two (female) roommates offered their home as a salon for **Harlem Renaissance** writers and artists. Anderson's plays include *Climbing Jacob's Ladder* (1931, about a lynching, inspired by the writing of **Ida B. Wells**), *Underground* (1932, about the Underground Railroad), *The Man Who Passed,* and *Matilda.* She also coedited the historical work, *Chronology of African-Americans in New York, 1621–1966* (1971).

REFERENCES: *AA:PoP. EB-BH-CD. MWEL. OCWW. WDAA.* Jefferson, Annetta, in *BWA:AHE.*

Andrews, Raymond (1934–11/25/1991)

Novels, essays

Andrews's novel *Appalachee Road* (1978) was awarded the first James Baldwin Prize for literature. His subsequent novels include *Rosiebelle Lee Wildcat Tennessee* (1980), *Baby Sweet's* (1983), *The*

Last Radio Baby: A Memoir (1991), *Jessie and Jesus and Cousin Clare* (1991), and *Once Upon a Time in Atlanta* (1997). His writing reflects the rich **oral tradition** of his Southern heritage. Emory University has his collected letters and memorabilia.

REFERENCES: Beaty, Freda R., in *OCAAL.*

Angelou, Maya (née Marguerite Johnson) (4/4/1928–)

Poems, autobiographies, plays; news editor

A native of St. Louis, Missouri, Maya Angelou is a prolific autobiographer, poet, and playwright, as well as an accomplished producer, director, actor, performer, and singer. Maya Angelou received national attention when she read her poem "On the Pulse of Morning" at President Clinton's inauguration in 1993. The author of several volumes of poetry, Angelou is nonetheless best known for *I Know Why the Caged Bird Sings* (1969), the first of her five autobiographical novels. Nominated for the National Book Award, this powerful and moving work chronicles Angelou's difficult childhood experiences.

The great-granddaughter of a woman born into slavery, Angelou spent her infancy in California. When her parents divorced in the early 1930s, her father sent her and her brother to live with his mother, who ran a black-owned general store in Stamps, Arkansas. The experience of living in the pre–civil rights, segregated South made a deep impression on Angelou, and she writes of the close-knit black community that somehow supported its members through the grueling hardships of the Depression and segregation.

For a time, Angelou went to live with her mother's family in St. Louis, where she was raped at age eight and became mute for several years thereafter. When she returned to the South, Angelou took refuge in her grandmother's store and immersed herself in books, reading voraciously and laying a foundation for her writing. As a teenager she moved back to California, finished high school, and gave birth to her only son, Guy Johnson.

The subsequent four volumes of Angelou's autobiography—*Gather Together in My Name* (1974), *Singin' and Swingin' and Getting Merry Like Christmas* (1976), *The Heart of a Woman* (1981), and *All God's Children Need Traveling Shoes* (1986)—show Angelou's political, spiritual, and psychological development as she became increasingly known as a

Maya Angelou on the set of Down in the Delta, *which she produced and directed, 1998 (Reuters/HO/Archive Photos)*

contemporary literary figure. The themes that emerge in the series are the struggle for civil rights in the United States and Africa, Angelou's involvement with the feminist movement, her ongoing relationship with her son, and her awareness of the difficulties of living in the U.S. lower classes. (EDITOR'S NOTE: Starting in 1961, Angelou lived in Cairo, Egypt for two years, where she was associate editor of the *Arab Observer,* an English-language news weekly. In 1963, she moved to Ghana, and the following year, she started work as a feature editor for *African Review,* which she continued until 1966, when she returned to the United States.)

I Know Why the Caged Bird Sings, generally considered the finest of the five autobiographical works, shows great moral complexity and has generated universal appeal. Critic Lynn Z. Bloom believes the decreasing popularity of subsequent volumes results from Angelou appearing "less admirable" as time passed. In *Gather Together in My Name,* for instance, Angelou nearly falls into a life of prostitution and drug addiction, a situation for which readers may not have been able to muster understanding or empathy. Bloom goes on to say Angelou "jeopardizes the maturity, honesty, and

intuitive good judgement toward which she had been moving in Caged Bird." Nonetheless, Angelou continued to receive praise from her critics for her strong sense of story and for her passionate desire to meet the challenges and injustices of her life with courage and an increasingly strong sense of self.

All God's Children Need Traveling Shoes, Angelou's latest work in the autobiographical series, looks to postcolonial Africa for ways black America can find intellectual, spiritual, and emotional sustenance in a poignant search for "home," both personally and metaphorically. For four years, Angelou lived and worked in Ghana as a freelance writer and editor. During this time, she explored the cultural similarities and differences between African and African-American society. She found much to admire about African culture yet affirmed that she is American and in some significant ways outside of traditional African culture. The critics praised this graceful exploration of African-American history and its connections to Africa as important.

Critics have not given the same high praise and attention to Angelou's poetry that they've given to her prose. Nonetheless, her many volumes of poetry—including 1972 Pulitzer Prize nominee *Just*

Give Me a Cool Drink of Water 'fore I Diiie (1971), as well as *And Still I Rise* (1976), *Shaker, Why Don't You Sing?* (1983), and *Life Doesn't Frighten Me* (1993)—have helped Angelou to establish her reputation. Most of Angelou's poetry consists of short lyrics with short lines, alliteration, and jazzy rhythms. Critics do not praise Angelou for her mastery of poetic form as much as for her embrace of the political. Angelou takes on social and political issues important to African Americans in her poems and challenges the sincerity of traditional American values.

EDITOR'S NOTE: Two of Angelou's additional poetry volumes are *Oh, Pray My Wings Are Gonna Fit Me Well* (1975) and *I Shall Not Be Moved* (1990). Her plays also include the screenplays *Georgia, Georgia* (1972) and *All Day Long* (1974).
                                                                                                 —*Lisa Bahlinger*

REFERENCES: Angelou, Maya (1994), *The Complete Collected Poems of Maya Angelou* (New York: Random House). *Discovering Authors Modules,* at http://galenet.gale.com. Lionnet, Françoise, in *OCAAL.* (See also *BDAA.*)

Anthony, Florence
See **Ai Ogawa, Florence**

Asante, Molefi Kete (né Arthur Lee Smith, Jr.) (8/14/1942–)
Scholarly writings

Arthur was the fourth child of Arthur and Lily Smith but their first son, and Arthur, Sr., gave him his name. Thirty years later, while Arthur Smith, Jr., was visiting Ghana, King Opoku Ware II gave Arthur the last name Asante, linking him to a Ghanaian tribe (once commonly referred to as the Ashanti). Then, Asante gave himself the first name Molefi, a Sotho name meaning "Keeper of the Traditions," and he chose as his middle name Kete, meaning "One Who Loves Music and the Dance." Asante's chosen first name aptly describes him, as he is the founder of the Afrocentric school of thought and a preeminent scholar of African-American history and traditions. A prolific writer, Asante has written at least 200 scholarly articles and has authored or edited nearly 40 books, including *Afrocentricity: The Theory of Social Change* (1980; 2nd ed., 1983); *African Culture: The Rhythms of Unity* (1985, edited with his wife, Kariamu Welsh Asante); *Afrocentricity* (1988); *Kemet, Afrocen-*

tricity and Knowledge (1990); *Malcolm X as Cultural Hero and Other Afrocentric Essays* (1993); *African American History: A Journey of Liberation* (1995); *African Intellectual Heritage: A Book of Sources* (1996, edited with Abu S. Barry); and *The Afrocentric Idea* (rev. ed., 1998).

Asante perfected his scholarship while earning his Ph.D. in communication in 1968 at the University of California at Los Angeles, where he served as president of the Student Nonviolent Coordinating Committee, a politically active organization in the struggle for civil rights. In addition to offering his numerous books, he has shared his knowledge with numerous students, first at the State University of New York at Buffalo, then (in 1984) at Temple University in Philadelphia. At Temple, Asante established the first Ph.D. program in African-American studies; since then, he has also chaired the Department of Africology. For Asante, the key to Afrocentric thought is an internal orientation, not merely an external manifestation, such as adopting an African name. Instead, "the Afrocentric school of thought," says Asante, "places Africans at the center of any analysis of ideas, concepts, or people." That is, "Afrocentricity is an orientation to data, which says that African people are ancient, and should be seen as agents, as subjects, in history, instead of as marginal players on the fringes of Europe."

In the mid-1990s, Asante was enstooled as a king among the Akan of Ghana, partly in recognition for his work on Afrocentricity and for increasing our knowledge and awareness of the history and culture of Africa's people.
                                                                                                 —*Tonya Bolden*

REFERENCES: *SMKC.* Interview between Molefi Asante and Tonya Bolden, summer 1998.

Ashe, Arthur (Robert), (Jr.) (7/10/1943–2/6/1993)
Nonfiction—memoir, sports history

Ashe's publications include his books *Getting Started in Tennis* (1977, with photographs by his wife **Jeanne Moutoussamy-Ashe**), *A Hard Road to Glory: A History of the Afro-American Athlete* (3 vols., 1988), *Days of Grace: A Memoir* (1993, with **Arnold Rampersad**), and *Arthur Ashe on Tennis* (with Alexander McNab, 1995).

REFERENCES: *BDAA. EB-BH-CD.* Robinson, Alonford James, Jr., in *EA-99.*

Attaway, William (11/19/1911–1986)
Novels, scripts

His novels include *Let Me Breathe Thunder* (1939) and *Blood on the Forge* (1941). Also a composer, Attaway wrote two books about songs: *Calypso Song Book* (1957) and *Hear America Singing* (1967). His scripts (written for radio, for television, and for film) include *One Hundred Years of Laughter* (1966, about African-American humor) and *The Atlanta Child Murders* (1985, about the tragic serial murders of numerous African-American boys).

REFERENCES: *NYPL-AADR*. Accomando, Christina, in *OCAAL*.

Aubert, Alvin (Bernard) (3/12/1930–)
Poems, short stories, dramas

Aubert's poems are often anthologized and published in periodicals; his poetry collections include *Against the Blues* (1972), *Feeling Through* (1975), and *South Louisiana: New and Selected Poems* (1985). As a college educator, he initiated a course on African-American literature. In 1975, he founded and edited *Obsidian: Black Literature in Review,* a periodical that included poems, essays, short stories, and literary reviews, as well as occasional dramatic pieces and bibliographies on specific authors or literary subjects. Although *Obsidian* ceased publication in 1982, in 1986, *Obsidian II* emerged and is still being published under different editorship.

REFERENCES: Vander, R. Goldman, in *OCAAL*.

B

Baker, Augusta (née Braxton or Braxston) (4/1/1911–2/23/1998)

Story anthologies, bibliography, lectures

A children's librarian for the New York Public Library (NYPL), Baker was a skillful storyteller and ardent advocate for children's literature, lecturing often on oral narratives (see **oral tradition**) and **folktales**. Her published works include the anthologies *The Talking Tree* (1960), *The Golden Lynx and Other Tales* (1960), and *The Young Years: Best Loved Stories and Poems for Little Children* (1960), as well as the bibliographic work *Books about Negro Life* (1957; revised and expanded to *The Black Experience in Children's Books,* 1971) and her guide, *Storytelling: Art and Technique* (1977, with Ellin Greene). She also helped create the **James Weldon Johnson** Memorial Collection of books at the Harlem branch of the NYPL (now named the **Countee Cullen** branch), and she initiated the radio series *The World of Children's Literature*. In addition to numerous other awards given to Baker, the American Library Association recognized her expertise with its first E. P. Dutton–John Macrae Distinguished Service Award. She was also consulted about children's literature for the *Sesame Street* television show.

REFERENCES: *EBLG.* Edwards, Roanne, in *EA-99.* Jenkins, Betty L., in *BWA:AHE.*

Baker, Houston A. (Alfred) (Jr.) (3/22/1943–)

Literary criticism, essays, poems, anthologies

As a literary critic, Baker was instrumental in proposing a "**black aesthetic**" for interpreting and evaluating literature. In the furtherance of this proposal, he has developed specific linguistic and sociohistorical strategies for studying the literature of persons from an oppressed culture living within a dominant culture. He has applied those strategies in several works of literary criticism, including *Black Literature in America* (1971); *Long Black Song: Essays in Black American Literature and Culture* (1972), which analyzed African-American linguistic patterns and folklore in the works of **Frederick Douglass, W. E. B. Du Bois, Richard Wright**, and others; *Singers of Daybreak: Studies in Black American Literature* (1974), essays on the works of **Paul Laurence Dunbar, Ralph Ellison, Jean Toomer**, and others; *The Journey Back: Issues in Black Literature and Criticism* (1980), examining both poetic and narrative language in African-American literature; *Blues, Ideology, and Afro-American Literature* (1984), probing the ways in which the blues have influenced and been influenced by African-American culture and how this idiom is expressed in literary phrasings and voice; *Modernism and the Harlem Renaissance* (1987), reflectively reassessing this period of surging African-American creativity; *Afro-American Poetics* (1988), in which he pays "special attention to the sociology, psychology, and entrancing sounding of race"; *Workings of the Spirit* (1991), assessing the literary contributions of African-American women writers such as **Zora Neale Hurston, Harriet Jacobs**, and **Toni Morrison**; and *Black Studies, Rap, and the Academy* (1993), extending Baker's distinctive analysis to the rap form. In addition, Baker has published collections of his own poems, such as *No Matter Where You Travel, You Still Be Black* (1979) and *Blues Journey, Home* (1985). He has also edited various anthologies and other works and has published numerous scholarly journal articles.

Baker earned his B.A. (1965) at Howard University (where he was Phi Beta Kappa) and his M.A. (1966) and Ph.D. (1968) from the University of California at Los Angeles. In addition to writing, he taught in the English and the Afro-American Studies Departments of the University of Virginia, as well as Yale, Cornell, and Haverford College. Since 1974, he has taught at the University of Pennsylvania, where he was given an endowed chair in 1982, and since 1986, he has directed the university's Center for the Study of Black Literature and Culture. More recently, his peers have recognized his singular leadership by electing him president of the prestigious Modern Language Association (1992).

REFERENCES: *EB-BH-CD. EBLG. OC20LE. TtW. WDAA.* Awkward, Michael, in *OCAAL.*

Baldwin, James (Arthur) (né Jones)
(8/2/1924–12/1/1987)
Novels, plays, poems, short stories, essays, children's book

When young Jimmy's mother, Emma Berdis Jones, married factory worker and evangelical preacher David Baldwin, Jimmy was just a toddler. David gave Jimmy his surname, but he never gave him his love, affection, or even his respect. Although Jimmy didn't know the underlying reason for his stepfather's scorn until years later, his stepfather always made it clear that he thought Jimmy was marked by the devil: a puny, ugly, and loathsome child. David also made sure Jimmy knew that he far preferred Jimmy's eight younger (step-)siblings over him; only later did Jimmy find out that David treated him like a bastard because he considered him one.

In this harsh home environment, whenever Jimmy was free of household chores and child-care duties, he escaped into literature, borrowing heavily from the public libraries near him in Harlem. His love of learning and reading were reinforced at school, where he found encouragement to write and to read further. At Frederick Douglass Junior High School, one of his teachers (and the adviser to the literary club he belonged to) was **Countee Cullen,** who further stimulated Jimmy Baldwin's interest in literature and in writing. There, he edited the school's newspaper, the *Douglass Pilot,* to which he also contributed a short story, some sketches, and some editorials. At De Witt Clinton High School, he coedited the school's newspaper, the *Magpie,* to which he contributed short stories.

Between ages 14 and 17, Baldwin also embraced religion with great fervor, serving as a teen preacher at the Fireside Pentecostal Assembly, a storefront church in Harlem. Although his stepfather had showed him the harsh, punitive side of religion, Mother Horn, an evangelist leader of the assembly, showed him the warmth and affection of Christian love. During this time, Baldwin developed his rhetorical style and his flair for swaying human emotions with his words, and he gained a large following of devout listeners. He also read the Bible intensively and followed the church's admonitions to abstain entirely from worldly pleasures. By his late teens, however, the burgeoning hormones and life forces of the young man led him to abandon his mission and turn to literature as the focus of his greatest passion.

After Baldwin graduated from high school (in 1942), he fled his stepfather's home in Harlem and took various jobs, including a well-paid construction job in New Jersey, where he encountered a brand of racism he had not known previously in Harlem. In the summer of 1943, within 24 hours, his stepfather died in a mental hospital, and a huge riot erupted in Harlem. These events spurred him to leave his stable but unpleasant job in New Jersey and move to Greenwich Village, determined to start his career in literature. Although he still had to earn a living in various war-related industries during the day, he worked on writing his first novel at night and on weekends.

In the winter of 1944–1945, Baldwin met his mentor, **Richard Wright,** whom he had admired since high school. Wright soon recognized Baldwin's budding talent and recommended him for the Eugene F. Saxton Memorial Trust Award, Baldwin's first professional recognition of his talent. This award helped pave the way for his first published essay in the *Nation,* which was soon followed by essays, reviews, short stories, and other articles in the *Nation* and other publications.

Meanwhile, Baldwin continued to work on his first novel. The work was progressing *very* slowly, in part because Baldwin needed to work out his thoughts and feelings about his own sexual and racial identity. He even considered marrying a woman at this time, and the couple made wedding plans. In 1948, he nixed the engagement and firmly acknowledged his homosexuality; all of his subsequent intimate relationships were homosexual, although he occasionally chose bisexual partners. That year, he was also granted a Rosenwald Fellowship, with which he bought a one-way ticket to France, leaving the country of his birth November 11, planning never to return.

In France, although he still encountered racism, he found much greater acceptance as an African-American, homosexual writer than he had in the United States. There, his friends included fellow African-American expatriate Richard Wright, American writers Saul Bellow and Truman Capote, and French writers Jean-Paul Sartre and Simone de Beauvoir. By 1952, he had also formed a long-lasting intimate relationship with Swiss native Lucien Happersberger. Sadly, by this time, the friendship between Baldwin and Wright had ruptured, and the two never reconciled.

Until the late 1950s, Baldwin remained in Paris, but when the civil rights movement heated up in the United States, Baldwin felt beckoned home, to participate actively in the struggle. He

James Baldwin, 1960s (Walter Daran/Archive Photos)

spent most of his time in the United States through most of the 1960s, dividing his time between the movement and his writing. (He even divided his interests geographically on occasion, living with the family of white writer William Styron in 1961 and with James Meredith and Medgar Evers in 1963.) Throughout this period, his writings eloquently elevated the discussion of civil and political rights, stirringly provoking his readers to reconsider their views on race in the United States. From the late 1970s through the mid-1980s, Baldwin lectured and taught at various colleges across the land (e.g., the University of California at Berkeley, Bowling Green State University), ending up as a professor of writing and of Afro-American studies at the University of Massachusetts at Amherst in 1983.

Baldwin's writings included plays, novels, short stories, poems, a children's book, and essays. In the middle of the twentieth century, Baldwin was one of the few African-American playwrights to have had more than one of his plays produced on Broadway. *Amen Corner,* his semiautobiographical work about a female evangelist, was first produced at Howard University (1954–1955) and later made it to Broadway, where it was modestly successful. *Blues for Mr. Charlie,* inspired by the outrageous lynching of Emmett Till and other African Americans in the deep South, reached Broadway in 1964 and received mixed reviews. Baldwin's other plays included *Woman at the Well* (1972) and *One Day When I Was Lost* (1972).

Baldwin's poems were collected in *Jimmy's Blues: Selected Poems* (1983); his short stories were collected in *Going to Meet the Man* (1965); and his children's book was titled *Little Man, Little Man: A Story of Childhood* (1976/1977, with Y. Cazac). Baldwin's best-known works, however, were his novels and his essay collections. The first of his novels, so long in the making, was *Go Tell It on the Mountain* (1953). He first started this novel in 1944, and he didn't finish it until 1952, while he was staying in Lucien's hometown in Switzerland. During this time, its title changed from "Crying Holy" to "In My Father's House" to its final version. Soon after Alfred Knopf published it, it was widely acclaimed as brilliant, and many critics still consider it Baldwin's finest work.

The main action of the first section of the book is compressed into a single day, the fourteenth birthday of a preacher's (step-)son. Through this compression, readers clearly see how the cruel preacher abuses all his family members, particularly his teenage stepson. In the middle section of the book, which takes place during a midnight prayer meeting, Baldwin uses flashbacks to share with readers the background that led to this day, showing the personal history of the preacher and his wife. In the final section, the teenager experiences surrealistic visions calling him to preach the gospel. Over time, the young man realizes that his conversion experience was not genuine, and he comes to believe that his hope for salvation is his emerging love for an older teenager, Brother Elisha.

Baldwin's next novel, *Giovanni's Room* (1956), frankly confronts issues of race and sexuality, so Knopf refused to publish it, and the book was first published in Britain until a U.S. publisher (Dial Press) was willing to publish it. The book is written from the viewpoint of a white American expatriate living in Paris, who is contemplating his engagement to a young woman and searching for his own sexual identity. While his girlfriend is away in Spain, he becomes embroiled in a homosexual love affair with a young Italian bartender (Giovanni). Because of his own homophobia, however, when his girlfriend joins him in Paris, he rejects Giovanni and makes plans to wed. When his girlfriend discovers him in a gay bar with a sailor, she breaks off the engagement and flees home to the United States. Meanwhile, a desperate Giovanni has been fired by the bar owner, who then offers to hire him back in exchange for sexual relations. After the bar owner fails to follow through on his promise, Giovanni murders him and is later convicted and about to be executed for murdering the bar owner. The protagonist is left to contemplate his role in Giovanni's plight, as well as his own sexual identity.

Although Baldwin worried that he might be categorized as a homosexual African-American writer, he didn't shun issues of sexuality and race— or controversy—in his next novel, *Another Country* (1962). The book included a variety of white and black characters; settings in Greenwich Village (New York), Alabama, and Paris; and a loosely structured plot that wove back and forth across time. Nonetheless, the lyricality of his narrative made this book, too, a best-seller. Baldwin's subsequent novels, chiefly centered in New York, are less widely acclaimed and have been criticized for being somewhat repetitive and argumentative. These novels include *Tell Me How Long the Train's Been Gone* (1968), about two African-American brothers living in the ghetto during the civil rights era;

If Beale Street Could Talk (1974), written from the perspective of an unwed teenager who is pregnant with the baby of a young African-American who has been unjustly imprisoned; and American Book Award–nominated *Just above My Head* (1979), about a homosexual gospel singer and his brother.

Baldwin's nonfiction includes several essay collections and a pair of conversations: *A Rap on Race* (1971) with European-American anthropologist Margaret Mead and *A Dialogue* (1973) with African-American poet **Nikki Giovanni**. His collections of essays, often written in the third-person plural voice, were probably the works that most firmly established him in the heart and soul of American literature—each one sold more than a million copies on publication. They certainly provoked thought and stirred controversy. Baldwin's critically acclaimed *Notes of a Native Son* (1955) and *Nobody Knows My Name: More Notes of a Native Son* (1961) gave a nod to his former mentor, Richard Wright (whose 1940 novel *Native Son* was probably his most celebrated work). Both works, and especially the second of these, eloquently indicted racism in the United States.

Baldwin's best-selling essay collection *The Fire Next Time* (1963) included essays on his experiences of abuse (by unscrupulous neighbors and by the police) as a teenager, his encounters with the Black Muslims, and his views on the civil rights struggle. The title for his book came from the words of a spiritual Baldwin knew well, which alluded to impending catastrophe. In Baldwin's view, the racial tensions of the 1960s seemed destined to erupt in violence, and the riots that burst forth across the nation during the late 1960s seemed to confirm Baldwin's warnings. Baldwin himself, however, had concluded his book with hope for blacks and whites to work together to end racial hatred and avert this disaster.

Baldwin's subsequent writings include *Nothing Personal* (1964), with photographs by Richard Avedon, a high-school chum; *No Name in the Street* (1972), in which he wrote, "We are responsible for the world in which we find ourselves, if only because we are the only sentient force which can change it"; *The Devil Finds Work* (1976); *Remember This House* (1980), his memoirs, mixed with biographical sketches of **Martin Luther King, Jr.**, **Malcolm X**, and Medgar Evers, assassinated leaders in the struggle for civil rights; *The Evidence of Things Not Seen* (1985), about the tragic serial murders of African-American boys in Atlanta,

Georgia, in the late 1970s and early 1980s; and *The Price of a Ticket: Collected Non-Fiction 1948–1985* (1985), a collection of all previous essays as well as some new ones.

Never one to shy away from lashing out at European Americans for their racist practices, Baldwin also never hesitated to express his views when they conflicted with the views being touted by African Americans of his day. Starting with his essay "Everybody's Protest Novel" (1949), Baldwin managed to irk many fellow African Americans with his distinctive views. Many of his essays provoked similar heated controversy among African-American political leaders.

One of Baldwin's last three books was his *Harlem Quartet* (1985), and when he died, he was still working on two never-completed projects: a play (*The Welcome Table*) and a biography of Martin Luther King, Jr. He died in France, shortly after the French government had named him a commander of the Legion of Honor, France's highest civilian award. At his memorial service, a who's who of African-American writers (e.g., **Maya Angelou**, **Amiri Baraka**, **Toni Morrison**) sang his praises and credited him with having profoundly influenced their work. Just a few of the pearls he shared include "Children have never been very good at listening to their elders, but they have never failed to imitate them" (*OTD*, 6/26); and "You think your pain and your heartbreak are unprecedented in the history of the world, but then you read. It was books that taught me that the things that tormented me most were the very things that connected me with all the people who were alive, or who had ever been alive" (cited on p. 97 of *Pearls of Wisdom: A Harvest of Quotations from All Ages*). Perhaps the most telling quote of his is the goal he stated in 1955: "I want to be an honest man and a good writer." He succeeded at both.

References: *1TESK. AA:PoP. AAW:AAPP. BAL-1-P. BDAA. BWA. EB-BH-CD. EBLG. EGW. G-97. OC20LE. PGAA. RG20. WDAA.* Harris, Trudier, in *OCAAL.* McKay, Nellie Y., in *WB-99.* Robinson, Lisa Clayton, in *EA-99.*

Baltimore Afro-American (1892–)

When it first appeared in 1892, the *Baltimore Afro-American* newspaper was published as a four-page sheet to advertise the church and community enterprises of Reverend William Alexander. John H. Murphy bought the paper from Alexander for

$200 in 1910 and merged it with the *Ledger.* Murphy worked at the *Afro-American Ledger* (later, the *Afro-American*) after 1917, and the circulation grew from 8,500 to 79,952 in 1937. By then it was the black paper with the greatest sales on the eastern seaboard. When Murphy died in 1922, his sons (see **Carl Murphy**) assumed leadership of the company and began to print editions in Washington and Philadelphia in the 1930s. The *Baltimore Afro-American,* along with the *Houston Informer* and several others, has been published continuously for more than 100 years. It is the oldest family-owned black newspaper in the United States. During its peak years between the two world wars, the newspaper printed 13 separate editions from New Jersey to South Carolina.

—*Lisa Bahlinger*

REFERENCES: *EAACH,* Vol. 1. Kellner, Bruce (Ed.) (1987) *The Harlem Renaissance: A Historical Dictionary for the Era* (New York: Methuen). Mack, Kibibi Vororia (Consulting Ed.) (1987), *The African American Encyclopedia Supplement* (Vol. 7), (New York: Marshall Cavendish).

Bambara, Toni (née) Cade
(3/25/1939–12/9/1995)
Anthologies, short stories, novels, essays, scripts

After introducing Toni to the delights of the Apollo Theater, Toni's father left her and her brother Walter in her mother's capable hands. Helen Cade encouraged both her children to behave well, to think clearly, to read read read, to learn about African-American history, to tell stories, to write, and to take time "to wonder, to dawdle, to daydream" (p. 28, *BWWW*).

In 1959, when Toni graduated from Queens College (B.A. in theater arts and English literature), she published her first short story, "Sweet Town," and started winning awards for her fiction and her essays. From 1959 to 1965, she worked in various social welfare positions, taking a little time off in 1961 to travel and study acting and mime in Italy and France.

After she earned her master's degree in African-American literature from City College of New York, CCNY (now CUNY) hired her to teach English and theater arts in the Search for Education, Elevation, Knowledge (SEEK) program there. From then on, she taught literature and theater arts at various colleges and universities—in addition to offering countless writers' workshops, readings, and lectures at prisons, museums, and so on. During the 1960s, Toni also started publishing short stories and essays in various magazines, newspapers, and journals (e.g., *New York Times, Ms., Essence*).

For Toni, 1970 was a highly productive—and reproductive—year. First, *Black Woman,* her stridently pro–civil rights, feminist anthology of poems, essays, and short stories, was published. *Black Woman* included consciousness-raising works by **Nikki Giovanni**, **Alice Walker**, **Audre Lorde**, and **Paule Marshall**, as well as pieces by some of her SEEK students. Ever since, many professors of literature, women's studies, and black studies have urged their students to read *Black Woman*. Although Toni's surname for *Black Woman* was Cade, she soon legally adopted the surname Bambara, taken from a signature on a sketchbook she found in her grandmother's trunk. In addition, Toni's only daughter, Karma, was born that year. Regarding how Bambara managed her personal life and her professional life, she said, "I have no shrewd advice to offer developing writers about this business of snatching time and space to work. . . . except to say that it will cost you something. Anything of value is going to cost you something" (p. 16, *BWWW*).

In 1971, Bambara produced *Tales and Stories for Black Folks,* which included stories by **Langston Hughes**, **Ernest Gaines**, and Alice Walker, as well as stories by her students. She compiled the volume chiefly to promote the study of cultural history, black folk traditions, and the richness of black English among African-American high school and college students. As with *Black Woman,* she succeeded in reaching a wide readership.

In 1972, Bambara published *Gorilla, My Love,* her first collection of her own short stories, which earned rave reviews. Of the 15 stories in the collection, 3 were original to this volume, and 12 had been written (and previously published) between 1950 and 1970. At that time, when stories included female characters, the females were usually helpless victims needing male rescuers—at best, females aided the male heroes. In contrast, most of Bambara's stories affectionately feature feisty teenage girls who tell their own stories, using their own African-American rhythms and styles of speech. These stories emphasize the strength and fortitude of memorable African Americans who learn about themselves, their families, and their communities. Bambara's stories also accentuate women's *interdependence* more than their independence, as her female characters support and nurture one another.

Bambara's trips to Cuba (1973) and to Vietnam (1975) broadened her view of interdependence and mutual support, fostering her increasing commitment to social activism and community organizing. The trips also deepened her ties between her writing and her sociopolitical beliefs and practices. "[In Cuba,] I learned what Langston Hughes and others . . . had been teaching for years—that writing is a legitimate way, an important way, to participate in the empowerment of the community that names me" (pp. 41–42, *BWW*). Her second collection of her own short stories, *The Sea Birds Are Still Alive* (1977), reflected both her cross-cultural experiences and her intense interest in community action. During the late 1970s, Bambara manifested the link between social organization and writing by cofounding the Southern Collective of African American Writers and participating in various other writers' guilds and organizations.

Bambara's first novel, *The Salt Eaters* (1980), is actually sort of a nonlinear patchwork of short stories about overlapping characters. The central character is Velma Henry, a burned-out community organizer, and the narrative thread tying the disparate pieces together is Velma's recovery from a suicide attempt. The community she had struggled to save, in turn, rallies to aid her recovery, offering her everything from traditional folk remedies, through the spiritual guidance of the elders, to modern medical miracles. On the one hand, many critics disdained Bambara's forward and backward movement through time and space and her diverse array of characters and settings. On the other hand, many readers have praised her deft handling of dialogue and her richly idiomatic use of language. Among those who have prized her work is **Toni Morrison**, the Nobel Prize–winning Random House editor who shepherded Bambara's novel through publication. Apparently, Morrison was not alone in her appraisal because the book won the 1981 American Book Award and the 1981 Langston Hughes Society Award, as well as additional awards. (After Bambara's death, Morrison edited a collection of Bambara's work, *Deep Sightings and Rescue Missions: Fiction, Essays, and Conversations* [1996/1999]).

Among Bambara's other novels are *If Blessing Comes* (1987), which addresses the tragic serial murders of boys in Atlanta, and *Raymond's Run* (1990). Her final novel, published posthumously in 1997, was given the preliminary title of *Ground Cover*. In recognition of her overall contribution to literature, she received a 1981 National Endowment for the Arts Literature Grant.

In the 1980s, Bambara returned to her interest in the performing arts by writing and narrating films and videos. She wrote nine screenplays, including *Tar Baby,* based on the novel by her friend and editor Toni Morrison. She also worked on various television documentaries and participated in adapting several of her short stories to film.

Bambara's most memorable contributions have remained her short stories, including her many contributions to feminist anthologies. Her essays and short stories continue to be widely anthologized, both in the United States and in European and Asian publications. She clearly succeeded in achieving her primary goal: "I work to tell the truth about people's lives; I work to celebrate struggle, to applaud the tradition of struggle in our community, to bring to center stage all those characters, just ordinary folks on the block, who've been waiting in the wings, characters we thought we had to ignore" (p. 18, *BWWW*). Of her writing, she observed, "Writing was/is an act of discovery" (p. 19, *BWWW*); her readers might answer that to read her writing offers an opportunity for discovery as well.

References: *BASS. BDAA. BI. BW:AA. BWW. BWWW. EB-98. EBLG. G-97. MWEL. NAAAL. OC20LE. RT. TWT.* Byerman, Keith E., in *OCWW.* Stanford, Ann Folwell, in *OCAAL.* Amazon.com, 1/2000.

Banneker, Benjamin
(11/9/1731–10/9/1806)
Almanacs, letters, essays, short narratives, poems

Although his maternal grandmother had taught him to read and write on the family farm in Maryland, Benjamin had no formal schooling until he was about 12 years old, when a Quaker opened a one-room school for boys of all races. Benjamin quickly mastered mathematics and various other subjects. During this time, he also adopted the plain clothing, the thinking, and many of the manners of Quakers.

While improving his mind, Banneker continued to help his family thrive, performing farm chores and making occasional trips to the coast to sell his family's tobacco crop. On one such trip, when he was about 22 years old, he met a man with a pocketwatch. Banneker was so obviously captivated by it that the owner gave him the watch. Banneker spent quite a while taking apart the watch and putting it back together. He then obtained a journal with a picture of a clock, a book on geometry, and Isaac Newton's *Principia*. Armed with these print materials, his own observations, a pocket knife, and some wood, he spent his free time for the next two years building his own clock, fashioning every single part from wood. By the time he was 24, he completed his clock—the first clock ever built entirely in America, of American-made parts—and his clock continued to tick accurate time until it was destroyed, a few days after his death.

When Banneker was about 28 years old, he inherited his father's farm and tried to gain the hand (and the freedom) of his beloved Anola, a neighbor's slave. Through a series of misfortunes, he was prevented from doing so, nearly dying in the attempt, and a disheartened Anola drowned herself. Banneker never again found anyone whom he wished to marry.

In 1772, when Banneker was about 41 years old, another Quaker influence entered his life: The Ellicott family moved into the area, and George Ellicott and Banneker struck up a close friendship. During this time, Ellicott frequently loaned his astronomy books, telescope, and some other scientific instruments to Banneker, and when Ellicott died, he bequeathed these things to Banneker. As a farmer, Banneker had always been vitally interested in the night sky, but with Ellicott's books and telescope, he became a dedicated astronomer.

Once his interest in astronomy soared, he sold his farm to the Ellicotts in exchange for a modest annuity and use of his cabin home and workshop. That done, he usually slept by day and watched the stars by night. In 1791, he used his astronomical observations to help Andrew Ellicott, the chief surveyor for mapping out the territory that was to become the nation's capital. Around that time, Banneker accurately predicted a solar eclipse, and his prestige as an astronomer was established. In 1792 (when he was 60), through contacts with abolitionist printers, he published the first of a series of almanacs, which prominently featured the *ephemerides* (astronomical tables) he had calculated. He also included weather forecasts for the year (vital for farmers), sunrise/sunset times, a Chesapeake Bay tide table, a list of holidays, lists of preventive medicines and

of curative remedies, recipes, poems, essays, proverbs, and other practical information for farmers. Banneker didn't author all of the items in the almanac (other than the ephemerides), but he did write some of the verses and short narratives.

Banneker's almanacs were widely read throughout the middle states, even gaining him international recognition. He took advantage of this popularity by including his opinions on slavery and racism, as well as his proposals for the betterment of society. For instance, his 1792 almanac included a proposal for establishing a national Department of Peace instead of a Department of War. His proposal also included suggestions for establishing free schools for all children "in every city, village and township of the United States" and for abolishing capital punishment.

Banneker also wrote more narrowly focused tracts on various naturalistic subjects, such as a dissertation on bees and an insightful paper postulating the 17-year cycles of locust plagues. Other than his almanacs, however, perhaps the most well-known document written by Banneker was his letter to Thomas Jefferson, addressing Jefferson's appalling unwillingness to apply the sentiments of the Declaration of Independence to all people—or at least to all men. An excerpt highlights Banneker's message:

> One universal Father hath given being to us all; and he hath not only made us all of one flesh, but he hath also, without partiality, afforded us all the same sensations and endowed us all with the same faculties; and that however variable we may be in society or religion, however diversified in situation or color, we are all in the same family and stand in the same relation to Him. . . . I freely and cheerfully acknowledge that I am of the African race and in that color which is natural to them of the deepest dye; . . . . Suffer me to recall to your mind that time in which the arms and tyranny of the British Crown were exerted with every powerful effort in order to reduce you to a state of servitude. This, Sir, was a time when you clearly saw into the injustice of a state of slavery and in which you had apprehensions of the horrors of its conditions.

Banneker accompanied the letter with a manuscript of his almanac to show Jefferson that he had indeed authored it. Jefferson's response was rather obtuse, agreeing with Banneker that he had espoused the values of freedom and that Banneker clearly had great intellectual power, but still managing to weasel out of acknowledging his own blatant hypocrisy in continuing to endorse slavery despite his protestations regarding the equal rights of all "men."

In Banneker's modest cabin home and workshop, he entertained visiting scholars and other distinguished scientists and artists. On his death, just a few days before his seventy-fifth birthday, he was honored by the French Academy of Sciences and in the English Parliament, but in the United States, he was honored only privately, by those who knew him or knew of him. He left his scientific instruments, his books, and his correspondence with Jefferson to Andrew Ellicott, the son of George, who had so fortuitously helped him to lift his eyes heavenward. Unfortunately, two days after his funeral, his humble home burned to the ground, and his wooden clock, as well as most of his other writings, went up in smoke.

REFERENCES: *AA:PoP. BAL-1-P. BDAA. BF:2000. BPSI. BWA. E-97. EB-98. EBLG. G-95. SMKC.* Born, Brad S., in *OCAAL.*

Baraka, Amiri (né Everett LeRoy Jones; pseudonym: LeRoi Jones) (10/7/1934–)
Poems, novels, plays, essays, anthologies, editorials

Amiri Baraka's activities and attitudes seem to be countercultural in any age, but they didn't start out that way. When writing in the late 1950s and early 1960s, Baraka used the name LeRoi Jones and was basically apolitical. Although Jones wrote his poetry in the vernacular language of ordinary people, he did not use his art to further any political ideals or principles. The general political activism within the United States and a trip to Cuba changed the tone of Jones's (Baraka's) work in the 1960s and 1970s. During this period, Baraka integrated his art with his political views, initiated the **Black Arts movement,** and founded the Black Arts Repertory Theatre. Since that time, Baraka has revised his politics, accepted a university teaching position, and continued to write and comment on society, culture, and poetry.

Born in Newark, New Jersey, LeRoy apparently had an ordinary middle-class upbringing. His mother, Anna Lois Russ Jones, was a social worker, and his father, Coyt LeRoy Jones, was a postal worker. LeRoy was a good student in high school and attended first Rutgers University and then Howard University, eventually flunking out of Howard. Jones then enlisted in the U.S. Air Force in 1954, where he served until receiving a dishonorable discharge, reportedly for submitting some of his poetry to what were considered communist publications.

After leaving the Air Force in 1957, Jones moved to Greenwich Village in New York City, where he began cultivating and using his writing talents more fully. He associated with and earned the respect of well-known artists in the area, including Allen Ginsberg. There, Jones met his first wife, Hettie Cohen, a white Jewish woman, and married her in 1958. Together, they edited *Yugen,* a literary journal that sought to publish works by struggling authors. Jones was invited to visit Cuba in 1960 because he was considered an important "Negro writer." This visit, along with the assassination of **Malcolm X**, the black power movement, and the Civil Rights Act of 1964, altered Jones's view of poetry, politics, and the black community. Jones began to realize that his poetry and other writings could become vehicles for political views and could serve as catalysts for social and political change. Consequently, he started taking an active interest in promoting black nationalism in the African-American community.

Jones initiated the Black Arts movement, encompassing the years 1965–1975. During this artistic and cultural movement, many African-American artists produced works calling for a rejection of white society and cultural norms and pride in African-American heritage and culture. This new political attitude struck Jones on a personal level, as well. He divorced his first wife, moved to Harlem and later Newark, and committed himself to raising a new level of consciousness within the black community. At this time, Jones also changed his name to Amiri Baraka and remarried, this time to an African-American woman, Sylvia Robinson (later known as Amina Baraka), with whom he eventually had five children.

Over time, Baraka decided that black nationalism was pandering to and imitating the white culture and power structure and therefore betraying black culture. His political awareness increased. Baraka had so far discovered that neither apolitical stances nor black nationalism would bring about the society he envisioned. This observation pushed him to make yet another ideological shift to a

Marxist-Leninist position. This shift led him to a vocal and public disagreement with controversial filmmaker **Spike Lee** about the making of *Malcolm X,* one of Lee's films.

To read Baraka's work in chronological order is to witness the personal and political evolution that he has experienced as a black man in the United States. Some scholars liken his personal political changes to the changes taking place within the larger black community. Baraka's first collection of poetry is *Preface to a Twenty Volume Suicide Note* (1961). This early poetry evokes a sense of jazz with its offbeat rhythms and gives hints of Baraka's emerging political views.

Baraka's first drama, Obie Award–winning *The Dutchman* (1964), is an overtly political one-act play condemning racist oppression and startling audiences into consciousness. Baraka's semiautobiographical novel, *The System of Dante's Hell* (1965), further raises the issue of trying to reconcile the conflicts inherent in being an African American in white America. Robert J. Forman notes that "Western culture attracts [Baraka] intellectually, yet it morally damns him," that he remains "somewhere between black and white cultures, accepted by neither and estranged from both."

Other books of poetry by Baraka include *The Dead Lecturer* (1964), *Black Magic: Sabotage—Target Study—Black Art: Collected Poetry, 1961–1967* (1969), *It's Nation Time* (1970), *In Our Terribleness* (1970), *Spirit Reach* (1972), *Hard Facts* (1975), *Poetry for the Advanced* and *Selected Poetry of Amiri Baraka/LeRoi Jones* (both in 1979); *Reggae or Not!* (1981); *Transbluesency: The Selected Poems of Amiri Baraka/LeRoi Jones (1961–1995)* (1995); and *Funk Lore: New Poems (1984–1995)* (1996).

In addition to poetry, Baraka wrote such dramas as *The Slave* (1964); *Slave Ship: An Historical Pageant, The Baptism,* and *The Toilet* (all in 1967); and *Four Black Revolutionary Plays* (1969). His other writings include *Home: Social Essays* (1966); *Raise Race Rays Raze* (1972); *Daggers and Javelins: Essays 1974–1979* (1984); *The Autobiography of LeRoi Jones/Amiri Baraka* (1984); and *The Music: Reflections on Jazz and Blues* (1987).

Throughout his work, Baraka often seems like a man on a mission. He is a man who has something to say, who will have his say, and who will flatten, circumvent, or bypass any obstacles he finds—all the while creating a path for others to follow.

—Janet Hoover, with Diane Masiello

REFERENCES: *EBLG. NAAAL.* Ansen, D., and F. Chideya (1991), "The Battle for Malcolm X," *Newsweek* 118(9), 52–55, *Magazine Academic Index Plus.* Brucker, Carl, "Dutchman," in *MAAL.* Draper, James P. (Ed.) (1992), "Amiri Baraka 1934–," in *BLC* (Vol. 1). Forman, Robert J., "System of Dante's Hell," *Masterpieces of Azine Index Plus.* Lacey, Henry C., "Baraka, Amiri," and *"Dutchman,"* in *OCAAL.* Nazareth, Peter (1997), "World Literature in Review: English," *World Literature Today, 97*(1), 154–156. Popkin, Michael (Compiler and Ed.) (1978), "Baraka, Amiri," *Modern Black Writers* (New York: Ungar). Serafin, Steven R. (Compiler and Ed.) (1995), "Amiri Baraka," *Modern Black Writers: Supplement* (New York: Continuum). Zlogar, Laura Weiss, "Poetry of Amiri Baraka," in *MAAL.*

Barber, Jesse Max (7/5/1878–9/20/1949)
Essays, articles; editor

A journalist, Barber was the sole managing editor of *Voice of the Negro,* a literary journal founded in Atlanta in January 1904. Initially, the journal included works by both accommodationists (e.g., **Booker T. Washington**) and radical activists (e.g., **W. E. B. Du Bois**), but with Barber's guidance, it soon had a reputation for progressive thinking, publishing works by **Charles Chesnutt**, John Hope, **Pauline Hopkins**, Kelly Miller, **William Pickens**, and **Mary Eliza Church Terrell**. In it, Barber also published works by poets such as **James D. Corrothers**, **Paul Laurence Dunbar**, and **Georgia Douglas Johnson**.

REFERENCES: *EA-99.*

Barnett, Claude Albert (?/1889–1967)
Founder, the Associated Negro Press

An entrepreneur, Barnett noticed that newspapers catering to African Americans would benefit from having a source for news affecting African Americans. In 1919, he founded the Associated Negro Press (ANP), modeled after the Associated Press news service. The ANP gathered, edited, and distributed articles to its member newspapers (about 200 of them by the start of World War II). After World War II, the press also included member newspapers in Africa, handling articles in French as well as in English. During the 1960s, the number of African-American newspapers declined, and shortly after Barnett's death, the ANP ceased to exist (leaving 112 newspapers without ANP as a resource).

REFERENCES: *BDAA. EA-99.*

Barnett, Marguerite Ross
See **Ross–Barnett, Marguerite**

Barrax, Gerald W. (William) (6/21/1933–)
Poems

Barrax's poetry collections include *Another Kind of Rain* (1970), *An Audience of One* (1980), *The Deaths of Animals and Lesser Gods* (1984), and *Leaning against the Sun* (1992).

REFERENCES: Scott, Daniel M. III, in *OCAAL*.

Bass, Charlotta (née) Spears
(10/?/1880–4/29/1969)
Journalist; newspaper publisher

From 1900 to 1910, Charlotta Spears had devoted herself to Rhode Island's *Providence Watchman,* exhausting herself physically and mentally. Her doctor told her to head West—and take some time out to rest, relax, and recuperate. She followed his suggestion to go West, but she didn't listen to his advice about resting. At first, she just sold subscriptions to the *Eagle,* the oldest African-American newspaper in the West, but by the end of two years, she owned it, published it, and was its managing editor.

Soon, Charlotta Spears also took on another big commitment: She married Joseph Bass, cofounder of the *Topeka Plaindealer,* whom she named as editor of her paper. She also renamed the paper the *California Eagle,* and through it, she protested against D. W. Griffith's 1915 white-supremacist film *The Birth of a Nation;* deplored the U.S. Army's unfair court-martial, conviction, and punishment of the soldiers in the 24th Black Regiment in Houston, Texas, in 1917; and bitterly challenged the unjust legal railroading of the innocent Scottsboro Boys in 1931.

After her husband died (in 1934), Charlotta Bass kept up the struggle through her *California Eagle* for another two decades. Starting in the 1940s, however, she increasingly turned to politics as a vehicle for social change. After running for city council, directing the western region of Wendell Wilkie's 1944 presidential campaign, and cofounding the Progressive Party in 1948, in 1952 Bass was chosen to run as Vincent Hallinan's vice-presidential running mate on that ticket. If you don't recall hearing about President Vincent Hallinan, you know that Bass and Hallinan lost the election. Nonetheless, they stimulated public discussion of war (stop the Cold War and the Korean War) and peace (ban the bomb), as well as the need to address issues of social equity (for women, all people of color, and all impoverished people).

In the 1950s, Senator Joseph McCarthy conducted his notorious witch hunt to punish and rebuke anyone who seemed remotely sympathetic to socialism, civil rights, or civil liberties—and Bass was certainly sympathetic to all three, so she suffered along with many others during McCarthy's Red Scare. In the long run, however, Bass fared well—we still remember her for her integrity and her willingness to make sacrifices for the benefit of other people.

\ —*Tonya Bolden*

REFERENCES: *BAAW.* Bass, Charlotta Spears (1960), *Forty Years: Memoirs from the Pages of a Newspaper.*

Bayley, Solomon (fl. c. 1800s)
Slave narrative

Bayley was one of the first to write his own spiritual slave autobiography, *A Narrative of Some Remarkable Incidents in the Life of Solomon Bayley, Formerly a Slave in the State of Delaware, North America; Written by Himself, and Published for His Benefit* (2nd London ed., 1825), rather than dictating it to an *amanuensis* (someone who writes down what another person dictates aloud).

REFERENCES: *BAL-1-P.* Shields, John C., "Literary History: Colonial and Early National Eras," in *OCAAL*, pp. 446–447.

Beasley, Delilah (9/9/1872–8/18/1934)
Nonfiction—history; columns

By age 12, Beasley had started writing for the *Cleveland Gazette,* and by age 15, she was a regular columnist for the Sunday edition of the *Cincinnati Enquirer.* About 1910, she started writing a column for the Sunday *Oakland Tribune,* which she continued to write for another 20 years. One of her themes was her adamant opposition to racial discrimination and stereotyping, such as in the use of the words "darky" and "nigger" in mainstream U.S. newspapers in her day. In addition, through her own archival research and collection of oral history, she gathered enough information on the history of African Americans in California to write *The Negro Trail-Blazers of California* (1919). Her self-published book was so highly respected by sociologists that it was nominated for inclusion in the *Guide to the Best Books*.

REFERENCES: *EA-99*. Crouchett, Lorraine J., in *BWA:AHE*.

Beckham, Barry (1944–)
Novels; book publisher

Beckham's novels include *My Main Mother* (1969) and *Runner Mack* (1972, nominated for the National Book Award). Beckham also wrote a "novelized biography," *Double Dunk* (1981), and a play, *Garvey Lives!* (1972). When he ran into difficulties publishing his *The Black Student's Guide to Colleges* (1982), he decided to start his own book-publishing company, Beckham House Publishers.

REFERENCES: Loeb, Jeff, in *OCAAL*.

Bell, James Madison (?/1826–1902)
Poems

Bell specialized in writing long (750–950 lines) verse orations on historical subjects, such as slavery, the Civil War, emancipation, and Reconstruction. His books included *A Poem* (1862), *A Poem Entitled the Day and the War* (1864), *An Anniversary Poem Entitled the Progress of Liberty* (1866), and *A Poem Entitled the Triumph of Liberty* (1870), as well as his entire collected works, *Poetical Works* (1901).

REFERENCES: Sherman, Joan R., in *OCAAL*.

Bennett, Gwendolyn B.
(7/8/1902–5/30/1981)
Poems, criticism, essays, columns, short stories

When Gwendolyn was eight years old, her schoolteacher parents divorced, and her father abducted her, moving frequently to avoid letting Gwendolyn's mother find them. Not until Gwendolyn was a junior in high school did her father and she settle in Brooklyn, where she then won numerous school awards and contests.

As Bennett finished college, the **Harlem Renaissance** flowered, and her budding talent blossomed. She started contributing to literary journals, creating covers and writing articles and poems for *Crisis* and *Opportunity*. Many of her poems (e.g., her best-known poem, "To a Dark Girl") celebrate the natural grace, physical loveliness, and emotional qualities of African-American females. Her lyrical poems were distinctively refreshing

during this time when many descendants of Mother Africa failed to appreciate their racial and cultural characteristics.

Between 1923 and 1928, Bennett wrote most of her stories, poems, and essays. During this highly productive period, she developed warm supportive relationships with her peers, especially **Langston Hughes** and **Countee Cullen**. To support her writing and her artwork, Bennett taught art and design at Howard University. She had no sooner begun teaching than she won a prestigious foreign-study award, which allowed her to study art in Paris from 1925 until 1926. While there, she kept corresponding with her peers in Harlem. They continually urged her to write for publication and told her of literary opportunities in the United States.

In 1926, Bennett returned to Harlem and joined Hughes and others to form the editorial board of *Fire!!,* a quarterly journal for work by young African-American artists. Sadly, soon after her return to the United States, much of her Parisian work went up in smoke—literally. From 1927 to 1928, she returned to teaching art at Howard but still kept in touch with her colleagues in Harlem. She drew on these contacts for her "Ebony Flute" column (1926–1928) in *Opportunity*, which she described as "literary and social chit-chat": influential essays and news about African-American literary and artistic trends and activities. Her column is often cited as having documented, supported, and shaped the Harlem Renaissance.

In May of 1928, Bennett left her teaching post to help her husband set up his private medical practice in Florida. Unable to tolerate the rigid segregation of the South, however, she finally convinced him to return to New York. Unfortunately, they arrived during the Great Depression, when support for the arts dried up, and the Harlem Renaissance shriveled up. Soon after, Bennett's husband died, and she had to turn from expressing her heart and soul to feeding her stomach. Eventually, she found a job suited to her artistic temperament, directing the Harlem Community Art Center. Unfortunately, in 1941, she was unfairly dismissed for suspected communist sympathies. Eventually she remarried and spent the rest of her life as a housewife and then a widowed antiques dealer.

REFERENCES: *BANP. EB-98. MWEL. NAAAL. RLWWJ. RT. TtW.* Govan, Sandra Y., in *OCAAL*.

Bennett, Hal (4/21/1930–)
Novels, short fiction

Bennett sold his first short story at age 15, started writing features for the Newark *Herald News* at age 16, and edited a newsletter for soldiers when he was in the U.S. Air Force during the Korean War. Bennett's novels include *A Wilderness of Vines* (1966), *The Black Wine* (1968), *Lord of Dark Places* (1970), *Wait until Evening* (1974), and *Seventh Heaven* (1976); his short fiction has been collected in *Insanity Runs in Our Family* (1977). In 1973, Bennett won the prestigious PEN/Faulkner Award for literature.

REFERENCES: Miller, James A., in *OCAAL.*

Bennett, Lerone, Jr. (10/17/1928–)
Nonfiction—history; journalist

Bennett's highly readable and well-researched books include the best-selling *Before the Mayflower: A History of the Negro in America, 1619–1962* (1962); *The Negro Mood, and Other Essays* (1964); *What Matter of Man* (1964, his biography of Martin Luther King, Jr.); *Confrontation: Black and White* (1965); *Black Power, U.S.A.: The Human Side of Reconstruction, 1867–1877* (1967); *Pioneers in Protest* (1968); *The Challenge of Blackness* (1972); *The Shaping of Black America: The Struggles and Triumphs of African-Americans, 1619 to the 1990s* (1975; 2nd ed., 1993); *Wade in the Water: Great Moments in Black History* (1979); *Listen to the Blood: Was Abraham Lincoln a White Supremacist? and Other Essays and Stories* (1994); and *Whipped into Glory: Abraham Lincoln and the White Dream* (1996). He also collaborated with **John H. Johnson** in writing Johnson's memoirs, *Succeeding against the Odds* (1989).

Bennett is also a journalist; after a brief stay as associate editor at *Jet* magazine (1953–1954), he moved to *Ebony* magazine, eventually becoming its executive editor (since 1987). In his magazine work, he has also promoted the appreciation of African-American history (e.g., developing the four-volume compilation, *Ebony Pictorial History of Black America,* 1971), often contributing his own articles on the subject for the magazine. In addition, Bennett has had several of his poems and short stories published.

REFERENCES: *EBLG.* Robinson, Lisa Clayton, in *EA-99.* Stone, Les, in *BH2C.*

Berry, Mary Frances (2/17/1938–)
Nonfiction—history

Among Berry's scholarly works of history are *Black Resistance/White Law: A History of Constitutional Racism* (1971; paperback 1995); *Military Necessity and Civil Rights Policy: Black Citizenship and the Constitution, 1861–1868* (1977); *Stability, Security, and Continuity: Mr. Justice Burton and Decision-Making in the Supreme Court, 1945–1958* (1978); *Long Memory: The Black Experience in America* (1982, with John W. Blassingame; paperback 1986); *Why the ERA Failed: Politics, Women's Rights, and the Amending Process* (1986); *Black Self-determination: A Cultural History of African-American Resistance* (2nd ed., 1993, with V. P. Franklin); *The Politics of Parenthood: Child Care, Women's Rights, and the Myth of the Good Mother* (1993); and her critically acclaimed *The Pig Farmer's Daughter and Other Tales of American Justice: Episodes of Racism and Sexism in the Courts from 1865 to the Present* (1999); as well as numerous articles in scholarly journals. In addition to the doctorate she earned from Howard University, she has received numerous honorary doctorates and many other awards in recognition of her scholarship.

REFERENCES: Glenshaw, Peter, in *EA-99.* McNeil, Genna Rae, in *BH2C,* and in *BWA:AHE.* Amazon.com, 8/1999.

Bibb, Henry (5/10/1815–1854)
Fugitive slave narrative, articles, lectures; newspaper founder

Bibb is best known for his self-published *Narrative of the Life and Adventures of Henry Bibb Written by Himself* (1849, 1st ed.; also published as *Narrative of the Life and Adventures of Henry Bibb, an American Slave*). In his account, he describes escaping and being recaptured several times, including this account of his final escape: "The swift running steamer started that afternoon on her voyage, which soon wafted my body beyond the tyrannical limits of chattel slavery. When the boat struck the mouth of the river Ohio, and I had once more the pleasure of looking on that lovely stream, my heart leaped up for joy at the glorious prospect that I should again be free" (p. 114, *BAL-1-P*). In his day, he and his narrative were not nearly as well received as were **Frederick Douglass** and Douglass's narratives, but contemporary scholars have affirmed his narrative as one of the most reliable accounts of slavery in Kentucky and the South.

In 1842, Bibb made his final, successful escape to Detroit, leaving behind his first wife and daughter. As a free man, he worked actively to defeat slavery, giving antislavery lectures and writing abolitionist articles. Following the 1850 passage of the Fugitive Slave Act, he and his second wife fled to Canada. There, in 1851, Bibb founded *The Voice of the Fugitive,* Canada's premier African-American abolitionist newspaper, which he edited. He also worked to aid the Underground Railroad and any other causes that would undermine or defeat slavery.

REFERENCES: *BAL-1-P. EA-99. NYPL-AADR.* Lowance, Mason I., Jr., in *OCAAL.*

Black Aesthetic (1960s–1970s)

Supporters of the **Black Arts movement** (lasting from the early 1960s to the mid-1970s) sought themes that arose from the context of African-American culture and provided their own frame of reference. This became known as "Black Aesthetic theory." It generated a remarkable amount of criticism and theory about African-American literature.

The spirit of the Black Arts movement was captured in 1968 by **Larry Neal** and **Amiri Baraka,** who edited *Black Fire: An Anthology of Afro-American Writing.* In examining how the political values of the black power movement found expression in the aesthetic of African-American artists, Neal and Baraka postulated that there were two Americas, one black and one white. A central theme of black power was that African Americans should define the world in their own terms. The black aesthetic viewed this concept from the vantage point of the artist. The artist's primary responsibility, according to Neal and Baraka, was to speak to the spiritual and cultural needs of black people: "Therefore, the main thrust of this new breed of contemporary writers is to confront the contradictions arising out of the Black man's experience in the racist West. . . . Implicit in this reevaluation is the need to develop a Black Aesthetic . . . the Western aesthetic has run its course: It is impossible to construct anything meaningful within its decaying structure. We advocate a cultural revolution in art and ideas."

Amiri Baraka amplifies the nature of the new aesthetic in his poem "Black Art," which ends with the lines

We want a black poem. And a
Black World
Let the world be a Black Poem

And Let All Black people Speak This Poem
Silently
or LOUD

—*Michael Strickland*

REFERENCES: *NAAAL.* Baraka, Amiri, and Larry Neal (1968), *Black Fire: An Anthology of Afro-American Writing* (New York: Morrow). Gates, Henry Louis, Jr. (1987), *Figures in Black: Words, Signs and the Racial Self* (New York: Oxford University Press). Gates, Henry Louis, Jr. (1992), *Loose Canons: Notes on the Culture Wars* (New York: Oxford University Press).

Black American Literature Forum (1967–)

This pioneering journal, also called *Negro American Literature Forum* and *African American Review,* was one of the first to highlight African-American literary issues, and throughout its history, it has been on the cutting edge of African-American literary and cultural studies, the first to focus on writing by and about African Americans, including women's writing, autobiography, biography, film and other artistic studies, critical theory, and science fiction.

In 1967, at Indiana State University, John F. Bayliss founded the *Negro American Literature Forum.* The journal originally focused on the teaching of literature, but as it evolved and came under the editorship of Hannah Hendrick and W. Tasker Witham (1973–1976), it began to concentrate more and more on critical analysis of literary texts.

In 1976, current editor Joe Weixlmann reorganized and reformatted the journal and renamed it *Black American Literature Forum,* focusing on literary studies, poetry, and related cultural disciplines, including theater, visual art, and music. In 1983, it received high praise from the Modern Language Association, an organization of literary scholars, which named it the official publication of the MLA Division on Black American Literature.

In the 1990s, interest in cultural studies swept the academy, and the journal moved with the times and began to include more and more essays on nonliterary topics. It also shifted away from critical essays and gave more space to publishing high-quality fiction and poetry. In the spring of 1992, the shift in focus led to another new name for the journal: *African American Review.* It continues to provide brilliant, insightful commentary on issues in African-American literature, media, and culture, including articles on the cultural studies

Leroi Jones (now known as Amiri Baraka), a leader of the Black Arts movement, 1975 (Bettmann-Corbis)

movement, critical theory, women's writing, and African-American autobiography, nonliterary essays, fiction, poetry, and other genres.

—*Diane Masiello and Lisa Bahlinger*

REFERENCES: Weixlmann, Joe, "*African American Review*," in *OCAAL*.

Black Arts Movement (1960s–1970s)

The Black Arts movement, the first major African-American artistic movement after the **Harlem Renaissance**, lasted from the early 1960s through the mid-1970s, while the civil rights movement was at its peak, as were new ways of thinking about African Americans. This movement formed the literary, cultural, aesthetic, and spiritual wing of the black power struggle. Movement participants sought to produce works of art that would be meaningful to the black masses.

For the most part, during this period African-American writers were very supportive of separatist politics and black nationalism. Acting more in the spirit of **Malcolm X** than of **Martin Luther King, Jr.,** they believed that artists had a responsibility to be political activists. Many adher-

ents viewed the artist as responsible for the formation of racially separate publishing houses, theater troupes, and study groups.

The term "Black Arts" is of ancient origin and had a negative meaning for centuries, similar to "black magic." It was first used in a positive sense by **Amiri Baraka** (formerly LeRoi Jones), a leader of the Black Arts movement. In 1965, Baraka founded the Black Arts Repertory Theatre in Harlem. In addition, Baraka and **Larry Neal** edited *Black Fire: An Anthology of Afro-American Writing* (1968), a collection of stories, plays, and essays by African-American writers, which helped define the movement.

Black Arts movement participants looked for inspiration in such sources as popular music, including John Coltrane's jazz and James Brown's rhythm and blues. The literature of the movement was confrontational in tone. In fact, some of the language used by these writers was intentionally vulgar and shocking, to show the vitality of their position. Black Arts writing generally used black English vernacular and addressed such issues as racial tension, political awareness, and the relevance of African history and culture to U.S. blacks.

Rebelling against mainstream society by essentially being antiwhite, anti–middle class, and anti-American, participants in the movement were radically opposed to any concept of artists that alienated them from their community. They moved from the Harlem Renaissance view of art for art's sake to their own view of art for politics' sake. Another organizer of the movement was **Ishmael Reed**, who later dissented from some Black Arts doctrines and became inspired more by black magic and spiritual practices of the West Indies.

Leading theorists of the Black Arts movement included **Houston A. Baker**; **Henry Louis Gates, Jr.**; **Addison Gayle, Jr.**, editor of the anthology *The Black Aesthetic* (1971); **Hoyt Fuller**, editor of the journal *Negro Digest;* and poet and essayist Don Lee (**Haki Madhubuti**). African-American women also played an important role in the movement. Poet and playwright **Sonia Sanchez** brought the often-overlooked female voice to the black nationalist movement.

Among the numerous other writers associated with the Black Arts movement were Obie Award–winning dramatist **Ed Bullins**; playwright Ben Caldwell; poets **Margaret Taylor Burroughs**, **Jayne Cortez**, and **Eugene Redmond**; and novelists **Toni Morrison**, **Ntozake Shange**, **Alice Walker**, and **June Jordan**. The movement, characterized by acute self-awareness, produced such autobiographical works as *The Autobiography of Malcolm X* (1965), cowritten by **Alex Haley**; *Soul On Ice* (1968) by **Eldridge Cleaver**; and *Angela Davis: An Autobiography* (1974).

The Black Arts movement served two functions significant to African Americans today. First, important African-American texts that had been ignored were discovered. Second, black literature was defined in terms that differed from those used by white writers. Black Arts supporters sought themes that arose from the context of African-American culture and provided their own frame of reference, based on **Black Aesthetic** theory. The movement generated a remarkable amount of criticism and theory about African-American literature and brought wide acclaim to many African-American writers, fostering the growth of black studies courses and departments in higher education around the country. It also fostered the inclusion of African-American literature in the curriculum of elementary, middle, and high schools.

—*Michael Strickland*

REFERENCES: *NAAL*. Baraka, Amiri, and Larry Neal (Eds.) (1968), *Black Fire: An Anthology of Afro-American Writing* (New York: Morrow). Gates, Henry Louis, Jr. (1987), *Figures in Black: Words, Signs and the Racial Self* (New York: Oxford University Press). Gates, Henry Louis, Jr. (1992), *Loose Canons: Notes on the Culture Wars* (New York: Oxford University Press).

Black Scholar (1969–)

Established in 1969 as the journal of the Black World Federation, the *Black Scholar* arose from the black-power movement and the movement's emphasis on self-determination and social struggle. The *Black Scholar* was intended to be a forum for discussing and critiquing African-American ideologies, and the journal published such writers as **Sonia Sanchez**, **Alice Walker**, **Maya Angelou**, **Gwendolyn Brooks**, **Gayl Jones**, **Clarence Major**, and John Stewart. The journal also published the work of black intellectuals and activists and sought to be a bridge between black academia and the black community by promoting black studies programs and printing community-service listings of rallies, events, conferences, and the like.

—*Lisa Bahlinger*

REFERENCES: *EAACH*, Vol. 1.

Black World
See *Negro Digest*

Bogle, Donald (3/?/1952–)
Film history

Young Donald's interest in films emerged early. By his own account (in *Blacks in American Films and Television: An Illustrated Encyclopedia*), "Black performers in movies and television cast a beguiling spell over me. . . . Even during those early years of my moviegoing and TV-watching experience, I think I was struggling to sort out incongruities of what I viewed, to clear up disparities. Always my curiosity and thirst for information led me to the library in search of some comment on a particular film, character, or personality. Usually, I returned home empty-handed, without any answers to some basic questions."

To our good fortune—and his—Bogle was able to make a living by informing himself—and us—about African Americans in American popular culture, with an emphasis on motion pictures and television. While satisfying his lifelong curiosity, he has become one of the nation's foremost authorities on this fascinating subject. Bogle shares what he has learned by

- Teaching (e.g., at Rutgers University, the University of Pennsylvania, and New York University's Tisch School of the Arts)
- Lecturing (at forums across the country)
- Commenting on film for television (e.g., HBO's *Mo Funny: Black Comedy in America* and the American Movie Channel's documentary on African Americans in the movies, *Small Steps, Big Strides*)
- Curating and cocurating several major film series in New York City (e.g., a retrospective on Sidney Poitier at the American Museum of the Moving Picture, and the Film Forum's *Black Women in the Movies: Actresses, Images, Films; Blacks in the Movies: Breakthroughs, Landmarks and Milestones;* and *Blaxploitation, Baby!*)
- Writing countless articles and reviews for various periodicals (e.g., *Freedomways, Essence, Spin,* and *Film Comment*)
- Writing books

For most of us, Bogle's books have been his most important contribution to what we know about African Americans involved in movies and television. Bogle's first book was the award-winning bestseller *Toms, Coons, Mulattoes, Mammies, and Bucks: An Interpretive History of Blacks in American Films* (1973; 3rd rev., updated ed., 1994). His next book, *Brown Sugar: Eighty Years of America's Black Female Superstars* (1980), was the basis for a documentary for the Public Broadcasting System, which he researched, adapted to film, and executive produced, and which the Association of American Women in Television and Radio named as one of the best documentaries of 1987. Bogle's other books include *Blacks in American Films and Television: An Illustrated Encyclopedia* (1988), comprising hundreds of entries, and *Dorothy Dandridge* (1997), a rich, vibrant biography of the much-celebrated actress of the 1940s and 1950s, with whom Bogle had been enraptured as a young boy.

If you're desperate to find a few more words by Bogle, you may find them in his foreword for Spike Lee's *Mo' Better Blues,* his introduction to John Kisch and Edward Mapp's *A Separate Cinema:*

Fifty Years of Black-Cast Posters, and a contemporary edition of Ethel Waters's 1951 autobiography *His Eye Is on the Sparrow.* Through all of these contributions, all those who share Bogle's curiosity about the history of African-American actors, producers, and directors can share in his abundant knowledge.

—*Tonya Bolden*

REFERENCES: *SMKC.*

Bolden, Tonya (3/1/1959–)
Biographies, juvenile books

Bolden's literary reviews and other articles have appeared in *Black Enterprise, Essence, New York Times Book Review, Small Press,* and *Washington Post Book World,* among other periodicals. She was also the book review columnist for *YSB* magazine from its inception in 1991 through its final issue in October 1996, and she was the editor of *Quarterly Black Review of Books* for its March 1994–June 1995 issues.

Bolden has authored, coauthored, or edited more than ten books. These include *The Family Heirloom Cookbook* (1990); *Mama, I Want to Sing* (1992, novel with Vy Higgensen, based on Higgensen's musical); *Rites of Passage: Stories about Growing Up by Black Writers from Around the World* (1994); *Just Family* (1996, novel); *The Book of African American Women: 150 Crusaders, Creators and Uplifters* (1996); *Through Loona's Door: A Tammy and Owen Adventure with Carter G. Woodson* (1997, illustrated by Luther Knox); *33 Things Every Girl Should Know: Stories, Songs, Poems, and Smart Talk by 33 Extraordinary Women* (1998, an ALA "Best Book for Young Adults"); *And Not Afraid to Dare: The Stories of Ten African American Women* (1998, a NYPL "Best Book for the Teen Age"); and *Strong Men Keep Coming: The Book of African American Men* (1999). She also collaborated with talk-show host Mother Love on *Forgive or Forget: Never Underestimate the Power of Forgiveness.*

REFERENCES: Personal communication (1/5/99, 5/31/99); vitae/résumé (1999).

Bonner (married name: Occomy), Marita (Odette) (6/16/1899–12/6/1971)
Essays, plays, short stories

After earning her B.A. in English and comparative literature from Radcliffe College (1922), she spent two years teaching at Bluefield Colored Institute in West Virginia, then moved to Washington, D.C., where she taught until 1930. In 1930, she married accountant William Almy Occomy, with whom she moved to Chicago, continued teaching, and raised three children (William Almy, Jr.; Warwick Gale Noel, and Marita Joyce).

Although Bonner never lived in Harlem, she was nurtured by fellow writers of the **Harlem Renaissance** period, especially those who congregated at the Washington, D.C., literary salon of **Georgia Douglas Johnson**, including such notables as **Countee Cullen**, **Jessie Redmon Fauset**, **Langston Hughes**, **Alain Locke**, **May Miller**, **Jean Toomer**, and **Willis Richardson**. In this stimulating and supportive environment, Bonner wrote two essays that aptly conveyed the spirit of the renaissance: In her autobiographical essay "On Being Young—a Woman—and Colored" (1925), she said, "You decide that something is wrong with a world that stifles and chokes; that cuts off and stunts; hedging in, pressing down on eyes, ears and throat. Somehow all wrong." Her militant essay "The Young Blood Hungers" (1928) warned of the dangers of continued racism.

In addition, Bonner wrote three plays: *The Pot Maker: A Play to Be Read* (1927), which indicts infidelity; *The Purple Flower* (1928), which provocatively suggests a revolt against racism; and *Exit, an Illusion: A One-Act Play* (1929), which probes multiracial ancestry. As the title of her first play suggests, she intended these plays to be read, and none were produced during her lifetime. In all of the plays, moral dilemmas challenge her characters.

Bonner also wrote numerous short stories, most of which were published in **Crisis** or in **Opportunity**, including "The Hands" (1925), "The Prison-Bound" (1926), "Drab Rambles" (1927), "Nothing New" (1928), "The Triple Triad on Black Notes" (1933), "Tin Can" (1934), "A Sealed Pod" (1936), "The Hongry Fire" (1939), "The Makin's" (1939), "The Whipping" (1939), and "Patch Quilt" (1940). "Tin Can" (the plot of which may have inspired **Richard Wright**'s *Native Son*) and several other stories won first- and second-place literary prizes from *Crisis* and from *Opportunity*. Through her stories, Bonner addressed issues of poverty, interracial and intergenerational conflicts and connections, class and gender differences, harmful effects of the urban environment, and infidelity, as well as the issue of beauty, which contemporary writers are again considering seriously. Many of her stories interconnected through her fictional "Frye Street," where ethnically diverse characters interacted with one another. Her final short story, "One True Love"

(1941), eloquently echoes the theme she described in her 1925 essay, on the double jeopardy of being African American and a woman. Following its publication, she turned her attention to her own family and her teaching career. Years after Bonner's death, her daughter Marita was instrumental in having *Frye Street and Environs: The Collected Works of Marita Bonner Occomy* (1987, edited by Joyce Flynn and Joyce Occomy Stricklin) published.

REFERENCES: *EA-99. NYPL-AADR.* Brown-Guillory, Elizabeth, in *BWA:AHE.* Dillon, Kim Jenice, in *OCAAL.*

Bontemps, Arna Wendell
(10/13/1902–6/4/1973)
Poems, novels, short stories, children's literature, anthologies, criticism, nonfiction—history, biography

Arna Bontemps was born in Louisiana, the eldest of two children of Paul Bismark Bontemps (a Roman Catholic brick mason) and Maria Carolina Pembroke Bontemps (a Methodist former schoolteacher), both of Creole descent. Maria encouraged her son (and his younger sister, Ruby Sarah) to love reading books, but Paul had little interest in—and little use for—literature of any kind. Paul could see no reason why his son would need literature while laying bricks, as he intended for Arna to do.

Paul Bontemps was a stern, strong-willed man, and when two drunk white men threatened him just for being black in their presence, he decided to move his family away from the South. When Arna was three, he and his family settled into a big home in a mostly white neighborhood in Los Angeles, California. Pretty soon, Arna's grandmother (his mother's mother), his grandmother's brother Uncle Buddy, and other family members had moved to L.A., too. When Arna was just a dozen years old, his much-beloved mother died, and he moved in with his grandparents, developing a close relationship with his Uncle Buddy, a tall-tale-telling, hard-drinking charmer. Uncle Buddy encouraged Arna to write, and he told Arna delightful preacher-and-ghost stories and slave-and-master stories in his rich, native Creole dialect.

During their time in California, Paul Bontemps had converted to the Seventh-Day Adventist faith, and pretty soon, he decided he didn't want his son to come under Uncle Buddy's influence any more. Before Arna reached his fifteenth birthday, he was

Arna Wendell Bontemps was writer-in-residence at Fisk University, 1973 (UPI/Corbis-Bettmann)

shipped off to a Seventh-Day Adventist boarding school, the San Fernando Academy. The school was mostly white, and before Arna left, Paul admonished him, "Now don't go up there acting colored." Instantly, Arna realized the appalling racial self-hatred embedded in that remark. When he later reflected on it, he challenged the very idea: "How dare anyone, parent, schoolteacher, or merely literary critic, tell me not to act *colored?*" Three school years later (in 1920, when Arna was 17), he graduated from the academy. From there, he went to the Seventh-Day Adventist's Pacific Union College, in Angwin, California, where he earned his B.A. (1923).

After graduating from college, Bontemps got a job working nights in a Los Angeles post office while taking a series of postgraduate courses at the University of California at Los Angeles. When he wasn't working or going to school, he was feverishly reading novels, biographies, dramas, poems, and anything else of interest from his local library. At work, he often discussed his readings with his coworker, **Wallace Thurman**. Soon, he was also writing poems of his own, sending them to various magazines, in hopes of having one of them published—to no avail. After noticing that **Jessie Redmon Fauset**, the editor of *Crisis* magazine, was interested in publishing the works of young African-American writers, Bontemps sent her "Hope," one of his poems rejected by other publishers.

Bontemps's hope was realized when his poem was printed in the August 1924 issue of the magazine. He quit his job at the post office and headed for Harlem to catch the blossoming of the **Harlem Renaissance**. To support himself there, he got a job teaching at the Seventh-Day Adventist Harlem Academy, where he was eventually made principal. In addition, he sought to deepen his own knowledge, taking courses at Columbia University, New York University, and the City College of New York.

On August 26, 1926, Bontemps married Alberta Johnson (a former student), who became his lifelong partner. In 1927, the couple had the first of their six children: Joan Marie Bontemps (Williams), followed by Paul Bismark Bontemps (II), Poppy Alberta Bontemps (Booker), Camille Ruby Bontemps (Graves), Constance Rebecca Bontemps (Thomas), and Arna Alexander Bontemps. This stable family man still managed to make time for his literary pursuits, however. As he said to a reporter for the *Nashville Tennessean* (February 18, 1951, quoted in *BH2C,* p. 81), "I've done some of my best books at home with the children playing . . . all around me. I just pull up the card table, close the door (if that's possible) and go to work." It also helped that he started work at 5:00 A.M. and he could compose his works directly on the typewriter (working on a card table in the living room), often completing his works in just one or two drafts. Bontemps also constantly took notes. His eldest son (Paul) later recalled, "I thought this was the normal way that people lived, with a note pad beside the bed. In the morning there'd be scribbles all over it" (quoted in *BH2C,* p. 81).

Soon after Bontemps had moved to New York, he met **Countee Cullen**. Cullen told him of the frequent meetings of writers at the 135th Street Branch of the New York Public Library and invited him to a gathering of writers at the home (and literary salon) of **Regina Anderson** and Ethel Ray Nance. There, he met numerous fellow writers of the renaissance, such as his editor Jessie Redmon Fauset and the foster father of many literary careers, **Alain Locke**.

Probably the most important contact Bontemps made, however, was with the honoree of the gathering, **Langston Hughes**, who became his lifelong literary soulmate and dear friend. Even when they lived in separate cities, the twosome maintained close ties, making frequent personal visits and exchanging about 2,500 letters until Hughes died (in 1967). According to Hughes biographer **Arnold Rampersad**, the two had "virtually a marriage of minds, that would last without the slightest friction" (quoted in *BH2C,* from Rampersad's *The Life of Langston Hughes*). Through their correspondence, they often proposed joint projects, shared project ideas and publishing tips, and encouraged one another in each of their solitary literary pursuits. In Bontemps's letters to Hughes, he frequently used the Creole dialect he had learned from his parents. (Their correspondence may be found in *Arna Bontemps–Langston Hughes Letters, 1925–1967* [1980], edited by Charles H. Nichols [New York: Dodd, Mead].)

By mid-1931, Bontemps's first novel, *God Sends Sunday,* was published. Bontemps's literary pursuits had always been a source of friction between him and his Seventh-Day Adventist supervisors at the Harlem Academy. At the end of the school year in 1931, when the Adventists closed the academy in Harlem, they sent Bontemps to the Adventists' Oakwood Junior College in Huntsville, Alabama, far removed from the literary circles of Harlem. Some sources have claimed that Bontemps was sent away from New York against his will, but Bontemps's autobiographical sketch at Fisk University suggests that he was not unwilling to go. With the onset of the Great Depression, many artists and writers of the Harlem Renaissance were having to seek jobs elsewhere, so Bontemps was ready to leave Harlem when he did.

At Oakwood, Bontemps was both a librarian and an English instructor. Although he didn't enjoy Oakwood or Alabama, he was highly productive during his stay there, churning out quite a few publications. He also had a chance to visit Fisk University in Nashville, Tennessee, where he discovered a treasure trove of **slave narratives** that had been virtually ignored until then. When his pal Langston Hughes visited him at Oakwood, the school's administrators admonished Bontemps against contact with Hughes. They further balked at his receiving so many books and spending so much time writing. Bontemps was a believer but not a fundamentalist fanatic, and when the school administrators ordered him to stop writing novels, to stop teaching students about them, and to burn all of his books that were not of a religious nature, Bontemps decided he should resign, effective at the end of the school year in May of 1934. Bontemps moved his wife and children to Los Angeles to live with his father and stepmother in their home. During the 1934–1935 school year, Bontemps studied dialects, analyzed children's books, and conducted other research in a local library; he also lectured to adults and held children's story hours there. During the summer of 1935, while he and his family were cooped up in his father's house, Bontemps wrote *Black Thunder,* which was to become his most celebrated novel.

As soon as a publisher gave Bontemps an advance on royalties for the novel, he moved his family to Chicago. There, he found work as a principal and teacher at the Seventh-Day Adventists' Shiloh Academy on the impoverished South Side of Chicago. He also found another blossoming bevy of talented African-American writers, such as **Margaret Walker** and fellow Seventh-Day Adventist **Richard Wright**. The critical acclaim given to Bontemps's *Black Thunder* (1936) won him entry into this literary circle, and Wright and Bontemps developed a mutual respect for one another's work. Bontemps also found a new locale for his program of self-education (the Hall Branch of the Chicago Public Library), and he embarked on a program of formal education, as well. In 1936, he enrolled at the University of Chicago, taking postgraduate courses in library science and in English.

Bontemps soon won a Rosenwald Foundation grant to write his third novel, *Sad-Faced Boy* (1937), and he used some of that money to travel to the Caribbean to conduct research for his fourth novel, *Drums at Dusk* (1939). In 1938, Bontemps left the Shiloh Academy to take a position as editorial supervisor and technical assistant (in charge of African-American students) to the Illinois state director of the Federal Writers' Project (FWP) in the Works Progress Administration (WPA). Richard Wright and other Chicago writers were also working for the FWP.

The same year that Bontemps started working for the FWP, **James Weldon Johnson** died, leaving vacant his position as professor of creative writing at Fisk University in Nashville, Tennessee. Soon after, the head librarian position there also became available. The Fisk administrators offered Bontemps these posts, but Bontemps felt he lacked the formal training needed to fill these positions. By 1943, Bontemps had used two additional Rosenwald fellowships to complete his master's degree in library science at the Graduate Library School, University of Chicago, writing his thesis on "the Negro in Illinois." The year he earned his degree, Bontemps felt ready to accept the position at Fisk.

As Fisk's head librarian, he established the James Weldon Johnson collection, as well as collections for the papers of his old Harlem Renaissance pals, Langston Hughes, Countee Cullen, and **Jean Toomer.** After retiring from Fisk in 1966, Bontemps returned to Chicago, where he was a professor of English at the University of Illinois (Chicago Circle) until 1969. In 1969, he moved on to Yale University, where he was instrumental in developing the African-American studies program and became curator of the James Weldon Johnson Memorial Collection in Yale's Beinecke Library. (Bontemps's own extensive correspondence with Langston Hughes is also housed there.) From 1970 until his death (1973), he returned to Fisk as writer-in-residence.

Bontemps wrote or edited more than 30 books, covering almost every literary genre: poems, plays, anthologies (of poems and of folklore), literary criticism, children's stories, novels, and nonfiction histories and biographies. Throughout his works, he reflects the nobility of the African-American cultural heritage, while realistically depicting the struggles African Americans have faced—and mixing in generous doses of humor. He also managed to use authentic dialect in his works without sounding stereotypical or being incomprehensible to those who spoke other forms of American English.

Starting with "Hope," Bontemps's earliest poems began appearing in *Crisis* (published by the National Association for the Advancement of Colored People) and *Opportunity* (published by the National Urban League) magazines from 1924 through 1931. In the mid-1920s, two of his poems ("Golgotha Is a Mountain" and "The Return") won *Opportunity* magazine's Alexander Pushkin prizes, and two ("A Black Man Talks of Reaping" and "Nocturne at Bethesda") won first honors from *Crisis*. Many of his poems were collected in his volume *Personals* (1936; 3rd ed., 1973). Although Bontemps's poems are entirely modern in their compactness, they clearly reflect his deep-seated Christian education and point of view. Critics often refer to his work as intellectually challenging yet graceful, meditative, and serene.

During this early period, Bontemps also wrote short stories, including his *Opportunity* prize–winning "A Summer Tragedy" (1932) about the hardships of sharecropping in the South. This and a dozen or so more stories were collected decades later in his *The Old South: A Summer Tragedy and Other Stories of the Thirties* (1973).

Bontemps's very first novel (*Chariot in the Cloud,* written in 1929), set in southern California and focusing on the main character's psychological growth, was never published. The first of his novels to be published, *God Sends Sunday* (1931), was probably inspired by Bontemps's observations of his Uncle Buddy, as it depicts high living in St. Louis during the 1890s. In it, Little Augie, a fun-loving African-American jockey, manages horses better than he manages people. Bontemps and Countee Cullen later (in 1937) adapted the novel to the stage, and the retitled *St. Louis Woman* enjoyed success as a musical comedy on Broadway in 1946. In 1952, Metro-Goldwyn-Mayer bought the movie rights to the play. Despite its popularity and acclaim, many critics found fault with it; among others, **W. E. B. Du Bois** chided Bontemps for highlighting various less-than-morally-upright aspects of the African-American experience.

Two of Bontemps's novels focused on slave revolts. When Bontemps was younger, he had been taught a narrow view of slavery, typical of his day, and he had long wondered why none of the slaves had ever revolted. When he was older, and he heard of slave revolts in Haiti and in the antebellum South, he decided to ensure that other young African Americans wouldn't suffer in ignorance as he had. His novel *Black Thunder: Gabriel's Revolt, Virginia 1800* (1936) tells the story of Gabriel Prosser and the slave rebellion he attempted about two centuries ago. Bontemps revealed how bad weather and deceit foiled Prosser's efforts. Although the novel won no prizes, it was widely acclaimed; critic **Sterling Brown** praised it as "one of the six best African-American novels ever written." Bontemps's novel *Drums at Dusk* (1939) describes an eighteenth-century (1794) slave revolt on the island of Haiti.

Haiti was also the locale for the first book Bontemps wrote for children: *Popo and Fifina: Children of Haiti* (1932). He wrote this book (in collaboration with Langston Hughes) while teaching at Oakwood, when his own children were very young. The success of that book led him to continue, and he ended up writing a total of 16 books for children and youths, including such fictional works as *You Can't Pet a Possum* (1934), about an eight-year-old farm boy and his old yellow hound dog; *Sad-Faced Boy* (1937), about three country boys in Harlem; *We Have Tomorrow* (1945), about the extraordinary achievements of a dozen ordinary African-American youths; and *Lonesome Boy* (1955), about a trumpet-playing youth. With Jack Conroy (a thorough researcher whom he knew from his early days in Chicago), he also wrote a few tall tales: *The Fast Sooner Hound* (1942); *Slappy Hooper, the Wonderful Sign Painter* (1946); and *Sam Patch, the High, Wide and Handsome Jumper* (1951). Bontemps also edited at least one poem anthology for youths: *Golden Slippers, an Anthology of Negro Poetry for Young Readers* (1941); one source suggests that his was the first such anthology for young people, and another source mentions that he edited another poetry volume for youths in 1968.

On his own, Bontemps also wrote quite a few nonfiction books intended for children and youths, including his Jane Addams Children's Book Award–winning *The Story of the Negro* (1948), which traced African roots back to ancient times, beginning with Egyptian civilizations. He wrote *Chariot in the Sky: A Story of the Jubilee Singers* (1951) while at Fisk University, enjoying their soulful songs. He also wrote biographies such as *Story of George Washington Carver* (1954); *Frederick Douglass: Slave, Fighter, Freeman* (1959; a brief biography, written for young readers); *Free at Last: The Life of Frederick Douglass* (1971; a full-length biography, written for youths and adults), and *Young Booker: The Story of Booker T. Washington's Early Days* (1972).

Bontemps also published his historical work for adults, *One Hundred Years of Negro Freedom* (1961), which chronicles the period of Reconstruction immediately after the Civil War, highlighting the key roles played by **Frederick Douglass**, W. E. B. Du Bois, **Booker T. Washington**, and others. With Jack Conroy, Bontemps wrote *They Seek a City* (1945; revised as *Anyplace but Here,* 1966), which more narrowly focused on the great migration from the deep South to the North following Reconstruction. This work drew heavily on the research materials Bontemps and Conroy had gathered while working for the FWP in Chicago. While Bontemps was still in Alabama, he ghostwrote *Father of the Blues: An Autobiography of W. C. Handy* (1941), and he wrote *W. C. Handy's Compositions.*

In addition to his own writing, Bontemps enjoyed collecting and highlighting the outstanding works of fellow writers. With Langston Hughes, he edited the anthologies *The Poetry of the Negro 1746–1949* (1949), *The Book of Negro Folklore* (1958), *American Negro Poetry* (1963), and *I Too Sing America* (1964). After his coeditor died (in 1967), Bontemps continued to compile memorable anthologies: *Hold Fast to Dreams: Poems Old and New* (1969), including poems written by both African-American and European-American writers; *Great Slave Narratives* (1969); and *Harlem Renaissance Remembered: Essays with a Memoir* (1972; reprinted 1984). Each of his anthologies has been touted as offering highly readable yet thorough and scholarly explanations of literary and historical traditions linking the various works.

In addition to the Rosenwald fellowships and the prizes he was awarded for individual works, Bontemps earned Guggenheim fellowships (1949, 1954) for creative writing and honorary degrees from Morgan State University (1969) and Berea College (1973). In addition, his birthplace and early childhood home in Alexandria, Louisiana, is now the Arna Bontemps African American Museum and Cultural Center (dedicated 12/12/1992) and was registered as the Arna Wendell Bontemps House on the National Register of Historic Places (9/13/1993).

REFERENCES: *AA:PoP. AAW:AAPP. BAL-1-P. BDAA. BWA. EA-99. EB-BH-CD. EBLG. G-97. NAAAL. OC20LE. WDAA.* Andrews, William L., in *WB-99.* Bader, Barbara, in *CBC.* James, Charles L., in *OCAAL.* Smith, Jessie Carney, in *BH2C.*

Bourne, St. Claire (Cecil) (2/16/1943–)
Documentary films

Bourne's father, St. Clair Bourne, Sr., was the editor of Harlem's *Amsterdam News* and a reporter for *People's Voice,* so young St. Clair grew up appreciating the value of documenting people's lives and events. The son, however, preferred to report his observations through film, rather than the printed word. Among other projects, Bourne's documentary films have included *Something to Build On* (1971); *Let the Church Say Amen!* (1973); *The Black and the Green* (1982, commissioned by the British Broadcasting Corporation); *In Motion: Amiri Baraka* (1982); *Langston Hughes: Keeper of the Dream* (1987); *Making "Do the Right Thing"* (1989); and participation in a Public Broadcasting System *American Masters* show, "Paul Robeson: Here I Stand." He has also directed other films, including a documentary executive produced and narrated by actor Wesley Snipes, *John Henrik Clarke: A Great and Mighty Walk* (1997).

REFERENCES: *EA-99.*

Boyd, Melba (Joyce) (4/2/1950–)
Poems, essays, biographies

Boyd's poems have been published in various periodicals (e.g., ***Black Scholar*** and *First World* [see ***Negro Digest***]) and anthologies. They have also appeared in her collections *Cat Eyes and Dead Wood* (1978) and two books published in both German and English: *thirteen frozen flamingoes* (1988) and *Song for Maya* (1989). In addition, she published *Discarded Legacy: Politics and Poetics in the Life of Frances E. W. Harper* (1994) and has been the assistant editor for the periodical *Broadside*.

REFERENCES: Bloom, Karen R., in *OCAAL*.

Bradley, David (Henry), Jr. (9/7/1950–)
Novels, essays, book reviews

A native of a rural coal-mining town, Bradley has spent most of his adult life in urban Philadelphia. After graduating summa cum laude from the University of Pennsylvania (1972), Bradley was awarded a Thouron Scholarship to attend the University of London (M.A., 1974). While there, he began work on his first novel, *South Street* (1975), about the observations and experiences of an African-American poet, an outsider who gets to know the habitués of Lightin' Ed's Bar and Grill, the Elysium Hotel, and the World of Life Church in an African-American neighborhood of Philadelphia. *South Street* was praised by critics for its characterizations. Bradley clearly relishes involving his readers in the lives of his characters: "When you sit down at your typewriter, you're having a good time. I can make you spend hours finding out about somebody that you would not invite to your dining table" (Blake and Millner, quoted in *NAAAL*, p. 2535).

By 1977, after teaching English elsewhere, Bradley joined the faculty at Temple University as a professor of English and creative writing, where he remained until 1996. While teaching, Bradley wrote his critically acclaimed PEN/Faulkner Award–winning second novel, *The Chaneysville Incident* (1981, Book of the Month Club alternate selection). The novel centers on a fictional history professor and the revelations he discovers while trying to understand the suicide of his biological father. In truth, much of the information on which Bradley based his novel was uncovered by his mother, Philadelphia historian Harriet M. Jackson Bradley. Among the true incidents on which the story is based is one in which fugitive slaves in danger of reenslavement chose instead to commit suicide. In addition to his novels, Bradley has written numerous essays, interviews, and book reviews (e.g., in *New York Times Book Review* and *Washington Post Book World*); and his writings have been anthologized in works such as **Terry McMillan**'s *Breaking Ice* and Gates and McKay's *Norton Anthology of African American Literature*.

REFERENCES: *EA-99. NAAAL*. Ensslen, Klaus, in *OCAAL*.

Braithwaite, William Stanley Beaumont (12/6/1878–6/8/1962)
Poems, criticism, anthologies; editor, publisher

William, the son of mixed-race parents, spent his first 12 years in a prosperous, well-cultured home. That changed when his father died, and William had to stop his formal education to help support his family. Fortunately, in one of his jobs, he set type for some lyric poetry by the British Romantics—and fell madly in love with lyric poetry. Soon, he started writing poems, using traditional lyrical forms.

By 1903, his verse and his literary criticism were being published in various prestigious periodicals. His criticism spotlighted the poetry of both European Americans and African Americans. In 1904 and 1908, he published two collections of his own poems: *Lyrics of Life and Love* and *The House of Falling Leaves, with Other Poems,* respectively. In 1912, Braithwaite launched his *Poetry Journal*—which folded soon after. Undaunted, his next venture succeeded: His esteemed *Anthology of Magazine Verse and Yearbook of American Poetry* was published annually from 1913 until 1929. These anthologies included a wide assortment of poems highlighting themes of eternal truths and spiritual beauty. Notably absent were didactic, polemical, or narrowly political poems. He complemented the poems with his critical literary analyses and sensitive reviews.

Braithwaite preferred relatively traditional lyrical poetry and was initially wary of dialect poetry and other unconventional poetic forms. Perhaps because of his own abbreviated formal education, he worried that nontraditional forms would perpetuate stereotypes that African Americans were uneducated, uncultured, or unsophisticated in their grasp or expression of poetry. He also avoided segregating talented African-American poets from other fine literary artists in his anthologies and carefully included poets of other races.

Braithwaite was not entirely averse to novel poetic forms or themes, however, as he praised such dialect poets as **Paul Laurence Dunbar**, and he favorably reviewed many poems expressing the distinctive African-American experience. He introduced many African-American poets to a wider readership than they might otherwise have enjoyed. Similarly, he gradually introduced readers to various innovative poetic forms while maintaining his fondest love for lyrical poetry. For his contributions to African-American literature, in 1918 he won the NAACP's prestigious Spingarn Medal.

Braithwaite continued to contribute to American literature over the next three decades. For six years (1921–1927), he was editor of a publishing company he founded. His own published works included at least two novels and a short-story collection. During the Great Depression, however, he, his wife, and their seven children struggled financially. From 1935 to 1945, he taught creative literature in Atlanta and served on the editorial board of *Phylon*. In addition, he continued to write for periodicals and wrote his autobiography (1941), his last collection of his own poetry (1948), and his biographical study of the Brontës (1950), and he edited his last poetry anthology (1959).

REFERENCES: *BANP. BWA. EBLG. OC20LE. NAAAL. TtW.* Schulze, Robin G., in *OCAAL.*

Brandon, Barbara (11/27/1958–)
Comic strip, beauty and fashion articles

When Barbara was about ten years old, her father, Brumsic Brandon, Jr., started publishing his comic strip, "Luther," in African-American newspapers across the country. His Luther was a city kid, like Barbara and her two older siblings. After Barbara Brandon studied illustration at Syracuse University, she created her "Where I'm Coming From" strip, featuring the perspectives and commentaries of a diverse set of nine young African-American women. At first, her strip was commissioned for *Elan,* a lifestyle magazine, but before it was published, the magazine folded. Although *Essence* didn't want Brandon's strip, it did hire her to write beauty and fashion articles. In the late 1980s, the *Detroit Free Press* decided to seek some African-American–oriented comic strips and asked Barbara's dad (who had stopped drawing "Luther" in the mid-1980s) whether he happened to know of any talented cartoonists. Guess what he answered. In 1990, the United Press Syndicate decided to

pick up Barbara Brandon's all-woman strip, thereby making her the first African-American woman to have her cartoons syndicated nationally in mainstream, white-owned newspapers.

In 1993, fans of Cheryl, Nicole, Lekesia, Sonya, and Brandon's other five talking heads got a treat with the publication of the book *Where I'm Coming From,* with a foreword by **Ruby Dee** and **Ossie Davis**. Brandon introduced a little girl, Brianna, to the crew in the anthology *33 Things Every Girl Should Know* (Tonya Bolden, Ed.).

—*Tonya Bolden*

REFERENCES: *33T. BAAW.* Thompson, Kathleen, in *BWA:AHE.*

Brawley, Benjamin (4/22/1882–2/1/1939)
Essays, textbooks, literary criticism, literary history, social history, biography

Among his works of scholarship are *The Negro in Literature and Art in the United States* (1918, with many subsequent editions), *A Social History of the American Negro* (1921), *New Survey of English Literature* (1925), *Early Negro American Writers* (1935), *Paul Laurence Dunbar: Poet of His People* (1936), *The Negro Genius* (1937, short biographies of African-American artists and writers), and *Negro Builders and Heroes* (1937, biographies). A prolific writer, Brawley also contributed extensively to the leading journals of his time. Although he was often critical of—and criticized by—writers of the **Harlem Renaissance**, his own writing skills were unimpeachable. A man of his times, his literary taste may now be viewed as bourgeois and Eurocentric.

REFERENCES: *EBLG.* Williams, Kenny Jackson, in *OCAAL.*

Braxton, Joanne M. (5/25/1950–)
Poems, criticism

Braxton's published work includes her poetry collection *Sometimes I Think of Maryland* (1977), her landmark work of feminist literary criticism *Black Women Writing Autobiography: A Tradition within a Tradition* (1989), and two edited works: *Wild Women in the Whirlwind: Afra-American Culture and the Contemporary Literary Renaissance* (1990, with Andree Nicola McLaughlin) and *The Collected Poetry of Paul Laurence Dunbar* (1993).

REFERENCES: Clark, Keith, in *OCAAL.*

Briggs, Cyril Valentine
(5/28/1888–10/18/1966)
Editorials; journal founder

An outspoken radical militant in his day, Briggs advocated armed self-defense for African Americans. When he was evicted from his post with the *Amsterdam News* (in 1919) for an editorial attacking the League of Nations, he turned his attention to the journal he had founded the previous year, the *Crusader.* Initially, Briggs aligned himself with **Marcus Garvey** but then turned against virulent anticommunist Garvey when he aligned himself with the Communist Party USA. In 1929, he went to work for the communist-aligned *Harlem Liberator,* but in 1938 his championing of black nationalism led to his being ejected from the Communist Party.

REFERENCES: *EA-99.*

Broadside Press (1965–)

Almost by accident, **Dudley Randall** founded Broadside Press. Initially, he founded it just to publish a *broadside* (publication on one [usually large] single sheet of paper) of one of his poems, to preserve his copyright for it. Since that first publication, Randall's press has published the work of more than 200 other poets, as well as more than half a dozen of his own poetry collections. In particular, at the height of the **Black Arts movement**, Broadside Press published the works of numerous important poets of that period (e.g., **Nikki Giovanni**, **Etheridge Knight**, Don Lee [**Haki Madhubuti**], **Audre Lorde**, **Sonia Sanchez**), including broadsides, chapbooks, full-length poetry collections, and even recordings of readings. He also published the works of poets from earlier literary periods, such as **Gwendolyn Brooks** and **Sterling Brown**. When Randall experienced a long-term illness, the press published very little. Briefly, the Alexander Crummell Center owned the press and published some works, but then it, too, stopped publishing. In 1985, Don and Hilda Vest took over ownership of the press and restructured it as a nonprofit press, which has been publishing new works and republishing backlist titles as "Broadside classics" ever since.

REFERENCES: Madgett, Naomi Long, in *OCAAL.*

Brooks, Gwendolyn (Elizabeth)
(6/7/1917–)
Poems, autobiographies

Poet—this one word describes every cell of Gwendolyn Brooks's being. It was always poetry—from her Chicago childhood to her 1950 Pulitzer Prize to her awakening social consciousness to her Illinois poet laureate status and through all the other honors and awards. It was always poetry—and few writers other than Brooks can speak volumes with so few words.

Born into a large and close-knit extended family, including memorable aunts and uncles whom Brooks later honored in her work, Brooks seems always to have been comfortable with herself. Her mother, Keziah Wims, met her father, David Anderson Brooks, in Topeka, Kansas, in 1914. They soon married and relocated to Chicago. Keziah returned to her family in Topeka to give birth to her first child, Gwendolyn. Keziah stayed in Topeka for several weeks before returning to her husband in Chicago with her infant daughter. Gwendolyn's only sibling, her younger brother Raymond, was born 16 months later. Brooks's mother had been a schoolteacher in Topeka, and her father, son of a runaway slave, had attended Fisk University for one year in hopes of becoming a doctor. Economic survival became more important, however, so his desires for a medical career were dashed, and he spent much of his life as a janitor. Despite financial constraints on the young family in Chicago, Brooks remembers a loving, family atmosphere throughout her childhood.

She had a more difficult time fitting in with her high school classmates, however, attending three high schools: Hyde Park, which was mostly white; Wendell Phillips, which was all black; and Englewood High School, the integrated school from which she eventually graduated in 1934. Two years later, she graduated from Wilson Junior College (1936). Even prior to her high school years, it became apparent to Brooks that she did not really fit in with her peers. She was a nonperson at Hyde Park and socially inept at Wendell Phillips. She kept her self-esteem, however, largely due to her strong family ties. Also, from early childhood, her mind had been someplace else. That place was poetry, which she had started writing at age seven. Her parents contributed to her love of language and story. As a former schoolteacher, Brooks's mother encouraged her daughter's interest, and her father often told stories and sang songs about his family's history with

Gwendolyn Brooks won the Pulitzer Prize, 1950 (Popperfoto/Archive Photos)

slavery. From her parents and her extended family, Brooks learned the honor and dignity found in living everyday life with love and integrity.

Her first published poem, "Eventide," appeared in *American Childhood Magazine* in 1930, when Brooks was 13. At 16, with her mother's help, Brooks met two prominent African-American writers, **James Weldon Johnson** and **Langston Hughes**. Although both writers read Brooks's work and told her that she had talent and should keep reading and writing poetry, only Hughes de-

veloped a long and enduring friendship with Brooks. She later wrote a poetic tribute to him, titled "Langston Hughes," published in her *Bean Eaters* collection. She also remembers him fondly and with great respect in her autobiography, *Report from Part One*. In the meantime, she contributed regularly to the *Chicago Defender,* having 75 poems published there in two years.

Brooks also pursued interests besides poetry, joining the Youth Council of the National Association for the Advancement of Colored People

(NAACP) in 1938. There she met her future husband and fellow writer, Henry L. Blakey III, whom she married in 1939. Marriage took Brooks from the comfort of her parents' home and into a kitchenette apartment, the setting for her first volume of poetry, *A Street in Bronzeville,* published in 1945. She gave birth to their first child, Henry, Jr., in 1940, and to their daughter, Nora, in 1951. Throughout this time, Brooks kept writing her poetry. She and her husband participated in a poetry workshop given by Inez Cunningham Stark, a reader for *Poetry* magazine. There, Stark and other workshop participants encouraged Brooks.

In 1943, Brooks received the Midwestern Writers' Conference Poetry Award, which proved to be the first of many for Brooks: In 1945, she was named one of *Mademoiselle* magazine's "Ten Young Women of the Year"; in 1946, she won the American Academy of Arts and Letters Award; in 1947 and 1948, she won Guggenheim fellowships; and in 1949, she won the Eunice Tietjens Memorial Award. Brooks published *Annie Allen* in 1949 and with it won the Pulitzer Prize for literature, becoming the first African American to do so. The awards and honors continued for years: She was invited to read at a Library of Congress poetry festival in 1962, at the request of then President Kennedy; named poet laureate of Illinois; nominated for the National Book Award in 1969; appointed poetry adviser to the Library of Congress in 1985; honored with a Lifetime Achievement Award in 1989 by the National Endowment for the Arts; named the 1994 Jefferson Lecturer by the National Endowment for the Humanities; and awarded the National Medal of Arts in 1995 and the Order of Lincoln Medallion given by the Lincoln Academy of Illinois in 1997. She has also received numerous honorary degrees and taught poetry at various colleges and universities in the United States. (EDITOR'S NOTE: She was also invited to join the American Academy of Arts and Letters and was the first African-American woman chosen to serve as poetry consultant to the Library of Congress.)

Brooks has also sponsored writing contests for students and has given scholarships and travel awards to Africa in an attempt to encourage young African-American writers. Throughout all this, Brooks has been a prolific writer. Her first published collection of poetry, *A Street in Bronzeville* (1945), garnered immediate national acclaim. The collection chronicles the life of poor urban blacks in a segregated setting reminiscent of Chicago's South Side—essentially a series of portraits of people who fled rural poverty and hopelessness only to find themselves trapped in an urban ghetto. Realistic yet compassionate, the poems unflinchingly examine the failed dreams and small hopes of the maids, preachers, gamblers, prostitutes, and others who live in "Bronzeville."

After Brooks received the Pulitzer for *Annie Allen,* her major works included *Maud Martha* (novel, 1953); *Bronzeville Boys and Girls* (1956); *The Bean Eaters* (1960); *Selected Poems* (1963); *In the Mecca* (1968); *Riot* (1969); *Family Pictures* (1970); *Aloneness* (1971); *A Report from Part One* (autobiography, 1972); *The Tiger Who Wore Gloves; or What You Are You Are* (1974); *Beckonings* (1975); *A Primer for Blacks* (1980); and *To Disembark* (1981). Brooks's work has always honored the everyday existence of African Americans. She did, however, change her style as the social situation in the United States changed. (EDITOR'S NOTE: Brooks also wrote two manuals for young readers: *Young Poet's Primer* and *Very Young Poets.* The second of her autobiographies, *Report from Part Two,* was published in 1996 by **Third World Press**.)

One catalyst for this change was her attendance at a writer's conference at Fisk University in 1967. There she met young black writers who were a part of the **Black Arts movement**, who wrote with overt anger and sometimes used obscenities. This event gave Brooks pause and called into question her own sensibilities of her blackness. After this event, Brooks started selling her work to smaller African-American publishing houses. Some have accused Brooks of becoming too much like the newer poets—too polemical, leaving behind her subtle and unique use of language and form as a way of seeing the world. Yet still others sense in Brooks's more recent work a renewed vision of what it means to be African American, a continuance of her abiding respect and awe for the wonders of everyday existence and of her unique way of finding universal truths within the specific lives and events of ordinary people.

—Janet Hoover, with assistance from Lisa Bahlinger

REFERENCES: *BLC-1. BW:SSCA,* pp. 64–65. *EBLG. NAAAL.* Lee, A. Robert, "Poetry of Gwendolyn Brooks," in *MAAL.* McKay, Nellie (1991), "Gwendolyn Brooks," *Modern American Women Writers* (New York: Scribner's). McLendon, Jacquelyn, in *AAW.* Melhem, D. H. (1987), *Gwendolyn Brooks: Poetry and the Heroic Voice* (Lexington: University Press of Kentucky).

Podolsky, Marjorie, "Maud Martha," in *MAAL*. Williams, Kenny Jackson, "Brooks, Gwendolyn," and "*Street in Bronzeville*," in *OCAAL*. http://www.black-collegian.com, "Gwendolyn Brooks." http://www.greatwomen.org, "Gwendolyn Brooks." http://www.sj-r.com/news/97/11/13, "Brooks brings 'free-verse kind of time' to UIS." (See also *BDAA*.)

Brown, Cecil (7/3/1943–)

Novels, short stories, scripts

Brown's novels include his landmark *The Life and Loves of Mr. Jiveass Nigger* (1969), noted for its insighful satire, and his *Days without Weather* (1982). His other works include his autobiography *Coming Up Down Home* (1993) and various articles, short stories, screenplays, and stage plays.

REFERENCES: Carson, Warren J., in *OCAAL*.

Brown, "Charlotte Eugenia" (née Lottie Hawkins) (6/11/1883–1/11/1961)

Nonfiction—manners; fiction

History books point to Brown for her work as the almost single-handed creator of a school, much like her contemporary Mary McLeod Bethune. She raised funds and invested her bountiful energy and hard work in building the Palmer Memorial Institute in Sedalia, North Carolina. Her institute was considered one of the best African-American schools in the South in the mid–twentieth century. During her day, however, across the nation, Mrs. Brown was known as the African-American Miss Manners because of her book *The Correct Thing to Do—to Say—to Wear* (1941).

Much of Brown's advice may seem quaint to us today (e.g., her "Earmarks of a Lady" chapter and her observation, "All food should be put into the mouth with the right hand"). Many of her suggestions seem very contemporary, however. For instance, she even recommends ways to save wear and tear on Mother Earth: "*Be saving*. Don't burn lights unnecessarily. Be sure that the hot water faucet is turned off. Don't leave the hose on too long in the back yard. Don't drive the automobile around the corner when you can walk. Don't turn the radio on in the morning and let it run all day. Don't leave the outside doors wide open when the furnace is going full blast." She also urges her readers to be thoughtful and considerate, such as by suggesting, "Don't save your table manners until company comes. You and your family are just as good and deserve just as much consideration as any of your friends or acquaintances." She even offers some good, sound, practical advice for young women: "[Do] not seek dark and secluded places in which to socialize."

Actually, Brown's book on the "social graces" was not her first venture into writing. She had published many articles and short stories. Her only short story published in book form, *"Mammy": An Appeal to the Heart of the South* (1919), was intended to shame former slaveholders who had allowed their former slaves to become totally destitute in old age.

—*Tonya Bolden*

REFERENCES: *AAWW. BAAW.* Thompson, Kathleen, in *BWA:AHE*. Vick, Marsha C., in *BH2C*.

Brown, Claude (2/23/1937–)

Essays, autobiography

Brown is best known for his best-selling autobiography *Manchild in the Promised Land* (1965), about his physically and psychologically brutal childhood and adolescence, including his own violent criminal activities in a youth gang. Brown also wrote *The Children of Ham* (1976), about the harsh realities and struggles of 13 African-American youths in a Harlem ghetto. Brown's essays and other articles have appeared in periodicals such as the *New York Times Magazine*. Despite his troubled youth, his adulthood included warm companionship and academic success: Brown married Helen Jones September 9, 1961, and four years later, he earned a bachelor's degree from Howard University (1965).

REFERENCES: *EA-99. EBLG. G-97.* Dudley, David L., in *OCAAL*.

Brown, Elaine (3/2/ or 3/3/1943–)

Memoir, songs

Brown's memoir of her childhood and of her experiences within the Black Panther Party (BPP), *A Taste of Power: A Black Woman's Story* (1992), offers a refreshingly candid account of the BPP as viewed from within. In addition, Brown wrote and recorded songs on two albums: *Seize the Time* (1969) and *Until We're Free* (1973).

REFERENCES: *EBLG. TAWH.* Brown, Angela D., in *BWA:AHE*.

Brown, Hallie Quinn

(3/10/1845–9/16/1949)

Biography, nonfiction—rhetoric, public speaking

Brown's birth year is in question—listed as 1845 in *EA-99;* c. 1845 in *BWA:AHE;* c. 1847 in *OCAAL;* and 1850 in *EB-98, EB-BH-CD, EWHA,* and *WDAW.* Because it was common prior to the mid–twentieth century to alter women's birth years to make them appear younger, the earliest year seems the most probable one. Brown's parents, Frances Scroggins Brown and Thomas Arthur Brown, had both been slaves and had used their resources to aid fugitive slaves on the Underground Railroad. The Browns taught Hallie and her five siblings the value of working with others to effect social change. A lifelong social activist, Brown worked ardently for temperance and suffrage, participated in church organizations, lectured throughout the United States and abroad, and led women's clubs (e.g., president of the National Association of Colored Women, 1920–1924).

The Browns also taught their children the importance of education, moving their family from Canada to Wilberforce, Ohio, so that Hallie and her brother could attend Wilberforce University (B.A., 1873). Brown was subsequently awarded an honorary master's degree (1890, Chautauqua Lecture School) and an honorary doctorate (1936, Wilberforce University). After graduating, Brown dedicated herself to the education of others, teaching elementary school, working as a dean for Allen University in South Carolina, administering an adult night school, working as dean of women ("lady principal") at the Tuskegee Institute, and then professing elocution at Wilberforce University. Wilberforce honored her in 1948 with the dedication of its Hallie Q. Brown Library, which houses her unpublished papers. Her numerous published works include *Bits and Odds: A Choice Selection of Recitations* (1880), *First Lessons in Public Speaking* (1920), *The Beautiful: A Story of Slavery* (1924), *Tales My Father Told* (1925), *Our Women: Past, Present, and Future* (1925), *Homespun Heroines and Other Women of Distinction* (1926), and *Ten Pictures of Pioneers of Wilberforce* (1937). Brown's *Homespun Heroines,* which included 60 illustrated biographies of important African-American women born between about 1750 and 1875, is still used as an important reference work.

REFERENCES: *EB-BH-CD. EWHA. PBW,* p. *xx. WDAW.* Fisher, Vivian Njeri, in *BWA:AHE.*

Moody, Joycelyn K., in *OCAAL.* Robinson, Alonford James, Jr., in *EA-99.*

Brown, Linda Beatrice (a.k.a. Linda Brown Bragg) (3/14/1939–)

Poems, novels

Brown's poems have been published in various literary journals and anthologies and have been collected in her *A Love Song to Black Men* (1974). Her novels include *Rainbow Roun Mah Shoulder* (1984, reissued in 1989) and *Crossing over Jordan* (1994).

REFERENCES: Brookhart, Mary, in *BWA:AHE.* Browne, Phiefer L., in *OCAAL.*

Brown, Sterling Allen

(5/1/1901–1/13?/1989)

Poems, folklore, criticism

Born a slave, Sterling Nelson Brown had long been deeply embedded in the well-educated middle class of Washington, D.C., by the time he and his wife had their son Sterling Allen Brown. Sterling Nelson Brown was a prominent, often-published professor of religion at Howard University, as well as a pastor; he counted **Frederick Douglass** and **Paul Laurence Dunbar** among his personal friends; and his wife had been the valedictorian of her graduating class at Fisk University. Young Sterling Allen Brown profited from this intellectually stimulating environment, attending public schools and graduating with honors (1918) from the prestigious Paul Laurence Dunbar High School, where he was taught by **Jessie Redmon Fauset** and **Angelina Weld Grimké,** among others.

His talents earned him a scholarship to Williams College in Williamstown, Massachusetts, where he was elected to the distinguished honor society Phi Beta Kappa and earned his baccalaureate with honors (1922). At Williams, he had been the only student awarded "Final Honors" in English, and he won the Graves Prize for his essay "The Comic Spirit in Shakespeare and Molière." After graduating, Brown went on to earn a master's degree in literature at Harvard University (1923). During his studies, he had been enthralled with the poetry of Carl Sandburg, Edwin Arlington Robinson, and Robert Frost, European-American poets who highlighted the voices and experiences of everyday folks in their own communities.

With his master's degree in hand, he took a series of teaching positions at various historically black colleges and universities in the South, including Virginia Seminary and College; Lincoln University in Jefferson City, Missouri (1926–1928); and Fisk University (1928–1929). He later recalled that this period marked his most important education, as he embarked on a self-directed program of studying the speech patterns, folklore, and folk wisdom of African Americans in the communities surrounding each of the colleges where he worked. He gathered sketches and anecdotes from the habitués of barbershops and **folktales** and other stories from farmers way out in the country. He collected work songs, **spirituals,** ballads, and blues songs in the street, in the farmhouse, and in juke joints. All the while, he absorbed the dialect and manner of speaking of the folks around him. While in Lynchburg, Brown also made another life-changing discovery: He wedded Daisy Turnbull, to whom he stayed married for more than 50 years.

In 1929, Brown started another long-term relationship: He began teaching English at the first university he had ever known—Howard University, where he was to stay for another 40 years. In 1931 and 1932, Brown returned to Harvard to work on his doctorate, but even with this credential, most of his English Department colleagues at Howard sneered at his appreciation for the folkways and speech patterns common among the everyday African Americans whom Brown had come to respect and admire. To this day, heated controversy continues to ignite discussions among African-American scholars regarding whether to celebrate or to scorn traditional African-American speech patterns and folk traditions within the context of American literature, scholarship, and education.

The English professors of Howard particularly disdained Brown's poetry, in which he occasionally dabbled in such traditional poetry forms as sonnets, villanelles, ballads, and children's songs, but more often used poetry forms reminiscent of work songs, spirituals, jazz riffs, blues rhythms and refrains, and other expressions rooted in the African-American folk and **oral tradition**s. For Brown, the language he was celebrating showed "tonic shrewdness, the ability to take it, and the double-edged humor built up of irony and shrewd observation" (quoted in *OCAAL*). He noted, "I was first attracted by certain qualities that I thought the speech of the people had, and I wanted to get for my own writing a flavor, a color, a pungency of speech. Then later, I came to something more important—I wanted to get an understanding of people, to acquire an accuracy in the portrayal of their lives" (quoted in *OCAAL*). Thus, his poetic themes addressed the everyday life experiences of ordinary African Americans and often incorporated African-American folklore (e.g., tall tales and folk sermons).

Despite his poems' poor reception at Howard, they were published in **Opportunity** and other literary publications and were widely anthologized (e.g., in **Countee Cullen**'s *Caroling Dusk,* 1927; and in **James Weldon Johnson**'s *The Book of American Negro Poetry,* 1931, which Brown helped to revise). In 1932, Brown's first collection of verse, *Southern Road,* was published. The critics and the general public praised it highly for its lyrical celebration of African-American speech patterns, ordinary African-American protagonists, and traditional African-American songs and verses. Noted critic **Alain Locke** extolled the virtues of Brown's freshly original compositions as echoing the lyricality of authentic folk ballads. Nonetheless, Brown's colleagues at Howard still frowned on his poems for their obvious ties to and roots in everyday African-American speech patterns, themes, and musical traditions.

As it turns out, during the Great Depression, publishers were unwilling to take a chance on a poetry book that departed too much from the literary traditions valued by the Howard English professors, so Brown couldn't find anyone to publish his second poetry collection, *No Hiding Place.* Hence, Brown turned away from poetry. His next collection didn't appear for another four decades: *The Last Ride of Wild Bill and Eleven Narratives,* published in 1975—the same year that *Southern Road* was reprinted. The poems from *No Hiding Place* weren't published until **Michael S. Harper** edited *The Collected Poems of Sterling A. Brown* in 1980; the literary community responded to those long-ago-rejected, long-neglected poems with the Lenore Marshall Prize for the outstanding volume of poetry published in the United States in 1980. Among the poems of Brown's that continue to be widely anthologized are his "Strong Men," "Slim in Hell," and "Southern Road."

Although he turned away from poetry, Brown did not stop writing. Instead, he turned toward writing literary criticism and historical analyses of African-American culture. During the late 1930s, Brown served as the national editor of Negro Affairs for the Works Progress Administration's Federal Writers' Project (the WPA's FWP). The job was a perfect match for Brown, as it provided federal government funding for him and other writers to collect authentic American folklore. In connection with that effort, Brown published two books in an Atheneum series called the "Bronze Booklets" (originally published in 1937, then reissued in the 1938 series): *The Negro in American Fiction* and *Negro Poetry and Drama,* short surveys of the existing works in those fields.

In 1939, Brown worked on the staff of a landmark study funded by the Carnegie Foundation and directed by Swedish sociologist and economist Gunnar Myrdal. Whereas the thrust of Myrdal's work was the detrimental effects of racism on African Americans, Brown focused on the ways in which African Americans have risen to the challenge of an often-hostile environment, using folk humor and other defense strategies.

In 1941, Brown collaborated with Arthur Davis and Ulysses Lee to edit the noted anthology *The Negro Caravan* (1941; reprinted 1969), which offered a wide array of African-American literature, much of which the editors obtained from unpublished manuscripts. Their text was groundbreaking at the time, a key reference text for decades after, and a valuable resource to this day.

From the 1940s on, Brown lectured at various colleges and universities (e.g., Atlanta University and New York University), in addition to his post at Howard. After three semesters of teaching at prestigious Vassar College, in 1945, he was offered a full-time position there. He turned it down, however, preferring to stay at Howard, where he had his professional and familial home. Also, although he felt less than welcome among his fellow English professors and suffered from periodic bouts of deep depression (sometimes requiring hospitalization), he was greatly loved and admired by his students there. Among those students were **Amiri Baraka**, **Stokely Carmichael**, **Ossie Davis**, and **Toni Morrison**. Brown felt that his greatest legacy was the effect he had had on his students. In 1969, he retired from Howard, and through his many celebrated students, he enjoyed a revival of interest in his poetry.

In 1971, he was awarded an honorary doctorate from Howard, and before he died, he had been awarded additional honorary doctorates from Williams College, Vassar College, Harvard University, and Brown University. He had also been named poet laureate of the District of Columbia

and elected to the Academy of American Poets. In 1979, Brown was invited to contribute a memoir of his experiences to the collection *Chant of Saints: A Gathering of Afro-American Literature, Art, and Scholarship.*

REFERENCES: *1TESK. AAW:AAPP. BAL-1-P. BWA. EB-BH-CD. EBLG. G-97. MWEL. NAAAL. OC20LE. WDAA.* Robinson, Lisa Clayton, in *EA-99.* Tidwell, John Edgar, in *OCAAL.*

Brown, William Wells (?/1814?–11/6/1884)
Novels, plays, autobiography, biography, travel, nonfiction—history

William failed in his first attempt to escape slavery, but his second attempt—aided by a Quaker couple, Mr. and Mrs. Wells Brown—succeeded. In appreciation of their help, he added their names to his own first name. From 1834 to 1843, he stewarded ships on the Great Lakes and was a conductor on the Underground Railroad. Meanwhile, he taught himself reading, writing, and other subjects, and he gained increasing confidence and skill as an abolitionist public speaker. In 1843, the Western New York Anti-Slavery Society (and other abolitionist societies) hired him to lecture around the country.

In 1847, his autobiography, *Narrative of William W. Brown, a Fugitive Slave, Written by Himself,* was published. In it, he modestly described his experiences, revealing himself to have been a slave trickster, who used realistic—if less than exemplary—means of survival. Although his narrative frequently flouted nineteenth-century morality, the book underwent four U.S. editions and five British editions before 1850.

In 1848, Brown published his poetry collection, *The Anti-Slavery Harp.* He spent 1849 through 1854 in Europe, delivering more than a thousand lectures to foster British support for abolition. His lectures led to his book *Three Years in Europe* (1852), credited as being the first published travel book by an African American. While in England, he also wrote and published *Clotel; or, the President's Daughter: A Narrative of Slave Life in the United States* (1853), believed to be the first novel published by an African American. As a contribution to African-American literature, its historical importance continues to outweigh its literary and aesthetic merit.

While Brown was abroad, several of his friends raised the funds to buy his emancipation, so he returned to the United States a fully free man. In 1856, he wrote the first dramatic work by an African American: *Experience; or, How to Give a Northern Man a Backbone,* which has since been lost. That year, he also wrote his second play, *The Escape; or, A Leap for Freedom,* about two slaves who secretly marry. This, his only published play, was the first play written by an African American to be published (in 1858).

He also wrote more than a dozen nonfiction books and pamphlets, including historical and biographical works such as *The Negro in the American Rebellion: His Heroism and Fidelity* (1867, the first military history of African Americans). Before the end of the Civil War, Brown had become a physician and continued his medical practice until he died.

REFERENCES: *1TESK. AA:PoP. BAL-1-P. BF:2000. BWA. E-98. EB-98. EBLG. G-97. MWEL. NAAAL.* Andrews, William L., in *OCAAL.*

Brownies' Book (1920–1921)

A magazine published especially for African-American children ages 6–16 years, the *Brownies' Book* was published by **W. E. B. Du Bois** and Augustus Granville Dill from January 1920 through December 1921. The magazine functioned as an independent counterpart to *Crisis,* the magazine of the National Association for the Advancement of Colored People (NAACP). The publication of the *Brownies' Book* is significant because it marks the beginning of African-American children's literature. With only one exception, black artists made all of the drawings of black children illustrating the magazine.

—*Lisa Bahlinger*

REFERENCES: Johnson-Feelings, Dianne, in *OCAAL.*

Bryan, Ashley F. (7/13/1923–)
Folklore, children's literature; illustrator

When Bryan was still in kindergarten, he created his first book—illustrating, binding, and distributing it himself. It was an alphabet book, and as he later recalled, "Number books, word books, sentence books followed" (*CBC,* p. 100). His large family (two parents, five siblings, and three cousins being raised by his parents) gave his self-published books "rave reviews." "Encouraged, I published books as gifts to family and friends on all occasions. By the time I was in third or fourth grade, I had

published hundreds of books." After earning degrees from Cooper Union Art School and Columbia University, Bryan has put together quite a few more books and taught painting and drawing at Dartmouth College, from which he is now retired.

Of the numerous children's picture books Bryan has illustrated and authored, he particularly revels in **folktales** and African-American **spirituals.** His first book of spirituals, which he considers "a gift from the musical genius of the Black people" (p. 100, *CBC*), was *Walk Together Children* (1974). *What a Morning: The Christmas Story in Black Spirituals* (1987/1996) celebrates the Christmas story through vivid paintings and five traditional spirituals. Bryan's *Climbing Jacob's Ladder: Heroes of the Bible in African American Spirituals* (1991) tells the stories of Noah, Abraham, Jacob, Moses, Joshua, David, Ezekiel, Daniel, and Jonah through illustrations, along with the lyrics and musical notation of spirituals for each biblical hero. In addition, he published *All Night, All Day: A Child's First Book of African-American Spirituals* (1991), which illustrates and provides the lyrics and musical notation for 20 spirituals. Bryan later observed, "With the birds trilling, my mother singing, and the general music-making that went on at home, it is only natural that I would one day do books of songs that had special meaning to me, the black American spirituals" (*BBG,* p. 16).

Other children's books by Bryan include various folktales, which he researches extensively, adapts to interest his readers, drafts as poems to be read aloud, and then illustrates vividly and appealingly. Bryan revealed his motivation for writing these books: "Stories are always a treasury of the history of people. African tales are a beautiful means of linking the living Africa, past and present, to our own present. What the African sees in his world, the questions he asks, and the things that he feels and imagines have all found their way into the stories" (*MAI-1,* p. 18). His first such book, *The Ox of the Wonderful Horns and Other African Folktales* (1971/1993), features a few **trickster tales.** His other books include *The Adventures of Aku* (1976), a folktale explaining how the trickster Ananse was instrumental in why cats and dogs fight like—well, cats and dogs; *The Dancing Granny* (1977), about a grandmother who deters the trickster Ananse from eating everything in her garden; his Coretta Scott King Award–winning *Beat the Story Drum, Pum-Pum* (1980; paperback 1987), with Nigerian folktales explaining how enmity emerged between other animals (e.g., bush cow versus elephant; frog versus snake); *Cat's Purr* (1985), about how the cat got its purr; *Turtle Knows Your Name* (1989), a West Indian folktale; *The Story of Lightning and Thunder* (1993, adapter/illustrator), Bryan's adaptation of a Nigerian folktale on the origins of rain, thunder, and lightning; *Lion and the Ostrich Chicks: And Other African Folk Tales* (1996), with four Coretta Scott King Honor–winning folktales, including the title tale about how a mongoose cleverly rescues six ostrich chicks from a lion; and *Ashley Bryan's African Tales, Uh-Huh* (1998), which includes 14 of the tales previously published in other volumes.

In addition to his spiritual books and his folktale adaptations, he has illustrated several poetry books for children, including *Greet the Dawn* (1978), with poems by **Paul Laurence Dunbar**; *Sing to the Sun: Poems and Pictures* (1992, author/illustrator), with about two dozen of Bryan's own illustrated poems on the ups and downs of life, families, and nature; *The Sun Is So Quiet: Poems* (1996), with 13 poems by **Nikki Giovanni**; *Ashley Bryan's ABC of African American Poetry* (1997, compiler/illustrator), with 25 poems by noted African Americans, selected, excerpted, and illustrated by Bryan; *Carol of the Brown King: Nativity Poems* (1998), by **Langston Hughes**; and *Jump Back Honey: Poems* (1999), with more poems by Dunbar. Bryan also illustrated *Fablieux* (1964); *Christmas Gif': An Anthology of Christmas Poems, Songs, and Stories Written by and about African Americans* (1963/1993, compiled by **Charlemae Hill Rollins**); *What a Wonderful World* (1995, song text by George David Weiss and Bob Thiele, popularized by Louis Armstrong); *Story of the Three Kingdoms* (1997, text by **Walter Dean Myers**); *The House with No Door: African Riddle-Poems* (1998, text by Brian Swann); *Why Leopard Has Spots: Dan Stories from Liberia* (1999, tales adapted by Won-Ldy Paye and Margaret H. Lippert); and numerous other books.

Bryan also practices reading poems aloud and lectures on African-American poetry; his readings may be heard on a pair of audiocassettes, *Ashley Bryan: Poems and Folktales* (1994). In addition, he creates puppets from driftwood and other objects he finds on his daily walks on the beach, and he paints, creates stained-glass panels from glass he finds on the beach, exhibits his works in various one-man shows, and plays musical instruments.

REFERENCES: *BBG. EBLG. MAI-1.* Ross, Ramon Royal, in *OCAAL.* S. H. H., in *CBC.*

Bullins, Ed (né Edward Artie)
(7/2/1935–)
Plays, novel, poems; magazine founder, editor

Bertha Marie Queen and Edward Bullins probably wanted their son to steer clear of gangs and to stay in school, but in the tough Philadelphia neighborhood where Ed grew up, it seemed a lot easier to join a gang than to join the chess club or the nerd squad at school. By the time Ed dropped out of school (at age 17), he had already been stabbed—and nearly died as a result—and he knew the ins and outs of marketing bootleg whiskey.

He escaped gang life by joining the U.S. Navy in 1952, and he spent the next three years going wherever the navy told him to go. When he was discharged in 1955, he returned to Philadelphia for a while, but by 1958 he felt the need to escape the violence again, so he fled to Los Angeles—the big city farthest from Philadelphia, as far as he knew. There, he earned his high school diploma and attended classes at Los Angeles City College. In college, he started reading extensively and began writing short stories and poems; he even founded a campus literary magazine, the *Citadel*. After a while, he decided to move on, and after roaming the country, in 1964, he settled in the San Francisco Bay area. There, he enrolled in the creative writing program at San Francisco State College and started writing plays. (It wasn't until 1994 that Bullins earned his M.F.A. from San Francisco State University, after having earned his B.A. from Antioch University, in Yellow Springs, Ohio, in 1989.)

Because Bullins's plays drew on the street violence he experienced in his youth, he found it difficult to find a theater company to produce his plays. Rather than quit writing, he started looking for ways to produce his work himself. With several others (including playwright **Amiri Baraka**), he cofounded the Black Arts/West in the Fillmore District of San Francisco, a militant African-American cultural and political organization that produced plays in coffeehouses, bars, lofts, and almost anywhere else people could gather in small groups. In August 1965, three of Bullins's one-act plays were produced: *How Do You Do?* (his first play); *Dialect Determinism, or The Rally;* and *Clara's Ole Man.*

From the Black Arts, Bullins (and Baraka) moved across the bay to Oakland. There, Bullins, Baraka, **Sonia Sanchez**, Black Panther Party (BPP) cofounders Huey Newton, Bobby Seale, and **Eldridge Cleaver**, and several other African-American theater artists and political activists joined forces to create Black House. For a short time, Bullins was the cultural director of Black House and the minister of culture for the BPP. After a while, however, the views of Bullins and the artistically oriented participants conflicted with those of the political activists. Although both groups valued theater as a means of expression and communication and shared similar political outlooks, they differed sharply as to the mission of theater: Should it be focused on art, from a given political perspective, or should it be focused on politics, with theater as one of the means for achieving political ends? In 1967, these divergent views led to a break, and Bullins accepted an invitation to move to Harlem, in New York City, the heart and soul of American theater.

The invitation had come from Robert Macbeth, a director who had read and liked Bullins's play *Goin' a Buffalo*. Macbeth and others were just establishing the New Lafayette Theatre in Harlem. By the time Bullins reached Harlem, he had also written and produced *In the Wine Time* (his first full-length play). At the Lafayette, Bullins started out as playwright-in-residence and eventually became the theater's associate director. After the Lafayette folded (in 1972), Bullins became playwright-in-residence at the American Place Theatre, also in New York City, in 1973. Meanwhile, he also edited *Black Theatre* magazine (1969–1974). In 1974, Bullins became the producing director of Surviving Theatre, and during most of the 1970s, he was on the staff of the Public Theatre's New York Shakespeare Festival.

In 1978, Bullins's son, Edward Jr., died tragically; soon after, Bullins returned to California, where he founded the Bullins Memorial Theatre and cofounded (later, with fellow playwright Jonal Woodward) the Bullins/Woodward Theater Workshop in San Francisco. Under Bullins's stewardship, in addition to offering theater workshops and playwriting seminars, the Theater Workshop staged plays. During this time, Bullins also started teaching at various colleges and universities, including Columbia University, Dartmouth College, and Northeastern University in Boston (where he has taught theater since 1995).

Even Bullins's earliest plays, produced at the New Lafayette, had earned critical praise (e.g., winning the Vernon Rice Drama Desk Award), although commercial success was slower in coming. Bullins was relentless in churning out dozens of plays throughout the 1960s and 1970s. By 1977,

Bullins had written more than 50 plays, more than 40 of which have been produced professionally. Between 1968 and 1980, 25 of his plays were produced in New York theaters, and 3 of those won Obie Awards: *In New England Winter* (1969), *The Fabulous Miss Marie* (1971), and *The Taking of Miss Janie* (1975; it also won the New York Drama Critics Circle Award as best U.S. play of 1974–1975). Although Bullins slowed down considerably after 1980, he has still continued to write and produce plays.

With his great number also comes great range, from gritty realism to surrealistic fantasy; from a focus on the distinctive urban black experience to a focus on brutal interactions with white society; from tragedy to humor-inflected drama. Some of his dramas also play with "the fourth wall," inviting audience members to interact verbally with the characters onstage.

In the Wine Time (produced in 1968) was the first of a projected cycle (series) of 20 plays Bullins decided to write about African Americans in the contemporary urban United States, titled his "Twentieth-Century Cycle." Many of these plays feature two young African-American half-brothers: Cliff Dawson and Steve Benson, both of whom (like Bullins) had served in the navy. Family relationships, friendships, and violence figure prominently in many of these dramas. Among the plays in this cycle are *The Corner* (produced 1968), *In New England Winter* (1969), *The Duplex: A Love Fable in Four Movements* (produced 1970, published 1971), *The Fabulous Miss Marie* (1971), *Home Boy* (1976), and *Daddy* (1977), as well as *Boy x Man* (1995). Bullins's other plays (not included in his cycle of plays) include *The Gentleman Caller* (1969), *The Pig Pen* (1970), and *Salaam, Huey Newton, Salaam* (1991). In addition, Bullins has written two children's plays (*I Am Lucy Terry*, 1976; and *The Mystery of Phillis Wheatley*, 1976); the books for two musicals (*Sepia Star* and *Storyville*, both 1977, and both in collaboration with European-American composer Mildred Kayden), and two antidrug plays (*A Teacup Full of Roses*, 1989; *Dr. Geechee and the Blood Junkies*, 1991). In addition, quite a few of his works have been collected in *New—Lost Plays by Ed Bullins* (1994).

Although Bullins is best known for his plays, he has also written poetry (e.g., *To Raise the Dead and Foretell the Future*, 1971), short stories (e.g., *The Hungered Ones, Early Writings*, 1971), and a novel (*The Reluctant Rapist*, 1973, about Steve Benson, from his cycle of plays). In addition, he has edited anthologies, including *Five Plays: New Plays from the Black Theatre* (1969); *The New Lafayette Theatre Presents, The Theme Is Blackness* (1973); and *Four Dynamite Plays* (1971). Occasionally, he has used the pseudonym Kingsley B. Bass, Jr.

In addition to his three Obies, his two New York Drama Critics Circle Awards (1975, 1977), and his Vernon Rice Drama Desk Award, Bullins has been awarded four Rockefeller grants, two Guggenheim fellowships, an honorary doctorate from Columbia College in Chicago, a National Endowment for the Arts grant, and a Creative Artists Public Service Program award.

REFERENCES: *AA:PoP. EB-BH-CD. EBLG. NAAAL. OC20LE. WB-99. WDAA.* Fay, Robert, in *EA-99.* Grant, Nathan L., in *OCAAL.* Marranca, Bonnie, in *G-97.*

Bunche, Ralph (Johnson)
(8/7/1904–12/9/1971)
Memoir; politics

Bunche, a delegate and then an undersecretary to the United Nations, helped write the United Nations Charter. Prior to that, in 1937, he had published *A World View of Race,* an anthropological view of the European colonization of Africa. He had also collaborated with sociologist Gunnar Myrdal in producing *An American Dilemma: The Negro Problem and Modern Democracy* (1938), considered a monumental landmark study of race relations in the United States. In addition, some of his insights and ideas may be seen in *Ralph J. Bunche: Selected Speeches and Writings* (1993/1995).

Bunche was the first African American to win the Nobel Peace Prize (in 1950), he won the NAACP's Spingarn Medal (in 1950), and he was awarded the presidential Medal of Freedom (in 1963), the highest honor given to civilians in the United States.

REFERENCES: *BDAA. EB-BH-CD. EBLG. G-97. PGAA.* Balfour, Lawrie, in *EA-99.* Warren, Nagueyalti, in *BH2C.*

Burroughs, Margaret (née) Taylor
(11/1/1917–)
Poems, short stories, children's books

A graduate of the Art Institute of Chicago (B.F.A., 1944; M.F.A., 1948), Burroughs has created prints, paintings, and sculpture, specializing in

portrayals of African-American heroes such as Crispus Attucks, **Harriet Tubman**, **Sojourner Truth**, and **Frederick Douglass**. Burroughs's interest in history goes far beyond art, however. In 1961, she and her second husband, Charles Burroughs, opened part of their Chicago-area home as the Ebony Museum of Negro History. She raised funds for their museum and continued to expand it, renaming it the DuSable Museum of African-American History in 1968. (Its namesake, black fur trader Jean Baptiste Pointe DuSable, was among the first to settle the territory encompassing present-day Chicago.) As you might expect from an artist, the museum hosts a nice collection of African-American art (especially from the 1940s to the 1960s) and both fine and folk art from Africa (which Burroughs gathered on trips to the Caribbean and to more than a dozen African nations). Nonetheless, the name accurately reflects its emphasis on African-American history, particularly focusing on the Midwest, especially Chicago.

Burroughs's writings also reflect her passionate interest in history. These writings include children's books, short stories, and poems. Her most celebrated piece is the title poem of her first collection of verse, *What Shall I Tell My Children Who Are Black?* (1968). Her other works include *Jasper, the Drummin' Boy* (1947); *Did You Feed My Cow? Rhymes and Games from City Streets and Country Lanes* (1955); *Whip Me Whop Me Pudding and Other Stories of Riley Rabbit and His Fabulous Friends* (1966); her anthology *For Malcolm: Poems on the Life and the Death of Malcolm X* (1967, edited with **Dudley Randall**); and her second poetry collection, *Africa, My Africa* (1970). Her literary legacy may be best expressed in her own words, from her poem "What Shall I Tell My Children Who Are Black?": "I must find the truth of heritage for myself / And pass it on to them. . . . For it is the truth that will make us free!"

—*Tonya Bolden*

REFERENCES: *BAAW.*

Burroughs, Nannie Helen
(5/2/1879–5/20/1961)
Columns, play, nonfiction—organizational management

In addition to writing provocative columns for several African-American newspapers (e.g., the *Christian Banner*), Burroughs produced a wide variety of other publications. These include her guidebook *What to Do and How to Do It* (1907); her play *Slabtown District Convention: A Comedy in One Act* (1908), and several religious works, including *Grow: A Handy Guide for Progressive Church Women* and *Making Your Community Christian*. She also chaired a commission responsible for a major study, *Negro Housing: Report of the Committee on Negro Housing* (1932).

REFERENCES: Higginbotham, Evelyn Brooks, in *BWA:AHE*. Jordan, Casper Le Roy, in *BH2C*. Robinson, Alonford James, Jr., in *EA-99*.

Butler, Octavia E. (Estelle) (6/22/1947–)
Novels, short stories

Laurice Butler, a shoeshining man, died before he saw his daughter Octavia take her first steps. With the help of her own mother, Octavia M. Guy Butler gave little Octavia a strict Baptist upbringing. The three females lived in a racially integrated neighborhood in Pasadena, California, so Octavia grew up believing that African Americans, Asian Americans, Hispanic Americans, and European Americans could all share a culturally diverse community. Even the boarders her mother and grandmother hosted in their home reflected the cultural diversity of their community. Only when she accompanied her mother to work (as a maid in other people's homes) did Octavia realize the harsh realities of racial discrimination and segregation.

Tall for her age, Octavia was shy and withdrawn, preferring the company of books and her own thoughts to that of other children. Although she was dyslexic, she read avidly. She later recalled, "When I discovered that my first-grade teacher expected me to be content with Dick and Jane, I asked my mother if I could have a library card. From the day she took me to get one, I was a regular at the fairy tale shelves. I also explored, read anything else that looked interesting, got hooked on horse stories for a while, then discovered science fiction" (quoted in *BWA:AHE*). Among her favorites were Harlan Ellison, Isaac Asimov, Robert Heinlein, Ursula Le Guin (e.g., her *Dispossessed*), and Frank Herbert (especially the first book in his Dune series). She also read the numerous science fiction magazines that were widely available during the era of the Cold War's race into space, and she enjoyed reading comic books (*Superman* and various superheroes in Marvel comics) and *Mad* magazine.

By age ten, Octavia had started writing her own stories, chiefly the same kinds of stories she was reading. When her reading shifted to science fiction, so did her writing. With the help and encouragement of her junior high science teacher, Butler began submitting her stories to some science fiction magazines, although they didn't end up in print.

After graduating from John Muir High School (1965) and from Pasadena City College (associate's degree, 1968), Butler started at California State University at Los Angeles (CSULA). She didn't stay long, though, because CSULA offered next to nothing in the way of creative writing courses. In 1969 and 1970, she took some writing classes at the University of California at Los Angeles and at the Writers' Guild of America West through its "Open Door" program, where she met her mentor, Harlan Ellison. In addition to giving her encouragement and candid, constructive suggestions for improving her work, he urged her to attend the six-week Clarion Science Fiction Writers' Workshop, held in Clarion, Pennsylvania, in the summer of 1970. The workshop's instructors were well-known writers and editors of science fiction, who offered practical advice and realistic tips for writing in this genre. She often cites this training as being the most valuable she has received for perfecting her writing craft.

At first, Butler patterned her own stories after the white male–dominated, technologically oriented science fiction stories that she was reading. After a while, however, it started to bother her that there were almost no people of color, no independent-minded leading women characters, and very few richly developed characters of any kind in the books she read. Soon, her own stories reflected the life experiences and the people she knew, and she offered fully developed characterizations in her work. Her novels and short stories have since become widely acclaimed—both by science fiction readers and by literary critics, and she has become one of the few women to achieve success in this white male–dominated genre.

Her road to success was not without hardship, however, as she had to overcome not only publishers' resistance to science fiction works centered on the experiences of African-American women, but also her family's pressures to get a job that would pay her a steady income and her own feelings of discouragement during financially difficult times. Nonetheless, she persevered, and her perseverance has since paid off.

By the mid-1990s, Butler had authored numerous novels and short stories and had won the two most prestigious awards given to works of science fiction: the Nebula and the Hugo. Her earliest works center around the ominous character Doro, a 4,000-year-old immortal Nubian who dominates his descendants through his supernatural psychic powers and his superhuman physical strength. Doro can invade other people's bodies whenever he wishes to, terrorizing his numerous descendants. Although he prefers the bodies of black males, he may choose to inhabit anyone, of any race or gender. He can even transcend time, inhabiting persons from various time periods. All Doro's descendants form a pattern of mentally linked individuals, so Butler calls this series her "patternist" novels. Other characters in these novels include several strong, self-confident females, such as Doro's daughter Mary, a highly gifted telepath; Alanna, an African-Asian feral child who has to survive in a hostile environment of warring aliens; and Anyanwu, an African woman with great healing powers. Through her patternist novels, Butler addresses race, gender, and class differences, as well as ethical, social, and political issues. Butler's patternist novels include *Patternmaster* (1976), *Mind of My Mind* (1977), *Survivor* (1978), *Wild Seed* (1980), and *Clay's Ark* (1984). Because these novels take place in the distant past as well as in the future, they may be more accurately called "speculative fiction" than "science fiction."

While working on the patternist series, Butler wrote *Kindred* (1979), which she originally intended to be part of the series, but which turned out to be too closely tied to reality to fit into the series. In the novel, Dana Franklin, an African-American woman living in a 1970s Los Angeles suburb, is celebrating her twenty-sixth birthday with her European-American husband when she is suddenly and unwillingly transported back in time. Much to her chagrin, she finds herself a slave on a Maryland plantation before the Civil War. It appears that she was summoned back by Rufus, an obnoxious, self-centered, hot-tempered white slaveowner who is her grandmother Hagar's father. Apparently, he called her back because his life was in danger, and he needed her help to save him. Because he is Dana's biological ancestor, he has the power to force her to do so. As the novel unfolds, and Dana moves back and forth across space and time, she discovers the true physical and psychological brutality of slavery, even losing an arm in the process.

After the patternist series, Butler started a new set of novels, her Xenogenesis trilogy. Following a nuclear holocaust, the surviving humans are rescued by a species of extraterrestrials, who crossbreed with the humans. The alien species appreciates the intelligence of humans but dislikes the human tendency to form hierarchies, class divisions, stereotypes, and other categories that lead to conflict and prejudice. These novels are *Dawn: Xenogenesis* (1987), *Adulthood Rites: Xenogenesis* (1988), and *Imago: Xenogenesis* (1989). Since writing this trilogy, Butler also wrote *The Parable of the Sower* (1993), about a twenty-first-century African-American teenage woman prophet in the midst of a spiritually decadent society where drug addiction has caused economic disintegration.

In addition to her novels, Butler has written numerous short stories, including her 1984 Hugo Award–winning "Speech Sounds" (1983), about an anarchistic world in which communications deficits are the norm. Butler's "Bloodchild" (1984), about a society in which aliens exploit human males for purposes of reproduction, won a 1985 Hugo Award, a 1984 Nebula Award, and the Locus Award. Both short stories were printed in *Isaac Asimov's Science Fiction Magazine*. In all her works, she addresses themes of enslavement, race relations, and class and gender differences. Although she carefully researches the most recent scientific advances in the social, biological, and physical sciences, her fiction highlights human thoughts and feelings and human (or human-alien) interactions, rather than technological or scientific wizardry. When not fully engaged in her writing, she volunteers her time helping others learn how to read. In 1995, Butler was awarded a MacArthur Foundation fellowship, often referred to as a "genius award."

REFERENCES: *AA:PoP. EA-99. EB-BH-CD. EBLG. NAAAL. OC20LE. WDAA.* Foster, Frances Smith, *"Kindred,"* in *OCAAL.* Govan, Sandra Y., in *OCWW.* Mickle, Mildred R., "Butler, Octavia E.," in *OCAAL.* Stevenson, Rosemary, in *BWA:AHE.*

Rowell, where it stayed nine years before moving to the University of Virginia in 1986 in a printing collaboration with Johns Hopkins University Press.

C *Callaloo* has dedicated whole issues to such authors as Chinua Achebe, Aimé Césaire, **Toni Morrison**, **Alice Walker**, and **Ernest Gaines**, as well as major younger writers such as **Yusef Komunyakaa**. The journal is contemporary with current trends in poetry, fiction, and drama.

—*Lisa Bahlinger*

REFERENCES: Keene, John R., in *OCAAL*.

Cabrera, Lydia
(5/20/1900–9/19/1991)
Short stories, nonfiction—cultural anthropology

Of mixed heritage herself (African American and Cuban American), Cabrera sought to enhance her readers' appreciation of Afro-Cuban culture. Among her many published works are two short-story collections offering insight into Afro-Cuban culture: *Cuentos Negros de Cuba* (1940) and *Por Qué: Cuentos Negros de Cuba* (1948). In addition, she wrote *El Monte: Notes on the Religion, the Magic, the Superstitions and the Folklore of Creole Negroes and the Cuban People* (1954, her study of Afro-Cuban folk culture); *Refranes de Negros Viejos* (1955, compiling Afro-Cuban proverbs); *Anagó: Vocabulario Lucumí* (1957, detailing the Yoruban vocabulary spoken in Cuba); *La Sociedad Secreta Abakuá* (1958, compiling an all-male secret society's legends and **folktales**); *Otan Iyebiye: Las Piedras Preciosas* (1970, on the ritual meanings of precious stones); and *Reglas de Congo* (1980, on Bantu rituals in Cuba). From 1970 until 1991, Cabrera published three more short-story collections and nine more anthropological investigations.

REFERENCES: Edwards, Roanne, in *EA-99*.

Callaloo (1976–)

First published in 1976 at Southern University in Baton Rouge, Louisiana, *Callaloo* is an African-American and African journal of arts and letters, established to ensure a creative outlet for the black Southern writing community that emerged in the late 1960s and early 1970s. (*See also* **Tom Dent**.) *Callaloo*'s editorial vision gradually expanded to include a wider range of writing, as well as visual art from Africa and the African diaspora, including original Afro-Brazilian poetry and West Indian and African literature. In 1977, the journal moved to the University of Kentucky with editor Charles H.

Campbell, Bebe Moore (1950–)
Novels, short stories, radio plays, memoir

Campbell's published work includes her memoir, *Sweet Summer: Growing Up with and without My Dad* (1989), and her novels, *Your Blues Ain't Like Mine* (1992), *Brothers and Sisters* (1994), and *Singing in the Comeback Choir* (1998). Her commentaries can often be heard on National Public Radio and other radio and television talk shows. Her compassion and humor resonate through all her work.

REFERENCES: *EBLG*. Amazon.com, 1/2000.

Campbell, James Edwin
(9/28/1867–1/26/1896)
Poems

Campbell's dialect poems predated those of his contemporary, **Paul Laurence Dunbar**. Specifically, many of Campbell's poems were written in the Gullah language of the South Carolina sea islands. Nonetheless, like Dunbar, he also published many poems written in standard English, although his dialect poems are generally considered his better work. Campbell's poetry collections include *Driftings and Gleanings* (1887) and *Echoes from the Cabin and Elsewhere* (1895). His dialect poems may have heralded those of the **Harlem Renaissance** in their racial awareness, sense of satire, and skepticism of religion, while reflecting the lyricality of his own time in their phrasing, rhyme, and rhythm patterns.

In his brief lifetime, he supported himself by working as a teacher in African-American schools in Ohio (1884–1887) and West Virginia (1887–1891) and as a school principal in West Virginia (1891–1894). In 1891, Campbell married schoolteacher Mary Champ. He also worked as a staff writer for the *Pioneer,* an African-American newspaper (starting in 1887), and for the *Chicago Times-Herald* (starting in 1894), and he contributed poems and articles to other periodicals as well. Sadly, he contracted pneumonia while visiting his parents for Christmas in Ohio, and it killed him early the following year.

REFERENCES: *BV. EBLG. NYPL-AADR.* Sherman, Joan R., in *OCAAL.*

Carmichael, Stokely (new name: Kwame Touré) (6/29/1941–11/15/1998)
Essays, speeches

Carmichael's best-known literary achievement is probably his having been credited with popularizing the term "black power." A graduate (with honors) from Howard University (1964), Carmichael is better known for his social activism as a Freedom Rider, a Congress of Racial Equality (CORE) activist, a Student Nonviolent Coordinating Committee (SNCC) voter registrar, and a Black Panther Party (BPP) leader. In each of these pursuits, Carmichael demonstrated a mastery of rhetoric, delivering powerful speeches to large audiences. His speeches were provocative in challenging the white establishment, opposing nonviolence as a strategy for political change and integration as a political goal, fostering racial pride, and promoting political and economic independence and power. Many of these speeches were gathered in *Stokely Speaks: Black Power Back to Pan-Africanism* (1965/1971), and he and political scientist Charles V. Hamilton coauthored *Black Power* (1967), published just before he left SNCC to join the BPP.

Two years later, he left the BPP to join a pan-African movement and moved to Guinea, West Africa, with his first wife, world-renowned South African singer Miriam Makeba (married 1968–1978). In 1978, he adopted the first name of Kwame Nkrumah and the last name of Sekou Touré, African leaders whom he admired. He later married Guinean physician Marlyatou Barry, with whom he had a son, Boca Biro, and whom he later divorced (in 1992). Although Carmichael's ever-evolving message appealed to many black men and women, whom he inspired to political activism, he also offended many women with his sexist attitudes, such as his assertion that the position of women in the civil rights movement should be "prone."

REFERENCES: *EB-BH-CD. EBLG.* Balfour, Lawrie, in *EA-99.* Leak, Jeffrey B., in *OCAAL.* Nicholson, Dolores, in *BH2C.*

Carroll, Vinnette (Justine) (3/11/1922–)
Plays

In collaboration with Micki Grant (née Minnie Perkins McCutcheon), Carroll wrote two Tony Award–nominated, award-winning plays: *Don't Bother Me, I Can't Cope* (1971) and *Your Arms Too Short to Box with God* (1975), as well as *When Hell Freezes Over I'll Skate* (1979).

REFERENCES: *EBLG. TAWH.* Perkins, Kathy A., in *BWA:AHE.*

Cary, Mary Ann (née) Shadd (10/9/1823–6/5/1893)
Pamphlets, news articles; newspaper founder and publisher

The eldest of 13 children of self-employed, free blacks Harriet and Abraham Shadd, Mary Ann Shadd learned responsibility and independence early on. She also learned a fierce dedication to abolition from her parents, who provided her with a Quaker education. Her father, a subscription agent for William Lloyd Garrison's *Liberator,* had been deeply involved in the Underground Railroad, and he fervently opposed the back-to-Africa movement of the 1830s, believing that African Americans should work to abolish slavery and to establish racial justice in the United States.

In the 1840s, Shadd applied her education to teaching African-American children, at first establishing her own school in Delaware and then accepting teaching jobs, first in New York and then in Pennsylvania. Through her teaching, she fostered her pupils' independence and personal responsibility. In 1849, she wrote a pamphlet touting her belief in the importance of self-reliance, *Hints to the Colored People of North America,* and she wrote articles for **Frederick Douglass**'s *North Star.*

When the Fugitive Slave Act passed in 1850, Shadd was persuaded (by **Henry Bibb** and his wife) to join the exodus of African Americans seeking sanctuary in the abolitionist country of Canada West (as the province of Ontario was called at the time). When she (and her brother) reached the promised land in Canada West, she established a school with financial support from the American Missionary Association and several

African-American families. Soon she decided to integrate the school, and she lectured and wrote, encouraging other African Americans to flee persecution in the United States and find safety in Canada West.

Bibb, publisher of the *Voice of the Fugitive,* favored separatism and urged African Americans to return to the United States as soon as slavery was ended. He refused to publish Shadd's articles favoring integration and encouraging African Americans to consider Canada their permanent home. At the time, Bibb owned the only printing press in town. In 1852, Shadd decided to publish her own 44-page pamphlet, *Notes on Canada West,* which included statistical data and other facts documenting the bounty of that country, including information on farming, schooling, and churches. Her pamphlet is considered the first by an African-American woman to have used a factual database as the foundation for a persuasive message.

Bibb vehemently denounced Shadd's views in his *Voice,* so the funding for Shadd's school dried up, and in 1853, she had to close it. That year, with Samuel Ringgold Ward, Shadd founded, published, edited, and contributed to the weekly newspaper the *Provincial Freeman,* thereby becoming the first African-American woman to own and operate a periodical of any kind. In her paper, she scolded Bibb for promoting charity-supported self-segregated communities of fugitive slaves and she promoted abolition, integration, and—most of all—her firm belief in the value of self-reliance.

In 1856, Shadd married Thomas F. Cary, with whom she had two children: their daughter Sarah and their son Linton. In 1858, while working hard for abolition, Mary Ann Shadd Cary attended an antislavery meeting at which John Brown described his bold plan. He and those he could convince to join him would raid the armory at Harpers Ferry, grabbing the weapons and distributing them to slaves. Brown firmly believed that once the slaves had weapons, they would then rise up en masse, throwing off their bonds and freeing themselves, their loved ones, and all others in bondage. At that meeting, Brown met two of Cary's pals: Osborne P. Anderson, whom he conscripted to accompany him, and **Martin Delany,** later known as the father of black nationalism. In 1859, Brown and Anderson executed their raid (for which Brown was later executed), and Anderson ended up being the only African American to escape capture when their plan was thwarted.

Thus, Anderson offered a distinctive eyewitness account of the historic event, detailed in *A Voice from Harpers Ferry,* which Cary edited and published in 1861.

The year of the Harpers Ferry raid, financial troubles caused Cary's paper to fold, and she returned to teaching. The following year, her husband died and she continued teaching, supporting herself and her children. In 1863, however, in the middle of the Civil War, she moved her family back to the United States. There, with the encouragement of Martin Delany, she became a recruitment officer, encouraging African Americans in Indiana to fight for the Union Army. Following the Civil War, she moved to Washington, D.C. There, she became a school principal and wrote articles for Frederick Douglass's *New National Era* and other periodicals while earning a law degree from Howard University. Although she earned the degree in 1871, Howard didn't grant her the degree for another decade, as the school officials feared negative publicity for giving a woman a degree. Needless to say, Cary became an ardent feminist and a suffragist. (She was one of just a few woman who voted in federal elections during Reconstruction, although voting didn't become legal until 1920.)

—Tonya Bolden and Shari Hatch

REFERENCES: *ANAD. BAAW.* Born, Brad S., in *OCAAL.* Calloway-Thomas, Carolyn, in *BWA:AHE.* Hudson, Peter, in *EA-99.* Shadd's papers have been collected at the Moorland-Spingarn Research Center at Howard University, as well as in the Public Archives of Canada in Ottawa, Ontario.

Cayton, Horace Roscoe, Jr.
(4/12/1903–1/22/1970)
Nonfiction—sociology

Working with collaborators, Cayton coauthored two key sociological studies of African Americans: With George S. Mitchell, he completed *Black Workers and the New Unions* (1939); and with **St. Clair Drake**, he wrote the award-winning sociological study of Chicago, *Black Metropolis* (1945). A columnist for the *Pittsburgh Courier,* Cayton was the son of publisher Horace Roscoe Cayton, Sr.

REFERENCES: Robinson, Alonford James, Jr., in *EA-99* (*see also* the excerpt, "The Black Bugs," *EA-99*).

Chapman, Tracy (3/20/1964–)
Songs

While being raised by her impoverished single mother, Chapman began singing and writing her own songs in sixth grade. Since then, her songs have included "Talkin' Bout a Revolution" and "Fast Car," and her albums have included *Crossroads* (1989), *Matters of the Heart* (1992), and *New Beginning* (1995).

REFERENCES: Tuttle, Kate, in *EA-99*.

Chase-Riboud, Barbara (née Dewayne)
(6/26/1939–)
Novels, poems

Vivian (a medical assistant) and Charles (a building contractor) Chase encouraged their only child, Barbara, to develop her talents and interests in the arts, including classical piano, dancing, drawing, sculpting, and—of course—writing poetry. At age 8, Barbara won her first prize for her artwork, and at age 15, she won a *Seventeen* magazine award and sold her prize-winning print to the Museum of Modern Art in New York. After high school, she went to the nearby Tyler Art School at Temple University (in Philadelphia, Pennsylvania), where she earned her B.F.A.(bachelor's in fine arts) in 1957. Awarded a John Hay Whitney Foundation fellowship, she spent the following school year (1957–1958) studying art in Egypt and at the American Academy in Rome. Back in the United States, she earned her M.F.A.(master's in fine arts) from Yale University (1960).

Over the next two decades, Chase exhibited her work in Europe, the Middle East, Asia, Africa, and the United States. During this time, she met and married (12/25/1961) French photojournalist Marc Riboud. Although the couple had two sons (David and Alexis), they managed to continue to travel extensively. After two decades of marriage, the couple divorced in 1981, and she later married art expert and broker, archeologist, historian, and publisher Sergio Tosi. By the mid-1990s, she and Tosi had established homes in Paris and Rome.

Chase-Riboud's artwork (drawings and sculpture) and her writings (poems and novels) both reflect the Asian, European, and African influences to which she has been exposed in her extensive travels. Through all her creative offerings, she expresses her hope for harmonious interactions among diverse races and cultures and between the sexes. Chase-Riboud's first poetry collection, *From Mem-*

phis and Peking (1974), reflected on her travels through Africa (e.g., Memphis, Egypt) and China (Peking). In the People's Republic of China, she was the first American woman to visit since the revolution of 1949. Her second poetry volume, *Portrait of a Nude Woman as Cleopatra* (1987), was inspired by a Rembrandt sketch with that title. In it, she tells Plutarch's story of Mark Antony and Cleopatra through an interwoven dialogue written in 57 sonnets.

Chase-Riboud's best-known novel is her story of the long-term relationship between Thomas Jefferson and his slave mistress Sally Hemings (a quadroon who was Jefferson's wife's half-sister). Chase-Riboud explored their relationship from various points of view and suggested its implications for gender relations, gender roles, race relations, and the role of each race in American society. As just one example, Chase-Riboud suggests that Jefferson's relationship with Hemings may have been at the root of his change in view about slavery. Although he had at first outspokenly opposed slavery, he eventually stopped opposing it, and Chase-Riboud suggests that perhaps part of his motivation was that the end of slavery would have meant that Hemings would have left Virginia, and he couldn't have borne to be parted from her.

When Chase-Riboud wrote the novel, based on the historical research of Fawn Brodie, this relationship was the subject of much controversy. Hemings's family members had long acknowledged the relationship, perhaps even before **William Wells Brown** wrote *Clotel* (1853), his novel about a relationship between Jefferson and one of his female slaves. Jefferson's white family members, however, had always repudiated the allegations of such a relationship. In the late 1990s, indisputable genetic evidence confirmed the relationship, forever putting the question to rest. Despite the controversy, *Sally Hemings* (1979) won the 1980 Janet Heidinger Kafka Prize for Fiction by an American Woman, and the book has been translated into at least eight languages.

Chase-Riboud's next novel was set at about the same time but was located in the Ottoman Empire during the late 1700s and early 1800s. In *Valide: A Novel of the Harem* (1986), Algerian pirates capture a Martinican woman and sell her to Sultan Abdulhamid I, who enslaves her in his harem. The women of the harem have little to do and lead self-indulgent lives, so they plot against one another to gain the favors of the sultan. Eventually, this woman's son becomes the sultan, so she becomes valide (queen mother), the highest position for a woman in the Ottoman Empire.

Chase-Riboud's third and fourth novels also address slavery but return to the United States as the location. Her *Echo of Lions* (1989) tells the fact-based story of Joseph Cinqué (Sengbe Pieh) and his fellow African slaves, who revolted against the crew of the slave ship *Amistad* (in 1839). Since the publication of her book, the story has been made into a movie. In her book and in the movie, the slave ship lands off the coast of Long Island, and the Africans are jailed for slaughtering most members of the slave ship's crew. Former U.S. president John Quincy Adams successfully defends the prisoners in the U.S. Supreme Court, citing the illegality of the slave trade and the absolute right of anyone to commit homicide in self-defense.

In *The President's Daughter* (1994), Chase-Riboud takes the Hemings story forward from Sally to her daughter Harriet, carrying the narrative through the Civil War and its aftermath. For her various artistic achievements, Chase-Riboud earned a National Endowment for the Humanities fellowship (1973), first prize in the New York City Subway Competition for architecture (1973), the Academy of Italy gold medal for sculpture and drawing (1978), and an honorary doctorate from her alma mater, Temple University (1981).

REFERENCES: *EBLG.* Bolden, B. J., in *BWA:AHE.* Robinson, Lisa Clayton, in *EA-99.* Stanford, Ann Folwell, in *OCWW.* Tarver, Australia, in *OCAAL.*

Chesnutt, Charles Waddell
(6/20/1858–11/15/1932)
Short stories, novels, biography, journals, essays

Charles was born with many choices not available to other African Americans of his era: Both he and his mulatto parents were free, and he was so light-skinned that he could have passed as white, although he chose not to do so. After the Civil War, Charles worked in his family's store while regularly attending school. By the time he was 14, however, Charles had to stop his formal education in order to help support the family, so he worked as a pupil-teacher at the school. At age 16, he started teaching full time, and in his late teens, he was appointed assistant principal at the school he had attended.

In 1878, Chesnutt married Susan Perry and then started a family (four children in all) soon after. When he was in his twenties, he was a promi-

nent principal with a wife and children, but he longed for a writing career. In 1879, he confided to his journal that he planned to move North to "get employment in some literary avocation, or something leading in that direction." Two years later, he confided to his journal, "Every time I read a good novel, I want to write one. It is the dream of my life—to be an author!" In the early 1880s, Chesnutt tried to work as a journalist in Washington, D.C., returned to North Carolina, then tried working in New York City, and finally moved his wife and children to Cleveland, Ohio, where he worked as a legal clerk–stenographer. He soon set up his own profitable legal stenography business while studying to pass the bar. In 1887, he was admitted to the Ohio bar and added a law practice to his stenography firm. In addition, in his spare time in the evenings, he wrote short stories.

He soon received some assurance that his efforts were worthwhile, when his story "The Goophered Grapevine" became the first short story by a black writer to be published in the highly revered *Atlantic Monthly.* Like the traditional plantation stories by white authors, Chesnutt's story centered around an ex-slave African–American storyteller, Uncle Julius McAdoo, who spun delightful antebellum recollections of Southern life. Unlike the white authors' narrators, however, Uncle McAdoo described a much less idyllic picture of the antebellum South and offered a much more realistic portrait of African-American folk culture. According to McAdoo, the slaves used trickery and deception to subvert their masters' dominance and brutality; they weren't cheerfully looking forward to complying with the kind requests of their masters.

The next year (1888), the *Atlantic Monthly* published Chesnutt's "Po' Sandy." Chesnutt continued to split his time between his literary pursuits and his legal career until the fall of 1899, when he closed his prosperous business to pursue writing as a full-time career. He felt certain that his book sales and his speaking engagements would suffice to support himself and his family, so he dedicated a few years to writing three novels. By the time he started writing his third novel, however, he realized that his particular books would not sell widely enough to sustain him and his family, so in 1902, he reopened his court-reporting business and his law practice.

Over his literary career, Chesnutt published more than 50 tales, short stories, and essays, and he wrote 4 novels and a biography. In 1899, he published his biography, *Frederick Douglass,* and 2 short-story collections. His first short-story collection, *The Conjure Woman,* illuminates the relationships between white employers (or slave owners) and black servants (or slaves), as seen through the eyes of a black man who is a servant to a white man who has moved from the North to the South. It sold so well that his publisher (Houghton Mifflin) rushed the publication (the same year) of his second short-story collection, *The Wife of His Youth and Other Stories of the Color Line.* This second collection studies color prejudice among blacks, as well as between blacks and whites, by examining the racial identity of mixed-race Americans.

Chesnutt's first novel, *The House behind the Cedars* (1900; originally called "Rena Walden"), dealt with interracial marriage and with a young girl's attempt to pass for white. Although it was generally well received, it didn't sell widely or well (although it did go to four printings rather quickly). His second novel, *The Marrow of Tradition* (1901), was based on a true incident and addressed the pervasive white supremacist activities and violence of the post–Reconstruction South. Despite the book's nationwide reviews touting it as a timely but disturbing study, the book did not sell well. Chesnutt's next literary venture was a romance novel, for which he couldn't find a publisher. His 1905 novel *The Colonel's Dream* (published by Doubleday) explored the problems of freed slaves struggling against prejudice and exploitation in a Southern town. When this novel sold poorly, too, Chesnutt lost faith in his ability to become rich and famous through his literary career, and he stopped writing novel-length fiction.

With two of his daughters in college and two younger children still at home, Chesnutt needed to realistically plan for the many demands on his financial resources. Perhaps he had also been unrealistic in his expectation that writing was likely to provide fame and fortune. For instance, he noted in his journal, "I want fame; I want money; . . . literature pays—the successful." Chesnutt also loved writing for its own sake, however: "There is a fascination about this calling that draws a scribbler irresistibly toward his room. He knows the chance of success is hardly one out of a hundred; but he is foolish enough to believe, or sanguine enough to hope, that he will be the successful one."

Although his career in writing proved less successful than he had expected, he was pleasantly surprised by the financial rewards of his legal career. Thus, contrary to his expectations, his other pursuits proved more financially rewarding than did writing. He still continued to write and speak on social and political issues of interest to him, but he wrote only a handful of short stories and an unpublished novel ("The Quarry") during the final 25 years of his life.

Although his financial rewards for writing may have fallen short of his expectations, his literary achievements were nonetheless important. For one thing, he is now widely recognized as one of the first American writers to realistically portray African-American experience. He is also generally considered the first major African-American novelist, though his short stories may have been a more valuable contribution to U.S. literature than his novels. In any case, Chesnutt was the first African-American writer to have mainstream white-controlled presses publish his candid writings about the racially oppressed lives of African Americans in the South.

Chesnutt used his fiction, rooted in African-American experience, to address social injustice, racial discrimination, and a wide array of other issues and problems in American life, particularly those among African Americans in the post–Civil War era. As he said, "The object of my writings would be not so much the elevation of the colored people as the elevation of the whites—for I consider [the unjust treatment of colored people] a barrier to the moral progress of the American people."

In 1928, the National Association for the Advancement of Colored People awarded Chesnutt its venerable Spingarn Medal for his "pioneer work as a literary artist depicting the life and struggles of Americans of Negro descent, and for his long and useful career as scholar, worker, and freeman of one of America's greatest cities." Despite poor health, he managed to publish his literary autobiographical essay, "Post-Bellum—Pre-Harlem" in 1931.

REFERENCES: *1TESK. AA:POP. BAL-1-P. BASS. BDAA. BV. BWA. E-98. EB-98. EBLG. G-95. MAAL. MWEL. NAAAL. OC20LE. SMKC.* Andrews, William L., in *OCAAL.*

Child, Lydia Maria (née Francis)
(2/11/1802–10/20/1880)
Abolitionist polemics, historical novels, biographies, history, advice book; editor, children's periodical founder and editor

Although of European-American ancestry, after marrying Boston abolitionist, attorney, and writer

David Lee Child (1794–1874) in 1828 and meeting William Lloyd Garrison in 1831, Child dedicated herself to fiercely opposing slavery, and most of her writings were in the service of abolition. She also edited the **slave narrative** of **Harriet Jacobs**, *Incidents in the Life of a Slave Girl* (1861). Her most noted work is her highly influential *An Appeal in Favor of That Class of Americans Called Africans* (1833, with her husband), which was probably the first published book denouncing slavery, segregation, and the mistreatment of African Americans. Her other antislavery writings include *Letters from New York* (1843), *The Duty of Disobedience to the Fugitive Slave Act* (1860), and *The Freedmen's Book* (1865). Child also edited the weekly periodical of the American Anti-Slavery Society, *National Anti-Slavery Standard* (1841–1843). She and her husband were separated during the 1840s but reunited in 1850.

Child's other writings include her highly popular *The Frugal Housewife* (1829, a practical guide on domestic thrift; 33 editions were printed); *Ladies' Family Library* (1830s, a five-volume set of biographies); *The History of the Condition of Women, in Various Ages and Nations* (1835, a feminist account of history); several historical novels (e.g., *Hobomok*, 1824; *The Rebels, or Boston Before the Revolution*, 1825; *A Romance of the Republic*, 1867); several books on behalf of Native Americans (e.g., *An Appeal for the Indians*, 1868); and the lyric "Boy's Thanksgiving" (1844), which begins, "Over the river and through the woods, to grandmother's house we go." She also founded and edited the first U.S. periodical for children, *Juvenile Miscellany* (1826–1834), from which she was ousted as editor because she had alienated her readers through the publication of her *Appeal*.

REFERENCES: *EB-98. G-97. MWEL. WDAA. WDAW.* Mills, Bruce, in *OCWW.* Woloch, Nancy, in *WB-99.*

Childress, Alice (10/12/1916–8/14/1994)
Plays, novels, children's literature, essays, columns

When Alice was just five years old, she was put on a train headed for Harlem; there, her grandmother Eliza welcomed her and raised her. Eliza encouraged Alice's artistic and intellectual development, taking her to museums, art galleries, libraries, theaters, and concert halls. The two of them often sat at their window, watching people pass by, while Eliza asked Alice to imagine what the passersby were thinking.

Although Alice dropped out of high school, her grandmother had ensured that she would never lack an education: "Grandmother Eliza gently urged, 'Why not write that thought down on a piece of paper? It's worth keeping.' . . . Jottings became forms after I discovered the public library and attempted to read two books a day. Reading and evaluating form, I taught myself to know the difference of structure in plays, books, short stories, teleplays, motion picture scenarios, and so forth" (*BWW*, p. 114).

Childress married young, had her daughter Jean, and divorced soon after, thereby having to work menial jobs (assistant machinist, domestic worker, salesperson, and so on) to support herself and her young daughter throughout the 1940s. These jobs helped her to keep in close touch with the working-class people she depicted in her plays and other fiction. Eventually, Jean fulfilled the dreams of the long line of Childress women, becoming the first college graduate in her mother's family.

In the early 1940s, Childress helped found the American Negro Theater (ANT), and she studied and worked with ANT both on and off Broadway until the early 1950s, participating in every aspect of producing plays. During that time, her longstanding friend Sidney Poitier raised the challenge that no one could write a strong play overnight. Childress took the challenge and in one night wrote her first play, *Florence*, a well-crafted one-act play centering on a black woman who comes to respect her daughter's pursuit of an acting career. What influences the mother? She happens to meet and converse with a white actress who presumes that she knows more about blacks than they know about themselves. As Childress observed, "Those who repress and exclude us also claim the right to instruct us on how best to react to repression. All too often we follow their advice" (*BWW*, p. 113). When ANT produced *Florence* in 1949, Childress directed it and starred in it.

Childress initially pursued a career in acting, but despite being nominated for a Tony award for her performance in the Broadway play *Anna Lucasta*, she found that racial prejudices limited her range of options. As she discovered, "I could more freely express myself as a writer" (*BWW*, p. 115). Thus, from the early 1950s until the late 1980s, Childress wrote a large number of plays, including several for juveniles, many for adults, and a few plays featuring music. Childress also set many of her plays within realistic African-American historical contexts, which she hoped might broaden the worldview of her viewers and readers, offering them new insights into how things came to be as they are.

Among literary critics, Childress was known for her skillful use of straightforward and direct language, her sensitively crafted characterizations, and her penetrating gaze into African-American lives. All of her plays involve realistic stories about everyday African Americans who courageously confront the debilitating effects of racism, sexism, and classism in the United States. Her heroes are not winners in the classical sense; instead, she writes "about those who come in second, or not at all . . . the intricate and magnificent patterns of a loser's life. . . . My writing attempts to interpret the 'ordinary' because they are not ordinary. Each human is uniquely different. . . . I concentrate on portraying have-nots in a *have* society" (*BWW*, p. 112, emphasis in original). Her protagonists, like Childress herself, inspire others as role models, not just for surviving but also for maintaining their dignity in trying circumstances. They, too, collaborate with others and seek out familial and community support in surmounting the obstacles they face.

In addition to *Florence,* Childress wrote more than nine plays examining racial and social issues, including her 1954–1955 Obie-winning *Trouble in Mind*. In this satiric indictment of racial stereotyping, staged as a play-within-a-play, the cast presumably rehearses a dramatic story about a lynching. How did Childress react when she discovered she was the first woman of any race to receive an Obie for a play? True to her convictions, she retorted that her honor merely highlighted the glaring absences of opportunities offered to other women of color.

Childress also wrote several plays that feature music (e.g., *Just a Little Simple,* 1950, based on **Langston Hughes**'s *Simple Speaks His Mind*) and two plays for juveniles, and she edited *Black Scenes* (1971), which excerpted various plays for children. Other major plays by her include *Wedding Band: A Love/Hate Story in Black and White* (1966/1973) and *Wine in the Wilderness: A Comedy-Drama* (1969).

Despite Childress's prodigious output of plays, many readers know her better for her juvenile fiction and children's literature than for her plays. Perhaps best known is her *A Hero Ain't Nothin' but a Sandwich* (1973), a novel written for adolescents about a teenage drug addict who overcomes his addiction. Her book urges African Americans to take greater responsibility for nurturing their youths, especially males. The book was made into an award-winning film in 1978, for which Childress wrote the screenplay, but both the book and the film have been banned by many school systems. (Many of her plays have also been banned in many states.) Less well known than *Hero* is her juvenile novel *Rainbow Jordan* (1981), which was named an outstanding book by *School Library Journal,* the Children's Book Council, and the *New York Times Book Review.*

For adults, Childress wrote *Like One of the Family: Conversations from a Domestic's Life* (1956, reprint 1986), which uses a series of witty and satirical monologues by Mildred, a domestic housemaid, who teaches her white employers to see their own inhumanity. This book led Childress to write a series of columns, "Here's Mildred," for the **Baltimore Afro-American,** from 1956 to 1958. More than two decades later, Childress wrote another fiction book for adults, *A Short Walk* (1979; nominated for a Pulitzer Prize), which explores twentieth-century African-American history from the **Harlem Renaissance** to the civil rights movement of the 1960s by chronicling the life experiences of a black woman. Childress's shorter fiction and dramas have been anthologized in Langston Hughes's *The Best Short Stories by Negro Writers* (1967) and other works. Perhaps her variety of written expression can best be understood by noting her observation, "I try to bend my writing form to most truthfully express content" (*BWW,* p. 114).

Little is known about Childress's private life as an adult. On July 17, 1957, she married Nathan Woodard, a professional musician and music instructor, with whom she was living in Long Island when she died of cancer in August of 1994. Tragically, her daughter had predeceased her on Mother's Day in 1990. When Childress died, she was working on her memoirs and on a sixth novel, never completed.

REFERENCES: *AA:PoP. AWA. BDAA. BWW. CBC. E-95. EB-98. EBLG. MAAL. MWEL. OC20LE. RT.* Brown-Guillory, Elizabeth, in *OCAAL.* Jennings, La Vinia Delois, in *OCWW.*

Chisholm, Shirley (Anita) (née St. Hill) (11/30/1924–)

Autobiographies

In 1970, Chisholm wrote her first autobiography, including an account of how she became the first African-American woman elected to the U.S.

Congress (in 1968, 12th Congressional District of Brooklyn, New York, a seat she held for several terms, leaving office in the early 1980s). In 1973, she thought she had a little something more to add about herself, so she wrote *The Good Fight,* describing her 1972 candidacy to become the Democratic nominee for President of the United States—the first woman and the first African American ever to do so. If you don't recall hearing about the Chisholm–Nixon debates, it is because there weren't any—the Democratic Convention didn't nominate her. As her book pointed out, though, she did manage to raise numerous issues of importance to African Americans and to women—child care (a former preschool teacher and child care center director herself), women's rights, employment opportunities and training, and civil rights, as well as the need for environmental protection, and her opposition to the Vietnam War and to the seniority system in Congress.

After she left office, Chisholm founded the National Political Congress of Black Women to continue to raise important political and social justice issues and to encourage more African-American women to pursue positions of leadership in society. In fact, Chisholm's presidential candidacy made lots of people think hard about who would want to hold high political offices and who might end up doing so. Partly as a result of her candidacy, many more women (and African Americans) entered politics and campaigned for various positions.

—*Tonya Bolden*

REFERENCES: *BAAW. E-94. G-94. PGAA.*

Clark, Kenneth B. (Bancroft)

(7/24/1914–)

Nonfiction—psychology

With his wife, **Mamie Phipps Clark**, Kenneth B. Clark wrote numerous influential studies on the impact of segregation on African-American youths, as well as on European Americans, which proved instrumental in winning the landmark *Brown v. Board of Education* Supreme Court decision of 1954. Born in the Panama Canal Zone, Clark and his sister had been brought to the United States by their mother, Miriam, a seamstress and labor activist. As a child, Clark had admired **Countee Cullen**, who had taught at his junior high school, and **Arthur Schomburg**, who curated the collection he amassed at the Harlem branch of the New York Public Library.

While Clark was still an undergraduate at Howard University, he met and married Mamie, his lifelong intellectual comrade, research collaborator, and domestic partner in rearing their two children. (See the entry on **Mamie Clark** for more on their collaborative efforts.)

From 1939 to 1941, Clark participated in research conducted by Swedish sociologist and economist Gunnar Myrdal, probing the problems of racial segregation and discrimination in the United States. During that time, Clark also earned his Ph.D. in psychology from Columbia University, the first African American to do so. In 1942, Clark was hired to teach at the City College of New York (CCNY), where he was made full professor in 1960, the first African American to earn that distinction there. (He retired from CCNY in 1975.)

In addition to numerous scholarly articles, Clark wrote *Prejudice and Your Child* (1953, 3rd ed., 1963), *Desegregation: An Appraisal of the Evidence* (1953), *The Negro Student at Integrated Colleges* (1963, with Lawrence Plotkin), *The Negro Protest* (1963, based on his televised interviews with **James Baldwin**, **Malcolm X**, and **Martin Luther King Jr.**), *Social and Economic Implications of Integration in the Public Schools* (1965), *Dark Ghetto: Dilemmas of Social Power* (1965), *The Negro American* (1966, coedited with Talcott Parsons), *A Relevant War against Poverty: A Study of Community Action Programs and Observable Change* (1968, with Jeannette Hopkins), *Crisis in Urban Education* (1971), *Pathos of Power* (1974), and *King, Malcolm, Baldwin* (1984). Among the honors he received for his work on behalf of civil rights and for fostering the well-being of African-American youths was the 1961 NAACP Spingarn Medal and the Gold Medal Award from the American Psychological Association (APA), of which Clark had been elected president.

In the mid-1940s, he and Mamie founded the Northside Testing and Consulting Center; more than a decade later, he founded Harlem Youth Opportunities Unlimited (HARYOU), to help youths avoid delinquency, stay in school, and get jobs; and in the 1970s, he and Mamie and their two children founded a consulting firm. Despite these impressive accomplishments and recognition, Clark has lamented the lack of progress in educating U.S. youths, observing in a 1993 *Newsweek* interview, "Children must be helped to understand the genuine meaning of democracy from the earliest grades; . . . to understand that one cannot keep others down without staying down with them;

and . . . to understand the importance of empathy and respect" (quoted in *BH2C,* p. 134).

REFERENCES: *EBLG. G-97.* Balfour, Lawrie, in *EA-99.* Banks, Michelle, in *BH2C.* Gutek, Gerald L., in *WB-99.*

Clark, Mamie (née Phipps)
(10/18/1917–8/22/1983)
Nonfiction—psychology

Mamie was one half of the legendary Clark-and-Clark team that provided research fundamental to the historic 1954 *Brown v. Board of Education* Supreme Court decision. While still Mamie Phipps, she met **Kenneth B. Clark** at Howard University in the 1930s. The two married in 1938, the year she earned her bachelor's degree and he (with his master's degree in hand) was working as a psychology instructor at Howard University. Later on, the couple moved to New York's Columbia University, where the two earned doctorates in psychology (his in 1940, hers in 1943), becoming the first African American (Kenneth) and the first African-American woman (and the second African American—Mamie) to do so. In fact, the Clarks were the first two African Americans to earn Ph.D.s of any kind at Columbia.

Given their primary status, were universities across the land rushing to make them inviting offers for the good life in the ivory tower? Well, if those towers were to preserve their ivory hue, apparently not. At last, Kenneth was hired as an assistant professor at Hampton Institute and at the College of the City of New York. Mamie wasn't. Apparently, her skin color was not the only physical barrier blocking her entry to academia. Still, she collaborated with Kenneth on his research, and in 1946 they founded the Northside Testing and Consulting Center, their Manhattan clinic for treating African-American children with special needs. Many of these children had been incorrectly identified as "retarded" by the public school system or suffered from emotional disturbance, learning disabilities, or personality disorders for which they were not receiving treatment.

By the mid-1950s, the Clarks had written numerous articles about their observations of children, such as "Racial Identification and Preference in Negro Children" and "Emotional Factors in Racial Identification and Preference in Negro Children." Some attorneys at the National Association for the Advancement of Colored People (NAACP) noticed one of their articles on the harmful effects of school segregation on African-American children. The NAACP chief counsel **Thurgood Marshall** asked the Clarks to conduct further research specifically to show those effects. They developed a study using white-skinned dolls and black-skinned dolls. When they asked children to identify the "bad dolls," both white children and black children chose the black dolls every time. Next, when they asked the children to choose the dolls with which they would want to play, most of the children—both white and black—chose the white dolls. Marshall asked Kenneth to give testimony on the Clarks' collaborative research in the Supreme Court. He did, and the justices overturned the "separate but equal" doctrine—and they did so just as unanimously as the children in the Clarks' studies had done when they labeled the black dolls as the "bad" ones.

Meanwhile, back at the center, Mamie served as executive director for more than three decades. As the center's reputation grew, it started drawing clients from all races and was renamed the Northside Center for Child Development. By the time Mamie stepped down (in 1979), the center had helped more than 16,000 children and their families. In 1973, Mamie had seen the need to provide schooling for emotionally disturbed and learning-disabled youngsters whom the public schools were not educating, so she founded the Northside Day School. In 1975, she and her husband and their two children, Kate Miriam Clark and Hilton Bancroft Clark, founded a consulting firm that guides corporations in implementing affirmative action programs for hiring African Americans and other nonwhites.

REFERENCES: *BAAW.* Banks, Michelle, in *BH2C.*

Clark, Septima (née) Poinsette
(5/3/1898–12/15/1987)
Autobiographies

Clark participated in the writing of at least two books on her life story: Grace Jordan McFadden's *Oral Recollections of Septima P. Clark* (1980) and Clark's autobiography *Ready from Within: Septima Clark and the Civil Rights Movement* (1986, edited by Cynthia Stokes Brown), which won the National Book Award in 1987. Why would the life of a humble schoolteacher deserve so much discussion?

On April 19, 1956, after she had taught school for 40 years, Septima Clark was told that she had a choice: Give up her membership in the National

Association for the Advancement of Colored People (NAACP) and her vocal protests for civil rights or give up not only her teaching job but also all of her retirement benefits. What would any sensible 58-year-old widow do in a situation like this? How on Earth could she give up her career, her livelihood, and her only means of supporting herself? If she could keep quiet and compliant for four more years, she could retire and do whatever she wanted to do. Well, the choice seemed obvious to anyone.

Well, it was obvious to her, too. She kept her NAACP membership, she kept up her protests—except that she did get a little louder—and she lost her job and was prevented from getting another one anywhere in South Carolina. Fortunately, when the Highlander Folk School in Chattanooga, Tennessee, found out about her situation, they invited her to be the school's director of education. Highlander already had a reputation for training community activists, and she had previously conducted a workshop for the school when she was hired. With Clark at the helm, the school had an excellent role model for how to live by your conscience when big issues are at stake. Among the people Clark inspired was a little-known bus-riding seamstress named Rosa Parks.

As an outgrowth of her work at Highlander, Clark founded various citizenship schools, designed to prepare African Americans to pass the citizenship tests required for them to become registered voters. A few of the people with whom she worked in the citizenship schools included Fannie Lou Hamer, John Lewis, and Andrew Young—all of whom went on to contribute significantly to the civil rights struggle.

—*Tonya Bolden*

REFERENCES: *BAAW.* Brown, Cynthia Stokes, in *BH2C.* Fay, Robert, in *EA-99.* McFadden, Grace Jordan, in *BWA:AHE.* Clark's papers have been collected at the College of Charleston, Robert Scott Small Library, in South Carolina.

Clarke, John Henrik
(1/1/1915–7/16/1998)
History books, essays, anthologies, short stories; journal founder, editor

As a young boy, Clarke so loved reading that in addition to the Bible, he would read tin-can labels, signs, and any other words he could lay his eyes on. He borrowed books from the personal libraries of white folks whose children could read but wouldn't, and he forged white people's names on notes to be able to borrow books from public libraries that followed Jim Crow policies.

This young word-hungry reader inspired many people to have faith in his promise, too: His mother, who saved 50 cents per week for his college education (but died when John was just ten years old); his father and his uncles, who pooled their money to pull together the $3.75 they needed to buy his schoolbooks each semester; and his beloved teacher, Evelena Taylor, about whom he later recalled, she "took my face between her hands and looking me straight in the eyes said, 'I believe in you.'"

Taylor and the others had good reason to believe in John. He was quick to learn, as well as quick to raise questions about peculiarities he noticed. For instance, why was Jesus depicted in the Bible as being a blue-eyed blonde, yet the Bible described him as having dark eyes and dark hair, like the other people of that region?

When John sought a book on the contributions of Africans in ancient history, a kindly white lawyer whose books he borrowed told him that there was no such book, implying that there were no such contributions. John wondered why no such book existed. Had Africans really made no contributions to world history at all—or had no one written about them—or had this attorney just been ignorant of the existing books and contributions?

By great good fortune, Clarke discovered the answer to that question while still in high school. While he was watching over the belongings of a guest speaker, he noticed a copy of *The New Negro,* an anthology compiled by **Alain Locke**. In it, he glimpsed an essay by **Arthur Schomburg**: "The Negro Digs Up His Past." Wow! Negroes had a past to dig up! As Clarke later remembered, he was thrilled to discover "I came from a people with a history older than the history of Europe. . . . [My people's] history was older than that of their oppressors."

Intrigued, Clarke tracked Schomburg to his native habitat, the Harlem branch of the New York Public Library. Schomburg encouraged Clarke in his pursuits and told him that he would need to study not only African history but also European and American history to figure out how Africa contributed to European culture, why Europeans developed the slave trade, and how the Americas figured into the picture. Clarke heeded Schomburg's advice—with vigor.

After a brief interruption while Clarke served in the Air Force, he returned to his self-designed program of informal study as well as formal studies at various universities (e.g., New York University, the New School for Social Research in New York, the University of Ibadan in Nigeria, and the University of Ghana). By the mid-1960s (and continuing through the mid-1980s), he was teaching his favorite subject around Harlem, in a variety of community centers as well as at various colleges and universities (e.g., Columbia, Cornell). Even after he settled into being a professor of black and Puerto Rican studies at New York's Hunter College (1966–1988), he continued to lecture across the country and to develop curricula, study guides, and teaching materials for others to use.

While teaching and studying, Clarke managed to churn out quite a few short stories (including "The Boy Who Painted Christ Black," the most widely anthologized of his stories) as well as myriad articles on African-American history, which he contributed to **Robert Abbott**'s *Chicago Defender*, **W. E. B. Du Bois**'s *Phylon,* the European Negritude journal *Présence Africaine* (founded by Senegalese author Alioune Diop), and numerous other periodicals. He was also cofounder and associate editor of at least two journals: *Harlem Quarterly* (1949–1951) and *Freedomways* (starting in 1962). His nonfiction books included *Africans at the Crossroads: Notes for an African World Revolution* (1991), *Christopher Columbus and the African Holocaust* (1992), and *African People in World History* (1995). He even wrote a book of verse, *Rebellion in Rhyme* (1948).

Rounding out this impressive output are all the books he edited, such as *Harlem U.S.A.: The Story of a City within a City* (1964); *American Negro Short Stories* (1966); *Malcolm X: The Man and His Times* (1969); *William Styron's Nat Turner: Ten Black Writers Respond* (1970); *Marcus Garvey and the Vision of Africa* (1973, with **Amy Jacques Garvey**); and *New Dimensions in African History: The London Lectures of Dr. Yosef ben-Jochanan and Dr. John Henrik Clarke* (1991).

Contemporary historians such as **John Hope Franklin** and Herb Boyd have recognized Clarke's contributions, and his life has been documented in the film *John Henrik Clarke: A Great and Mighty Walk* (1997), directed by **St. Claire Bourne** and executive produced and narrated by actor Wesley Snipes. Fortunately, for those of us who follow in his absence, the proceeds from the film's premiere helped pay for cataloging and preserving the John Henrik Clarke Collection at the Schomburg Center for Research in Black Culture.

—*Tonya Bolden*

REFERENCES: *EA-99. EBLG. SMKC.* Boyd, Herb (1998), "The Griot of Our Time," *New York Amsterdam News,* July 23–29. Mix, Dusty (1998), "Coming Home," *Ledger-Enquirer* (Columbus, GA), July 26.

Cleage (married name: Lomax), Pearl (Michelle) (12/7/1948–)

Plays, essays and articles, poems, novel, short stories

A prolific playwright, Cleage has had many of her plays produced in New York, Washington, D.C., and Atlanta (e.g., *Hymn for the Rebels,* 1968; *Duet for Three Voices,* 1969; her audience attendance-record-breaking *puppetplay,* 1983; her award-winning one-act *Hospice,* 1983; *Banana Bread,* 1985; *Porch Songs,* 1985; *Chain,* 1992; *Late Bus to Mecca,* 1992; and *Flyin' West,* 1994). Many of her plays have also been published, such as those in her *Flyin' West and Other Plays* (1999), and she has been named playwright-in-residence (1983) and artistic director (1987) of the Just Us Theater Company and playwright-in-residence at Spelman College (1991).

The daughter of a politically activist family, Cleage writes powerful, candid, thought-provoking columns for the *Atlanta Tribune,* as well as other essays addressing issues of sex and race in the United States. Close to three dozen of her essays have been collected in *Deals with the Devil and Other Reasons to Riot* (1993), the first of her books to garner popular and critical acclaim. Since then, her *What Looks Like Crazy on an Ordinary Day: A Novel* (1997; audiocassette abridgment read by the author, 1998; large-print edition, 1999) earned much-coveted inclusion in Oprah's Book Club (see **Oprah Winfrey**). Cleage's other publications include *Mad at Miles: A Blackwoman's Guide to Truth* (1991), *The Brass Bed and Other Stories* (1991), and her poetry collections *We Don't Need No Music* (1971), *Dear Dark Faces: Portraits of a People* (1980), and *One for the Brothers* (1983). Also, in 1987, she founded the magazine *Catalyst.*

REFERENCES: *EBLG.* Marsh-Lockett, Carol P., in *OCAAL.* Amazon.com, 7/1999.

Cleaver, (Leroy) Eldridge
(8/31/1935–5/1/1998)
Essays and letters

After a troubled youth involving numerous incarcerations for drug deals and thefts, in 1954 Cleaver was imprisoned for two-and-a-half years for possessing marijuana. In prison (Soledad, Folsom, and San Quentin prisons in California), he completed high school and began reading the works of Karl Marx and of **W. E. B. Du Bois**. After his release, he was again convicted and imprisoned in 1958, this time for rape and for assault with intent to commit murder. During this lengthier prison term, he joined the Black Muslims, enthusiastically following the teachings of **Malcolm X**. Following Malcolm's break with the Nation of Islam, Cleaver left, too, joining X's secular Organization of Afro-American Unity (OAAU).

Cleaver also started trying to have some of the essays he was writing published. When his essay "Notes of a Native Son," a homophobic assault on **James Baldwin**, was published in *Ramparts* magazine (a leftist publication), he gained the attention of various intellectuals, who helped him win parole in 1966. While writing and editing for *Ramparts,* he came to know Black Panther Party (BPP) cofounders Huey Newton and Bobby Seale. They named Cleaver the BPP's minister of information, and he was soon traveling nationwide promoting the message of the BPP. Within two years, he had published *Soul on Ice* (1968), a collection of his essays and letters reflecting on his criminal behavior, his experiences in prison, and the situation of African Americans within American culture, as well as gender relations and other topics. Just a couple months after *Soul on Ice* was published, Cleaver was arrested for assault and attempted murder following an armed confrontation between the police and BPP members. When it looked as though he would be returning to prison, he asserted that he feared for his life, jumped bail, and fled the United States, spending the next several years in Cuba, Algeria, and France. Cleaver's new wife and fellow Panther Kathleen Neal joined him abroad, and the couple had two children (their son Maceo, born in Algiers; and their daughter Joju, born in North Korea).

At first, Cleaver continued to write leftist articles for such publications as *Black Panther, Ramparts,* and **Black Scholar**, and he wrote *Eldridge Cleaver: Post-Prison Writings and Speeches* and *Eldridge Cleaver's Black Papers* (both published in 1969). He also completed his autobiographical novella *Black Moochie* (1969), which he had begun writing while he was writing for *Ramparts.* Over time, however, he became disenchanted with leftist politics. By 1975, when he returned to the United States to face the charges against him, he had become a fundamentalist right-wing Christian. With his newfound religious and political beliefs, he was able to get the attempted murder charges dropped in exchange for pleading guilty to the assault charges, for which he was given just five years probation and 1,000–2,000 hours of community service, with no prison time. (Ironically, many of his earlier speeches and writings were published a year later in the collection *The Black Panther Leaders Speak: Huey P. Newton, Bobby Seale, Eldridge Cleaver, and Company Speak Out through the Black Panther Party's Official Newspaper.*) Cleaver eventually joined the Republican Party, unsuccessfully running for the GOP's nomination for the U.S. Senate.

Cleaver wrote an account of his conversion experiences in *Soul on Fire* (1978). His religious beliefs did not suffice to keep him from turning to drugs, however, as he was arrested again in 1994 for intoxication and possession of cocaine. In addition to the aforementioned publications, he wrote poems, short stories, and pamphlets. His lasting testament appears to be his early writings in *Soul on Ice,* however, as it is still prompting readers to praise or scorn him (Amazon.com, 7/1999).

REFERENCES: *EB-BH-CD. EBLG. NAAAL.* Balfour, Lawrie, in *EA-99.* Berger, Roger A., in *OCAAL.* Stone, Les, in *BH2C.* Weinstein, Henry, "Life on the Line: Conversation with Cleaver," 1969, quoted in *EA-99.* Amazon.com, 7/1999.

Cliff, Michelle (11/2/1946–)
Novels, poems, short stories, essays

Cliff's heritage is a blend of African, Native American, and European ancestry, and her life experiences combine the influences of Jamaica and the United States. Born in Jamaica, she lived in New York City with her mother and sister from ages three until ten, becoming a naturalized U.S. citizen; she has maintained her citizenship even after returning to Jamaica as a young girl. There, light-skinned Michelle attended a private girls' school, where she saw firsthand the pernicious influence of a caste system based on color. Jamaica's colonial past had led to intraracial cruelty, oppression, and even violence; societal privileges were distributed according to color, and Michelle's darker-skinned compatriots suffered condemnation and alienation in their homeland.

After completing school, Cliff left Jamaica to study in London, then earned her B.A. in European history at Wagner College in Staten Island, New York (1969). The year she graduated, she started working as a researcher and then a production supervisor for New York publisher W. W. Norton. In the early 1970s, Cliff returned to London, where she earned her M.Phil. (master's in philosophy) from Warburg Institute (1974), writing her thesis on languages and comparative historical studies of the Italian Renaissance. Back in New York, she returned to publishing, working as a manuscript and production editor (specializing in history, politics, and women's studies) for the Norton Library Series. In the early 1980s, she and poet Adrienne Rich coedited and published a lesbian feminist journal.

While writing has been Cliff's main focus, she has also worked as a reporter and researcher and has lectured and taught extensively at various colleges and universities on both U.S. coasts, including Stanford University in Palo Alto, the New School for Social Research (New York), Hampshire College and the University of Massachusetts at Amherst, Norwich University (Northfield, Vermont), the Martin Luther King, Jr., Public Library (Oakland), the University of California at Santa Cruz, and Trinity College (Hartford, Connecticut).

By the late 1970s, Cliff's essays, poems, and short stories were starting to appear in print. Her essay "Notes on Speechlessness" was published in the lesbian feminist magazine *Conditions II* in 1977. Her essays often address themes of racial tension and of sexual identity. Two of her books include both essays and poems: *Claiming an Identity They Taught Me to Despise* (1980) and *The Land of Look Behind: Prose and Poetry* (1985). Many of her short works have been widely anthologized. In each of these works, she explores issues of colonialism, class struggle, sexual identity, racism, and feminist consciousness. Cliff also edited *The Winner Names the Age: A Collection of Writing by Lillian Smith* (1978).

Cliff's *Bodies of Water* (1990) has been called a short-story collection, but it may also be viewed as a novel, as the characters appear across different stories, and their stories interweave, making use of folk myths and legends as well as history. Prior to *Bodies of Water,* Cliff wrote two novels (*Abeng,* 1984; *No*

Telephone to Heaven, 1988) featuring as their central character Clare Savage, a fair-skinned, middle-class Jamaican who must come to terms with her mixed cultural heritage and the privileges accorded to her because of her light complexion.(Sound familiar?) In *Abeng,* Clare and her dark-skinned friend Zoe confront a situation that highlights the difference in their status on the Caribbean island, and their friendship collapses under the weight of these disparities. By the end of the book, Clare is fleeing to the United States, leaving Zoe behind in Jamaica. *No Telephone to Heaven* continues Clare's story, weaving back and forth in time as well as between the United States and Jamaica. Through both novels, Cliff explores the difficulties of affirming multiple aspects of a mixed cultural heritage. Cliff's third novel, *Free Enterprise* (1993), tells the story of a fictitious nineteenth-century woman abolitionist who helps fugitive slaves escape through the Underground Railroad.

In her writings, Cliff blends broad aspects of history with autobiography, offering deeply personal insights within a richly detailed historical context. A fluent speaker of multiple languages, Cliff also intermingles the patois of the Caribbean with the speech patterns of standard American English. In appreciation of her work, Cliff has been awarded fellowships from the MacDowell Colony and the National Endowment for the Arts (1982) and the Massachusetts Artists Foundation and the Yaddo Writers Colony (1984).

REFERENCES: *EBLG. NAAAL. OC20LE.* Fonteneau, Yvonne, in *BWA:AHE.* Robinson, Lisa Clayton, in *EA-99.* Wagner-Martin, Linda, in *OCWW.*

Clifton, Lucille (née Thelma Lucille Sayles) (6/27/1936–)
Poems, children's books, memoir, novels, essays, short stories, screenplays

Lucille Clifton probably couldn't help becoming a poet and storyteller: Although neither of her parents had a formal education, Lucille grew up observing how to write poems and tell stories. Her mother, a professional laundress and dedicated amateur poet, often read or recited poems to Lucille and her siblings. Her father, a steel worker by vocation and griot by avocation, frequently told his children stories about their African ancestors and their history in this country. In Clifton's own words, "I grew up a well-loved child in a loving family and so I have always known that being very poor ... had nothing to do with lovingness or familyness or character or any of that" (*BWW,* p. 137).

When Lucille was just 16 years old, she won a full scholarship to study drama at Howard University (with fellow students **Amiri Baraka** and **Sterling Brown**). When she transferred to another college, she joined a drama group and met novelist **Ishmael Reed** and poet **Langston Hughes** (who later anthologized some of her poems). After a while, however, she became so absorbed in writing that she dropped out of college before earning a degree. Hardly a typical dropout, however, she eventually received two honorary doctorates in humane letters (1980).

During the 1950s, in addition to writing, she worked for several years as a civil servant. In 1958, her mother died, Lucille married Fred Clifton, and she gave birth to their first child—quite a year! Over the next eight years or so, the couple had five more children. When the youngest of her children was a teenager (about a year before her husband Fred died, in 1984), she explained her priorities: "At home I am wife and mama mostly. My family has always come first with me" (*BWW,* p. 138).

Her children didn't prevent her from writing, however. In fact, she credits her four daughters and two sons with having inspired much of her work, and a large proportion of her literary output has been about children or addressed to them. Nonetheless, her children have often been less than encouraging about her poems and her books for young readers. When she was invited to share her children's books with classes all over the country, her own children begged her not to come to their classes—or if she *had* to come, they begged her, "You know how you walk? Don't walk that stupid walk. You know how you talk? Don't talk like that. Don't laugh your laugh. Don't wear your clothes" (*LoL,* p. 94). Although she may have felt a little hurt by their comments, her good humor got her past them, as shown in her poem "Admonitions": "Children / When they ask you / why your mama so funny / say she is a poet / she don't have no sense" (*BWW,* p. 142).

In the 1970s, Clifton began holding various positions as a lecturer, a poet in residence, and a professor at several colleges and universities in Maryland and nearby Washington, D.C. After her children were grown and she was widowed, she accepted positions farther afield.

Lucille Clifton was the poet laureate of Maryland, 1988 (Chris Felver/Archive Photos)

Clifton's poetry uses simple vocabulary and syntax to convey complex and subtle messages. As she has noted, "I am interested in being understood not admired" (*NAAAL,* p. 2219). Her voice is both realistic and optimistic, chiefly focused on everyday experiences and feelings. Her poetry illuminates the commonplace. For instance, she begins her poem "an homage to my hips," "these hips are big hips. / they need space to / move around in. / they don't fit into little / petty places. / these hips / are free hips."

Clifton has a hopeful, positive, life-affirming outlook, even when she writes about challenges and emotionally daunting experiences (as she often does). She describes difficult times without minimizing their fearsomeness or even their cruelty, yet she highlights the ways people face and get past the obstacles in their paths. Even when the ordinary people in her poems cannot entirely overcome the troubles they see, they do their best. As she has said, "Acting when you *are* afraid, *that's* where the honor is" (*LoL,* p. 95).

She particularly focuses on the responsibility and "response-ability" of humble heroes. She rails against injustice without fostering hatred and she argues for taking personal responsibility without preaching to her readers. By recognizing in herself and others both their vulnerability and their strength, Clifton encourages and empowers her readers as they confront their own problems. For instance, in concluding "Daddy," a poem she wrote to her father after his death, she said, "When his leg died, he cut it off. / 'It's gone,' he said, 'it's gone / but I'm still here'" (*BWW,* p. 147).

Besides triumph over difficulties, Clifton's other dominant theme is continuity across generations. After her parents died, she carried on her father's griot tradition and wrote a memoir about her family titled *Generations* (1976). Through all of her writing, she nudges her readers to acknowledge their indebtedness to generations past as well as their obligation to generations to come. She asks readers to affirm the past—even when it is painful, such as in the experiences of slavery or of sexual molestation—to observe its effects in the present, and then to focus on moving forward into the future.

Clifton has authored more than ten poetry collections and is widely anthologized in other people's collections. Many of her readers have never seen these works, however, knowing her solely through her children's books. These books focus on the everyday struggles of family life in the inner city. Perhaps her favorite central character is Everett Anderson, a six- or seven-year-old boy who lives with his single working mother in an inner-city neighborhood. Through him and other characters, Clifton shows that poverty and other material circumstances do not determine who you are or who you can become.

Clifton's stories encourage children to be proud of themselves and to act in ways that will make them proud of themselves. She describes no goody-two-shoes children, however. She realistically addresses children's difficulties with moral and social dilemmas. Rather than demanding (or trying to show) perfection, she shows lovably flawed children trying to do the best they can with whatever they have. With a loving family (of whatever size) and through conscientious effort, each child can be an ordinary hero. To date, she has written more than 16 books of fiction and poetry for young readers, about half of which feature Everett Anderson; several others spotlight history. In addition to her poetry, her memoir, and her children's books, she has written novels, essays, short stories, and screenplays.

Clifton has received many awards for her writing (e.g., National Endowment for the Arts fellowships, Pulitzer Prize nominations, an Emmy Award, and dozens of others), but she generally shies away from celebrity. When she was first invited to become the poet laureate of Maryland, she asked **Gwendolyn Brooks** (poet laureate of Illinois) how the position would affect her life and how it would benefit her people. When Brooks told her that the honor was "what you make of it," Clifton decided to accept the award. She has since commented on celebrity, "I wish to celebrate and not be celebrated (though a little celebration is a lot of fun)" (*BWW,* p. 137).

When asked about her own life experiences, Clifton has responded, "I don't know if I think I've had a hard life, but I *have* had a challenging life. . . .but I was blessed with a sense of humor, . . . which has saved me on occasion. I can also see what I have gained from being challenged in my life" (*LoL,* pp. 81–82).

REFERENCES: *AWAW. BWW. CBC. LoL. MAAL. MWEL. NAAAL. PC:PEL. Q:P. TTS. TtW. TWT.*

Cobb, Charles E., Jr. (1943–)
Poems, essays, travel writings

Cobb's poetry collections include *In the Furrows of the World* (1967) and *Everywhere Is Yours* (1971). He has also written articles for various journals and became a *National Geographic* staff writer in 1985. In addition, Cobb published *African Notebook: Views on Returning Home* (1971), on his experiences during an extended sojourn in Tanzania.

REFERENCES: Greene, Michael E., in *OCAAL.*

Cobb, Jewell (née) Plummer
(1/17/1924–)
Nonfiction—cell biology

Although Cobb has published extensively in scholarly journals on her scientific research, she has also published some articles on social issues involving women and minorities. For instance, in her article "Filters for Women in Science" (1979), she describes how women are more commonly filtered out of scientific careers than are men.

REFERENCES: *EWS.* Robinson, Lisa Clayton, in *EA-99.* Thompson, Kathleen, in *BWA:AHE.*

Cobb, William Montague
(10/12/1904–1990)
Nonfiction

In addition to writing more than 600 scholarly articles on physical anthropology and contributing to several standard reference works in medicine (e.g., *Gray's Anatomy*), Cobb wrote books on African-American medical care and on jobs in medicine, including *The First Negro Medical Society: A History of the Medico-Chirurgical Society of the District of Columbia* (1939).

REFERENCES: Fay, Robert, in *EA-99*.

Coleman, Wanda (née Evans)
(11/13/1946–)
Drama, poems, short stories

Coleman had published several poems by age 15 and has since published several books of her works, including *Art in the Court of the Blue Fag* (1977), *Mad Dog Black Lady* (1979), *Imagoes* (1983), *A War of Eyes and Other Stories* (1988), *Dicksboro Hotel and Other Travels* (1989), *African Sleeping Sickness: Stories and Poems* (1990), *Heavy Daughter Blues: Poems and Stories* (1991), and *Hand Dance* (1993). For her work, Coleman has been awarded an Emmy and grants from the National Endowment for the Arts and the Guggenheim Foundation. On June 13, 1999, Coleman came in second at the World Poetry Bout Association's contest in Taos, New Mexico, losing to Sherman Alexie.

REFERENCES: *NAAAL*. Stanley, Sandra K., in *OCAAL*. http://www.fallsapart.com.

Colón, Jesús (1/20/1901–1974)
Anthologies, sketches, articles, columns

In 1923, Colón started writing for the Puerto Rican prolabor paper *Justicia*, and soon after, he was regularly writing columns for *Gráfico* and the *Daily Worker*. Many of his sketches and essays were collected in *Puerto Rican in New York and Other Sketches* (1961) and *The Way It Was and Other Writings* (1993, published nearly two decades after his death).

REFERENCES: Vega-Merino, Alexandra, in *EA-99*.

Colored American Magazine (1900–1909)

First published in 1900, *Colored American Magazine* was the most widely distributed black journal before 1910. This monthly featured articles of general interest to African Americans. It was important at the beginning of the century in encouraging and promoting the work of African-American writers. For instance, the fiction and nonfiction of **Pauline Hopkins** often appeared in the journal and she was an editor of the magazine during its early years. Hopkins, who regarded herself as a race historian, pursued a politically risky agenda and sought to discredit **Booker T. Washington** as overly accommodating. She was fired in 1904 when Washington's ally, Fred Moore, purchased the magazine and moved its offices to New York. It ceased publication in 1909.

—Lisa Bahlinger

REFERENCES: Gruesser, John C., in *OCAAL*.

Conwell, Kathleen (3/18/1942–9/?/1988)
Plays, screenplays, novel

Conwell's screenplays have included *Losing Ground* (1982), *Madame Flor* (1987), and *Conversations with Julie* (1988) and have been aired on the Learning Channel and on the Public Broadcasting System. Her stage plays include *In the Midnight Hour* (1981), *The Brothers* (1982), *The Reading* (1984), *Begin the Beguine* (1985), *Only the Sky Is Free* (1985), *While Older Men Speak* (1986), and *Looking for Jane* (198?). She finished writing her novel *Lollie: A Suburban Tale* the year she died.

REFERENCES: Keough, Leyla, in *EA-99*. Amazon.com, 1/2000.

Cooper, Anna Julia (née Haywood)
(8/10/1859–2/27/1964)
Essays, addresses

After earning her bachelor's and master's degrees from Oberlin College, Cooper started teaching at Wilberforce University. She often went against the accepted wisdom of the day, insisting on the value of a liberal arts education, contrary to **Booker T. Washington**'s emphasis on vocational training. In pursuit of her own liberal arts education, she earned her Ph.D. at age 67 at the Sorbonne in Paris, writing her dissertation on "The Attitude of France toward Slavery during the Revolution." She was the fourth African-American woman to garner the doctorate. Throughout her life, Cooper gave addresses and contributed essays, which we now have inherited in her *A Voice from the South by a Black Woman of the South* (1892), often cited as the first book-length work of African-American feminism.

Among other feminist writings in her book are her "The Higher Education of Women" and "The Status of Woman in America."

—*Tonya Bolden*

REFERENCES: *AAWW. BAAW.* Guy-Sheftall, Beverly (Ed.) (1995), *Words of Fire: An Anthology of African-American Feminist Thought* (New York: New Press).

Cooper, J. (Joan) California
(c. mid-1900s–)
Short stories, novels, plays

A prolific writer, Cooper has written numerous plays (at least 17 by the mid-1990s, including *Everytime It Rains; System, Suckers, and Success; How Now; The Unintended; The Mother; Ahhh; Strangers;* and *Loners*), many of which have been produced on live stage, on radio, and on public television; and some of which have been anthologized. Despite her success as a playwright, Cooper may be better known for her short stories, having published several short-story collections (*A Piece of Mine,* 1984, published by **Alice Walker**'s publishing company and including a foreword by Walker; *Homemade Love,* 1986, winner of a 1989 American Book Award; *Some Soul to Keep,* 1987; *The Matter Is Life,* 1991; and *Some Love, Some Pain, Sometime,* 1995). She has also written three novels: *Family* (1991), her Civil War–era novel about a slave and her family; *In Search of Satisfaction* (1994), about the black daughter and the mulatto daughter (and granddaughter) of a former slave from Reconstruction through the 1920s; and *The Wake of the Wind* (1998), a family saga that begins in Africa in the 1760s when two friends are captured, enslaved, and brought to the United States, where their descendants' lives intersect in the troublesome and confusing period during and immediately following the Civil War. In addition to awards for her individual works, in 1988 Cooper was named a Literary Lion by the American Library Association and garnered the James Baldwin Writing Award.

In many of her works, Cooper shows the ways in which women offer one another support through times of abuse, neglect, economic difficulties, and other struggles. Despite the challenges they face, Cooper's characters show optimism, humor, and a strong spirit. They also tend to reinforce feminist family values and Cooper's firm belief that true happiness comes from within, often as a result of helping others. Some critics suggest that she tends toward preachiness, but others praise her clear moral stands. In her narratives, Cooper uses authentic dialogue and first-person accounts, offering one woman's insights into her own life crises or into the experiences of those whom she observes at close range. Readers frequently feel as though the narrator is speaking directly to them, using a folksy, chatty voice. Cooper's birth date is nowhere to be found in available resources about her, and she closely guards her private life, but it is known that she has a daughter, Paris A. Williams, to whom she has dedicated her fiction.

REFERENCES: *EBLG. RP.* King, Lovalerie, in *OCAAL.* Yohe, Kristine A., in *OCWW.* Amazon.com, 7/1999.

Cornish, Samuel E. (?/1795–?/1858)
Journalist; newspaper founder

In 1822, Samuel Cornish was ordained as an evangelist by the New York Presbytery and spent the next quarter of a century as a minister in various Presbyterian churches. In March of 1827, he and **John Brown Russwurm** made history when they printed the first edition of *Freedom's Journal,* the first African-American weekly newspaper, which the pair had cofounded. The paper's motto was "We Wish to Plead Our Own Cause"—the cause being abolition in the South and civil rights in the North. As part of pleading their own cause, the founders hired African Americans to print and run the paper. Cornish also strongly opposed the policies of the American Colonization Society, which urged freed (or fugitive) slaves to emigrate to Africa to establish a colony of free African Americans in Liberia.

By the fall of 1827, Cornish felt that his duties as coeditor of the newspaper were taking him away from his ministry, so he resigned as coeditor, leaving the paper in Russwurm's hands. Much to Cornish's chagrin, Russwurm shifted the editorial policy of the paper away from fighting for abolition and civil justice in this country and toward emigration and resettlement (colonization) in Liberia. By the time of the paper's two-year anniversary, Russwurm had despaired of achieving any reforms in the United States and joined the American Colonization Society, embracing its aims. He turned the newspaper back to Cornish's control and moved to Liberia. Russwurm's editorial policies had damaged the paper's credibility as an advocate of abolition and social justice for

African Americans in the United States, and even though Cornish renamed the paper the *Rights of All,* he was unable to revive it, and on October 29, 1829, he folded up shop.

In January 1837, Cornish started editing the *Weekly Advocate,* which changed its name to the *Colored American* (cf. ***Colored American Magazine***) in March of that year. Cornish continued editing the periodical until April of the following year. Cornish's work as a journalist and a minister was not his only social and political involvement. He also worked with the American Anti-Slavery Society, the African Free Schools, and the American Missionary Society, cooperating with others to oppose slavery, promote abolition, and evangelize his Christian beliefs. Perhaps he worked so hard to help others, in part, to divert himself from his personal troubles: his son William's emigration to Liberia, his wife Jane Livingston's death (1844), his daughter Sarah's death (1846), and his daughter Jane's mental collapse (1851).

REFERENCES: Button, Marilyn D., in *OCAAL.*

Corrothers, James D. (1869–1917)
Poems, sketches, autobiography

In addition to having his poems and sketches published in various periodicals, his sketches were collected and published as *The Black Cat Club* (1902), and his autobiography, *In Spite of Handicap,* appeared in 1916.

REFERENCES: *NYPL-AADR.* Bruce, Dickson D., Jr., in *OCAAL.*

Cortez, Jayne (5/10/1936–)
Poems; book publisher

Born on her father's army base at Fort Huachuca, Arizona, Jayne Cortez grew up in Watts, then an African-American ghetto of Los Angeles. Cortez grew up in a family of bibliophiles (book lovers), and from an early age, she was reading children's books and Bible stories. Soon, she was keeping notebooks full of new words she found in dictionaries, encyclopedias, and other reference books, and writing down the stories her family members enjoyed telling. Her literary interests expanded to include newspapers and the writings of African-American poets (e.g., **Langston Hughes** and **Sterling Brown**) as well.

Cortez also grew up savoring the sounds of music, especially her family's huge collection of jazz and blues albums, as well as the songs her mother sang to her. By the time she reached her teens, she was taking piano lessons, and she learned to play the bass and the cello and studied music harmony and theory. Often, while listening to local musicians at their jam sessions, she wrote and drew, inspired by the rhythms she was hearing. In 1951, she met avant-garde saxophonist Ornette Coleman; in 1954, she married him; in 1956, the twosome had their son Denardo; and in 1960, the couple divorced.

After her divorce, Cortez returned to writing poetry and started studying drama. In the summers of 1963 and 1964, she worked with the Student Nonviolent Coordinating Committee (SNCC) to register African-American voters in Mississippi. Back in Los Angeles, she cofounded the Watts Repertory Theater and served as its artistic director, starting in 1964. By 1972, Cortez and her son had moved to New York, where she founded Bola Press. (*Bola* means "successful" in Yoruba.) Through Bola Press, she published not only her poetry collections but also sound recordings of performances of her pieces, such as *Celebrations and Solitudes* (1975). From 1977 until 1983, she worked as writer-in-residence at Livingston College of Rutgers University in New Jersey. She lives in New York City with her second husband, artist Melvin Edwards, but she also travels extensively to perform her pieces and give readings.

Cortez's poetic themes reflect her political concerns for justice and civil rights and her opposition to racial prejudice and political oppression. Her poetic forms reflect her lifelong enchantment with music, particularly jazz and blues. In fact, music is often the theme of her poems (e.g., her often-quoted "How Long Has Trane Been Gone," an elegy to jazz saxophonist and composer John Coltrane). Although Cortez may be considered a performance poet—her works are most effective when spoken aloud—her poems also visually dance across the page in printed form, and they have been widely anthologized and translated into multiple languages.

In Cortez's first collection of poetry, *Pisstained Stairs and the Monkey Man's Wares* (1969), she used her poetic artistry to celebrate the aesthetic expressions of African-American jazz musicians, thus firmly establishing herself as a poet of the **Black Arts movement**. Cortez's second collection, *Festivals and Funerals* (1971), affirmed her appreciation of African-American culture, traditions, and language patterns. Starting with her third collection, *Scarifications* (1973), Cortez self-published her works through her Bola Press. Her subsequent collections include *Mouth on Paper* (1977), *Firespitter* (1982), *Coagulations: New and Selected Poems* (1984), *Poet Magnetic* (1991), and *Somewhere in Advance of Nowhere* (1996).

In addition, Cortez has produced various recordings of her poetic readings accompanied by music. The music is performed by her jazz group, the Firespitters, which includes her son, Denardo Coleman, on the drums; on at least one of her albums (*Maintain Control*), her former husband Ornette Coleman played the sax. Her recordings include *Celebrations and Solitudes* (1975), *Unsubmissive Blues* (1980), *There It Is* (1982), *Maintain Control* (1986), *Everywhere Drums* (1990), and *Taking the Blues Back Home: Poetry and Music* (1996). She and the Firespitters have also released a videotape of their performance. In addition to her published works (which have been translated into 28 languages), Cortez has lectured and performed her work in Europe, Africa, and North and South America.

Cortez's achievements have earned her two National Endowment for the Arts fellowships, a Before Columbus Foundation American Book Award for excellence in literature (1980), and the New York Foundation for the Arts award for poetry (1987).

REFERENCES: *EA-99. EBLG. OC20LE. WDAA.* Wilkinson, Michelle J., in *OCAAL.* Woodson, Jon, in *OCWW.*

Cosby, Bill (William Henry) (Jr.)
(7/12/1937–)
Humor, children's fiction, memoir

As a high school student, Bill was asked to join a class for gifted students, but family and work responsibilities led him to repeat the tenth grade and eventually to drop out of school. In 1956, he joined the U.S. Navy, where he earned his high school equivalency certificate and won awards for his athletic performance on the track. After his four-year stint in the Navy ended, he enrolled in Temple University on an athletic scholarship and majored in physical education.

While still in college, Cosby also worked as a bartender, continuing to develop the sense of humor that had helped him through difficult times in his early life. Occasionally, when the regular stand-up comedian didn't show, Cosby was asked to fill in. The money for that job was much better than what he earned as a bartender, so he started to seek other stand-up comedy jobs elsewhere. His exquisite timing, warm and friendly manner, and relaxed style of communicating made him appealing to audiences. By 1962, Cosby decided that he could earn pretty good money doing stand-up, so he left Temple in his sophomore year and worked in clubs in New York City, Chicago, and elsewhere. At first, he borrowed heavily from other successful comedians, but pretty soon, he was writing all his own material. In 1963, he recorded the first of about 30 comedy albums, which have cumulatively sold millions of copies.

That same year, Cosby met Camille Hanks through mutual friends, and despite the objections of her family, they wedded January 25, 1964. In part, Camille's parents objected because they foresaw that she would leave school to follow him as he rambled around the country for his career, which Camille's parents saw as offering less than a promising lifestyle for their daughter. Since then, the Cosbys had five children: Erika Ranee, Errin Chalene, Ensa Camille, Evin Harrah, and their only son, Ennis William, who was tragically murdered January 16, 1997. Within days after their son's death, while the Cosbys were still in shock with profound grief, a young woman attempted to extort millions from Cosby, claiming that she was his daughter through an extramarital relationship.

After gaining national attention on Johnny Carson's *Tonight Show* and other venues, in 1965 Cosby landed a contract to star in *I Spy* (costarring Robert Culp), which aired until 1968. Through this role, Cosby became the first African American to star in a dramatic role on network television, and he earned a few Emmys in the process. *I Spy* was followed by other television series: several *Bill Cosby Specials* (1968–1971, 1975), his sitcom the *Bill Cosby Show* (1969–1971), regular appearances on the educational *Electric Company* (1971–1976), his children's cartoon *Fat Albert and the Cosby Kids* (1972–1984; later called *The New Fat Albert Show*), his variety show *New Bill Cosby Show* (1972– 1973), *Cos* (1976), his sitcom *The Cosby Show* (1984–1992), the game show *You Bet Your Life* (1992–1993), his detective show *The Cosby Mysteries* (1994), his sitcom *Cosby* (1996–present), and the children's talk show *Kids Say the Darndest Things* (1997–present). In addition, Cosby has appeared in numerous films and television commercials.

Cosby's books include several books for adults: his best-selling *Fatherhood* (1986; named the all-time best-selling nonfiction book by an African American [in *AABL*]), *Bill Cosby's Personal Guide to Power Tennis* (1986), *Time Flies* (1987, about aging), *Love and Marriage* (1989), *Childhood* (1991), and *Congratulations! Now What? A Book for Graduates* (1999). In addition, through Scholastic's Cartwheel Books, he has published numerous "Little Bill Books for Beginning Readers" for elementary school children (ages seven to ten), including *The Best Way to Play* (1997), *The Meanest Thing to Say* (1997), *The Treasure Hunt* (1997), *Money Troubles* (1998), *Shipwreck Saturday* (1998), *Super-Fine Valentine* (1998), *The Day I Was Rich* (1999), *Hooray for the Dandelion Warriors* (1999), *My Big Lie* (1999), *One Dark and Scary Night* (1999), and *The Day I Saw My Father Cry* (2000). As you might expect from the creator of Cliff Huxtable, these books humorously accept children's foibles while encouraging them to show prosocial behavior. Cosby also has numerous audiocassettes and audio CDs available, including *200 mph* (1980), *I Started Out as a Child* (1980), *Wonderfulness* (1980/1998), *To Russell, My Brother* (1980/1998), *Bill Cosby Is a Very Funny Fellow* (1988), *Bill Cosby at His Best* (1993), and *Why Is There Air* (1998).

In addition to his extensive work, Cosby managed to return to college, earning his master's degree (1972) and his doctorate in education (1977) from the University of Massachusetts at Amherst. Later on, his wife Camille, who had also dropped out of college to support her husband's career, also earned her doctorate from the University of Massachusetts. The Cosbys have also given millions to colleges ($1.3 million to Fisk in 1986; $1.3 million to be shared among Central State at Wilberforce [Ohio], Howard University, Florida A&M State University, and Shaw University; $1.5 million to be shared between Meharry and Bethune-Cookman Colleges; and $20 million to Spelman; among others). Among the many honors he has received for his numerous achievements and contributions, he was awarded the NAACP's prestigious Spingarn Medal in 1985.

REFERENCES: *AABL. EB-BH-CD. EBLG. PGAA.* Bennett, Eric in *EA-99*. Smith, Jessie Carney, in *BH2C*. Amazon.com, 1/2000.

Coston, Julia (née) Ringwood
(fl. late 1800s)
Nonfiction—fashion magazines

In 1886, Julia Ringwood married minister and writer William Harry Coston and moved with him from Washington, D.C., to Cleveland, Ohio. In Ohio, in 1891, she started publishing the very first—ever—fashion magazine for African-American women, *Ringwood's Afro-American Journal of Fashion.* In 1893, she started up her second magazine, *Ringwood's Home Magazine,* another African-American women's first. Sadly, we know little else about Ringwood and nothing about either magazine after 1895.

—Tonya Bolden

REFERENCES: *BAAW.*

Cotter, Joseph Seamon, Jr. (1895–1919)
Poems; journalist

The son of poet **Joseph Seamon Cotter, Sr.**, Cotter set off on his own poetically. Although his father and their family friend **Paul Laurence Dunbar** wrote lyrical dialect poems, Cotter experimented with free verse as well as traditional poetic forms (e.g., a 19-sonnet sequence "Out of the Shadows"). While still a college student, Cotter worked for the *Fisk Herald,* a monthly published by Fisk University's literary societies. In his second year at Fisk, he contracted tuberculosis, so he returned home, where he served as editor and writer for the *Louisville Leader* newspaper. Before tuberculosis took his life when he was just 23 years old, he wrote the poems in his collection *The Band of Gideon* (1918) and the poems later gathered in *Joseph Seamon Cotter, Jr.: Complete Poems* (1990, edited by James Robert Payne). In addition, his one-act play *On the Fields of France,* about World War I being fought in Europe, was published in *Crisis* magazine.

REFERENCES: Payne, James Robert, in *OCAAL.*

Cotter, Joseph Seamon, Sr.
(2/2/1861–3/14/1949)
Poems, plays, short stories

Fortunately, Joseph Cotter had learned to read at age 3 and lived with a mother who was a gifted poet, storyteller, and playwright, because by age 8, he had to leave school to earn money for his family. At age 22, he was able to return to school and quickly learned enough to begin teaching; his career as an educator (public school teacher and administrator) lasted more than 50 years. Although Cotter is remembered best for his poetry, he also wrote several plays (e.g., his blank verse four-act play *Caleb, the Degenerate,* 1901 or 1903), a short-story collection (*Negro Tales,* 1912), a pamphlet on his civic leadership, and a collection of miscellany (*Negroes and Others at Work and Play,* 1947). His eclectic poetry collections include *A Rhyming* (1895), *Links of Friendship* (1898), *A White Song and a Black One* (1909), *Collected Poems of Joseph S. Cotter, Sr.* (1938), and *Sequel to the "Pied Piper of Hamelin" and Other Poems* (1939). Among the poems that continue to receive scholarly attention are his "The Negro's Loyalty," on the loyalty of an African-American soldier during the Spanish American War when lynchings were widespread in the American South; and his "Sequel to the 'Pied Piper of Hamelin,'" in response to Robert Browning's poem, "The Pied Piper." (NOTE: Robert Browning's mother was a dark-skinned Creole from St. Kitts in the Caribbean.) In 1894, Cotter and poet **Paul Laurence Dunbar** began a social and literary friendship, which prompted Cotter to experiment more with dialect poems. Tragically, Cotter's son, fellow poet **Joseph Seamon Cotter, Jr.**, predeceased him by 30 years.

REFERENCES: *EBLG.* Payne, James Robert, in *OCAAL.*

Craft, William (c. 1826–1900)
Fugitive slave narrative

After William Craft and his wife Ellen daringly escaped from slavery, he chronicled their escape in *Running a Thousand Miles for Freedom* (1860).

REFERENCES: *NYPL-AADR.* Nelson, Dana D., in *OCAAL.*

Crayton, Pearl (1930–)
Poems, short stories

Crayton's short stories and poems have been widely published in various journals and anthologies; for her work, she has been awarded the California Arts Council Poet in the Schools Fellowship (1987–1990).

—*Tonya Bolden*

REFERENCES: *RP.*

Crews, Donald (8/30/1938–)
Children's picture books

In addition to illustrating many children's picture books for other writers, Crews has written and vividly illustrated numerous books for young children, including *Ten Black Dots* (1970s; revised edition, 1986), *Freight Train* (1978; Caldecott Honor), *Truck* (1980; Caldecott Honor), *Light* (1981), *Carousel* (1982/1987), *Parade* (1983), *School Bus* (1984), *Bicycle Race* (1985), *Flying* (1986/ 1989), *Harbor* (reprinted 1987), *Bigmama's* (1991/ 1998), *Shortcut* (1992), *Sail Away* (1995), *Night at the Fair* (1998), *Cloudy Day Sunny Day* (1999), and *Chicken Coop* (2000). Most of Crews's books simply and boldly illustrate an aspect of the environment that appeals to young children. As he has observed, "Once I become fascinated with a subject, I'll do some freewheeling sketches. . . . thinking it through and exploring the visual possibilities. . . . I really believe in the idea of a *picture*-book. A picture-book is a book that really ought to tell the story with pictures" (*MAI-1,* pp. 24–25, emphasis in original). Crews also uses pictures and words to tell a narrative, as in his *Bigmama's* and *Shortcut,* which nostalgically take readers back to Crews's own visits to the home of his grandmother.

REFERENCES: *CBC. MAI-1.* AMAZON.COM, 1/2000.

Crisis (1910–)

The official magazine of the National Association for the Advancement of Colored People (NAACP), *Crisis* was founded in 1910 by **W. E. B. Du Bois**. Originally called the *Crisis: A Record of the Darker Races,* the magazine is historically important as the register of African-American history, thought, and culture. Du Bois said the reason for publishing *Crisis* was "to set forth those facts and arguments which show the danger of race prejudice, particularly as it is manifested today toward colored people. . . . The editors believe this is a critical time in the history of the advancement of men." After **Booker T. Washington**'s death in 1915, Du Bois assumed a role of national leadership through *Crisis.* The monthly magazine published literature, editorials, reports of NAACP activities, feature articles, and so on. Du Bois served as editor for 24 years, retiring in 1934. Among its contributors, *Crisis* published work by George Bernard Shaw, Mahatma Gandhi, Sinclair Lewis, **Langston Hughes**, and others. Though the circulation dropped dramatically when Du Bois retired, by 1988, the circulation had risen again to 350,000 subscribers. The *Crisis* continues to publish writing by contributors from all walks of life from clergy to lawyers, doctors, academics, and others.

—*Lisa Bahlinger*

REFERENCES: *AAW. EAACH* (Vol. 2).

Crosswaith, Frank Rudolph
(7/16/1892–1965)
Nonfiction

A native of the West Indies, Crosswaith edited the *Negro Labor News* and coauthored two books on African-American labor: *True Freedom for Negro and White Workers* and *Discrimination Incorporated*.

REFERENCES: Fay, Robert, in *EA-99*.

Crouch, Stanley (12/14/1945–)
Essays, criticism

Touted by the renowned writer Tom Wolfe as "the jazz virtuoso of the American essay, the maestro of startlingly original variations and improvisations upon familiar themes," and by **Henry Louis Gates, Jr.,** as "a moment, or embodiment, of hard earned integrity and insight . . . among our generation of writers," Stanley Crouch is one of the most critically acclaimed jazz and cultural critics of our era. He is a contributing editor to the *New Republic,* a Sunday columnist for the *New York Daily News,* and a frequent guest on *The Charlie Rose Show.* He has written three extremely well-received books of essays. He was a jazz critic and staff writer for the *Village Voice* for a number of years and is also artistic consultant for jazz at Lincoln Center.

It is remarkable that he rose to such heights, considering that his childhood was beset by extremely difficult circumstances. He was born in 1945 in Los Angeles to a father who was a heroin addict and a mother who worked long hours as a domestic. Despite her long working hours, she nevertheless managed to find time to teach him to read before he entered school—and may have set up a program of independent learning that he carried with him throughout his life. Although he attended Los Angeles Junior College and Southwest Junior College, he never received a degree—he is instead a self-educated man, but no less a writer for his lack of a diploma.

In the 1960s, Crouch was involved in the theater, working as an actor, director, and playwright. He also was a drummer in his own jazz band and

even recorded an album. During that time, he was interested in black nationalism, but upon reading the works of **Ralph Ellison** and **Albert L. Murray** began to distance himself from that movement.

Today some call him a "race traitor" because of his conservative views that include criticizing the civil rights movement. His critical writing is said to be extremely harsh and biting—as almost all satire is—but with a wit that has led writer Saul Bellow to characterize him as "jazzy, breezy and playful" yet "willing to reject the taboos which restrict the free discussion of racial and other social questions." Despite his critics, he speaks his mind and denounces "all forms of cant, quackery and nonsense."

—*Diane Masiello*

REFERENCES: Crouch, Stanley (1998), *Always in Pursuit: Fresh American Perspectives, 1995–1997* (New York: Pantheon Books). Early, Gerald, in *OCAAL*.

Crummell, Alexander
(3/2/1819–9/10/1898)
Sermons, political writings

Crummell gained his early education in schools operated by African-American clerics and in integrated schools run by white abolitionists. (His schoolmates included **Henry Highland Garnet** and Ira Aldridge, later an internationally renowned actor.) When racist policies barred him from gaining the pastoral and theological education he sought, Crummell entered a program of self-study and of training in the Episcopal Seminary in Boston, and in 1844, he was ordained an Episcopal priest. When he found it impossible to raise enough money to build a church in New York City for his impoverished parishioners, he went to England to raise funds. During the three years he traveled around Britain raising his church-building funds, he was also studying with a tutor, who prepared him to enter Queen's College in Cambridge. There, Crummell earned his baccalaureate (1853), but instead of returning to the United States, he moved to the newly independent (in 1847) African nation of Liberia, where he served as an Episcopalian missionary for the next 20 years. In Liberia, he faced many challenges, such as founding numerous churches and encouraging the moral uplift of his parishioners, but not the U.S. ones of slavery, the Civil War, and the early Reconstruction era.

Although Crummell visited the United States several times to encourage African Americans to emigrate to Liberia and to raise funds for Liberian schools, churches, and other worthy causes, he did not return to live in the United States until political upheaval in Liberia forced him to flee there in 1872 or 1873. He then founded and pastored St. Luke's Episcopal Church in the nation's capital.

In 1894, he retired from the ministry to teach theology at Howard University (1895–1897). After that, he founded the American Negro Academy (1897), which included such celebrated scholars as **W. E. B. Du Bois** and **Paul Laurence Dunbar**, and he was the Academy's first president. It was his hope that this premier scholarly society for African Americans would promote the publication of scholarly works on African-American history and culture.

Crummell's own publications included *The Relations and Duties of Free Colored Men in America to Africa* (1861) and *The Future of Africa* (1862), which encouraged Africans and African Americans to appreciate a shared resistance to the oppression they suffered; *The Greatness of Christ* (1882), a collection of sermons preaching the need for Christians to do good deeds as well as to accept Christ as their savior; and *Africa and America* (1891, collecting speeches and essays from the 1860s), on the relationship between the continent and the nation, particularly focusing on Africa's descendants in this country. Whatever he wrote or preached, he was always advocating on behalf of the civil rights and voting rights of Africans and of African Americans, although he often emphasized the need for developing moral character more than political action as a means to that end. He often urged fellow African Americans to lift themselves up through education (especially vocational training)—thereby anticipating **Booker T. Washington**'s emphasis on vocational education. He also urged the well-educated African-American elite, the "talented tenth," to lift up their race through service to others, thereby anticipating the views of Washington's intellectual adversary, W. E. B. Du Bois, who made famous Crummell's phrase as the basis for his personal philosophy.

REFERENCES: *AAW. BDAA. BWA. EA-99. EB-BH-CD.* West, Elizabeth J., in *OCAAL.*

Cruse, Harold Wright (3/18/1916–)
Nonfiction essays and books

Cruse's thought-provoking books on politics include *The Crisis of the Negro Intellectual: A Histor-*

ical Analysis of the Failure of Black Leadership (1967); his collection of essays, *Rebellion or Revolution?* (1968); and *Plural but Equal* (1982).

REFERENCES: Balfour, Lawrie, in *EA-99.*

Cullen, Countee (né Countée LeRoy Porter) (3/30/1903–1/9/1946)
Poems, essays, children's books, plays

Little is known about Countee's childhood, and he failed to provide much information himself. (EDITOR'S NOTE: He may have lived with his mother's mother until 1918, when she died. There is also some question as to his birth date, as some sources list May 30 and others list March 30.) In 1918, Countee LeRoy Porter was adopted by Reverend Frederick Cullen and his wife, Carolyn, leaders of one of the largest and most influential churches in Harlem (the exact date and circumstances of the adoption are unknown). His birthplace has been reported to be Louisville, Baltimore, and New York City. Cullen is said to have claimed New York as his birthplace after he achieved celebrity for his work, but scholars believe that Louisville is correct, as Cullen himself wrote on official college documents; in addition, others who knew him well, such as his second wife, affirmed the Louisville origin.

Cullen was an excellent student, and he began writing poetry in elementary school. In high school, he achieved his first writing success by winning a citywide contest, and he was a published poet before he graduated. While still a college undergraduate, Cullen wrote most of the poems that were published in his first three books of poetry (*Color,* 1925; *Copper Sun,* 1927; *The Ballad of the Brown Girl,* 1927). He also won many poetry awards during this time. Cullen graduated with honors from New York University, where he earned a teaching degree, and he earned his master's degree from Harvard in 1927. After college, Cullen returned to school—as a teacher, inspiring countless students to become creative writers and thinkers (e.g., **James Baldwin** and **Kenneth Clark**).

Cullen is one of the earliest black writers (preceded by **Phillis Wheatley** and **Paul Laurence Dunbar**) to garner several important writing awards and widespread—though not unanimous—respect for his work. Cullen's poetry is most strongly characterized by bridges: His poetic aesthetic was founded on the belief that art could bridge the differences between white and black

Countee Cullen, poet of the Harlem Renaissance (Culver Pictures)

American cultures. Unlike some of his contemporaries writing during the **Harlem Renaissance**, he believed that black writers should attempt to work within English conventions rather than modeling their work on African arts. Eschewing experimentation with jazz, blues, or free verse forms, which characterize the work of many of his peers, he focused on writing in traditional lyric modes. He felt it was unnecessary to attempt to create distinctions between white and black poetry, believing, as he said in his foreword to *Caroling Dusk: An Anthology of Verse by Negro Poets* (1927), that "Negro poets, dependent as they are on the English language, may have more to gain from the rich background of English and American poetry than from any nebulous atavistic yearnings toward an African inheritance."

This aesthetic did not prevent Cullen from strongly indicting U.S. racism in his work. In poems such as "Heritage," "Atlantic City Waiter," "Incident," "Tableau," and "Ballad of a Brown Girl," Cullen expresses tremendous anger and frustration at the unfairness of racism. Though racial in nature, these poems, like his others that focus on more traditional romantic themes of love and

death, were geared at reaching Cullen's main aims—to show that blacks could write traditional poetry as well as anyone, to help bring more harmonious racial relations to the United States, and thus to achieve a complete sense of colorblind artistic freedom in this country. In addition to the aforementioned volumes, Cullen published the collections *The Medea, and Some Poems* (1935), *The Lost Zoo (A Rhyme for the Young, but Not Too Young)* (1940), and *On These I Stand: An Anthology of the Best Poems of Countee Cullen* (1947, published after Cullen's death in 1946).

Ironically, because of his attempts to bridge African-American and European-American cultures and poetic expression, Cullen was criticized by many of his literary contemporaries who asserted that the rigid structure of his traditional literary forms could not address the radical ideas that needed to be addressed. Many also denounced him for being too quiet in his rejection of the white status quo, and although many of his poems clearly attack racism, Cullen himself has been quoted as saying that he did not strive to be a "Negro poet" but rather just a poet. Also, according to one scholar, Cullen completely abandoned racial themes after writing *The Black Christ and Other Poems* (1929). In addition to these apparent contrasts, Cullen felt conflicts about his sexual orientation and about his own spirituality. His spiritual conflict served as the basis for many of his works, including *The Black Christ*. In this and other works, he both rejects and accepts Christianity and a Christian god.

Although Cullen's poetic star dimmed later in his life, when the Great Depression drew attention and funding away from the work of the Harlem Renaissance, he stayed very active in teaching and turned his creative energy elsewhere. He wrote one novel, *One Way to Heaven* (1932), which deals with two different kinds of life in Harlem—that of the lower-middle-class church attendees that populated his father's church and that of the people of the intellectual circles in which he ran as a young man. Critics panned it as uneven and mediocre, so he abandoned novel writing to become quite an accomplished dramatist, working with **Arna Bontemps** to adapt Bontemps's novel into the play *St. Louis Woman*.

Cullen died before the play premiered on Broadway but left behind a luminous record of achievement. Though he is remembered most vividly for his early poetry, his less famous work as a teacher and an astute and fair literary critic was equally brilliant and more consistent. His resilience and determination to succeed despite setbacks in both poetic and novelistic endeavors make him not only one of the great artists but also one of the great men of his time.

EDITOR'S NOTE: In 1927, Cullen was awarded a Guggenheim fellowship and a Harman Foundation award for his poetry. With that money in hand, he planned to study in Europe. Before leaving, however, he wed the daughter of **W. E. B. Du Bois,** Yolande. The marriage ended in divorce in 1930. A decade later, Cullen married Ida Mae Roberson, to whom he was still married when he died. (See *BDAA*.)

—*Diane Masiello and Janet Hoover*

REFERENCES: *AAL. BW:SSCA. DANB.* Bloom, Harold (1994), "Countee Cullen, 1903–1946," *Black American Prose Writers of the Harlem Renaissance: Writers of English, Lives and Works* (New York: Chelsea), "Countee Cullen, 1903–1946," *BLC-1.* "Countee Cullen, 1903–1946," and "Harlem Renaissance, 1919–1949," in *NAAAL.* Early, Gerald, in *OCAAL.* Lewis, David Levering (1994), *Harlem Renaissance Reader* (New York: Viking). Shackelford, D. Dean, "Poetry of Countee Cullen," in *MAAL.*

Cuney-Hare, Maud
See **Hare, Maud Cuney**

Curtis, Christopher Paul (5/10/1953–)
Juvenile novels

Thus far, Curtis has produced just two novels for young readers, each of which has won two awards from the prestigious American Library Association: *The Watsons Go to Birmingham, 1963* (1996) won a Coretta Scott King Honor and the John Newbery Medal (and was named among the best books of 1995 by the *New York Times Book Review, Horn Book,* and *Publishers Weekly,* among others), and *Bud, Not Buddy* (1999) won both the Coretta Scott King Award and the Newbery Medal. In Curtis's first book, ten-year-old Kenny Watson, a native of Flint, Michigan, must accompany his family to his grandparents' home in Birmingham, Alabama, where he views the civil-rights struggle up close. Kenny's story offers humor and compassion, as well as frank insights into the terrifying realities of Southern racism during that era.

Curtis's second book, set during the Great Depression, tells the compelling story of a ten-year-old orphan who flees his foster home in Flint, hoping to find a father he has never known. His only clues come from some old flyers advertising a jazz band. The Newbery Award selection committee chair noted, "This heartfelt novel resonates with both zest and tenderness as it entertains questions about racism, belonging, love, and hope. Bud's fast-paced, first-person account moves with the rhythms of jazz and celebrates life, family and a child's indomitable spirit." For Curtis, however, "the highest accolade comes when a young reader tells me, 'I really liked your book.' . . . That is why I write" (http://www.randomhouse.com/teachersbdd. curt.html).

Like his protagonists, Curtis grew up in Flint, Michigan, where he worked for 13 years on an auto assembly line and attended the Flint branch of the University of Michigan. Curtis recalled, "I used to write during breaks because it took me away from being in the factory. . . . I was probably very young when I knew I wanted to write; but as a profession, that didn't come until [much, much later]. . . . The best advice I can give to any aspiring writer is to write. Write anytime you have the opportunity. . . . like any other skill, you have to work at it and you have to practice." Nowadays, Curtis does most of his writing in the library, having discovered it as a haven when he was still a young boy.

Curtis and his wife, Kaysandra, live in Windsor, Ontario, Canada, with their two children, Steven Darrell and Cydney McKenzie.

REFERENCES: Gross, Terry, Interview on National Public Radio, Fresh Air, 1/27/2000. *NPR-ME,* 2/6/2000. http://www.ala.org/newbery.html. http://www.ala.org/news/newberycaldecott2000. html. http://www.randomhouse.com/teachersbdd. curt.html. amazon.com, 1/2000.

Damas, Léon-Gontran

(3/28/1912–1/22/1978)
Poems, travel writings

A native of French Guiana, Damas was comfortable in France, Africa, and the United States (spending the last years of his life here). He was one of three main poets to found and champion the Negritude movement, which celebrated the achievements of persons of African descent, particularly highlighting the work of French-speaking writers. (The other two were Aimé Césaire and Léopold Sédar Senghor.) His own writings include the travel book *Retour de Guyane* [Return from Guiana] (1938); the poetry collections *Pigments* (1937), *Graffiti* (1952), *Black-Label* (1956), and *Névralgies* (1966); and the anthology he edited, *Poètes noirs d'expression française* [Black Poets in the French Language] (1948).

REFERENCES: *EA-99. NYPL-AADR.*

Danner, Margaret (Essie or Esse)

(1/12/1915–1984)
Poems

Caleb and Naomi Danner raised their daughter Margaret in Chicago, where she won her first poetry prize when she was still in the eighth grade. After graduating from Englewood High School, she went on to study poetry at Loyola College, Roosevelt University, and Northwestern University. We know little of Danner's private life: She married Cordell Strickland, and the pair had a daughter, whom they named Naomi after Margaret's mother; Danner later married again, to Otto Cunningham, and she had at least one grandchild: her grandson, Sterling Washington, Jr., who inspired Danner to write what she called her "muffin poems." Even the spelling of her middle name is disputed, spelled differently in different sources.

During the 1940s, Danner was still writing poems, as she was awarded second prize in the poetry workshop of the Midwestern Writers Conference in 1945. From the 1950s through the 1970s, Danner's life as a writer became more public. From 1951 to 1957, she worked for *Poetry: The Magazine of Verse,* published in Chicago. She started out as an editorial assistant, and in 1956, she became the first African-American assistant editor there. At *Poetry,* she worked with Karl Shapiro and Paul Engle, who encouraged her as a poet; she later recalled her experiences there as being among the most rewarding she ever had. Her series "Far from Africa: Four Poems" was printed in a 1951 issue of the magazine, and it is still widely anthologized. The series also won her the 1951 John Hay Whitney fellowship, which was to help pay for her to travel to Africa. It ended up being about a decade and a half before she finally made the trip.

By 1961, Danner had left Chicago and moved to Detroit, where she became the first poet-in-residence at Wayne State University. The following year, she convinced Dr. Boone, the minister of Detroit's King Solomon Church, that his parish needed a community arts center, and she persuaded him to let her convert an empty parish house into the Boone House for the Arts. Soon other notable African-American poets were also involved in Boone House, including **Dudley Randall**, **Robert Hayden**, and **Naomi Long Madgett**.

Both Boone House and Randall's **Broadside Press** helped make Detroit a major center of the **Black Arts movement** and made Danner's poetry a prominent feature in that movement. In 1962, Broadside published Danner's *To Flower.* Four years later, Broadside published Danner and Randall's *Poem Counterpoem* (1966), which provided matched poems on facing pages, one written by each author. The poems treated a variety of subjects from each author's distinctive perspective and poetic viewpoint. That year, Danner finally made it to Africa, when she went to Dakar, Senegal, to present her work at the World Exposition of Negro Arts. She returned to the United States with a deepened commitment to highlighting African traditions among African Americans.

In 1968, Broadside Press published Danner's *Impressions of African Art Forms.* As the title suggests, many of her poems celebrated Africa's many gifts to African Americans and encouraged African Americans to prize their African heritage. During the 1968–1969 academic year, Danner was poet-in-residence at Virginia Union University (in Richmond), and during the 1970s, she was poet-in-residence at LeMoyne-Owens College (in Memphis, Tennessee). During this period, Danner's poetry collections included *Iron Lace* (1968) and *The Down of a Thistle: Selected Poems, Prose Poems, and Songs* (1976). *The Down of a Thistle,* perhaps her most important collection, was dedicated to Robert Hayden and included poems illustrated with African images as well as poems protesting against white racism and its effects on African Americans. Danner also participated in the 1973 **Phillis Wheatley** Poetry Festival, a gala event rejoicing in poetry written by African-American women.

REFERENCES: *AAW:AAPP. BAL-1-P. EBLG.* Aldridge, June M., in *OCWW.* Carson, Sharon, in *OCAAL.* Thompson, Kathleen, in *BWA:AHE.*

Danticat, Edwidge (1/19/1969–)
Short stories, novels

Danticat's writings include the novels *Breath, Eyes, Memory* (1994) and *The Farming of Bones* (1998) and her short-story collection *Krik?Krak!* (1995), all of which reflect her experiences as a Haitian American.

REFERENCES: Cantave, Sophia, in *EA-99.*

Dash, Julie (10/22/1952–)
Screenplays, documentaries

Dash's documentaries include *Working Models of Success* (1973), *Four Women* (1978, focusing on experimental dance), *Illusions* (1983, about African-American women in the film industry), *Breaking the Silence: On Reproductive Rights* (1987), *Preventing Cancer* (1987) and a documentary on **Zora Neale Hurston** as well as two music videos (1992, 1994). In addition to these works, the film scripts she has written include *Diary of an African Nun* (1977, based on an **Alice Walker** short story) and *Daughters of the Dust* (the first full-length general-release film by an African-American woman). *Daughters of the Dust,* written primarily in Gullah patois with occasional American English subtitles, premiered at the celebrated Sundance Film Festival in 1991 and aired nationally on Public Broadcasting System's *American Playhouse* series in 1992.

REFERENCES: *EA-99.* Goodall, N. H., in *BWA:AHE.*

Davis, Angela Yvonne (1/26/1944–)
Essays, autobiography

During the 1970s, scholar and militant political activist Angela Davis wrote a memoir (*If They Come in the Morning: Voices of Resistance,* 1971) and her best-selling autobiography (*Angela Davis: An Autobiography,* 1974/1989) about her experiences. In the 1980s, she wrote several books on how women fit into our social, political, and economic structure, including *Women, Race, and Class* (1981) and *Women, Culture and Politics* (1989). Other books of hers include *Blues Legacies and Black Feminism: Gertrude "Ma" Rainey, Bessie Smith, and Billie Holiday* (1998) and the *Angela Y. Davis Reader* (1998, edited by Joy James).

Despite her many contributions to scholarship, Davis may be best remembered for her Marxist rhetoric, her membership in the Communist Party and in the Black Panther Party, and her link to **George Jackson,** one of the Soledad Brothers who was charged with murdering guards at Soledad Prison. At Jackson's trial, there was an aborted attempt to help him escape from a California courtroom, which ended up killing Jackson's brother, a trial judge, and two other people. Davis was accused of conspiring in the disastrous attempt, and she fled from prosecution. Placed on the FBI's most-wanted list, within two months, Davis had been arrested, denied bail, and imprisoned while she waited . . . and waited for a trial. At the end of the years-long process, an all-white jury acquitted her of all charges. Barred from teaching at any publicly funded institutions in California (by then-governor Ronald Reagan), she sought positions at various private institutions. In the early 1990s, Davis managed to regain a position teaching philosophy at the University of California at Santa Cruz.

—Tonya Bolden

REFERENCES: *BAAW. BDAA. EB-98. G-97.* Elliott, Joan C., in *OCAAL.*

Davis, Frank Marshall
(12/31/1905–7/26/1987)
Poems, memoir; journalist

From 1930 until 1955, Davis, who never earned a college degree, worked as a feature writer, editorial writer, sports reporter, theater and music critic,

Angela Yvonne Davis, author and political activist, 1970 (Archive Photos)

correspondent, contributing editor, editor, managing editor, and executive editor for several Chicago-based African-American periodicals, including the *Evening Bulletin,* the *Whip,* and the *Star,* and for various other periodicals, such as the *Atlanta World,* the *Gary* (Indiana) *American,* and the *Negro Digest,* as well as the Associated Negro Press. He also wrote short fiction for some of these periodicals.

Other than journalism, Davis's chief literary love was poetry, which at first seemed to love him back. Davis's first poetry collection, *Black Man's Verse* (1935) was acclaimed by such notable critics as Stephen Vincent Benét, **Sterling Brown**, and **Alain Locke**, some of whom compared his poems to those of American folk poets Walt Whitman and Carl Sandburg. His next two poetry collections (*I Am the American Negro,* 1937; *Through Sepia Eyes,* 1938) were less well received. Although his *47th Street: Poems* (1948) is considered by some to be his best effort, after his 1948 move to Hawaii, he seemed to fade into oblivion, operating a wholesale paper business and writing a weekly column for the *Honolulu Record.* Later on, he published his autobiographical narrative poem *Sex Rebel: Black*

(1968) and his collection *Awakening, and Other Poems* (1978).

In the late 1960s and early 1970s, however, poet and historian **Margaret Taylor Burroughs**, literary critic Stephen Henderson, and publisher and poet **Dudley Randall** rediscovered his work, and soon Davis was giving readings and lectures at black colleges around the country. His existing poems were reprinted, and he wrote many new poems, which were gathered in his *Jazz Interlude* (1985). After his death, his *Livin' the Blues: Memoirs of a Black Journalist and Poet* was published in 1992.

REFERENCES: *BV. EBLG. G-97. TtW.* Tidwell, John Edgar, in *OCAAL.*

Davis, Ossie (12/18/1917–)

Plays, scripts, novel, memoir

When Ossie was a wee little boy in Cogdell, Georgia, his father, Kince Charles Davis, was threatened by Ku Klux Klan (KKK) members. The Klan didn't go too far, however, because the white folks in the area needed his skills: He was a self-taught (though illiterate) railway-construction engineer who was willing to work for a black man's wages. Davis later commented that the KKK incident motivated him to become a writer in order to tell the world the truth about the African-American experience.

Because there were no schools in Cogdell, when Ossie was five years old, he had to move 23 miles away to live with the father and stepmother of his mother (Laura Davis) in Waycross, where he could go to school. In high school, Ossie started writing plays as well as acting in them. When he went on to Howard University (1935–1939), he studied under drama critic **Alain Locke**, who encouraged him to go to New York City to make his career in the theater. In New York, Davis joined the Rose McClendon Players of Harlem, making his stage debut with them in 1941. Meanwhile, Davis continued to write plays in his off hours.

World War II prompted Davis to take a temporary leave from the theater, while he served in the medical corps and in special services for the U.S. Army. Even in the military, he continued to write for the stage. He wrote and produced the musical variety show *Goldbrickers of 1944* while he was posted in Liberia. In 1945, following his discharge, he returned to New York right away. There, he was awarded the title role in *Jeb* (1946, written by Robert Ardrey), costarring with a talented young actress, **Ruby Dee**. Numerous other stage performances (e.g., *A Raisin in the Sun,* 1959) followed—as did his (December, 1948) marriage to Ruby Dee, with whom he has shared his life ever since. (Davis and Dee have three children.)

Davis has also performed on television, such as his 1969 Emmy-winning performance in *Teacher, Teacher,* for which he wrote the script; his regular role on *Evening Shade,* 1990–1994; and countless other appearances. He has also acted in movies (e.g., the film version of *Raisin* and several **Spike Lee** features, such as *Do The Right Thing,* 1989) and has directed them. Among the films he has directed are these for which he also wrote the screenplays: *Cotton Comes to Harlem* (1970, written with Arnold Perl, based on a **Chester Himes** novel), *Black Girl* (1972; coscripted), and *Countdown at Kusini* (1976). Davis also coproduced *Countdown* with Dee; it was the first American feature film that was filmed entirely in Africa, using only black professionals. Among the other television programs by Dee and Davis are "The Ruby Dee/Ossie Davis Story Hour" (1974) and the Public Broad-

casting System arts education television series *With Ossie and Ruby* (1981).

Davis and Dee have also been partners in civil rights activism. In fact, during the 1950s, their activism cost them many opportunities to work, when they were blacklisted by the ruthless, right-wing anticommunists of the paranoid McCarthy era. During the 1960s, the red scare had subsided, and Davis and Dee's careers were resurrected. As they gained celebrity, they used their fame and popularity to promote civil rights causes. Davis acted as master of ceremonies for the 1963 March on Washington and delivered memorable and moving eulogies for both **Martin Luther King, Jr.**, and **Malcolm X**. In 1972, Davis chaired the fund-raising drive to pay for **Angela Davis**'s defense against conspiracy charges, of which she was later acquitted.

Davis's earliest plays include *The Mayor of Harlem* (1949), *Point Blank* (1949), *Clay's Rebellion* (1951), *What Can You Say, Mississippi?* (1955), and *Montgomery Footprints* (1956), about the civil rights movement. Another of his early works was his one-act play *Alice in Wonder* (1952), which he then expanded into his full-length *The Big Deal* (1953); the story centers around the moral dilemma of an African-American television performer who is asked either to testify against his brother-in-law during a McCarthy-era witch hunt or to face being unable to find work in his field.

Davis's first commercially successful play was his satirical *Purlie Victorious* (1961), about an African-American preacher who seeks to build a racially integrated church in the South. When the play debuted on Broadway, Davis played the title role. He later adapted the play to make the feature film *Gone Are the Days* (1963). Davis even adapted the play into a musical version, *Purlie* (1970), in collaboration with Philip Rose, Peter Udell, and Gary Geld. (In 1993, the play was published as *Purlie Victorious: A Commemorative*.) Decades later, Davis adapted another work to the musical form: William Brashler's book *Bingo Long's Traveling All Stars and Motor Kings* (1985), about a baseball team during the days of the old Negro League.

Some of Davis's other plays honor the lives of important African Americans, such as *Curtain Call* (1963), about Shakespearean actor Ira Aldridge; *Escape to Freedom: The Story of Frederick Douglass, A Play for Young People* (1976; published by Viking Junior Books, 1978; republished in 1990 as *Escape to Freedom: A Play about Young Frederick Douglass*); and

Langston: A Play (1982), about poet **Langston Hughes**. Other plays by Davis include *Alexis Is Fallen* (1974) and *They Seek a City* (1974). In 1992, Davis wrote a novel intended for youths ages 10–14: *Just Like Martin,* set around the time of the 1963 March on Washington. The book centers on the relationship between an embittered father and his idealistic teenage son, who admires Martin Luther King, Jr.'s nonviolent means of effecting social change and achieving civil rights.

In 1998, Davis and Dee published their collaborative memoir *With Ossie and Ruby: In This Life Together,* in honor of their fiftieth wedding anniversary. The authors wrote the book in alternating chapters, starting with Dee in Chapter 1 and Davis's recollection of the KKK incident in Chapter 2. A *New York Times Book Review* critic observed that the book is "a conversation studded with anecdotes . . . inspiration, wisdom and gossip." In addition to their personal experiences, their family life, and their careers in entertainment, a central theme in their work is their participation in "The Struggle" for civil rights for all Americans.

Among Davis's numerous awards are the Hall of Fame Award for outstanding artistic achievement (1989) and the Image Award for best performance by a supporting actor for the film *Do the Right Thing* (1989) from the National Association for the Advancement of Colored People, the National Medal for the Arts (1995), and the Presidential Medal for Lifetime Achievement in the Arts.

REFERENCES: *AA:PoP. EBLG. G-97.* Davis, Ossie, and Ruby Dee (1998), *With Ossie and Ruby: In This Life Together* (New York: William Morrow). Edwards, Roanne, in *EA-99.* Jackson, Cassandra, in *OCAAL.* Amazon.com, barnesandnoble.com, 7/1999.

Davis, Thulani (c. mid-1900s–)
Poems, novels, articles, libretti

In addition to her regular contributions to New York City's *Village Voice,* Davis's published works include her poetry collections, such as *Playing the Changes* (1985); novels, such as *1959* (1992); libretti, such as *X: The Life and Times of Malcolm X* (1986); and the text accompanying a photograph book, *Malcolm X: The Great Photographs* (1995).

REFERENCES: *EBLG.*

Dee, Ruby (née Ruby Ann Wallace) (10/27/1924–)
Children's books, poems, stories, plays, memoirs, columns; editor

Ossie Davis, her husband since 1948, introduced her in *My One Good Nerve: Rhythms, Rhymes, Reasons* (1986) with this observation:

Here is a mind that diddles with nursery rhymes, that turns popular themes upside down in unexpected stories and poems that are serious without half trying as they pay tribute, embrace or criticize. For example, the nursery rhymes—behind the chuckles—are comments about unemployment, loneliness, racism, housing, abortion, love and death. The stories are fantasies about overpopulation, growing old, looking for a handout from heaven, or eating pork. Some seem almost autobiographical as she writes about childhood memories or an experience in Hollywood. There is a real appreciation here of the people she salutes in poetry and prose.

You may know Dee better for her acting, which she started doing in the early 1940s, along with Sidney Poitier, Harry Belafonte, and the man whom she was to claim as her own, Ossie Davis. She has won an Obie for her stage work and an Emmy for her movie work (she has acted in more than 25 silver-screen and made-for-TV movies since the 1950s, and she and Davis had their own PBS series, *With Ossie and Ruby* in 1981). More importantly, she managed to create a fine acting career even though she consistently chose her conscience over opportunities to enhance her career. She consistently refused to keep quiet, restrain her protests, and refrain from supporting **Malcolm X**, the Black Panthers, or any other militants who asserted their rights and pursued freedom.

For the world of literature, long before she published her *My One Good Nerve,* she started contributing poems to Harlem's *Amsterdam News* when she was still a teenager. Since then, she has edited poetry collections (e.g., *Glowchild and Other Poems,* 1972) and written children's books (e.g., *Two Ways to Count to Ten* and *Tower to Heaven*), stories, and plays, including the script for the musical *Take It from the Top.* In 1989, she received a Literary Guild Award for her body of work.

EDITOR'S NOTE: Dee has also written columns for the *Amsterdam News* and has been an associate editor for *Freedomways.* Dee's one-woman show,

Ruby Dee and Ossie Davis starred in Seven Times Monday, *1960s (Archive Photos)*

based on *My One Good Nerve,* opened in New York in 1998. That year, Dee and Davis published *With Ossie and Ruby: In This Life Together,* which they coauthored. The twosome has three children and numerous grandchildren.

—*Tonya Bolden*

REFERENCES: *BAAW. EA-99.* Pagan, Margaret D., in *BWA:AHE.* Amazon.com, 7/1999. (See also *BDAA.*)

Delaney, Sara ("Sadie") Marie (née) Johnson (2/26/1889–5/4/1958)
Nonfiction articles—library sciences, bibliography

Delaney's published works include her articles on bibliotherapy (e.g., "Bibliotherapy in a Hospital," 1938, **Opportunity** magazine) and on the need for books about African Americans (e.g., "The Negro and His Books"), but perhaps her major contribution to literature was her initiation and promotion of books as a therapeutic means of recovery for African-American war veterans, in her role as chief librarian of the U.S. Veterans Administration Hospital in Tuskegee, Alabama (where she expanded the library's collection from 200 to 4,000 books, as well as other materials). Prior to her work at Tuskegee, Delaney had worked at the New York Public Library branch in the center of the **Harlem Renaissance**, where she learned firsthand about noteworthy African-American authors.

EDITOR'S NOTE: Sara's birth surname was Johnson, her first married surname was Peterson, and her second married surname was Delaney.

—*Tonya Bolden*

REFERENCES: *BAAW.*

Delany, (Annie Elizabeth) "Bessie" (9/3/1891–9/25/1995)
Memoir, inspirational advice

The third of ten children, Bessie Delany, like all her other siblings, worked her way through college. Initially, Bessie graduated from St. Augustine's College in Raleigh, North Carolina. With that start on her education, she taught school for a little more than two years, when a confrontation with an intoxicated white man just about got her lynched. Soon after, she and her sister Sadie left the Jim Crow South and moved to New York City, where she enrolled in dentistry courses at Columbia University in 1919. In 1923, she was awarded her doctorate of dental surgery and became the second African-American woman to become a licensed dentist in New York City. When she retired from her practice in 1950, she was still charging the same rates she had charged when she started her practice. After all, she said, she "was getting by OK. I was always proud of my work, and that was enough for me." After hours, political activists such as family friend **W. E. B. Du Bois**, sociologist **Edward Franklin Frazier**, and NAACP leader **Walter White** frequently met at her dental office.

Bessie Delany's chief contribution to literature is the book she wrote with her sister Sadie, *Having Our Say: The Delany Sisters' First 100 Years* (1993, with *New York Times* reporter Amy Hill Hearth). In their book, these two centenarians vividly and charmingly chronicled more than 100 years of their lives and of distinctive American experiences across the span of the twentieth century. Although they drop names (e.g., fellow Harlemite **Adam Clayton Powell** and various celebrities of the **Harlem Renaissance**), they do so with humor and grace. Camille Cosby (see **Bill Cosby**) purchased the film, stage, and television rights to their runaway best-seller, which became the basis for a Broadway play, which was subsequently made into a full-length TV movie. By popular demand, the two sisters then wrote *The Delany Sisters' Book of Everyday Knowledge* (1994, with Amy Hill Hearth), in which they offered uplifting inspiration and down-to-earth advice (e.g., they recommended reading the newspaper and watching Public Television's news-hour show each day, praying twice daily, doing yoga exercises, eating lots of vegetables and garlic every day, and taking cod-liver oil and vitamin supplements).

REFERENCES: *EB-98.* Browne, Phiefer L., in *BH2C* and in *PBW.* Amazon.com, 7/1999.

Delany, Clarissa (née Scott) (?/1901–1927)
Poems, essays

In association with the Urban League and the Women's City Club of New York, Delany published a study, "Delinquency and Neglect among Negro Children in New York City." Unfortunately, many of Delany's writings were unpublished and thereby lost to posterity when members of her immediate family died. Nonetheless, we do still have some of her works, which were published in anthologies and literary periodicals, including her essay "A Golden Afternoon in Germany" and poems "Interim," "The Mask," "Solace," and "Joy." Of these, the best known is her very long prize-winning poem "Solace," published in the Urban League's *Opportunity* magazine in 1925.

—*Tonya Bolden*

REFERENCES: *BAAW.*

Delany, Martin R. (Robison)
(5/6/1812–1/24/1885)
Novel, nonfiction books and articles; publisher

One of the first African Americans to enter Harvard Medical School, Delany is better known for his writing, for which he is often called the "father of black nationalism." In the mid-1840s (1843–1847), Delany launched *Mystery,* his weekly abolitionist, feminist, and civil rights newspaper. Even with his focus on abolition and civil rights, many of the articles he printed were later reprinted in white-owned newspapers because of the high quality of the writing and the journalism. In the late 1840s (1847–1849), he stopped publishing his own paper and joined **Frederick Douglass** as coeditor of Douglass's *North Star,* another abolitionist weekly newspaper. At the end of the 1840s, he turned his attention to medical school and to his medical practice for a time, but by the early 1850s, he once again made time for his political views.

In 1852, Delany alienated—and infuriated—his fellow abolitionists with his *The Condition, Elevation, Emigration and Destiny of the Colored People of the United States, Politically Considered,* in which he appealed to African Americans to abandon hope of eliminating slavery and oppression in the United States and to emigrate to Africa instead. In 1856, he moved his family (which would eventually include seven children, all named after admirable Africans and African Americans) to Chatham, Ontario (the "Canada West" **Mary Ann Shadd [Cary]** described so invitingly and a hotbed of revolutionary abolitionism). There, in 1859, he published his highly popular insurrectionist, pan-African novel, *Blake, or The Huts of America,* considered to be the first black nationalist novel. Sadly, in the copies still extant today, the last six chapters are missing.

Starting in the spring of 1859, Delany practiced what he preached, sailing to Africa and exploring Liberia and the Niger Valley for three fourths of a year. He published his account of that sojourn in his *Official Report of the Niger Valley Exploring Party*

in 1861 (reprinted in 1969 by the University of Michigan Press). During the Civil War, Delany returned to the United States and served as surgeon for the 54th Massachusetts Volunteers. He also recruited numerous soldiers for the Union Army and became the first African American to receive a regular army commission (as a major, awarded by President Abraham Lincoln) for his efforts.

Delany also wrote essays on international and national policy and politics, reflections on the Civil War, scholarly articles on botany, and *Principia of Ethnology: The Origins of Races and Color with an Archaeological Compendium of Ethiopian and Egyptian Civilizations* (1879), his study of African history from biblical times to his times, highlighting African achievements and contributions to ancient civilization. The first book *about* Delany, *Life and Public Services of Martin R. Delany* (1868), was authored by **Frances A. Rollin (Whipper)**.

—*Tonya Bolden*

REFERENCES: *BAAW. EB-98. PGAA.* Austin, Allan D., in *OCAAL.* Sellman, James Clyde, in *EA-99.* (See also *BDAA.*)

Delany, Samuel ("Chip") R. (Ray) (Jr.)
(4/1/1942–)
Short stories, novels, nonfiction, criticism, memoirs

Young Samuel was the namesake of his father, the prosperous owner of Levy and Delany, a Harlem funeral parlor, and he was the only child of Samuel Sr. and his wife, Margaret Carey Boyd Delany, a clerk on the staff of the New York Public Library. Samuel Sr. and Margaret provided their son with rich cultural experiences, including lessons in playing the violin and the guitar, acting, and ballet dancing. From 1947 through 1956, they sent him to the progressive Dalton elementary school, a private school where his chums were primarily upper-class liberal European Americans and Jewish Americans; even his summers were spent in racially integrated youth camps in upstate New York. Even given these advantages, Samuel Jr. suffered from dyslexia, which wasn't diagnosed at the time, so he always had to struggle with his schoolwork, despite being intellectually gifted and culturally advantaged. Nonetheless, he read widely, including the writings of numerous African-American authors, classical mythology, fantasies, and science fiction. He particularly enjoyed the stories of Ray Bradbury, Robert Heinlein, Jules Verne, and later those of Arthur C. Clarke and others as well.

In 1956, Delany enrolled in the prestigious public school, the Bronx High School of Science. There, he excelled in math and science (especially physics), and he met Jewish poet and child prodigy Marilyn Hacker. Delany was quite prodigious himself, singing folk songs, writing a violin concerto, keeping a journal, and writing science fiction. Before he reached his teens, he had written some sword-and-sorcery fantasies in his journals; in his teens, he wrote quite a few never-published novels (from 1954 to 1961). His adolescence was not problem free, however, as it included some unsettling sexual experimentation, a troublesome relationship with his father, and counseling sessions with a psychiatrist.

After graduating from high school, Delany attended the City College of New York (1960, 1962–1963). At age 19 he married Hacker, and she encouraged him to submit his manuscript to Ace Books, where she was working. While still 19, he published his novel *The Jewels of Aptor* (1962). Hacker went on to become a National Book Award–winning poet, and Delany and she coedited the first four issues of the speculative fiction quarterly *Quark*. (Eventually, however, after the couple had a daughter together, their relationship disintegrated; they separated in 1975 and divorced in 1980. Since then, Delany has openly identified himself as homosexual.)

During the 1970s, Delany lived in the Heavenly Breakfast commune in New York City and played in a rock band. In 1975, Delany was named Visiting Butler Chair Professor of English at the State University of New York at Buffalo. In 1977, he moved on to become senior fellow at the Center for Twentieth Century Studies at the University of Wisconsin at Milwaukee. Since 1988, he has been a professor of contemporary literature at the University of Massachusetts at Amherst.

Although Delany is best known for his novels as well as his nonfiction, he has also written comic book scripts, a film screenplay (the half-hour film *The Orchid,* which he also directed and edited), and short stories. His short stories include "Aye, and Gomorrah" (1967), which won a Nebula Award from the Science Fiction Writers of America; and "Time Considered as a Helix of Semi-Precious Stones" (1969), which won both a Nebula Award and a Hugo Award (at the World Science Fiction Convention at Heidelberg). His short stories have been collected in *Driftglass, Distant Stars,* and *Driftglass/Starshards.*

Literary critics have divided Delany's novels into two periods: his early novels, which have been described as "space operas"; and his later novels, which are considered more complex and fully developed. His early novels used highly literary language, but though his tales were original and his characters included females and blacks, the books still relied heavily on conventions typical of the science fiction genre, such as exotic, futuristic settings with heavy emphasis on aliens, intergalactic conflicts, spaceships, and other technological gee-whiz gadgets. These novels include *The Jewels of Aptor* (1962), *Captives of the Flame* (1963), *The Towers of Toron* (1964), *The Ballad of Beta-2* (1964), and *City of a Thousand Suns* (1965). In 1965, Delany suffered a nervous breakdown, following which he tried to slow down the speed with which he whipped out his novels. In 1966, he published *Babel 17,* which featured an artist as its protagonist and explored the ways in which language shapes human experience. *Babel 17* earned him the first of his five Nebula Awards and marked the beginning of his recognition as a major science fiction writer. It was followed by *Empire Star* (1966), Nebula Award–winning *The Einstein Intersection* (1967), and *Nova* (1968), sometimes considered the best of his space-opera novels.

His later novels offer greater complexity and can be read on multiple levels. In these works, he addresses issues of race and gender, freedom and slavery, and sexual desire and sexual identity. He once observed, "The constant and insistent experience I have had as a black man, a gay man, as a science fiction writer in racist, sexist, homophobic America, with its carefully maintained tradition of high art and low, colors and contours every sentence I write" (quoted in *OCAAL*). Delany also textures these later novels by using anthropology, linguistics, and philosophy to explore language and meanings, mythology and power. In addition, these novels reflect a greater mastery of his craft, with a sophisticated narrative structure and rich literary allusions. These novels include *The Tides of Lust* (1973, also published as *Equinox*), *Dhalgren* (1975), *Triton* (1976), *Stars in My Pocket Like Grains of Sand* (1984), *The Splendor and Misery of Cities* (1985), *They Fly at Ciron* (1992), and *Atlantis: Model 1924* (1995).

Starting in the 1980s, Delany also returned to a genre he had enjoyed while still in his teens: sword-and-sorcery fantasies. Between 1979 and 1987, he wrote the four-volume *Return to Neveryon* series: *Tales of Nevèryon* (1979), *Neveryóna: Or the Tale of Signs and Cities* (1983), *Flight from Neveryóna* (1985), and *The Bridge of Lost Desire* (1987). The books are set in a prehistoric, precivilized, preindustrial empire.

Since the mid-1970s, Delany has also written numerous nonfiction works, including some books of literary criticism (sometimes using the aliases K. Leslie Steiner and S. L. Kermit for these works): *The Jewel-Hinged Jaw: Notes on the Language of Science Fiction* (1977), *The American Shore* (1978), *Starboard Wine: More Notes on the Language of Science Fiction* (1984), *The Straits of Messina* (1989), and *Longer Views: Extended Essays* (1996). He has also written the autobiographical books *Heavenly Breakfast* (1979), about his experiences in communal living during the late 1960s; and *The Motion of Light in Water* (1988), about his experiences in the 1960s, when the counterculture of New York met the gay subculture. In addition, Delany published *Silent Interviews: On Language, Race, Sex, Science Fiction and Some Comics* (1994), which included many of the written interviews he had previously published in various journals.

In addition to his Hugo and Nebula awards, Delany has been given the Pilgrim Award for excellence in science fiction criticism from the Science Fiction Research Association (1985) and the Bill Whitehead Memorial Award for Lifetime Excellence in Gay and Lesbian Literature (1993).

REFERENCES: *AA:PoP. EB-98. EBLG. G-97. NAAAL. OC20LE. WDAA.* Govan, Sandra Y., in *OCAAL.* Smethurst, James, in *EA-99.*

Delany, (Sarah Louise) "Sadie"
(9/19/1889–1/25/1999)
Memoir, inspirational advice

The second of ten children, Sarah ("Sadie") Delany and all her siblings earned their own way through college. For Sadie, that meant graduating from St. Augustine's College in Raleigh, North Carolina, after which she taught school for a while and then took on the job of county school superintendent, chauffeuring **Booker T. Washington** to show him the schools she supervised. When the brutality of Jim Crow laws confronted Sadie and her younger sister Bessie, the pair moved to New York, where Sadie graduated from the two-year program at the Pratt Institute, followed by a bachelor of science degree (1920) and then a master's degree (1925) from Columbia University. With

her degrees in hand, while the Great Depression was making jobs scarce for everyone, she was appointed to teach at an all-white school. By evading a white-face-to-black-face interview with school personnel, she had become the first African-American woman home-economics ("domestic science") teacher in New York, where she taught for 30 or so years. Both she and Bessie (one of the first African-American women dentists) devoted their lives to their careers, rather than to marrying and to raising children.

When they were both centenarians, Sadie and her sister Bessie wrote *Having Our Say: The Delany Sisters' First 100 Years* (1993, with *New York Times* reporter Amy Hill Hearth), their spirited observations on 100 years of living well in the midst of turbulent times—from lynchings and the imposition of Jim Crow policies, through the **Harlem Renaissance**, the Great Depression, and the civil rights movement, to the last decade of the twentieth century. This long-running best-selling book was the basis for a Broadway play and a full-length TV movie, and it inspired such reader demand that the sisters subsequently wrote *The Delany Sisters' Book of Everyday Knowledge* (1994, with Amy Hill Hearth). After Bessie's death in 1995, Sadie wrote *On My Own at 107: Reflections on Life without Bessie* (1997, with Amy Hill Hearth), in which she lovingly recalled her memories of her sister while affirming life on her own.

REFERENCES: Brown, Phiefer L., in *BH2C,* and in *PBW.* Amazon.com, 7/1999.

Demby, William (12/25/1922–)
Novels, nonfiction

William Demby and Gertrude Hendricks had firsthand experience with racial discrimination, having been barred from entering college (in Philadelphia), to study architecture and medicine, respectively. They were also aware of the race riots and the all-too-frequent lynchings of African Americans during the post–World War I era. After the couple married, William Sr. got a white-collar job in a munitions factory (and later in a natural gas company), and they moved to Pittsburgh, where young William and his siblings were born. There, they lived in a middle-class culturally diverse community, where families of first-generation immigrants (from Ireland, Poland, or Italy) mingled with African-American families. Much to the pleasure of the Dembys, members of this community understood that pride in being an American could coexist with pride in a cultural heritage from a distant land.

At Langley High School, young William became a jazz musician, a writer, and a socialist. He also observed how pride of ethnicity, religion, and political affiliation could lead to conflict. After William graduated (1941), his family moved to Clarksburg, West Virginia, a nearly all-black community, which offered William a captivatingly new way of looking at the world. Demby started attending West Virginia State College, where he studied music, philosophy, and literature, taking writing classes from poet-novelist **Margaret Walker**. His love of playing jazz music also led him to the Cotton Club (in South Carolina), and soon he was skipping classes to play there (or to sleep in after playing the previous night). Eventually, he had missed so many classes that he wasn't making progress in school, and he decided to join the army, to help the Allies in World War II.

He spent some of his time in military service in North Africa, but for most of his two-year tour, he was stationed in Italy. During that time, he wrote for the military newspaper *Stars and Stripes*. After his discharge from the service, he returned to college. This time, he enrolled in Fisk University, took his studies seriously, and delved into writing. While Demby was in his senior year at Fisk, poet **Robert Hayden** started teaching at Fisk and shepherding the militantly antifascist student newspaper the *Fisk Herald*. Hayden also encouraged Demby to contribute to the paper, which Demby did.

One of the stories Demby contributed to the *Herald,* "Saint Joey," was the basis for his first novel, *Beetlecreek* (published in 1950), set in an economically (and perhaps spiritually) depressed town in West Virginia. The novel centers around the rather desperate lives of three individuals: a reclusive elderly white man, a gang-affiliated black teenager, and an artist who gets involved with an unsavory woman. Mondadavi, one of Italy's most prestigious publishers, produced this internationally acclaimed novel.

After Demby graduated from Fisk (B.A., 1957), he returned to Rome. There, he supported himself by playing the alto saxophone in jazz groups and working for the Italian film and television industry (writing screenplays and adapting Italian screenplays for English-speaking audiences). In his free time, he studied literature at the University of Rome, wrote, painted, and traveled extensively. During this time, he also married Italian poet-

writer Lucia Drudia, with whom he had a son, James, who composes music.

While in Italy, Demby wrote some nonfiction pieces and completed his second novel, *The Catacombs* (1965), set in the area surrounding the Roman catacombs. In it, Demby includes himself as a fiction writer telling about a love affair between an African-American actress/dancer and an Italian count.

Around the time that *Catacombs* was published, Demby returned to the United States to live. For a while, he worked in public relations at a New York ad agency; then in 1969, he started teaching at the College of Staten Island of the City College of New York. In 1978, Demby published *Love Story Black* (1978), in which he again places himself in the novel, as Professor Edwards, the author of the novel. In the novel, Professor Edwards ends up in the fantasy life of an 80-year-old ex-vaudeville performer who is writing her memoirs. In 1979, Demby published *Blueboy,* and in 1996, he was working on a novel about an army cook he knew when he was in the military.

REFERENCES: *BAL-1-P. BWA. EBLG.* Smith, Virginia Whatley, in *OCAAL.*

Dent, Tom (né Thomas Covington Dent) (3/20/1932–)
Poems, essays, oral histories, dramas; journal founder

A native of New Orleans, Dent edited his college's newspaper (c. 1952) and later (c. 1960) wrote for the African-American weekly, the *New York Age*. While in New York, at the inception of the **Black Arts movement** in 1963 and 1964, he, **Calvin Hernton**, and David Henderson produced the poetry journal *Umbra* as an outgrowth of the Umbra Workshop writing collective they had founded. After returning to New Orleans (1965), he wrote his most famous play, *Ritual Murder* (1967), and continued working with other writers (e.g., **Kalamu ya Salaam**). He also cofounded the literary journals *Nkombo* (in 1969) and *Callaloo* (in 1975). His reviews and essays have appeared in numerous African-American periodicals, and his poetry was collected and published in *Magnolia Street* (1976) and *Blue Lights and River Songs* (1982). In addition, Dent has been deeply involved in collecting oral histories about New Orleans jazz, about the civil rights movement, and about the American South in the late twentieth century.

REFERENCES: Ward, Jerry W., Jr., in *OCAAL.*

Derricotte, Toi (4/12/1941–)
Poems, memoir

Derricotte's poetry includes her collections *The Empress of the Death House* (1978), *Natural Birth* (1983), and *Captivity* (1989; reprinted in 1991 and 1993). In addition, her secret childhood journals serve as the basis for her *The Black Notebooks,* about her experiences.

REFERENCES: Richardson, James W., Jr., in *OCAAL.*

Deveaux, Alexis (9/24/1948–)
Poems, short stories, children's story, biography, plays, novels, essays; editor

In addition to writing, Deveaux has taught English to students at the State University of New York at Buffalo and other colleges, and she has edited for *Essence* magazine. Internationally renowned, she has had her writings published in several languages (e.g., Dutch, Japanese, Serbo-Croatian, and Spanish), and she has lectured and performed on five continents and across the United States.

Deveaux has published in almost every genre. Across genres, Deveaux writes as an urban, African-American woman whose experiences are personal yet relevant to other African-American women. Deveaux raises social and political issues of worldwide concern (e.g., racial, gender, and economic inequities) in both her fiction and her nonfiction, her poetry and her prose. While considering the big issues, she sensitively and caringly focuses on the distinctive experiences of an individual woman and her personal relationships (e.g., parent-child relationships or lesbian relationships). In addition, as she noted herself, "Music is also a great influence on my work. Each piece has a different rhythm" (*BWWW,* p. 53).

Deveaux's award-winning 1973 children's book, *Na-Ni,* set in Harlem, compassionately tells the story of an impoverished child's longings in the face of urban crime and a callous social welfare system. In her 1973 novel *Spirits in the Street,* she interweaves her own surrealistic drawings throughout her narrative about a young African American's experiences in Harlem during the turbulent 1970s. Deveaux's 1980 biography *Don't Explain: A Song of Billie Holiday* candidly puts the reader into the mindset of this talented and troubled singer. In 1985, Deveaux published her collection *Blue Heat: Poems and Drawings,* and in 1987,

she published another children's book, *An Enchanted Hair Tale.* Meanwhile, her poems, essays, and short stories have continued to appear in national journals, magazines, and anthologies.

Deveaux's play *Circles* was produced for KCET-TV, *Tapestry* was produced in New York City on PBS, and *A Season to Unravel* was produced by the Negro Ensemble Company in New York City. These and her other plays explore family and intimate relationships. In addition to these works, Deveaux was involved in a video documentary, "Motherlands: From Manhattan to Managua to Africa, Hand to Hand." In all her works, as she has noted, "I try to listen to language. I'm very interested in how words work. I try to write each piece in the language of the piece, so that I'm not using the same language from piece to piece."

In addition to her writing, Deveaux managed to cofound a theater company, a writing workshop, and an art gallery, which has exhibited some of her own paintings. She has also been given numerous awards, including two Coretta Scott King awards, a National Endowment for the Arts fellowship, two Unity in Media awards, a Fannie Lou Hamer Award for Excellence in the Arts, a PBS grant, and the Lorraine Hansberry Award for Excellence in African-American Children's Literature.

REFERENCES: *BFC. BWWW. EBLG.* King, Lovalerie, in *OCAAL.* Wilkerson, Margaret B., in *OCWW.*

Diddley, "Bo" (né Otha Elias Bates) (12/30/1928–)
Songs

Initially a rhythm-and-blues guitarist, Diddley took to rock 'n' roll right away and soon had written and performed about a dozen hit songs, including "I'm a Man" and "Who Do You Love?" In 1987, he was inducted into the Rock and Roll Hall of Fame.

REFERENCES: *EA-99.*

Dodson, Owen (Vincent) (11/28/1914–6/21/1983)
Plays, poems, novels

Young Owen was the ninth child in a Brooklyn family that was always short on cash but rich on intellectual stimulation. Owen's dad, a freelance journalist, directed the National Negro Press Association; through his contacts, he introduced Owen to noteworthy African Americans of that era, including the philosophical adversaries **Booker T. Washington** and **W. E. B. Du Bois**. After attending outstanding public schools, Owen went on to Bates College (in Lewiston, Maine, 1932–1936), where he earned his bachelor's degree, and then to Yale University School of Drama (in New Haven, Connecticut, 1936–1939), where he earned his M.F.A. (master's in fine arts) in playwriting. His master's thesis was the manuscript of his play *Divine Comedy* (1938), which was produced at Yale, as was his play *The Garden of Time* (1939).

After Yale, Dodson served in the U.S. Navy and taught theater and literature at several colleges and universities, including the historically black Atlanta and Hampton universities. During this time, he also wrote and directed *New World A-Coming* (1944), about African-American contributions during World War II. In 1947, Dodson started teaching drama at Howard University and directing the Howard University Players. Through his work at Howard, he influenced an entire generation of African-American theater professionals.

In addition to teaching drama, Dodson wrote nearly 40 plays and operas, almost 30 of which have been produced, and 2 of those at the prestigious Kennedy Center in Washington, D.C. His thesis play, *Divine Comedy* (1938), was a verse drama about the lives of people who are drawn to a charismatic religious leader such as Father Divine. His *The Garden of Time* (1939) was also a verse drama, offering a new interpretation of the ancient Greek myth of Medea, a vengeful sorceress who kills her own children when their father betrays her. Dodson's other plays include *Bayou Legend* (1946) and *Media in Africa* (1964).

In addition to his dramas, Dodson also wrote poetry, some of which was collected in *Powerful Long Ladder* (1946). Dodson regarded as his finest work *The Confession Stone* (1970), a series of verse monologues uttered by members of the Holy Family about Jesus's life. Through simple language, Dodson communicates the speakers' humanity. In 1970, James Earl Jones used his rich, mellifluous voice to dramatically read and record Dodson's *The Dream Awake*. In 1978, Dodson's poetic captions accompanied funeral photos taken by celebrated photographer James Van Der Zee in *The Harlem Book of the Dead*. Although Dodson's final poetry collection, "Life on the Streets," was never published, it was performed onstage at the New York Public Theatre in May 1982. Probably his most

critically praised poem is his "Yardbird's Skull," an homage to renowned jazz musician and composer Charlie "Yardbird" (or simply "Bird") Parker.

Dodson even tackled the novel form in *Boy at the Window* (1951), published by the esteemed Farrar, Straus and Giroux. In this semiautobiographical novel, a nine-year-old boy in Brooklyn suffers the death of his much-beloved mother and must cope not only with his grief but also with his guilt, for he believes that if he had undergone a religious conversion, her life might have been spared.

Dodson has also won several major grants for his writing, including a General Education Board grant (1937), Rosenwald (1943) and Guggenheim (1953) fellowships, and a Rockefeller grant (1968). In 1964, President Lyndon Johnson invited Dodson to the White House to celebrate the four hundredth anniversary of fellow dramatist Shakespeare's birth. In recognition of his lifetime contributions to American drama, in 1974 the Black Repertory Theater (Washington, D.C.) honored him with a pastiche of his writings, titled *Owen's Song*.

REFERENCES: *BAL-1-P. BWA. EBLG. G-97. MWEL. WDAA.* Hatch, James, in *OCAAL.*

Domino, (Antoine) "Fats" (2/26/1928–)
Song lyrics

Domino's distinctive boogie-woogie piano work underscored his dynamic rhythm-and-blues and rock 'n' roll songs, including "Ain't It a Shame," "My Blue Heaven," and "Blueberry Hill." Although several popular white performers stole and marketed several of his songs, he managed to sell more than 65 million records in a dozen years (1950–1962), with at least 13 songs on the Top Ten charts. In 1986, he was inducted into the Rock and Roll Hall of Fame.

REFERENCES: Myers, Aaron, in *EA-99.*

Dorsey, Thomas (Andrew) (7/1/1899–1/23/1993)
Songs—gospel and blues lyrics and tunes

From his earliest days, Dorsey was drawn to "the Lord's music," singing His praises in church, as well as to "the devil's music," getting low-down and funky in juke joints, honky-tonks, and houses of ill repute. The first blues composition he copyrighted (in 1920) was "If You Don't Believe I'm Leaving, You Can Count the Days I'm Gone." After a while, earning his living by playing the blues, he suffered a severe attack of the blues.

While his mother nursed him back to health, she also urged him back into the church, where he saw a new kind of music emerging, called "gospel music"; it melded traditional **spirituals** and shouts of praise with the contemporary jazzy, bluesy beats he had been enjoying outside the church. Soon, he had written his first sacred song, "If I Don't Get There"; along with his "Someday, Somewhere," it was printed in Willa A. Townsend's edited work, *Gospel Pearls* (1921), produced by the National Baptist Convention.

In the early 1920s (1921–1926), however, he strayed again from sacred music, composing and arranging jazzy, bluesy music for such notables as **"Ma" Rainey**. For a time, it looked as though the "Father of Gospel Music" was going to be a son of the blues, instead. In the late 1920s (1926–1928), however, he suffered another severe depression, teetering on the deadly precipice of suicide more than once. Once again, he was brought back from the edge, and again, he turned to sacred songs in giving thanks for his recovery.

Making a living at gospel songs was tough going at first: Many church-goers rejected his jazzy rhythms as too secular, but folks outside the church rejected his sacred lyrics. On occasion, to put bread on his table, he still wrote decidedly "worldly" songs (e.g., "It's Tight Like That").

At last, in 1930, his "If You See My Savior, Tell Him That You Saw Me" hit big among Baptist church choirs, and Dorsey's career as a gospel songwriter was finally on its way. In 1931, Dorsey founded the first gospel music publishing company, and he organized some church choirs to spread the gospel. A personal tragedy led to Dorsey's most beloved gift to gospel music: In 1932, his wife died in childbirth, and his newborn daughter died soon after. After three days of deep despair, Dorsey rose up with "Precious Lord, Take My Hand." Eventually, Dorsey was to compose more than 1,000 songs, about half of which were gospel songs, such as "The Lord Will Make a Way Somehow," "There'll Be Peace in the Valley for Me," "Walking Up the King's Highway," "If We Never Needed the Lord Before, We Sure Do Need Him Now," and "Search Me Lord."

—*Tonya Bolden*

REFERENCES: *EAACH. EA-99. PGAA. SMKC.*

Douglass, Frederick (né Frederick Auld) (?/?/1818–2/20/1895)

Autobiographies, editorials; newspaper founder and publisher

Frederick Douglass stands forth as a shining example of American achievement and ingenuity. Although he was born a slave in Maryland in 1818, in 1895 he died a free man who not only had bought his own freedom with the money he earned from his publications and public speaking tours but also had risen to the highest position an African American had ever held in the U.S. government. He became one of the most influential African Americans of the nineteenth century and throughout his lifetime earned the respect not only of his friends and supporters but also of the entire nation and the federal government. By the time of his death he had in many ways become an example both to newly freed black Americans and to white Americans—he showed black Americans that their color need not stand in the way of their achieving great things, and he made whites more aware of their obligation to allow black Americans access to the same opportunities that they were making available to their own children.

Frederick Douglass received no such opportunities—he was, in the purest sense, a self-made man, having received little help from anyone in securing his freedom or making his way in life. He was born of a slave, Harriet Bailey, and an unknown white man; his name was originally Frederick Auld, as he bore the last name of the man who owned him. He spent a large part of his life trying to find information about his birth, but to little avail (although recent historical scholarship has placed it as around 1818). In his biography he records that his resentment at not knowing his birthday was one of the earliest forces behind his desire to break out of slavery. The beatings he witnessed during his youth were another major force behind his dissatisfaction as a slave, although he never received such abuse himself. During his childhood he suffered less from violence than from deprivation—in his biography he claims that as a young boy he was not so much beaten as deprived of food, clothing, and human contact, his mother having died when he was very young.

He was given his first tool to use in fighting his way out of slavery in 1826, when he was sent to work for his master's son-in-law's brother, Hugh Auld. There, Auld's new bride, Sophia, who had just moved to Maryland from the North, took it as her Christian duty to help Douglass learn to read. When Hugh Auld returned home one day to find her giving Frederick reading lessons, he forcefully forbade his wife to continue, telling her that teaching slaves was both illegal and unsafe. He told her that teaching a slave to read would give him ideas, and that since a slave should think of nothing but his master's wishes, teaching him to read would only make him unhappy and unmanageable and thus less valuable. Although Hugh's words effectively put an end to Sophia's lessons, they inspired Douglass to teach himself how to read and write. Hugh's words showed Douglass the power that could be gained from the ability to read ideas and write them down, and he became wholeheartedly determined to acquire that power.

Douglass's determination to break free of slavery increased when, in 1833, he was returned to the Maryland farm on which he was born because of a quarrel between Hugh and his brother. By this time, Douglass had become increasingly resentful of his masters, and his owner decided to send him to work at the farm of Edward Covey, a local slave breaker. While Douglass was working on the farm, Covey used brutal whippings, unrelenting work, and terrible humiliations to break Douglass's spirit so that he would become an obedient worker. This physical and mental brutality actually had an opposite effect on the 16-year-old Douglass—instead of submitting and becoming more obedient, he fought back, intimidating Covey to such a great extent that the slave breaker refrained from ever touching Douglass again.

Frederick tried to escape from slavery for the first time in 1836 but failed. His master sent him to Baltimore to work in the shipyards. This setting provided him with a perfect opportunity to escape, and escape he did. In 1838, with some of the money he earned from working in the yards, as well as the assistance of Anna Murray, the woman who would become his wife, he posed as a free black merchant sailor and boarded a train bound for New York. Although he arrived in New York the next day, his freedom was by no means secure, as the Fugitive Slave Act of 1793 imposed stiff penalties on those who aided in the escape of a slave or abetted an escaped slave. Despite the fact that the Northern states had passed personal freedom laws to protect escaped slaves, many men and women were returned to slavery in the South after their escape.

Nevertheless, Douglass remained free for the rest of his life. Although he did not know it right

Frederick Douglass, revered abolitionist and suffragist (Culver Pictures)

away, he had effectively escaped from slavery on September 3, 1838. Within a month, Anna Murray joined him, and they married. They moved to a thriving African-American community in New Bedford, Connecticut, and he changed his surname from Auld to Douglass to protect himself. Within three years, he had joined the abolitionist movement led by William Lloyd Garrison, beginning his career as a full-time lecturer in 1841 during an antislavery meeting in Nantucket. He became an eloquent and powerful speaker and in those days was known more as an orator than as the brilliant writer for which we know him today.

He began his career as a writer in 1845 when he published his life story, *Narrative of the Life of Frederick Douglass, an American Slave, Written by Himself.* Although he was not the first slave to publish his story, his book was the most successful of all **slave narratives** of the time, selling over 30 million copies in five years. The success could be attributed to any number of things—his clear, direct, first-person narrative style that made the story both powerful and accessible; the belief that his story well represented the experience of slavery; the highly compelling portrait he painted of African-American selfhood; or the fact that the book was "*Written by Himself*" and thus disrupted many expectations and conventions, as many previous slave narratives were transcribed by amanuenses who recorded the narrators' oral tales. This desire to overturn conventions was in many ways deliberate—Douglass specifically designed this biography and his future writings to create an image of himself that is nothing less than heroic, so as to break social stereotypes in the minds of both whites and blacks.

Yet before those stereotypes could be overturned, Douglass knew he needed first to help to topple the institution of slavery. However, he was still very much afraid he would be captured and returned to his master, more so now that he was receiving a large amount of attention because of the popularity of his book. So, after the book was published he went on a two-year speaking tour of Great Britain and Ireland. He returned to the United States in 1847 and, with the money he had earned from his book and his lecture tour, bought his freedom. Then he started publishing his own newspaper, the *North Star,* both to show that a newspaper run by a black man could succeed and to give himself a forum to express himself freely without needing the approval of other abolitionists. He not only edited and managed the paper, but also wrote most of the articles and editorials. It was in this paper that he first published his novella, *The Heroic Slave.* (EDITOR'S NOTE: In 1847, **Martin R. Delany** joined Douglass in editing the *North Star.* After he left, Douglass's paper was called *Frederick Douglass' Paper* and then *Douglass' Monthly.*)

In the early 1850s, Douglass fought with his close associate William Garrison, an abolitionist leader. After they split, Douglass did a great deal of reflection and soul-searching and came to the realization that, although progress was still possible, the abolitionists had not yet helped him to fully reach his goals as a free man. Instead, he felt he needed to turn to the Northern black community in order to feel a truly liberated sense of self. This period of reflection and realization culminated in Douglass's 1855 publication of his second autobiography, *My Bondage and My Freedom.* In this book, Douglass reevaluates his life after 15 years of being free, reflecting on his goals as a reformer and setting out his realizations about the Garrisonian abolitionists.

Soon after the publication of his second autobiography, in 1859, Douglass had to flee to Canada because he was publicly linked to John Brown, who had initiated the raid on Harpers Ferry. While Douglass was in Canada, Abraham Lincoln was elected president, and after the Civil War broke out, Douglass began lobbying Lincoln to allow black men to fight. In 1863, African-American men began to be recruited into the Union Army, and Frederick Douglass delivered inspirational speeches to get men to join it. (EDITOR'S NOTE: After the Civil War, from 1870 to 1874, Douglass published the *New National Era,* addressing newly freed former slaves.)

After the war ended in 1865, Douglass turned his efforts toward getting President Andrew Johnson to pass a national voting rights act that would make it possible for black men to vote in all states. As a result of his political involvement and his loyalty to the Republican Party, he was appointed to the positions of federal marshal (1877–1881) and recorder of deeds (1881–1886) for Washington, D.C.; assistant secretary of the Santo Domingo Commission; U.S. minister to Haiti (1889–1891); and president of the Freedman's Bureau Bank. These were, at the time, the highest offices that any African American had ever won.

As a result of these political appointments and the income from his books and lectures, he earned enough money to live in comfort for the last 20 years of his life. He published his last memoir, *Life and Times of Frederick Douglass,* in 1881 and published an expanded version in 1892. Although the book did not garner the critical or economic success that his earlier autobiographies earned, it enunciates the ending of a life of great achievement—what he called a "life of victory, if not complete, at least assured." It also serves as a conclusion of a life that inspired African-American writers such as **Booker T. Washington** and **W. E. B. Du Bois**, who were greatly influenced by Douglass in writing their own biographies. Douglass's life serves as a model of heroism, self-advancement, self-liberation, and self-reliance to this day.

EDITOR'S NOTE: Anna Murray Douglass and Frederick had three sons—Charles Remond; Frederick, Jr.; and Lewis Henry—and two daughters—Rosetta and Annie. Anna also provided a home life that facilitated Frederick's career successes. Frederick recognized the value of women's contributions and advocated for women's suffrage and other civil rights, and the couple's four granddaughters were active suffragists and feminists during the twentieth century. Douglass nonetheless had a traditional marriage and held that the rights of women (including African-American women) would have to be subordinate to the rights of African Americans. He further confounded his biographers with his second marriage (following Anna's death in 1882) to a white woman, Helen Pitts, in 1884. (*See* Martin, Waldo E., Jr., "Douglass, Frederick," in *BWA:AHE;* see also *BDAA*.)

—*Diane Masiello*

REFERENCES: *NAAAL.* Andrews, William L., in *OCAAL.* (See also *BDAA*.)

Douglass, Sarah (née) Mapps
(9/9/1806–9/8/1882)
Articles, essays

Raised as a Quaker, Douglass was a regular contributor to William Lloyd Garrison's abolitionist *Liberator* newspaper. Through her antislavery efforts, she became close pals with fellow abolitionists, including both the **Forten** sisters (prominent African Americans) and the **Grimké** sisters (prominent European-American Quakers). Her correspondence with the Grimké sisters remains a testament of insightful abolitionist sentiments. A well-educated teacher herself, she was instrumental in promoting education among African-American youths.

REFERENCES: *TAWH.* Lerner, Gerda, in *BWA:AHE.* Robinson, Lisa Clayton, in *EA-99.*

Dove, Rita (Frances) (8/28/1952–)
Poems, a novel, short stories, essays, verse drama, editor

Rita's parents, Ray and Elvira Dove, prized education, but they recognized that the material rewards of education may not be immediately forthcoming, particularly to African Americans: Even though Ray was at the top of his class when he earned his master's degree, he had to work as an elevator operator at Goodyear for several years before he became one of the first African-American chemists in the U.S. tire and rubber industry. Elvira and Ray raised their four children to be proud of their racial heritage, to be wary of the evils of racism, and to watch for changing times, when their abilities and knowledge would be recognized.

As Dove noted in *The Poet's World,* "Education was the key: That much we knew, and so I was a good student. . . . I adored learning new things and looked forward to what intellectual adventures each school day would bring; some of the luckiest

magic was to open a book and to come away the wiser after having been lost in the pages" (Library of Congress, 1995, p. 75). "I read everything I could get my hands on. . . . Our parents allowed me and my siblings to read whatever we wanted to read. Some of my most wonderful memories are of wandering along the bookshelves in our house thinking, 'What book am I going to read this time'" (*LoL*, pp. 118–119).

Rita also showed an early interest in writing plays, stories, and poetry (inspired by Robert Frost and other poets). When one of her high school teachers took her to a local writers conference, her desire for a career in writing blossomed. In an interview for the *Chicago Tribune,* Dove noted, "When I told my parents that I wanted to be a poet, they looked at me and said 'OK.' They didn't know what to make of it, but they had faith in me."

After high school, Dove graduated summa cum laude from Ohio's Miami University (1973), accepted a Fulbright/Hays fellowship to study modern European literature at the University of Tübingen in Germany (1974–1975), and completed her M.F.A. (master of fine arts) at the University of Iowa (1977). While she was in Iowa, she met and married German novelist Fred Viebahn, with whom she since had a daughter, Aviva (b. 1983). This international family loves to travel, and Dove roams extensively in Europe, northern Africa, and Israel. She considers travel "a good way to gain different perspectives and to avoid becoming complacent" (quoted from *Contemporary Authors,* p. 115).

As a writer, Dove came of age a decade after the **Black Arts movement** had peaked, and her poetry differs markedly from poems produced during that era. Unlike the loose, improvisational, jazz style of that era, her poetry style shows tremendous discipline and technically precise lyricality. Similarly, she rejected the narrow focus of that movement in favor of a more inclusive, encompassing worldview and a broader perspective on human experience. Her lovingly crafted work offers deep insights into universal themes through precise depictions of specific individuals at particular moments.

This is not to say that Dove shies away from complex racial issues. Rather, such issues don't form the central focus of her work. Her works often highlight the experiences of African-American individuals, both past and present, but she sets them within a larger context of history, culture, and world literature. As she noted in a 1991 interview

Rita Dove, U.S. poet laureate and Pulitzer Prize winner, 1987 (Reuters/Bettmann)

(in *Callaloo*), "I would find it a breach of my integrity as a writer to create a character for didactic or propaganda purposes." She tries "very hard to create characters who are seen as individuals—not only as Blacks or as women, or whatever, but as a Black woman with her own particular problems, or one White bum struggling in a specific predicament."

Following is a brief chronology of her literary output: From 1977 through 1988, she produced four chapbooks. In 1983, she published *Museum,* her first of several poetry collections, which was favorably received. In 1986, *Thomas and Beulah,* a volume of narrative verse tracing the life experiences of her maternal grandfather and grandmother, was published. In 1992, she published her novel *Through the Ivory Gate,* which tells the life story of a talented young African-American woman, interweaving present experiences and flashbacks to past incidents. Her verse drama, *The Darker Face of the Earth,* was first published in 1994 and produced in 1996. In 1995, she published *Mother Love,* her sixth book of poetry, written chiefly in sonnet form and focusing on the mother-daughter relationship; and her first collection of essays, *The Poet's World.* In addition, her work is often published in periodicals and anthologies.

Dove's academic career may be chronicled as follows: Starting in 1981, she began as an assistant professor at Arizona State University (ASU) at Tempe. From there, she spent a year as writer-in-residence at the Tuskegee Institute before returning to ASU and staying there until 1989. In 1989, she joined the faculty at the University of Virginia Center for Advanced Studies and in 1993 was promoted to endowed Commonwealth Professor of English at the University of Virginia, where she still teaches creative writing. Meanwhile, she has served on the literary advisory panel for the National Endowment for the Arts (NEA), has been named chair of the poetry grants panel for the NEA, and has served on the board of directors of the Associate Writing Programs (serving as its president, 1986–1987). In 1987, she became linked to two key institutions of African-American culture: as the associate editor of *Callaloo,* a journal of criticism and the arts known for publishing contemporary poetry; and as commissioner of the Schomburg Center for Research in Black Culture.

In addition to being the 1993–1995 poet laureate of the United States (the first black person, the first woman, and the youngest person to hold that post), Dove has received numerous other honors: Starting in 1970, she was awarded a Presidential scholarship and was invited to the White House. She since has been awarded a National Achievement Scholarship, a Fulbright/Hays scholarship, literary grants from the NEA, numerous fellowships (including Guggenheim and Mellon grants), a Pulitzer Prize in poetry (the second African American to receive that honor, following **Gwendolyn Brooks**), at least eight honorary doctorates, a Bellagio residency, citation as a Literary Lion of the New York Public Library, appointment to numerous prestigious panels (e.g., the National Book Award poetry panel), an invitation to read at the White House and to speak at the two hundredth anniversary celebration of the U.S. Capitol, and many, many more honors.

REFERENCES: *1TESK. AAP. AA:PoP. BF:2000. E-98. EB-98. EBLG. G-95. LoL. MAAL. MWEL. NAAAL. OC20LE. PBW. RT. TtW.* Stanford, Ann Folwell, in *OCWW.* Williams, Kenny Jackson, in *OCAAL.*

Drake, St. Clair (1/12/1911–6/14/1990)
Nonfiction—anthropology, sociology

With **Horace Cayton**, Drake coauthored the classic sociological study of Chicago's South Side (known as "Bronzeville"), *Black Metropolis* (1945). While working to found one of the preeminent African-American studies departments in the United States (at Stanford University), he wrote his two-volume work, *Black Folk Here and There* (1987–1990).

REFERENCES: Balfour, Lawrie, in *EA-99.*

Driskell, David (6/7/1931–)
Nonfiction—art

A painter and art curator, Driskell's books have been written and published as companions to art exhibitions he has curated, such as *Two Centuries of Black American Art* (1976) and *Hidden Heritage: Afro-American Art* (1985).

REFERENCES: *EA-99.*

Du Bois, Shirley (Lola) (née) Graham (11/11/1896?–3/27/1977)
Biographies, plays, libretti, nonfiction; journal cofounder

By the time she reached her mid-twenties, Shirley was the widow of Shadrack McCanns, with two young boys to support. With help from her parents, she managed to complete her training as a musician and to earn her bachelor's degree in music (1934) and her master's degree in music history and fine arts (1935).

In the 1930s and 1940s, Shirley Graham wrote several plays. First was her one-act play *Tom-Tom,* which she developed into the opera *Tom-Tom: An Epic of Music and the Negro* (1932), the first major opera written and produced by a woman, featuring an all-black cast. She also wrote several other plays while a Julius Rosenwald Fellow at the Yale University School of Drama (following a brief stint with the WPA's Federal Theater Project); these plays included *Deep Rivers* (1939, a musical), *It's Morning* (1940, a one-act tragedy set in the brutal times of slavery), *I Gotta Home* (1940, a one-act drama), *Track Thirteen* (1940, a radio script), *Elijah's Raven* (1941, a three-act comedy), and *Dust to Earth* (1941, a three-act tragedy). In recognition of her work, she was given a National Institute of Arts and Letters Award in 1950.

Starting in the 1940s, Graham also began writing biographies of important African Americans, Africans, and others, such as *Dr. George Washington Carver, Scientist* (1944); *Paul Robeson: Citizen of the World* (1946); *There Was Once a Slave: The Heroic Story of Frederick Douglass* (1947); *Your Most Humble Servant* (1949, about **Benjamin Banneker**); *The Story of Phillis Wheatley* (1949); *The Story of Pocahantas* (1953); *Jean Baptiste Pointe du Sable: Founder of Chicago* (1953); *Booker T. Washington: Educator of Hand, Head, and Heart* (1955); *His Day Is Marching On* (1971, a memoir of **W. E. B. Du Bois**); *Gamal Abdel Nasser, Son of the Nile* (1972); *Julius K. Nyerere: Teacher of Africa* (1975); and *A Pictorial History of W. E. B. Du Bois* (1976). She also wrote a novel, *Zulu Heart* (1974), giving her distinctive view of whites in South Africa.

While she was gaining awareness of important contributors to African-American history, she was also becoming increasingly politically active, as is evident in her articles for progressive periodicals such as *The Masses* and *The Harlem Quarterly* during the late 1940s and the 1950s. During this time, she had grown closer to **W. E. B. Du Bois**, whom she had known since she was a teenager (and he was nearing 50) and with whom she had corresponded since 1936. In 1951, a year after the death of Nina Du Bois, W. E. B.'s wife of 55 years, Graham married him. For the next dozen years, Shirley Du Bois virtually stopped her own writing

and dedicated herself to aiding him with his, helping him to write what would have been his magnum opus, the *Encyclopedia Africana.*

Throughout the 1950s and into the 1960s, however, the red scare (anticommunist frenzy) inflamed the U.S. government's zeal for persecuting civil rights activists and anyone else suspected of communist sympathies. In 1961, Shirley and her husband emigrated to Ghana. They still kept in touch with the politics of the United States, however. In the early 1960s, she, her husband, and **Paul Robeson** cofounded the cultural and literary journal, *Freedomways,* which called itself "a journal of the Freedom Movement." The U.S. government repeatedly barred the Du Boises from returning to this country (other than for Shirley's visits in 1971 and 1975), and she (like her husband) died in exile.

—*Tonya Bolden*

REFERENCES: *BAAW.* Brown-Guillory, Elizabeth, in *BWA:AHE.* Edwards, Roanne, in *EA-99.* Warren, Nagueyalti, in *OCAAL.*

Du Bois, W. E. B. (William Edward Burghardt) (2/23/1868–8/27/1963)
Essays, novels, biography, autobiography, nonfiction—political and social issues, history; journal founder and editor

Any serious student of African-American culture, history, and intellectual life finds much to glean from the life and work of William Edward Burghardt Du Bois, and his influence remains strong today. A superbly well-educated man and a prolific writer, Du Bois played an integral role in the African-American community's call for racial equality and social justice. Du Bois believed that the African-American community needed to be intellectually astute and politically active. His own political activity sometimes brought him into conflict with other black and white leaders of the time, however, including **Booker T. Washington**.

Du Bois was born in Great Barrington, Massachusetts, into a family of free blacks whose ancestors had never been slaves, but instead had roots in the American Revolution. Du Bois lived with his mother, Mary Slyvina Burghardt Du Bois, for much of his childhood, as his father, Alfred Du Bois, left his wife and son soon after the boy's birth. Du Bois grew into a fine student, graduating first in his 1884 high school class. Others recognized his intelligence and encouraged his intellectual talents. Du Bois enjoyed life in Massachusetts,

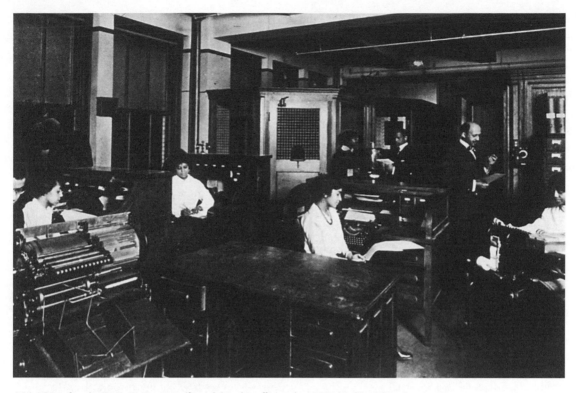

NAACP cofounder W. E. B. Du Bois (far right) in his office, early 1930s (Archive Photos)

remembering no discrimination, even though the town was by and large populated by whites. He and his mother attended the First Congregational Church as the only black members. His mother died soon after Du Bois graduated from high school, and at that time, he apparently had no plans or money for college, although he was industrious, always attending the annual town meetings and writing for the *New York Globe*. Eventually, the members of his family's church provided the money for his fees to attend Fisk University in Nashville, Tennessee, in 1885.

After graduating from Fisk in 1888, Du Bois received a scholarship to Harvard University, earning a second bachelor's degree in 1890 and a master's degree in 1891. Du Bois continued with his studies, spending two years at the University of Berlin and gaining his Ph.D. from Harvard in 1896. Du Bois holds the distinction of being the first African American to receive this degree from Harvard. Additionally, Du Bois's doctoral dissertation, *The Suppression of the African Slave-Trade to the United States of America, 1638–1870,* was published in 1896 as volume 1 of Harvard's multivolume *Historical Series.*

Du Bois found a teaching post in Ohio at Wilberforce University, and while he was there, he met his future wife, Nina Gomer, marrying her in 1896. That same year, Du Bois was hired by the University of Pennsylvania to teach and to conduct a sociological study of blacks. His work culminated in *The Philadelphia Negro* (1899), the first work of its kind. Du Bois's innovative and serious academic work earned him another job offer: He was invited to head the sociology department at Atlanta University. Du Bois continued to study African-American life and to teach in Georgia until 1910. While at Atlanta, Du Bois continued to produce groundbreaking sociological works about the lives of African Americans.

In Atlanta, Du Bois also wrote his most famous and enduring work, *The Souls of Black Folk* (1903). This book landed Du Bois right in the middle of the fight for equality. It also landed him in the middle of a long controversy with the most prominent black leader at the time, Booker T. Washington. During his early years, Du Bois had had no firsthand experience with the racial inequities so prevalent in many areas of the United States, yet when he attended Fisk, Du Bois saw a new side to the world—and he did not like what he saw. Washington, too, did not like the situation in the United States. What separated the two intellectual giants was not the goal of equality but the method by which to achieve it.

Du Bois believed that Washington, who was closely allied with the more practical Tuskegee Institute in Alabama, promoted methods for achieving equality that were submissive, focusing on the common economic self-interests of blacks and whites instead of demanding equality based on rational and philosophical grounds. Du Bois argued that African Americans needed to be highly educated and then serve as ladders to help others achieve similar status. Thus, *The Souls of Black Folk* directly challenged Washington, and Du Bois gained both popularity and notoriety.

Washington's political stance continued to gain popularity with blacks and whites alike, however. Du Bois responded by founding the Niagara Movement in 1905. Although the organization folded in 1910, some consider it to be the first African-American protest movement of the twentieth century. Du Bois went on to become the only African-American founding officer of the National Association for the Advancement of Colored People (NAACP) in 1910.

While with the NAACP, Du Bois started the organization's journal *Crisis,* which Du Bois also edited and wrote for. Although Du Bois published new black writers, such as **Countee Cullen** and **Langston Hughes**, he became frustrated by what he considered their lack of commitment to political action. After 24 years, Du Bois resigned from the NAACP because of a conflict with its executive board. He returned to Atlanta University in 1934, heading the sociology department there until his forced retirement when he was 76 years old. Du Bois then returned to the NAACP in 1944, engaged in more conflict with the leadership over his renewed interest in and promotion of communism, and was fired in 1948. (EDITOR'S NOTE: Du Bois also founded the literary journal *Phylon* in 1940 and served as its editor-in-chief until 1944.)

In 1950, Du Bois ran for the Senate as a Labor Party candidate and lost. Du Bois later led the Peace Information Center and stirred up more controversy. He was indicted by a grand jury in 1951, which accused him of being a foreign agent, and he had to forfeit his U.S. passport in the process. Although a judge threw the case out of court, it took some time for Du Bois to regain his passport. When he did, however, he traveled to Europe, including the Soviet Union. (EDITOR'S NOTE:

About this time, Du Bois's wife Nina died [in 1950], and about a year later [in 1951], he married **Shirley Graham [Du Bois]**, nearly 30 years his junior. The Du Boises, **Paul Robeson,** and others later cofounded *Freedomways: A Quarterly Review of the Negro Freedom Movement.*)

Du Bois saw an international community in the world's future and continued to be frustrated by the tiny steps of progress toward racial equality within the United States. Years earlier, Du Bois had accurately identified two conflicts in the United States that continue to this day: (1) The concept of "double consciousness" questions whether African Americans can be true to both their cultural heritage and their national identity, and (2) as Du Bois noted, "The color line" will be the problem of the twentieth century. (EDITOR'S NOTE: Perhaps it will be the problem of the twenty-first century, as well.)

Du Bois's frustration grew until he eventually left the United States in 1961, moving to Ghana. He became a naturalized citizen of Ghana and died there in 1963. Ironically, Du Bois died on the exact date when **Martin Luther King, Jr.**'s famous March on Washington took place. To some, it seemed as if the baton had been passed. Others mourned the loss of one of the African-American community's greatest intellectuals. All, however, agree that Du Bois's legacy, work, and influence will not soon be forgotten.

In addition to the works previously mentioned, Du Bois published the following: *John Brown* (1909, a biography); *The Quest of the Silver Fleece* (1911, a novel); *The Negro* (1915, pan-African history); *Darkwater: Voices from within the Veil* (1920, a collection of prose and verse); *The Gift of Black Folk: Negroes in the Making of America* (1924); *Dark Princess* (1928, a novel); *Black Reconstruction in America* (1935, a massive treatise); *Dusk of Dawn: An Essay toward an Autobiography of a Race Concept* (1940, an autobiography); *In Battle for Peace: The Story of My Eighty-Third Birthday* (1952, a memoir); a novel trilogy, *The Black Flame* (comprising *The Ordeal of Mansart,* 1957; *Mansart Builds a School,* 1959; and *Worlds of Color,* 1961); and *The Autobiography of W. E. B. Du Bois: A Soliloquy on Viewing My Life from the Last Decade of Its First Century* (1968), published posthumously.

EDITOR'S NOTE: Du Bois's work was made much easier by Nina Gomer, his wife of 55 years, and by his second wife, Shirley Graham Du Bois, who followed him to Ghana to spend his last years with him there. Shirley also helped him with his massive work, *Encyclopedia Africana,* which was incomplete at the time of his death.

—*Janet Hoover*

REFERENCES: *EBLG.* Blight, David W. (1990), "Up From 'Twoness': Frederick Douglass and the Meaning of W. E. B. Du Bois's Concept of Double Consciousness," *Canadian Review of American Studies, 21*(3) Online, EBSCO Host. Coates, Rodney D., "Autobiography of W. E. B. Du Bois: A Soliloquy on Viewing My Life from the Last Decade of Its First Century," in *MAAL.* Cunningham, George P., in *AAW.* Franklin, Robert Michael (1990), "W. E. B. Du Bois and the Strenuous Person," *Liberating Visions: Human Fulfillment and Social Justice in African-American Thought* (Minneapolis: Fortress). "From 1909 to the Great Depression: A Partial Chronicle" (1994), *Crisis, 101*(1) Online, EBSCO Host. Rampersad, Arnold, in *BLC*-1 and in *OCAAL.* Richardson, Ben, and William Fahey (Eds.) (1976), *Great Black Americans* (2nd rev. ed.; formerly titled *Great American Negroes*) (New York: Thomas Crowell). Townsend, Kim (1996), "'Manhood' at Harvard: W. E. B. Du Bois," *Raritan, 15*(4), Online, EBSCO Host.

Dumas, Henry L. (7/20/1934–5/23/1968)
Poems, short stories

Born in Sweet Home, Arkansas, Dumas spent the early years of his childhood in the South before his family moved to Harlem when he was ten years old. Dumas's short fiction reflects his deep understanding of the African-American experience both in the rural South and in the urban North. After graduating from high school, Dumas enrolled in the City College of New York, but he soon left to join the U.S. Air Force (1953–1957). While in the Air Force, he married Loretta Ponton (September 24, 1955), and he contributed poems and short stories to Air Force periodicals, winning creative writing awards for his efforts. After his military service, he enrolled at Rutgers University, but family responsibilities for his sons David (born in 1958) and Michael (born in 1962) led him to quit school and focus on earning a steady income.

In 1967, Dumas was invited to teach, counsel students, and direct language workshops at Southern Illinois University. There, he met **Eugene Redmond**, a fellow teacher and poet who was to become his friend and literary conservator. In the late spring of 1968, when his literary career seemed so promising and his young family was so needful of his promise, Dumas's life was tragically ended in a violent clash with a New York City transit officer on a subway platform, who mistakenly shot him.

Much of Dumas's work centered on the theme of the metaphorical clash between African- and European-American cultures. Other important influences on his writings were religion, supernatural phenomena, folk traditions (e.g., African-American music and lore), and the struggle for civil rights. After Dumas's death, Redmond edited several collections of his works, including his short-story collections *Ark of Bones and Other Stories* (1974, edited by Hale Chatfield and Eugene Redmond), *Rope of Wind and Other Stories* (1979), and *Good-bye Sweetwater: New and Selected Stories* (1988), which included stories from his previous collections as well as excerpts from his unfinished novel *Jonoah and the Green Stone* (published in 1976); and his poetry collections *Poetry for My People* (1970; republished as *Play Ebony, Play Ivory,* in 1974) and *Knees of a Natural Man: Selected Poetry of Henry Dumas* (1989).

REFERENCES: *EB-BH-CD. EBLG. G-97. WDAA.* Harris, Trudier, in *OCAAL.*

Dunbar, Paul Laurence
(6/27/1872–2/9/1906)
Poems, essays, short stories, novels; newspaper founder and editor

Although slavery had ended years before Paul was born, both of Paul's parents had known well the oppressive burden of slavery. His father, Joshua Dunbar, had escaped slavery to join a black regiment during the Civil War, and after the war, he had worked as a plasterer. Paul's mother, Matilda Glass, had worked as a launderer after gaining her freedom. Both Joshua and Matilda enjoyed telling their young son stories of their experiences on the plantations of the South. Sadly, however, while Paul was still young, his parents divorced, and his father died soon afterward.

The only African American in his Dayton, Ohio, Central High School class, young Paul already showed literary talent: He was named class poet, president of the literary society, and editor-in-chief of the school newspaper. Although he couldn't afford to continue his education after high school, within two years after graduating he had some of his poems published in the *Dayton Herald.* Soon after, Wilbur Wright (one of the two first-flight brothers) financed Dunbar's founding of the *Dayton Tattler,* which Dunbar also edited. When the

Tattler folded, Dunbar sought jobs with local news-papers, but not one was willing to hire an African American, regardless of his talent. With that avenue closed to him, he got work as a hotel elevator op-erator, which allowed him time for writing.

In 1892, one of Dunbar's former teachers asked him to address the Western Association of Writers in Dayton. At that meeting, Dunbar was intro-duced to James Newton Matthews, who was to become another of his champions. For starters, Matthews wrote to an Illinois newspaper singing Dunbar's praises, and Matthews's letter was widely reprinted in other newspapers across the land. One of the people who read of Dunbar was poet James Whitcomb Riley. Intrigued, Riley read numerous poems by Dunbar, and he, too, started singing the young poet's praises.

With the financial help of Wilbur Wright, Dun-bar self-published his first collection of poems, *Oak and Ivy* (1893). Many of these poems were written in standard English (e.g., "Ode to Ethiopia," a poem celebrating the achievements of African Americans; "Sympathy," a somber verse about the dismal plight of African Americans). In addition, many of the poems in this volume were written in plantation dialect, which reflected the Southern slaves' speech patterns Dunbar had learned at his parents' knees. The poems in *Oak and Ivy* were well received, and attorney Charles A. Thatcher offered to help pay for Dunbar to attend college. Appre-ciative of the offer, Dunbar nonetheless decided to turn him down to pursue writing ever more dili-gently. Apparently, Dunbar's refusal was gracious, as Thatcher continued to promote Dunbar's work in Ohio, helping him find opportunities to read his poems at various gatherings, such as at meetings in libraries. At this point, however, Dunbar's writings did not free him (or his mother) from having to earn money by other means.

While doing odd jobs at the 1893 World's Columbian Exposition in Chicago, Dunbar met **Frederick Douglass**, who was working as the commissioner in charge of the Haitian exhibit there. Douglass immediately recognized Dunbar's talent and inscribed one of his books to Dunbar, "From Frederick Douglass to his dear young poet friend Paul Dunbar, one of the sweetest songsters his race has produced and a man of whom I hope great things" (Bryan, 1978, p. 7). Douglass also paid Dunbar $5 a week (out of his own funds) to work as his clerical assistant during the fair. At the exhi-bition's Colored Americans Day, Douglass invited

Paul Laurence Dunbar, poet and prose writer (Culver Pictures)

Dunbar to sit on the platform with him and other celebrities and to read his own poetry.

Another of Dunbar's supporters was psychia-trist Henry A. Tobey, who helped him distribute *Oak and Ivy* and sent him money from time to time. Tobey and Thatcher then collaborated in helping Dunbar to publish his next book, *Majors and Minors,* published in 1895. The "Majors" were complex poems written in standard English, and the "Minors" were his dialect poems. The standard English poems absorbed most of his attention dur-ing these early years, and they reflected his vora-cious appetite for reading the English Romantic poets (e.g., John Keats, William Wordsworth, Samuel Taylor Coleridge) and many contemporary European-American poets (e.g., Riley, John Greenleaf Whittier, Henry Wadsworth Longfel-low). Perhaps surprisingly, Dunbar's dialect poems were actually more popular among his readers, most of whom were European Americans. It was chiefly these dialect poems that earned him na-tional fame. They also earned him the friendship and affection of fellow writer Alice Ruth Moore, with whom he began a lengthy correspondence.

Thatcher and Tobey also introduced Dunbar to a literary agent, who secured many more opportunities for Dunbar to give readings and even gained Dunbar a literary contract. With this contract, Dunbar published *Lyrics of Lowly Life* (1896). Most of the poems in this collection had previously appeared in his *Oak and Ivy* and his *Majors and Minors* collections.

On Dunbar's twenty-fourth birthday, he received an unexpected gift: The prestigious journal *Harper's Weekly* published an essay by novelist and celebrated literary critic William Dean Howells, praising Dunbar's poetry. At that time, Dunbar was still working as an elevator operator in a hotel in Dayton, Ohio. Afterward, Dunbar was widely recognized as the first important African-American poet, and according to Mabel Smythe (1976, p. 48), he had a greater impact than any other African-American writer of his time. More than two decades later, **James Weldon Johnson** called him the first true African-American master of writing and recognized him as the first to earn and keep high honors for what he wrote (1922, p. 34). Perhaps the best evidence of his acclaim, however, is that after the publication of his book, he was able to eke out a (humble) living based solely on his writing—a feat that remains difficult to this day.

To begin with, Dunbar started a six-month tour of England, giving readings of his poetry. While there, he found a British publisher for *Lyrics of Lowly Life,* and he earned the friendship of musician Samuel Taylor Coleridge, with whom he wrote an operetta, *Dream Lovers.*

In 1897, Dunbar returned to the United States, but not to the Midwest. Instead, he gained work as a clerk for the Library of Congress in Washington, D.C. With this stable income in hand, he and Moore wedded the next year (in secret, over the objections of her family and friends) (see **Alice Ruth Dunbar Nelson**). The continual exposure to dust from the library shelves caused Dunbar respiratory difficulties, and his health began to suffer. Nonetheless, he continued to write, and in 1898, he published *Folks from Dixie,* his first short-story collection, and *The Uncalled,* his first novel. That year, he left the Library of Congress and toured the country giving readings. Although his health continued to decline, he still published *Lyrics of the Hearthside* in 1899.

In the spring of 1899, he was diagnosed with tuberculosis and fled to the mountains to rest and recuperate. In the early 1900s, Dunbar published his collection of tales *The Strength of Gideon and Other Stories* (1900) and three more novels. After the publication of his fourth novel, *The Sport of the Gods* (1902), his respiratory problems (including a bout of pneumonia) worsened, and Dunbar exacerbated his health problems by abusing alcohol. That year, he and Alice separated. The following year, Dunbar suffered a nervous breakdown, followed by yet another attack of pneumonia.

Despite being so ill he could barely walk, Dunbar managed to continue writing, publishing *Lyrics of Love and Laughter* (1903), *When Malindy Sings* (1903), *Li'l Gal* (1904), *Howdy, Honey, Howdy* (1905), and *Lyrics of Sunshine and Shadow* (1905), one after another. Ultimately, however, tuberculosis was the death of him, at just 33 years of age.

Although Dunbar wrote several outstanding novels, short stories, essays, and many poems in standard English, his literary reputation has always chiefly rested on his "dialect poems," written to reflect the speech patterns of African-American folks living on antebellum plantations. During his lifetime, this poetry was praised widely among both European Americans and African Americans. Following World War II, however, critics lamented his use of dialect and whined about his stereotypes of plantation life, often depicting African Americans as being servile. During the early 1960s, critics viewed Dunbar as a victim of circumstance, who muted his protest against injustice and tempered his praise of African Americans to please his European-American patrons, publishers, and readers.

Starting in the late 1960s, however, Dunbar's work was once again viewed in a new light. The 1972 Centenary Celebration on Paul Laurence Dunbar at the University of California at Irvine reflected a new appreciation of this preeminent poet, given the postslavery Reconstruction era in which he emerged and his own struggle to survive as a writer. Dunbar was recognized for awakening U.S. readers to dialect poetry and to the valuable contributions Africans and African Americans had made to U.S. culture. Dunbar's "Little Brown Baby" and other lyrical poems have uplifted countless young African Americans (e.g., see **Patricia McKissack**) and have been hailed as inspirational by numerous subsequent African-American poets, such as **Nikki Giovanni**, who named him a "natural resource" of his people (Giovanni, 1988, p. 122).

Evidence of Dunbar's continuing importance may be seen in the fact that following the 1913 publication of his *Complete Poems of Paul Laurence Dunbar,* this volume has remained in print, year

after year, continually rediscovered by new generations of Americans who appreciate the skill with
which he expressed the yearnings and the fears, the
humor and the turmoil of African Americans at
the turn of the twentieth century.

—*Michael Strickland*

REFERENCES: Bontemps, Arna (1976), "The Black
Contribution to American Letters," in Mabel M.
Smythe (Ed.), *The Black American Reference Book*
(Englewood Cliffs, NJ: Prentice-Hall). Bryan, Ashley
(1978), *I Greet the Dawn: Poems by Paul Laurence
Dunbar* (New York: Atheneum). Giovanni, Nikki
(1988), in *Contemporary Authors* (Vol. 124), (Detroit:
Gale Research). Johnson, James Weldon (1922),
Book of American Negro Poetry (Orlando: Harcourt,
Brace and World). Smythe, Mabel M. (Ed.) (1976),
The Black American Reference Book (Englewood
Cliffs, NJ: Prentice-Hall).

Dunbar Nelson, Alice Ruth (née Moore)
(7/19/1875–9/18/1935)
*Novel, poems, essays, short stories, literary
criticism, edited volumes, diary; journalist,
newspaper publisher*

Alice excelled in school, both as a student
(through her master's degree) and as a teacher at
the elementary, secondary, and college levels. *Vio-
lets, and Other Tales,* Alice's first book, was published
privately in 1895. This collection of sketches, reviews, stories, poems, and essays expresses her
characteristic fascination with language and with
various literary forms. It also introduced her recurring themes: class differences, ambivalent attitudes toward women's roles, and romance. Her
writing also notably neglects issues of racial identity, perhaps reflecting her conflicts regarding how
her own Creole cultural and racial heritage and
her fair skin affected her self-concept and her sociopolitical outlook.

The year her first book was published, **Paul
Laurence Dunbar** was attracted to one of her poems and began corresponding with her. Alice analyzed the contrast between her writing and his in a
letter she wrote to him: "You ask my opinion about
the Negro dialect in literature? Well, frankly, I believe in everyone following his own bent. If it be so
that one has a special aptitude for dialect work why
it is only right that dialect work should be a specialty. But if one should be like me—absolutely de-
void of the ability to manage dialect, I don't see the
necessity of cramming and forcing oneself into that
plane because one is a Negro or a Southerner."

In 1898, she married Dunbar in secret, over the
objections of her family and friends. In 1899, her
14-tale collection *The Goodness of St. Rocque, and
Other Stories* was published as a companion piece
to Dunbar's *Poems of Cabin and Field*. Some critics
consider these stories to be her finest work, establishing her reputation for skillful depiction of Creole culture. In 1902, Paul Dunbar's extensive
travel, poor health, and alcohol abuse led Alice and
him to separate, but they remained friends until
his death.

Alice then moved to Wilmington, Delaware,
where she taught English for 18 years. During this
time, she married again—and again: In 1910, she
married a fellow teacher, whom she soon divorced, then in 1916, she married journalist
Robert J. Nelson, with whom she spent the rest of
her life. Alice and Robert owned and operated the
Wilmington Advocate, a civil rights newspaper. In
addition, her interest in public speaking and oratory led to two edited volumes: *Masterpieces of Negro Eloquence* (1914) and *The Dunbar Speaker and
Entertainer* (1920).

During the 1920s and early 1930s, Dunbar
Nelson was primarily known for her poems,
which were precisely crafted, incisive, romantic,
and traditional in form. These works appeared in
Crisis and **Opportunity** magazines and were often
anthologized. In addition, her literary reviews influenced fellow poets, such as **Langston Hughes**.
She continued to write steadily throughout the
Harlem Renaissance period, but much of her
work (including her diary) was not published until after her death.

REFERENCES: *1TESK. BANP. EB-98. EBLG.
NAAAL. OC20LE. RLWWJ. RT.* McKoy, Sheila
Smith, in *OCWW.* Titus, Mary, in *OCAAL.*

Dunham, Katherine (6/22/1909–)
Nonfiction—anthropology, autobiography

Although Dunham is most widely known for
her dancing, her direction of her dance troupe, and
her choreography, she is well regarded in scholarly
circles for her anthropological study of dance.
Dunham's love of dance had begun before she
graduated from high school, and she took dance
lessons while attending Joliet Junior College. Her
brother, Albert, persuaded her to transfer to the
University of Chicago, where she supported herself by giving dance lessons as well as assisting in
the library. In Chicago, she studied various kinds of

dance and formed an African-American dance troupe. During this time, she also met **Langston Hughes** and other luminaries of the **Harlem Renaissance**, and she met and married fellow dancer Jordis McCoo, who worked nights at the post office, while she attended school by day.

At the university, her ethnology professor Robert Redfield inspired her interest in anthropology by emphasizing the role of dance in the social and ceremonial life of a culture. Perhaps also, she was already primed to be interested in cultural diversity, as her own ancestry included West African, Malagasyan, French Canadian, and Native American heritage. With encouragement from psychologist Erich Fromm and sociologist **Charles (Spurgeon) Johnson**, she was soon awarded a Julius Rosenwald Foundation fellowship to do fieldwork in the West Indies (Haiti—observing the Vaudun ceremonies, Jamaica—the Accompong, and Martinique and Trinidad). As her research continued, she also received a Rockefeller Foundation fellowship.

Eventually, this research led to her receiving bachelor's and master's degrees in anthropology from the University of Chicago and a doctorate from Northwestern University, based on her doctoral thesis on the dances of Haiti. With her impressive credentials and distinctive knowledge, she gave lectures on her investigations at Yale, the Royal Anthropological Society of London, and other institutions throughout the United States, Europe, and South America.

Dunham has also demonstrated a lifelong commitment to civil rights, justice, and freedom from oppression. As just one example, despite pressure from the U.S. State Department, she and her troupe toured internationally performing her dance *Southland,* which dramatized a lynching, following the outrageous lynching of young Emmett Till. In 1992, she also went on a 47-day fast to publicize the despicable U.S. policies toward Haitian refugees in the United States.

While working for the Federal Theatre Project in the 1940s, Dunham met Anglo-Canadian artist and set and costume designer John Pratt. After divorcing her first husband, on July 10, 1939, she married 24-year-old Pratt, to whom she remained married until his death in 1986. In 1952, Pratt and Dunham adopted a daughter, a mixed-heritage French Martinican 5-year-old, Marie Christine Columbier, who is now a designer herself, living in Rome. Almost a decade before adopting her, in 1943, Dunham had opened the Katherine Dunham School of Arts and Research in New York. There, in addition to studying dance and theater arts, students learned about literature and world cultures until the school closed in 1955. Her students had included actors Marlon Brando and James Dean, dancer Eartha Kitt, and choreographer Arthur Mitchell.

Dunham's dance troupe toured internationally from 1940 to 1963, and her last U.S. performance was in 1965 at the Apollo Theatre. After that, Dunham spent two years involved in dance in Senegal (1965–1967). On returning to the United States, she opened the Performing Arts Training Center of Southern Illinois University, where she again encouraged cross-cultural understandings through dance, literature, and other arts. In association with the center, Dunham has been involved in a children's workshop and the Katherine Dunham Museum. She has won numerous honorary degrees and other awards from U.S. institutions (e.g., the Kennedy Center Award for Lifetime Achievement in the Arts, 1983; the Distinguished Service Award of the Anthropological Association, 1986) and from the Haitian government.

In addition to writing numerous scholarly journal articles and popular magazine essays, Dunham has contributed short stories to various popular magazines, sometimes using the nom de plume Kaye Dunn. Dunham's book-length publications include her Jamaican observations, *Journey to Accompong* (1946, 1971 reprint titled *Katherine Dunham's Journey to Accompong*); her first memoir, *A Touch of Innocence: Memoirs of Childhood* (1959/1994); her Haitian observations written while she was living in Senegal, *Island Possessed* (1969/1994); her fiction set in Senegal, *Kassamance, a Fantasy* (1969); and her authoritative work based on her doctoral thesis, *Dances of Haiti* (1949/1983). She is said to be working on her second volume of memoirs.

REFERENCES: BDAA. EB-BH-CD. EBLG. PGAA. WDAW. Aschenbrenner, Joyce, in *BWA:AHE*. Jackson, Gregory, in *OCAAL*. Keough, Leyla, in *EA-99*. Odom, Selma Landen, in *WB-99*. Tobias, Tobi, in *G-95*. Wood, Phyllis, in *BH2C*. Amazon.com, 7/1999. Dunham's papers, films, and artifacts are archived at the Missouri Historical Society in St. Louis.

Edelman, Marian (née) Wright
(6/6/1939–)
Inspirational/motivational books of child advocacy, memoir

The parents of Marian, her sister, and her three brothers prized education and cherished children. Although they lacked many financial resources, every one of the Wright children went to college, and the Wrights raised 12 foster children in addition to their own children. Marian's daddy, a Baptist minister (Marian is "the aunt, daughter, granddaughter, and sister of Baptist ministers"), built a playground and snack bar behind his church to ensure that the black children of the neighborhood, barred from white play areas in Jim Crow South Carolina, would have somewhere to enjoy themselves, to belong, and to feel safe. In 1954, when Marian was 14 years old, the U.S. Supreme Court case *Brown v. Board of Education* was a major topic of conversation in her household. Sadly, her father died the week before the decision was handed down, so he never knew how that case would affect future generations of African-American children. By the time Marian's father died, she had already learned to rely on her religion to guide her to serve those in need.

Early on, Marian Wright was active in the civil rights movement. For instance, she was among 14 students arrested at an Atlanta sit-in. After she earned her baccalaureate from Spelman College (1960) and while a student at Yale University Law School, she spent the summer working on the voter-registration campaign in Mississippi. In 1963, after she graduated from Yale, she became a staff attorney for the National Association for the Advancement of Colored People (NAACP) Legal Defense and Education Fund, which helped release students jailed for their civil rights activities. She put her beliefs to the test when assaulted by Southern sheriffs' fire hoses and attack dogs and when incarcerated in Southern jails. During that time, she became the first African-American woman to pass the Mississippi bar (at age 26). She also joined the board of the Child Development Group of Mississippi, a major Head Start program.

During the Mississippi Freedom Summer of 1964 and her battles for Head Start in 1965, Wright observed the tremendous hunger, homelessness, and illiteracy of children (and their families), and she determined that local, specific actions seemed ineffectual in addressing those needs. As a result, she conceived of a broader, more encompassing organization that could address these needs on a national level. In 1968, she was awarded a Ford Foundation grant, which she used to start the Washington Research Project to investigate national policies and investment strategies that might address the needs she saw. Following a brief stint (1971–1973) as director of the Harvard University Center for Law and Education, she returned to Washington and built on the foundation she had laid for the Washington Research Project to found the highly esteemed Children's Defense Fund (CDF), a nonprofit organization lobbying on behalf of children's issues. She has since presided over the CDF, tackling such issues as child care and youth employment. One of the most widely recognized CDF programs is its nationwide multimedia and community-based campaign to prevent or reduce teen pregnancy.

Meanwhile, Marian's personal life also came to center around children. In 1967, in Mississippi, she met her husband, the grandson of Russian Jews, who shared her dedication to civil rights. In 1968, they married, and fairly soon after, they had three sons (Josh, Jonah, and Ezra). As she said in her 1992 book, *The Measure of Our Success: A Letter to My Children and Yours,* she has been fortunate to have a job that allowed her to ensure that her children "came first in any crunch." Not only was she *able* to put her own children ahead of her work for the nation's children, however, but she also *chose* to do so, such as ensuring that when one of her children was sick, either she or her husband stayed home with them. She also attended most school parent meetings and baked her share of cookies and brownies—and then she went to work the next morning, to fight for the well-being and education of other people's children.

Marian Wright Edelman, president of the Children's Defense Fund, 1983 (Corbis/Bettmann-UPI)

Among the numerous leadership awards she has been given is a 1985 MacArthur fellowship (nicknamed a "genius grant"). Her numerous appointments to prestigious and influential bodies include positions on the Council on Foreign Relations and on the board of trustees of Spelman College. She was soon the first African American and the second woman to chair the college's board of trustees.

In addition to countless legal documents and other advocacy writings, she has written at least four books: Her 1987 book, *Families in Peril: An Agenda for Social Change,* shows how poverty is the most pressing national problem and urges readers to ensure support for poor mothers and children of all races. Her 1992 *The Measure of Our Success: A Letter to My Children and Yours* warmly describes her own interracial family life and spells out her beliefs regarding how we as a society can best promote the well-being of our children and youths. Her 1995 *Guide My Feet: Prayers and Meditations on Loving and Working for Children* offers prayers by the author and by others, intended to cry out for help to protect and care for our children. Also, her 1999 memoir *Lanterns: A Memoir of Mentors* highlights those who have inspired her and illuminated her path.

REFERENCES: *1TESK. AA:PoP. AAB. BF:2000. EBLG. G-95. H.* Edelman, Marian (1992), *The Measure of Our Success: A Letter to My Children and Yours* (Boston: Beacon Press). Amazon.com, 8/1999.

Edmonds, Kenneth ("Babyface")
(4/10/1959–)
Songs

Among award-winning songwriter Edmonds's many hits are "Tender Lover," "Unbreak My Heart," "Take a Bow," and "Change the World," and Grammy winners "I'll Make Love to You" and "When Can I See You," recorded by such singers as Whitney Houston, Madonna, and Eric Clapton.

REFERENCES: Crockett, Kenneth, in *BH2C.*

Elder, Lonne, III (1931–1996)
Plays, screenplays

Elder's stage plays include his highly celebrated *Ceremonies in Dark Old Men* (1969), as well as *Charades on East Fourth Street* (1967) and his first—still unpublished—play, *A Hysterical Tale in a Rabbit's Race* (1961). His screenplays include episodes of *NYPD* (for ABC-TV, 1967–1969) and of *McCloud*

(for NBC-TV, 1970–1971) and the films *Sounder* (1972, based on the novel by William Armstrong), *Day of Absence* (1975, adapted from **Douglas Turner Ward**'s stage play), *Melinda* (c. 1972), *The Terrible Veil* (1963), and *A Woman Called Moses* (1978). Elder's first mentor, who inspired him to write, was poet **Robert Hayden**; his second was the Harlem Writers Guild cofounder and patron saint **John Oliver Killens**. His roommate, Douglas Turner Ward, was also instrumental in pointing his writing toward the theater.

REFERENCES: Frye, Karla Y. E., in *OCAAL.*

Ellison, Ralph (Waldo)
(3/1/1914–4/16/1994)
Novels, essays, short stories; editor

A descendant of slaves, Ralph (Waldo) Ellison was named after nineteenth-century European-American philosopher and writer Ralph Waldo Emerson. Lewis Alfred Ellison, a construction worker and small-time entrepreneur, gave his son that name in the hope that young Ralph would someday become a writer. Lewis was an avid reader and was exposing his son to books by the time Ralph started learning to walk. Lewis and Ida Millsap Ellison had moved to Oklahoma City, Oklahoma, from the deep South, in the hope that this western frontier state would be a land of greater opportunities for African Americans to prosper. Even after Lewis died, when Ralph was just three years old, the Ellisons held fast to their belief in limitless possibilities.

Ida worked as a domestic servant, a custodian, and occasionally even a cook to earn enough to support Ralph and his brother Herbert. She also moved herself and her sons into the parsonage of a local church and continued to organize for the Socialist Party, enlisting African Americans. Ida often brought home discarded popular magazines, books, and records from the white householders for whom she worked. Ralph, an avid reader like his father, later recalled, "These magazines and recordings . . . spoke to me of a life that was broader and more interesting and although it was not really a part of my own life, I never thought they were not for me because I happened to be a Negro. They were things which spoke of a world which I could some day make my own" (quoted in *NAAAL*). Ida always affirmed Ralph's youthful beliefs about his possibilities for fulfillment. Even his wider community seemed to affirm these possibilities, as everywhere

Novelist Ralph Ellison, 1967 (Bernard Gotfryd/Archive Photos)

he saw African Americans courageously rising to challenges they faced.

In 1920, young Ralph started attending the segregated public schools in town. By the time he finished high school, in 1931, he had studied music theory and classical music and had started playing the trumpet and several other brass instruments. At that time, Oklahoma City was a haven for jazz and other music, so the blacks-only schools emphasized music education. In addition, Ralph made every effort to find places where he could listen to jazz music—which wasn't hard in Oklahoma City. To ensure that this talented young African American would not try to attend one of the whites-only colleges in Oklahoma, the state gave Ellison a scholarship to attend the Tuskegee Institute (in Alabama). The scholarship wasn't enough to pay for his living expenses in Alabama, however, so it was two years before Ellison had saved enough money to attend Tuskegee. In 1933, he hitched a ride (like a hobo) on a freight train headed to Alabama and entered Tuskegee to study music composition.

In his second year at Tuskegee, a sophomore English class opened Ellison's eyes and ears to the world of modern literature, such as T. S. Eliot's poem *The Waste Land,* with its jazzlike rhythms. Increasingly, he found himself spending more and more time in the library, delving into literature and history, while continuing his music major. For him, European-American poets such as T. S. Eliot and Ezra Pound wrote poems more closely linked to jazz than did the African-American poets of the 1930s. Through their works, he started realizing that his interests in literature and in music could be merged, and a career in writing gained appeal for him. During this time, he met literary critic **Alain Locke**, who also encouraged him to think about writing as a career. Ellison developed an intense interest in sculpture, too.

Over time, the relatively anti-intellectual college life at Tuskegee, centered around campus politics and athletics, appealed to him less and less. The school's accommodationist philosophy also grated on Ellison, who had grown up believing in limitless possibilities, not quiet acceptance of whatever constraints white society imposed on him. Each summer, Ellison had to work to earn money for living expenses the following year. After his junior year (summer of 1936), he decided to find work in New York City, where he thought he might also pursue his interest in sculpture. In New

York, he contacted Locke again; Locke introduced him to **Langston Hughes** and **Arna Bontemps**. Enraptured by the pro-intellectual literary haven of New York City, Ellison never returned to Tuskegee. The following year, Ellison's mother died, and Ellison spent half the year with his brother, grieving, hunting, and reading. When he returned, Ellison knew that New York City was his home, and his career aim was to become a writer.

In 1937 (the year Ellison's mother died), **Richard Wright** moved from Chicago to New York, and Hughes and Bontemps introduced Ellison to Wright. Wright proved to be a tremendous mentor to Ellison, encouraging Ellison to read widely, including European novelists (e.g., James Joyce, Joseph Conrad, Fyodor Dostoyevsky) and European-American novelists (e.g., Henry James, Ernest Hemingway). He also urged Ellison to work on perfecting his writing craft. Wright even allowed Ellison to see a master artisan at work, while Wright was writing his most widely acclaimed novel, *Native Son.* Ellison shared many of Wright's political views, too, although he never joined the Communist Party, and he was always much more optimistic about the possibilities for change than Wright was. (The optimism Ellison had learned from his parents had apparently become deeply ingrained.) Nonetheless, Wright was pretty much the literary center of Ellison's universe at that time.

Wright also urged Ellison to contribute writings to the *New Challenge,* a Marxist literary magazine that Wright had started editing in Harlem. The sole issue of *New Challenge* included Ellison's review of *These Low Grounds* by **Waters Turpin**, and Ellison's short story "Hymie Bull": Ellison could officially call himself a writer. The late 1930s were nothing like the 1920s (the era of the **Harlem Renaissance**), however, so writing for a living was pretty tough. Most writers had to earn a living doing menial jobs that left them little time for writing after work. Fortunately, one of the New Deal programs was the Federal Writers' Project (FWP), which employed quite a few writers to conduct research and write reports on their findings. Through Wright, Ellison managed to get an FWP job in 1938, earning $103 each month to gather and record folklore and oral histories through extensive interviews with Harlem residents. In 1940 and 1941, Ellison wrote a couple of essays on the value of African-American folklore in African-American fiction, and he continued to contribute short stories, essays, and articles to *New Masses* and other periodicals.

Ellison's earliest short stories (e.g., "Slick Gonna Learn," 1939; "The Birthmark," 1940) closely paralleled Wright's literary style and political outlook; far from being flattered, Wright rebuked Ellison for his derivative work, and their close relationship grew distant. Soon, Ellison started finding his own voice, style, and aesthetic and political outlook, and his writing became distinctively his own. In 1942, Ellison started editing *The Negro Quarterly,* and by 1944, he had written almost five dozen published articles (including a *New York Post* article on the 1943 Harlem riot), more than half a dozen stories, and various sketches and book reviews. No longer working for the FWP, he also started working on a novel, which was to be his masterpiece.

In 1943, Ellison joined the U.S. Merchant Marine, serving as a cook while continuing to write. After the war ended and he left the service, he planned to start writing a novel about a Tuskegee Airman captured by the Nazis during World War II, based on his 1944 short story "Flying Home." Instead, he found himself developing a novel based on a few words he had scribbled on a sheet of paper: "I am an invisible man." Fortunately, a publisher encouraged him to write it, and a Rosenwald fellowship provided him enough money to do so. About seven years later, he completed his best-selling *Invisible Man* (1952).

The complex novel is seen through the eyes of an unnamed idealistic and naïve young black male who seeks his identity and his place in the world. On graduating from high school, the young man goes off to a well-respected college, where he hopes to find his way but instead finds himself invisible in a college much like Tuskegee, where neither the accommodationist founder nor the white patrons can see African Americans as an integral part of American society, instead seeing them only in terms of preconceived roles. After failing to find what he seeks in the South, the young man moves to Harlem, where he is again invisible as an individual and is instead urged to define himself in terms of various political stances (e.g., black nationalism, communism). Throughout the novel, the young man yearns for respect and equality, and only at the end of the book does he realize that he has wrongly sought to define himself through others— others to whom he is invisible as an individual. Instead, he must define himself through a solitary quest for self-awareness and self-knowledge, drawing on his own intellect and cultural heritage. Only then is he ready to enter a society full of possibilities for him, ready to forge his own identity and to create his own place (as a writer) in the world.

Although some African-American activists and scholars criticized the work for Ellison's response to militant African-American political activists, most literary critics of all races lauded the work. Among the many awards Ellison received for the book was a 1953 National Book Award for fiction, making him the first African American to win it. At the awards ceremony, Ellison credited the richness of African-American speech as central to his writing.

Ironically, one of several colleges and universities to award Ellison an honorary degree was his alma mater, the Tuskegee Institute, which he had left without graduating and which he had not too subtly indicted in his novel; in 1963, Tuskegee awarded him an honorary Ph.D. in humane letters. In 1974, Harvard University awarded him an honorary doctorate as well. In 1967, the Oklahoma State Legislature recognized him for his "outstanding contribution to the creative arts." In 1969, President Nixon awarded Ellison the Presidential Medal of Freedom, the highest civilian honor. Perhaps the most remarkable honor, however, was awarded in 1965, when a poll of 200 book critics, editors, and authors named *Invisible Man* "the most distinguished American novel written since [the end of World War II]." The poll, published in *Book Week,* was taken more than a decade after the book was published and was based on the assessment of critics who had read countless books each year, including books by J. D. Salinger, Mary McCarthy, Norman Mailer, Joseph Heller, Jack Kerouac, Truman Capote, and Eudora Welty.

In the mid-1950s, Ellison went to Europe, lecturing in Germany and Austria; in 1955, he was awarded the Prix de Rome by the American Academy of Arts and Letters; the prize money paid for him to live in Italy for a while. When he returned to the United States, numerous colleges and universities invited him to lecture, teach, and work as writer-in-residence. Between 1958 and 1964, he taught at Bard College (in New York) and the University of Chicago; he was a writer-in-residence at Rutgers University (in New Jersey); he was a visiting fellow at Yale University; and he lectured at such prominent colleges and universities as Antioch, Bennington, Columbia, Fisk, Oberlin, Princeton, and the University of California at Los Angeles. In 1970, he was named the

Albert Schweitzer Professor of Humanities at New York University, from which he retired after 1979.

In addition to the novel on which his literary reputation rests, Ellison wrote short stories and essays, which have been widely anthologized. A couple of years after his death, many of Ellison's short stories were collected in *Flying Home: And Other Stories* (1996). Of the thirteen short stories in the collection, six were found after his death and had never been published before. All the stories were written between 1937 (his return to New York) and 1954 (before he left for Europe), including "Flying Home"; "Hymie Bull," his first published short story; four humorous stories about Buster and Riley, adventurous preteens; and "A Party Down at the Square," a white Northern boy's observation of a lynching in the South.

When Ellison died, two volumes of his essays had been published: *Shadow and Act* (1964) and *Going to the Territory* (1986). Ellison dedicated *Shadow and Act* to Monteza Sprague, the English teacher at Tuskegee who had opened his eyes to the world of modern literature. Both collections include autobiographical observations of his own emergence as a writer, literary reviews and criticism, and essays, speeches, and interviews on the African-American experience (jazz and blues music, art and culture, and social issues). *Shadow and Act* included sections on literature and folklore ("The Seer and the Seen"), music ("Sound and the Mainstream"), and African Americans in a social, cultural, and societal context ("The Shadow and the Act"). *Going to the Territory* also included excerpts from his second novel, still incomplete at the time of his death. *The Collected Essays of Ralph Ellison* (1995, edited by John F. Callahan) includes all the works from both collections, along with nearly two dozen previously uncollected or newly discovered works. His other major nonfiction work, also published posthumously, is *Conversations with Ralph Ellison* (1995; edited by Amritjit Singh and Maryemma Graham).

Ellison started his long-awaited second novel in the mid-1950s. Sadly, after he had worked on the manuscript for more than a year, a fire at his summer home in Plainsfield, Massachusetts, made ashes of his masterwork. For the next three decades or more, Ellison had to try to re-create what he had written and then further develop the manuscript. At the time of his death, at least eight excerpts had been published (in his essay collection, in literary journals, and in readings during Ellison's appearances on television or on college campuses), but the work was still considered incomplete.

Ellison's literary executor, John F. Callahan, pulled together numerous sections of his work (about one third of the 2,000-page manuscript Ellison had written) to create the novel *Juneteenth,* published in 1999. Many critics have hailed its arrival as a major achievement, while others have decried both the completed work and even the effort to complete a work that Ellison himself was unable to finish during his lifetime. In *Juneteenth,* U.S. Senator Adam Sunraider, a white-complected racist, suffers a fatal gunshot wound while delivering a speech to fellow senators. To the great surprise of all who thought they knew him, on his deathbed, Sunraider asks to see Reverend Alonzo ("Daddy") Hickman, a black revivalist preacher. Apparently, the two have a long history together, and their lives are intertwined in ways that had never been revealed before.

Although Ellison made himself highly accessible to college students, he enjoyed his privacy. He and his wife, Fanny McConnell (whom he had married in 1946), lived in a flat in Manhattan, where he enjoyed listening to music, playing the jazz trumpet, making furniture, and experimenting with photography. He recognized his own way of contributing, however, when he observed, "[writing] offers me the possibility of contributing not only to the growth of the literature but to the shaping of the culture as I should like it to be." Ellison also commented, "What moves a writer to eloquence is less meaningful than what he makes of it" (from "The World and the Jug," quoted in *NAAAL*).

REFERENCES: *1TESK. AA:PoP. AAW:AAPP. BAL-1-P. BF:2000. BWA. EB-BH-CD. EBLG. EGW. NAAAL. OC20LE. RG20. WDAA.* Early, Gerald, "Decoding Ralph Ellison," in *EA-99.* Gayle, Addison, in *G-97.* McKay, Nellie Y., in *WB-99.* Reckley, Ralph, Sr., in *OCAAL.* Robinson, Lisa Clayton, in *EA-99.* Amazon.com, barnesandnoble.com, 8/1999.

Equiano, Olaudah (a.k.a. Gustavus Vassa) (c.1745–3/31/1797)
Slave narrative, verse

In the mid-1700s, Olaudah was born into the Ibo tribe in the village of Essaka (or Benin) in the kingdom of Benin (what is now southeastern Nigeria), West Africa. When Olaudah was 11 (or

12) years old, he and his sister were captured and kidnapped by black slave raiders. Shortly after their abduction, he and his sister were separated, and he spent months in the service of a black chieftain, whose treatment of him was mild compared with the brutality of the British slave traders to whom he was sold soon after. The slave traders then took him to Barbados in the West Indies, but he was not sold there, so he was taken to America. In America, he was purchased by a Virginia plantation owner.

Fortunately for Olaudah, he was soon sold to a British Royal Navy officer (a captain or a lieutenant), who renamed him Gustavus Vassa, after the sixteenth-century Swedish king and freedom fighter. Olaudah worked for the navy officer either as a personal servant or as a ship steward, and he traveled widely with the officer to many countries and colonies on the North Atlantic and the Mediterranean. Several friendly white sailors helped him learn to speak, read, and write English, and they introduced him to Christianity.

By the early 1760s, when Equiano reached adulthood, he had spent several years on various vessels, engaged mostly in commerce but sometimes in naval warfare. In 1762, he was sold to a West Indian trader, who soon sold him to Robert King, a Philadelphia Quaker and merchant. King taught him about seagoing commercial enterprises and allowed him enough free time to work at other enterprises to earn enough money to purchase his freedom. Finally, on July 10, 1766, Equiano had put aside enough money not only to purchase his freedom but also to start his own business career, working on commercial vessels and occasional scientific expeditions to Central America and the Arctic regions.

In 1767, Equiano moved to England to start an entirely new career, working as a hairdresser for affluent Londoners (at a time when wigs for men and women were quite popular). He also learned how to play the French horn, expanded his knowledge of math, and experienced a long, intense spiritual conversion, at least in part a result of his much earlier introduction to Christianity. He joined the Methodists, known for their opposition to slavery.

In 1773, Equiano returned to the sea to join a scientific expedition to the Arctic and the North Pole. This trip started his return to working on ships, traveling to Europe, the Middle East, the Caribbean, and North, Central, and South America. During his seafaring experience, he handled a variety of tasks and situations: taking charge of a ship during a storm, serving as parson when needed, governing a vessel when the captain died and then conducting it safely into port, and even overseeing slaves on occasion. Whenever he visited England, however, he further pursued his education, and eventually, in 1777, he decided to settle in England.

In the 1780s, the British Parliament debated whether to end the slave trade. Equiano became an active abolitionist, lecturing against slavery and petitioning the British Parliament, calling for abolition. Among other things, he railed against the cruel practices of British slaveowners in Jamaica. In 1787, he was appointed commissary of provisions and stores aboard the *Vernon,* which was carrying 500–600 male and female impoverished freed slaves to Freetown, Sierra Leone, on the west coast of Africa, to establish a colonial settlement there. Some disputes with the venture management led to his returning to England rather than settling back in his native land.

Back in England, British abolitionists paid for Equiano to publish his thick two-volume autobiography, *The Interesting Narrative of the Life of Olaudah Equiano, or Gustavus Vassa, the African* (1789, England; 1791, United States), in order to document and to offer evidence on the sufferings of slaves. His narrative is credited with being the prototype for the **slave narrative** genre. Although some critics trace his distinctive autobiographical form highlighting spiritual conversion to Saint Augustine's *Confessions* (c. 400), his addition of the element of social protest makes the form of his book distinctive. Specifically, he paralleled the three-part structure of a life of sin, a conversion experience, and an emergence into a spiritually awakened life with a life in slavery, a struggle for freedom, and then freedom from the physical bonds of slavery. Stylistically, Equiano's narrative interweaves a direct, straightforward, graphic style (especially in describing his personal experiences and adventures) and an elaborate, elevated style (especially in relation to his spiritual awakening).

Although Equiano wasn't the first African-born former slave to *tell* his life experiences of enslavement and emancipation, he was the first to write his life story himself, without help or direction from white ghostwriters, amanuenses, or editors. Perhaps for this reason, his slave narrative much more compellingly indicts slavery as the brutal institution it was, emphasizing the atrocities of slavery and adamantly urging its total and immediate abolition. His autobiography is so compelling a narrative, so insightful a spiritual awakening, and so forceful an indictment of slavery that John Wesley, the founder of Methodism, the religion to which Equiano had converted, had the book read to him on his deathbed.

His book also included an idealized, sentimental, affectionate description of his early life in Benin. He describes his fellow Africans as having simple manners, highly just moral values, and a profoundly harmonious society. In contrast, he describes the terror he felt on seeing the mean-faced white men with long hair and red faces, who packed him and fellow slaves as human cargo to be crammed into the dark hulls of slave ships. His account was the first to show the extreme brutality (suffocating stench, filth, disease, sexual abuse, near starvation, and physical tortures) of the journey of the Middle Passage, from Africa to the Americas.

Another highlight of Equiano's book was his revelation of the effects of slavery on the master as well as on the slave. He also mixed personal remembrances with his wide range of reading in the areas of history, geography, religion, politics, and commerce. His account powerfully describes his dichotomous feelings of terror and awe during his first contacts with Europeans and European Americans. He concludes his account with two goals: to lobby for the abolition of the slave trade and to become a Christian missionary to Africa. After his book was published in 1789, he traveled extensively throughout England and Ireland promoting it—and the abolition cause. In 1792, he married an Englishwoman, Susanna Cullen, in England, and the couple had two daughters. His book was so popular that by 1794, there had been eight editions printed in England and one in the United States. The book was also translated into Dutch (1790), German (1792), and Russian (1794). By the middle of the nineteenth century, about 20 or more editions had been produced in the United States and Europe. The book has also been printed in several new editions since the 1960s.

In his autobiography and his later *Miscellaneous Verses,* Equiano idealized his African past, taking pride in his race yet condemning those Africans who trafficked in slavery. While being transported to the slave ship on the coast, he further observed how European intrusion into African societies had a corrupting influence on them, such as by introducing the new weaponry of war and by fostering

hostilities and greed to elicit the Africans' aid in the Europeans' barbarous venture. He further showed appreciation of King's kindness and of the English abolitionists and others who had befriended him.

REFERENCES: *1TESK. AA:PoP. BAL-1-P. BWA. CSN. EB-98. EBLG. MAAL. NAAAL.* Costanzo, Angelo, in *OCAAL.*

Evans, Mari (7/16/1923–)
Poems, children's books, anthologies, essays, plays, short stories, reviews, lectures, criticism, biographies

A native of Toledo, Ohio, Evans credits her father with encouraging her literary development. As she said in "My Father's Passage," her autobiographical essay in the volume she edited, *Black Women Writers* (1984, p. 165), "No single living entity really influenced my life as did my father." For instance, he had saved her first printed story, written when she was in the fourth grade and printed in the school newspaper. As she recalled, her father had "carefully noted on it the date, our home address, and his own proud comment" on her achievement.

Evans attended Toledo public schools and studied at the University of Toledo, where she studied fashion design—a career she never pursued after college. As she noted, "I moved from university journalism to a by-lined column in a Black-owned weekly and, in time, worked variously as an industrial editor, as a research associate with responsibility for preparing curriculum materials, and as director of publications for the corporate management of a Job Corps installation." Her "industrial editor" job involved being an assistant editor at a local chain-manufacturing plant, where precise language and discipline in writing were essential. Although her supervisor was wary of having a young black woman working for him, he knew how to write well, and his own example and demands for her work encouraged her to revise endlessly. Eventually, she was able to turn out prose as precise as he demanded, and he allowed her some creative freedom.

By the end of her three years working with him, she fully understood "that writing is a craft, a profession one learns by doing. One must be able to produce on demand, and that requires great personal discipline. . . . I cannot imagine a writer who is not continually reaching, who contains no discontent that what he or she is producing is not more than it is. . . . discipline is the foundation of the profession" (p. 167). She added, "I have always written, it seems. I have not, however, always been organized in my approach. Now, I find I am much more productive when I set aside a specific time and uncompromisingly accept that as commitment."

Beginning in 1969, Evans started teaching at a series of U.S. universities and lecturing widely and frequently as a much-sought-after speaker (e.g., at the biennial National Black Writers Festival held at Medgar Evers College). These appointments included the following:

- 1968–1973—producer, writer, and director, *The Black Experience,* a WTTV, Channel 4, Indianapolis TV show
- 1969–1970—instructor of African-American literature and writer-in-residence at Purdue University
- 1969–1970—consultant, Discovery Grant Program, National Endowment for the Arts
- 1970–1973—consultant in ethnic studies, Bobbs-Merrill Co.
- 1970–1978—assistant professor and writer-in-residence at Indiana University, Bloomington
- 1972–1973—visiting assistant professor, Northwestern University, Evanston, Illinois
- 1975—fellowship residency at the MacDowell Colony, Peterborough, New Hampshire
- 1975–1980—member, board of management, Fall Creek Parkway YMCA
- 1976–1977—chair of Literary Advisory Panel, Indiana Arts Commission
- 1978–1979—member, Indiana Corrections Code Commission
- 1978–1980—visiting assistant professor at Purdue University, West Lafayette, Indiana
- 1980—visiting assistant professor at Washington University, St. Louis
- 1981–1984—visiting assistant professor and distinguished writer, Africana Studies and Research Center, Cornell University
- other appointments as visiting professor at SUNY Albany and at Spelman College

Evans's literary career has primarily involved poetry and plays, but she has also published many short stories, essays, book reviews, children's books, articles, and works of literary criticism and biography. Many of her writings have been translated into Swedish, French, Dutch, Russian, German, and Italian for use in countless textbooks and anthologies. Her poetry has also been choreographed and used on record albums, filmstrips, calendars, radio, television specials, and two off-Broadway productions. She has even attempted to write a novel.

Starting in 1963, her poetry was published in **Phylon, Negro Digest,** and *Dialog.* Thereafter, her work has been published in *Black World* (see *Negro Digest*), *Okike,* **Callaloo***, Essence, Ebony, Black Collegian,* and myriad other journals and magazines. By the time she published her first poetry collection, *Where Is All the Music?* (1968), addressing various aspects of intimate love affairs, she was already able to craft tight verse.

Her second poetry collection, *I Am a Black Woman* (1970), begins with the theme of romantic love but expands into a more complex volume, embracing historical and political themes. She progresses from the intimate relations between two African Americans to the entire African-American community, and then she further extends her embrace to encompass others who have been impoverished and oppressed, whether here in the United States or elsewhere in the world. In it is her oft-anthologized poem "Who Can Be Born Black": "Who / can be born black / and not / sing / the wonder of it / the joy / the / challenge / Who / can be born / black / and not exult!" As in her second collection, her third collection, *Nightstar: Poems from 1973–1978* (1981), is patterned as an ever-widening progression from the personal and individual to the political and global, but in it she uses more innovative rhetorical devices and more complex poetry techniques. In both this work and her *A Dark and Splendid Mass* (1991 or 1992), she deftly shows the uncommon courage of ordinary black folks, using authentic African-American voices.

Her plays, featuring vividly realistic characters and richly textured details, highlight the valor and strength of African Americans who face many small and large challenges. Evans's *Rivers of My Song* (first performed, 1977) incorporates poetry and prose, music and dance in a distinctively African-American drama. Her *Portrait of a Man* (1979) intersperses episodes showing the struggles of both a young and an old African-American man, whom the viewers soon realize are one and the same. Her other plays include *Boochie* (1979) and *Eyes* (1979), her screenplay for a musical adapted from **Zora Neale Hurston**'s *Their Eyes Were Watching God.*

Although Evans is widely known for her poems and plays, many readers know her best for her children's books, which include *I Look at Me!* (1974), *Rap Stories* (1974), *JD* (1973/1975), *Singing Black: Alternative Nursery Rhymes for Children* (1976), *Jim Flying High* (1979), and *The Day They Made Biriyani* (1982). (Evans is divorced and has two sons of her own, as well.) Her books highlight a nurturant, positive perspective of the African-American community and foster a positive self-concept among African-American youths. Although she sometimes introduces words unfamiliar to young readers, she does so in a self-explanatory context.

The other literary work for which Evans is well known is her landmark critical analysis *Black Women Writers (1950–1980): A Critical Evaluation* (1984, editor). The volume covers 15 poets, novelists, and playwrights, including for each author an autobiographical commentary on her own literary development, two critical essays (offering differing perspectives), and a brief biographical summary and list of key publications. This book celebrates the diversity of African-American women writers, offering a broad spectrum of critical approaches to their writings.

Among the numerous awards she has been given are a John Hay Whitney fellowship (1965); a Woodrow Wilson grant (1968); the Most Distinguished Book of Poetry by an Indiana Writer (for her *I Am a Black Woman*) (1970); the Indiana University Writers' Conference Black Academy of Arts and Letters First Poetry Award (1975); MacDowell fellow, MacDowell Colony, Peterborough, New Hampshire (1975); Outstanding Woman of the Year, Alpha Kappa Alpha Sorority graduate chapter, Indiana University, Bloomington (1976); Builder's Award, **Third World Press,** Chicago (1977); Indiana Committee for the Humanities grant for *Eyes* (1977); Commins Engine Company Foundation grant (stage project) (1977); Black Liberation Award, Kuumba Theatre Workshop Tenth Anniversary, Chicago (1978); an honorary doctorate of humane letters degree from Marian College (1979); Copeland fellow, Amherst College, Amherst, Massachusetts (1980); Black Arts Celebration Poetry Award, Chicago (1981); and a National Endowment for the Arts grant (1981).

Her body of work celebrates African-American culture and shows a strong sense of social responsibility. She passionately combats oppression on both personal and institutional levels and illuminates the heroic struggles of ordinary African Americans. The simplicity of her lyrical verse eloquently expresses her straightforward themes; her plays have been produced repeatedly over the years; her children's books are praised for their constructive values and positive view of the African-American community; and her essays logically and coherently reveal her deeply held political beliefs. Evans's beliefs have also led her to political action and community activism, championing such causes as prison reform and opposing various forms of oppression, such as capital punishment.

REFERENCES: *AA:PoP. BAL-1-P. BDAA. BV. BWA. BWW. EB-98. EBLG. MWEL. NAAAL. TtW. TWT.* Dorsey, David F., Jr., in *OCAAL.* Wagner-Martin, Linda, in *OCWW.*

Evers-Williams, Myrlie (Louise) (née Beasley) (3/17/1933–)

Memoirs

The widow of civil rights activist Medgar Evers, Myrlie Evers-Williams cowrote *For Us, the Living* (1967, with William Peters), a candid account of her life with Evers and their three children. Through her persistent efforts, the killer of Evers was caught, prosecuted, convicted, and imprisoned on February 5, 1994—about 30 years after Evers was assassinated. Since then, Evers-Williams wrote a second memoir (which she has called "an instructional autobiography"), *Watch Me Fly: What I Learned on the Way to Becoming the Woman I Was Meant to Be* (1999, with Melinda Blau), which documents her childhood and youth, her up-and-down relationship with Evers, her valiant struggle to raise her children as a single mother following his assassination, her experiences as she welcomed her second husband into her life and her heart— and then shared his final fight against terminal cancer, her rise to chairing the National Association for the Advancement of Colored People, and her triumphs in business. Evers-Williams also participated in two other book projects: She wrote the introduction to Steven Kasher's *The Civil Rights Movement: A Photographic History, 1954–68* (1996), and she participated in writing *No Mountain High Enough: Secrets of Successful African American Women* (1997).

REFERENCES: *EA-99. EB-BH-CD. G-99. WB-99.* Assensoh, A. B., in *BH2C.* Bailey, Ronald, in *BWA:AHE.*

F

Fabio, Sarah (née Webster)

(1/20/1928–11/7/1979)

Poems

Sarah Webster studied poetry under **Arna Bontemps** at Fisk University and then paused for almost two decades to marry Cyril Fabio and raise their five children. After earning her master's degree in language arts and creative writing, she helped establish a black studies department at the University of California at Berkeley in the late 1960s. Her writings mirror the **Black Aesthetic** of the **Black Arts movement**, during which she published the books *Saga of a Black Man* (1968); *A Mirror, a Soul* (1969); *Dark Debut: Three Black Women Coming* (1966); *Return of Margaret Walker* (1966); *Double Dozens: An Anthology of Poets from Sterling Brown to Kali* (1966, editor); *No Crystal Stair: A Socio-Drama of the History of Black Women in the U.S.A.* (1967); and her seven-volume poetry collection *Rainbow Signs* (1973).

REFERENCES: Warren, Nagueyalti, in *OCAAL*.

Fauset, Jessie Redmon

(4/27/1882–4/30/1961)

Novels, essays, poems, short stories, children's nonfiction; literary editor

Jessie was born in Camden County, New Jersey, the youngest of seven children born to Annie Seamon Fauset and Reverend Redmon Fauset, an Episcopal minister. Both of her parents were well educated and literary but not as well off financially as they were intellectually. Sadly, Jessie's mother died when Jessie was a small child, leaving her father as sole provider and role model for her and her siblings. As if seven children weren't enough to care for, Reverend Fauset then married a widow with three children, and the couple went on to have three children of their own. Far from living a life of privilege, her younger half-brother, Arthur Huff Fauset (b. 1899), described their family as "dreadfully poor." (As an adult, Arthur wrote short stories, biographies, and nonfiction books as well as essays and articles, for such journals as *Crisis* and *Opportunity;* he was also a public school teacher, a school principal, a noted anthropologist, and a businessperson. He earned a Ph.D. from the University of Pennsylvania.)

By the time Jessie started high school, her family was living in Philadelphia. Jessie responded to her family's emphasis on the importance of education, excelling in her studies at a public high school (the High School for Girls) known for its high academic achievers. When she graduated, in 1900, based on her outstanding scholarship, she applied to Bryn Mawr College. That school managed to avoid permitting a black girl to enter by obtaining a scholarship for her to attend Cornell University. In 1905, she earned her B.A. from Cornell University (when she was about 23 years old). She was the first black woman to be elected to the Phi Beta Kappa honor society at Cornell, and she was probably the first—or at least one of the first—black woman to be given a Phi Beta Kappa membership key in the United States. Even after she began her career, she continued her education, earning her master's degree at the University of Pennsylvania in 1919 and spending six months studying at the world-renowned Sorbonne University in Paris during 1925 and 1926.

Upon graduating from Cornell, she spent the next 13 years (1905–1918) teaching high school. Initially, she sought a teaching position in Philadelphia but was barred from having one because of her race. Hence, she moved to Baltimore to teach at Douglass High School for a year. The next year, she started teaching French and Latin at Dunbar High School, an all-black high school in Washington, D.C., where she continued to teach until she decided to return to college to complete her master's degree.

Starting when she was in her thirties, Fauset had begun to write articles for the NAACP's *Crisis* magazine, then edited by **W. E. B. Du Bois**. After a bit, she became one of the magazine's four staff editors. After Fauset finished her master's degree, when she was in her late thirties, Du Bois convinced her to move to New York and become *Crisis*'s literary editor at a crucial epoch in African-American literary history: the first blossoming of the **Harlem Renaissance** (1919–1926). This accident of timing put her in a position to shape the literature emerging in this exciting, dynamic period. Specifically, she chose the literary selections for each magazine and was thereby able to mentor many young writers (e.g., **Countee Cullen**, **Nella Larsen**, **Claude McKay**, **Jean Toomer**). In fact, **Langston Hughes** said she was one of "the three people who midwifed the so-called New Negro literature into being" during the Harlem Renaissance. With her knack for discovering talented writers and her willingness to work long and hard, she managed to bring to full bloom the literary careers of many a budding writer. She often encouraged them through letters and through invitations to her home. There, her guests would read poetry aloud, discuss literature, and converse in French. Meanwhile, she continued her own writing projects, such as essays and works of fiction.

When Du Bois began his short-lived (1920–1921) monthly periodical for African-American children, *Brownies' Book*, he asked Fauset to edit the periodical and to do much of the writing for it. The periodical featured historical biographies of notable African Americans, such as Denmark Vesey and **Sojourner Truth**, as well as articles on current events, Africa, and games, riddles, and music.

In 1926, Fauset quit her position as literary editor for *Crisis*, hoping to turn her attention to her own writing as a full-time occupation. (There may also have been some tension in her relationship with Du Bois, and a decline in the magazine's circulation may have contributed to her decision.) During this time, she traveled and lectured, wrote poetry, and explored her new role as a wife: At age 47 (in 1927), she married insurance broker Herbert E. Harris. Unfortunately, however, she was unable to sustain a living from her writing, so she returned to teaching and wrote only three more novels after she left *Crisis*.

From 1927 until 1944, Fauset (Harris) returned to teaching (starting at DeWitt Clinton High School in New York), which she continued throughout the rest of her working life. As a teacher, she decried the lack of nonwhites in classroom curricula, textbooks, and other reading materials; denounced the absence of positive role models; and urged the creation of biographical materials on important African Americans. She intended to write some herself, but her teaching duties took up her time, and she never got around to writing the biographies she wished to see. A few years after she retired from teaching high school, she worked briefly (September 1949–January 1950) as a visiting professor at the Hampton Institute. When she retired, she was still living with her husband in Montclair, New Jersey, until he made her a widow in 1958. After he died, she left New Jersey and returned to Philadelphia, to live with her stepbrother, Earl Huff, with whom she lived until her death, in 1961, of heart disease.

Between the 1910s and the early 1930s, Fauset wrote numerous essays, poems, and short stories, which were published in various periodicals of the day as well as in anthologies such as those edited by Countee Cullen and **Alain Locke**. Between 1924 and 1933, Fauset produced four novels, each of which reflected her belief in the importance of self-acceptance as a key to personal success. Most of her characters are light-skinned, well-educated, middle-class African Americans. For them, self-hatred posed a greater challenge than did racial prejudice and discrimination, which have more profoundly oppressed darker-skinned, less-educated, working-class African Americans. By focusing on mulattos and African Americans who can pass for white, Fauset explored issues of identity and race, class, and gender differences.

Fauset's 1924 novel *There Is Confusion* centers on an African-American family confronting racial discrimination. *Plum Bun: A Novel without a Moral* (1928 or 1929) features Angela Murray, a light-skinned young black artist who constantly seeks to "pass" as white among white New York artists. Only when she eventually stops posing, embraces her African-American heritage, and accepts her ties to the African-American world does she succeed in finding happiness. Her 1931 novel *The Chinaberry Tree: A Novel of American Life* deals with interracial marital relationships and is not considered her finest effort. Her best-known novel is *Comedy: American Style* (1933), in which the black female protagonist, Carey, longs to be white and hates being black, but her son and her husband take pride in their African-American cultural heritage.

REFERENCES: *AA:PoP. AWA. BANP. BDAA. BF:2000. BFC. EB-98. EBLG. MAAL. NAAAL. OC20LE. RLWWJ. RT.* McLendon, Jacquelyn Y., in *OCAAL.* Wagner, Wendy, in *OCWW.*

Feelings, Tom (5/19/1933–)
Children's books, book illustrations, comic strip

Since childhood, Tom had immersed himself in art, studying graphic arts in vocational school, specializing in cartooning and illustration at the School of Visual Arts, and even serving in the U.S. Air Force as a graphic artist. While he was still an art student, his comic strip "Tommy Traveler in the World of Negro History" started being regularly published in the *New York Age*. (More than 30 years later, his "Tommy Traveler" materials led to his book, *Tommy Traveler in the World of Black History*, 1991, featuring **Frederick Douglass** and other notables.)

From the mid-1960s through the early 1970s, Feelings lived abroad, creating illustrations for the Ghanaian government's printing house and for *African Review* and directing a children's book project while teaching art in Guyana. During the 1970s, he and his first wife, writer Muriel Feelings, collaborated on three award-winning children's books inspired by their experiences in Africa: *Zamani Goes to Market* (1970), *Moja Means One: Swahili Counting Book* (1971), and *Jambo Means Hello: Swahili Alphabet Book* (1974). During this time, he also wrote his autobiographical *Black Pilgrimage* (1972).

In addition, Feelings has illustrated books for such distinguished authors as **Julius Lester** (*To Be a Slave*, 1968; *Black Folktales*, 1969), **Eloise Greenfield** (*Daydreamers*, 1981), and **Maya Angelou** (*Now Sheba Sings the Song*, 1987). Other books he has illustrated include celebrations of African lore and crafts, *Tales of Temba: Traditional African Stories* (1969, with text by Kathleen Arnot) and *African Crafts* (1970, with text by Jane Kerina). In his *Soul Looks Back in Wonder* (1993), he offers lively paintings of children engaged in various activities—from dreaming to daring—as his vision of poems written by noteworthy authors such as **Lucille Clifton** and **Mari Evans**.

His most masterful piece, however, is almost surely his *The Middle Passage: White Ships/Black Cargo* (1995). Comprising more than 60 magnificent black-and-white paintings of the nightmare that was the slave trade, his pièce de résistance took him about two decades—and a great deal of emotional, physical, and intellectual energy—to create.

—*Tonya Bolden*

REFERENCES: *SMKC*. C. H. S., in *CBC*.

Fields, Julia (1938–)
Poems, short fiction, plays, children's books

As a young girl growing up on an Alabama farm, Julia reveled in biblical verses and works by British poets such as Robert Burns, Lewis Carroll, William Shakespeare, and William Wordsworth. When she was just 16 years old, her poem "Horizons" was published in *Scholastic* magazine.

After earning her bachelor's degree at Knoxville (Tennessee) College and studying (perhaps earning her master's degree) at Breadloaf College in Middlebury, Vermont, Fields taught for a while in Alabama and then went to the University of Edinburgh to study in Robert Burns's homeland. In Britain, she met **Langston Hughes** and South African writer Richard Rive. On returning to the United States, **Georgia Douglas Johnson** and **Robert Hayden** offered her inspiration, and for two years, she spent countless hours in the Library of Congress.

In 1966, one of Fields's plays, *All Day Tomorrow*, was produced at Knoxville College. Two years later, Fields published her first book of poetry, aptly titled *Poems* (1968); wrote her eulogy of the fallen leaders Medgar Evers, **Malcolm X**, and **Martin Luther King, Jr.**, titled "Poem"; and had her short story "Not Your Singing, Dancing Spade" anthologized in LeRoi Jones (later **Amiri Baraka**) and **Larry Neal**'s landmark *Black Fire* (see the **Black Arts movement**). Fields's book-length works include her critically acclaimed poetry collection *Slow Coins* (1981) and her verse picture book for children, *The Green Lion of Zion Street* (1988). Fields and her husband also raised two daughters of their own, both adults now.

REFERENCES: *BAL-1-P*. Hauke, Kathleen A., in *OCAAL*. Wald, Gayle, in *OCWW*. Amazon.com, 7/1999.

Fire!! (1926)

Published in 1926, this avant-garde journal was intended to be a quarterly dedicated to the second generation of the **Harlem Renaissance**. Unfortunately, only one issue was published by editor **Wallace Thurman**, who was chosen for the position by **Langston Hughes**. Hughes had wanted the journal to be by and for black artists, a break from the social commentary of the day's established journals. Several associate editors included **Zora Neale Hurston** and **Gwendolyn Bennett**. The journal failed due to a lack of financing, poor distribution, and bad luck—most copies of *Fire!!* burned in an actual apartment fire. Two years later, Thurman tried again with *Harlem: A Forum for Negro Life*, but it also failed after its premier issue.

—*Lisa Bahlinger*

REFERENCES: *AAW*. White, Craig Howard, in *OCAAL*.

First World
*See **Negro Digest***

Fishburne, Laurence, III (7/30/1961–)
Play

A prominent film actor, Fishburne wrote, directed, and starred in *Riff Raff,* a one-act play.

REFERENCES: *EA-99.*

Fisher (married name), Abby (c. 1832–?)
Cookbook

Fisher's *What Mrs. Fisher Knows about Old Southern Cooking* (1881, containing 160 recipes) is probably the first published cookbook authored by an African-American woman. Because Fisher could neither read nor write, she dictated her 160 recipes, based on more than 35 years of experience in cooking. Apparently, her evident expertise was much admired and desired, given the book's popularity.

—*Tonya Bolden*

REFERENCES: *BAAW.* Fisher, Abby (1881/1995), *What Mrs. Fisher Knows about Old Southern Cooking, Soups, Pickles, Preserves, Etc.* (reprint, with historical notes by Karen Hess) (Applewood Books).

Fisher, Rudolph (John Chauncey) ("Bud") (5/9/1897–12/26/1934)
Novels, short stories

Born in Washington, D.C., but raised in Providence, Rhode Island, Fisher was an outstanding scholar at Brown University (B.S., 1919; M.S., 1920) in Providence, and he earned high honors from Howard University Medical School (M.D., 1924) in Washington, D.C. After graduating, Fisher spent a year interning at the Freedman's Hospital and then garnered a fellowship for postgraduate study in the medical school at Columbia University (ending in 1927). After completing his studies, Fisher opened his medical practice in New York.

While attending Brown, Fisher had met **Paul Robeson**, whose singing he would accompany on the piano. During the early 1920s, the pair toured the eastern seaboard, earning money to pay for their college tuition. After earning his M.D., Fisher also managed to meet (1924) and then marry (1925) Jane Ryder, and the couple soon completed their family with the birth of their son Hugh (1926). Quite a busy fellow, Fisher also managed to write and have published some of his short stories (e.g., "The City of Refuge," 1919, in *Atlantic Monthly;* "High Yaller," 1926, Amy Spingarn Prize for fiction) during this time.

While practicing medicine as a roentgenologist (X-ray specialist) during the **Harlem Renaissance,** Fisher wrote two novels—*The Walls of Jericho* (1928) and *The Conjure-Man Dies: A Mystery Tale of Dark Harlem* (1932)—now considered classic texts of the 1920s era among African-American New Yorkers. Fisher's first novel satirizes class and race distinctions through his portraits of black and white New Yorkers of each class. His second novel is widely recognized as the first African-American detective novel and might also be considered an early psychological thriller: Its central character is a Harvard-educated psychiatrist from Africa who uses his knowledge of deviant psychology (especially paranoia) to catch a killer. Although almost all of Fisher's short stories (e.g., "Common Meter," "The Conjure Man Dies," "Miss Cynthie") were published individually during his all-too-brief lifetime, it wasn't until more than half a century after his death that his stories were collected and published in *The City of Refuge* (1987). Sadly, Fisher died at age 34, due to complications of a digestive-tract disorder.

REFERENCES: *EBLG. G-97.* McCluskey, John, Jr., in *OCAAL.*

Folktales

In the past, many white scholars contended that African Americans had a poor, shallow literary tradition imitative of white culture. These scholars studied only British and Anglo-American influences on African-American tradition, pointedly ignoring the influence of Africa and the Caribbean. To the contrary, the African-American folk tradition is actually rich and diverse, drawing on oral and written traditions from the West Indies, West Africa, and Europe, as well as white America. The distinctive qualities of the African-American folk tradition are well illustrated in folktales, where many cultural strands are interwoven.

In fact, folktales are part of a long, continuing **oral tradition** of creating and passing on the stories, customs, rituals, and lifestyle patterns of a culture. When slaves were brought to America from Africa, they carried a literary tradition with them—an oral one that had been passed down in towns and villages through many generations. Because African-American folktales come from the common people's storytelling tradition brought over by slaves, many elements of folktales—the characters, motifs, styles of telling, and story types—strongly resemble the stories told in sub-Saharan and western Africa. As time passed, however, and African Americans came in contact with the folktales of other cultures—Native Americans as well as European Americans—they assimilated elements of other cultures into their own stories. African-American folktales thus contain an amalgam of many different cultural ideas and views.

A major distinction between African-American folktales and their African counterparts is the institution of slavery. The slaveholders' attempt to obliterate the African identities of the slaves (their language, cultural traditions, and ways of seeing and ordering the world around them) was effected by forbidding slaves to learn how to read or write. The only way slaves could preserve their stories and cultural views was by word of mouth. In doing so, African Americans passed on their stories as a form of underground rebellion against their masters. Thus as **Nikki Giovanni**, a scholar of African-American folktales, says, African-American folktales were "built and focused on a quest for freedom and equality."

Also, in many ways, African-American folktales resemble the folktales of many other cultures—they mirror people's hopes and fears, explain relationships, interpret the nature of the world, ask and answer questions of existence and origin, and clarify people's doubts about life. They order the world and create both a foundation on which to construct reality and a filter through which to process daily events. They convey people's culture, religion, and social customs, while imparting history, explaining the inexplicable, expressing values, identifying acceptable and unacceptable behavior, exposing fears and dreads, and communicating aspirations and goals. They are stories to live by but are also lived through—they not only teach but also provide their listeners with hope.

African-American folktales fall into seven categories: tales of origins (how things came to be as they are); stories dealing with trickery and trouble (with people getting into each other's business, with varying consequences); tales of noble black figures triumphing over natural and supernatural evils; funny stories that gladden the heart; mothers' narratives for teaching about expectations of marriage, family, and parenthood; ghost stories; and master-slave stories in which the clever slave outwits the foolish master (most of the time).

Many African-American folktales are *animal tales* in which the main characters are animals with human characteristics. Such tales can be seen to contain, in varying forms, all seven categories already mentioned. Many of these stories deal with origins—"How the Snake Got His Rattles," "The Story of the Skunk and Why He Has Such a Bad Smell," and "Why Hens Are Afraid of Owls." Origin stories across all cultures emerge because most people have lacked the scientific knowledge to explain why things are as they are, such as why animals behave and look as they do. The need for these stories in African-American culture was exaggerated because of the slave trade, which thrust slaves into a land with creatures and plants they had never seen before.

Nonetheless, most animal tales deal less with origins and more with teaching morality, for as time passed, African Americans had less need to make the unfamiliar landscape explainable and instead needed tales to provide entertainment and instruction. One of the most famous characters in the moral animal tales is Brer Rabbit—a wise and shrewd trickster who regularly outwits and gains victory over a physically stronger adversary. In some stories, the function of Brer Rabbit is that of teacher—in outwitting his adversary, he implicitly teaches the right way to treat others and the punishment that may befall any creature who fails to do so. In many stories, however, Brer Rabbit can be seen as a powerless slave who outwits a powerful master, making such stories into tales of rebellion in which a clever slave uses trickery to undermine the system of slavery by which the slave had seemed insurmountably trapped. Such tales can also be cautionary tales to warn potential tricksters to be wary of overestimating their own shrewdness. (See **trickster tales.**)

Another genre of tale that serves to caution and even scare children into proper behavior are the supernatural stories—tales of monsters (the bogeyman being the most famous), witches, devils, and evil spirits who plague wayward children who are too curious, wander too far from home, disobey their parents and other elders, lie, talk back, get too lazy to do their chores, or try to be something they are not. These tales are based largely on remembered stories of supernatural beings from African homelands but are set in the lands of rural America—the woods, swamps, mountains, rivers, and, of course, cemeteries.

Some of the stories are set in times before the advent of humans, and some even take place as recently as postslavery eras, but most are set either during the time of slavery or in ancient times. The ancient legends focus mostly on teaching proper ways of behaving and show brave black figures triumphing over supernatural tests and temptations. The tales set in times of slavery derive mostly from actual historical events in which African Americans took part. In these tales, the supernatural activity does not turn against wayward children but instead punishes a cruel, evil, greedy, or abusive master. Such stories serve not only as warnings but also as a release—a fantasy in which cruel people get the punishment they deserve but do not seem to receive in real life.

Release, relief from frustration, and diverting entertainment are among the most common features of all African-American folktales. The tales that serve this purpose most clearly are the humorous tales, designed purely to make folks laugh. Such tales are set in every time period from preslavery days to the present and have existed since slaves first arrived. **Langston Hughes** said that slaves would joke about their food, their masters, their bodies, their preachers, and even the devil, all because "they were laughing to keep from crying." Unlike all other genres of folktales—the animal tales, the ghost stories, the fables—humorous folktales are not really meant to teach anything. They focus less on moralizing and more on entertaining, while giving listeners a way to celebrate cultural traditions and make political statements.

Jokes are one form of humorous tales enjoyed widely by both urban and rural African Americans. In the African-American tradition, jokes have often taken the form of verbal jesting and games that tested people's verbal skill. These verbal contests had firm rules; the loser was the person who permitted his or her emotion to interfere, allowing an impersonal insult to become personalized. Another form of verbal play in the African-American tradition is jive. *Jive* is a playful way to communicate that excludes most whites. Some of the words African Americans have brought into the English language are "jazz," "boogie," "gumbo," and "okra," as well as the expressions "uh-huh" and "unh-uh" for yes and no.

Jokes and humorous tales can be found in the performances of such contemporary black comedians as Eddie Murphy, **Whoopi Goldberg**, Sinbad, and **Bill Cosby**. These comedians carry on the tradition of the humorous folktale by taking pieces of everyday life and, through exaggeration, showing the subtle psychological relationships that go on between people in any slice of life. In many ways, they also serve to heal their listeners, helping them laugh at their hardships.

In addition to the work of contemporary African-American comedians, African-American folktales have inspired many contemporary African-American writers, such as **Arna Bontemps**, **Sterling Brown**, **Paul Laurence Dunbar**, **Ralph Ellison**, **Virginia Hamilton**, Langston Hughes, **Zora Neale Hurston**, **James Weldon Johnson**, **Julius Lester**, **Paule Marshall**, **Toni Morrison** (whose *Song of Solomon* was inspired by tales of flight such as "All God's Chillen Had Wings"), **Jean Toomer**, **Alice Walker**, and **Richard Wright**. In fact, not only did Hughes, Hurston, and Lester gather inspiration from folktales, but they also compiled collections of them that are still available today—Zora Neale Hurston's *Mules and Men* represents one of the earliest efforts to accurately record the oral tradition of African-American communities, and Langston Hughes and Arna Bontemps's *The Book of Negro Folklore* holds a wonderful collection of stories, as do Lester's *Black Folktales* (1969), *The Knee-High Man and Other Tales* (1972), and his numerous Brer Rabbit books.

The readers of African-American folktales, however, must realize that the written versions differ in many ways from the tales as told orally. The written versions do show that such folktales are often told in a combination of languages, with African words translated into English either directly or told as asides, and text notes may inform readers that tales are often told with rhythmic chants and wails, as well as with various instruments, but such notes cannot immerse readers in the experience of listening to oral storytelling.

When the tales are told orally, the storyteller may incorporate music, costume, voices, chanting, screaming, and rhythmic language, as well as emotion, humor, and wisdom in order to hold the attention of the listeners. In oral tellings, the listeners are just as important as the teller, for the audience in many ways directs how the story will go by asking questions, making comments, and responding in other ways. When a storyteller has a specific audience, he or she may also make topical references to people in the audience, drawing parallels between the tale being told and things that have occurred in the community. Many of these elements are lost when the tales are written down, but in the hands of the best storytellers (whether oral or written) African-American folktales still maintain their main characteristic—as tales that are not so much heard as experienced.

In addition to being interwoven as a subtext for storytelling, music is often a vehicle for storytelling, particularly as it emerged on plantations before emancipation. In work songs, hollers, story songs, and **spirituals,** slaves were able to hold onto their hopes and to affirm their faith in God and in their own self-worth. By acknowledging their sorrows, despair, and feelings of worthlessness through shared song, slaves were able to transcend these feelings, comforting themselves and others. These songs later paved the way for blues, jazz, gospel, and rap lyrics and music.

The folktale tradition continues to develop today in so many ways, through the written works of contemporary authors, through contemporary music, and through preaching. There is a need for more serious scholarship of the African-American folk tradition, to preserve and pass on the beauty and art of this tradition for future generations.

—*Diane Masiello and Lisa Bahlinger*

REFERENCES: *AAL. NAAAL.* Abrahms, Roger D. (1985), *Afro-American Folktales: Stories from Black Traditions in the New World* (New York: Pantheon Books). Bristow, Margaret Bernice Smith, "Hamilton, Virginia," in *OCAAL.* Coffin, Tristram Potter, "Folktales," in *E-98.* Goss, Linda, and Marian E. Barnes (1989), *Talk That Talk: An Anthology of African American Storytelling* (New York: Simon and Schuster). Harris, Trudier, "Folk Literature," in *OCAAL.* Hughes, Langston, and Arna Bontemps (1958), *The Book of Negro Folklore* (New York: Dodd, Mead and Company). Hurston, Zora Neale (c. 1935/1978), *Mules and Men* (Bloomington: Indiana University Press). Olson, Ted, "Folklore," in *OCAAL.*

Forrest, Leon (1/8/1937–)
Novels

Forrest supported himself as a journalist (e.g., for *Muhammad Speaks,* the Nation of Islam newspaper) while working on his first novel. For that book, *There Is a Tree More Ancient than Eden* (1973), **Toni Morrison** was his editor at Random House. Forrest's other novels include *The Bloodworth Orphans* (1977), *Two Wings to Veil My Face* (1984), and *Divine Days* (1992).

REFERENCES: *WDAA.* Miller, James A., in *OCAAL.*

Forten, James
See **Fortens, Grimkés, and Purvises**

Forten (Purvis), Sarah (Louisa)
See **Fortens, Grimkés, and Purvises**

Fortens, Grimkés, and Purvises

The Fortens, the Grimkés, and the Purvises were highly literary families who played vital roles in political and social activism as well as literature throughout the 1800s and the early 1900s. The patriarch of the Forten family was JAMES FORTEN, SR. (9/2/1766–3/4/1842), born the son of free African-American parents in Philadelphia. As a boy, he had studied in a school run by a Quaker abolitionist, Anthony Benezet, but James had quit at age 15 to serve in the Navy during the American Revolution. When the British captured his vessel, they imprisoned him for months, during which time he met leading British abolitionists.

After the war, he was apprenticed to a sailmaker, and by 1798, he had purchased the sailmaking business. After inventing—and patenting—a special sail-positioning device, his company prospered, and by 1832 he was a wealthy employer of 40 European- and African-American workers. Forten used much of his fortune to promote abolition, women's suffrage, civil rights, and temperance. His home gave birth to the American Anti-Slavery Society (in 1833), and he often hosted abolitionists such as William Lloyd Garrison (whose publication the *Liberator* he helped to fund) and the poet John Greenleaf Whittier (who dedicated a poem "To the Daughters of James Forten").

Probably the most noteworthy of the social- and political-activist pamphlets he wrote was his 1813 pamphlet of protest against a Pennsylvania bill barring free African Americans from immigrating into the state. In addition, Forten and his second wife, CHARLOTTE VANDINE FORTEN (1784–1884), raised five strongly abolitionist children, including their daughters Margaretta, Sarah, and Harriet (and their sons James Jr. and Robert Bridges), as well as his granddaughter Charlotte Forten Grimké. Charlotte Forten and her daughters were charter members of the Philadelphia Female Anti-Slavery Society.

MARGARETTA FORTEN (1808–1875) taught for years in a private school her father and **Sarah Mapps Douglass** had opened for African-American children in Philadelphia, leaving it only to start her own grammar school. When SARAH (LOUISA) FORTEN (PURVIS) (1814–1883) was only 19 or 20, using the pen name Ada (for her protest poems) or Magawisca (for her fiery essays), she began contributing to antislavery journals such as William Lloyd Garrison's *Liberator.* Composer Frank Johnson even set to music her poem "The Grave of the Slave," which became kind of an abolitionist anthem. She found it bitterly ironic that her father and many others had fought so fervently for liberty only to have slavery embraced by the new nation, as the following excerpt shows (*PBW,* p. 254):

> Where—where is the nation so erring as we,
> Who claim the proud name of the "HOME
>   OF THE FREE"? . . .
> Speak not of "my country," unless she shall be,
> In truth, the bright home of the "brave and
>   the free."
> Till the dark stain of slavery is washed from
>   her hand,
> A tribute of homage she cannot command.

Early in 1838, Sarah married Joseph Purvis, the younger brother of her sister's husband Robert. After her marriage, bearing and rearing eight children (alone after Joseph left her a widow) took most of her time, but she still managed to write some antislavery verses and prose. Sarah's sister HARRIET FORTEN (PURVIS) (1810–1875) had been highly active in numerous abolitionist organizations and conventions before marrying Robert Purvis. Afterward, she and he offered their home as a way station (complete with a specially designed room with a hidden trapdoor) for the Underground Railroad and as a hostel for fellow abolitionists.

ROBERT PURVIS (SR.) (8/4/1810–1898), the son of a wealthy white English immigrant and his freeborn mulatto mistress, was well educated, among the first African Americans to attend Amherst College. After his father's death, Robert and his brother Joseph, both residents of Philadelphia by this time, each inherited a fortune. Soon after, when Robert was about 20 years old, he met fervent abolitionists William Lloyd Garrison and Benjamin Lundy, who encouraged him to embrace antislavery causes. In addition to his work for the Underground Railroad, he supported the "Free Produce Movement," buying, eating, and serving only food that had been planted and harvested by free laborers, not slaves. He joined fellow

abolitionist James Forten in opposing Pennsylvania's fugitive slave legislation. His main literary contributions include essays, letters, speeches, petitions, and eulogies (e.g., James Forten's). He also wrote pamphlets trying to prevent the disenfranchisement of African-American men of Pennsylvania. **William Still** recalled that "he gave with all his heart his money, his time, his talents" to the antislavery cause. Purvis also advocated on behalf of women's rights, civil liberties and rights, temperance, prison reform, and the education of all African Americans. For instance, when his local township tried to bar African-American children from attending public schools, Purvis threatened to withhold his considerable school taxes unless they reintegrated the schools.

Two contemporaries of the Fortens and the Purvises were two European-American sisters, the daughters of South Carolinian slaveowners: SARAH (MOORE) GRIMKÉ (11/26/1792–12/23/1873) and ANGELINA (EMILY) GRIMKÉ (WELD) (2/20/1805–10/26/1879). The main literary contributions of these sisters were essays, pamphlets, and lectures. Although raised with riches, they were denied formal education because of their gender. Nonetheless, the two girls would sneak into their father's ample library. Sarah furtively studied law, although she was prevented from practicing because she was female. The two sisters rebelled against these constraints, and when Sarah (and later Angelina) converted to the Religious Society of Friends (Quakerism), the sisters embraced abolition, as they had long been aware of the injustices of slavery. In 1821, Sarah moved to Philadelphia, and her sister Angelina joined her in 1829. In the 1830s, the sisters started touring New England and lecturing against slavery, thus becoming the first white women to speak to "promiscuous audiences" (containing both men and women). (**Maria W. Stewart** was the first woman of any color to do so.) As former slaveowners, they provided candid insights into the abuses of slavery.

In addition to their lectures, the sisters wrote abolitionist essays and pamphlets. Angelina's best-known work is her *An Appeal to the Christian Women of the South* (1836), urging Southern women to rise up and oppose slavery. Sarah's best-known work is her *An Epistle to the Clergy of the Southern States* (1836), pleading for Southern ministers and other clerics to fight against slavery and to encourage their parishioners to abolish it. Copies of these works were burned in the South, and the sisters were threatened with imprisonment if they ever returned to South Carolina. In contrast, Sarah Forten (Purvis) began corresponding with Angelina and welcomed the sisters' writings with her own "Lines Suggested on Reading *An Appeal to the Christian Women of the South* by A. E. Grimké," praising Grimké and urging other white feminists and Southern women to join her in opposing slavery.

Soon afterward, the sisters persuaded their mother to deed over the family slaves as their part of the family estate after their father's death. She did so, and the sisters immediately freed the slaves. The sisters are less well known for Sarah's 1838 *Letters on the Equality of the Sexes, and the Condition of Woman* and Angelina's 1837 *Letters to Catherine Beecher in Reply to an Essay on Slavery and Abolitionism Addressed to A. E. Grimké,* among the first American writings calling for women's rights. Although Sarah opposed marriage, turning down two proposals, her sister Angelina relented, marrying outspoken abolitionist Theodore Weld in 1838. The marriage signaled the end of the sisters' careers as lecturers, and they turned their attention toward helping Weld run liberal schools in New Jersey. Nonetheless, Sarah continued to write on abolition and women's rights. After the Civil War, at ages 78 (Sarah) and 65 (Angelina), the sisters led a suffrage demonstration, going out in a severe snowstorm to cast symbolic votes in a separate ballot box.

Before the Grimké sisters were able to free their family's slaves, their brother Henry and his slave Nancy Weston had parented ARCHIBALD HENRY GRIMKÉ (8/17/1849–2/25/1930) (author of essays, biographies, and scholarly works; newspaper founder), FRANCIS J. (JAMES) GRIMKÉ (1850–1937) (author of sermons), and JOHN GRIMKÉ. The Grimké sisters sponsored Archibald's education at Lincoln University in Pennsylvania (B.A., 1870; M.A., 1872) and then at Harvard Law School, where he earned his L.L. B. degree in 1874. Five years later, he married Sarah Stanley, a white Bostonian writer whose father opposed the marriage. Soon after, the couple had a daughter, ANGELINA WELD GRIMKÉ, but Sarah Stanley soon abandoned her husband and daughter, never to see them again. Archibald and his young daughter moved in with his aunts Sarah and Angelina.

In addition to his law practice, Archibald was founding editor of the *Boston Hub* newspaper, the first African-American newspaper in New England. Archibald also served as an executive officer of the National Association for the Advancement of Colored People (NAACP) (1883–1886), a consul to the Dominican Republic (1894–1898), president of the American Negro Academy (which his brother Francis founded), and recipient of the NAACP's prestigious Spingarn Medal. An active abolitionist, Archibald wrote major biographies of William Lloyd Garrison (1891) and Charles Sumner (1892). He continued to publish extensively throughout his life, including some writings seeking to heal the divisions in African-American leadership erupting as a result of **Booker T. Washington**'s accommodationist policies.

Like his older brother, Francis J. (James) Grimké was educated at Pennsylvania's Lincoln University, then his aunts paid for him to attend Princeton Theological Seminary, from which he graduated in 1878. After graduating, Francis married into the Forten family, wedding James Forten's granddaughter (and the niece of Sarah Forten Purvis and of Robert Purvis) Charlotte ("Lottie") L. Forten (Grimké), who was 13 years older than he. A noted theologian and outspoken integrationist, he served as a Presbyterian minister in Washington, D.C. Renowned historian **Carter G. Woodson** collected Francis's writings into *The Works of Francis James Grimké* (4 vols., 1942).

When CHARLOTTE ("LOTTIE") L. FORTEN (GRIMKÉ) (8/17/1837?–7/23/1914) was a child, her mother died, so she was raised in various Forten (and Purvis) households and immersed in political activism. Her primary literary contributions were diaries, poems, and essays. Although Philadelphia schools were segregated, she was well educated, learning from private tutors until she was old enough to go to integrated schools in Massachusetts (see **Sarah Parker Remond**), attending grammar school, and then studying to become a teacher. While in New England, she began the first of her five journals, recording her impressions of political activists, abolitionists, and intellectuals (e.g., **Frederick Douglass**, John Greenleaf Whittier, William Lloyd Garrison, **William Wells Brown**, **Lydia Maria Child**, Ralph Waldo Emerson, and Wendell Phillips), as well as political events and her own experiences. For instance, she wrote of being barred from Philadelphia ice cream parlors and from Boston museums. Although her white classmates treated her kindly enough while in the school setting, they ostracized her when they met outside school in public settings. Charlotte also wrote essays and poems, and her *Parting*

Hymn was chosen as the class song from among about 40 entries.

After Forten graduated, though she was ill with tuberculosis, she became the first African American to teach white students in Massachusetts (starting in 1856). In 1858, she returned to Philadelphia to restore her health. Once she had recovered somewhat, at the encouragement of family friend William Lloyd Garrison, she journeyed to South Carolina in 1862 to participate in South Carolina's Port Royal Experiment. There, on the sea islands, she was to teach former slaves freed by the advancing Union Army. She shared virtually no life experiences with her illiterate, ill-fed, ill-clad, ill-housed, and impoverished students. Because of the isolation of the islands, their cultural experiences much more closely resembled those of their African homeland than those of this well-educated Northerner. She didn't even share a language with them, as most of them spoke a distinctive dialect developed in isolation from both Africa and the U.S. mainland. Young Charlotte faced a formidable challenge, which she recorded in her journal. During nearly two years on those islands, she experienced many setbacks but ultimately succeeded. (She even had some fun occasionally, such as when she met **Harriet Tubman** and listened to her recount her tales of life along the Underground Railroad.) In addition to her journal records, she wrote many firsthand accounts of her work for several Northern periodicals. Her two-part essay "Life in the Sea Islands" appeared in the prestigious *Atlantic Monthly.*

On her return to Philadelphia in 1864, Charlotte served as a nurse for "contraband" slaves and Union soldiers (including the all-black 54th Massachusetts Volunteers, defeated so resoundingly at Fort Wagner). She also wrote and published more poems and essays (often using a pseudonym) and translated a novel, but she took a 20-year hiatus from her journal.

When Forten was in her mid-thirties, she moved to Washington, D.C. There, when she was 41 years old, she married Reverend Francis J. Grimké and devoted herself to being a minister's wife and hosting the African-American intellectual elite of Washington, D.C. Sadly, their only child, Theodora Cornelia, died six months after her birth. Afterward, Charlotte focused her motherly love on being the cherished aunt of Angelina Weld Grimké. She returned to her journals again from 1885 to 1892 but was silent again until her death. Her insightful, politically revealing journals

(*The Journal of Charlotte L. Forten: A Free Negro in the Slave Era*) were published in 1953, nearly 40 years after her death.

Charlotte Forten Grimké unifies the politically active literary families of the Grimkés, the Fortens, and the Purvises. Her grandfather was James Forten; her aunts were his famous daughters Sarah, Margaretta, and Harriet, who was married to Robert Purvis. Her husband, Francis Grimké, and his brother, Archibald Grimké, were the nephews of abolitionists Sarah Moore Grimké and Angelina Grimké Weld. Her brother-in-law Archibald was the father of her niece, the talented Angelina Weld Grimké. Got it?

Archibald pampered his motherless daughter, but he demanded a great deal in return. Born in Boston, ANGELINA WELD GRIMKÉ (2/27/1880–6/10/1958) was educated at the finest liberal, integrated schools in New England as well as the Carleton Academy in Minnesota. Angelina's primary literary contributions were poems, plays, essays, and short fiction. In 1902, she graduated from what was later to be a part of Wellesley College. After graduating, she taught English during the school year in Washington, D.C., while taking summer classes at Harvard University for several years. In Washington, D.C., she lived with her father and her uncle Francis and her aunt Charlotte. She continued teaching school until 1926, when poor health led her to retire. After her father died (1930), she moved to Brooklyn, where she lived until her own death.

Angelina showed early promise as a writer, first publishing a poem in 1891, in her community's *Gazette.* Her essays and her prose were highly polished and expressed her familial inclination for political activism. Her plays and short stories similarly expressed her social and political awareness, particularly of racism. Unfortunately, she was writing at a time when African Americans—and especially African-American women—were not often published, although her works did occasionally appear in magazines such as **Crisis** and **Opportunity**. The **Harlem Renaissance** was blooming just as poor health was inhibiting her literary output. Thus, although she longed for a full-time literary career, ultimately, she was unable to support herself on her writing, and many of her works have yet to be published. Nonetheless, because of her lyrical skills and her distinctive African-American woman's perspective, many of her verses are frequently anthologized (e.g., in **Alain Locke**'s

1925 *The New Negro* and **Countee Cullen**'s 1927 *Caroling Dusk*).

Grimké's earliest verses follow conventional lyrical forms and themes (e.g., love, longing, and loss; motherhood; nature; philosophy; poetic tributes), but in the early 1900s she started experimenting a little with both the form (e.g., brief, with vivid images) and the content (politics, race) of her poems, anticipating the trends of the Harlem Renaissance. Though best known for her poetry, Grimké also wrote a play, *Rachel* (first produced in 1916 and published in 1920) and some short stories. *Rachel,* which addressed lynching and the effect of racism on a middle-class African-American family, gained attention as the first successful full-length drama written by an African-American woman and performed by African-American actors, for a European-American audience. The NAACP even sponsored several productions of the play as a means of dispelling some of the racist myths perpetuated by D.W. Griffith's racist film *The Birth of a Nation* (1915). Grimké's second drama, *Mara* (unpublished), also explored the effects of racism, as did her short story "The Closing Door" (published in 1919). In this story, after a lynching, a hysterical mother murders her own newborn son. Although Weld was not well known for her short stories, this story was well received.

REFERENCES: *1TESK. AA:PoP. ANAD. BAAW. BF:2000. BFC. BWA. E-98. EB-98. EBLG. G-96. MWEL. NAAAL. RT. TtW.* Bruce, Dickson D., Jr., "Grimké, Archibald," and "Grimké, Francis J.," in *OCAAL.* Bruce, Dickson D., Jr., "Grimké, Angelina Weld," in *OCWW.* Campbell, Jane, "Grimké, Sarah Moore, and Angelina Grimké Weld," in *OCWW.* Carruth, Mary C., "Grimké, Angelina Weld," in *OCAAL.* Cobb-Moore, Geneva, "Forten, Charlotte," in *OCAAL.* "Forten, Charlotte L.," "Forten, James, Sr.," and "Grimké, Archibald Henry," in *BDAA.* Hubbard, Dolan, "Grimké, Charlotte Forten," in *OCWW.*

Fortune, Amos (1710?–11/17/1801)
Enthusiastic appreciation

After purchasing his freedom from slavery—at age 60—Fortune was able to earn a good living by working as a tanner. His only published work was probably his epitaph ("Sacred to the memory of / Amos Fortune / who was born free in Africa / a slave in America / he purchased liberty / professed Christianity / lived respectfully / and died hopefully"). Nonetheless, he made an important contribution to literature by helping to found the public library in Jaffrey, New Hampshire (1/28/1796), and using his skills to bind the library's books.

REFERENCES: Liander, Margit, in *EA-99.*

Fortune, T. (Timothy) Thomas
(10/3/1856–6/2/1928)
Journalist; newspaper founder

Born a slave and a son of slaves, Thomas observed the Civil War as a young child and attended a Freedmen's Bureau school for a while after the Civil War. His father was a prominent Republican politician during Reconstruction; this status enabled Thomas to hold various patronage positions when he was a teenager. Although he started his studies at Howard University, he didn't have enough money to finish and he left after a year or two in order to begin a career in journalism. Within a short time, he had become a compositor for an African-American newspaper in Washington, D.C., and had married Carrie Smiley of Jacksonville, Florida. (He and Carrie later had children, two of whom survived past infancy, including a son who grew up to become a surgeon.)

In 1878, the young couple moved to New York City, and Thomas worked as a printer for the *New York Sun* and wrote articles for various white and black publications. The *Sun* editor appreciated his writing skills and promoted him to the paper's editorial staff. By 1882, he was editor and publisher of a daily African-American newspaper called the *New York Globe.* A militant defender of African Americans' civil rights, he urged African Americans to question their loyalty to Abraham Lincoln's party, which didn't seem to be serving their interests. When he came close to endorsing Grover Cleveland, conflicts with the management led to the death of the paper in 1884. He then founded the *New York Freeman,* which was essentially the old *Globe* with a new name and a new owner. This paper, renamed the *New York Age* in 1887, became the leading African-American newspaper at that time. From 1887 until 1907 (with some interruptions), he was also editor of the paper. (During this period, he also briefly coedited the *Voice of the Negro,* with May Barber.)

To get a feel for Fortune's brand of editorial, a contemporary of his once said, "He never writes unless he makes someone wince." Fortune expressed it this way: "Let us agitate! *Agitate! AGITATE!* until the protest shall awake the nation from its indifference." Among his causes was the segregation of children into separate schools for black and white schoolchildren—a cause that wasn't addressed nationally until the *Brown v. Board of Education* case in 1954. Needless to say, the white press didn't welcome his commentaries, and he was labeled a firebrand. In his widely read editorials, Fortune spoke out stridently against racial discrimination and segregation and defended African Americans' civil rights in both the North and the South. He also coined the term "Afro-American" and used it instead of the term "Negro" in his New York newspapers.

Fortune also wrote *The Negro in Politics* while he was still in his twenties. In 1884, he published *Black and White: Land, Labor, and Politics in the South,* in which he decried the exploitation of black labor by both agriculture and industry in the post-Reconstruction South, and he advocated for blacks to ally with white laborers to promote labor unionism.

In 1890, he conceived of and established the Afro-American League to promote African-American autonomy and to develop African-American political thinking. Essentially, this organization was the ideological forebear of the Niagara Movement of 1905, which was the basis for the National Association for the Advancement of Colored People (NAACP). Unfortunately, the league became inactive after a few years.

In 1895, both his newspaper and he were in financial difficulties, and he solicited and received both personal loans and subsidies for the *Age* from **Booker T. Washington**. As a result of his link to Washington, whose accommodationist views were opposed by **W. E. B. Du Bois** and others, Fortune's influence as a militant defender of civil rights declined. Many prominent militants felt that Fortune had compromised his principles by lending Washington moral support in exchange for Washington's financial support. In 1900, Fortune helped Washington organize the National Negro Business League.

Not too long after, however, Fortune's relationship with Washington became strained—both personally and politically—and in 1906, Fortune denounced Washington's support for President Theodore Roosevelt's actions following the Brownsville affair (in which an entire regiment of black troops was wrongly dishonorably discharged for inciting a riot; they were exonerated in 1972). In 1907, his relationship with Washington had de-

teriorated to the extent that Washington and his allies forced Fortune to sell them the *Age.* That same year, shortly before Fortune was forced to sell the *Age,* he had suffered a mental breakdown induced by marital discord and alcoholism. From then until 1917, Fortune was virtually destitute—and definitely depressed—barely supporting himself by editing several short-lived newspapers and writing columns for the *Age* every once in a while.

Fortune's association with another prominent African-American leader—**Marcus Garvey**—also involved mixed sentiments and yielded mixed fortunes for Thomas. Prior to 1923, Fortune absolutely rejected the notion of allegedly repatriating African Americans to Africa. From 1923 until his death, however, he worked as chief editorial writer of Garvey's *Negro World.* He never fully endorsed Garvey's views or joined Garvey's Universal Negro Improvement Association, but he still appreciated Garvey's ability to garner support from the masses through his dramatic message. Fortune also shared Garvey's aversion to Du Bois and the rest of the NAACP leadership, and when Garvey was charged with stock fraud, Fortune defended him against the charges.

REFERENCES: *AA:PoP. EB-98. G-95.* Fitzgerald, Michael W., in *OCAAL.*

Franklin, J. E. (Jennie Elizabeth) (1937–)
Plays, memoir

A schoolteacher and civil rights activist, Franklin started writing plays as a means to interest her students in reading. Her plays include *A First Step to Freedom* (1964), *Prodigal Daughter* (c. 1965), *The In-Crowd* (1965), *Mau Mau Room, Two Flowers,* her highly acclaimed *Black Girl* (1971), and her musical *The Prodigal Sister* (1976). She adapted her *Black Girl* as a screenplay, which **Ossie Davis** directed for film. In addition, she has written a nonfiction book on her experiences as a playwright, *Black Girl, from Genesis to Revelations* (1977), as well as numerous unpublished writings.

REFERENCES: Houston, Helen R., in *OCAAL.*

Franklin, John Hope (1/2/1915–)
Nonfiction—history, biography, essays

Born the son of a lawyer in the all-black town of Rentiesville, Oklahoma, Franklin grew up to be one of the leading scholars of U.S. history, illuminating the Civil War era and the civil rights movement. He earned his A.B. from Fisk University, in Nashville, Tennessee, in 1935; his A.M. from Harvard University in 1936; and his Ph.D. in history from Harvard in 1941. He went on to teach at Howard University in Washington, D.C. (1947–1956); at Brooklyn College (1956–1964); at the University of Chicago (1964–1982); and at Duke University (1982–1985; now emeritus), where he was the James B. Duke Professor of History and a professor of legal history at the university's law school. During his academic career, he also taught at Fisk and at North Carolina Central University.

Although he may be best known to history for helping to shape the legal brief for the landmark *Brown v. Board of Education* Supreme Court decision (1954), Franklin also presided over several historical organizations, including the American Studies Association, the Southern Historical Association, and the American Historical Association. He has also received numerous major honors and awards, including the National Association for the Advancement of Colored People's Spingarn Medal and the Presidential Medal of Freedom, the highest honor a civilian can be given by a grateful nation, both of which he received in 1995. In 1997, his nation further recognized his value when President Clinton appointed Franklin the chair of the advisory board for the Initiative on Race and Reconciliation. The honorary degrees he has received now number more than 100.

Franklin's most acclaimed text was his *From Slavery to Freedom* (1947; a seventh, revised edition, coauthored with Alfred A. Moss, Jr., extends the coverage through the early 1990s). Probably the preeminent textbook on African-American history, it traces the story of African Americans from the beginnings of civilization through the early 1990s. In it, he explicates the history, cultures, and peoples of Africa and ties them to the experiences of African Americans and other people of African descent in Latin America, the West Indies, and Canada. He also insightfully analyzes the ways in which African Americans have influenced and been influenced by American history and culture. The book also offers an extensive bibliography, an appendix of numerous important documents, and illustrative graphics such as maps and photographs.

Franklin's other publications include *The Free Negro in North Carolina, 1790–1860* (1943); *The Militant South, 1800–1861* (1956); *Reconstruction: After the Civil War* (1961 or 1962); *The Emancipation Proclamation* (1963); *Racial Equality in America*

(1976); and *The Color Line: Legacy for the Twenty-first Century* (1993). In addition, he edited three other books on the Civil War period as well as *Color and Race* (1968) and *Black Leaders of the Twentieth Century* (1982). He also published *Race and History: Selected Essays, 1938–1988* (in 1989 or 1990). Among scholars, Franklin may be best known for his *George Washington Williams: A Biography* (1985). This biography culminates 40 years of Franklin's scholarly research into the life and the achievements of pioneering nineteenth-century African-American historian **George Washington Williams.**

REFERENCES: *EB-98. EBLG. G-95. SMKC.*

Frazier, Edward Franklin
(9/24/1894–5/17/1962)
Nonfiction—sociology

Frazier's influential yet controversial sociological works include *The Free Negro Family* (1932), *The Negro Family in the United States* (1939), the textbook *The Negro in the United States* (1949), *Black Bourgeoisie* (1957/1997), *Race and Culture Contacts in the Modern World* (1957), *The Negro Church in America* (1963), and *On Race Relations: Selected Writings* (1968). Frazier never hesitated to challenge white Americans to think about race and to prod black Americans to think about socioeconomic class.

REFERENCES: Balfour, Lawrie, in *EA-99.*

Freedom's Journal (3/16/1827–1829)

Founded in 1827 in New York City, *Freedom's Journal* was the first black weekly newspaper, established by **Samuel E. Cornish**, a minister, and **John Brown Russwurm**, to respond to racist commentary in local white papers in New York. *Freedom's Journal* used current events, anecdotes, and editorials to convey a message of moral reform and other issues of interest to Northern free blacks, such as prejudice, slavery, and the threat by the American Colonization Society to expatriate free blacks to Africa. The newspaper was widely supported by blacks outside of New York City. Russwurm was gradually convinced of the idea of colonization, which damaged the paper's credibility. *Freedom's Journal* ceased publication in 1829, and Russwurm departed for the American Colonization Society's settlement in Liberia. Cornish was unable to revive the newspaper under a new name, the *Rights of All.*

EDITOR'S NOTE: Other cofounders included **Richard Allen, Alexander Crummell**, James Varick, and **Peter Williams, Jr.**

—*Lisa Bahlinger*

REFERENCES: *EAACH* (Vol. 2). Wagner, Wendy, in *OCAAL*.

French, William P. (Plummer)
(2/19/1943–1/14/1997)
Bibliographies, anthology, biography

While working in a bookstore specializing in African Americana and catering to noteworthy collectors **Arthur Schomburg** and **Arthur Spingarn**, French became expert on African-American books and bibliography. Based on his expertise, he compiled two biographical pamphlets on African-American poets and coedited a bibliographical book, *Afro-American Poetry and Drama, 1760–1975*. In recognition of his work, Harvard University's Afro-American Studies department has commemorated him with a book-collecting prize.

REFERENCES: Newman, Richard, in *EA-99*.

Fuller, Charles H. (Henry) (Jr.)
(3/5/1939–)
Plays, short stories, essays, poems

This son of Lillian Anderson Fuller and Charles H. Fuller, a prosperous printer, developed an early love of reading and writing at least partly because of his father's occupation. For one thing, his father sometimes asked young Charles to proofread some of his printing projects. In addition, his parents exposed him to a constant stream of different personalities and lifestyles, as they offered their home to foster children.

As a high school student, Charles was stage-struck when he saw a Yiddish-theater play starring Molly Picon and Menasha Skulnik at the Old Walnut Street Theater: He didn't understand a word being spoken, but "it was live theater, and I felt myself responding to it." His college education began at Villanova University (1956–1958); was briefly interrupted by some time in the U.S. Army, when he was stationed in Japan and in South Korea (1959–1962); and finished up at La Salle College while he worked at various jobs (1965–1967).

From 1967 until 1971, Fuller cofounded and served as director of the Afro-American Arts Theatre in Philadelphia. He also wrote and directed "Black Experience" on WIP radio station in Philadelphia. Meanwhile, he was developing his playwriting skills, evolving from writing dialogue-filled short stories to writing skits to writing one-act plays and finally into creating full-length dramas. In 1968, while he was working as a housing inspector in Philadelphia, Princeton University's McCarter Theatre offered to produce *The Village: A Party,* his drama about intermarriage and racial tensions. He now refers to it as "one of the world's worst interracial plays," but he nonetheless profited from this experience, as he met members of the Negro Ensemble Company (NEC) while that play was being produced. In 1974, his *In the Deepest Part of Sleep* was produced by NEC, and throughout the 1970s, he wrote plays for New York's Henry Street Settlement theater.

In 1975 or 1976, Fuller wrote his hit play *The Brownsville Raid* for NEC's tenth anniversary. The play is based on the historic Brownsville, Texas, incident of 1906, in which an entire regiment of African-American U.S. Army troops was dishonorably discharged on President Theodore Roosevelt's orders, after being falsely accused of inciting a riot that led to fatalities. (The soldiers were exonerated in 1972.) Although Fuller describes himself as a playwright who happens to be black, rather than a black playwright, he addresses issues of race realistically and sensitively, never hesitating to approach society's cruelty in a humanistic yet forceful light.

Fuller's next play was *Zooman and the Sign* (produced in 1980, published in 1982), an Obie Award–winning melodrama in which a father searches for the murderer of his daughter in Philadelphia. His best-known work, however, was his fourth play, *A Soldier's Play* (1981), for which he won the 1982 Pulitzer Prize for drama (only the second African-American playwright to win this award). In it, an African-American army officer (Captain Richard Davenport) investigates the murder of an African-American army sergeant (Sergeant Vernon C. Waters) at an army base in Fort Neal, a backwater of New Orleans, Louisiana, in 1944, during World War II. You may have seen this play as it was adapted (by Fuller) to a screenplay, produced in 1984, by Columbia Pictures, retitled *A Soldier's Story*. Fuller crafted the play as a series of interviews by Davenport, in which each enlisted man's story is revealed; one character also often tells the story of another character. In addition to the Obie and the Pulitzer Prize, Fuller has been awarded a Guggenheim fellowship, a Rockefeller fellowship, and a National Endowment for the Arts and CAPS playwrighting fellowship. Since 1988, Fuller has also been professor of Afro-American Studies at Temple University.

REFERENCES: *1TESK. AA:PoP. EB-98. EBLG. MWEL. MAAL.* Macon, Wanda, in *OCAAL.*

Fuller, Hoyt (1923–1981)
Criticism, editorials

Although Fuller's only book was his collection of essays, *Return to Africa* (1971), he played a major role in the **Black Arts movement**. Chiefly, he shaped the movement through his work as editor of **Negro Digest**, later renamed *Black World*. After *Black World* folded in 1976, Fuller moved from Chicago to Atlanta, where he worked with the First World Foundation to start *First World*, a magazine of opinion, scholarship, and literature. While still in Chicago, Fuller helped found the African-American writers' collective Organization of Black American Culture (OBAC), which nurtured the careers of **Haki Madhubuti** (Don L. Lee), **Carolyn Rodgers**, **Nikki Giovanni**, and **Angela Jackson**.

REFERENCES: *AAW:AAPP.* Long, Richard A., in *OCAAL.*

Gaines, Ernest J. (James)

(1/15/1933–)

Novels, short stories

The son of Manuel and Adrienne Gaines, Ernest was born on River Lake Plantation in Point Coupée Parish County, Louisiana, where his father worked and where later, he, too worked cutting sugarcane and digging potatoes for about half-a-dollar a day during his childhood. His aunt Augusteen Jefferson, who literally had no legs to stand on but had an iron will and tremendous courage and determination, raised him until he turned 15 years old. Because the parish had no high school for African-American youths, Ernest was sent to live with his mother and stepfather in Vallejo, California, to attend high school and then junior college there.

Homesick for Louisiana, Gaines tried to find books on the African-American, Anglo-American, Creole (Spanish- or French-African-American), and Cajun (French-Canadian-American) people whom he had known growing up—to no avail. Failing that, he read American (e.g., Ernest Hemingway and William Faulkner), Russian (e.g., Leo Tolstoy, Ivan Turgenev, and Nikolai Gogol), French, and Anglo-Irish authors who talked about rural ways of life across the country and around the world. Though these writers spoke of rural and peasant experiences similar to his own, they lacked the flavor of the down-home front-porch stories he had heard while growing up. It seemed that if he was to read such stories, he would have to write them himself. Although Gaines has spent most of his adolescence and adulthood in the San Francisco Bay area, his writings continue to reflect his roots in the potpourri of Louisiana's cultures.

In 1953, after a couple of years of junior college, Gaines was drafted into the army, where he served for two years. After his discharge, he went to San Francisco State College (now University), where he earned a bachelor's degree in English in 1957. During the mid- to late 1950s, San Francisco was a haven for writers of the Beat generation, and Gaines responded to this stimulating environment enthusiastically. While still in college, in 1956, he started having his short stories published—at first in the *Transfer,* a tiny campus periodical. A white literary agent, Dorothea Oppenheimer, saw one of his first stories and decided he had promise. With her support, in 1958 he was awarded a Wallace Stegner Creative Writing Fellowship to study creative (fiction) writing at Stanford University's graduate school.

Eventually, Oppenheimer also helped Gaines get a contract with Dial Press to publish his first novel, *Catherine Carmier* (1964), a third-person narrative about a star-crossed couple (an African-American man and a Creole woman whose father opposes their relationship). Ever since, he has spent part of his time writing and part of his time teaching or working as writer-in-residence at various colleges, including Denison and Stanford universities. In 1983, he was named professor of English at the University of Southwestern Louisiana at Lafayette, where he resides part of each year, spending the rest of his time in California, writing.

Through the process of "knowing the place, knowing the people," Gaines vividly describes the rural Louisiana settings of his stories, using authentic speech in dialogues and in first-person narratives. For many readers, this setting and these people might seem foreign if they were to visit, but through Gaines's narratives, they feel intimately engaged with his characters and become familiar with their settings and experiences. Through Gaines's compassion for the people in his stories, readers, too, care deeply about his characters. Also, even in the most desperate of circumstances, Gaines satisfyingly incorporates humor as it would naturally emerge in the real lives of courageous people. His characters face racism, other forms of oppression, and personal tragedies and difficulties with dignity and determination—and with the love and support of their family and their community.

Gaines's second novel, *Barren Summer,* was completed in 1963 but has never been published. His second published novel, *Of Love and Dust* (1967), tells a story of forbidden (i.e., interracial) love. This novel uses Gaines's characteristic first-person narration, such that the reader observes the events in the life—and death—of Marcus Payne as seen through the eyes of Jim Kelly. This novel gained Gaines some critical notice, but the novel that roused the literary world to attend to Gaines was his next novel, *The Autobiography of Miss Jane Pittman* (1971). In it, the centenarian Miss Pittman tells her own story, describing more than 100 years of her personal experiences while revealing an intimate account of slavery, Reconstruction, Jim Crow policies and practices, and the civil rights movement. The best-selling novel was even made into an Emmy Award–winning (nine Emmys!) made-for-TV movie (1974). Almost certainly his most memorable character, Pittman honors the qualities Gaines treasured in his beloved aunt: resourcefulness, integrity, stamina, determination, and loving compassion.

His next book, *In My Father's House* (1978), returned to third-person narration and was set chiefly in a town instead of in the countryside. This novel wasn't as widely acclaimed or as popular as the novel before it or the novel that followed it, *A Gathering of Old Men* (1983). In the opening of that book, a white Cajun farmer is murdered, and the white folks in town decide that a black man must pay—with his life. The reader hears the story through the first-person narratives of more than a dozen older African-American men, who act together to defend the black man targeted by the white folks. They do so by having each old man admit his guilt and accept responsibility for the murder. Although the actual events of the story are compressed into a single day, heightening their drama, each storyteller helps the reader see that these events are embedded within the context of a long history of racial injustice. This novel, too, was made into a movie (1987). Both *Miss Pittman* and *Gathering* won gold medals from the Commonwealth Club of Northern California.

Gaines's subsequent novel, *A Lesson Before Dying* (1993), was also made into a television movie. Readers view the novel through the eyes of Grant Wiggins, a teacher who was raised by his elderly aunt. As the story opens, a young African-American man is wrongly convicted of participating in a robbery that leads to murder. In a futile attempt to spare the young man's life, the youth's (European-American) lawyer says that the barely literate young man shouldn't be executed because to do so would be the equivalent of executing a hog, as the youth's mental level is no different than that of a hog. As the young man awaits execution, his elderly godmother asks Wiggins's aunt to get Wiggins to help

the youth realize his own worth and to see that he has human dignity much greater than that of a hog. Wiggins is unenthusiastic about this task, to say the least, and the young man has no great interest in Wiggins, either. In deference to his aunt, however, Wiggins grudgingly complies, and the young man agrees to do so out of respect for his godmother's wishes. Over time, Wiggins succeeds in helping the young man to read and to write in a journal, recording his increasingly philosophical thoughts and feelings. By the time the youth is executed, he has come to acknowledge his worth, and his journal reflects his tremendous dignity. The critically acclaimed novel won Gaines a National Book Critics Circle Award in 1994.

In addition to these works, Gaines has published many short stories, some of which have been collected in *Bloodline* (1968), comprising five different first-person narratives, one of which ("The Sky Is Gray") was made into a TV movie, and in *A Long Day in November* (1971). He also wrote a novel for young people: *A Warm Day in November*. In addition to the awards previously mentioned, Gaines has been honored with the Joseph Henry Jackson Literary Award (1959) and a MacArthur Foundation fellowship (often called a "genius grant") (1993) in appreciation for his many literary contributions.

REFERENCES: *AA:PoP. AAL. BWA. EB-BH-CD. EBLG. G-97. NAAAL. OC20LE. WDAA.* Lang, John, in *OCAAL.* Robinson, Lisa Clayton, in *EA-99.*

Garland, Hazel B. (née Hazel Barbara Maxine Hill) (1/28/1913–4/5/1988)
Journalist, editor

The eldest of the 16 children in her family and a bright student who loved learning and excelled in school, Garland was urged by her father to drop out of high school. Why? To make it easier for her younger brother to finish school. As she later recalled (quoted in *PBW,* p. 97), "My father was a dear soul. I loved him dearly. But his idea was, 'Why waste your money on sending a girl to college? She's going to get married. Save your money for the boys.' I used to go to the library where I would read and read. . . . I lived in libraries. I read everything." On January 26, 1935, she did exactly as her father predicted: She married (wedding business owner and photographer Percy A. Garland), and a little over nine months later, she had her only child (her daughter Phyllis) and settled down to homemaking.

With encouragement from her mother-in-law, Janey Garland, Hazel started getting involved in various civic organizations, including the local Young Women's Christian Association. As the club's reporter and a member of the publicity committee, Garland wrote up the event herself when a *Pittsburgh Courier* reporter got lost on the way to a club function. Editors at the *Courier* were impressed with her writing skills and her journalistic intuition, so they invited her to work for them as a "stringer"— a freelance reporter who got paid ($2) for each item she wrote but received no salary otherwise. She was to cover local events in various nearby communities. Pretty soon, Garland was turning in so many items that the editors encouraged her to combine her items into a column, titled "Tri-City News," starting in 1943. When the *Courier* offered training for the stringers, Garland made good use of the opportunity, and pretty soon she was filling in for staff reporters whenever they went on vacation. In 1946, she was invited to join the staff full time, and her column's title was changed to "Things to Talk About." Garland's highly popular column was published in various editions of the *Pittsburgh Courier* until her death in 1988.

In 1952, Garland won a prestigious regional journalism competition, beating out many white journalists and at least one Pulitzer Prize winner. The same year, when the *Courier* decided to start a new magazine section, the paper named Garland to be its associate editor. In 1955, she started writing another column, her weekly "Video Vignettes," which she also continued writing until the year she died. In it, she praised TV networks, producers, and executives that provided positive images of African Americans, put African Americans in front of the camera, and addressed issues of concern to African Americans—and she scorned them when they canceled those programs, dismissed those performers, or showed negative images of African Americans. To drive home her point, she often sent copies of her column to the TV executives and station managers she was honoring or scolding. She was the first African-American journalist to start a column critiquing television, and when she died, hers was one of the longest-running newspaper columns about television ever published.

When the magazine section was phased out, Garland became the woman's editor, and then in 1960 her job expanded to include being the entertainment editor as well. When the newspaper started having grave financial woes in the mid-1960s, and staffers' checks started to bounce, Garland's commitment never flagged. As she later recalled, "I loved the *Courier.* It was everything to me. I had spent the greater part of my life there, so I wanted to work even if I didn't get paid. I thought maybe we could keep on and hold it together." In 1966, *Chicago Defender* publisher John Sengstacke (**Robert Sengstacke Abbott**'s nephew) bought the *Courier,* adding it to his chain of African-American newspapers.

Sengstacke, a savvy publisher, promoted Garland—a woman—to city editor, considered a management-level position at a newspaper. In that position, Garland influenced the newspaper's policies and staff assignments. In 1972, Sengstacke further promoted her to editor-in-chief, making her the first woman to head a nationally circulated African-American newspaper chain. In that role, Garland reorganized the paper into different sections, developed new "beats" for the paper, and emphasized various features. In 1974, the National Newspaper Publishers Association named her "Editor of the Year." That same year, poor health forced her to step down as editor-in-chief, but she continued on as assistant to the publisher, so she still had a hand in editorial operations and decisionmaking. In 1977, Garland retired from her full-time position at the paper, but she still continued working for the paper as an editorial coordinator and consultant. In addition to working one day a week doing editing and layouts, she kept writing her columns and occasional feature articles, which she continued to do until three weeks before her death. In both 1978 and 1979, she was chosen to serve as a juror of journalism's most prestigious prize: the Pulitzer. In thinking about success, Garland commented, "We must not let anything turn us aside. And to be truly successful, we must always reach back and try to lift someone else as we climb" (quoted in *TAWH,* p. 100).

REFERENCES: Garland, Phyl, in *PBW. TAWH.*

Garnet, Henry Highland
(?/1815–2/13/1882)
Sermons, abolitionist writings; publisher

In 1824, Henry's father George, a descendant of a Mandingo chieftain, resisted slavery by absconding with his family—including 9-year-old Henry—from Maryland's eastern shore to New York City. Thereafter, Henry grew up not knowing the constraints of slave life, though he was never far removed from racial hatred and discrimination. When he was just 14, he went to sea as a cabin boy, but on his return to his home port, he found that his sister had been caught by slave hunters and the rest of his family had been forced into hiding to avoid capture. From then on, he carried a large knife, although his friends did manage to persuade him to hide on Long Island, rather than openly trying to defend himself from the slave hunters.

As a boy and a youth, Henry had attended the New York African Free School and then the Canal Street High School. As a young man, Garnet, **Alexander Crummell,** and Ira Aldridge (later to become a world-renowned Shakespearean actor) enrolled in the Noyes Academy in Canaan, New Hampshire, which had been all white prior to their enrollment. As if that weren't enough to rile the locals, the daring young Garnet and Crummell began speaking against slavery in a local church. An outraged mob of white neighbors to the school used a fleet of oxen to drag the school's main building into a nearby swamp. Undaunted, Garnet continued his schooling at Oneida Theological Institute, from which he graduated in 1839 or 1840.

Following his graduation, Garnet gained his own pastorship at a Presbyterian church, which soon was a center of abolitionist activity, as well as the location for a grammar school. In addition to his speeches from the pulpit, he lectured widely and wrote and edited numerous pieces for newspapers. In an 1843 address to the National Convention of Colored Citizens (also called the "National Negro Convention") in Buffalo, New York, he urged his listeners to take whatever steps they needed to in order to resist and oppose slavery, admonishing them, "THEREFORE IT IS YOUR SOLEMN AND IMPERATIVE DUTY TO USE EVERY MEANS, BOTH MORAL, INTELLECTUAL, AND PHYSICAL THAT PROMISES SUCCESS. . . . Brethren arise, arise! Strike for your lives and liberties. . . . Let your motto be resistance! *resistance!* RESISTANCE! . . . What kind of resistance you had better make, you must decide by the circumstances that surround you, and according to the suggestion of expediency."

In 1848, Garnet published *The Past and Present Condition, and the Destiny, of the Colored Race,* which detailed his views on abolition and his op-

position to emigration to Africa. At that time, he noted that many racist whites supported emigration because they feared that abolition was more likely to occur if freed African Americans remained in the United States to advocate and work for abolition. He also believed that if African Americans emigrated, they would be abandoning their legitimate claim to the fruits of their labor in the United States. He later (by the late 1850s) changed his mind and advocated emigration to Africa and the Caribbean.

In 1849, Garnet published *David Walker's Appeal in Four Articles; Together with a Preamble, to the Coloured Citizens of the World, but in Particular, and Very Expressly, to Those of the United States of America,* with which he included his 1843 speech. The combined effect of Walker's appeal and his own was to inspire countless slaves to revolt by whatever means they had available, including the murder of their masters if necessary. These two abolitionists' ideas also influenced sympathetic whites, such as William Lloyd Garrison (editor of the *Liberator*) and John Brown, who offered Garnet financial aid in this publication, and who was later to become rather famous himself at the little town of Harpers Ferry.

From 1850 to 1855, Garnet left the United States to lecture against slavery in Great Britain and Germany as well as to do missionary work in Jamaica. Meanwhile, in the United States, abolitionist sentiments were gaining ground, and Garnet's ideas about slave resistance and violence—and his opposition to emigration—were becoming increasingly acceptable to militant abolitionists. Even **Frederick Douglass**, who had denounced Garnet's violence in 1843, agreed that nonviolent moral suasion was unlikely to succeed in abolishing slavery and that violent means might be necessary to achieve abolition.

When Garnet returned to the United States in 1855, he became the pastor of Shiloh Presbyterian Church in New York City. During the Civil War, he offered aid to persons who were displaced and distressed because of the Civil War. In 1864, while he was pastor of the 15th Street Presbyterian Church in Washington, D.C., he urged President Lincoln to enlist African-American troops, and he helped recruit African Americans for the Union Army.

Another of Garnet's speeches also made history: On February 12, 1865, he became the first African-American minister to deliver a sermon to the U.S. Congress. In it, he admonished the representatives to "emancipate, enfranchise, educate, and give the blessings of the gospel to every American citizen." After the Civil War, Garnet supported government workers in developing programs to benefit former slaves. He also outspokenly advocated on behalf of civil rights, such as by urging land reform to get rid of the land monopolies held by white Southerners. In addition, his reach extended beyond the American continent, as he championed Cuban independence, maintained an interest in the West Indies, and promoted strong ties to Africa. Although Garnet married (two times, actually—first to Julia and second to women's rights activist Sarah Thompson), his primary devotion was to abolition, and his second was to his church and followers, leaving little for his personal life.

During his later years, he became increasingly disillusioned about the possibilities for African Americans in the United States and became interested in emigrating to Africa. In 1881, an appointment as minister to Liberia (established as a free state in Africa during the era of U.S. slavery) offered him a way out. Exactly 17 years after his groundbreaking speech to the Congress, within two months of his arrival in Liberia, he died there. He was buried on African soil, as was his wish, in a Liberian cemetery overlooking the Atlantic Ocean.

REFERENCES: *1TESK. AA:PoP. BAL-1-P. BF:2000. BWA. G-95. EB-98. NAAAL. OCAAL. SMKC. VBA.*

Garvey, Amy (Euphemia) (née) Jacques
(12/31/1896–7/25/1973)
Nonfiction—history, biography, editorials; journalist

A native of Jamaica, Amy Euphemia Jacques's main claim to fame is her link to fellow Jamaican and black nationalist leader **Marcus Garvey**, whom she wedded July 27, 1922, and with whom she had two sons (Marcus, Jr., born in 1930; and Julius Winston, born in 1933), raising them alone after Marcus widowed her in 1940. Before marrying Garvey, Amy Jacques had migrated to the United States in 1917, had joined the United Negro Improvement Association (UNIA) in 1918, and had worked as Garvey's private secretary and office manager. Eventually, she became the associate editor of UNIA's *Negro World* newspaper, edit-

ing the women's page and writing her own column, "Our Women and What They Think." When they married, Marcus was already under indictment for mail fraud, and when he was convicted and jailed, she ardently campaigned for his release through her editorials in *Negro World* and by giving speeches throughout the United States. She also compiled and edited Marcus Garvey's writings in the *Philosophy and Opinions of Marcus Garvey, or Africa for the Africans* (Vol. 1, 1923; Vol. 2, 1925) and two volumes of Marcus's poems in *The Tragedy of White Injustice* and *Selections from the Poetic Meditations of Marcus Garvey* (both published in 1927). In addition, decades after his death, she wrote her own account of Garveyism in *Garvey and Garveyism* (1963) and *Black Power in America* (1968).

REFERENCES: Martin, Tonya, "Marcus Garvey," in *BH2C*. Taylor, Ula, in *BWA:AHE*. Amy Garvey's papers are collected in the Marcus Garvey Memorial Collection at Fisk.

Garvey, Marcus (Moziah)
(8/17/1887–6/10/1940)
Essays, poems, speeches, commentary; newspaper and magazine founder and editor

During his lifetime and continuing to this day, Marcus Garvey has been a controversial character. There is even disagreement as to whether Garvey's middle name may have been Moziah (per *EB-98* and *EBLG*), Mosiah (per *EA-99, BDAA,* and *BH2C*), or even Mozian Mannasseth (per *BF:2000*). The son of a bold, brilliant, and book-loving stonemason, Garvey was born and raised in Jamaica. In Garvey's *Philosophy and Opinions of Marcus Garvey* (quoted in *BH2C*, p. 253), he said of his mother that she was "a sober and conscientious Christian, too soft and good for the time in which she lived."

After a superb elementary education, Garvey was apprenticed as a printer for his godfather during his early teens. At age 16, he had learned the trade well enough to go to Kingston and get work as the youngest foreman printer in Jamaica. While in Kingston, he printed his periodical *Garvey's Watchman* and his political club's newsletter, *Our Own.* In his early twenties, Garvey left Jamaica, traveling through Central and South America and Europe, everywhere observing the exploitation of African-descended workers and the appalling living conditions of African descendants on the American and European continents. After a while, he settled down in London for a couple of years, where he worked for the *Africa Times and Orient Review,* the leading pan-African journal of that time, and attended law lectures at the University of London. Increasingly, Garvey became outraged at the suffering of African people everywhere, including the people in African nations subject to European imperial rule, as well as African descendants whom the diaspora had scattered across the globe.

Before leaving London, Garvey read **Booker T. Washington**'s *Up from Slavery,* after which he was inspired to become "a race leader," destined to lead Africans everywhere to join him in uplifting his race. Within days of returning to Jamaica in 1914, he founded the pan-African organization Universal Negro Improvement and Conservation Association and African Communities League, usually called the Universal Negro Improvement Association (UNIA). UNIA's aim was to unite "all the Negro peoples of the world into one great body to establish a country and Government absolutely their own" (quoted in *BWA,* p. 566). Garvey began corresponding with Washington and embarked on a program to affirm a bond (which he called "confraternity") among Africans everywhere, aid the needy, establish education facilities like Washington's Tuskegee Institute, and improve the status of women.

Early in 1916, Garvey made a fund-raising tour to the United States, where he was able to inspire a much greater following than he had in Jamaica. During this time, many African Americans were migrating from the rural South to the urban North, only to find segregated housing, job discrimination, and other forms of racism, so Garvey's message of racial pride and economic independence was welcome indeed. By 1918, Garvey moved the UNIA headquarters to Liberty Hall in Harlem, and he established UNIA branches in numerous other large African-American ghettos of the urban North. He also founded his weekly newspaper, *Negro World,* through which he communicated to followers across the nation and around the world, and through which he gave voice to many writers of the **Harlem Renaissance**. By 1919, Garvey had attracted at least a million followers (estimates range from 1 million to 11 million; the exact number of UNIA members was never certain) in North America, the West Indies, Central and South America, West Africa, and England. (In 1919, Garvey married his secretary, Amy Ashwood, but they divorced three years later.)

Through his speeches (delivered weekly in UNIA headquarters at Liberty Hall) and his newspaper articles, poems, and essays, he told of the "new Negro," one who was no longer servile but rather proud of a triumphant African heritage. Garvey regaled his followers with accounts of the great achievements of African culture and the historic contributions of African Americans. He promised, "I shall teach the black man to see beauty in himself" (quoted in *BWA,* p. 565)—and he did so. While working toward the establishment of an independent nation in Africa, Garvey urged his followers to develop an independent, self-sustained African-American economy within European-American capitalist societies. Toward these ends, he formed the Black Star Line Steamship Corporation and the Negro Factories Corporation, which employed more than 1,000 African Americans to produce dolls, tailor clothes, and run a printing press, a hotel, and various restaurants, grocery stories, and laundries.

Among Garvey's many ardent supporters were **T. Thomas Fortune**, editor of *Negro World,* and Amy Jacques, associate editor of the newspaper, whom he married in 1922 soon after divorcing the first Amy Garvey. Not everyone in the black community supported Garvey, however. Labor leader **A. Philip Randolph** and National Association for the Advancement of Colored People (NAACP) leader **W. E. B. Du Bois** opposed Garvey's championing of segregation (which linked him to the Ku Klux Klan) and of racial purity (a troublesome goal for almost all Americans). Others criticized Garvey's haphazard, slapdash business practices, and still others found his flamboyant manner to be pompous and arrogant. In 1922, his inattention to minding his own businesses led to his being indicted for mail fraud (in connection with sales of Black Star Line stock); in 1923, he (and some other UNIA members) was convicted and sentenced to five years in prison (by a judge who was an NAACP member); and in 1925, after a failed appeal, he started serving his sentence in a federal penitentiary in Atlanta. In 1927, President Calvin Coolidge commuted his sentence, and Garvey was deported as an undesirable alien.

On returning to Jamaica in 1927, he established another newspaper, the *New Jamaican,* and a monthly magazine, *The Black Man.* His wife Amy also gave birth to his sons Marcus, Jr., and Julius while there. Garvey also tried to participate in the political process in Jamaica, but he ran into legal difficulties, and in 1934 he left Jamaica for England. While living in a cottage in London, he still published *The Black Man* for a few years, although he ended up dying in relative obscurity. Since his death, however, he has been much honored (with numerous roads, schools, and other buildings named after him; his likeness produced on statues, coins, and postage stamps; and his story told through songs and poetry). Ironically, despite his wide travels and his lifelong aim to establish a settlement in Africa, Garvey ended up never setting foot on African soil.

While Garvey was in prison, Amy campaigned for his release and compiled and edited his writings in the *Philosophy and Opinions of Marcus Garvey, or Africa for the Africans* (Vol. 1, 1923; Vol. 2, 1925). Two years later, Amy compiled two volumes of Garvey's poems in *The Tragedy of White Injustice* and *Selections from the Poetic Meditations of Marcus Garvey* (both published in 1927). In 1937, Garvey gave his top UNIA organizers his *Message to the People: The Course of African Philosophy,* which was published for wider circulation in 1986 (as the seventh title in "The New Marcus Garvey Library" series).

Although Garvey failed in his avowed goal for UNIA and in his business dealings, he achieved great success in stirring millions of African Americans to take pride in their African heritage (e.g., motivating the Jamaican Rastafarian movement), in prompting subsequent movements to establish economic independence for African Americans (e.g., the Nation of Islam), and in inspiring many African-American writers to create poetry and prose, fiction and nonfiction reflecting a proud people with a grand heritage. The red, green, and black colors that now symbolize liberation for African peoples were originally the colors of the UNIA flag. Even today, Garvey's words continue to arouse and embolden his readers:

> The time has come for the Negro to forget and cast behind him his hero worship and adoration of other races, and to start out immediately to create and emulate heroes of his own. We must canonize our own saints, create our own martyrs, and elevate to positions of fame and honor black men and women who have made their distinct contributions to our racial history. . . . We must

inspire a literature and promulgate a doctrine of our own without any apologies to the powers that be. (from his "African Fundamentalism," quoted in *BH2C,* p. 257)

In the 1930s, he had aptly prophesied, "I am only the forerunner of an awakened Africa that shall never go back to sleep" (quoted in *BWA,* p. 567).

REFERENCES: *AAW:AAPP. BAL-1-P. BF:2000. BWA. EB-BH-CD. EBLG. PGAA.* King, Martha, in *EA-99.* Martin, Tony, in *BH2C.* Williams, Patricia Robinson, in *OCAAL.*

Gates, Henry Louis, Jr. (9/16/1950–)
Scholarly literary criticism

Currently the W. E. B. Du Bois Professor of Humanities and chair of the Afro-American Studies Department at Harvard University, Gates is one of the leading U.S. literary and cultural critics. In *Figures in Black: Words, Signs, and the Racial Self* (1987), a seminal work of literary criticism, he tells how being the first black student in English at Cambridge, or at least the first in anyone's recollection, was all-important to him: "I had allowed myself to be in fantasies of meeting a certain challenge for 'the race,' in literature just as **W. E. B. Du Bois** had done in sociology at Heidelberg, or as **Alain Locke** had done in philosophy at Oxford" (p. xvi). Since his days in graduate school, Gates has drawn on the extraordinarily rich body of contemporary literary theory, using it to analyze the writings of a wide range of African-American and African authors published in English between the eighteenth century and the present.

Gates grew up in Piedmont, West Virginia, a backwoods town of about 2,000 people. He spent a year at a junior college before applying to Yale. After graduating from Yale summa cum laude, he received a fellowship to Cambridge. Gates physically limped through both universities. At age 14, he had suffered a hairline fracture while playing touch football at a Methodist summer camp and his joint calcified and began to fuse over the next 15 years. Despite aspirin, ibuprofen, heating pads, and massages, Gates couldn't escape the tremendous pain. "My leg grew shorter, as the muscle atrophied and the ball of the ball and socket joint migrated into my pelvis" (Gates, 1992a, p. 633). When Gates turned 40, doctors finally agreed to replace his hip, and after surgery, he ceremonially trashed his corrective shoe and began wearing matching normal

Henry Louis Gates, Jr. (Mark Alcarez/Corbis)

pairs for the first time. He describes this experience in his essay "A Giant Step" (1992a).

Although his legs were weak at Cambridge, Gates's intellectual ambition was strong: "It is somewhat embarrassing to admit this today, but I felt as if I were embarked upon a mission for all black people, especially for that group of scholars whom our people have traditionally called 'race men' or 'race women,' the intellectuals who collect, preserve, and analyze the most sublime artifacts of the black imagination" (Gates, 1987, p. xvii).

At Cambridge Gates met Nigerian writer Wole Soyinka, who encouraged him to study African-American literature. Soyinka had been recently released from a two-year confinement in a Nigerian prison. He was on campus to deliver a lecture se-

ries on African literature. In *Loose Canons: Notes on the Culture Wars* (1992), Gates tells the story of how African writing was not seen as a legitimate area of literary study when Soyinka had come to the university in 1973. Soyinka had been pursuing a two-year lectureship in English but was forced to accept an appointment in social anthropology instead. Gates contended that moving the African material to this area blatantly devalued the African work from the perspective of literary theory.

Shortly after he heard Soyinka's story, Gates asked the tutor in English at Clare College, Cambridge, why Soyinka had been treated this way. Gates told the tutor, as politely as he could, that he would very much like to write a doctoral thesis in "black literature." The tutor replied with great consternation, "Tell me sir, . . . what is black literature?" Gates said that when he responded to the tutor "with a veritable bibliography of texts written by authors who were black, [the tutor's] evident irritation informed me that I had taken as serious information what he had intended as a rhetorical question" (Gates, 1992b, p. 88).

Gates overcame this sort of suspicion, hostility, and skepticism, however, to pursue black literature at Cambridge. He eventually encountered professors there who, while professing their ignorance of the topic, worked with him on his thesis in African-American literature. Gates had to intellectually begin anew, abandoning his undergraduate training in history.

In 1977, he developed a close relationship with Professor John Holloway. Holloway allowed Gates to experiment by letting contemporary literary theories inform his close readings of black texts. The theories came from French, Russian, Anglo-American, British, and other perspectives. Most of his later work was shaped by those experimental exercises with Holloway.

After he completed his Ph.D. in English, Gates returned to Yale, this time as a professor. He has also taught English, comparative literature, and African Studies at Cornell and held an appointment at Duke before joining the faculty at Harvard.

Gates has a reputation as a literary archeologist. While looking at books in a Manhattan bookstore, he came across a copy of *Our Nig.* The autobiographical text was written in 1859 by **Harriet E. Wilson**, a free black woman. After investigating, Gates showed that this was the first novel published by a black person in the United States. Gates wrote the first extensive critical commentary of *Our Nig* in *Figures in Black,* along with a biography of Wilson. It was only the second time Wilson's work had been written about. (EDITOR'S NOTE: Some scholars have raised questions about Wilson's authorship and her primacy, though Gates's claims remain widely accepted in the literary community.)

Gates has written extensively on the African-American vernacular. His writings also tackle topics ranging from the contentious issue of multiculturalism to the idea of race as a meaningful category in the study of literature and the shaping of critical theory. Gates won the American Book Award for *The Signifying Monkey: A Theory of Afro-American Literary Criticism* (1988). His other publications include *Bearing Witness* (1991) and *Colored People: A Memoir* (1994). In 1996, he published *The Future of the Race*

with **Cornel West**, who is a close colleague and professor of Afro-American studies and the philosophy of religion at Harvard. That year, Gates also published *Africa: The Art of a Continent.*

In 1981, Gates was chosen by the MacArthur Foundation as one of the exceptionally talented individuals to receive a research award. He has garnered many other awards, including the Zora Neale Hurston Society Award for Cultural Scholarship, a Ford Foundation National Fellowship, and grants from the National Endowment for the Humanities.

Gates has written numerous articles and edited a number of books. He is known as an expert on African-American–Jewish relations. He is the general editor of the *Schomburg Library of Nineteenth Century Black Women Writers* (1991) and of the *Norton Anthology of African American Literature* (1992). In the latter text, he attempts to define the canon of African-American literature for instructors and students at any institution. Gates said that he was especially driven to complete the book so that no one could ever again use the excuse of unavailability of texts in order not to teach about writings by African Americans. The book brings together the central authors who are essential for understanding the shape and shaping of the tradition. "A well marked anthology functions in the academy to define and create a tradition, as well as to define and preserve it," Gates said. "A Norton anthology opens up literary traditions as simply as opening the cover of a carefully edited and ample book" (Gates, 1992b, pp. 31–32).

EDITOR'S NOTE: Gates also edited *Classic Slave Narratives* (1987), a foundational work for U.S. literary scholarship. Other works of note are *Black Literature and Literary Theory* (1984) and *Encarta Africana* (1999). (See *BDAA, EA-99,* and *OCAAL.*)

—*Michael Strickland*

REFERENCES: Gates, Henry, Louis, Jr. (1987), *Figures in Black: Words, Signs and the Racial Self* (New York: Oxford University Press), pp. xvi, xvii. Gates (1992a), "A Giant Step," in William L. Andrews et al. (Eds.), *African American Literature* (Austin, TX: Holt, Rinehart and Winston). Gates (1992b), *Loose Canons: Notes on the Culture Wars* (New York: Oxford University Press), pp. 31, 32, 88.

Gayle, Addison, Jr. (6/2/1932–10/?/1991)
Literary criticism, essays, biographies, autobiography

Gayle's dedication to his literary endeavors started early: He completed a 300-page novel by the time he finished high school and wrote numerous short stories and poems before a single work of his was published. At last, in the 1960s, his works started to appear in **Hoyt Fuller**'s *Black World* (see **Negro Digest**). Later, he published anthologies of literary criticism he edited, *Black Expression: Essays by and about Black Americans in the Creative Arts* (1969) and *The Black Aesthetic* (1971). In his introduction to *The Black Aesthetic,* he wrote, "The question for the black critic today is not how beautiful is a melody, a poem, or a novel, but how much more beautiful has the poem, the melody, play, or novel made the life of a single black man." He also authored his essay collection, *The Black Situation* (1970); his literary history of African-American novels, *Way of a New World* (1975); his three literary biographies, *Oak and Ivy: A Biography of Paul Laurence Dunbar* (1971), *Claude McKay: The Black Poet at War* (1972), and *Richard Wright: Ordeal of a Native Son* (1980); and his autobiography, *Wayward Child: A Personal Odyssey* (1977).

REFERENCES: *AAW:AAPP.* Donaldson, Bobby, in *OCAAL.*

Geddes, Norman Bel (né Norman Melancton Geddes)

(4/27/1893–5/8/1958)
Autobiography, nonfiction

Geddes's books include his design for a revolutionary national traffic system, *Magic Motorways* (1940), and his autobiography, *Miracle in the Evening* (1960, edited by **William Kelley**).

REFERENCES: *E-97. EB-98.*

Gerima, Haile (3/4/1946–)

Screenplays

Gerima's films include *Harvest: 3,000 Years* (1974, filmed in his native Ethiopia), *Bush Mama* (1976), the documentary *Wilmington 10–USA 10,000* (1977), *Ashes and Embers* (1982), the documentary *After Winter: Sterling Brown* (1985), and *Sankofa* (1994). Films still in the works at the end of the twentieth century include *The Death of Tarzan, Donald Duck and Shirley Temple* (working title, about African film history), and *In the Eye of the Storm* (working title, about European colonization of Africa).

REFERENCES: Heath, Elizabeth, in *EA-99.*

Gibson, P. J. (Patricia Joann)

(c. mid-1900s–)
Plays

By the end of the twentieth century, Gibson had written at least 26 plays, many of which have been produced in countries around the globe. Some of these include *The Black Woman* (1971, as a one-act play; 1972, as a three-act play), companion one-act plays *Void Passage* and *Konvergence* (1973), *Miss Ann Don't Cry No More* (1980), *Brown Silk and Magenta Sunsets* (1981), and *Long Time Since Yesterday: A Drama in Two Acts* (1992). Other literary forms she has tried include poems, short stories, and a novel.

REFERENCES: Brown, E. Barnsley, in *OCAAL.*

Giddings, Paula (11/16/1948–)

Nonfiction—history; editor

In addition to serving as the Paris bureau chief for Encore America and Worldwide News, Giddings edits the *Afro-American Review.* Her work has also been anthologized and she has written such books as *When and Where I Enter: The Impact of Black Women on Race and Sex in America* (1984; 2nd ed., 1996), a history of African-American women, using primary documents (letters, speeches, diaries) written by such celebrated women as **Ida B. Wells**, **Zora Neale Hurston**, and **Shirley Chisholm**; *In Search of Sisterhood: Delta Sigma Theta and the Challenge of the Black Sorority Movement* (1994), a history of this prestigious organization of college-educated women; *Climbing Jacob's Ladder: The Enduring Legacy of African-American Families* (1994, with Andrew Billingsley), a history of African-American families, from their roots in Africa through slavery to the present; and *Regarding Malcolm X: A Reader* (1995, with **Cornel West**).

REFERENCES: *EBLG. TAWH.* Amazon.com, barnesandnoble.com, 8/1999.

Giovanni, Nikki (née Yolande Cornelia Giovanni, Jr.) (6/7/1943–)

Poems, essays, children's poetry books; publisher

> If I could come back as anything, I'd be a bird first, but definitely the command key is my second choice.
>
> —*Nikki Giovanni*

A small woman with towering talent, Nikki Giovanni is one of America's most respected poets.

Nikki Giovanni, 1973 (Archive Photos)

She is one among many notable African-American artists and writers who emerged from the 1960s **Black Arts movement**, a loose coalition of African-American intellectuals who wrote politically and artistically about black rights and equality. Like much of the literature of the 1960s and 1970s, Giovanni's poetry was colorful and combative. Her early poems dealt with the black social revolution, whereas her later works are more personal, focusing on the themes of childhood, family, and love. During the civil rights movement, her popularity soared and she became known as a poet of the people.

Born in Knoxville, Tennessee, Yolande Cornelia Giovanni, Jr., was the second child of Jones Gus, a probation officer, and Yolande Cornelia Giovanni, a social worker. In August of 1943, the family moved to the Lincoln Heights neighborhood of Cincinnati, Ohio, a place Giovanni still calls home. There, she remained in close contact with her maternal grandmother, Emma Louvenia (Luvenia Terrell) Watson, and spent summers and holidays with her in Knoxville.

Giovanni grew up in a happy, close-knit family. She was especially close to her older sister, Gary, who studied music and inherited her strong sense of racial pride from her grandmother, who instilled in her an intense admiration for and love of her race. Giovanni's grandmother Emma spoke her mind and was extremely intolerant of the way blacks were treated by whites. Once, her husband, John Brown, had to smuggle her and the rest of the family out of Albany, Georgia, because Emma's outspokenness had given them cause to worry that her life was in danger. The family finally settled in Knoxville, the first town they found to be large enough for them (Pellow, 1992).

At age 17, Giovanni enrolled in the all-black Fisk University in Nashville, Tennessee. There, eventually, her strong will and independent nature caused her to abide by her own rules, and she became involved in a conflict with the school's dean of women and was asked to leave (Giovanni, 1994, p. 179). Determined to receive her degree, in 1964, she returned to Fisk and became a dedicated student. She also joined the Writer's Workshop and restored Fisk's chapter of the Student Nonviolent Coordinating Committee (SNCC). As a teenager, Giovanni had been conservative in her outlook. In college, however, a roommate named Bertha succeeded in persuading Giovanni to adopt revolutionary ideals (Giovanni, 1994, p. 150).

In 1967, Giovanni graduated from Fisk with honors and a degree in history. Two years later, she gave birth to a son, Thomas Watson Giovanni. She later told *Harper's Bazaar,* "I can't imagine living without Tommy, but I can live without the revolution."

At age 25, Giovanni published her first volume of poetry, *Black Feeling, Black Talk* (1968/1969), which was later followed by *Black Judgement* (1968/1970) and *Re: Creation* (1970). These early poetry collections were highly popular among black audiences. They also established her as a prominent new voice in black poetry and led to numerous poetry readings and speaking engagements. (EDITOR'S NOTE: In 1970, Giovanni founded her own publishing company, Niktom— for Nikki and her son Thomas.)

In 1971, Giovanni began experimenting with sound recording, which led to *Truth Is On Its Way,* her best-selling spoken-word album of that time. The album features Giovanni reading her poetry accompanied by gospel music. She remarked to *Ebony* magazine that she chose this genre because she wanted to make something her grandmother would listen to. With the success of *Truth,* Giovanni went on to make subsequent recordings, as well as audio- and videotapes in which she discussed poetry and African-American issues with famous writers such as the legendary **James Baldwin**. (EDITOR'S NOTE: In 1973, Giovanni and Baldwin published *A Dialogue: James Baldwin and Nikki Giovanni,* which addressed race and gender issues among other topics.)

Giovanni is beloved for her poetry for children and has published several volumes of children's poetry: *Spin a Soft Black Song* (1971), *Ego-Tripping and Other Poems for Young People* (1973), *Cotton Candy On a Rainy Day* (1978), and *Vacation Time* (1979/1980). In fact, the places where she grew up often provide her with subject matter for much of her poetry for children. She has a sweet, mesmerizing ability to relate to children. When Nikki Giovanni speaks to kids, she hits that perfect pitch between irreverence and sincerity, humor and sensitivity, toughness and approachability (Pilson, 1997).

Her essays are popular as well. In 1988, she published *Sacred Cows . . . and Other Edibles,* a book of essays. *Racism 101,* her provocative collection of essays about race relations, was published in 1994, and she edited *Grand Mothers: A Multicultural Anthology of Poems, Reminiscences, and Short Stories about the Keepers of Our Traditions,* a heartwarming collection of essays about the special relationship between grandmothers and granddaughters. She published a collection of her works in *The Selected Poems of Nikki Giovanni* (1996). Her most recent book, *Love Poems* (1997), a tender collection of emotionally candid poems, features 20 new poems, including "All Eyez On You" written for the late rapper, **Tupac Shakur**.

Giovanni has been honored as woman of the year by such magazines as *Ebony, Essence,* and *Mademoiselle* and has received numerous other prestigious awards. She writes frequently for national magazines and scholarly journals, makes many stage and TV appearances, and gives inspirational lectures. She lives in Roanoke (Christiansburg), Virginia, and is a professor of English at Virginia Polytechnic Institute and State University in Blacksburg, Virginia. Today, her work remains an international treasure.

—*Brenda Pilson*

REFERENCES: Giovanni, Nikki (1994), in *Contemporary Authors New Revision Series* (Vol. 41, pp. 150, 179) (Detroit: Gale Research). Pellow, Arlene Clift, in *NBAW* (p. 404). Pilson, Brenda (1997), "The Reason She Applauds Reading," *Creative Classroom,* May/June, p. 31.

Goines, Donald (occasional pseudonym: "Al C. Clark")
(12/15/1937–10/21/1974)
Novels

In his novels, Goines wrote authoritatively about the life of crime and drug use in the streets of Detroit. A high school dropout, he had lied about his age to join the U.S. Air Force. While serving in Japan during the Korean War, Goines became addicted to heroin and remained addicted for the rest of his short life (except while he was in prison). Arrested 15 times, Goines was in prison six and a half years, serving seven different prison sentences for crimes he committed to support his addiction. While in prison, Goines started writing fiction. At first, he tried his hand at westerns and other novels, but he soon found these genres unsuitable. After reading **Iceberg Slim**'s *Trick Baby,* however, he turned to writing his novels about criminals and drug users in the ghettos of Detroit.

The first novel he wrote, *Whoreson: The Story of a Ghetto Pimp* (1972), was his most autobiographical work and the only one he wrote in the first person. Although *Whoreson* was the first novel he wrote, the first of his novels to be published was *Dopefiend: The Story of a Black Junkie* (1971), about the power of a drug dealer to rule the life of a drug user. In his next novel, *Black Gangster* (1972), he showed how American society makes it difficult for African-American males to succeed in legitimate business endeavors and revealed the temptations to turn to illegal ones instead. His next books were *Black Girl Lost* (originally published in 1973, reprinted in 1995), his only book written from a woman's point of view; *Street Players* (1973/1996); and *White Man's Justice, Black Man's Grief* (1973/1988), about the injustices of the bail bond system in a racist society.

For his next nine books, Goines's publisher (Holloway House) asked him to use a pseudonym, which he did, using his friend's name, Al C. Clark. These books included *Crime Partners* (1974/1995), *Cry Revenge* (1974/1996), *Daddy Cool* (1974/1996), *Deathlist* (1974/1996), *Eldorado Red* (1974/1992), *Kenyatta's Escape* (1974/1992), *Kenyatta's Last Hit* (published posthumously in 1975, reprinted in 1998), *Never Die Alone* (1974/1995), and *Swamp Man* (1974/1995). His last novel was *Inner City Hoodlum* (posthumously published 1975, reprinted in 1992). Goines's life was cut short when he and his live-in lover, Shirley Sailor, were both shot and killed at home. His books have never gone out of print, and, in fact, all of his works were reprinted as mass-market paperbacks in the 1990s, more than two decades after his death. Goines's publisher once claimed that he was the best-selling African-American author, and the fact that his books are still being reprinted for a mass market speaks volumes about his continuing popularity.

REFERENCES: *EBLG.* Matthews, Valerie N., in *OCAAL.* Amazon.com, 7/1999

Goldberg, Whoopi (née Caryn Johnson)
(11/13/1949–)
Comic sketches, memoir

Young Caryn was bright but dyslexic, so she had difficulties in school, but she excelled as a performer. A native of New York City, she had been a child actor (1958–1960) and had acted on Broadway in various plays. In 1974, she moved to California, where she was a founding member of the San Diego Repertory Theatre, adopted the stage name Whoopi Goldberg, and joined Spontaneous Combustion, an improvisational comedy troupe. Acting jobs for an African-American woman were difficult to find, however, and she increasingly worked on developing her own repertoire as an improvisational comedian.

Over time, Goldberg developed a series of distinct characters, through whom she offered her distinctively refreshing insights into contemporary life. In 1983–1984, she had developed her character monologues into a one-woman show, titled *The Spook Show,* and she took it on tour throughout the United States and Europe. Celebrated producer-director Mike Nichols saw her show in New York and got it moved to Broadway, where she expanded it and renamed it *Whoopi Goldberg* (1984–1985). Between the time Nichols saw her show and the time it opened on Broadway, Goldberg won a Bay Area Theatre Award for her show *Moms,* her one-woman play (cowritten with Ellen Sebastian) about deceased comedian Moms Mabley.

In 1985, Stephen Spielberg saw her show and invited her to star in *The Color Purple,* based on **Alice Walker**'s novel, for which Goldberg received a best actress Academy Award nomination, a Golden Globe award, and an NAACP Image Award. Through the rest of the 1980s and the 1990s, Goldberg performed and starred in dozens of films, some light (e.g., *Jumpin' Jack Flash,* 1986), some serious (e.g., as a housekeeper struggling to get by in the segregated South of the 1950s, in *The Long Walk Home,* 1990; and as **Myrlie Evers** in *Ghosts of Mississippi,* 1996). She also starred in a short-lived television program based on the film *Bagdad Café* and had a recurring part as a humanoid bartender on *Star Trek: The Next Generation.*

Although Goldberg won a Grammy for best comedy album in 1985, her successful acting career has led to neglect of her career as a comedian. Nonetheless, she continues to give performances for charitable events, such as *Comedy Relief* (which she, Billy Crystal, and Robin Williams cofounded), and as an emcee, such as for the Academy Awards. Her charming, vibrant live performances have not translated well to the printed page, however, and her books (e.g., her memoir *Book* [1997], some recipe books, and some children's story books) have not been well received. From her first (brief) marriage, Goldberg has a daughter, Alexandrea Martin.

REFERENCES: *G-97*. Bennett, Eric, in *EA-99*. Simmons, Simmona E., in *BH2C*. Thompson, Kathleen, in *BWA:AHE*.

Golden, Marita (1950–)
Novels, poems, memoirs, anthology

At age 29, Golden started writing her first memoir, *Migrations of the Heart* (1983); a little more than a decade later, she published a book on her experiences in raising her son, *Saving Our Sons: Raising Black Children in a Turbulent World* (1994). Soon after it was published, she started publishing her novels *A Woman's Place* (1986), *Long Distance Life* (1989), and *And Do Remember Me* (1992). She also edited an anthology, *Wild Women Don't Wear No Blues: Black Women Writers on Love, Men, and Sex* (1993). As of 1999, she was also president and chief executive officer of the Hurston/Wright Foundation.

REFERENCES: Browne, Phiefer L., in *OCAAL*. "African-Americans in the Publishing Industry," Book TV, C-SPAN2, 9/25/1999.

Gomez, Jewelle (1948–)
Poems, novels, short stories, essays

The works of **Nikki Giovanni**, **Audre Lorde**, and **Ntozake Shange** inspired Gomez to write about her own experiences and those of other African-American women. Her published works include her poetry collections *The Lipstick Papers* (1980) and *Flamingoes and Bears* (1987), her first novel *The Gilda Stories* (1991, winner of two Lambda literary awards), and her essay collection *Forty-three Septembers* (1993).

REFERENCES: Shockley, Ann Allen, in *OCAAL*.

Gordone, Charles
(10/12/1925–11/17/1995)
Plays

A native of the Midwest, Gordone has a mixed racial heritage, including French-, Irish-, African-American, and Native American ancestry. He felt accepted by neither the whites who dominated his home town nor the blacks whom he knew there. Still, he was an outstanding student and athlete and started at the University of California at Los Angeles before leaving school to serve in the air force. After the military, he studied music at Los Angeles City College and then earned a B.A. in drama from the state college in Los Angeles (1952). With his diploma in hand, he moved to New York City, where he waited on customers in a Greenwich Village bar while trying to make his way in the theater. For a time, he even managed his own theater, the Vantage, in Queens.

Meanwhile, Gordone was also writing plays. His *No Place to Be Somebody* (1969) was set in a bar similar to the Greenwich Village bar in which he had worked. That play was produced on Broadway and earned him a 1970 Pulitzer Prize for drama, making him the first African American to win this prize. Gordone's other dramas include *Gordone Is a Mutha* (1970), *Baba Chops* (1975), *The Last Chord* (1976), *Anabiosis* (1979), and two incomplete works: "Roan Brown and Cherry" and "Ghost Riders." In 1987, Texas A&M University named him a distinguished lecturer, and he taught English and theater there until he died.

REFERENCES: *EB-98*. Leonard, Charles, in *OCAAL*.

Graham, Lorenz (1/27/1902–1989)
Children's and juvenile literature, novels, short stories, folklore, biography

Among Graham's story collections are *How God Fix Jonah* (1946, including twenty-one biblical stories related in West African speech patterns); *Tales of Momolu* (1946); and *I, Momolu* (1966). His award-winning juvenile ("young adult") novels include his four-volume *South Town* series (*South Town*, 1958; *North Town*, 1965; *Whose Town?* 1969; *Return to South Town*, 1976) and a quartet of novelettes (1972). He also wrote an African tale, *Song of the Boat* (1975), and a biography, *John Brown: A Cry for Freedom* (1980). Graham's *How God Fix Jonah* included an introduction by **W. E. B. Du Bois**, who subsequently came to be Graham's brother-in-law (see **Shirley Graham Du Bois**).

REFERENCES: Williams, Kim D. Hester, in *OCAAL*. A. Q., in *CBC*.

Graham, Shirley (Lola)
See **Du Bois, Shirley (Lola) (née) Graham**

Granville, Evelyn (née) Boyd
(5/1/1924–)
Nonfiction—math

In addition to her scholarly publications, Granville coauthored *Theory and Application of*

Mathematics for Teachers (1975, with Jason Frand), a textbook widely used in colleges.

—*Tonya Bolden*

REFERENCES: *BAAW.* Kenschaft, Patricia Clark, in *BWA:AHE.*

Green, J. (Jacob) D. (?/1813–?)
Autobiography, slave narrative

Green's 43-page fugitive **slave narrative** is *Narrative of the Life of J. D. Green, a Runaway Slave* (1864), in which he candidly describes his three attempts at escape, the last of which proved successful due to his clever trickery.

REFERENCES: *NYPL-AADR.* Andrews, William L., in *OCAAL.*

Greenfield, Eloise (5/17/1929–)
Poems, short stories, children's books, memoir, biography

A versatile writer, Greenfield has produced several famous, critically acclaimed, award-winning books for children and has written an extensive list of honored picture books, biographies, essays, collections of poetry, and novels. Among the prestigious awards she has earned is the Carter G. Woodson Award for her biography, *Rosa Parks* (1973). Her *Paul Robeson* (1975) won the Jane Addams Children's Book Award. Three of her picture books received major citations: *She Come Bringing Me That Little Baby Girl* (1974) won the Irma Simonton Black Award, *Africa Dream* (1977) won the Coretta Scott King Award, and *Me and Neesie* was an American Library Association Notable Book.

Greenfield is also a master poet. Her verse collections include *Honey, I Love and Other Love Poems* (1978), *Under the Sunday Tree* (1988), and *Nathaniel Talking* (1988). The poems in *Nathaniel Talking* celebrate the life of an African-American boy, who shows the deep, gentle, and joyful feelings to which all children relate. Greenfield's recording of *Honey, I Love* has been widely praised by critics. Her first attempt at poetry, the book was twice named a Notable Book by the American Library Association and is the most popular of all Greenfield's books.

Greenfield was born in Parmele, North Carolina, at the beginning of the Great Depression. When she was four months old, her family moved to Washington, D.C. Her father had gone ahead a month earlier, looking for work. Once he found a job, he sent for Greenfield, her mother, and her brother, and she has lived there ever since.

Greenfield believes that during her early years, when she loved the words that she read, writing was being stored (Greenfield, 1983, p. 137). She dreaded writing but loved the sounds and rhythms of words while reading. Greenfield even liked strange things about language, such as homonyms and silent letters. The future author also grew fond of books and movies. It was by channeling her love of words into love for the craft of writing that Greenfield went on to become one of the most renowned modern authors for children.

The path to this high level of artistry was not easy, but the strife is what inspired Greenfield the most. Washington, D.C., was segregated when Greenfield grew up, and she regularly faced racist treatment. While her parents explained that the rude people were ignorant, the experience of oppression for being African American engendered in the author a serious commitment to uplift her community. Greenfield later described how she educated herself in her poor surroundings: "Until I was 14, there was no library within close walking distance of our house, so every few weeks my father would take us in the car to the nearest one to get a supply of books. Finally, though, a branch of the public library was opened in the basement of a nearby apartment building. For the next few years, I practically lived there, and I worked there part-time during the two years that I was in college" (1980, p. 143). Later on, on her way to becoming an outstanding prose artist and poet, she attended Miner Teacher's College. (EDITOR'S NOTE: Additional information about Greenfield's personal experiences may be found in her memoir, *Childtimes: A Three-Generation Memoir,* 1979.)

Part of Greenfield's overall inspiration came from music, which is still very important in her life. Greenfield took piano lessons and sang in her school's glee club. Early on, her only goal was to be the teacher in charge of plays and singing. Greenfield abandoned that limited career track as she grew into adulthood. In her early twenties, she began a search for satisfying work, which she later found in writing. The craft combined her enjoyment of sounds and rhythms with her interest in story and words. In a May 23, 1975, speech to the International Reading Association, she talked of this connection: "If you love home and you love music and you love words, the miracle is that the poet chose those words and put them together in that order, and it is something to shout about. I [feel] like the Southern Black preachers who, in reciting from the Scriptures, would suddenly be surprised by an old, familiar phrase and would repeat it over to savor and to celebrate this miracle of words."

Greenfield's bountiful spirit led her to make the change to a writing life in the 1960s, when she was married (husband, Robert) and raising two children (Monica and Steve) while holding a full-time civil service job. During that time, her husband and her children were the central focus of her life. Nonetheless, Greenfield's passion for writing continued to emerge. She believed that there were far too few books that told the truth about African Americans.

Bored with her civil service job as a clerk typist, Greenfield decided to write three stories. If none of them sold, she would give up writing and try something else. She received three rejection slips and thought she had no writing talent. During this time, Greenfield wrote in solitude, nervously avoiding discussion of her work with other writers. Eventually, she began to believe that talent must have direction. She pored over books about the craft, sought the ideas of other writers, and realized that she needed a knowledge of techniques in order to utilize her talent. Over the next several years, she read and spoke with many people about writing.

Greenfield's first publication was a poem that appeared on the editorial page of the *Hartford Times*. She then began to publish stories in the **Negro Digest**. Greenfield wrote one or two stories a year until she began writing for children. As an influential writer, she has also contributed to *Ebony Jr.!, Ms., Horn Book Magazine,* and *Interracial Books for Children Bulletin.*

In 1990, Greenfield received the Recognition of Merit Award presented by the George G. Stone Center for Children's Books in Claremont, California. Many other organizations have officially praised her, including the Council on Interracial Books for Children, the District of Columbia Association of School Librarians, and Celebrations in Learning.

Greenfield's work is shared and loved in schools and homes across the country. In addition, she has often found time to work with other writers. She headed the adult fiction and children's literature divisions of the D.C. Black Writer's Workshop. The group, which no longer exists, encouraged the writing and publishing of African-American literature. She does most of her workshops in the D.C. area but travels also, sometimes giving free workshops on writing African-American literature for children.

Greenfield is now a member of the African American Writers Guild. She was awarded grants from the D.C. Commission on the Arts and Humanities, for which she has taught creative writing to elementary and junior high students. Greenfield believes that the value of a book comes from its application. In keeping with this philosophy, she has taped her works for the blind and visits schools regularly. Greenfield told the *Washington Post* (Trescott, 1976) that "seeing the reaction to the words and the realism and respect that you have touched makes you feel like continuing."

EDITOR'S NOTE: See also *MAI-2,* for quotes and further information about Greenfield's writing and about her childhood.

—*Michael Strickland*

REFERENCES: Greenfield, Eloise (1983), in Sally Holtze (Ed.), *Fifth Book of Junior Authors and Illustrators* (New York: W. H. Wilson), p. 137. Greenfield (1980), in *Something about the Author,* Vol. 19 (Detroit: Gale Research), p. 143. Greenfield "Something to Shout About," speech given at the International Reading Association—Children's Book Council Preconvention Institute: Books Open Minds, in New York, May 23, 1975. Trescott, Jacqueline (1976), "Children's Books and Heroes," *Washington Post,* Friday, October 29.

Greenlee, Sam (7/13/1930–)
Poems, novels, essays, screenplays

Greenlee's published works include his novels *The Spook Who Sat by the Door* (1969, Meritorious Service Award) and *Baghdad Blues* (1976), his poetry collection *Blues for an African Princess* (1971), and his miscellany collection *Ammunition: Poetry and Other Raps* (1975).

REFERENCES: Macon, Wanda, in *OCAAL.*

Gregory, "Dick" (Richard Claxton) (10/12/1932–)
Comedy sketches, autobiography, political writings

After his father left his mother ("Momma") alone to raise Dick and his five siblings (three brothers and two sisters), Momma used the "relief" money from the "welfare" agencies—and a healthy dose of hope and humor—to raise all six children as ably and skillfully as she could. Dick described how she managed in his autobiographical book *Nigger* (p. 25): "Like a lot of Negro kids, we never would have made it without our Momma. When there was no fatback to go with the beans, no socks to go with the shoes, no hope to go with tomorrow, she'd say, 'We ain't poor, we're just broke.' Poor is a state of mind you never grow out of, but being broke is just a temporary condition. . . . She taught us that man has two ways out in life—laughing or crying. There's more hope in laughing."

Although his mother made sure he stayed in school, Dick had to begin earning money by shining shoes and doing sundry other jobs to help his mother support his siblings. Despite his impoverished circumstances, however, he "never learned hate at home, or shame." As he said, "I had to go to school for that" (*Nigger*, p. 29). In high school, Dick became involved in a variety of sports and social causes. His skill as a middle-distance runner earned him a 1951 athletic scholarship to Southern Illinois University. On the one hand, while there, he was welcome to participate in all athletic endeavors, and he was named the university's outstanding student athlete in 1953. On the other hand, he was prohibited from eating a celebratory meal with his white teammates in a local restaurant, and he was banned from sitting in the orchestra section (instead of the balcony) at the local movie house with his date.

In 1954, Gregory was drafted into the U.S. Army, where he spent two years. His natural sense of humor caught the attention of his colonel, who called Gregory into his office and said, "Gregory, . . . you are either a great comedian or a goddamned malingerer. There is an open talent show at the service club tonight. You will go down there, and you will win it. Otherwise, I will court-martial you. Now get the hell out of here" (*Nigger*, p. 90). Gregory won that show and the two shows after that, and then he was transferred to Special Services and thereafter hosted and performed comedy routines in military shows. By the time he got out of the military in the spring of 1956, he was an experienced stand-up comic. Although he briefly returned to his alma mater, he soon started his professional career in the private sector. By 1958, Gregory was serving as a master of ceremonies at various Chicago nightclubs.

Around April of 1958, Gregory met Lillian Smith, a secretary at the University of Chicago, after one of his nightclub acts. He saw her a few times, and then that summer, when he was hospitalized with jaundice for six weeks, she visited him. Over the next several months, they developed an on-again, off-again relationship. Then according

to Gregory, on Thursday, January 29, 1959, "I went to see Lillian Smith. . . . She had quit her job at the University and she was leaving town. I had to ask her twice before she told me why. 'I'm pregnant, Greg. I'm going to have a baby.'" Recalling his own fatherless childhood, he quickly decided what to do. "I asked Lil to marry me. She refused. She said she didn't want to do anything to stand in my way. This time I didn't ask her, I told her . . . , and on Monday, February 2, 1959, I was a married man" (*Nigger*, pp. 115–116). By 1964, Dick and Lil had four children: Michele, Lynne, and the twin babies Pamela and Paula. Sadly, however, their infant son, Richard, Jr., had died suddenly in 1962.

The year before his son's death, on January 13, 1961, Gregory got his big career break: What was meant to be a one-nighter at the Chicago Playboy Club ended up being a six-week gig, which netted him a prized appearance on the highly acclaimed *Jack Paar Show*, as well as a profile in *Time* magazine. From that point on, he was invited to appear on television, in nightclubs, on college campuses, and wherever his brand of comedy could be showcased.

Gregory avoided slapstick, stereotypical jokes, and personal jibes, and instead, his satirical sketches and routines bitingly attacked poverty, segregation, and racial discrimination.

Following is an outline of his sketch, as he described it in *Nigger*, pp. 132–133: First, he started out with a self-mocking comment, such as "Just my luck, bought a nice white suit with two pair of pants today . . . burnt a hole in the jacket." Next, he poked fun at the contemporary racial situation: "They asked me to buy a lifetime membership in the NAACP, but I told them I'd pay a week at a time. Hell of a thing to buy a lifetime membership, wake up one morning and find the country's been integrated." Then he'd get the members of the mostly white audience to laugh at themselves: "Wouldn't it be a hell of a thing if all this was burnt cork and you people were being tolerant for nothing?" After that, he could talk about virtually anything he wanted to—as long as he didn't stray into talking about sex, which would put him back into being stereotyped as a black comedian.

Once Gregory had achieved national prominence (e.g., being listed in the 1963 edition of *Who's Who in America*), he used his fame to benefit civil rights causes. During the 1960s, he participated in numerous demonstrations, was arrested for civil disobedience several times, and was even jailed for his activities. **Martin Luther King, Jr.**, never hesitated to call on Gregory to focus attention on civil rights activities, and Gregory was a close associate of Medgar Evers. Ironically, Evers was the person who had told Richard that Richard, Jr., had died, and soon after Gregory had buried his son, he got the call telling him that Medgar Evers had been murdered.

During the 1960s and 1970s, Gregory wrote several books, reflecting both his comedic outlook and his political views. For instance, he published *From the Back of the Bus* (1962); *Nigger: An Autobiography by Dick Gregory* (1964, with Robert Lipsyte); *Write Me In* (1968); *The Shadow That Scares Me* (1968); *No More Lies: The Myth and the Reality of American History* (1972); *Dick Gregory's Political Primer* (1972); *The Murder of Dr. Martin Luther King, Jr.* (1977); and *Code Name "Zorro"* (1978). Gradually, Gregory's focus shifted away from comedy and toward politics (although he briefly returned to the comedy circuit in the mid-1990s). In 1966, he ran for mayor of Chicago, and in 1968, he ran for president of the United States on the Peace and Freedom Party ticket. During the 1970s, he broadened the range of issues he opposed to include war and other forms of violence, capital punishment, drug abuse, and poor health care. Gregory also began fasting to call attention to the problems of world hunger, and he started to promote vegetarianism as a statement of nonviolence.

During the 1980s, he returned to distance running, and he taught himself to become an expert on nutrition. After he developed his own nutritional product, the "Bahamian Diet," he founded Dick Gregory Health Enterprises, both as a successful entrepreneurial enterprise and as a vehicle for promoting better health and longer life expectancy among African Americans.

REFERENCES: *EB-98. EBLG. G-95. WB-98.* Gregory, Richard (with Robert Lipsyte) (1965), *Nigger: An Autobiography of Dick Gregory* (New York: Pocket Books, paperback; New York: E. P. Dutton, 1964, hardcover).

Griggs, Sutton E. (Elbert)
(6/19/1872–1/3/1933)
Novels, essays, biographies; publisher

Among Griggs's 33 published books were 5 novels (*Imperium in Imperio*, 1899; *Overshadowed*, 1901; *Unfettered*, 1902; *The Hindered Hand*, 1905; *Pointing the Way*, 1908). Although Griggs's novels

and other works are little known now, his books sold well in his day, in part because this Baptist minister established his own publishing house (Orion Publishing Company, Nashville, Tennessee, 1908–1911) to promote their sale.

REFERENCES: *NYPL-AADR.* Elder, Arlene A., in *OCAAL.*

Grimké, Angelina Weld
See **Fortens, Grimkés, and Purvises**

Grimké, Angelina (Emily) (married name: Weld)
See **Fortens, Grimkés, and Purvises**

Grimké, Archibald Henry
See **Fortens, Grimkés, and Purvises**

Grimké, Charlotte L. Forten
See **Fortens, Grimkés, and Purvises**

Grimké, Francis J.
See **Fortens, Grimkés, and Purvises**

Grimké, Sarah (Moore)
See **Fortens, Grimkés, and Purvises**

Guinier, Lani (4/19/1950–)
Nonfiction—social and political issues

This provocative civil rights lawyer has published at least three books: *The Tyranny of the Majority* (1994), *Becoming Gentlemen: Women, Law School, and Institutional Change* (1997), and *Lift Every Voice: Turning a Civil Rights Setback into a New Vision of Social Justice* (1998). Guinier also cofounded the nonprofit organization Commonplace, dedicated to stimulating enlightened discussion of racial issues.

REFERENCES: *EA-99.* Amazon.com, 7/1999.

Guy, Rosa (née) Cuthbert (9/1/1925 or 1928–)
Novels—juvenile, play, anthology

Soon after Rosa was born, her parents, Audrey and Henry Cuthbert, emigrated to the United

States, leaving Rosa and her sister behind in Trinidad. Seven years later, the two girls emigrated to Harlem, New York City, to join their parents. Their family reunion was short-lived, however, as in 1933, their mother became ill, and the two girls were sent to live with a Garveyite cousin in Brooklyn. The next year, their mother died, their father remarried, and the girls returned to Harlem to live with their father and his new wife. Even this period of a blended family life was not to last long, however, as their father died in 1937, abandoning his daughters to life in an orphanage. When Rosa was only 14 years old, she left school to work in a brassiere factory in the garment district.

When Rosa was only 16—and still working in the factory—she met and married Warner Guy in 1941. The next year, Rosa gave birth to her only child, Warner, her husband's namesake. While she attended to Warner the younger (and continued to work in the factory), her husband was serving in the military in World War II. Rosa continued to work in the factory but sought creative ways to express herself. Young and energetic—and in need of creative and intellectual outlets—Rosa started attending classes at New York University (NYU). At about the same time, one of her coworkers introduced her to the relatively newly formed American Negro Theater (ANT). Rosa did not perform in any of the ANT productions (despite her youthful energy, the need to work and care for her child did impose *some* limits), but she did study acting with ANT. Her association with ANT and with NYU led her to start writing plays and short stories.

When the war ended and the soldiers returned home, Rosa, her husband, and her son moved to Connecticut. Sadly, Rosa was not able to forge a lasting family life in Connecticut to replace the family she missed as a child. In just five short years, her marriage disintegrated, and she and her son returned to New York, where she returned to work in a clothing factory. Unfortunately, by that time, her ANT family had also dispersed, but another organization, the Committee for the Negro in the Arts, had appeared in its place. The goal of the committee was to rid the arts of racial stereotypes. It was through Rosa's interactions with this group that she wrote and performed in her first play, *Venetian Blinds* (1954), a one-act play successfully produced off-Broadway by ANT at the Tropical Theater.

Through the committee, Guy also met various other writers, including **John Oliver Killens**, who was to play an important role in her life. In 1951, she and Killens founded a workshop for African-American writers, which soon became known as the Harlem Writers Guild. Among the many notable participants were **Maya Angelou**, **Audre Lorde**, **Paule Marshall**, and **Douglas Turner Ward**. In fact, some have estimated that at least half of all the African-American writers of note between 1951 and 1970 were linked to the guild's workshop. Both Killens and the guild offered Guy (the guild's president from 1967 to 1978) the nurture and encouragement she needed to pursue her writing craft while overcoming her lack of education and continuing to handle her responsibilities as a single parent and factory worker.

Although Guy may lack formal education, she clearly loves exploring language, and her mastery of it reflects both her natural talent and her lifelong self-education. In addition to speaking English, Guy speaks French and Creole, and she enjoys researching African languages as a relaxing pastime. She has further expanded her grasp of language as well as culture and folkways through her travels to Africa and to two Caribbean countries with deep roots in Africa: Haiti and her native Trinidad.

Guy's writing also reflects her personal history as a cultural outsider, a family outsider, and an urban dweller struggling to survive and to come into her own identity. Most of her books are centered around African-American or West-Indian–American youths who are facing great adversity in the inner city. After writing and publishing a couple of short stories, Guy tackled the novel form. *Bird at My Window* (1966), her tragic first novel, written for adults and dedicated to **Malcolm X**, despairingly showed how her protagonist, Wade Williams, was eventually crushed by oppressive poverty and racism in a Harlem ghetto. Although Guy wrote two other novels for adults—*A Measure of Time* (1983) and *The Sun, the Sea, a Touch of the Wind* (1995)—her focus shifted chiefly to young adults.

Like many other Americans, Guy was shaken by the assassinations of Malcolm X and of **Martin Luther King, Jr.**, and she decided to investigate how African-American youths (ages 13–23 years) viewed their world during the turbulent 1960s. She ventured into the American South, interviewed numerous youths, and then returned North to edit her volume *Children of Longing* (1970), a collection of essays synthesizing the firsthand accounts of young people's experiences, aspirations, and fears.

After finishing her essay collection, Guy traveled in the Caribbean and lived for a time in Haiti and in Trinidad, and several of her subsequent novels reflected her cultural experiences on these islands. Her trilogy *The Friends* (1973), *Ruby* (1976), and *Edith Jackson* (1978) describes the psychological development of three young girls within the context of race, gender, class, and cultural discrimination. As the trilogy opens, two sisters (Ruby and her younger sister, Phyllisia) emigrate from the West Indies to join their parents in Harlem. In Harlem, their mother is dying, so the two girls feel ill at ease at home and they feel like outsiders at school. (Wonder where she got that idea?) Edith Jackson, an outcast orphan herself, offers Phyllisia her friendship, but Phyllisia's father discourages that relationship. In the second novel, after Phyllisia and Ruby's mother dies, their domineering father raises them, and each of the girls finds her own path to escape from their situation. The third novel centers on young Edith, who vainly strives to keep her three younger sisters with her. Each of the novels was named the Best Book of the Year by the American Library Association at the time of publication.

Guy followed this dramatic trilogy with a trilogy of detective stories centered on Imamu Jones, a 16-year-old Brooklyn probationer who is trying to do well: *The Disappearance* (1979), *New Guys around the Block* (1983), and *And I Heard a Bird Sing* (1987). Guy also produced a variety of other books for young readers: *Mother Crocodile* (1981), a picture book adaptation of an African fable; and *My Love, My Love: Or the Peasant Girl* (1985), an adaptation of Hans Christian Andersen's "The Little Mermaid," set in the Caribbean. She also wrote several other novels for youths: *Paris, Pee Wee, and Big Dog* (1984), *The Ups and Downs of Carl David III* (1989), and *Billy the Great* (1991). In addition, Guy wrote *Caribbean Carnival: Songs of the West Indies* (1992), a collection of songs for children, *Mirror of Her Own* (1981), and *The Music of Summer* (1992).

REFERENCES: *AA:PoP. CBC. EB-98. EBLG. MAAL. MWEL. OC20LE.* Warren, Nagueyalti, in *OCAAL.*

Haley, Alex (Alexander Murray Palmer)
(8/11/1921–2/10/1992)
Autobiographical/biographical novels; reportage

Simon Henry Haley and Bertha George Palmer were both students in Ithaca, New York, where they met, married, and had young Alex. The young family soon moved to Henning, Tennessee, where Alex and his two brothers spent most of their childhoods. Although both of his parents were educators (his father a professor of agriculture and his mother a grade school teacher), Alex was less captivated by his schooling than he was by the stories of his ancestors, as told by his mother's mother, her sisters, and the other members of his large extended family. At age 15, he graduated from high school, started attending college in Mississippi, and then transferred to a teachers college in North Carolina. After a couple of years there, in 1939, he enlisted in the U.S. Coast Guard.

While in the Coast Guard, Haley started writing articles and short stories. After several years of writing and submitting his works for publication, he eventually started having some of his short stories printed in magazines such as *Coronet, Reader's Digest, Atlantic,* and *Harper's.* By 1952, the Coast Guard recognized his writing talents, and he was given a new title as chief journalist, handling public relations for the Coast Guard. After putting in his 20 years of service, Haley retired from the Coast Guard in 1959.

After retiring, Haley moved to New York City to pursue a writing career, with his Coast Guard pension as a financial safety net. As a freelance writer, he started out with assignments for *Reader's Digest,* and then went on to initiate a series of interviews (e.g., with Miles Davis, **Martin Luther King, Jr.**, Cassius Clay [later Muhammad Ali], and **Malcolm X**) for *Playboy* magazine. His interview with Malcolm X proved crucial to Haley's career,

as the two eventually established a collaboration that led to the writing of Malcolm's autobiography.

Although the famous Muslim leader was initially reticent to reveal much to Haley, over time Haley earned his trust, and through intensive interviews, he elicited from Malcolm the frank and engaging story of his life. Haley chronicled Malcolm's terrifying early childhood experiences as the son of a militant Garveyite preacher, his youth as an unrepentant criminal, his prison conversion to Islam as manifested by the Black Muslims, his increasing prominence as a spokesperson for the Black Muslims, and his eventual spiritual awakening to traditional Islam during his pilgrimage to Mecca. Tragically, Malcolm X (renamed El-Hajj Malik El-Shabazz following his sojourn to Mecca) was assassinated (by Black Muslims) before the book went into print, so he never saw how profoundly his autobiography influenced Americans of both black and white races. Nor did he know that his critically acclaimed book sold more than 6 million copies; was required reading in many college classes in literature, African-American studies, and contemporary history; was translated into at least eight languages; and was made into a popular movie (in 1992).

The success of Haley and Malcolm X's collaboration firmly established Haley's writing career, and he continued to publish short articles, including a *Saturday Evening Post* exposé of Elijah Muhammad and the Nation of Islam. When Haley considered what major project to tackle next, he soon recalled the stories of his ancestors, which his mother's mother's family members recounted to him during his childhood. With the success of *The Autobiography* and his military pension, Haley could afford to spend the time—and pay for research assistance—to probe his family's history and genealogy.

Haley ended up spending the next 12 years of his life investigating his family's past. His explorations took him to many libraries (e.g., the Library of Congress and the Daughters of the American Revolution Library) and archives, as well as to several countries in Africa and elsewhere. He even followed the approximate route that a slave ship might have taken from Africa to America, across the Atlantic Ocean. Haley was soon giving lectures about his research in the United States and Great Britain, and he was publishing numerous magazine articles on his findings. He was even awarded

Alex Haley received an honorary degree from the U.S. Naval Academy as President George Bush looked on, 1989 (UPI/ Corbis-Bettmann)

several honorary doctorate degrees recognizing his scholarship in African-American history and genealogy.

As might be imagined, there were many times when the research bogged down, when it was difficult to know how to proceed, or when Haley might have felt a little discouraged. On the other hand, he was encouraged when he found many of the people identified in his grandmother's stories listed in U.S. census records in our National Archives. He was able to trace much of his family's history in this way. How was he to trace his family back to Africa, however? Africa is a huge continent, and there is no continental archive listing all Africans who left for America.

Haley thought that perhaps the few words and expressions carried through the generations might be one way of finding out the *part* of Africa from which his ancestor originated. With a little diligence, he found someone who had studied African languages extensively. When he told this scholar the terms he had learned from his grandmother,

the scholar identified the terms as being Mandinka, a language spoken in modern-day Gambia and Senegal.

With that bitty clue in hand, Haley went to Gambia and searched for the equivalent of national archives: a griot, a storyteller whose job it is to memorize and recall the history of the persons in each village. After interviewing various village griots, he found one in the village of Juffure whose narrative matched what he knew of his own ancestor. The griot told of a youth named Kunta Kinte, whose capture and kidnapping matched the story relayed to Haley by his grandmother. The griot provided Haley with rich information on Kunta's biography in Africa, which complemented what Haley had heard and had been able to find out about Kunta after he left Africa. The story of Kunta Kinte formed the major part of Haley's historical novel *Roots:* We last read of Kunta Kinte, as his daughter Kizzy is torn from his arms, on page 453 of 729 pages. The remaining pages tell the story of Kizzy and her descendants, in addition to about 20 pages documenting Haley's own investigation into his family's history.

Initially, Haley's story was excerpted in *Reader's Digest* in 1974, so when it was finally published in the fall of 1976, the critics had already heralded its arrival, and *Roots: The Saga of an American Family* (1976) succeeded phenomenally well, winning special citations from the Pulitzer Prize and National Book Award committees and the National Association for the Advancement of Colored People's Spingarn Medal in 1977, being translated into 26 languages, and selling millions of copies. When the book was adapted to television as a miniseries (in 1977), about 130 million Americans watched at least one of the several episodes of the series, making it one of the most popular television shows in U.S. history. In recognition of *Roots,* the U.S. Senate passed a resolution honoring Haley, and a *Scholastic Magazine* survey of 4,000 college and university deans and department heads named Haley "America's foremost achiever in the literature category." Perhaps the greatest honor awarded to Haley was that his work prompted tremendous popular interest in Africa and in African-American genealogy and history among everyday Americans. Haley also reinforced the literary tradition of having his characters speak in the vernacular of the larger African-American community.

Not everyone praised Haley, however. At least two published authors (**Margaret Walker**, author of *Jubilee;* and Harold Courlander, author of *The African*) accused Haley of plagiarism. Haley eventually gave Courlander a large settlement, saying that his researchers had provided him with any of the questionable passages without citing Courlander as the source. Other critics have found serious flaws in his genealogical research, pointing to many discrepancies in his data and problems in his research methods. Others have pointed out that the griot Haley encountered may have known what Haley wanted to hear and therefore may have fabricated some of the story told to Haley. Further, the final book contains no bibliographical citations and did not show the rigorous type of research that would be expected for a scholarly work. Regardless of how we view the legitimacy and importance of these criticisms, Haley's story will continue to be a significant contribution to African-American literature, and its role in stimulating a national discussion of African-American history cannot be questioned.

Following *Roots,* Haley chiefly focused on various television productions (e.g., *Roots: The Next Generation* [1979], a sequel to the original *Roots* miniseries; *Roots: The Gift,* a story about a Christmas Eve slave escape involving two of the principal characters from *Roots*). When Haley died, he left several unfinished manuscripts; one of them, *Alex Haley's Queen* (1993), about the ancestors of his paternal grandparents, was subsequently finished and then published by David Stevens. A TV miniseries about the story was shown at about the time the book was published.

In addition to his manuscripts, Haley left his family behind. While in the Coast Guard, Haley had married Nannie Branch in 1941, and the pair had two children. In 1964, he divorced her and then married Juliette Collins, with whom he had one daughter. After they divorced, Haley eventually remarried for a third time, although he had no additional children. After Haley died of cardiac arrest, he was buried on the grounds of the Alex Haley Museum in Henning, Tennessee.

REFERENCES: *1TESK. ADD. BDAA. BF:2000. DA* (for *Roots* and for *Malcolm X*). *E-97. EB-98. EBLG. G-95. MAAL. OC20LE.* Berger, Roger A., in *OCAAL.*

Hamilton, Virginia (3/12/1936–)
Children's picture books and novels

Virginia Hamilton is a prolific children's author who has been honored with every prestigious award for writers of children's books. She is best known for her novel *M. C. Higgins, the Great* (1971), the first book to win both the National Book Award and the John Newbery Award. The Newbery Award is given annually for the most distinguished contribution to literature for children published in the United States. Hamilton raised the standards for children's literature. Her graphic descriptions of emotional and physical landscapes give the reader views of the real world and the fanciful world with equal and exceptional clarity.

Hamilton has attended to the heritage, culture, and pride of African-American history, writing or editing stories for many more than 30 children's books, including contemporary novels about teenagers and biographies of such historical figures as **Paul Robeson** and **W. E. B. Du Bois**. She has produced collections of African-American folklore and slavery-era "liberation" stories of people, including **Harriet Tubman**, **Sojourner Truth**, and **Frederick Douglass** as well as their lesser-known contemporaries such as Henry Box Brown.

Hamilton grew up on a small farm near the college town of Yellow Springs, Ohio, located just 60 miles north of the Ohio River—the legendary boundary between slave states and free ones. The town is an old station on the Underground Railroad where her maternal grandfather, Levi Perry, had settled after escaping from slavery in Virginia by crossing the Ohio River to freedom. Born into a big farm family, Virginia was the daughter of Kenneth James and Etta Belle (Perry) Hamilton. In addition to two older brothers and two older sisters, she was also surrounded by a large extended family of cousins, uncles, and aunts and by the sights, sounds, and smells of rural America. These experiences later played a large role in the children's stories Hamilton was to spin as an adult.

Nonetheless, the fact that her own parents were storytellers was probably the biggest influence on the author, whom *Entertainment Weekly* called "a majestic presence in children's literature." In her acceptance speech for the 1988 Boston Globe/Horn Book Award for nonfiction, Hamilton said, "The past moves me and with me, although I remove myself from it. Its light often shines on this night traveler: and when it does, I scribble it down. Whatever pleasure is in it I need pass on. That's happiness. That is who I am." Young Virginia, named for her grandfather's home state, listened at her mother's and father's knee: "My mother said that her father sat his ten children down every year and said, 'I'm going to tell you how I escaped from slavery, so slavery will never happen to you.'"

Hamilton received a full scholarship to Antioch College and after 3 years transferred to Ohio State University. She went on to the New School for Social Research in New York City where she continued her study of writing. In New York, she fell in love with a young poet, Arnold Adoff, whom she married in March 1960. The couple's honeymoon in Africa was another influence on her work. They began a life together in New York City and settled there for 15 years, writing as much as possible and making a living however they could. During those early years, Hamilton has related, she worked at such varied jobs as cost accountant for an engineering firm, nightclub singer, and museum receptionist. Virginia and Arnold have two children: a daughter, Leigh, and a son, Jaime Levi. In 1967, Virginia published her first book, *Zeely,* and shortly thereafter, she and her family moved back to Yellow Springs.

Zeely was praised for its promotion of racial un-

derstanding. The novel tells the story of 11-year-old Elizabeth ("Geeder") Perry, who sees a portrait of a beautiful Watusi queen. She fantasizes that her six-and-a-half-foot-tall neighbor, Zeely Tayber, is also a Watusi queen, only to find out that she actually is. Geeder watches the beautiful Zeely walk at night, and she frightens her brother with stories about night travelers. Zeely helps Geeder understand the difference between fantasy and reality, and she leads Geeder to an even greater understanding of herself and the beauty of being who you are.

"*Zeely* was one of the very first books where black characters are simply being people and living; it's not a problem book about integration," Hamilton said. As a result, *Zeely* attracted considerable attention. Written during an era when racial strife roiled the country, along with a rising credo of "black is beautiful," the time was right for the novel.

In 1968, Hamilton published *The House of Dies Drear,* a mystery centering on the Underground Railroad. Rich with the historical research that would characterize many of Hamilton's subsequent works, the story of this house, which held an incredible secret, reflected the stories of liberation Hamilton grew up with in Yellow Springs. The book earned Hamilton the Edgar Allan Poe Award for best juvenile mystery of the year.

The isolated individual is the focus of *The Planet of Junior Brown* (1971), a story of urban life in New York in which lonely people find support in each other. In contrast, family is the emphasis of *M. C. Higgins, the Great* (1971); in fact, family is an important theme in most of Hamilton's books. This novel is set in southern Ohio, where 13-year-old Cornelius Higgins and his close-knit family live on old family property just beneath a slag heap (created by strip miners). The slow-moving heap threatens to engulf their home, and M. C. dreams of moving his family to safety. He surveys the world from a bicycle seat perched atop a 40-foot steel flagpole, his place of refuge. From there, M. C. sees a "dude" he imagines will make his mother a singing star and enable them to move. Another outsider, Luthreta, who is hiking through this section of Appalachia, awakens M. C. to the reality that he is never going to solve his problems by daydreaming about them. This moves M. C. to finally take a small but symbolic action.

In many of her books, Hamilton mixes realism, history, and folklore. *Justice and Her Brothers* (1978), *Dustland* (1980), and *The Gathering* (1981) are fantasy novels composing the "justice" trilogy. They deal with time travel, clairvoyance, and global disaster. *The Time Ago Tales of Jadhu* (1969) mimics traditional **folktales** while containing elements of fantasy. Other Hamilton books include *Bells of Christmas* (1990), *The Dark Way: Stories from the Spirit World* (1993), and *Plain City* (1993), a book in which Hamilton takes up the issues of homelessness and racial prejudice; *Jaguarundi* (1995), a picture book for young children, in which an animal tale offers an environmental slant on Hamilton's liberation theme; *Her Stories, African American Folktales, Fairy Tales, and True Tales* (1995), which won the Coretta Scott King Award; and *When Birds Could Talk and Bats Could Sing* (1996). (EDITOR'S NOTE: Three of the many other books by Hamilton are her *The People Could Fly: American Black Folktales* [1985], her Newbery Honor Book *In the Beginning: Creation Stories from Around the World* [1988], and her *Many Thousands Gone: African Americans from Slavery to Freedom* [1993], each of which is a narrative for juveniles.)

Hamilton has also edited numerous publications of the United States Committee for Refugees and writes reviews of books related to the history of the American South. She was awarded a MacArthur Foundation grant in 1995 and was the first African-American writer to receive the John Newbery Award (in 1967). She has also earned the American Book Award, the Boston Globe–Horn Book Award, the National Book Award, the Laura Ingalls Wilder Medal (in 1995), and the most prestigious of all, the Hans Christian Andersen Medal. Her books are frequently placed on the American Library Association's list of Notable Books and Best Books for Young Adults.

Hamilton has been instrumental in filling the glaring lack of children's literature about the ethnic experience that existed until recent years. One way she has helped do this has been by lending her name to an annual conference on multicultural children's literature, which helps writers to follow her lead.

—*Michael Strickland*

REFERENCES: *MAI-2.* Cullinan, Bernice E., and Lee Galda (1994), *Literature and the Child* (Orlando, FL: Harcourt Brace). *Entertainment Weekly,* February 5, 1993. Hamilton, Virginia (1967), *Zeely* (New York: Macmillan). Hamilton, Virginia (1974), *M. C. Higgins, the Great* (New York: Macmillan). Hamilton, Virginia (1996), "Home Page Away from Home," http://www.cris.com/~Bonfire2/index.shtml.

Huck, Charlotte S., Susan Helper, Janet Hickman, and Barbara Z. Kiefer (1997), *Children's Literature in the Elementary School* (Dubuque, IA: Brown and Benchmark Publishers).

Hammon, Briton (fl. 1700s)
Memoir

All we know of Briton Hammon is contained in his 14-page memoir, *A Narrative of the Uncommon Sufferings, and Surprising Deliverance of Briton Hammon, A Negro Man—Servant to General Winslow* (printed in Boston in 1760). From it, we learn that he lived as a slave, obtained permission to leave his master's service to go to sea, and sailed to Jamaica on Christmas Day, 1747. On his return to the mainland, his ship—heavily laden with wood—got caught on a reef off the coast of Florida. The captain refused to dump any of the cargo, choosing instead to send some of his crew ashore in a small boat. When a landing party approached the shore, natives from the mainland chased them back to the ship and killed the captain and all his fellow crew members. He managed to escape being killed, only to be held captive by them. Although he describes them as "barbarous and inhuman Savages" and "Devils," his description of their treatment of him is rather mild, noting that they fed him what they ate and "us'd me pretty well." After a time, some Spaniards helped him to escape to Havana, where the "Indians" pursued him. The Cuban governor refused to turn him over to them. Following a series of misadventures (including several years of wrongful detainment), Hammon managed to make his way to England. Next, he got work on a vessel headed back to Boston, only to find that his old master was a passenger, too. Hammon expressed his gratitude that "Providence" delivered him back into the hands of his master. Although this narrative is often cited as the first African-American **slave narrative**, many have questioned whether Hammon himself authored it.

REFERENCES: *BAL-1-P.* Williams, Roland L., Jr., in *OCAAL.*

Hammon, Jupiter (10/17/1711–c. 1806)
Poems, essays, political writings

A slave all his life, Hammon was well educated, and his intellect was given free expression within the circumstances to which he had adapted. A modest man who had become a deeply religious and devout Christian, Hammon wrote profoundly religious poems and essays. For a slave to be well educated and to write poetry was quite unusual, but Hammon went on to do something even more unusual: He had his writings published. The first literary work written by an African American and published in the United States was Hammon's 88-line "An Evening Thought. Salvation by Christ with Penitential Cries: Composed by Jupiter Hammon, a Negro belonging to Mr. Lloyd of Queen's Village, on Long Island, the 25th of December, 1760." The poem was published as a *broadside* (a work printed on single large sheet of paper) in 1761. Although he probably wrote many poems in the interim, the next published poem of Hammon's that survives to this day was written for the other famous African-American poet of his day: "An Address to Miss Phillis Wheatly [*sic*], Ethiopian Poetess, in Boston, who came from Africa at eight years of age, and soon became acquainted with the gospel of Jesus Christ" (1778). As is so often the case with trailblazers, he is better known for being first than for being foremost. His poems are simple and straightforward, focused on a single theme; subsequent literary critics have compared his verse rather unfavorably with that of his contemporary **Phillis Wheatley** as well as with those who followed him.

Actually, **Lucy Terry [Prince]**'s poetry predates the work of both Hammon and Wheatley, and she is therefore the first African American to have written poems that survive to this day, but her poetry was published after that of both Hammon and Wheatley. Thus, Hammon was the first African American to have his writings published, and Wheatley was the first African-American woman to have her works published. Two other poems of Hammon's are still extant: "A Poem for Children with Thoughts on Death" (1782) and "A Dialogue Entitled the Kind Master and Dutiful Servant" (1786). From the title of the 1786 poem, you may correctly infer that he recommended that slaveowners be kind to their slaves, but he also urged slaves to be patient in waiting for the bonds of slavery to be lifted. After all, he believed, they would be free forever in the world hereafter. He expressed these views in his *Address to the Negroes of the State of New York,* presented at the September 24, 1786, meeting of the African Society in New York City (published in 1787 and again in 1806). He did lament, however, that the patriotic African Americans who had fought in the Revolutionary War

were not freed following the war, and he wished that slaveowners would free their young slaves. Hammon's prose works include *A Winter Piece: Being a Serious Exhortation, with a Call to the Unconverted* (c. 1782); *A Short Contemplation on the Death of Jesus;* and *An Evening's Improvement, Showing, the Necessity of Beholding the Lamb of God* (c. 1783). In addition, *An Essay on the Ten Virgins* was advertised in a December 1779 issue of the *Connecticut Courant* but has still not been found in printed form.

REFERENCES: *AAW:AAPP. BAL-1-P. BWA. EBLG. G-97.* O'Neale, Sondra, in *OCAAL.* Robinson, Lisa Clayton, in *EA-99.*

Handy, W. C. (William Christopher)
(11/16/1873–3/28/1958)
Songs, musicology, autobiography

A masterfully musical horn man, Handy realized that he would do better to publish his own music than to have someone else publish it, giving him just a small portion of the profits. Hence, in 1908, he and lyricist Harry H. Pace cofounded the song-publishing outfit Pace and Handy Music Company. Their company published countless blues and ragtime songs, including many he wrote himself (e.g., "Memphis Blues," reportedly the first blues song to be published as sheet music; as well as "Aunt Hagar's Children's Blues," "Joe Turner's Blues," "Beale Street Blues," and "St. Louis Blues"). He was able to claim the title "Father of the Blues" not only for the blues he wrote and played, but also for his writings, including *Blues: An Anthology* (1926), *Book of Negro Spirituals* (1938), and *Father of the Blues* (1941, his autobiography).

EDITOR'S NOTE: In 1898, Handy married his long-time girlfriend Elizabeth Price, and they raised their six children together before she died in 1937. In 1954, Handy married Irma Louise Logan. For much of his adult life, he was partially or totally blind. (See *BDAA.*)

—*Tonya Bolden*

REFERENCES: *DANB. EAACH. EA-99. SMKC.*

Hansberry, Lorraine (Vivian)
(5/19/1930–1/12/1965)
Plays, essays, news articles, poems, reviews; editor

Lorraine Hansberry's writing was profoundly influenced by her family elders. Her uncle Leo Hansberry was a scholar of African history at Howard University, so Lorraine learned from an early age to link the experiences and challenges of African Americans with those of Africans struggling for liberation in their native land. Lorraine's mother, Nannie Perry Hansberry, was a schoolteacher, an influential politician, and a prominent society matron (entertaining in their home such cultural luminaries as poet **Langston Hughes**, scholar **W. E. B. Du Bois**, actor **Paul Robeson**, musician Duke Ellington, and novelist **Walter White**). The educational and cultural opportunities Lorraine's mother provided enriched the texture of Lorraine's writing.

When Lorraine was a young girl, her father, Carl Augustus Hansberry, Sr., was a realtor who specialized in subdividing large houses vacated by whites and selling the subdivided kitchenette units to African Americans migrating from the South. He was also a civil rights activist, and these two roles combined to have a tremendous impact on Lorraine's childhood experiences. When Lorraine was just eight years old, the National Association for the Advancement of Colored People (NAACP) sponsored her father to challenge Chicago's discriminatory housing covenants—written agreements that prohibited African Americans and other people of color from moving into segregated European-American neighborhoods. With that support, Carl moved his wife and children into Hyde Park, a wealthy whites-only Chicago neighborhood. Needless to say, the Hansberrys weren't greeted with a welcome wagon at their front door. Instead, threats and curses were hurled at the family members, and bricks were tossed at—and into—their home, one brick (thrown through the front window) just barely missing young Lorraine. The NAACP even had to provide armed guards to protect the family for a time. Not long after, an Illinois court evicted the Hansberrys from the home they had purchased, enforcing the city's covenants. This eviction started a two-year-long judicial crusade, which ended up in the U.S. Supreme Court. At last, the most exalted court in the land upheld the Hansberrys' right to live in whatever neighborhood they chose, and it overturned Chicago's segregationist covenants as being unconstitutional.

Unfortunately, the precedent of the *Hansberry v. Lee* decision was not widely applied until further court cases broadened its applications. The whole experience so deeply discouraged Carl Hansberry that he was preparing to move away from an America he deemed hopelessly racist to go to Mexico, when a cerebral hemorrhage suddenly

Lorraine Hansberry, first African-American woman to have a play on Broadway, 1959 (UPI/Corbis-Bettmann)

killed him at age 51. The integration experience also profoundly affected Lorraine, who never forgot the daily hostility she felt as she walked to and from the local school. Once the Hansberrys returned to a working-class community, Lorraine and her two older brothers and older sister attended public schools. Although the Hansberry children continued to enjoy cultural and financial privileges unknown to their working-class schoolmates, their parents taught them to take pride in their race and to admire the courage shown by their working-class peers. The Hansberry children were also encouraged to show civic responsibility, challenging discriminatory practices wherever they met them—such as at local stores and restaurants.

After high school, Lorraine decided not to follow the family tradition of attending a black college, and she enrolled at the University of Wisconsin at Madison, a predominantly white university, to study journalism (as well as theater and the visual arts). At Madison, she integrated an all-white women's dormitory and was soon active in leftist politics, becoming the president of the Madison campus chapter of the Young Progressive Association. She also saw a production of Sean O'Casey's *Juno and the Paycock,* which portrayed the struggles, hopes, and dreams of Irish peasants; his play inspired Hansberry to consider how to depict dramatically the strivings, hopes, and dreams of working-class African Americans. Meanwhile, she noticed she was more interested in stage design than in other subjects, so she decided to pursue painting more rigorously, studying art at Chicago's Art Institute and in a school in Guadalajara, Mexico. After exploring her talents at art, however, she decided that she wasn't talented enough to make it her chief occupation, so she quit studying art and moved to New York.

In New York, Hansberry found odd jobs to support herself while she perfected her skill as a writer. She frequently published articles, essays, reviews, and poetry in progressive periodicals such as Paul Robeson's *Freedom*. *Freedom* soon hired Hansberry as a reporter and then as associate editor. When Robeson was unable to attend an' international peace conference in Uruguay (because the U.S. State Department had revoked his passport), Hansberry went in his place. During this time, her civil rights activism intensified, and she read ever more widely the works of African Americans (e.g., W. E. B. Du Bois, **Frederick Douglass**, and Langston Hughes). She also studied whatever she could find about African-American history, politics, and culture, and she increasingly spoke out at public rallies and meetings, attacking U.S. policies she deemed racist or imperialist.

While participating in a civil rights demonstration at New York University (NYU), Hansberry met Robert Barron Nemiroff, the son of Russian Jewish immigrants, who had just earned his master's degree at NYU. The two courted briefly, then married on June 20, 1953, and moved to Greenwich Village. While Nemiroff pursued a career as a songwriter and music publisher, Hansberry left *Freedom* to write more creatively, such as sketches about the people and lifestyles she observed in Greenwich Village. Nemiroff also encouraged Hansberry to pursue her goal of writing a play. When one of Nemiroff's ballads became an instant hit, he offered financial support as well as emotional and intellectual support to Hansberry. Freed from having to earn a living, Hansberry devoted herself fully to writing her first play: *A Raisin in the Sun*. (In the early 1960s, after Hansberry had recognized and acknowledged her own lesbianism, she and Nemiroff divorced, but the two remained close friends.)

By 1957, Hansberry completed her play. Her title comes from Langston Hughes's collection *Harlem:* "What happens to a dream deferred? / Does it dry up / Like a raisin in the sun . . . ?" Fortunately, after she read her play to a friend of hers, her friend agreed to produce it. The play was a smash hit in its trial runs in New Haven, Philadelphia, and Chicago, and the rave reviews helped her garner enough financial support to produce the play on Broadway in 1959, starring Sidney Poitier, **Ruby Dee**, and other outstanding actors.

What was the underlying story of this smash hit? The play was set in Chicago in the 1940s and showcases a working-class black family contemplating a move from a Chicago ghetto to a white-dominated Chicago suburb. The play opens as the recently widowed Lena Younger realizes that the payment from her deceased husband's insurance policy is enough to fulfill her husband's lifelong wish to buy a home in an upscale neighborhood. Lena's son, Walter, has other plans for the money. He sees it as his once-in-a-lifetime chance to take advantage of a business opportunity. The play revolves around these hopes and dreams of the principal characters, as well as the feelings and longings of Walter's sister Beneatha, his wife Ruth, and his son Travis.

In addition to Hansberry's expert crafting of the drama, the play arrived at a propitious time in U.S. history, closing out a decade in which African Americans were celebrating the *Brown v. Board of Education* Supreme Court decision (1954) and the successful Montgomery (Alabama) bus boycott (1955–1956), and heralding a decade of civil rights activism among both whites and blacks, including student sit-ins, Freedom Riders, and Freedom Summer. For all these reasons, *Raisin* instantly achieved critical, popular, and financial success. The play's 538 performances across 19 months made *Raisin* the longest-running play by an African American on Broadway. At age 29, Hansberry became the youngest person, the first African American, and the fifth woman to win the New York Drama Critics Circle Award for the Best Play of 1959, surpassing plays by Tennessee Williams and Eugene O'Neill. The play was later (1961) made into a movie starring Poitier (which won a special award at the Cannes film festival) and into a Tony Award–winning musical (in 1973).

Following Hansberry's success with *Raisin,* NBC commissioned her to write a drama commemorating the one-hundredth anniversary of the Civil War. The network executives judged her resulting drama, *The Drinking Gourd,* "superb," but because of her frank treatment of slavery, the executives decided not to produce it. Another of Hansberry's works, *What Use Are Flowers?* (written in 1962, published in 1972), about the aftermath of nuclear war, was also never produced.

The next play of Hansberry's to be produced was *The Sign in Sidney Brustein's Window* (1964). She set the play in Greenwich Village, the racially (and religiously) mixed community in which she lived. The title character is a Jewish liberal intellectual who continually fluctuates between his political conviction and commitment to action and his sense of disillusionment and existentialist apathy. This play opened in mid-October 1964, earning mixed reviews, and it closed on January 12, 1965—the same day that Hansberry died of cancer.

When Hansberry died at age 34, she left several unfinished plays, including *The Arrival of Mr. Todog,* a satire of Samuel Beckett's *Waiting for Godot;* a play about the eighteenth-century feminist Mary Wollstonecraft; and *Les Blancs.* Hansberry left her works in good hands, designating her ex-husband, Robert Nemiroff, the literary executor of her estate. Nemiroff took his role very seriously and spent the rest of his life devoted to completing, publishing, and producing her works. Among other works, he gathered her essays and articles against racism, homophobia, war, and oppression into the books *To Be Young, Gifted and Black* and *The Movement: Documentary of a Struggle for Equality.* Hansberry's legacy lives on through the work of others, as well. **Woodie King, Jr.,** discovered that two thirds of the contemporary playwrights he questioned acknowledged that Hansberry had either aided them directly or influenced them in their work.

REFERENCES: *1TESK. AA:PoP. BF:2000. BDAA. E-97. EB-98. EBLG. G-95. MAAL. NAAAL. OC20LE. RLWWJ. WB-98.* Clark, Keith, in *OCWW.* Wilkerson, Margaret B., in *OCAAL.*

Hansen, Joyce (1942–)
Novels

While teaching middle school students identified as learning disabled, Hansen was reminded of the importance of having interesting, motivating reading materials for students who found reading to be burdensomely difficult. Dissatisfied with the relative paucity of stimulating stories about nonwhite youths from low-income areas, she decided to write her own. Her novels—known for their realistic experiences and settings, their authentic dialogue, and believable characters—include *The Gift-Giver* (1980), its sequel *Yellow Bird and Me* (1982), and *Home Boy* (1982). Her historical novels include *Which Way Freedom?* (1986), its sequel *Out from This Place* (1988), and *The Captive* (1994). Hansen also published a nonfiction history book, *Between Two Fires: Black Soldiers in the Civil War* (1994).

REFERENCES: Foster, Frances Smith, in *OCAAL.*

Hare, Maud (née) Cuney
(2/16/1874–2/13/1936)
Play, anthology, criticism, columns, nonfiction—music, history, folklore, biographies

Coming from a musical family and following her own talent, Maud Cuney studied at the New England Conservatory of Music. After the conservatory, one of her first jobs was to direct music at the Deaf, Dumb, and Blind Institute in Austin. When she was in her early thirties, she married William P. Hare and returned to New England.

Over the next three decades, Hare contributed greatly to music history and criticism as well as to literature, writing a regular column for ***Crisis***. She poured into her writings the wealth of folk songs and dances she had collected in Mexico and the Caribbean, tracing the African origins of many works. In her masterwork *Negro Musicians and Their Music* (1936, published just one month before her death), she provides priceless information on African-American performers, shows how many African-American musical expressions have African origins, and even offers an appendix of African musical instruments. Her medley of other offerings illustrates the breadth and range of this talented woman, including her biography of her father, *Norris Wright Cuney: Tribune of the Black People* (1913); her anthology of poems, *The Message of the Trees: An Anthology of Leaves and Branches* (1918); her musicological text, *Creole Songs* (1921); and her play, *Antar of Araby* (1929).

—*Tonya Bolden*

REFERENCES: *BAAW.* Koolish, Lynda, in *OCAAL.* Roses, Lorraine Elena, in *BWA:AHE.*

Hare, Nathan (4/9/1934–)
Nonfiction—sociology, psychology; journal founder

In addition to founding ***Black Scholar*** and the *Journal of Black Studies and Research* (in 1969), Hare started the African-American studies department at San Francisco State University. Hare has also published several books. For instance, he coedited *Pan-Africanism* (1974) and wrote *The Black Anglo-Saxons* (1965). With his wife, writer Julia Reed Hare, he wrote *The Endangered Black Family: Coping with the Unisexualization and Coming Extinction of the Black Race* (1984), *Bringing the Black Boy to Manhood: The Passage* (1987), and *The Hare Plan to Overhaul the Public Schools and Educate Every Black Man, Woman, and Child* (1991).

REFERENCES: *EBLG*.

Harlem Renaissance (1919–1940)

Within the African-American community, a cultural movement called the Harlem Renaissance emerged in the United States during the 1920s. The renaissance called for greater awareness, increased artistic activity, and overt political commentary by African Americans about racial discrimination, racial disparities in policy and practice, and insulting caricatures of blacks. Black artists consequently saw an opportunity and responsibility to influence prevailing views about themselves and their community through art. During the renaissance, many African-American artists moved to urban areas, including Harlem, New York, and Chicago, and produced an unprecedented amount of creative, culturally affirming works. These works are of varying genres, but all attempted to use art to highlight oppression and prejudice while promoting African Americans and their culture in a logical, artistic fashion.

The Harlem Renaissance, generally considered the first significant movement of black writers and artists in the United States, emerged during the Great Migration from the rural South to the urban North following the end of World War I, and these two events contributed to its emergence. By 1920, a series of agricultural crises, coupled with a labor shortage in the Northern industrial centers, had led approximately 2 million African Americans to move from the rural South to the urban North in search of jobs and a better life. Their participation in the urban industrial workforce resulted in greater racial cohesiveness and economic independence. This met with resistance from some conservative whites, provoking a revival of the Ku Klux Klan and an outbreak of racial violence.

This period of social conflict and upheaval inspired black intellectuals to reexamine their role in American society and their unique cultural heritage. Lured by the promise of employment, African Americans migrated to cities such as Chicago, Cleveland, Detroit, Philadelphia, and—especially—New York City. African Americans had fought in World War I to make the world safe for democracy but returned home to be confronted with racism, unemployment, and poverty. Furthermore, their racial identity had been solidified by their experiences in Europe, which had made them more aware of this country's prejudices. "The war to end all wars" had made them more eager than ever to change their condition. After World War I, African Americans began to fully recognize that racism and poverty could not take away their culture, which they prized increasingly.

First called the New Negro Movement, the Harlem Renaissance was a dramatic upsurge of creativity in African-American literature, music, and visual art. The word *renaissance* means rebirth, but the Harlem Renaissance was more of a birth, unprecedented in its variety and scope, than a rebirth. Its participants celebrated the uniqueness of African-American poetry, fiction, drama, essays, music, dance, painting, and sculpture. Such flowerings of unusually fertile cultural activity are often referred to as times of renaissance.

The celebration of African-American culture came at a time in U.S. history when the restraints of the Victorian era were giving way to the boldness of the Roaring Twenties. During this period, the first influential African-American literary journals were established, and African-American authors and artists received their first serious critical appraisal and widespread recognition. New and established African-American writers published more fiction and poetry than ever before.

Many young African-American writers came into prominence during the Harlem Renaissance. Both black and white readers were eager to experience a slice of African-American life, and the literature of the time provided that experience. The most popular and prolific poet of the 1920s was **Langston Hughes**, whose work delves into the lives of the black working class. **Arna Bontemps**'s poems "The Return" and "Golgotha Is a Mountain" won awards given by *Opportunity* magazine. Another major figure of the period, **Countee Cullen**, wrote poems exploring the problem of racism and the meaning of Africa for African Americans. Among fiction writers, **Claude McKay** stands out as author of *Home to Harlem* (1928), the first commercially successful novel by a

Harlem, site of the Harlem Renaissance in the early twentieth century (UPI/Corbis-Bettmann)

black writer. Other notable novels of the era include **Nella Larsen**'s *Passing* (1929), which focuses on sophisticated middle-class black women who are unable to escape the restrictions of racism; and **Jean Toomer**'s innovative novel *Cane* (1923), which demonstrates a strong identification with poor blacks. Many other authors, including poet **James Weldon Johnson**, folklorist **Zora Neale Hurston**, novelist **Rudolph Fisher**, poet **Georgia Douglas Johnson**, poet and critic **Sterling Brown**, and editor and novelist **Jessie Redmon Fauset**, received recognition for their poetic short stories, dramas, and novels. Essayist **Eric Walrond**, novelist **Walter White**, and poet William Waring Cuney are just some of the other writers associated with the Harlem Renaissance.

To carve a niche for themselves in the literary scene, young, educated African Americans traveled to New York City, in particular to Harlem, which was the cultural and artistic center for African Americans. Something approaching cultural revolution took place. Although a few other centers

approached Harlem's significance, they served chiefly to accentuate the importance of the Harlem Renaissance as a racial awakening on a national and perhaps even a world scale. The national scope of the phenomenon has led some to dispute the very existence of the Harlem Renaissance, with some downplaying its identification with one district in New York City. Nonetheless, the term *Harlem Renaissance* has remained popular.

Much of the extraordinary creativity took place in Harlem, the gathering place for what black leader, sociologist, and historian **W. E. B. Du Bois** had labeled the "talented tenth." Du Bois envisioned that this 10 percent of African-American intellectuals and artists would lead African Americans in the United States. In Harlem, these intellectuals and artists debated about the future of African Americans. The impulse of artists was to create boldly expressive, high-quality art as a response to their social conditions. Younger, radical African Americans believed that a "realistic" view of African-American life had to be presented because it was art. Some conservative African-American critics believed that literature should instead "uplift" the race by showing African Americans only in a positive light. A common goal and theme was an affirmation of African-American dignity and humanity in the face of poverty and racism.

Most publishers and readers in the United States were still white, however, and a controversy developed over the degree to which the perceived expectations of the white establishment should be met. Many African-American writers felt that whites, interested only in stereotypical portrayals of blacks as primitive, were unduly fascinated by the more sensational aspects of Harlem and African-American sexuality. Although this primitivism was rejected by some African-American authors as a destructive stereotype, it was actually fostered by others, who considered it a continuation of African custom and a defiance of white Puritanism. Among the poets who embraced primitivism was Bontemps.

The Harlem Renaissance was formally recognized as a movement in 1925 with the publication of **Alain Locke**'s anthology *The New Negro: An Interpretation,* in which he described the "New Negroes" of the 1920s. According to scholar **Arnold Rampersad**, *The New Negro* is the Harlem Renaissance's "definitive text, its Bible. Most of the participants in the movement probably held the book in similar regard." *The New Negro* "represents the triumph of the compiler's vision of a community and a nation changing before its eyes," Rampersad contended. It offered a definition of the cultural movement.

The Harlem Renaissance artists took on the self-appointed challenge to communicate the ills of racism through art rather than argument. They sought to chisel out a unique, African-centered culture for blacks and to simultaneously improve relations with whites. With his influential anthology of verse, *Book of American Negro Poetry* (1922), James Weldon Johnson set the manipulation of language and other patterns of signification as the heart of the African-American poetic enterprise. Thus, literature of the era was marked by a shift away from moralizing and political ideals, which had been characteristic of much post-Reconstruction writing.

At the same time, growing interest among white Americans in jazz and blues and the discovery of some African sculpture by modernist artists broadened the audience for African-American writing. Some black critics, including Du Bois and **Benjamin Brawley**, welcomed the increase in white patronage and stressed the value of literature in fostering racial equality. Others, including Alain Locke and **Charles W. Chesnutt**, decried such overt use of literature for propaganda purposes. Although few black critics asserted the complete independence of art from social concerns, most believed that literature could best promote racial equality by showing that black writers could produce works rivaling or surpassing those of their white counterparts.

During the Harlem Renaissance, New York City provided a wide variety of publishing opportunities. Major publishing companies began soliciting and publishing literary works by black writers. Several agencies had magazines that published work by young black writers and sponsored writing contests. Two such periodicals were *Crisis,* published by the National Association for the Advancement of Colored People (NAACP) and edited by Du Bois, and *Opportunity,* published by the National Urban League and edited by **Charles (Spurgeon) Johnson**. Independent magazines such as *The Messenger*—a militant socialist journal edited by **A. Philip Randolph** and **Chandler Owen**—published up-and-coming African-American writers. Some writers, such as **Wallace Thurman**, Langston Hughes, Zora Neale Hurston, Aaron Douglas, John P. Davis, **Richard Bruce Nugent**, and **Gwendolyn Bennett**, even tried to start their own literary journal—*Fire!!*—which lasted only one issue.

Du Bois, continuing work he had started at the beginning of the century, produced books and essays on the position of African Americans in this country and on the steps African Americans needed to take to achieve equality. The appearance of African-American journals such as Du Bois's *Crisis* and Johnson's *Opportunity* made it much easier for black writers to publish in a style that suited their tastes.

The Harlem Renaissance writers reflected both the uplifting theme of the conservative African-American critics and the realistic art movement of the younger, more radical African-American critics. Both sides succeeded in showing African Americans and the world that their culture was a worthy literary topic, that it was beautiful—a theme that would reemerge during the black power movement of the mid-1960s and early 1970s.

—*Janet Hoover and Michael Strickland*

REFERENCES: *EBLG.* Baker, Houston A., Jr. (1987), *Modernism and the Harlem Renaissance* (Chicago: University of Chicago Press). Bassett, John E.

(1992), *Harlem in Review: Critical Reactions to Black American Writers, 1917–1939* (Selinsgrove, PA: Susquehanna University Press). Bloom, Harold (1994), *Black American Prose Writers of the Harlem Renaissance: Writers of English, Lives and Works* (New York: Chelsea). Britannica Online—Biographies, Audio/Video, *Bibliography: Harlem Renaissance,* http://blackhistory.eb.com/micro/259/32.html. Encarta Schoolhouse (1997), "The Harlem Renaissance," http://www.encarta.com/schoolhouse/Harlem/harlem.asp. "Harlem Renaissance, 1919–1949," in *NAAAL.* Lewis, David Levering (1981), *When Harlem Was in Vogue* (New York: Knopf).

Harper, Frances Ellen (née) Watkins
(9/24/1825–2/22/1911)
Poems, novels, short stories, columns, letters, essays, speeches; journalist

Frances was born free, the only child of free parents, in the slave state of Maryland. Sadly, her mother and father died before she was old enough to have any memories of them. Luckily, she was raised by her uncle William Watkins and his wife and their children. The William Watkins Academy for Negro Youth had an excellent reputation for rigorous instruction in vocational subjects (such as seamstress training), academic subjects (such as languages and oratory), and moral leadership (such as abolition, radical politics, and biblical studies). Unfortunately, as was common at that time, financial pressures forced Frances to stop her formal education at age 13 and to start working as a housekeeper. Fortunately, her employers owned a bookstore, so in her spare time, she was able to read widely to advance her own self-education.

While still a teenager, Frances began writing poetry, and when she was about 20, her early poems were gathered into the collection *Forest Leaves,* published in about 1845. (The collection has since gone out of print, and no known copies remain.) When Watkins was about 25 years old, she put into practice her self-teaching and her talent for public speaking, becoming the first female instructor (teaching "domestic science") at the Union Seminary (later a part of Wilberforce University) in Columbus, Ohio. In 1853, Maryland passed a law prohibiting any free blacks from entering or returning to that state. Thereafter, if she had been caught in her home state of Maryland, she risked being either imprisoned or enslaved. That law inflamed Watkins's abolitionist passions. Hence, after

Watkins had spent a couple of years teaching in Ohio and in Pennsylvania, **William (Grant) Still** easily persuaded her to join the Underground Railroad and to begin speaking out for abolition.

Watkins started lecturing for the Maine Anti-Slavery Society, delivering her fiery oratory throughout the northeastern United States and in Canada. Despite the difficulties of transportation during that era, she carried out a grueling schedule of lectures, often lecturing in a new city every other day, commonly giving more than one lecture in each city. She spiced her speeches with her own original poems, which she managed to jot down while on the road. Although most of her poems addressed the issue of slavery, she also focused on feminist issues and topics such as religion, racial pride, and African-American history. While frantically scurrying from city to city, she virtually created the genre of protest poetry. This energetic, enthusiastic orator published her poems, essays, anecdotal sketches, and letters in various periodicals.

In 1854, Watkins's volume *Poems on Miscellaneous Subjects,* including both poems and essays, was published in both Boston and Philadelphia. It sold briskly, easily establishing her reputation as the most popular African-American poet of the era and going through 20 more editions over the next 20 years. Following is an excerpt from just one of the poems in that volume, from her well-regarded "Bury Me in a Free Land" (quoted in *BWA,* p. 225):

> Make me a grave where'er you will,
> In a lowly plain, or a lofty hill;
> Make it among earth's humblest graves,
> But not in a land where men are slaves.
> [three stanzas] . . .
> I'd shudder and start if I heard the bay
> Of bloodhounds seizing their human prey,
> And I heard the captive plead in vain
> As they bound afresh his galling chain.
> [two stanzas] . . .
> I ask no monument, proud and high,
> To arrest the gaze of the passers-by;
> All that my yearning spirit craves,
> Is bury me not in a land of slaves.

Also in that volume was her poignant poem "The Slave Mother":

> Heard you that shriek? It rose
> So wildly in the air,
> It seemed as if a burdened heart

was breaking in despair.
[two stanzas] . . .
He is not hers, although she bore
For him a mother's pains;
He is not hers, although her blood
Is coursing through his veins!
He is not hers, for cruel hands
May rudely tear apart
The only wreath of household love
That binds her breaking heart.
[four stanzas] . . .

This poem of devastating separation at the slave auction block is among the most frequently anthologized of Harper's poems.

With **Frederick Douglass** and several other notables, Watkins coedited and contributed to the *Anglo-African Magazine,* probably the earliest African-American literary journal. In that journal, in 1859, she published "The Two Offers," generally believed to be the first short story by an African American to appear in print. Although not her best literary effort, the work was revolutionary in its message that conscientious, smart women may choose options for their lives other than marriage.

In November 1860, Watkins made the choice to marry Fenton Harper, a widower with three children, and she used the proceeds from her book sales to buy a farm. Meanwhile, Frances continued to write. Considered one of the most popular African-American poets and most prolific women writers of the nineteenth century, she continued to publish her stories, poems, letters, and essays in various abolitionist and African-American periodicals. Nonetheless, she, Fenton, and the children settled into domestic life, and after a time, Frances gave birth to their new daughter, Mary. Less than four years later, Fenton died, and after creditors claimed the farm and most of their other belongings, Frances was left penniless with four children to support.

Harper hit the lecture circuit again, with full vigor (and her infant daughter Mary). She spent the next five years traveling throughout the post–Civil War South, lecturing to whites and blacks—separately and in integrated forums—in every southern state but Texas and Arkansas. She prodded whites to fully integrate Negroes into the mainstream of American life, and she urged former slaves to build up their race by enhancing their own lives, such as by mastering reading, writing, political participation, and home management.

While in the South, she also wrote for Northern newspapers, exhorting their readers to lend their financial, moral, and physical support for Reconstruction.

Soon after she returned to the lecture circuit, she joined the newly founded American Equal Rights Association (1866). (Fellow members included abolitionists and suffragists Frederick Douglass, **Harriet Forten Purvis** and **Robert Purvis**, **Sojourner Truth**, Susan B. Anthony, Lucretia Mott, and Elizabeth Cady Stanton.) Much to her dismay, these passionate idealists ended up parting company over whether the Fifteenth Amendment to the U.S. Constitution should extend the right to vote to blacks *and* to women, to black men (but not to women), or to white women (but not to blacks). She rejected both the racism underlying the focus on women and the sexism underlying the focus on blacks. Unless the franchise was extended to both blacks and women, Harper would not have the right to vote. Nonetheless, most agreed that the amendment stood little chance of passing at all if the white men in the U.S. Congress and in state legislatures were asked to extend the voting privilege so broadly.

Harper tried to negotiate some agreement between the factions, often reminding them, "We are all bound up together in one great bundle of humanity." Despite her tremendous oratory gifts and persuasive charms, Harper was unable to unify the conflicting parties and ended up having to divide her attentions between increasingly separate interest groups. She spoke out fervently in opposition to lynching and in support of educational and economic opportunities for blacks; she lectured widely for the American Woman Suffrage Association, and she railed against alcohol for the Woman's Christian Temperance Union. As in her youth, whenever she spoke, she lectured without notes, but she often pulled poems, short stories, or anecdotal sketches from her writings to make particular points or to highlight her commentary.

In addition to her lectures, essays, letters, and poems, Harper managed to write four novels. In all genres, Harper attended to the aesthetics of her writing, manipulating form and technique to suit her purpose. Her purpose was vital, too, however, as all her writing was intended to uplift her people. In the late 1860s, she published her blank verse allegory, *Moses: A Story of the Nile,* which narratively addresses the hopes and strivings of African Americans in the era of Reconstruction. At about the same time, she used the Moses allegory in her serialized novel, *Minnie's Sacrifice,* which encouraged African Americans to dedicate themselves to high ideals for elevating the race. She also dedicated her late 1860s novel *Sowing and Reaping: A Temperance Story,* serialized in the *Christian Recorder,* to the temperance movement.

In the 1870s, she published her collection simply entitled *Poems,* followed soon after by her collection *Sketches of Southern Life* (1872). In *Sketches,* she addressed the difficulties of Southern blacks through a series of dialect poems allegedly narrated by "Aunt Chloe." Aunt Chloe valiantly survived slavery and models the best in what African-American women could achieve in a postslavery era. She summons the courage she needed to survive slavery to take on a monumental task at age 60: learning to read. In other verses, Aunt Chloe poetically gives an oral history of her life under slavery, and she describes her current political and community activism (e.g., helping to build churches and schools and encouraging the menfolk to vote conscientiously). Like other African-American women of her era, Aunt Chloe may never have considered herself a feminist, but she exemplifies feminist thought and womanly strength in all she does and says.

Shortly after *Sketches* was published, Harper started writing a newspaper column in which she created the characters of Jenny, a recent college graduate and aspiring poet, and her Aunt Jane, a socially conscientious woman who encourages Jenny's aspirations while reminding her to shape them toward societal improvement. Through their "conversations" and activities, Harper discussed issues of aesthetics, politics, social reform, economics, and morality. Following her example, **Langston Hughes** used his character Simple as a vehicle for exploring twentieth-century social issues. Several other journalists have similarly followed suit.

In the late 1880s, Harper published *Trial and Triumph,* her temperance novel that refuted the myths of the happy slave, the chivalrous plantation owner, and the treacherous black freedman being propounded by Southern white plantation-school literature. In 1892, she published her novel *Iola Leroy: Or, Shadows Uplifted* (1892), telling the melodramatic story of an octoroon who initially passes for white, then is discovered to be black, and is sold into slavery. During the Civil War, she becomes a nurse. When a white doctor proposes marriage to her, contingent on her willingness to

again pass for white, she refuses him. She later meets and marries an African-American doctor who shares her devotion to social reform and racial uplift. Although Harper's mulatta suffers, she is not a typical tragic mulatta: She is not martyred for her race but she dedicates herself to working to uplift it. Further, Harper's fiction does not equate lightness of skin with nobility or accomplishment. Though she was a product of her time, Harper's feminism, positive values, and racial pride heralded sentiments that were not to be more fully appreciated for nearly a century.

In addition to her fiction, between 1890 and 1901, Harper published several poetry collections, including *The Sparrow's Fall and Other Poems, Atlanta Offering: Poems, Martyr of Alabama and Other Poems, Poems,* and *Idylls of the Bible* (1901). More recently, Harper's poems have been anthologized in *Complete Poems of Frances E. W. Harper* (1988) and *A Brighter Coming Day: A Frances Ellen Watkins Harper Reader* (1990).

When Harper was in her mid-seventies, her health began to fail, and she had to slow down and eventually stop lecturing. Her daughter Mary, a social worker, continued to lecture until Mary died in 1909. Two years later, the heart that had so vigorously sustained the life—and the liveliness—of Frances Ellen Watkins Harper gave out. Though she did not survive, her literary descendants live on. Her protest poetry can be seen in the writings of **Nikki Giovanni**, **Sonia Sanchez**, and **Audre Lorde**; her early feminist themes can be found today in the works of **Alice Walker** and **Gloria Naylor;** her biblical and literary allusions and her love of lyrics are today expressed in the work of **Margaret Walker** and **Rita Dove;** and her journalistic legacy has lived on through the work of **Ida B. Wells** and of contemporary African-American reporters, correspondents, and newspaper publishers.

REFERENCES: *1TESK. AA:PoP. BAL-1-P. BF:2000. BWA. EB-98. EBLG. MAAL. MWEL. NAAAL. PBW. RT. TtW. WB-98.* Campbell, Jane, in *OCWW.* Foster, Frances Smith, in *OCAAL.*

Harper, Michael S. (Steven) (3/18/1938–)
Poems, anthologies

Born in Brooklyn, Michael Harper grew up in a mostly white area in western Los Angeles. His parents, Walter Warren Harper (a postal supervisor) and Katherine Johnson Harper (a medical stenographer), provided their son with middle-class comforts (e.g., an extensive record collection and lots of books)—and expectations. When Michael was in junior high school, his asthma prevented him from participating much in gym class, so his gym teacher flunked him. That failing grade kept him from being on the school's honor roll, and Michael lost his enthusiasm for studying. At Dorsey High School, a school counselor started to put Michael in classes on the vocational-education track. Walter Warren Harper would have none of that, and he soon made it clear that his son was destined for a career in medicine, not for a career in industrial arts. Michael's own interests, however, inclined more toward writing poems than toward probing human physiology.

In 1955, Michael enrolled at Los Angeles City College and then transferred to Los Angeles State College. At first, he compliantly took pre-med courses—until his zoology professor advised him that no African American would be able to get into medical school. In the face of this racist advice, he turned to literature, studying the letters of poet John Keats, the philosophical writings of **W. E. B. Du Bois**, and **Ralph Ellison**'s *Invisible Man*—and earning a bachelor's degree from Los Angeles State College (1961). Meanwhile, he also worked in the post office, where many of his coworkers were well-educated African-American men much like his father. They told him how racial prejudice had blocked their progress and encouraged him to continue his education further.

Harper went on to attend the prestigious Iowa Writers' Workshop in the winter of 1961. While there, he was obliged to live in segregated housing, apart from fellow students, and he was the only African American in his poetry and fiction classes. Despite these affronts, Harper began writing poetry in earnest there. After leaving Iowa, he taught for a year at Pasadena City College (1962), then he returned to Iowa to earn his master's degree in English (1963). From there, he taught at Contra Costa College (1964–1968) and at California State College (now University, 1968–1969). Since the early 1970s, Harper has been on the faculty of the renowned Ivy League college Brown University, where he has taught literature and creative writing. His former students include novelist, playwright, and poet **Gayl Jones**.

Harper is best known for his poetry, which draws heavily on his lifelong love of African-American music, especially jazz rhythms and blues lyricality. By his own account, Harper has said,

"I'm trying to write a poem for the ear as well as the eye" (quoted in *NAAAL*). His poems are intended to be read aloud so that the listener can hear his offbeat rhythms and cadences, his bluesy refrains and repetitions, and his off-balance improvisations. Although his messages often allude to philosophical abstractions, he uses concrete imagery to make them accessible to his readers' senses. While Harper readily confronts racism in his writings, he offers messages of hope through human creativity and encourages Americans to embrace multiple cultures, rather than focus on either/or dualisms. He often celebrates and honors African Americans in his poems, especially highlighting the lives of musicians such as John Coltrane, who was also a close friend of Harper's.

When Harper was first launching his teaching career, he was already publishing his poems in various literary journals. His first poetry collection, *Dear John, Dear Coltrane* (1970) was nominated for the 1971 National Book Award, and thus Harper's very first book established his national reputation as a writer. Since then, numerous other poetry collections have followed, including *History Is Your Own Heartbeat: Poems* (1971), which earned him the Poetry Award of the Black Academy of Arts and Letters; *Photographs: Negatives: History as Apple Tree* (1972), published as a limited edition; *Song: I Want a Witness* (1972), which responds to religion, history, and other literary works; *Debridement* (1973), which is dedicated to his children; *Nightmare Begins Responsibility* (1975), which considers personal experiences in a literary and historical context; *Images of Kin: New and Selected Poems* (1977), which earned the Melville-Cane Award and was nominated for the 1978 National Book Award; *Rhode Island: Eight Poems* (1981); *Healing Song for the Inner Ear: Poems* (1984), which reflects on the thinking of **Frederick Douglass**, **Booker T. Washington**, and W. E. B. Du Bois; *Songlines: Mosaics* (1991), another limited-edition publication; and *Honorable Amendments: Poems* (1995).

His other works include his recording, *Hear Where Coltrane Is* (1971), and edited collections of works by other poets, *The Collected Poems of Sterling A. Brown* (1980) and a limited edition of **Robert Hayden**'s *American Journal*. Harper has also edited some anthologies: *Heartblow: Black Veils* (1975); the contemporary literary classic *Chant of Saints: A Gathering of Afro-American Literature, Art, and Scholarship* (1979, with Robert B. Stepto); *Every Eye Ain't Asleep: An Anthology of Poetry by*

Afro-Americans Since 1945 (1994, with Anthony Walton), and *The Vintage Book of African American Poetry* (2000, with Anthony Walton).

In recognition of his literary contributions, he has received the National Institute of Arts and Letters Creative Writing Award (1972), a Guggenheim fellowship (1976), a National Endowment for the Arts grant (1977). In 1988, he was named the first poet laureate of Rhode Island.

REFERENCES: *AAW:AAPP. EBLG. LoL. MWEL. NAAAL. OC20LE. VBAAP. WDAA.* Leonard, Keith D., in *OCAAL.* Robinson, Lisa Clayton, in *EA-99.*

Harrington, Oliver ("Ollie") Wendell
(2/14/1912–11/7/1995)
Cartoons, comic strips; journalist

By the time Harrington was 20 or so, his comic strips were being published in such African-American newspapers as the *Pittsburgh Courier,* (Harlem's) *Amsterdam News,* and **Baltimore Afro-American**. His most famous cartoon character, "Bootsie," soon took on a life of its own, and he ended up publishing a collection of Bootsie comic strips in *Bootsie and Others* (1958). Harrington also worked as a war correspondent, journalist, and illustrator of books (e.g., classic novels).

REFERENCES: *EA-99.*

Harris, Joel Chandler
(12/9/1848–7/3/1908)
Humorous trickster tales, short stories, novels, folklore, children's books; journal founder

A journalist of European-American ancestry, Harris took a profound interest in the **trickster tales** told by African Americans in the rural South (see also **oral tradition**). Based on his extensive study of this oral literature, Harris's "Negro Folklore: The Story of Mr. Rabbit and Mr. Fox, as Told by Uncle Remus" first appeared in the *Atlanta Constitution* on July 20, 1879. The story was enthusiastically received, and he continued to publish more stories. The following year, Harris collected various Brer Rabbit stories in *Uncle Remus, His Songs and His Sayings* (1880). This collection was followed by seven more, including *Nights with Uncle Remus* (1883) and *Uncle Remus and His Friends* (1892), as well as his posthumously published *Uncle Remus and the Little Boy* (1910).

In these stories, Harris was conscientious in retaining the authentic dialect of the many African-American storytellers whom he interviewed, and he remained true to the folktales they told, yet he set these stories within a context reflecting his European-American Southern background: He has the storyteller, Uncle Remus, tell these stories to the blue-eyed, blond son of his former master (and current employer), rather than telling them to his family and friends, which would have been much more believable. Further, as a white Southerner, Harris found it difficult to avoid perpetuating stereotypes of African Americans, such as portraying Uncle Remus as a jovial old man, content with his lot in life. Nonetheless, Harris's efforts to preserve this important aspect of African-American oral literature deserve credit, and because of his efforts, many others were inspired to pay attention to this important body of literature. In addition to the Uncle Remus stories, Harris published other short-story collections, such as *Mingo, and Other Sketches in Black and White* (1884), *Free Joe and Other Georgian Sketches* (1887), and *On the Wing of Occasions* (1900). He also wrote novels, including *Sister Jane, Her Friends and Acquaintances* (1896) and *Gabriel Tolliver* (1902). His other children's books included *Little Mr. Thimblefinger and His Queer Country* (1894), *The Story of Aaron* (1896), and *Aaron in the Wildwoods* (1897). Harris also published *On the Plantation* (1892), his autobiography, and in 1907, he and his son Julian cofounded *Uncle Remus's Magazine,* which he edited until his death.

REFERENCES: *EB-98. WDAA.* Gribben, Alan, in *WB-99.* P. R., in *CBC.* Paulsen, Frank M., in *G-97.*

Haskins, James S. (9/19/1941–)
Biography, children's literature, juvenile and adult nonfiction, criticism, diaries

Barred from using the public library in the Jim Crow South in which he grew up, Haskins spent his free hours lazily poring over the encyclopedias his mother had purchased one volume at a time. These childhood explorations fostered in him a love of learning and of reading about what's true. Years later, with his college degrees in hand, Haskins sold ads for the *New York Daily News* and sold stocks on Wall Street. After a while, though, he decided to earn a living with his love of learning, becoming a teacher in 1966. A lifelong diarist, Haskins wrote his first book based on his experiences as a special education teacher in a public school, *Diary of a Harlem Schoolteacher* (1969). While teaching, he saw the need for outstanding nonfiction books for children and youths. By 1995, Haskins had written and published more than 110 nonfiction books for children and adults, making him one of the most prolific authors in the country.

Haskins writes on a wide assortment of topics (e.g., the Underground Railroad, gambling, the Special Olympics, civil rights, the Civil War, the Vietnam War, India, ghost stories, labor history, boat people of Cuba and of Vietnam, the Statue of Liberty, werewolves, Methodism, and alcoholism). One of his most beloved topics, however, is music, as can be seen in his biographies of legendary singers Nat King Cole, Scatman Crothers, Lena Horne, Michael Jackson, and Diana Ross, and in his award-winning books *The Story of Stevie Wonder* (1976; Coretta Scott King Award), *Scott Joplin: The Man Who Made Ragtime* (1978, with Kathleen Benson), *Black Music in America: A History through Its People* (1987; the National Council for Social Studies' Carter G. Woodson Book Award), and *Black Dance in America* (1990). His books have also been commended by the Child Study Association, and his *The Sixties Reader* (1988) was named the American Library Association's Best Book for Young Adults. His adult book *The Cotton Club* (1977) was honored as only Hollywood can do it: It was made into Francis Ford Coppola's movie by that name.

Haskins has also written numerous biographies, including biography collections on African-American entrepreneurs, inventors, military heroes, and political and governmental leaders. In addition, he has written individual biographies on civil rights activists **Martin Luther King**, **Jr.**, Rosa Parks, and Bayard Rustin; as well as biographies of other leading African Americans such as astronaut Guion Bluford, diplomat **Ralph Bunche**, **Shirley Chisholm**, **Bill Cosby**, **Katherine Dunham**, **Langston Hughes**, **Jesse Jackson, Jr.**, **Barbara Jordan**, **Spike Lee**, **Thurgood Marshall**, politician **Adam Clayton Powell, Jr.**, former head of the Joint Chiefs of Staff Colin Powell, **Malcolm X**, photographer James Van Der Zee, politician Andrew Young, several sports stars, and many more. He has also written biographies of other prominent people, such as Corazón Aquino, Shirley Temple Black, Christopher Columbus, Indira and Rajiv Gandhi, and Winnie Mandela. He also wrote a series of counting books on the Arab lands, Brazil,

China, France, Greece, India, Ireland, Israel, and Italy, as well as a dictionary of African cultures.

Haskins's books for adults include *The Psychology of Black Language* (1973, with Hugh Butts), *Black Manifesto for Education* (1973, editor), *Snow Sculpture and Ice Carving* (1974), *Voodoo and Hoodoo: Their Tradition and Craft as Revealed by Actual Practitioners* (1978), and several biographies (e.g., of Scott Joplin, Mabel Mercer, and Richard Pryor). In addition, Haskins has written numerous critical essays and reviews of literature for scholarly journals and other periodicals. While being so prolific, Haskins has also managed to teach English since 1970, working as a full-time professor at the University of Florida since 1977.

REFERENCES: *EBLG*. Fikes, Robert, Jr., in *OCAAL*. L. F. A., in *CBC*.

Hawkins Brown, "Charlotte Eugenia" (née Lottie)

See **Brown, "Charlotte Eugenia" (née Lottie Hawkins)**

Hayden, Robert (né Asa Bundy Sheffey) (8/4/1913–2/25/1980)
Poems

Although Robert Hayden described himself as "a poet who teaches to earn a living so that he can write a poem or two now and then," history will record him as being much more than that. Although he did teach English at various universities for more than 30 years, he was an artist of the highest caliber whose remarkable poetic ability led him to be named consultant in poetry to the Library of Congress. This honor is equivalent to the distinction of poet laureate in England, and in both nations, the poets named to these positions are seen as the representative poets of the nation. Hayden was the first black poet to achieve this distinction in the United States.

At birth, the up-and-coming poet was named Asa Bundy Sheffey by his parents, Ruth and Asa Sheffey, but after his parents' marriage fell apart and his mother left to get her life together, he was raised by his foster parents, Sue Ellen and William Hayden. Although his mother did come by periodically to visit, he considered the Haydens his parents and took their name as his own. Nearsighted from an early age, he was a reclusive child who preferred indoor pastimes such as reading and writing to outdoor sports. In 1932, at 18 years of age, he published his first poem and began attending Detroit City College, where he majored in foreign languages.

After graduating in 1936, he joined the Federal Writers' Project, where he did research on black history—specifically the Underground Railroad and the antislavery movement—and black folk culture. He left the Federal Writers' Project in 1938 and married Erma Morris in 1940—the same year he published his first volume of poetry, *Heart-Shape in the Dust*. He then enrolled in the University of Michigan, where he pursued a master's degree and studied under a world-famous modern poet, W. H. Auden. He received his master's degree in 1944 and began teaching at Fisk University in Tennessee, where he stayed for 22 years. In 1968, he gained a position at the University of Michigan at Ann Arbor, where he worked until his death in 1980.

During his lifetime, he produced eight volumes of poetry, and although he is best known for the poems that focus on African-American historical figures, he cannot be classified as a historical poet. Indeed, as a poet, his expansive array of work, written in a wide variety of forms, deals with a great diversity of topics and themes, so he defies classification. Some critics have described his work as "kaleidoscopic" because the patterns in his work are always shifting, never focusing on the same themes, ideas, images, or styles twice. In each successive poem or collection of poems, Hayden finds ways to integrate new material, ask new questions, and add new perspectives. It is hard to find one thematic or stylistic preoccupation in even a majority of his works. This is very rare, as most poets, either because of the lives they have led or because of their general interests, tend to return to the same topics, themes, or ideas over and over again.

Part of the reason that Hayden avoids such repetition has to do with his philosophy about poetry. He believed that for a poet to focus on his own personal or racial identity in his work would limit the poetry and that poetry should never be constrained by such concerns. Although he acknowledged that poetry, because it comes from the mind of a living, breathing person, is unavoidably rooted in personal concerns, he also believed that the poet is responsible for moving the ideas of the poems from dealing with the personal to communicating something universal. Thus, one of his poems, "Monet's Waterlilies," begins with his feelings about

Robert Hayden, undated photo (Pach/Corbis)

the Vietnam War and the fact that he by chance catches a glance of Monet's famous painting, then it continues to make a statement about the way to escape history through contemplating art.

This theory of poetry occasionally earned him censure from some critics of his time. This criticism largely arose because, as William Meredith wrote in his foreword to Hayden's *Collected Prose,* "Hayden declared himself . . . an American rather than a black poet, when for a time there was posited an unreconcilable difference between the two roles." At the time, critics were advancing the notion that black poetry could only be understood in terms of black themes, black feelings about life, black speech, and black music. Hayden, in his belief that poetry should transcend the personal (which included not just personal experiences but also racial identity), vehemently disagreed with such ideas. He felt such notions put boundaries around the artist, confining the poet's reality to a very narrow space. He wanted to be an American writer and would not settle for anything narrower.

He also disagreed with many powerful critics as to how African-American art should be judged. At the time, it was said that black poetry should be judged by separate ethnic criteria. He believed that, although his poems originated in the real facts

of his "blackness," his race was really only "a point
of departure into that magic realm where all artists
of unmistakabl[e] . . . merit" become so all-inclusive
as to affect the whole world. He said that he
wanted his poetry to be "human rather than racial,"
to "speak . . . to other human beings and . . . not [be]
limited by time and place and not limited by the
ethnic."

Hayden's decision to prevent his work from being classified along racial lines was probably inspired by his adherence to the Baha'i faith. This
Eastern religion shaped many of his ideas about
identity, poetry, the personal, and the universal. Baha'is have faith in a coming world civilization and
believe that all people and all religions are united
by an essential oneness. The assertion of this spiritual unity led him to believe that humankind
would overcome divisiveness, and he certainly
didn't want his poetry adding to that separation by
being classified as "black poetry" or being judged
by different standards than other poetry of the English literary tradition.

Despite his desire to transcend classification,
Hayden is nevertheless best known for his poetry
that deals with African-American history and experiences. After reading "John Brown's Body," a
poem written by white poet Stephen Vincent
Benét, he was struck by Benét's admission that he
could not adequately "sing" the "black-skinned
epic" because he had "too white a heart," but that
he hoped "some day, a poet will rise to sing you /
And sing you with . . . truth and mellowness."
These words inspired Hayden to write a "black
epic," and throughout the 1940s he published poems that adhere to his desire to sing African-
American history.

"The Middle Passage" is known as one of Hayden's best poems and can be seen in and of itself as
a black epic. In this poem, Hayden uses a lot of the
research that he had done while working for the
Federal Writers' Project after college. The poem
deals with the stories of the African slave trade,
specifically the story of the *Amistad* mutiny and
the legal battle that followed it. It is told through a
montage of elements ranging from straight narration, to tales told by a variety of voices and characters, to log entries from the ships, to hymns sung
by the slaves in the belly of the ship, to testimony
of the mutineers of the *Amistad*. Even within the
poem, Hayden refuses to be pinned down to one
style, but rather uses the entire gamut of forms at
his disposal.

Although "The Middle Passage" is his best-
known work, he also wrote poems about **Harriet
Tubman** and the Underground Railroad, **Nat
Turner**, **Frederick Douglass** (all of which use
research he unearthed during his time at the Federal Writers' Project), and **Malcolm X**. All of these
topics would lead one to think that Hayden did
become what he never wished to be—a racial
poet. However, even within these poems, Hayden
slips away from such classification largely because
the historical poems do not really focus on the past
but always end with something—words or actions—that point toward the future. In closing this
way, Hayden meant to show that the hero is not
gone but is still a force to contend with, that the
heroes of the past are still acting on us today,
whether in the facts of our day-to-day life or in
our imagination.

In many ways, the historical figure becomes a
symbol—something that serves a dual purpose by
having its own characteristics but also standing for
something else. For instance, "The Middle Passage" deals with the character Cinque, who has a
physical presence in the history of the *Amistad* but
who also stands for a kind of spiritual emancipation that overcomes physical bondage. The poem
then becomes a work that not only is about the
African-American slave experience but also speaks
to anyone who has been enslaved or anyone who
has found spiritual freedom. It fails to fall into the
category of "historical poetry" or "racial poetry"
but instead moves to a more universal arena—one
that deals with the struggle between humans' spiritual and imaginative nature and the realities of life
on Earth.

For this, in essence, was Robert Hayden's project—to write works of art that are meant to delight
the senses and allow the spiritual side of humans to
flourish. Although he acknowledges that people are
tied to the real world and have their possibilities
limited by the tragedies of everyday life and the
evils of the world, he nevertheless will not give up
on the idea that people can overcome those limits.
This transcendence can be achieved not by escaping the horrors but by rising above them in such a
way that the tragedies and evils are changed into
something beautiful, good, and sacred.

—*Diane Masiello*

REFERENCES: *AAW. BW:SSCA. EA-99. OCAAL.*

Haynes, Elizabeth (née) Ross
(7/30/1883–10/26/1953)
Nonfiction—sociology, biographies

Haynes's publications included sociological essays on African-American women workers and two biographies, including *The Black Boy of Atlanta* (1952, about college president and banker Richard Robert Wright).

REFERENCES: Robinson, Lisa Clayton, in *EA-99*. Wilson, Francille Rusan, in *BWA:AHE*.

Haynes, Lemuel (7/8/1753–9/28/1833)
Nonfiction—theology

The primary publication of cleric and theologian Haynes was *Universal Salvation, a Very Ancient Doctrine,* published in about 70 editions. Although he was no abolitionist activist, he also wrote a manuscript, "Liberty Further Extended," urging that the freedoms and principles underlying the American Revolution be extended to liberate slaves.

REFERENCES: *EA-99*. Saillant, John, in *OCAAL*.

Heard, Nathan C. (Cliff) (11/7/1936–)
Novels, articles

While Heard was in prison, a fellow inmate introduced him to **Langston Hughes**, **Amiri Baraka**, **James Baldwin**, and other writers, and he soon started writing himself. Initially, he wrote about music and about African history. By 1963, he had written the manuscript for his first novel, *To Reach a Dream* (1972). His other novels include *Howard Street* (1968), *A Cold Burning* (1974), *When Shadows Fall* (1977), and *House of Slammers* (1983). A musician, educator, TV host, and actor, Heard has also written numerous articles.

REFERENCES: Banks, Marva O., in *OCAAL*.

Henson, Matthew Alexander
(8/8/1866–3/9/1955)
Adventure memoir

A key member of Robert Peary's 1909 expedition to the North Pole, Henson wrote *A Black Explorer at the North Pole* (1912), describing his role as navigator and as translator for the four native Inuits (often called "Eskimos" by outsiders) who accompanied him and Peary.

REFERENCES: *BDAA. EA-99. EB-BH-CD.*

Hernton, Calvin C. (Coolidge)
(4/28/1934–)
Nonfiction, novels, poems, criticism; magazine founder

After earning a B.A. in social science (Talladega College, 1954) and an M.A. in sociology (Fisk, 1956), Hernton taught history and sociology at four different colleges across the south from Florida to Louisiana (1957–1960). He then briefly left teaching to get hands-on experience as a social welfare counselor in New York City (1960–1961), and he cofounded *Umbra* magazine in 1963. Next, Hernton wrote his first major literary work, his thought-provoking treatise *Sex and Racism in America* (1965; with a new introduction, 1988; 1992), in which he reflected on case studies and his own understanding to propose how racism and sex are interrelated in American society. In his view, the puritanical beliefs of white men prevented them from viewing white women as sexual beings, so they pursued black women as objects of sexual desire; in turn, white men's guilt over their lust for black women led them to fear that black men felt lust for white women. Thus, according to Hernton, "all race relations tend to be, however subtly, *sexual* relations" (quoted in *OCAAL,* p. 353). This thesis permeates much of Hernton's other writings. Starting in 1965, Hernton studied with radical therapist R. D. Laing as a research fellow at the London Institute of Phenomenological Studies (*phenomenology* is an aspect of philosophy concerning human consciousness and self-awareness). After returning to the United States in 1969, he became a writer-in-residence at Oberlin College in Ohio, where he was invited to be a tenured professor in 1973.

While in London, Hernton wrote his essay collection *White Papers for White Americans* (1966), reviewing the events of the civil rights movement up to that time. At Oberlin, he wrote his analysis *Coming Together: Black Power, White Hatred, and Sexual Hang-ups* (1971), his novel *Scarecrow* (1974), his poetry collection *Medicine Man: Collected Poems* (1976), and *Sexual Mountains and Black Women Writers: Adventures in Sex, Literature, and Real Life* (1987).

REFERENCES: *EBLG. TtW.* Boelcskevy, Mary Anne Stewart, in *OCAAL*. Amazon.com, 7/1999.

Herron, Carolivia (7/22/1947–)
Novels, short fiction, children's fiction, edited book

Herron edited the *Selected Works of Angelina Weld Grimké* (1991), a book in the Schomburg Library series on nineteenth-century African-American women writers; she has also written a novel, *Thereafter Johnnie* (1991), and short stories. She has received a Bunting Award and a Fulbright, among other honors. More recently, Herron published *Nappy Hair* (1997), a picture book for young children, exuberantly celebrating a young girl's nappy hair, narrated in enthusiastic call-and-response format.

REFERENCES: NPR-WA, 7/22/1999. Coleman, Alisha R., in *OCAAL*. Amazon.com, 1/2000.

Heyward, (Edwin) DuBose
(8/31/1885–6/16/1940)
Novels, poems, plays, children's books, nonfiction

European-American writer DuBose Heyward often collaborated with his wife Dorothy (née) Kuhns Heyward (1890–1961), who had studied at Harvard University, married Heyward in 1923, had a play of her own produced on Broadway (1924), and collaborated with other writers as well as with her husband. Dubose Heyward's most famous work is his best-selling novel *Porgy* (1925), which he and his wife Dorothy dramatized in the Pulitzer Prize–winning play *Porgy* (produced in 1927, published in 1928). George Gershwin, in turn, spent a summer with the Heywards adapting their play to create Gershwin's popular opera *Porgy and Bess* (1935), for which DuBose Heyward and Ira Gershwin wrote the libretto (lyrics). A quarter of a century later, the opera was made into a movie, *Porgy* (1959).

Although Heyward was European American— his family directly descended from a signer of the Declaration of Independence, Thomas Heyward— his work sensitively yet unsentimentally portrayed the experiences of African Americans living in Charleston and on the sea islands of South Carolina. Because Heyward's family was impoverished, although he had been crippled by polio as an infant and suffered poor health all his life, he had to leave school at age 14 in order to earn money for his widowed mother and family. His jobs included employment as a retail clerk in a hardware store, as a dock worker, as a checker in a cotton warehouse, and for an insurance company until grave health problems forced him to stop. In many of these jobs, Heyward worked alongside African Americans as an equal coworker.

Heyward's other works include the novels *Angel* (1926); *The Half-Pint Flask; Mamba's Daughters: A*

Novel of Charleston (1929; reprinted 1995), about the efforts of three generations of an African-American family to improve their economic situation, which he and his wife Dorothy adapted into a play (1939); *Peter Ashley* (1932), a Civil War chronicle; *Lost Morning* (1936); and *Star-Spangled Virgin* (1939), about the economic struggles of African Americans in the Virgin Islands. In addition to the plays he and Dorothy adapted from his novels, he wrote the play *Brass Ankle* (1931), about a mixed-race romance. His poetry collections include *Carolina Chansons: Legends of the Low Country* (1922, with Hervey Allen), *Skylines and Horizons* (1924), and *Jasbo Brown and Selected Poems* (1931). He also wrote an outstanding children's book, *Country Bunny and the Little Gold Shoes* (1939; reprinted in 1949 and 1974 and available on audiocassette in 1999). His book was far ahead of its time, showing that a clever, kind, wise, poor, hard-working, brown mother of 21 (rabbits) can do whatever she sets out to do, even when big, brawny, rich, white males try to thwart her efforts. He also cowrote a nonfiction work, *Fort Sumter* (1938, with H. R. Sass).

REFERENCES: *EB-98. OC20LE. RG20. WDAA.* French, Warren, in *G-97*. Hitchcock, Bert, in *WB-99.* San Diego Summer Pops program, 8/28/1998.

Hill, Anita Faye (7/30/1956–)
Memoir

As an attorney who had worked for Clarence Thomas, Hill came forward during the hearings for Thomas's nomination to the U.S. Supreme Court, asserting that he had sexually harassed her while he was her supervisor as head of the Equal Employment Opportunity Commission. She has since written *Speaking Truth to Power* (1997) about her experiences in regard to the Thomas matter.

REFERENCES: *SEW.* Keough, Leyla, in *EA-99*.

Himes, Chester (Bomar)
(7/29/1909–11/12/1984)
Novels, autobiography, short stories

To get a feel for how Himes viewed his life, we might glance at these titles: *The Quality of Hurt: The Autobiography of Chester Himes* (1972) and *My Life of Absurdity: The Autobiography of Chester Himes* (1976). Following a troubled childhood, he spent his young adulthood in prison (sentenced to 20–25 years, starting at age 19). In prison, he started writing, and after a while, his stories began being published in the **Baltimore Afro-American,** *Abbott's Monthly,* and other African-American periodicals of the 1930s. In 1934, he sold "Crazy in the Stir" to *Esquire* magazine, his first professional story to appear in a mainstream white-owned periodical. Two years later, he was paroled.

Nearly a decade later, he started publishing his largely autobiographical novels *If He Hollers Let Him Go* (1945), *Lonely Crusade* (1947), *Cast the First Stone* (1952), *The Third Generation* (1954), and *The Primitive* (1955). Of these, his first two are often cited as his best, and all are sometimes cited as "protest novels." By the mid-1950s, Himes started pumping out his crime-thriller novels featuring Coffin Ed Johnson and Grave Digger Jones, cop-detectives in Harlem. These novels include *For Love of Imabelle* (1957, a.k.a. *A Rage in Harlem,* 1965), *The Crazy Kill* (1959), *All Shot Up* (1960), *Cotton Comes to Harlem* (1965), *The Heat's On* (1966), and *Blind Man with a Pistol* (1969). If you think you recognize the name of one of them, it's probably because it was adapted to a 1970 film, directed by **Ossie Davis**: *Cotton Comes to Harlem.* (*The Heat's On* was also adapted to film as *Come Back, Charleston Blue,* but this 1972 picture didn't do well at the box office.) Whereas his first two novels are deemed his greatest literary achievements, his last eight were definitely his greatest popular and financial successes.

In addition to his early novels and his detective novels, Himes wrote the novels *A Case of Rape* (1963) and *Be Calm* (1961); a satire on sexual attraction between whites and blacks, *Pinktoes* (1961); and his collection *Black on Black: Baby Sister and Selected Writings* (1973). Also, after his death, his short stories were gathered into *The Collected Stories of Chester Himes* (1990).

—*Tonya Bolden*

REFERENCES: *EAACH. EBLG. SMKC.* Sanders, Mark A., in *OCAAL.*

Hine, Darlene Clark (2/7/1947–)
Nonfiction—history, biography, edited works

Hine has interviewed history watchers and storytellers, dug around in archives and libraries, plumbed the depths of basements, and climbed the heights of attics to gather information on her primary passion: African-American history, particularly the special contributions of African-American women. As a result of her long hours of research,

she has written and edited numerous works. The books she has authored include *When the Truth Is Told: A History of Black Women's Culture and Community in Indiana, 1875–1950* (1981); *Black Women in White: Racial Conflict and Cooperation in the Nursing Profession, 1890–1950* (1989); *Black Victory: The Rise and Fall of the White Primary in Texas* (1979); *Hine Sight: Black Women and the Re-Construction of American History* (1994); and *A Shining Thread of Hope: The History of Black Women in America* (1998, with Kathleen Thompson). Her edited works include *The State of Afro-American History: Past, Present, and Future* (1986); the 16-volume collection *Black Women in United States History: From Colonial Times to the Present* (1990); the 2-volume *Black Women in America: An Historical Encyclopedia* (1993, with Elsa Barkley Brown and Rosalyn Terborg-Penn, comprising 641 biographical essays and 163 essays on various topics relevant to African-American women's history); and *"We Specialize in the Wholly Impossible": A Reader in Black Women's History* (1995, with Wilma King and Linda Reed). In addition, her contributions to periodicals are too numerous to count.

—*Tonya Bolden*

REFERENCES: *BAAW.*

Hoagland, Everett H., III (12/18/1942–)
Poems, columns

Hoagland's poetry collections include *Ten Poems: A Collection* (1968), *Black Velvet* (1970), and *Scrimshaw* (1976). His poems are frequently anthologized, and he received a fellowship from the National Endowment for the Humanities (1984). Hoagland also wrote a weekly column for the *New Bedford Standard-Times* (1979–1982).

REFERENCES: Halil, Karen Isabelle, in *OCAAL.*

Holiday, Billie (née Eleanora Fagan) (4/7/1915–7/17/1959)
Songs, autobiography

With journalist William Duffy, jazz singer "Lady Day" wrote her somewhat self-mythologizing autobiography *Lady Sings the Blues* (1956/1984). The book, which she had wanted to title *Bitter Crop* (from the last line of her signature song, "Strange Fruit"), emphasizes her personal tragedies—often inaccurately—and gives short shrift to her musical talents and career. For instance, both the book and the 1972 movie made from the book neglect her talent as a songwriter (e.g., "God Bless the Child" and "Don't Explain").

REFERENCES: *BDAA. EB-BH-CD.* Cook, Susan, in *BWA:AHE.* Griffin, Farah Jasmine, in *OCAAL.* Sellman, James Clyde, in *EA-99.*

hooks, bell (née Gloria Jean Watkins)
(9/25/1952?–)
Feminist and social criticism, nonfiction books and essays, children's book, memoirs

Rosa Bell and Veodis Watkins raised young Gloria, her brother, and her five sisters in a segregated, working-class Southern neighborhood. At home, her parents taught her the same patriarchal, patriotic values her teachers and textbooks were teaching her in all-black public-school classrooms. At home and at school, she learned that African-American girls were of little worth. How did she respond to such belittlement? She enlarged her mind by escaping into a world of literature, particularly the verses of Walt Whitman and the romantic poets. Secretly, she scribbled her own poems, too.

When Gloria stepped onto the Stanford campus, she entered an integrated environment. For the first time, she was interacting continuously with whites. At about this time, the campus women's movement was starting to raise people's consciousness of sexism, and Gloria started to question the patriarchal values she had known all her life. She soon started to question many other values she had been taught. As she extended her questioning further, she noticed a distinct absence of African-American women and other women of color in the women's movement. Women's studies was usually white women's studies. (Similarly, black studies was usually black male studies.) In her academic studies, her white (mostly male) professors engaged in covert racism, ignoring their nonwhite students, perhaps without even realizing they were doing so. After earning her B.A. (1973) in English literature from Stanford, she went on to earn her M.A. (1976) from the University of Wisconsin and her Ph.D. (1983) from the University of California at Santa Cruz.

At age 19, while still earning her undergraduate degree, she began her first book project, a full-length book, *Ain't I a Woman: Black Women and Feminism*. This book harshly criticized the feminist movement for its unwillingness to explore issues of race and class as well as issues of sexism as they apply uniquely to women of color. She provided a feminist analysis of the history of African-American women from the days of slavery through the 1970s. Her analysis asserted that nineteenth-century African-American women had developed greater feminist consciousness than contemporary African-American women seem to evidence. Both men and women involved in the struggle for black liberation have ignored the distinctive plight of African-American women.

When she was ready to publish her first book, Gloria Jean Watkins changed her name to bell hooks. She took the name from her maternal great-grandmother, an outspoken woman whom bell describes as "a sharp-tongued woman, a woman who spoke her mind, a woman who was not afraid to talk back." In addition to her admiration for her grandmother, she chose the name to pay homage to matriarchal legacies. If outspoken clarity is the criterion, bell hooks has indeed honored her namesake. She spells her name in lowercase letters as a symbol of her devaluing of ego and celebrity.

Needless to say, the blunt and irreverent bell hooks had trouble finding a publisher for her book, as even the feminist presses and independent black publishers were less than enthusiastic about it. At last, when speaking at a feminist bookstore, she was put in touch with South End Press, which published *Ain't I a Woman: Black Women and Feminism* (in 1981) and all her subsequent books. Academics didn't welcome her book with open arms, but many others responded favorably to it. A reviewer in *Publishers Weekly* called the book one of the "twenty most influential women's books of the last twenty years."

While she was still earning her doctorate, hooks lectured in English and ethnic studies at the University of Southern California. Once she had her doctorate, she became an assistant professor at Yale, teaching African and African-American studies and English literature there. She left Yale to become an associate professor of American literature and women's studies at Oberlin College (the first college to admit women as well as men). She has also taught English at the City College of New York. A popular lecturer, her courses in African-American women's fiction and the politics of sexuality are always filled to capacity.

Her subsequent books have further elaborated hooks's analysis of feminism. For instance, in *Feminist Theory from Margin to Center* (1984; 2nd ed., 2000), she posited that mainstream feminism has put middle-class white women at the center of the movement and has marginalized working-class women and women of color. In *Talking Back: Thinking Feminist, Thinking Black* (1989), she prodded women of color to start speaking out to advocate liberation of the oppressed. Her *Yearning: Race, Gender and Cultural Politics* (1990) questioned sexism, classism, and racism in the arts (especially cinema), winning the Before Columbus Foundation's American Book Award. She and **Cornel West** coauthored a dialogue, *Breaking Bread: Insurgent Black Intellectual Life* (1991), which probes the challenge of African-American intellectuals who emerge from working-class backgrounds. In *Black Looks: Race and Representation* (1992), she questions the manipulation of dominant cultural images of African-American women and the ways in which those images reinforce inequality. Her *Sisters of the Yam: Black Women and Self-Recovery* (1993) shares its name with a support group for black women, which hooks established in the 1980s. In *Outlaw Culture: Resisting Representation* (1994), she critiques various facets of American culture; in *Teaching to Transgress: Education as the Practice of Freedom* (1994), she prods young men and women of color to participate fully and actively in their own education. She also wrote *Art on My Mind: Visual Politics* (1995), some essays on modern art; *Killing Rage: Ending Racism* (1995); *Reel to Real: Race, Sex, and Class at the Movies* (1996); and *Bone Black: Memories of Girlhood* (1996), her memoir. More recently, hooks has written two books about her experiences as a writer—*Wounds of Passion: A Writing Life* (1997) and *Remembered Rapture: The Writer at Work* (1999)—and a book on her reconceptualization of love, *All about Love: New Visions* (2000) as well as her children's picture book, *Happy to Be Nappy* (1999), reminiscent of **Carolivia Herron's** *Nappy Hair.*

REFERENCES: *1TESK. EB-98. EBLG. G-95. PBW.* Chay, Deborah G., in *OCAAL.* Amazon.com, 1/2000.

Hopkins, Pauline (Elizabeth)

(?/1859–8/13/1930)
Novels, short stories, essays and other nonfiction, plays; journalist, editor, publisher

While still a teenager, Hopkins won an essay contest, for which **William Wells Brown** awarded her the $10 prize. After finishing public school, Hopkins toured the country, singing with her mother and stepfather in their group Hopkins' Colored Troubadours for a dozen years. While touring, she wrote and performed her first two plays: *Slaves' Escape; or, The Underground Railroad* (also called *Peculiar Sam;* written 1879, produced 1880), a musical lauding **Harriet Tubman, Frederick Douglass**, and other slaves who escaped to freedom; and *One Scene from the Drama of Early Days,* about the biblical character Daniel. Eventually, she grew tired of having no steady income and no home, so she left the family business to get a civil service job as a stenographer for the Massachusetts Decennial Census in the Bureau of Statistics during the 1890s.

In 1900, she started her professional association with the newly founded Colored Cooperative Publishing Company in Boston, becoming a shareholder and a member of the company's board of directors. That year, the company started publishing *Colored American Magazine*. In the first issue were Hopkins's first published short story, "The Mystery within Us," and an announcement that Hopkins was to be the first editor of the magazine's women's department. In October, the company published Hopkins's first novel, *Contending Forces: A Romance Illustrative of Negro Life North and South* (1900), about a multigenerational mixed-race family. The novel followed the family members from their enslavement in Bermuda in 1790 through slavery in North Carolina and the brutality of the post–Civil War era to their experiences in Boston late in the nineteenth century. In it, Hopkins highlights strong women characters who embody the role of mothers as keepers and conveyors of culture, and who demonstrate the value of education and employment for women.

While working as editor, Hopkins also contributed numerous short stories, essays, editorials, social and political commentaries, and biographical sketches of famous African-American men (e.g., William Wells Brown, Frederick Douglass) and women (e.g., **Sojourner Truth**, Harriet Tubman) as well as serialized versions of her novels. The only literary form this great-grandniece of poet **James Monroe Whitfield** did not contribute was poetry. Whatever literary form she used, all of her works reflected her aims of racial pride, social justice, racial and gender equality, and protest against Jim Crow racist policies and practices. Worried that her own name was appearing too often in the magazine, she sometimes used her mother's maiden name, Sarah A. Allen, as a pseudonym for her works. Her serialized novels included her traditional romances *Hagar's Daughter: A Story of Southern Caste Prejudice*

(1901–1902, using her pseudonym), about an upper-class woman who discovers she has African ancestry, and *Winona: A Tale of Negro Life in the South and Southwest* (1902), about a mulatta's struggle to resist and escape slavery; and her fantasy *Of One Blood; or, the Hidden Self* (1902–1903), which highlights the splendorous achievements of ancient African civilizations. In her short stories, she dabbled in westerns, detective stories, and other popular genres of her day.

Through all her fiction—even her traditional romance novels—Hopkins explored racial and social themes, including such issues as miscegenation and racial intermarriage, racial politics, pseudoscientific theories about race, segregation, and racial inequities. In 1903, Hopkins was named the magazine's literary editor, and many of her male colleagues resented having a woman in such an important role on the magazine. In that role, she exerted powerful influence on the magazine's editorial policies, helping to ensure that racial uplift and protest against racism were reflected in the magazine's articles, editorials, and fiction items. (Male literary critics of her day and subsequent male historians may have underestimated her influence in this regard.)

Hopkins's outspoken views eventually reached the eyes and ears of **Booker T. Washington**, who was outraged by her opposition to his accommodationist, segregationist policies and beliefs. In 1904, Washington's supporters bought the *Colored American Magazine,* and a month after they bought it, the magazine announced that "ill health" had forced Hopkins to resign. Poor, sickly Hopkins was actually in such vibrantly good health that she soon started publishing articles in the *Voice of the Negro* (edited by **Jesse Max Barber** and **T. Thomas Fortune**), including her series of articles "The Dark Races of the Twentieth Century," which predicted that the two major crises of that century would be the "Negro Problem" and the conflict between laborers and capitalists. Quite prescient. Income from her articles in *Voice of the Negro* wasn't enough to support her and her aging mother, however. In 1905, she founded her own publishing company, P. E. Hopkins and Co., which published her *A Primer of Facts Pertaining to the Early Greatness of the African Race,* making use of her extensive knowledge of ancient African civilizations. A decade later, she tried to found another journal, which she hoped would become the equivalent of the *Colored American Magazine* she had known and

loved, but only two issues of her *New Era* were published before financial difficulties forced her to stop. Her last publication was her novella *Topsy Templeton,* published serially in 1916. That same year, she returned to working as a stenographer, employed by the Massachusetts Institute of Technology. This incendiary writer was killed by a fire in her home in Cambridge, Massachusetts; any remaining unpublished manuscripts that she may have written went up in smoke with her.

Hopkins was not as well known as many of her male contemporaries, and it was not until 1972 that **Ann Shockley** rediscovered her works, and by the 1980s, her works started being recognized more widely. Since then, some of her works have been republished in paperbacks, and biographers frequently identify her as a pioneer in African-American literature.

REFERENCES: *EB-BH-CD. EBLG. MWEL. NAAAL. OC20LE. WDAA.* Campbell, Jane, in *BWA:AHE* and in *OCWW.* Robinson, Lisa Clayton, in *EA-99.* Tate, Claudia, in *OCAAL.* Hopkins's papers are archived at Fisk University Library.

Horton, George Moses (?/1797?–1883?)
Poems

When George was a young boy, music prompted him to sing out his own poems, and as soon as he could, he struggled to learn to read a few words in the hope that someday, he might write down his own verses. Some of his first verses were inspired by Scripture and by Methodist hymns. Particularly appealing were verses on freedom, which he had never known but had always longed for.

When Horton was leaving his teen years behind, and he was hawking his master's produce at the University of North Carolina (UNC) in Chapel Hill, he started reciting some of the verses he had composed within earshot of some of the students there. Pretty soon, he was being commissioned to make up verses for the students. He wrote some of these on the eight-mile walk to and from the university each Sunday—or while taking care of his farm chores during the week, or perhaps just before his weary mind slipped into unconsciousness in his bed each night. He might charge a quarter—or even two or three—for writing a special love poem or a poem centered around the letters of a sweetheart's name. In any case, he always received a cash payment, upon delivery, when he recited the poem to the patron. After a while, people started calling him the "Colored Bard of North Carolina," perhaps mockingly at first but then with reverence. His patrons also became his coaches, providing him with classical poetry from Byron to Shakespeare, with stops for Homer and Milton along the way.

When he was making up verses on his own self-chosen themes, frequent subjects were freedom—and his longings to enjoy it—and slavery—and the depredations of that institution. Soon, the wife of one of the UNC professors, writer Caroline Hentz, started rallying support for gaining him his liberty. She sent some of his poems to the *Lancaster* (Massachusetts) *Gazette,* which published two of them, and in the summer and fall issues, ***Freedom's Journal*** was urging every African American in New York to donate a penny toward Horton's manumission. In 1829, his *The Hope of Liberty, Containing a Number of Poetical Pieces,* was published, becoming the third book of poetry by an African American published in the United States (see **Phillis Wheatley** for the first) and the first book of any kind authored by an African American, which was published in the South. In 1830, able to see a bright new life for himself, he married; later on, the couple had two children: their daughter, Rhoda, and their son, Free. At about this time, he also mastered reading and writing, so from the early 1830s forward, he could read poetry and write down his own verses.

Although his hope of liberty was not extinguished, he was unable to raise enough money to buy it despite the efforts of his supporters. After a few years, his owner recognized that Horton was far better suited to poetry than to farming, thereafter allowing Horton to buy his own time for a quarter a day. When he couldn't earn the money by selling poems, he did odd jobs at UNC. Still, despite all his efforts, he couldn't buy more than a day of freedom at a time. Discouraged with waiting for his freedom, in the mid-1830s, Horton decided that liquor was quicker in easing his troubled mind.

At last, toward the end of the 1830s, his *Hope of Liberty* was printed twice more, retitled *Poems by a Slave* in 1837, and as an addition to the reprint of *Memoir and Poems of Phillis Wheatley* in 1838. In 1843, after Horton's lifelong owner died, and the owner's son was Horton's new owner, the son started charging Horton two quarters a day for his freedom. At that rate, freedom for more than a day or two seemed a long way off.

He decided to step up his efforts. In addition to taking on as many wage-earning jobs as he could, he sold subscriptions to his second book of poetry, for which he charged 50 cents a subscription. Once he had gathered enough money, he published his *Poetical Works of George M. Horton, the Colored Bard of North Carolina, to Which Is Prefixed the Life of the Author, Written by Himself* (1845). He firmly believed that if he could sell just 100 copies of his book, with a final (nonsubscription) price of $2, he would be able to buy his freedom. Just as he was reaching his goal, in 1852, his new owner told him that the full sale price for his body and soul was now $250. So near, but yet so far. Throughout his struggle for freedom, Horton also summoned the financial aid of prominent white abolitionists, such as *Liberator* publisher William Lloyd Garrison and Horace Greeley. By all accounts, neither obliged him. Why not? Because the person who was to have posted these summons, new UNC president (and future North Carolina governor) David Swain failed to send the summons.

After decades of dedicated labor to free himself, in April 1865 Horton (and his fellow slaves) were liberated by Captain Will Banks and the entire Union Army's 9th Michigan Cavalry. Horton's poor new master didn't get a dime for his "property." Over the next several months, Horton wrote poem after poem about being enslaved, being at war, leading the Yankees, leading the Rebels, and even about writing poetry. By September of that year, Banks compiled Horton's new poems—and a few of his previously published ones—into a new volume, *Naked Genius.*

The following year, Horton moved to Philadelphia, parting company with Banks and leaving behind his wife and children. Sadly, the "Colored Bard of North Carolina" never received in freedom anything close to the "celebrity" he had while in bondage.

—*Tonya Bolden*

REFERENCES: *SMKC.* Sherman, Joan R. (Ed.) (1997), *The Black Bard of North Carolina: George Moses Horton and His Poetry* (Chapel Hill: University of North Carolina Press). Sherman, Joan R. (Ed.) (1989), *Invisible Poets: Afro-Americans of the Nineteenth Century* (2nd ed.) (Urbana and Chicago: University of Illinois Press).

Houston, Charles (Hamilton)
(9/3/1895–4/22/1950)
Nonfiction—legal matters; editor

Although we know of no books he authored, Charles Houston's writings made history. Yes, he was the first African-American editor of the *Harvard Law Review,* and yes, he wrote a seminal report on constitutional law funded by a Rockefeller grant, "The Negro and His Contact with the Administration of the Law" (1928). He also headed Howard University's law school, turning it upside down to make it the finest he could make it, and by 1932, it was fully accredited and approved by the American Bar Association and the Association of American Law Schools.

On leave from Howard as the full-time special counsel to the National Association for the Advancement of Colored People (NAACP), he wrote columns for various periodicals such as the *Baltimore Afro-American.* Those columns were important for rallying support for the battle he was starting to wage. His historic writings, however, were his legal briefs for the NAACP's series of Supreme Court cases, designed to force the nation to obey its own laws, especially the equal protection clause of our Constitution's Fourteenth Amendment. His writing also influenced two life-or-death decisions (in 1935 and 1938) in the cases of two African-American men; for each, his death sentence was reversed when Houston showed the Court that their trials had been unfair because African Americans had been specifically barred from serving on their juries.

By the time Houston turned over his NAACP job to his protégé (and former student) **Thurgood Marshall**, he had guided Marshall well in how to write a persuasive brief. Houston went on to serve as counsel to various union and governmental organizations, and he continued to advise his colleagues at the NAACP. One of his last services for the NAACP was to file a brief for a case involving segregated schools in Washington, D.C. That case was later subsumed, along with several others, into the case now known as *Brown v. Board of Education* (1954), which Thurgood Marshall fought and won. As Marshall readily acknowledged, Houston had taught him well.

—*Tonya Bolden*

REFERENCES: *BH2C. EAACH. SMKC.* McNeil, Genna Rae (1983), *Groundwork: Charles Hamilton Houston and the Struggle for Civil Rights* (Philadelphia: University of Pennsylvania Press). Tushnet,

Mark V. (1987), *The NAACP's Legal Strategy against Segregated Education, 1925–1950* (Chapel Hill: University of North Carolina Press).

Houston, Drusilla (née) Dunjee
(1876–1941)
Nonfiction—history, cultural anthropology, paleontology, archeology

As a child, Drusilla had loved roaming through history in her father's massive library. As a young woman, she wrote history-related columns while working with her brother, Roscoe Dunjee, founding editor of the *Black Dispatch,* a weekly newspaper. Later still, she applied her historical research and expertise to writing a masterwork of African history. As celebrated bibliophile **Arthur Schomburg** said of her self-published *The Wonderful Ethiopians of the Ancient Cushite Empire* (1926/ 1985), "I can assure everyone that the author must have used considerable oil in her lamp represented by her extensive research, the indefatigable labor that resulted in the astonishing compilation before me." At a time when few others were studying Africans and African Americans, Houston embarked on a planned massive three-volume survey of ancient sub-Saharan African history, highlighting its gifts to Western civilization. Sadly, she was able to publish only this first of the three before her death, and the manuscripts for the other two have been lost.

—*Tonya Bolden*

REFERENCES: *BAAW.* Coates, W. Paul, in *BWA:AHE.*

Hughes, (James) Langston
(2/1/1902–5/22/1967)
Poems and news columns, short stories, novel, plays, screenplay, autobiographies, children's books, anthologies

James Langston Hughes was born in Joplin, Missouri, and grew up in Lawrence, Kansas, with his maternal grandmother, Mary Langston. Young Langston moved to Lawrence with his mother, Carrie Langston Hughes, when his father and mother separated. His father, James Nathaniel Hughes, moved to Mexico to practice law in a place where he would not be discriminated against because of racism, leaving his family behind. Hughes was often lonely as a boy, left with his grandmother while his mother was frequently away looking for work and pursuing a dream of being an actress. Growing up with his grandmother was difficult. They were poor, and Hughes's grandmother did not want him to play with children who lived nearby.

She did read to him, though, sometimes from the Bible, and she often told Langston stories, many of them true stories about the brave history of Langston's family. She told him about her first husband, Lewis Sheridan Leary, who had ridden with John Brown and was killed at Harpers Ferry in the struggle to end slavery. Langston's grandfather, her second husband, was also a militant abolitionist. John Mercer Langston, a brother of Langston Hughes's grandfather, was one of the best-known black Americans in the nineteenth century. She also told him about two uncles who were heroes, "buffalo soldiers," as the Native Americans called them because of their curly hair. Native Americans considered the buffalo soldiers to be the bravest of the brave. Langston's grandmother herself helped fugitives on the Underground Railroad, and she told him stories about helping slaves escape to the safety of the North. She may have been poor, but she knew and claimed a rich and proud history for her grandson. She knew how to feed his imagination and his dreams with real-life heroes.

As Langston's grandmother grew older, she withdrew into herself, becoming silent for long periods of time. In his loneliness, Langston Hughes discovered new possibilities for his life in books: "Then it was that books began to happen to me, and I began to believe in nothing but books and the wonderful world in books—where if people suffered, they suffered in beautiful language."

By the time Hughes enrolled at Columbia University in New York, he had already published his first poem, "The Negro Speaks of Rivers," in *Crisis* magazine, edited by **W. E. B. Du Bois**. He had also realized that he wanted to write, and to write specifically about being an African American in the United States. Hughes left Columbia in 1922 and spent the next three years working menial jobs as well as traveling abroad. Hughes moved frequently, working on a freighter on the west coast of Africa, living for a time in Paris, and working as a busboy in Washington, D.C. By 1924, when he returned to the United States, he was known in African-American circles as a gifted young poet.

Though Hughes wrote in many genres, he is best known for his poetry. In his early work, he embraced jazz and blues rhythms and the cadence of vernacular speech. Hughes's poetry was often written in free verse or loosely rhymed verse, reflecting the poet's admiration for Walt Whitman and Carl Sandburg. Hughes had an ear tuned to the music of black speech, however, and came to see black American culture as his primary influence and black Americans as his most important audience.

Hughes's first two books, *The Weary Blues* (1926) and *Fine Clothes to the Jew* (1927), established Hughes as a major poet of the **Harlem Renaissance**. With the fame came a great deal of criticism in the middle-class black press for dwelling on lower-class black culture and for taking as his subject matter sexuality, poverty, loss, sorrows, and violence. In 1926, Hughes published an essay titled, "The Negro Artist and the Racial Mountain" in the *Nation,* which became a manifesto for the young artists and writers who were determined to claim the freedom to write about racial issues from a perspective of racial pride.

In a search for more stability in his life, Hughes enrolled at Lincoln University, a historically black college in Pennsylvania, from which he graduated in 1929. Two years earlier, in 1927, Hughes had met Mrs. Charlotte Mason, or "Godmother," an older white woman who became his patron until 1930. During the period of her patronage and under her intense encouragement and meticulous editing, Hughes wrote his first novel, *Not without Laughter* (1930). When she suddenly withdrew her friendship for reasons still not known today, Hughes was devastated and became ill. He fled to Cuba and Haiti with $400 from the Harmon Prize for Literature. He spent several weeks on Haiti's northern coast, evidently reviewing his life choices and direction for the future.

When Hughes returned, his politics had become leftist, so he spent the following year in the Soviet Union (1932–1933), during which he wrote his most radical verse. His poetry was no longer lyrical and blues based; the poem "Goodbye Christ," published without his knowledge in Germany, attacked American imperialism and Christianity in favor of communist/Marxist values. He would later repudiate this work. He spent the following year (1934) in Carmel, California, under the sponsorship of Noel Sullivan, a liberal patron of the arts. Despite the friendship of his white patron, Hughes wrote *The Ways of White Folks,* his satiric, bleak, and cynical collection of short stories about race relations in the United States. While the

Langston Hughes (Archive Photos)

collection was unprecedented in its harshness and bitter portrayal of whites in their confused and insincere dealings with blacks, it established Hughes as a fiction writer, which helped him to live solely by his writing.

When Hughes's father died in 1934, Hughes went to Mexico, spending several months there, translating the work of several short pieces by young Mexicans for possible publication in the United States. U.S. editors had no interest in this material, however, and Hughes returned in 1935, almost broke, to live with his mother in Oberlin, Ohio, where her parents had lived during their youth before the Civil War.

Hughes then wrote *Mulatto,* a dramatized account of U.S. race relations in the segregated South, with its disastrous denial of the humanity of blacks and their essential role in the country. Despite harsh reviews, *Mulatto* remained on Broadway longer than any play by a black playwright until **Lorraine Hansberry's** *A Raisin in the Sun*

many years later. After *Mulatto* opened on Broadway in 1935, Hughes wrote other plays: *Little Ham* (1936), *Troubled Island* (1936), *Joy to My Soul, Front Porch, Soul Gone Home,* and *Don't You Want to Be Free?* In 1938, Hughes published his only collection of socialist poetry, *A New Song,* with an introduction by Mike Gold, a radical writer. Most of Hughes's plays made virtually no money, so throughout the 1930s, he struggled financially.

In 1939, he worked in Hollywood as a writer on *Way Down South,* a movie set on a plantation in the days of slavery, written for the popular young singer Bobby Breen. Unfortunately, and to Hughes's dismay, the movie was denounced in liberal circles when it opened. In 1940, a major luncheon in Pasadena, California, to present Hughes's new autobiography, *The Big Sea,* was canceled due to picketing by an evangelical group that accused Hughes of communism and atheism. The basis for their outrage was Hughes's poem "Goodbye Christ" from 1932. Hughes then repudiated the poem as a youthful error, thereby ending his reputation as a socialist.

During World War II, Hughes completed his withdrawal from leftist politics. *Shakespeare in Harlem* (1942) took him back to the blues as a theme for his work. In *Jim Crow's Last Stand* (1943), he attacked racial segregation. In what may have been his finest literary achievement during the war, however, he began writing a weekly column in the *Chicago Defender* in 1942, which continued for 20 years. The column introduced Jesse B. Semple, or Simple, a character from Harlem who commented on racism, race, and other matters. Simple was Hughes's most beloved character and became the subject of five collections edited by Hughes, beginning with *Simple Speaks His Mind* (1950). Two postwar books of poetry, *Fields of Wonder* (1947) and *One-Way Ticket* (1949), were not well received, but *Montage of a Dream Deferred* (1951) was an important work, blending poetry with the new bebop jazz in a discordant reflection of the despair of many urban blacks living in the North.

In 1953, Senator Joseph McCarthy subpoenaed Hughes to testify about his politics. Humiliated and frustrated, Hughes cooperated with McCarthy, though he had no respect for McCarthy or his aims. Hughes testified that he had never been a Communist Party member but admitted that "Goodbye Christ" had been ill advised. Some leftists criticized Hughes for cooperating with McCarthy, but overall, Hughes's career was not hurt by this episode, unlike that of **Paul Robeson** and **W. E. B. Du Bois**. Soon McCarthy himself was discredited. Hughes then wrote *I Wonder as I Wander* (1956), an account of his year in the Soviet Union and an admired second volume to his autobiography.

In the 1950s, Hughes was finally able to break free from the seemingly endless poverty he had lived in all his life. Becoming prosperous, he bought a home in Harlem. He looked to the stage again, first with a show based on the Simple books, *Simply Heavenly* (1957), which met with some popularity. His next show, *Tambourines to Glory* (1963), was a gospel musical, but it failed badly. Some critics accused Hughes of caricaturing black Americans. Hughes went on to write other gospel-based stage shows, including *Black Nativity* (1961) and *Jericho-Jim Crow* (1964).

Versatile and prolific, Hughes also wrote a dozen children's books throughout his career, beginning with *Popo and Fifina: Children of Haiti*

(1932, written with **Arna Bontemps**), which drew on Hughes's visit to Haiti in 1931. Many of his children's books sought to introduce children to various aspects of black culture or black Americans, such as *The First Book of Jazz* (1957), one of a series of "first" books, and *Famous American Negroes* (1954).

Hughes also edited and anthologized the work of others in books such as *The Poetry of the Negro 1746–1949,* which included work of Caribbean writers; *New Negro Poets USA* (1964); and *The Best Short Stories by Negro Writers* (1967), which included the first published story of **Alice Walker**.

Hughes was distinctively able to write for the needs of his black audience, as he held to a vision of a more inclusive America. His work celebrates and lifts up the lives and dreams of average black Americans, who in turn praised and celebrated him. His poetry, with its jazz rhythms and blues influence, is some of the best and most influential of any written this century by any black poet. "The Negro Speaks of Rivers," "Mother to Son," and "Harlem" are anthems of black America.

Langston Hughes died in a New York hospital, still hard at work on various projects until just before his death. *The Panther and the Lash* (1967), a collection of poetry published posthumously, focuses on the civil rights and black power movements. To this day, Langston Hughes is considered one of our most creative and prolific African-American poets.

—*Lisa Bahlinger*

REFERENCES: *AAW. EA-99.* Haskins, James S. (1976), *Always Movin' On: The Life of Langston Hughes* (New York: Watts). Rampersad, Arnold (1986), *The Life of Langston Hughes, 1902–1941: Vol. 1.: I, Too, Sing America* (New York: Oxford University Press). Rampersad, Arnold, in *OCAAL.*

Hunter, Alberta (4/1/1895–10/17/1984)
Songs

Chiefly known as a blues singer, Hunter wrote many of her own songs such as "Downhearted Blues" (1922), recorded by fellow blues singer Bessie Smith. From 1955 until 1977, Hunter retired from singing and songwriting to work as a nurse, but when she returned to singing at age 82, she once again returned to the fore in her profession.

REFERENCES: *EA-99. EB-BH-CD. WDAW.* Meadows, Eddie S., in *BWA:AHE.*

Hunter (married name: Lattany), Kristin Eggleston (9/12/1931–)

Novels, children's/juvenile novels, short stories, dramas, screenplays, columns, articles; advertising copywriter

Mabel and George Lorenzo Eggleston planned that their only child would become a schoolteacher like them. Although Kristin's family home held a wealth of books and her parents encouraged her to read, she was rarely allowed to speak in this "children-were-seen-and-not-heard household." As Hunter has said (*BWWW*, p. 85), "I escaped into books very early. When I picture myself as a child, I see myself somewhere reading, usually hiding and reading." She also learned early that if she wished to express herself, she would have to do so through writing. In retrospect, Hunter has noted, "I always knew I wanted to be a writer" (*BWWW*, p. 85).

When Kristin was 14 years old, her aunt helped her get work writing a youth column for the *Pittsburgh Courier*. After a bit, she started writing feature articles for the paper. During her six-year association with that paper, she also had some of her poems and "a short story or two" published, and she graduated from the University of Pennsylvania (in 1951). On graduation, she briefly tried to fulfill her parents' wishes for her to teach in public school. After teaching third grade for less than a year, however, she realized that she needed to follow her own goals, not her parents' dreams for her. She resigned her teaching job to seek a career as a writer.

At first, she worked as an advertising copywriter and pursued other kinds of writing after hours. In 1955, she won a national Fund for the Republic Award competition for a television script, having submitted her script *Minority of One*. Her script involved black-white school integration, but by the time the teleplay aired, the CBS network had transformed the script into a story about a French-speaking immigrant starting out in an all-Anglo school.

Hunter continued to write fiction at night and on weekends while working as a copywriter, an information officer, and a freelance writer (e.g., with articles in *Philadelphia Magazine* and other publications) by day. In 1964, Hunter had another breakthrough when her social criticism novel *God Bless the Child* was published. The central character, Rosie Fleming, tragically believes that because her poverty has oppressed her, the secret to happiness must be to achieve high financial status and

success at all costs. She ends up sacrificing her relationships with loved ones and even her own health in the effort. The next year, Hunter's play *The Double Edge* was produced, and in 1966, her novel *The Landlord* was published. In her novel, a young wealthy white landlord buys a black-ghetto apartment building and starts to try to shape the lives of his tenants. Over time, however, his tenants have far more influence on him than he has on them. The novel was made into a 1970 movie, which portrayed a far harsher view of the landlord and the tenants than Hunter had described.

In the late 1960s, Hunter turned to writing novels for young adults. Many readers now know her primarily as an author of these works. Her first young adult novel was *The Soul Brothers and Sister Lou* (1968), centered around Louetta Hawkins. "Lou" forms a singing group whose rise in popularity carries them up and out of their urban ghetto. In this work, Hunter uses the authentic speech of African-American urban youths, a relatively novel approach at the time. The Council on Interracial Books recognized this book with its 1968 Children's Prize, and the book sold more than 1 million copies. Hunter's other novels (and novelettes) for young readers include *Boss Cat* (1971), *The Pool Table War* (1972), *Uncle Dan and the Raccoon* (1972), and her sequel *Lou in the Limelight* (1981). She also wrote a short-story collection for young adults, *Guests in the Promised Land* (1973), for which she became a National Book Award finalist and was awarded the 1973 Chicago Tribune Book World Prize for juvenile literature.

Hunter also continues to writes novels for adults, including *The Survivors* (1975), about a friendship between a lonely middle-aged dressmaker and a neglected, homeless, 13-year-old boy. Her 1978 novel *The Lakestown Rebellion* tells the story of how a small community of blacks cleverly sabotages a powerful corporation's attempt to bulldoze through their town to build a highway. Clearly along the lines of the **trickster tales** tradition in African-American and world literature, the protagonist Bella Lake leads the residents of the town to innovatively create comical disruptions that foil the plans of the out-of-towners. Hunter noted that her account is fictional, but she based it on an actual rebellion.

Once Hunter had established her writing career, she ended up returning both to the University of Pennsylvania campus and to teaching in 1972, offering instruction in creative writing and

African-American literature there. She enjoys "working with young people, finding out what's on their minds, seeing them develop. It's a source of energy even though it drains the writing energy" (*BWWW,* p. 86). Although teaching also provides needed income, she finds that it inhibits her writing, particularly if she teaches more than two courses per semester. Hunter is also married and has children. When her children were youngsters around the house, she had to create a room of her own in which to work.

Although Hunter's own experiences have been centered in the middle class, she writes both realistically and optimistically, with sensitivity, warmth, and humor, about the black urban ghetto. In an interview, Hunter observed, "I don't think I'll ever run out of ideas. I may run out of energy. Stories are waiting to be written. It's whatever grabs my imagination. It finds form, as a novel, as a short story. What is most urgent I do first. I have a dozen more stories I haven't done yet. You see this box of future projects; it's full" (*BWWW,* p. 84).

REFERENCES: *BI. BWWW. EBLG. G-95. MAAL. MWEL.* Collier, Eugenia W., in *OCWW.* Tate, Claudia, in *OCAAL.*

Hunter, Latoya (6/13/1978–)
Memoir

Hunter's *The Diary of Latoya Hunter: My First Year in Junior High School* was published when she was just 12 years old. Since then, she has continued to write and aspires to be a journalist.

—*Tonya Bolden*

REFERENCES: *33T.*

Hunter-Gault, Charlayne (2/27/1942–)
Memoir; journalist

At age 12, Charlayne already knew she wanted to be a journalist like her comic strip heroine Brenda Starr. In high school, she was editor of her school newspaper, but her guidance counselor tried to dissuade Charlayne from journalism because of her double jeopardy: being both female and black. Undaunted, Charlayne decided to attend a college with an outstanding journalism program; the one she chose (with a little nudging from the National Association for the Advancement of Colored People [NAACP]) was the all-white University of Georgia. That started her two-year legal battle to become the first African-American

woman to attend the University of Georgia since its start 176 years earlier. While her NAACP lawyers were working her case through the legal system to the Supreme Court, Charlayne started studying journalism at Wayne State University in Detroit. At last, in January of 1961, the court ordered that Charlayne Hunter and Hamilton Holmes be admitted as the first two African Americans to desegregate the University of Georgia. That's when the real battle began, with white racists violently protesting her presence. She later observed, "There was conflict and there was pain. . . . But I emerged as a whole person and the university came out the better for it" (quoted in *TAWH,* p. 189). A short time before she graduated (B.A. in journalism, 1963), she married fellow (white) student Walter Stovall, and a few years later, the couple had a daughter, Susan. (Although the marriage didn't last, the two have stayed friends.)

After graduating, Hunter-Stovall started out as a secretary for *New Yorker* magazine, began contributing items for the magazine's "Talk of the Town" column, and was soon promoted to a writing position on the staff. In 1967, she studied social science through a Russell Sage Fellowship and started working for *Trans-Action* magazine. The magazine sent her to cover the Poor People's Campaign in Washington, D.C., and soon she was anchoring and reporting the local evening news for WRC-TV there. In 1968, she joined the staff at the *New York Times,* where she founded and managed the paper's Harlem bureau. She has since observed, "I have never apologized for doing black stories, being interested in black stories, and insisting that every institution that I work for report black stories" (quoted in *RWTC,* p. 43). While working for the *Times,* she took time out to codirect the Michele Clark Fellowship program for minority students at Columbia University's school of journalism. In 1971, Hunter married a second time, to African-American banker Ronald Gault, with whom she has a son, Chuma.

In 1978, Hunter-Gault joined the *MacNeil/ Lehrer Report,* and in 1983, she became the program's national correspondent when it expanded to the one-hour *MacNeil/Lehrer NewsHour.* In 1997, she left the *NewsHour* to take a job as South Africa bureau chief for National Public Radio, during the critical times of that nation's history. Among Hunter-Gault's awards are the prestigious George Foster Peabody Award for Excellence in Broadcast Journalism (1986), the Journalist of the

Year Award from the National Association of Black Journalists (1986), the National Urban Coalition Award for Distinguished Urban Reporting, the *New York Times* Publisher's Award, the American Women in Radio and Television Award, and two national news (outstanding coverage of a single breaking story and outstanding background/analysis of a single current story) and documentary Emmy Awards. In addition to writing numerous articles for national publications (e.g., *Essence, Life, New York Times Magazine, Saturday Review*), Hunter-Gault wrote her autobiography *In My Place* (1992), and she has coauthored and contributed to other volumes.

REFERENCES: *EBLG. EWJ. RWTC. TAWH.* Garza, Hedda, in *G-97.* Robinson, Lisa Clayton, in *EA-99.* Smith, Jessie Carney, in *BWA:AHE.* Amazon.com, 7/1999.

Hurston, Zora Neale
(1/7/1891?–1/28/1960)
Essays, short stories, novels, nonfiction—anthropology, folklore, autobiography

Zora Neale Hurston is probably best known as the author of *Their Eyes Were Watching God* (1937) and as one of the most prolific participants in the **Harlem Renaissance**. She has influenced such writers as **Ralph Ellison**, **Toni Morrison**, **Gayl Jones**, and **Toni Cade Bambara**. The author of four novels and a number of short stories, essays, and other nonfiction works, Hurston is also acknowledged as the first African American to collect and publish African-American folklore.

Hurston was raised in the first incorporated African-American town—Eatonville, Florida. Eatonville had a mayor, a charter, a marshal, and a council. She described it as the first attempt at self-government on the part of African Americans. A rich source of African-American cultural tradition, the locale inspired most of her fiction.

Hurston's mother, Lucy Potts Hurston, a former schoolteacher, died when Zora was about nine years old. Her father, John Hurston, was a carpenter, a Baptist preacher, and three-term mayor of Eatonville. The fifth of John and Lucy's eight children, Zora Neale Hurston had a rocky relationship with her family. Her father remarried shortly after Lucy's death, and Hurston's dislike of her stepmother caused her relationship with her father to deteriorate.

Hurston was taken out of school at age 13, and she left home to take a job as a wardrobe girl in a repertory company touring the South. Eighteen months later, she left the troupe in Baltimore, Maryland, and an employer later arranged for her to complete her primary education. She completed her high school requirements at Morgan Academy in Baltimore. She went on to Howard Prep School and Howard University, where she earned an associate's degree. She completed her undergraduate education at Barnard College and Columbia University, becoming a member of Zeta Phi Beta. In college, she studied under esteemed anthropologist Franz Boas, an experience that influenced her work.

While in New York, Hurston became a part of the Harlem Renaissance literati, making regular company of artists such as **Langston Hughes**, **Wallace Thurman**, and **Jessie Redmon Fauset**, and calling the black literati the "niggerati." She became well known not only for her writing but also for her outspokenness, her distinct way of dress, and her refusal to be ashamed of her culture.

Ironically, several members of the "niggerati" harshly criticized Hurston for her rugged individualism. Like many other black artists of the period, she received funds from white patrons and philanthropic organizations to do her work. She was very adept in her quest for funds. To some of her contemporaries, however, this was just another reason to criticize her, even though many of them relied on the same patrons and organizations for their livelihood.

From 1927 to 1931, Hurston collected African-American folklore in Alabama and Florida, working on a private grant. She also traveled to the Caribbean and Latin America for her folklore writings. Her most active years were the 1930s and early 1940s. During that time, she was awarded a Guggenheim fellowship, joined the Federal Writers' Project in Florida, published four novels and an autobiography, and worked as a story consultant for Paramount Pictures.

Hurston drew on the folklore material for her plays, musicals, short stories, and novels. In *Zora Neale Hurston: A Literary Biography* (1977), Robert Hemenway quotes Hurston's definition of folklore: "Folklore, Hurston said, is the art people create before they find out there is such a thing as art; it comes from a folk's 'first wondering contact with natural law'—that is, laws of human nature as well as laws of natural process, the truths of a group's experience as well as the principles of physics."

Zora Neale Hurston, 1935 (Corbis)

Hurston's search for the "inner heart of truth," which she believed could be found in folklore, led her on many perilous adventures. Her study of African-American folklore took her into the secret world of hoodoo (voodoo), and because she believed in personally participating in her research, she learned how to conjure. Albert Price III, a man to whom Hurston was married for a short time, claimed that she had supernatural powers and could "fix him." The belief in voodoo features in Hurston's fictive Eatonville, which is often controlled by seemingly supernatural forces.

Fearing for her life, Hurston fled Haiti shortly after writing *Their Eyes Were Watching God,* which is an intense blend of black folklore and Western literary tradition. Her intensive study of voodoo, which she believed to be rooted in African mysticism, came to an abrupt end. According to Hemenway, "She had gone deeply enough into the Caribbean night."

Hurston embraced hoodoo for artistic inspiration because it freed her of the institutional restraints that restricted the freedom of a black woman in a white patriarchy. *Their Eyes Were Watching God,* considered Hurston's best work by many critics, tells the story of her protagonist Janie's quest for fulfillment and liberation. In the novel, when Tea Cake, Janie's third husband, becomes ill after being bitten by a rabid dog, he fears that he has been conjured. He is suspicious that Janie wants to be free of him so that she can marry a lighter-skinned man. In an attempt to quell his fear, Janie says, "Maybe it wuz uh witch ridin' yuh, honey. Ah'll see can't Ah find some mustard seed whilst Ah's out."

Hurston's novel *Jonah's Gourd Vine* (1934) combines her knowledge of folklore with biblical themes. Her nonfiction work *Mules and Men* (1935) incorporates **folktale** elements drawn from her hometown culture. In *Moses, Man of the Mountain* (1939), an allegorical novel of American slavery, Hurston made use of her studies in voodoo in New Orleans. Her autobiography *Dust Tracks on a Road* was published in 1942.

Hurston's individualism was mixed with a strong sense of optimism. In *Dust Tracks on a Road,* she recalled her mother urging her eight children to aim high: "Jump at de sun. . . . We might not land on the sun, but at least we would get off the ground." She shocked many, while delighting others, by living her life as she pleased.

In an essay called "How It Feels to Be Colored Me," Hurston said, "I am not tragically colored. There is no great sorrow dammed up in me or lurking behind my eyes. I do not mind at all. I do not belong to the sobbing school of Negrohood who hold that nature somehow has given them a lowdown dirty deal and whose feelings are all hurt about. . . . No, I do not weep at the world—I am too busy sharpening my oyster knife."

Hurston was raised to be a Christian but became a pagan. Educated to be a scholar, she believed in the integrity of the genius of black vernacular. She was an African-American woman who achieved fame in a white man's world, and she was an artist, an urban New Yorker, and a rural Floridian. In "How It Feels to Be Colored Me," Hurston described herself as "a brown bag of miscellany propped against a wall."

During the mid-1940s, Hurston began to publish less and less. It was not that she did not produce work, but her work was rejected with increasing frequency, and she had to find other ways to make a living. During the remaining years of her life, she worked variously as a newspaper reporter, librarian, and substitute teacher. For a while in 1950, she worked as a maid in Rivo Island, Florida. During that period, she published an article in the *Saturday Evening Post.* She moved to Belle Glade, Florida, late that year, and she continued to write and publish, including another article in the *Saturday Evening Post.*

Her finances and her health faltered, however. Like many other artists who were before their time, Hurston lived her last few years in relative obscurity. In 1959 she suffered a stroke and had to enter the St. Lucie County Welfare home. She died there penniless and was buried in an unmarked grave in a segregated cemetery in Fort Pierce, Florida. In 1973, writer **Alice Walker** discovered Hurston's grave and put a gravemarker on the site. Walker published the essay "In Search of Zora Neale Hurston" in *Ms.* magazine in March 1975 and resurrected the literary world's interest in Hurston. Since 1989, there has been an annual festival in her honor in Eatonville.

—*Michael Strickland*

REFERENCES: *EBLG.* Hemenway, Robert E. (1977), *Zora Neale Hurston: A Literary Biography* (Chicago: University of Chicago Press). Hooks, Rita (1996), "Conjured into Being, Their Eyes Were Watching God," http://splavc.spjc.cc.fl.us/hooks/ Zora.html. Hurston, Zora Neale (1979), "How It Feels to Be Colored Me," in Alice Walker (Ed.), *I Love Myself*

When I Am Laughing . . . and Then Again When I Am Looking Mean and Impressive (Old Westbury, NY: Feminist Press). Hurston, Zora Neale (1937), *Their Eyes Were Watching God* (New York: Harper and Row).

Hutson, Jean (née) Blackwell
(9/7/1914–2/3/1998)
Nonfiction—bibliography

A frequent contributor to bibliographic works, particularly on African-American writers and writings, Hutson also wrote short stories and the introductions to numerous books. Nonetheless, she is chiefly known for her work as a librarian. After working for the New York Public Library a dozen years, in 1948, Hutson was appointed curator of the Arthur A. Schomburg Collection within the Harlem branch of the library. By 1972, she had so expanded the collection that she was appointed chief of the collection, now known as the Schomburg Center for Research in Black Culture. When Hutson took over the collection, it comprised Schomburg's 15,000-book library and was located in a small, decaying Carnegie library building. For the next eight years, she raised funds and elevated public awareness of the collection, now considered the preeminent research center of its kind, comprising more than 5 million separately catalogued items, housed in a spacious new facility. She also supervised the development of the *Dictionary Catalog* of the entire Schomburg collection, a massive undertaking. This notable bibliophile was married for a time to lyricist **Andy Razaf**, and then to library security guard John Hutson, with whom she adopted a daughter, Jean, Jr., who died in 1992.

—*Tonya Bolden and Shari Dorantes Hatch*

REFERENCES: *BAAW.* Gunn, Arthur, in *BWA:AHE.* Newman, Richard, in *EA-99.*

Mama Black Widow (1969), *Airtight Willie and Me* (1979), *The Long White Con* (1977), and *Death Wish* (1976) and numerous essays and poems.

REFERENCES: Oliver, Terri Hume, in *OCAAL*.

I

Iceberg Slim (né Robert Beck)
(1918–1992)
Essays, novels, autobiography, poems

Despite earning a scholarship to the Tuskegee Institute and studying there for two years, Slim ended up spending the next 25 years of his life either imprisoned or involved in street crime, as noted in his autobiography *Pimp: The Story of My Life* (1967). From then on, for the next quarter of a century, he wrote the novels *Trick Baby* (1967),

Ice-T (né Tracey Morrow)
(2/16/1958–)
Rap lyrics, opinion

Considered one of the most prolific and outspoken rap artists, Ice-T named himself in deference to **Iceberg Slim**, whom Ice-T knew personally. Despite his "bad-boy" image and his provocative "gangsta rap" lyrics, Ice-T has been noted for speaking out against gang violence, drug abuse, and censorship. In addition to his numerous rap lyrics (e.g., "The Coldest Rap," "Colors," "Cop Killer"), Ice-T's literary contributions include his book *The Ice Opinion* (1994).

REFERENCES: *EA-99*.

J

Jackson, George Lester
(9/23/1941–8/21/1971)
Memoir, letters

The Soledad Prison writings of Jackson, compiled in his *Soledad Brother: The Prison Letters of George Jackson* (1970), had tremendous impact at the time of their publication, sparking heated controversy and much admiration among revolutionary thinkers of the early 1970s.

REFERENCES: *EA-99*.

Jackson, Angela (1951–)
Poems, plays, other fiction

It was during the **Black Arts movement** that Jackson's poetry emerged, and her poetry continues to reflect her roots in this movement. Her writing career was nurtured by the Chicago-based Organization of Black American Culture (OBAC) founded by **Haki Madhubuti**, **Carolyn Rodgers**, **Johari Amini**, and **Hoyt Fuller**, whom she succeeded as OBAC's coordinator. Among her published works are her poetry collections *Voodoo/Love Magic* (1974), *The Greenville Club* (1977), *Solo in the Boxcar* (1985), and *Dark Legs and Silk Kisses: The Beatitudes of the Spinners* (1993); several short stories; her poetic dramas *Witness!* (1978), *Shango Diaspora: An African-American Myth of Womanhood and Love* (1980), and *When the Wind Blows* (1984); and *Cowboy Amok* (1992). More recently, Jackson published her collection *And All These Roads Be Luminous: Poems Selected and New,* which has been described as "passionate and brimming with poetic surprises," characterized by "compassion, grace, and daring."

REFERENCES: Patterson, Tracy J., in *OCAAL*. Amazon.com, 1/2000.

Jackson, Elaine (1943–)
Plays

Jackson's plays include *Toe Jam* (1971), *Cockfight* (1976), *Paper Dolls* (1979), and *Birth Rites* (1987), as well as a musical version of *Birth Rites* (with composer-lyricist Martin Weich) and a new play, *Puberty Rites.*

REFERENCES: Manora, Yolanda M., in *OCAAL*.

Jackson, Jesse (1/1/1908–4/14/1983)
Juvenile fiction and biography

This Jesse Jackson never ran for U.S. president or preached in a pulpit, but he has influenced many youths nonetheless. Following three years at Ohio State University's School of Journalism (1927–1929), Jackson left school and started working for the *Ohio State Press*. After that, he took a variety of jobs, including that of juvenile probation officer (1936). While working with African-American adolescents, he saw a need for young adult novels relevant to their experiences. In Jackson's first novel, *Call Me Charley* (1945), the title character, Charles Moss, strives for acceptance and respect—a difficult task for a black youth living in an all-white neighborhood and attending an all-white public school. Jackson's book was among the first young adult books to address racial prejudice as a central theme. At the time, this book blazed a trail that many others were to follow. (For example, the *Brown v. Board of Education* decision was not handed down until 1954, the Little Rock Nine didn't integrate Central High School until 1957, and James Meredith didn't integrate the University of Mississippi until 1962.) In light of contemporary experiences and understandings, however, many critics question the tremendous forbearance Charley shows in responding to the racial insults to which he is subjected.

Jackson's subsequent books for young adults include two sequels to his first novel (*Anchor Man,* 1947; *Charley Starts from Scratch,* 1958); *Room for Randy* (1957); and *Tessie* (1968) and *Tessie Keeps Her Cool* (1970), about a young African-American girl in Harlem who earns a scholarship to attend an all-white private school.

In addition, Jackson wrote nonfiction for young adults, including two biographies of Stonewall Jackson, *The Sickest Don't Always Die the Quickest*

(1971) and *The Fourteenth Cadillac* (1991), as well as his two Carter G. Woodson Award–winning books, *Black in America: Fight for Freedom* (1971) and *Make a Joyful Noise unto the Lord! The Life of Mahalia Jackson, Queen of the Gospel Singers* (1974). In 1974, he started working as a lecturer, instructor, and writer-in-residence at Appalachian State University, where he continued to work until his death.

REFERENCES: *EBLG*. Lowe, Barbara, in *OCAAL*.

Jackson, Jesse (Louis), Jr. (10/8/1941–)
Political commentary, speeches, autobiography

What makes Jesse Jackson such an effective political and religious leader? His ability to craft words and deliver them with gusto. From his earliest days as a student sitting-in in Greensboro, North Carolina, through his U.S. presidential campaigns in 1984 and 1988, he has given eloquent voice to the pleas and the demands of those who suffer oppression, poverty, and injustice. He has cried out for us in our despair at losing **Martin Luther King, Jr.**, whose blood stained his shirt; he has exclaimed jubilantly for us at the March on Washington; and he has triumphantly urged us to proclaim, "I am somebody," always including those whom many others disparage, ignore, and neglect.

Always one to lead with words but never one to stop with them, he has organized boycotts, led corporations to do good, stirred support for African-American entrepreneurship, spearheaded enrichment programs for youths, and negotiated peaceful international win-win settlements when it seemed everyone was about to lose. Through his Operation PUSH (People United to Save Humanity) and his Rainbow Coalition, he has accomplished a great deal. Just what does he want to be the outcome of his words and his actions? No one says it better than he does. In his address to the 1984 Democratic National Convention, he said, "We are not a perfect people. Yet we are called to a perfect mission: to feed the hungry, to clothe the naked, to house the homeless, to teach the illiterate, to provide jobs for the jobless, and to choose the human race over the nuclear race."

In addition to giving speeches and writing forewords and introductions to numerous books, Jackson authored *Time to Speak: The Autobiography of Reverend Jesse Jackson* (1988) and coauthored *Keep Hope Alive: Jesse Jackson's 1988 Presidential Campaign: A Collection of Major Speeches, Issue Papers, Photographs, and Campaign Analysis* (1989, with Frank Clemente and Frank E. Watkins) and other books.

REFERENCES: *EAACH*. *SMKC*. Williams, Nicole L. Bailey, in *BH2C*.

Jackson, Joseph Harrison (9/11/1900–8/18/1990)
Opinion

Jackson is perhaps best known for being an African-American Baptist minister opposed to civil disobedience and the civil rights movement, favoring instead economic independence and self-development, as expressed in his book *Unholy Shadows and Freedom's Holy Light*.

REFERENCES: Newman, Richard, in *EA-99*.

Jackson, Mae (1946–)
Poems

Jackson's poems, reflective of the **Black Arts movement**, have frequently been published in literary journals and anthologies. Her poetry has also been collected in her *Can I Poet with You?* (1969/1972).

REFERENCES: Lindberg, Kathryne V., in *OCAAL*. Amazon.com, 1/2000.

Jackson, Mahalia (10/26/1911–1/27/1972)
Autobiography

Jackson, a world-renowned gospel singer, wrote her autobiography *Movin' On Up* (1966) with the help of writer Evan Wylie. Perhaps her most memorable performance was at the 1963 rally in Washington, D.C., at which **Martin Luther King, Jr.,** gave his world-renowned "I Have a Dream" speech. Two decades after her death, Oxford University Press published an account of her life, *Got to Tell It: Mahalia Jackson, Queen of Gospel.*

REFERENCES: *EA-99*. *EB-98*. *SEW. WDAW.* Jackson, Joyce Marie, in *BWA:AHE*.

Jackson, Mattie J. (c. 1843–?)
Autobiography

With her *amanuensis* (a person who writes down dictation), Dr. L. S. Thompson (the second wife of Mattie's mother's second husband), Jackson authored her book, *The Story of Mattie J. Jackson* (1866), describing her family's valiant struggle for freedom from slavery. She dictated the book at age 20 to pay for obtaining a formal education—with which she might write her own words in her own hand.

REFERENCES: Moody, Jocelyn K., in *OCAAL*.

Jackson, Rebecca (née) Cox
(?/1795–1871)
Autobiography

Following a religious conversion, Jackson became an evangelist and wrote a spiritual autobiography describing her experiences with prophetic visions, religious revelations, and spiritual healings. After she was excommunicated from the African Methodist Episcopal (AME) church for heresy (women preachers were considered heretics), she embraced the Shaker faith and became an eldress in that church. In 1981, Jean McMahon Humez compiled and edited Jackson's spiritual writings into the volume *Gifts of Power: The Writings of Rebecca Jackson, Black Visionary, Shaker Eldress.*

REFERENCES: Humez, Jean McMahon, in *BWA:AHE*. Moody, Jocelyn K., in *OCAAL*.

Jacobs, Harriet Ann (pen name: "Linda Brent")* (c. 1813–3/7/1897)
Slave narrative, letters

Whatever we know of Harriet Jacobs, we have learned from Harriet herself. Born into slavery in Edenton, North Carolina, she was allowed to live with her family until she was six years old. Her family included her mother (Delilah), her father (Elijah or Daniel, a skilled carpenter, who was the son of a white farmer and who was enslaved by a doctor), and her brother William ("Willie" or John), who was two years younger than she. Sadly, her mother died when Harriet was just six years old, and Harriet was sent to live with Margaret Horniblow, who had "owned" her mother. For the next six years, her new "mistress" was kindly toward young Harriet, teaching her to sew, to read, and to spell and letting her run outside to gather berries or flowers from time to time.

When Harriet was 12, however, Margaret Horniblow died, and instead of freeing Harriet, Margaret bequeathed her "property" to her sister's daughter, Mary Matilda Norcom, a 5-year-old white girl. At first, Harriet was treated fairly well in the Norcom household, but as she ascended into puberty, she became the victim of Dr. James Nor-

com's sexual harassment. By the time she was 15 years old, she was subject to unrelenting sexual aggression. In an attempt to gain an ally against this aggression, when Harriet was just 16 years old, she initiated an intimate relationship with a young white neighbor, attorney Samuel Tredwell Sawyer.

By the time Jacobs reached her early twenties, she had moved into the home of her grandmother, baker Molly Horniblow, who had been freed in 1828 when Hannah Pritchard purchased Molly's freedom. Jacobs had fled there to try to escape the Norcoms—both the doctor and his wife, who was furious with jealous rage toward Jacobs. At her grandmother's house, Jacobs had borne two children with Sawyer: her son Joseph (born c. 1829) and her daughter Louisa Matilda (c. 1833–1913). Outraged that Jacobs had these children by another man, James Norcom sent Jacobs away from Edenton to his son's plantation out in the country, where the working conditions were harsh. When Jacobs heard that Norcom planned to sell her children to a plantation owner, she made plans to escape, hoping that either her own father (who had, by then, purchased his freedom) or her children's father would be able to purchase and then free her children once Norcom believed that Jacobs was gone altogether.

In June of 1835, Jacobs escaped from Norcom's grasp, hiding in sympathetic white and black neighbors' houses and in a nearby snake-riddled swamp until her grandmother and her uncle had built a tiny (3 feet high by 9 feet long by 7 feet wide) hiding place for her above her grandmother's porch. Jacobs later reflected that her strong, dignified, compassionate "good old grandmother" was a "special treasure," about whom she had "tender memories" (quoted in *CSN* and in *BWA:AHE*). Later in 1835, Sawyer was allowed to buy their children, as well as Jacobs's brother—but he didn't free them, although he let them live with Jacobs's grandmother. For nearly seven years, Jacobs was confined to her grandmother's crawlspace, writing letters that she would have other people mail to Norcom from Boston or New York.

In 1842, abolitionists helped her escape to the North, where she soon was reunited with her children. In 1849, she moved to Rochester, New York, where she joined her brother, an abolition activist and associate of **Frederick Douglass**. There, she told her story to her friend Amy Post, a feminist Quaker, who urged Jacobs to write it down, as Post believed the story would incite the sympathies of Northern women, thereby aiding the abolitionist cause.

In 1850, the year the Fugitive Slave Law was passed, Norcom died, but his daughter Mary continued to try to capture Jacobs. For quite a while, Jacobs did domestic work for writer Nathaniel Parker Willis and Cornelia Grinnell Willis. Mary Norcom sent agents to New York to try to kidnap Jacobs from their home. In 1852, Ms. Willis began arranging for Jacobs's freedom to be purchased, which it was in 1853. Although Jacobs was relieved to be free from fear of recapture, she bitterly resented having her wrongful enslavement sanctioned through the exchange of money.

Meanwhile, Jacobs was mulling over Post's suggestion, and she practiced her writing skills by contributing letters to the *New York Tribune*. From 1853 to 1861, Jacobs corresponded with Amy Post about her narrative, starting with her initial conception of the book and concluding with its publication. At first, she had hoped that **Harriet Beecher Stowe** would serve as her amanuensis and would record her story as she dictated it to her. Instead, Stowe had offered to incorporate some of Jacobs's experiences into her fictional sequel to *Uncle Tom's Cabin* (1851), *The Key to Uncle Tom's Cabin* (1853).

Somewhat reluctantly, but with determination, Jacobs decided to write her own life story—with continuing encouragement from Post. For the next several years, she worked on the manuscript whenever she had completed her child care and other domestic duties for the day. When at last she had completed her manuscript, she had great difficulty finding a publisher, perhaps largely because of her candor in revealing the sexual abuse she had suffered. She even sought letters of introduction from Boston abolitionists and took the letters to England in the unrewarded hope of getting British abolitionists to publish the work. At last, in 1860, African-American author **William C. Nell** introduced her to European-American author **Lydia Maria Child**. Child agreed to edit the work (which Child described as "making minor grammatical alterations"), to add an introduction to the work, and to act as Jacobs's literary agent in getting the work published.

At last, in the spring of 1861, *Incidents in the Life of a Slave Girl: Written by Herself* was published. Jacobs was the first to reveal the truth of how African-American slaves had been sexually exploited as well as physically abused. She also frankly described the racial prejudice she encountered in the North, the horrors of the Fugitive Slave Law, and the support she received from other women.

Only Child's name appeared on the title page (listed as the book's editor), and Jacobs used a pseudonym both for herself ("Linda Brent") and for the people in her book (e.g., Norcom became "Dr. Flint"). Among other concerns, Jacobs feared that her candor about her sexual exploitation might make life very difficult for her—a single mother—and for her children. Unfortunately, although the book was well received in the abolitionist press, her book's publication preceded the outbreak of the Civil War by just a month or so, and potential readers—North and South—were otherwise distracted.

During the war, with the support of Quakers and other abolitionists, Jacobs and her daughter Louisa worked behind the Union Army lines to offer emergency relief. They also helped establish the Jacobs Free School (owned and operated by African Americans), to teach freed slaves in Union-occupied Alexandria, Virginia. After the war, mother and daughter did similar work in Savannah, Georgia. Jacobs continually supplied the Northern press with reports on their activities. In 1868, the mother-daughter team went to England to raise funds to build an old-age home and orphanage in Savannah. On their return, however, white rage erupted in the post–Civil War South, and Harriet and Louisa fled North again, moving to Cambridge, Massachusetts. There, Harriet managed a boarding house for students and faculty members of Harvard University.

From 1877 to 1897, Harriet and Louisa lived in Washington, D.C., where Harriet continued her work on behalf of freed slaves, and Louisa taught at Howard University and other schools. A few years before she died, Harriet sold the house and lot that her grandmother had owned, where she had found refuge so many decades before.

When Jacobs's book was first published, abolitionists believed it was an authentic narrative written by an African-American woman. As time went by, however, scholars questioned both its authenticity and its authorship. In 1981, however, literary historian Jean Fagan Yellin did a thorough examination of the evidence, including correspondence documenting Jacobs's work on the manuscript. In 1987, Yellin published an annotated edition of Jacobs's book, thereby establishing the widespread acceptance of Jacobs's authorship and of the work's authenticity. Some skeptics remain (e.g., John

Blassingame), who question the plausibility of some of the events and who find many of her descriptions melodramatic. Despite the skeptics, however, Jacobs's autobiography has become an important part of the canon of American literature, telling a key aspect of American history.

REFERENCES: *1TESK. CSN. G-97. NAAAL.* Robinson, Lisa Clayton, in *EA-99.* Woodard, Helena, in *OCWW.* Yellin, Jean Fagan, in *BWA:AHE* and in *OCAAL.*

Jeffers, Lance (né Lance Flippin)
(11/28/1919–7/19/1985)
Poems, novel

After graduating from high school in 1938, Jeffers attended a series of colleges and then joined the army in 1942. After his discharge from the army (1946), he graduated with honors and earned his master's degree from Columbia University. Starting in 1951, he began teaching at various colleges and universities (from California to North Carolina). In 1974, he finally joined the faculty at North Carolina State University in Raleigh, where he continued to teach until he died.

Jeffers's first poetry collection, *My Blackness Is the Beauty of This Land* (1970), highlights the courage and endurance of African Americans who face racial oppression; and his second collection, *When I Know the Power of My Black Hand* (1974), expands this theme to embrace the oppression of other American minorities, such as Native Americans, and other oppressed people around the globe, such as the Jews of the Buchenwald concentration camp (during World War II) and the people of Vietnam (during the Vietnam War). His subsequent collections include *O Africa, Where I Baked My Bread* (1977) and *Grandsire* (1979). In his poetry, Jeffers employed *anaphora* (repetition of the initial words and phrases in sequential poetic lines), *alliteration* (repeated initial sounds in the words of a poetic line or stanza), *litany* (repeated phrasings reminiscent of chanting), and *metaphor* (figurative speech), which reflect the African-American **oral tradition**. Jeffers also often coined compound words such as "bluecool" and "corpse-head." Although Jeffers's work is not as widely read as that of many of his contemporaries more strongly identified with the **Black Arts movement**, his work has appeared in numerous literary journals and has been widely anthologized (e.g., in the definitive **Black Aesthetic** volume *Black Fire* by LeRoi Jones [later **Amiri**

Baraka] and **Larry Neal**), and his last three collections are still in print. Jeffers dedicated three volumes of his poetry to his second wife, Trellie James (whom he married in 1959). With Trellie, he had three daughters; with his first wife, social worker Camille Jones, he had a son.

In addition to his poetry, Jeffers wrote the novel *Witherspoon* (1983), about a minister who tries to spare the life of a convict facing execution.

REFERENCES: *EBLG. TtW.* Harris, Trudier, in *OCAAL.* Amazon.com, 7/1999.

Joans, Ted (7/4/1928–)
Poems, stories

A jazz musician since age 13, and a surrealist painter who earned his bachelor of fine arts (1951, Indiana University), Joans moved to Greenwich Village in New York during the heyday of the Beat Generation. There, his jazz, his artwork, and his poems were appreciated, and in 1959 he published his collection *Jazz Poems.* Soon, however, he became disillusioned with how the Beat Generation was being commercialized, and in 1961 he published *All of Ted Joans and No More,* bidding adieu to the Beat phase of his career to travel through Europe and Africa. While abroad, he published *Black Pow-wow: Jazz Poems* (1969), which revealed his link to the American **Black Arts movement**. On returning to the United States, he published *Afrodisia: New Poems* (1970), which he had written abroad; *A Black Manifesto in Jazz Poetry and Prose* (1979); a German-English volume *The Aardvark-Watcher: Der Erdferkelforscher* (1980); and *Sure, Really I Is* (1982). More recently, Joans published *Teducation: Selected Poems* (1999). Joans married and became the father of three sons and one daughter.

REFERENCES: *EBLG. TtW.* Lindberg, Kathryne V., in *OCAAL.* Amazon.com, 7/1999.

Johnson, Amelia E. (Etta) (née Hall)
(?/1858–?/1922)
Novels, short stories, articles

Johnson is best known for her three novels (*Clarence and Corinne, or God's Way,* 1890; *The Hazeley Family,* 1894; *Martina Meriden, or What Is My Motive?* 1901), but she also started an eight-page monthly magazine, *Joy* (1887), and she published poems, short stories, and articles in various periodicals.

REFERENCES: *NYPL-AADR.* Fabi, M. Giulia, in *OCAAL.*

Johnson, Charles (Richard) (4/23/1948–)

Novels, short stories, essays, screenplays, literary criticism, cartoons

Starting when Johnson was just 17 years old, he was drawing editorial cartoons for various newspapers (e.g., the *Chicago Tribune, Black World* [see **Negro Digest**]). With more than 1,000 of his drawings already published in newspapers, he published two collections of his cartoons (*Black Humor,* 1970; *Half-Past Nation Time,* 1972). While he was still a college student, he had his own how-to-draw show on PBS, *Charley's Pad* (1971, comprising 52 segments). During this time, he also wrote several "apprentice" novels, sailing along on the inspiration of writers he deeply admired—**James Baldwin**, **John A. Williams**, **Ralph Ellison**, **Jean Toomer**, **Richard Wright**, Albert Camus, Hermann Hesse, Jean-Paul Sartre, Nathaniel Hawthorne, Thomas Mann, and Herman Melville, among others.

While Johnson was a doctoral student in phenomenology (an aspect of philosophy) and literary aesthetics, he published his surrealistic first novel, *Faith and the Good Thing* (1974), which built on literary traditions from African-American folklore and on his predilection for philosophical inquiry. Johnson constructed his next novel, *Oxherding Tale* (1982), on the basis of African-American **slave narratives** (especially **Frederick Douglass**'s first autobiography), which continued to reflect his philosophical explorations. Meanwhile, he started teaching English at the University of Washington in Seattle (since 1976), and he wrote some biographical screenplays for PBS (*Charlie Smith and the Fritter Tree,* 1978, about an African-American cowboy; and *Booker,* 1984, about **Booker T. Washington**).

Johnson's next major publication, *The Sorcerer's Apprentice: Tales and Conjurations* (1986), made even more obvious his enthusiasm for experimenting with various literary forms. The eight stories in this collection addressed Johnson's philosophical questions through different literary genres, including sci-fi ("Popper's Disease") and horror ("Exchange Value"). The prestigious literary guild PEN nominated Johnson's collection for a PEN/Faulkner Award in recognition of his achievement.

Next, Johnson addressed literature directly through his nonfiction book of literary criticism, *Being and Race: Black Writing since 1970* (1988). The next genre he took on was the sea adventure, through his novel *Middle Passage* (1990). Johnson

had conducted extensive research (e.g., reading ship logs, dictionaries of nautical terms and of Cockney slang, and "every sea story that I could get my hands on") before writing the book. He was rewarded for his effort with the 1990 National Book Award for fiction (only the second African American to receive the award; **Ralph Ellison** was the first in 1953). In 1990, he also tackled another literary form, with his play *All This and Moonlight,* and in 1993, he completed a screenplay for a film version of *Middle Passage.*

In Johnson's next novel, *Dreamer* (1998), he integrated his love of philosophy, his interest in biography, and his fascination with the novel form. The dreamer of whom he speaks is, of course, **Martin Luther King, Jr.** Perhaps more than a fictionalized biography, it is a fictional exploration of King's Christian philosophy. Johnson investigates how King lived and breathed his philosophy of nonviolence as an outgrowth of unconditional love, founded on his soul-deep Christian beliefs. The same year Johnson's *Dreamer* appeared in print, Johnson himself was given an award that will allow him to pursue his own dreams—the John D. and Catherine T. MacArthur Foundation's $300,000 so-called genius award. Doubtless, he will find still newer ways to use his genius to explore the objects of his passion: literature and philosophy.

—*Tonya Bolden*

REFERENCES: *G-96. SMKC.* Nash, William R., in *OCAAL.*

Johnson, Charles (Spurgeon)

(7/24/1893–10/27/1956)

Nonfiction—sociology; journal founder

Charles H. Johnson had been educated alongside the son of his parents' master. He then went on to earn a divinity degree at the Richmond Institute, later named the Virginia Union University (VUU). On receiving his degree in 1890, Reverend Johnson and his wife, Winifred Branch Johnson, established a pastorate in Bristol, Virginia, where the couple raised five children, the eldest of whom was Charles Spurgeon Johnson. In Bristol, Reverend Johnson's congregation built him a fine big church. When it came time for Charles the younger to go to college, he was sent to Wayland Baptist Academy (affiliated with VUU). Within three years, he had earned his degree, with distinction (B.A., 1916). At Wayland, he started to believe that racism often interrelates with economic hardship and social deprivation. To investigate this notion further, he went on to the University of Chicago to do postgraduate work (Ph.D., 1918) with the esteemed trail-blazing urban sociologist **Robert Ezra Park**.

While Johnson was studying with Park, Park was president of the Chicago Urban League and helped Johnson get a position directing research and records for the league. This position permitted Johnson to study the Great Migration of African Americans from the rural South to the urban North. In response to a race riot (July 1919), Chicagoans established the Chicago Commission on Race Relations to investigate the origins of the riot, and Johnson was asked to direct the commission (1919–1921). The commissioners gathered sociological data based on surveys of blacks and whites in the area. The commission's report, chiefly Johnson's effort, comprehensively analyzed the underlying causes of the riot, particularly focusing on flaws in the social infrastructure such as in employment, housing, education, and social services. The report further warned that if these conditions did not change, further riots were entirely possible. The final report was published in 1922 as *The Negro in Chicago: A Study in Race Relations and a Race Riot*.

In 1921, the National Urban League appointed Johnson to direct research for the league in New York City. In that role, he founded *Opportunity: A Journal of Negro Life,* in 1923. He served as the league's magazine editor and director of research until 1928. Johnson's timing was flawless, as he was editing *Opportunity* when it was one of the two most important literary magazines publishing work by African-American writers and artists during the height of the **Harlem Renaissance**. (The other was the NAACP's journal, *Crisis*.)

In 1928, Johnson left the Urban League to accept a position as professor of sociology at Fisk University in Nashville, Tennessee, where he chaired the department of social sciences until he was named president of Fisk in 1946, the first African American to take the helm of that historically black university (established in 1867). Johnson also continued to probe the ways in which economic and social conditions influence race relations in this country. As an expert in that field, he was consulted by Presidents Franklin D. Roosevelt, Herbert Hoover, and Dwight D. Eisenhower. Johnson also served in the League of Nations (1930), worked with the U.S. Department of Agriculture (1936–1937), and helped Japanese educa-

tors reorganize the Japanese educational system following World War II.

Among his many publications are myriad articles and 17 or so books, including *The Negro in American Civilization* (1930), *Economic Status of the Negro* (1933), and *Shadow of the Plantation* (1934; reprinted 1996), about the near-serfdom of tenant cotton farmers in Macon County in Alabama, which interwove sociological data with commentaries from oral interviews with the tenant farmers. That work was followed by *The Collapse of Cotton Tenancy* (1935, with Will Alexander and Edward Embree, director of the Julius Rosenwald Fund), *The Negro College Graduate* (1936), and *Growing Up in the Black Belt* (1941), which argued that race relations in the United States did not truly form a caste system, as social protest and progressive governmental action would erode the castelike boundaries between the races. Johnson's *Patterns of Negro Segregation* (1943) continues to be consulted as a sociological reference work on the insidious ways that segregation harms Americans. He also wrote *Educational and Cultural Crisis* (1951) and *Bitter Canaan* (published posthumously in 1987), a sociological history of Liberia. Johnson's son Robert continued his father's interest in sociology, and Johnson and his wife, drama and music teacher Marie Antoinette Burgess Johnson, had three other children: Charles II, Patricia, and Jeh.

REFERENCES: *AA:PoP. BDAA. BF:2000. EA-99. EB-BH-CD. G-97. MWEL.* Robbins, Richard, in *BH2C*. Toppin, Edgar Allan, in *WB-99*.

Johnson, Fenton (5/7/1888–9/17/1958)
Poems, short stories, articles, essays, plays; magazine founder

Elijah H. Johnson (a railroad porter) and his wife Jesse (Taylor) Johnson were among the wealthiest African-American families in Chicago, and their son Fenton started writing fiction when he was just nine years old. His first published poem appeared in a Chicago-area newspaper in 1900. After graduating from Chicago public schools, he had intended to become a cleric, but after enrolling at the University of Chicago (in 1910), he realized that his interests had changed. After studying at Northwestern University for a while, he moved to New York (around 1913) to study at the highly acclaimed Columbia University School of Journalism. During college, he also wrote for the *New York News* and for the Eastern Press Association. After college, he taught at a private African-American Baptist-owned college in Louisville, Kentucky, but after a year, he decided to turn his attention to magazine editing and publishing. During this decade, he also married Cecilia Rhone.

In 1916, Johnson moved back to Chicago, where he founded *Champion Magazine* and *Favorite Magazine,* but by the end of the decade, financial difficulties and other problems drove the magazines out of business. He also wrote and self-published several collections of his own works. His *A Little Dreaming* (1913; reprinted 1969) includes both poems written in standard English and poems written in language expressing traditional African American speech patterns; all of the poems were conventional in form, including his lyrical 300-line blank verse poem "The Vision of Lazarus."

Between this collection and the next, Johnson's poetry changed dramatically. He left behind conventional forms and embraced irregular rhythms and unrhymed lines, keeping his poems closer to actual speech and to realistic urban situations, rather than the more romantic expressions of his earlier works. These poems also echo a much more profound sense of despair than he expressed in his earlier poems. He also began using more deviant spellings and nonstandard syntax in these works. In addition, Johnson started incorporating more elements of African-American musical forms such as **spirituals** (reminiscent of the rural South) and blues (representing the urban North). His last two volumes were *Visions of the Dusk* (1915; reprinted 1971) and *Songs of the Soil* (1916; reprinted 1969). After Johnson's death, about 40 of his poems were collected and published posthumously by the Works Progress Administration's "Negro in Illinois" program. Johnson also published collections of his short stories, *Tales of Darkest America* (1920), and of his essays, *For the Highest Good* (1920).

In addition, Johnson wrote plays. By the time he was 19 years old, some of his plays had been produced at the old Pekin Theatre in Chicago. In 1925, his *The Cabaret Girl* was performed at the Shadow Theatre there. None of the scripts for his plays have survived.

Perhaps Johnson was just a little too far ahead of his time, for by the middle of the next decade, the **Harlem Renaissance** was blooming in Chicago just as much as in Harlem. What was poor timing for Johnson, however, proved invaluable for literary historians, as his work bridges the gap between the turn-of-the-century writings of African Americans

and those of the renaissance. Quite a few of Johnson's poems are repeatedly anthologized, representing that narrow window between the two highly productive periods in African-American literature. Among his poems that are most widely anthologized are "The Scarlet Woman" (1922), "The Minister," and "Tired" (1919). By the end of the renaissance period, Johnson's only contact with the artistic community was his continuing correspondence with **Arna Bontemps**.

REFERENCES: *AAW:AAPP. BAL-1-P. BWA. EBLG. G-97. NAAAL.* Engelhardt, Elizabeth Sanders Delwiche, in *OCAAL.* Johnson's unpublished poems and papers are collected at Fisk University.

Johnson, Georgia (Blanche) Douglas (née Camp) (9/10/1877–5/14/1966)
Poems, short stories, plays, columns, novel

There are questions about the year in which Georgia Camp was born—given variously as 1877, 1880, and 1886, with more than one source citing each year. During her era, it was common practice for women to have their birth years moved forward somewhat by the women themselves and by their parents, so it seems safest to assume that the earliest of these dates is probably the most accurate. Georgia's heritage reflects America's diversity well, as her father, George Camp, had African-American and English ancestry, and her mother, Laura (Jackson) Camp, had African-American and Native American ancestry.

When Georgia was attending public schools in Atlanta, Georgia, she was often her teachers' favorite, although she was quite shy and reserved. She chose her friends carefully, often preferring her own company. She also considered music to be a great companion and taught herself to play the violin. After high school, she studied music extensively at Atlanta University's Normal School, where she met her future husband, Henry Lincoln Johnson (the son of former slaves, born in 1870). The university had been a haven for her, and she was sorry to leave it when she graduated in 1896. She went on to study musical composition at Howard University in Washington, D.C., and then she traveled even farther from her home in Georgia to study at the Oberlin Conservatory of Music and the Cleveland College of Music, in Ohio. When she finished her studies, she returned to Georgia, where she taught and worked as an assistant principal in the public schools. By the time she married "Link" Johnson (September 28, 1903), she had shifted her main interest from composing music to composing lyric poetry.

For a few years, Georgia and Link remained in Atlanta, where he was a prominent attorney and an up-and-coming Republican politician. By the end of the decade, his interest in politics attracted him to Washington, D.C. There, Georgia settled into her roles as a wife and the mother of two sons (Henry Lincoln, Jr., and Peter Douglas), and Link was soon embedded in Republican politics, appointed as recorder of deeds by President Taft (in 1912). Link definitely had traditional expectations that Georgia would assume full responsibility for the home and primary responsibility for bringing up their two sons. In his view, if she wanted to write, it would have to be *after* she had taken care of these duties. Georgia, however, far preferred reading and writing to cooking and cleaning, which sometimes caused friction in their relationship. Nonetheless, he financially supported all of her creative pursuits, even if he did not endorse them altogether.

During this period, Georgia wrote numerous poems and short stories. When Kelly Miller (see **May Miller**), a dean at Howard University, read her work, he encouraged her to continue writing. She occasionally submitted some of her writings to newspapers and magazines, but it wasn't until 1916 that her poems were first published in the NAACP's journal *Crisis*. Her love of music is evident in the lyricism of all her poems, which tend to center on emotional, often romantic, themes. Any of her poems that address sociopolitical issues do so through personal, emotion-laden experiences. For instance, in her poems "Black Woman," "The Mother," and "Shall I Say, 'My Son, You're Branded,'" she explores the feelings of enslaved women who face the abomination of bearing a child who will be enslaved for a lifetime.

Two years after Johnson's first poem was published, her poems were collected in *The Heart of a Woman and Other Poems* (1918). Celebrated poet and poetry critic **William Stanley Braithwaite**, whom she greatly admired, praised the volume for offering unique insights into the experiences of African-American women. Other critics and intellectuals acknowledged her gift for language and her lyricality, but they lambasted her for failing to focus on racism, racial issues, and race-centered experiences.

Johnson's next collection, *Bronze: A Book of Verse* (1922), focused chiefly on racial themes (including racism, racial prejudice, integration, interracial romance, and children of mixed racial heritage) while continuing to address gender issues and motherhood—issues closely tied to her own experiences. **W. E. B. Du Bois**, **Jessie Redmon Fauset**, and other critics and commentators of the day lauded this work. Johnson, however, felt that these were not her best works; she preferred to write on more intimate, romantic, sentimental human themes, as she confided in a letter to **Arna Bontemps**.

Eighteen days before Georgia and Link would have celebrated their twenty-second wedding anniversary, he died, leaving Georgia to find a way to support herself and her two teenage sons and to pay for their college educations. By hook and by crook, she managed to send her son Peter Douglas through Williston Seminary, Dartmouth College, and Howard University's medical school, and she sent Henry Lincoln, Jr., to Asburnham Academy, Bowdoin College, and Howard University's law school. At first, she shifted from job to job (e.g., substitute teacher, civil service file clerk), always having to work very long hours for very little pay. Fortunately, Link's political contacts led to her gaining an honorary post in President Calvin Coolidge's administration, as commissioner of conciliation in the Department of Labor. In that job, she investigated the living and working conditions of laborers in various places across the land.

Despite her long work hours, Johnson managed to continue writing, and she traveled across the country giving lectures and readings of her writings; in her travels, she also met with other writers (e.g., Carl Sandburg in Chicago, **Charles Chesnutt** in Cleveland). Meanwhile, the **Harlem Renaissance** was in full swing, and Johnson made her home at 1461 S Street, N.W., the Washington, D.C., outpost of the renaissance, hosting a literary salon in her home. In addition to offering writers' workshops there, she hosted the "Saturday Nighters' Club," a weekly open house for writers, such as **Countee Cullen**, W. E. B. Du Bois, **Alice Dunbar Nelson**, Jessie Redmon Fauset, **Angelina Weld Grimké**, **Langston Hughes**, **Zora Neale Hurston**, **Alain Locke**, **Anne Spencer**, and **Jean Toomer**. In addition, artists, politicians, and other intellectuals often attended. Douglas kept up correspondences with prisoners, and when they were released from prison, they too were invited to attend the weekly gatherings. She called her house "Half-Way Home," allegedly for two reasons: She saw her home as a common ground for anyone who was willing to meet halfway, and she offered her home to visiting writers (e.g., Hurston, Hughes), paroled prisoners, and anyone else who was willing to fight halfway to make it.

Johnson's unflagging encouragement of writers (young and old, female and male), parolees, and others in need made her one of the most beloved and cherished of renaissance poets. During this time, she produced the collection often cited as her finest work: *An Autumn Love Cycle* (1928). In this volume, she returned to focusing on women's experiences, especially regarding romantic love, but she also took steps in a new direction, exploring free verse rather than the more traditional forms she had used in her earlier volumes. The collection made Johnson the first African-American woman since **Frances Ellen Watkins Harper** to gain national attention for her poetry. It included Johnson's oft-anthologized "I Want to Die While You Love Me," which playwright and poet **Owen Dodson** read at her funeral.

Johnson had dedicated her *Autumn Love Cycle* collection to Zona Gale, a European-American writer who had prompted Johnson to give playwriting a try. From the mid-1920s to about 1940, Johnson did just that, completing 28 plays—most of which, sadly, are no longer available. Regarding the plays that remain, critics have praised Johnson's ability to express the drama through authentic folk speech rather than stereotypical dialect. Her plays, unlike her poems, focus on race issues such as the harmful impact of racism, interracial relationships, the need for harmony between the races, and the distinctive experiences of African Americans. Apparently, at least some of her plays were produced during the 1920s, and several more won literary prizes.

Johnson's *Plumes: Folk Tragedy, a Play in One Act* (1927), about modern medicine versus folk customs, won first prize in a contest for best new play of the year held by the National Urban League's **Opportunity** magazine; the play was also anthologized by **Alain Locke** in 1927 and published as a single work in 1928. Her controversial play *Blue Blood* (1926) also won honorable mention in an *Opportunity* contest. *Blue Blood,* in which an African-American woman is raped by European-American men, was performed in New York City (by the Krigwa Players) in the fall of 1926 and was published in 1927. Even more controversial was Johnson's *A Sunday Morning in the South* (1928;

written in 1925), in which an innocent black teenager is lynched in the throes of Southern white hysteria. The play also showed how the Ku Klux Klan and the police conspired to create—and to cover up—the atrocity. That play was included in a 1974 anthology. After 1928, Johnson continued to write poems and plays, but she found it harder and harder to get her work published as the Great Depression descended on the country. Still, she was able to publish a series of newspaper columns: *Homely Philosophy,* which was syndicated in 20 newspapers across the country (1926–1932); *Wise Sayings; Beauty Hints;* and an interracial news column for the *New York Amsterdam News.*

In 1934 Douglas lost her job in the Department of Labor, and from then on, she struggled to find clerical jobs and whatever other jobs she could find, and for three decades she applied for numerous fellowships to get funding for her writing. None of these efforts were rewarded, and she continued to struggle to produce poems, short stories, and plays in spite of her financial difficulties. Fortunately, her son, attorney Henry Lincoln, Jr., and his wife, moved in with her, so they helped her financially; she also continued to show generosity toward any writers, artists, or other needy souls to whom she could offer shelter despite her limited financial resources. From 1930 to 1965, she founded and managed an international correspondence club, and for some time, she sponsored a lonely-hearts club.

During this period, Johnson wrote several historical plays, including *Frederick Douglass* (1935), *William and Ellen Craft* (1935), and *Frederick Douglass Leaves for Freedom* (1940). She also wrote two more lynching-related plays, in association with the Federal Theater Project: *Blue-Eyed Black Boy* (1935) and *Safe* (1936). The plays were never chosen for production by the project—in all likelihood because of their controversial subject matter. In the late 1940s, Johnson also collaborated on a musical work with composer Lillian Evanti, the only specifically musical composition resulting from her early musical training.

In the early 1960s, Johnson compiled a "Catalogue of Writings," listing her more than 200 poems, 28 plays, and 31 short stories. Many of her short stories were probably never published, and only 3 of them have been found: "Free," "Gesture," and "Tramp"; the last 2 were published in **Dorothy West**'s journal *Challenge* in 1936 and 1937 under the pseudonym "Paul Tremaine." Like her poems, her short stories focus on intimate human relationships rather than race relations. The catalogue also mentions an unpublished biography she wrote about her late husband, *The Black Cabinet;* a novel, *White Men's Children;* and a book-length manuscript about the literary salon she hosted during the 1920s and 1930s. Her final work, *Share My World* (1962), was a small poetry collection she published privately. Douglas never stopped writing, however, and to the end, she was known for wearing a tablet around her neck, so she could quickly and easily jot down any idea that came to mind.

In addition to the awards she received for her individual works and the awards she received from various organizations for her work, in 1965 she received an honorary doctorate from her alma mater, Atlanta University. Sadly, soon after she died, workers cleaned out her house, discarding her numerous unpublished manuscripts and other documents, depriving the literary world of ever knowing what else she may have had to contribute.

REFERENCES: *1TESK. AAL. AA:PoP. EBLG. NAAAL. OC20LE. RLWWJ.* Collier, Eugenia W., in *OCWW.* Donlon, Jocelyn Hazelwood, in *BWA:AHE.* Honey, Maureen, in *OCAAL.* Robinson, Lisa Clayton, in *EA-99.*

Johnson, Helene (née Helen)
(7/7/1906–1995)
Poems

After finishing high school and briefly attending Boston University, 18-year-old Helene Johnson and her cousin **Dorothy West** left Massachusetts to embrace the literary reawakening of the **Harlem Renaissance** in New York. There, Johnson attended classes in journalism at Columbia University, although she never earned a degree. From 1925 to 1927, the founding editor of the National Urban League's *Opportunity* magazine, **Charles (Spurgeon) Johnson** (no relation), published many of Helene Johnson's poems. About Helene's prize-winning work, Charles said, "Helene Johnson has a lyric penetration which belies her years, and a rich and impetuous power" (quoted in *OCWW,* p. 448). Her use of vernacular language and themes of racial pride led others to sing her praises as well, including poet **Countee Cullen**, novelist and *Fire!!* editor **Wallace Thurman**, and novelist and critic **Carl Van Vechten**. From 1928 to 1934, Johnson published only about a dozen poems, and after she married William

Hubbell (from whom she later separated) and had her daughter, Abigail, she stopped writing poems altogether and didn't start writing them again until the 1960s. Her poems have never been collected in a single volume, although they have appeared in numerous periodicals and anthologies.

REFERENCES: Ferguson, Sally Ann H., in *OCAAL.* Keough, Leyla, in *EA-99.* Patterson, Raymond R., in *OCWW.*

Johnson, James Weldon (né James William Johnson) (6/17/1871–6/26/1938)
Poems, novels, criticism, lyrics, editorials, anthologies, autobiography; newspaper publisher

As the celebrated lyricist of what is now called the "Black National Anthem," "Lift Every Voice and Sing," James Weldon Johnson's talent and influence seem unending. He is perhaps most well known for his Broadway productions and the compositions written with his brother, John Rosamond Johnson, and their partner, Bob Cole.

Writing lyrics, however, was only one of James Johnson's accomplishments. He also served as a United States diplomat to Venezuela and Nicaragua, started a newspaper, was the first African American since the end of Reconstruction to be admitted to the bar in Florida, and served as an officer in the National Association for the Advancement of Colored People (NAACP), as well as being a poet, novelist, editor, principal, and English professor. Johnson played a vital role in the **Harlem Renaissance**, and his untiring enthusiasm, activism, and talent took him to various areas of interest and places where he never failed to distinguish himself.

Johnson was born in Jacksonville, Florida, as was his younger brother, Rosamond. Their parents, James and Helen Louise Dillet Johnson, had moved to Florida from the Bahamas after a hurricane destroyed their sponge fishing and hauling businesses in 1866. Initially, Helen taught James at home. He then attended and graduated from the Stanton School at age 16 and went on to Atlanta University, writing poetry and graduating in 1894. Johnson then returned to Florida and served as principal of the Stanton School.

During this time, Johnson started writing poetry and also published the *Daily American,* a newspaper for which Johnson did most of the work. The content of the newspaper focused on issues important to the African-American community,

James Weldon Johnson, undated (Corbis)

including racial injustice. Unfortunately, the paper had financial difficulties and lasted only a year. Continuing as principal of the Stanton School, Johnson then studied law, passed the Florida bar, and built up a successful law practice in Jacksonville. Practicing law did not satisfy Johnson, however, and when his brother Rosamond returned to Jacksonville after completing studies at the New England Conservatory of Music (1897), the two collaborated, with James's poems serving as lyrics to Rosamond's music. One of the brothers' most famous compositions, "Lift Every Voice and Sing," was written in 1900 for the students at the Stanton School to sing during a celebration of Abraham Lincoln's birthday. Apparently, the Johnson brothers did not intend a broader audience for their song. Yet after the song was published, it took root with students all over the South, finally culminating in the NAACP adopting it as the "Negro National Anthem" around 1920. The brothers had a successful partnership and split their time between New York and Jacksonville for several years before both moved permanently to New York City.

In New York, the brothers met Bob Cole and the three of them wrote more than 200 songs,

often for Broadway productions. One production, *The Shoo-Fly Regiment,* was a musical comedy staged in 1906 with an all-black cast. James also met his future wife, Grace Nail, while in New York. As Bob and Rosamond started to travel with a successful vaudeville act, James stopped songwriting to accept two successive government posts, first as consul to Venezuela (1906) and then as consul to Nicaragua (1909).

While a diplomat, Johnson wrote the novel *The Autobiography of an Ex-Coloured Man* (1912). When the book was published, the reading audience perceived it as the true story of an African-American male who is light-skinned and consequently can choose whether to move within the white world or the black world. Ultimately, out of fear, the main character chooses to turn away from his African heritage and pass as white. Johnson originally had the novel published anonymously, though in 1927 he admitted that he had written the book and that it was a work of fiction. The book was subsequently republished with Johnson's name on it. (EDITOR'S NOTE: In 1913, Johnson changed his middle name from William to Weldon.) Carolyn Dirkson notes that *Autobiography* was the first of its kind, in that it chronicles the black perspective of white society, describes the tension within the black community about fair-skinned and dark-skinned blacks, and provides insights into the black community. This was a groundbreaking work at the time and opened the door for future African-American writers to explore similar subjects.

Johnson switched careers again in 1913, taking a job as editorial writer for the *New York Age* newspaper. (His editorials have since been collected into a book, published in 1995 by Oxford University Press and edited by Sondra Kathryn Wilson.) Johnson also moved into the larger public sphere by taking a post with the NAACP in 1920.

During the next several years, Johnson produced numerous written works, including authoring *Fifty Years and Other Poems* (1917) and editing *The Book of American Negro Poetry* (1922), *The Book of American Negro Spirituals* (1925), and *The Second Book of American Negro Spirituals* (1926). In 1927, one of Johnson's most famous works, *God's Trombones: Seven Negro Sermons in Verse,* was published. Additionally, Johnson chronicled the achievements of African Americans on the New York artistic scene in *Black Manhattan* (1930).

Johnson's autobiography, *Along This Way,* was published in 1933 while Johnson was teaching at

Fisk University, a post he had accepted a couple of years earlier. In part, Johnson was motivated to write his autobiography to settle any confusion that had occurred as a result of *Autobiography* being published. *Negro Americans, What Now?,* his last major literary contribution to the world, was published in 1934. He was killed in a car accident in 1938 and is buried in Brooklyn, New York.

When examining Johnson's work and life, it seems clear that he worked hard to preserve African-American culture and heritage, highlight the positive influence of blacks on the United States in general, and encourage young black writers to pursue their talents and choices of vocations. All of these things he did with grace and diplomacy in an attempt to bridge the differences between blacks and whites in the early twentieth century and to produce a more humane society for all.

—*Janet Hoover*

REFERENCES: *BLC-2. EBLG. NAAAL.* Beavers, Herman, in *OCAAL.* Dirkson, Carolyn, "The Autobiography of an Ex-Coloured Man," in *MAAL.* Fleming, Robert E. (1997), "Reviews," *African American Review,* 31(2), 351–352, *Magazine Academic Index Plus.* Morgan, Thomas L. (1997), "Bob Cole, J. Rosamond Johnson, and James Weldon Johnson," http://www.redlt.com/jass/c&j.html.

Johnson, John H. (Harold) (né Johnnie Johnson) (1/19/1918–)

Autobiography; magazine founder and publisher, book publisher

Born and raised in desperate poverty in Arkansas, Johnson has amassed a vast fortune by publishing materials of interest to African-American readers. After his family moved to Chicago, Johnson started high school, edited the *Phillipsite* (his school's newspaper), and was the class president of his junior and senior classes. A frequent visitor to the public library, Johnson read whatever he could find on African-American history and literature, including the works of **W. E. B. Du Bois**, **Booker T. Washington**, and **Langston Hughes**. After high school, Johnson got a job working for Supreme Life Insurance, intending to work his way through the University of Chicago. In 1939, Johnson was promoted to editor of the company's monthly newsletter, the *Guardian,* and he quit college.

After several years of editing the Supreme publication, Johnson decided that the news he was gathering for Supreme's top executives might interest other African Americans, so he used his mother's furniture as collateral to borrow $500 with which to start his own magazine. With that capital, he sent out mailings to Supreme's client list and sold 3,000 advance subscriptions to his proposed magazine (for $2 apiece). At last, in 1942 he began publishing his 68-page **Negro Digest**, patterned after the highly popular *Reader's Digest,* and reprinting articles from both white and black periodicals. After distributing copies to his subscribers, he had to sell 2,000 more copies to be able to pay his bills and print the next issue. Through his hard work and industry in finding outlets for his magazine, he made money on his first issue—so there could be a second issue.

Starting in 1943, Johnson also included original articles and essays in the digest. By late 1943, Johnson had made enough money to be able to buy his first building: a three-story apartment building with an apartment for his mother and stepfather as well as for himself and his wife Eunice Walker (with whom he has two biological children and an adopted daughter, broadcaster and Johnson Publishing Company president Linda Johnson Rice).

Until 1944, Johnson's only employee was a full-time secretary (although he fudged the masthead with names of some of his relatives), but after that he hired his mother (whom he employed until her death in 1977) and other staffers. With *Negro Digest* running smoothly, in 1945 Johnson started publishing *Ebony* magazine, a photo-rich periodical showcasing African Americans in news articles about current events and in feature articles. (It was similar in format to *Life* magazine, a popular magazine of that time.) Its first printing of 25,000 copies sold out within hours, and the second printing of 25,000 sold out, too. In no time at all, *Ebony* had outsold *Negro Digest* to become the most widely circulated African-American magazine. Among the talented African Americans he hired were **Era Bell Thompson** and Moneta Sleet, Jr. (who was the first African American to win a Pulitzer Prize for photography). That year, Negro Digest Publishing Company also published its first—and its last—book, *The Best of Negro Humor,* which Johnson edited himself.

In 1949 Johnson renamed his company the eponymous Johnson Publishing Company. In 1951 he suspended publication of *Negro Digest* (see **Negro Digest** for more on the ups, downs, and various rebirths of this periodical), which had a circulation of about 60,000. That same year, he launched *Jet,* a small-format (5.25-inch-by-4-inch) news magazine that predated *USA Today* in offering bite-sized news features and articles on politics, sports, and entertainment. Almost immediately, its circulation passed 300,000, and by the late 1990s, its circulation was more than 1 million, including subscribers in more than 40 countries. Other Johnson magazine ventures have included *Tan Confessions* (a true-confessions magazine), *Proper Romance, Beauty Salon, Ebony Man,* and *Ebony South Africa,* as well as *Ebony, Jr.!,* a monthly magazine for African-American children.

In 1962, in addition to its periodicals, Johnson Publishing Company started publishing books, such as **Lerone Bennett, Jr.**'s *Before the Mayflower: A History of the Negro in America, 1619–1962* (1962). The book division now also publishes books for children as well as for adults. Johnson's enterprises also expanded to include many other business ventures (e.g., radio stations, clothing, cosmetics, wigs, and vitamins). His numerous awards include being named one of the U.S. Junior Chamber of Commerce's top ten young men (1951), the NAACP's prestigious Spingarn Medal (1966), induction into the Black Press Hall of Fame (1987), and various honorary degrees. In 1993, Johnson published his autobiography *Succeeding against the Odds* (with Lerone Bennett, Jr.).

REFERENCES: *EB-BH-CD. G-97. PGAA.* Fay, Robert, "Johnson Publishing Company," in *EA-99.* Smith, Jessie Carney, in *BH2C.* Toppin, Edgar Allan, in *WB-99.*

Johnson, Kathryn Magnolia
(12/15/1878–5/?/1955)
Memoir; putting books into thousands of readers' hands

A well-educated schoolteacher, in 1910 Johnson started selling subscriptions to **Crisis,** the National Association for the Advancement of Colored People (NAACP) journal **W. E. B. Du Bois** had started, promoting NAACP membership in the process. Although she had done quite well for the NAACP, after she started outspokenly denouncing their inclusion of whites in leadership positions, she was asked to take her services elsewhere— which she did, for the Young Women's Christian Association (YWCA).

During World War I, the YWCA asked her, Addie Waites Hunton, and another woman to go to France to watch over the rights and the well-being of segregated African-American soldiers fighting for their own country in that country. When Johnson and Hunton returned, they published an account of their travels and their experiences, *Two Colored Women with the American Expeditionary Forces* (1922). That done, Johnson returned to the road, selling the "Two-Foot Shelf of Negro Literature," the 15 books then published by the Association for the Study of Negro Life and History and its Associated Publishers. One of the best-selling authors on the shelf was the "Father of Black History," **Carter G. Woodson**, who had founded both the association and its publishing affiliate. By mid-1928, Johnson had traveled more than 9,000 miles and had sold more than 15,000 books.

—*Tonya Bolden*

REFERENCES: *BAAW. TAWH.* Arnold, Thea, in *BWA:AHE.*

Johnson, William (?/1809–1851)
Diaries

Johnson's 13-volume set of diaries cover his life experiences as a freed slave in Mississippi. His diaries began October 12, 1835, initially as a record of his income and outgo; they expanded in scope to consider social, economic, and political events; and they continued until his death 16 years later. Considered the longest and most detailed narrative of the antebellum South written by an African American, Johnson's diaries offer deep and broad insights into that period. (*See also* **Slave Narratives**.)

REFERENCES: Andrews, William L., in *OCAAL.*

Jones, Gayl (Amanda) (11/23/1949–)
Novels, short stories, poems, plays, criticism

Young Gayl grew up in a storytelling family: Her grandmother wrote plays for her church, and her mother constantly made up stories to entertain the children and other family members. As Gayl recalls, "I began to write when I was seven, because I saw my mother writing, and because she would read stories to my brother and me, stories that she had written" (*BWW,* p. 234).

Although Gayl received little encouragement for her storytelling and her writing in school, she continued to write. Finally, while earning her bachelor's degree in English from Connecticut College, she was awarded several prizes for her poems. After graduation, she sought her graduate degrees in creative writing (M.A., 1973; D.A., 1975) at Brown University, an Ivy League school. As she later noted (*BWW,* p. 234), "The individuals who have influenced my work are my mother, Lucille Jones; [and] my creative writing teachers, **Michael Harper** and William Meredith," with whom she studied at Brown.

As soon as Jones earned her D.A., she moved to the University of Michigan, where she taught creative writing and African-American literature as an associate professor of English (1975–1983). Her academic interests have included African-American folklore, narrative strategies, fictional forms, and **oral tradition**. Although Jones enjoyed teaching and found that "teaching other writers can make you think more about certain themes, literary techniques, and strategies, which I think can be helpful" (*BWW,* 235), she also found that full-time teaching detracted from her writing.

The year Jones earned her D.A. and started teaching, she also published both her play *Chile Woman* and her first novel, *Corregidora*. *Corregidora* tells the story of a blues singer whose foremothers' abuse under slavery mirrors the contemporary abuse she receives from her husband. Jones credits her editor, **Toni Morrison**, with helping to shape the work. In her next novel, *Eva's Man* (1976), the protagonist Eva tells how she ends up being imprisoned in an institution for the criminally insane. In it, Eva reports having poisoned her abusive lover and then biting his penis. Through the story, Jones experiments with the definitions of sanity and psychosis, reality and fantasy. Jones further explores psychological distortions in her short-story collection *White Rat* (1977). Another of her novels, *Palmares,* published in the early 1980s, explores man-woman relationships, set in seventeenth-century Brazil. More recently, she wrote *The Healing* (1998), about a beautician who becomes a traveling faith healer, and *Mosquito* (1999) a free-wheeling novel about a woman truck driver.

Although best known for her gothic novels of violence and sexual aggression, Jones also writes in other genres. In the early 1980s, she started publishing her poetry collections: *Song for Anninho* (1981), *The Hermit-Woman* (1983), and *Xarque and Other Poems* (1985) thematically center on the resistance to slavery, particularly focusing on a slave revolt that occurred in eighteenth-century Brazil. Her nonfiction includes her critical exploration of the African-American oral tradition, *Liberating*

Voices: Oral Tradition in African American Literature (1991), about which she has said, "I am very much interested in form and structure. I am as interested in *how* things are said as I am in what is said" (*BWW,* p. 235). For her poems and her fiction, she has been recognized with many grants and other awards, including a National Endowment for the Arts grant in writing (1976–1977) and the *Mademoiselle* Award for Fiction (1975).

Jones's personal life sometimes seems to imitate her art; in the 1990s, her husband's suicide was followed by her own hospitalization for an apparent nervous breakdown. By the end of the decade, however, Jones had returned to her writing with renewed productivity.

REFERENCES: *AA:PoP. BI. BWW. BWWW. EBLG. MAAL. OC20LE. RT.* Byerman, Keith E., in *OCWW.* Gottfried, Amy S., in *OCAAL.* Amazon.com, 1/2000.

Jones-Meadows, Karen (1953–)
Stage plays, screenplays

Starting in 1985, Jones-Meadows managed to have *Henrietta,* the second play she wrote, produced off-Broadway by the Negro Ensemble Company. Since then, she has written *Tapman* (1988), *Major Changes* (1989), *Crystals* (1994), *Mystery Cycle Plays* (1989), *In the Name of the Woman* (1993), and *Harriet's Return!* (1994). She has also written two stage plays for young adults—*Private Conversations* (1991–1992) and *Everybody's Secret* (1994), as well as several television and film scripts.

REFERENCES: Brown, E. Barnsley, in *OCAAL.*

Jordan, Barbara (Charline)
(2/21/1936–1/17/1996)
Autobiography, speeches, political writings

Best known as a politician, Jordan became the first African-American state senator in Texas since 1883, the first woman state senator ever (1966–1972), and the first African-American congresswoman from the South (1972–1978). Despite her status as a groundbreaker, Jordan announced, "I am neither a black politician nor a female politician, just a politician" (quoted in *EA-99*). In 1974, she was a member of the House Judiciary Committee during the Nixon impeachment hearings, and her eloquent and explicit observations were among the most memorable and stirring during that historic time. For instance, she noted, "My faith in the Constitution is whole. It is complete. It is total. I am not going to sit here and be an idle spectator in the diminution, the subversion, and the destruction of the Constitution" (quoted in *BH2C,* p. 398). In 1976 (and again in 1992), she delivered the keynote address to the Democratic National Convention, the first woman and the first African American ever to do so. Again, she inspired her listeners with her observation, "That this [keynote address] is possible is one additional bit of evidence that the American Dream need not forever be deferred" (quoted in *TAWH,* p. 87).

In 1978, Jordan left Congress and taught social sciences (specializing in political ethics and public policy) at the University of Texas at Austin. A decade later, she revealed that she was diagnosed with multiple sclerosis (a neuromuscular disorder). Her published works include her autobiography, *Barbara Jordan: A Self-Portrait* (1979, with Shelby Hearon); *Local Government Election Systems* (1984, with Terrell Blodgett); *The Great Society: A Twenty-Year Critique* (1986, edited with Elspeth Rosto), and a collection of her speeches, *Selected Speeches* (1999, edited by Sandra Parham). Among Jordan's numerous awards are the Eleanor Roosevelt Humanities Award (1984), the National Association for the Advancement of Colored People's Spingarn Medal (1992), the presidential Medal of Freedom (1995), and more than 20 honorary doctorates from prominent U.S. universities. She also cofounded and served on the board of People for the American Way, a liberal organization that opposes censorship.

REFERENCES: *BDAA. EB-BH-CD. EBLG. G-97. TAWH.* Duckworth, James, in *BH2C.* Edwards, Roanne, in *EA-99.* Hamilton, Charles V., in *WB-99.* Pitre, Merline, in *BWA:AHE.* Amazon.com, 7/1999.

Jordan, June (7/9/1936–)

Poems, novels, essays, children's books, dramas, columns, short stories, anthologies, libretti

Granville and Mildred Jordan had emigrated from a life of desperate poverty in Jamaica to the Bedford–Stuyvesant neighborhood of Brooklyn before their daughter June was born. June's mother, a nurse, had longed to be an artist but had to abandon her dreams to address more practical concerns. As an adult, June Jordan reflected back on the situation of her mother in her essays "Notes of a Barnard Dropout" and "Many Rivers to Cross" (1985) and in poems such as "Getting

Down to Get Over" (1977). In these works, she places her mother's situation and eventual suicide (in 1966) in the historical context of other black women whose longings and aspirations have been unfulfilled and whose voices and creative works have been ignored. June's relationship with her father, a postal clerk, was complicated: He beat her savagely—to the point of scarring her physically as well as emotionally. Yet he also shared with June his love of literature, especially the verses of the Bible, Shakespeare, Poe, and **Paul Laurence Dunbar**.

At age seven, June started writing her own poems. Over the years, her changing interests in poets (the major Romantic poets, African–American male poets, women poets, and so on) influenced shifts in her own poetry. Both her parents worked hard to ensure that young June would have what they considered an outstanding education. In most of the schools she attended, she was among a small minority of blacks—in Midwood High School, a long commute from Bedford-Stuyvesant, she was a minority of 1 black among 3,000 students. To say that she felt unwelcome would be to understate the situation. For that matter, the situation wasn't much different at the Northfield School for Girls (in Massachusetts) or at Barnard College (in New York City).

In each of these exclusive schools, Jordan was faced with a white male–oriented curriculum, which in no way related to her, her family, her friends, her community, or her cultural background. Although she had once been turned on to literature through the works of white males, as a youth, she resisted the exclusive focus on a heritage and life experiences she did not share. On her own, she sought out African-American writers such as **Margaret Walker**, **Robert Hayden**, and **Langston Hughes**.

While Jordan was still an undergraduate at Barnard College, she married Michael Meyer, a white liberal graduate student at Columbia. They wedded in 1955, when interracial marriage was actually illegal in 43 states—and was reviled in all 50. When Meyer went on to the University of Chicago, June followed him to that university, taking a year off from Barnard. The following year, she returned to Barnard for a year, but she dropped out the following year, and the next year (1958), she and Michael had a son, Christopher David Meyer.

After leaving college, Jordan tried out several different jobs, including assistant movie producer. She also worked closely with innovative architect

Buckminster Fuller, developing a plan for renovating Harlem, for which she was awarded a 1970 Prix de Rome in environmental design. She also took her young son with her and rode to Baltimore, Maryland, with the Freedom Riders, despite her husband's fear that she and her son would be in danger by doing so. As she became increasingly involved in the civil rights movement in New York, and he became increasingly involved in his work in Chicago, the couple drew apart, and in 1966 (the same year her mother committed suicide), the two divorced. While June (she kept the surname Meyer until 1969) did freelance journalistic writing to support herself and her son, she also wrote poems every day.

Supporting a son on freelance writing proved difficult, and starting in 1967, Jordan (Meyer) began teaching literature, English, African-American literature, and writing at several colleges in Connecticut (e.g., Yale) and in New York (e.g., City College of New York). She also accepted positions as poet- and playwright-in-residence, children's workshop leader, and lecturer at various schools and institutions. In 1989, she was named professor of African-American Studies and Women's Studies at the University of California at Berkeley. At the same time, she started writing political columns for *The Progressive* magazine. At Berkeley, Jordan directs a forum for aspiring poets, the Poetry for the People program, which seeks to develop the poetic talents of students and community members.

In the academic community, Jordan has attempted to rectify the educational flaws she observed in her own schooling. Hence, she has fervently advocated for including African-American and Third World studies within the university curricula. She has also championed the use of Black English (or Ebonics) as an acceptable, lovely, and efficacious form of English language expression. She has also argued that the resistance to Black English centers more on the power dynamics in the mainstream culture than on any qualities intrinsic to either Black English or Standard American English.

Jordan has applied her own use of language to a variety of genres, including more than eight poetry collections, five children's books, three plays, four books of essays, novels, and countless short stories and news columns, and she has edited several anthologies. Jordan's free verse poems have been widely published and anthologized. In *Who Look at Me* (given the American Library Association's Notable Book Award in 1969), she interwove her

dialect poem into a series of paintings depicting the history of blacks in the United States. *Some Changes,* her first poetry collection followed in 1971, including highly personal poems as well as poems that addressed political, social, and racial issues and even poems responding to aesthetic questions.

Her subsequent poetry publications include *Poem: On Moral Leadership as a Political Dilemma (Watergate, 1973)* (1973), *New Days: Poems of Exile and Return* (1974), *Things That I Do in the Dark: Selected Poetry* (1977), *Passion: New Poems, 1977–1980* (1980), *Living Room: New Poems, 1980–1984* (1985), *Lyrical Campaigns: Selected Poems* (1989), *Naming Our Destiny: New and Selected Poems* (1989), and *Haruko/Love Poems* (1993/1994). These collections reflect Jordan's expanding sense of inclusiveness, as she first embraces African Americans, then other U.S. ethnic groups, women around the globe, and all people who are struggling everywhere. As she wraps her poetic attention around humanity throughout the world, she still moves in close to give readers an intimate view of universal experiences.

In addition to her poetry, Jordan has written plays and the libretti (lyrics) for more than one opera. She is perhaps better known, however, for her juvenile fiction works. Her books for youths include the novel *His Own Where—* (1971), a National Book Award finalist, written entirely in Black English, about a youthful protagonist who undertakes an urban renewal project to renovate his neighborhood. Her historical novel *Dry Victories* (1972) and her biography *Fannie Lou Hamer* (1972) explore African-American history from the Reconstruction era through the civil rights movement. Jordan also recorded the narratives of children directly, in the reader she edited with Terri Bush, *The Voice of the Children: Writings by Black and Puerto Rican Young People* (1970/1974). Other works for juveniles include *New Room, New Life* (1974/1975) and *Kimako's Story* (1981).

More recently, Jordan's writings have included works of nonfiction, including the essay collections *Civil Wars* (1981), *On Call* (1985), *Moving towards Home* (1989), and *Technical Difficulties: African-American Notes on the State of the Union* (1992). As in her poetry, Jordan frequently addresses international issues and themes in her work. She doesn't hesitate to address tough questions to her own situation, either. For instance, she observes how her own experiences and worldview as a black vacationer in the Caribbean differ from those of the black women and men who make her bed and serve her drinks.

Throughout her career, Jordan has received numerous awards for her activism and for her writing, including a 1969 Rockefeller grant in creative writing, a 1982 National Endowment for the Arts fellowship, and a 1984 National Association of Black Journalists Award.

REFERENCES: *AA:PoP. EB-98. EBLG. G-95. LDW. MAAL. MWEL. NAAAL. OC20LE. TtW. TWT.* Johnson, Ronna C., in *OCAAL.* Zevenbergen, Susan J., in *OCWW.*

Josey, E. J. (Elonnie Junius) (1/20/1924–)
Nonfiction—library sciences, bibliography

Among the many volumes Josey has edited are *The Black Librarian in America* (1973) and *The Black Librarian in America Revisited* (1994), and he has coedited such books as *What Black Librarians Are Saying* (1972, with **Ann Shockley**), *Ethnic Collections in Libraries* (1983, with Marva L. DeLoach), and *Politics and the Support of Libraries* (1990, with Kenneth D. Shearer).

REFERENCES: *EBLG.*

Just, Ernest Everett
(8/14/1883–10/27/1941)
Nonfiction—biology

Just sped through the Kimball Academy (prep school, four-year course completed in three years, graduated with honors, 1903) and Dartmouth College (B.S. in biology, with minors in Greek and in history, magna cum laude, 1907) and started teaching English and rhetoric at Howard University. Fortunately for science, in 1909 Howard needed an instructor of biology, zoology, and physiology for its newly expanded science curricula, and it pressed Just into service. In 1912, Just married fellow Howard instructor Ethel Highwarden, and later on, the couple had three children.

While developing the science program from fall through spring, Just spent his summers at the world-renowned Marine Biological Laboratory (MBL) in Woods Hole, Massachusetts. Frank R. Lillie, the director of the MBL, also headed the zoology department at the University of Chicago, and he took an interest in the bright and hard-working Just. With Lillie's encouragement, Just earned his Ph.D. in 1916 from the University of Chicago while maintaining his teaching duties at Howard and continu-

ing to work at MBL each summer. Before Just even received his doctorate, he had started publishing scientific articles on his research (e.g., "The Relation of the First Cleavage Plane to the Entrance Point of the Sperm," 1912, a well-regarded study). In 1915, the National Association for the Advancement of Colored People (NAACP) recognized his contributions and his potential by awarding him the first NAACP Spingarn Medal. They knew what they were doing when they awarded it, as Just went on to publish about 60 research papers in various scientific journals during his more than 30-year career at Howard. Most of these papers focused on the life of normal and abnormal cells, which Just believed held the promise of giving insight into how various diseases (such as cancer) came into being—and could possibly be eradicated.

Because Just's true passion was his research, he viewed his teaching duties as a distraction. He loved to get research grants that would take him to Europe and other places, so that he could be free of his teaching duties and could focus solely on his research. (Needless to say, his wife and children weren't thrilled to have him be away so much; the couple eventually divorced.) In 1939, he published *The Biology of the Cell Surface,* which revolutionized biologists' view of cells by showing that the life of the cell depended just as much on the activities in the *ectoplasm* (the outer part of the cell) as on the functions of the cell *nucleus* (the figurative heart and brain of the cell).

The year after his revolutionary book appeared in print, Just was studying at a biological research arm of the prestigious Sorbonne University in France. By that time, he had remarried, having wedded a biology graduate student whom he had met previously in Germany. His health was failing, but he never flagged in his dedication to his work. In June, the Germans invaded France and interred him in a prison camp until his new wife's father intervened and had him released. The Justs quickly escaped to the United States. By the end of the following year, Just was dead, having succumbed to a disease caused by abnormal cell growth: cancer. Given his dedication to his work, he probably died saying to himself, "If only I could have unlocked a few more secrets of the cell. . . ."

—Tonya Bolden

REFERENCES: *EAACH. SMKC.* Manning, Kenneth R. (1983), *Black Apollo of Science: The Life of Ernest Everett Just* (New York: Oxford University Press). Tuttle, Kate, in *EA-99.*

K

Keckley, Elizabeth (née Hobbs) (c. 1824–5/26/1907)
Memoir

More than a century before Monica Lewinsky's book hit the newsstands, Elizabeth Hobbs Keckley published her tell-all memoir of her experiences with folks in the White House. Keckley's memoir wasn't her first show of industry and initiative, however. Born and raised a slave in St. Louis, Missouri, she had become quite handy with a needle. When the person who owned Elizabeth and her elderly mother threatened to hire out Elizabeth's frail mother, Elizabeth offered to hire out her own services as a seamstress. Within three years, she had not only provided an income for 17 people but also had been able to buy freedom for herself and her son (the product of a rape by a white man). For $1,200, including her own savings and some money she borrowed from her clients, she was free to leave St. Louis and set up shop in Baltimore, Maryland.

In Baltimore, Elizabeth met and married the disreputable James Keckley. In less than a year, she left the swindler behind and moved to Washington, D.C., where she set up yet another seamstress shop, employing up to 20 women at times. In no time at all, many of the best-dressed and most esteemed women of Washington were seeking her services. The wives of Stephen Douglas (Lincoln's proslavery rival for the presidency) and of Jefferson Davis (soon to be president of the Confederacy) were among her patrons. When Mary Todd Lincoln, the First-Lady-to-be, spilled coffee on her inaugural gown, Mrs. McClean (General Charles Sumner's daughter) suggested she seek the help of Elizabeth Keckley. After rescuing the future First Lady, Keckley was soon the only fashion designer to work for Mrs. Lincoln.

Just as nowadays many barbers, hairdressers, and "personal trainers" become the confidantes of their clients, in those times, dressmakers heard all the juicy details of the lives of their patrons. Even after Abraham Lincoln died, Keckley continued her close relationship with Mary Todd Lincoln. At first, she even followed Lincoln to Chicago, but when it seemed apparent that her business would do better back in the nation's capital, Keckley returned to D.C. When Lincoln decided to auction off her White House wardrobe, she asked Keckley to help her in this mission. Unfortunately, the auction netted Lincoln more ridicule than cash.

In some ways, the same could be said for Keckley when, in 1868, she published her memoirs, *Behind the Scenes: Or, Thirty Years a Slave and Four Years in the White House.* In it, she included quite a few letters Mary Todd Lincoln had written to her, as well as many recollections from confidences Lincoln had shared with her in person. Although Keckley protested that she had written her book to stir up public sympathy for Mrs. Lincoln, Mary was outraged, perceiving that her privacy and her friendship had been betrayed. Robert Todd Lincoln, the only surviving (and oldest) son of the Lincolns, tried to have booksellers remove the book from their shelves. When that effort failed, he rather fruitlessly tried to remove them by buying up as many copies as he could.

Needless to say, Keckley's business suffered, too. For the 1892–1893 school year, she taught domestic arts at Wilberforce University in Ohio. The following year, she retired to D.C., where her failing health eventually overshadowed her other troubles.

—*Tonya Bolden*

REFERENCES: *BAAW.* Keckley, Elizabeth Hobbs (1868), *Behind the Scenes: Or, Thirty Years a Slave and Four Years in the White House.*

Kelley, Emma Dunham (fl. late 1800s)
Novels

Some research suggests that Kelley's *Megda* (1891; reprinted in 1988, with an introduction by Molly Hite) may have been the first novel by an African-American woman published in this country; others (e.g., **Henry Louis Gates, Jr.** and David Curtis) have said that **Harriet Wilson**'s *Our Nig* (1859) predates Kelley's work, based on evidence they gathered in the mid-1980s. In the late 1990s, however, other scholars (e.g., Charles Blockson) have raised questions about whether Wilson's work was actually written by an African-American woman. Regardless of whether Kelley's novel is the first or the second one to be published, written by an African-American woman, it is an important early contribution to African-American literature.

Megda was originally published under the pseudonym "Forget-Me-Not," and Kelley's second novel, *Four Girls at Cottage City* (1895; reprinted in 1989, with an introduction by Deborah McDowell), was published under the name Emma Dunham Kelley-Hawkins, presumably her married name. Both of Kelley's novels focus on young women coming of age, who move beyond devil-may-care adolescence, and accept an evangelical Protestant, Christ-centered orientation to their lives. The Christian spiritual development of Kelley's young women accompanies their maturation and prompts their peaceful acceptance of their womanly duties of marriage followed by motherhood, as interpreted by nineteenth-century norms and values.

REFERENCES: Schwartz, Meryl F., in *OCAAL*.

Kelley, William Melvin (11/1/1937–)
Novels, short stories, essays, edited works

Young William Kelley grew up in an Italian-American Bronx neighborhood in New York. As a young man, he went to a private prep school, Fieldston School, in New York, and then he went on to attend Harvard University. At Harvard, his instructors included Archibald MacLeish and novelist John Hawkes. While still an undergraduate, Kelley was awarded the Dana Reed Prize for his writing (1960). After college, he garnered grants from the New York Writers' Conference, the Bread Loaf Writers' Conference, the John Hay Whitney Foundation, and the Rosenthal Foundation of the National Institute of Arts and Letters, which he used to write his first novel, *A Different Drummer* (1962).

A Different Drummer, often named his best novel, centers around an intriguing what-if: What would happen if all the black residents of a Southern state left the state in a mass exodus? What would happen to the blacks who left (e.g., those of the Caliban family) and to the whites who were left behind (especially those of the Willson family)?

Kelley's next novel, *A Drop of Patience* (1965), tracks the life story of Ludlow Washington, a blind saxophone-playing jazz musician, starting in his childhood and progressing through his adulthood. In the story, Ludlow ends up in a misguided sex-

ual relationship with a white woman, who becomes pregnant by him and then abandons him, thereby driving him to madness. *A Drop of Patience* is loosely connected to *A Different Drummer* in that Ludlow's daughter Bethra ends up marrying a member of the Caliban family.

Kelley dedicates his next novel, *dem* (1967), to "the Black people in (not of) America" (quoted in *BWA*). The novel is narrated by Mitchell Pierce, whose wife, Tam, gives birth to fraternal twins: one white and one black. This rather surrealistic novel satirizes white family life in relation to that of African Americans. Kelley's *Dunfords Travels Everywheres* (1970) has been compared to James Joyce's *Finnegans Wake* because of its dream sequences, fantasy, and playful linguistic experimentation. In the novel, Kelley compares and contrasts the two main characters—Chig Dunford, a middle-class writer, and Carlyle Bedlow, a working-class hustler.

Kelley's short-story collection, *Dancers on the Shore* (1964), also includes many stories involving the Dunfords and the Bedlows. Of the 16 stories in the collection, 6 focus on the Dunfords (e.g., "A Visit to Grandmother," "Saint Paul and the Monkeys," "Christmas with the Great Man") and 4 focus on the Bedlows. Kelley also forms links between the stories and his other novels. For instance, one of the characters in his first story, "The Only Man on Liberty Street," is the illegitimate daughter of a white (former slaveowning) member of the Willson family. In the last story, "Cry for Me," Wallace Bedlow (a refugee from the mythical Southern state who knows the Calibans) flees to New York, where he gets to know his nephew Carlyle, who was an important character in *dem* and in *Dunfords Travels Everywheres*.

In addition, Kelley has written numerous essays about the African-American experience, which appeared in various national periodicals throughout the 1960s (e.g., *New York Times Magazine, Esquire, Mademoiselle,* and **Negro Digest**). He also edited **Norman Bel Geddes**'s autobiography, *Miracle in the Evening* (1960).

In addition to his writing, Kelley has taught at the New School for Social Research in New York and both taught and worked as writer-in-residence at the State University of New York at Geneseo. He has also taught literature and writing at the University of Paris at Nanterre, and has lived in France, Italy, and Jamaica.

REFERENCES: *AAL. BAL-1-P. BWA. G-97.*
Fleming, Robert E., in *OCAAL*.

Kennedy, Adrienne (Lita) (née Hawkins)
(9/13/1931–)
Plays, memoirs

Adrienne's parents were Cornell Wallace Hawkins, executive secretary of the Young Men's Christian Association (YMCA), and Etra Haugebook Hawkins, a teacher. Their first child (and their only daughter), she was quite gifted, learning to read when she was just three years old. After Adrienne turned four, her family moved from Pittsburgh, Pennsylvania, to an integrated, middle-class neighborhood in Cleveland, Ohio. In Cleveland, she attended public schools, where her own racial heritage was part of the multiethnic blend of the community. Her strict parents always stressed the importance of both education and religion. While still a youth, Adrienne saw Tennessee Williams's play *The Glass Menagerie,* which dramatically portrays the emotional dynamics in a troubled family. As she later recalled, seeing that play was "when the idea of being a writer and seeing my own family onstage caught fire in my mind" (quoted in *OCAAL,* from her memoir). As time went on, she recalled, "I often saw our family [as] if they were in a play" (quoted from *NAAAL*). She compensated for a certain rigidity in her childhood by developing a dramatic inner life.

In 1949, Adrienne entered Ohio State University to study writing. There, she faced tremendous racial hostility, which she had never before encountered in the multiethnic community of her childhood. Nonetheless, many good things came out of that experience, not the least of which were a B.A. in education (1953) and meeting the man she married two weeks after graduating: Joseph C. Kennedy. Within six months, she was pregnant, and Joseph was on his way to Korea, courtesy of the U.S. Army. While Joseph was in Korea, Adrienne moved back in with her parents, and she started writing her earliest plays.

When Joseph returned, he and Adrienne—and their infant son Joseph C., Jr.—moved to New York so that Joseph Sr. could further his education at Columbia's Teachers College. Soon, Adrienne, too, returned to school at Columbia, where she studied drama and creative writing. She also continued to write, including her autobiographical play *Pale Blue Flowers* (1955) and some other unpublished autobiographical fiction. In 1958, she started studying at the American Theatre Wing of the New School for Social Research in New York.

In 1960, Adrienne accompanied her Josephs (Sr. and Jr.) to Ghana, where Joseph Sr. was to do research. On board the ship to Ghana, Adrienne wrote her short story "Because of the King of France," which was published in 1963 under the pseudonym Adrienne Cornell in *Black Orpheus: A Journal of African and Afro-American Literature.* During this trip, she also gained a sense of connection to African culture and came in contact with the writings of Africans Chinua Achebe and Wole Soyinka.

This trip also inspired Adrienne to start writing her play *Funnyhouse of a Negro* (which was produced in 1964). In addition to being productive, she was reproductive, and when her pregnancy with her second child proved difficult, she and Joseph Jr. went to Rome. There, she could have easy access to physicians and other conveniences while she awaited the birth of Adam Patrice (named after Patrice Lumumba, an African leader who had been assassinated, whom Adrienne also included as a character in *Funnyhouse*) while Joseph Sr. completed his research.

When she returned to New York, Adrienne submitted *Funnyhouse* to Edward Albee's playwriting workshop at Circle-in-the-Square Theatre. The theater produced this surrealistic play featuring many outstanding actors of the day as historic characters in nightmarish dreamscapes. Albee liked the play well enough to option it for an off-Broadway production at the East End Theatre, where it ran for 46 performances and won a *Village Voice* Obie Award for distinguished play of 1964 and a Stanley Drama Award. Her very first play made her an instant hit as a playwright.

Kennedy's favorite play was her next one, *The Owl Answers* (1965), a one-act play in which she uses composite characters to portray multiple aspects (and selves) of a black woman's search for identity in a white man's world. She went on to write several more one-act plays by the end of the 1960s: *A Beast Story* (1966); *A Rat's Mass* (written in 1963, named one of the best plays of the season when it was produced in 1966), in which humans are transformed into rats; *A Lesson in a Dead Language* (1968), which surrealistically depicts pubescent sexual maturation as a rite of passage in a classroom setting; *Boats* (1969); and *Sun: A Poem for Malcolm X Inspired by His Murder* (commissioned in 1968, produced in 1969 and 1970, published in 1971 and 1972), in which a male voice dominated the drama. *The Owl Answers* and *A Beast Story* were produced together at the New York Shakespeare Festival (by Joseph Papp) as *Cities in Bezique* (1969), again using surrealistic dreamscapes and composite characters to highlight the inhumanity of humans in relation to beasts.

To create her surrealistic effects, Kennedy often uses nontraditional music, masks, religious symbols (both pagan and Christian), rich imagery, and other theatrical devices. She also has some characters played by more than one actor, has some characters transform into other characters, and includes composite characters. Many of her composite characters include members of her immediate family as well as other people from her childhood, along with historical figures. Her use of nonlinear narratives, unconventional plots, and dreamlike sequences furthers the surrealism of her work. She also adds to her works' complexity by infusing the plays with poetic, figurative language, which can convey multiple levels of meaning.

In 1967, Kennedy worked with John Lennon and Victor Spinetti to dramatically adapt Lennon's writings into Kennedy's first full-length play, *The Lennon Play: In His Own Write* (first produced in 1967; published in 1968 and 1973). Her subsequent plays include *Evening with Dead Essex* (1973), about a Vietnam War incident involving a sniper; *A Movie Star Has to Star in Black and White* (1976), her best-known full-length play, which probes dysfunctional family relationships through the lens of movie stars' fantasy lives; *Orestes and Electra* (1980), a commissioned adaptation of the Greek tragedies; *A Lancashire Child* (1980), her first play for children, a commissioned musical based on the memoirs of Charlie Chaplin; *Diary of Lights* (1987), a music-inspired play about an idealistic young African-American couple living in New York City's Upper West Side; and *Sleep Deprivation Chamber* (1991), about an incident involving the beating of her son Adam by outlaw police officers.

In 1992, Kennedy came out with *The Alexander Plays,* a set of four one-act plays about a character named Suzanne Alexander: *She Talks to Beethoven* (first produced in 1989); *The Ohio State Murders,* in which the protagonist acts out some of the wrenching experiences Kennedy had during her undergraduate studies at Ohio State; *The Film Club: A Monologue;* and *The Dramatic Circle,* in which the action of *The Film Club* is dramatized. Each of the four plays tells a story resolved in one act, and they were published together in *Plays in One Act* (1991). In 1993, Kennedy came out with

a fifth Suzanne Alexander story: *Letters to My Students on My 61st Birthday by Suzanne Alexander.* Kennedy actually introduced Suzanne Alexander to readers in her mystery novella (with two solved puzzles), which incorporated journal entries from her experiences in London (between 1966 and 1969), *Deadly Triplets: A Theatre Mystery and Journal* (1990).

Kennedy has also written several plays for children; her memoir, *People Who Led to My Plays* (1987), which lists both fictional characters and actual persons who influenced her in her early years, thus extending the surrealistic quality of her plays into her memoir; and *Adrienne Kennedy in One Act* (1988). In addition, many of her plays have been anthologized in various collections. In thinking about how she writes, Kennedy has said, "I think about things for many years and keep loads of notebooks, with images, dreams, ideas I've jotted down" (quoted in *NAAAL*).

Some time between the mid-1960s and the mid-1970s, Adrienne and Joseph divorced. Meanwhile, she started teaching and lecturing at Yale University, where she was a fellow at the Yale School of Drama and a visiting professor (1972–1974); after that she became a visiting professor at Princeton University (1977), at Brown University (1979–1980), at the University of California at Davis, at the University of California at Berkeley (1986), and at Harvard University (1990–1991). She was also invited to serve as playwright-in-residence for the 1995–1996 season with the Signature Theater Company in New York, where previous honorees include Pulitzer Prize–winning playwrights Horton Foote and Edward Albee.

Kennedy has also received numerous grants, including a Guggenheim Memorial Fellowship (1968), several Rockefeller grants (1967–1969, 1973–1974, 1976), a National Endowment for the Arts grant (1973), a CBS Fellowship at the School of Drama (1973), a Creative Artists Public Service Grant (1974), a Yale Fellowship (1974–1975), and a New England Theatre Conference Grant. She also received an American Book Award in 1990 and a Lila Wallace–Reader's Digest Fund's Writers Award in 1994.

REFERENCES: *EBLG. NAAAL. OC20LE.* Carter, Steven R., in *OCWW.* King, Lovalerie, in *OCAAL.* Robinson, Lisa Clayton, in *EA-99.*

Killens, John Oliver

(1/14/1916–10/27/1987)

Novels, essays, juvenile biographies, plays, screenplays

Young John was exposed early to a love of literature. Every week, his father read aloud **Langston Hughes**'s newspaper column, and his mother presided over the Macon, Georgia, Dunbar Literary Club. Going even farther back in the family, John's great-grandmother used to tell him stories about living under the burden of slavery and about her first taste of freedom.

Though Killens longed to be a writer, a career as a lawyer seemed a lot more practical. He pursued the law, but when World War II broke out, he took time out for a tour of duty in the South Pacific. On returning home, he took to labor relations, union work, and political activity. By the late 1940s, Killens was living in New York and taking classes at Columbia University and New York University, studying how to write well. Pretty soon, he came into contact with **W. E. B. Du Bois**, Langston Hughes, and **Paul Robeson**, and he started thinking that a writing career might be possible for him. Soon he was writing for Du Bois and Robeson's *Freedomways* magazine and Robeson's newspaper, *Freedom*.

Realizing the value of writers supporting one another, Killens joined up with **John Henrik Clarke**, Walter Christmas, and **Rosa Guy** to form the writing workshop later known as the Harlem Writers Guild. During the 1950s and beyond, some of the writers whose careers were bolstered by the guild included **Maya Angelou**, **Alice Childress**, **Ossie Davis**, **Joyce Hansen**, **Paule Marshall**, **Walter Mosley**, and **Brenda Wilkinson**, to name just a few.

Killens was also the first to show that the guild could produce publishable outcomes. In 1954 he published his first novel, *Youngblood,* revealing the agony of staying down home in Georgia, suffering under Jim Crow, while many blacks were fleeing North. His subsequent novels included *And Then We Heard the Thunder* (1962, a Pulitzer Prize nominee about racism in the U.S. armed forces during World War II), *'Sippi* (1967, about the one-man-one-vote struggle in the South), *Slaves* (1969), and *The Cotillion; or, One Good Bull Is Half the Herd* (1971, a Pulitzer Prize–nominated satire on social class climbing and assimilation within the African-American community). In the 1970s, Killens wrote inspiring biographies for young readers: *Great Gittin' Up Morning: A Biography of Denmark Vesey* (1972) and *A Man Ain't Nothin' but a Man: The Adventures of John Henry* (1975). He also wrote a novel about Russian novelist Alexandr Pushkin, *The Great Black Russian: A Novel on the Life and Times of Alexander Pushkin,* which wasn't published until after Killens's death (1989). Killens even tackled the essay form in his collection, *Black Man's Burden* (1965), and he wrote numerous plays and screenplays, including adaptations of his novels *Slaves* and *The Cotillion,* as well as *Winter Soldier* and *Odds against Tomorrow.*

—Tonya Bolden

REFERENCES: *BAAW. EA-99. EAACH. EBLG. SMKC.*

Kincaid, Jamaica (née Elaine Potter Richardson) (5/25/1949–)

Novels, essays, short stories; journalist

Born and raised in the West Indies British colony of Antigua, young Elaine—a prolific reader—was taught that all the greatest literature had been written in Britain prior to 1900. Although she had won scholarships to colonial schools in Antigua, at age 16 Elaine fled to New York City to be an au pair, earning her room and board by doing domestic work for a white family.

Elaine had intended to go to college to become a nurse, but she ended up studying photography and then working as a secretary. She soon started doing freelance writing for various magazines. As a freelancer, she gained some recognition for an interview of Gloria Steinem, which she reported to *Ingenue* magazine. After a time, she was invited to write a "Talk of the Town" piece for *New Yorker* magazine, and in 1976, she was hired for a *New Yorker* staff position. In that position, she changed her name to Jamaica Kincaid, in recognition of her Caribbean island heritage.

Much of Kincaid's work is autobiographical fiction, particularly centered around a feminist exploration of her intensely emotional relationship with her mother. She explores this relationship within the context of her childhood experiences in the West Indies and her adolescent and young adult experiences as a U.S. immigrant. During her career, she has written a few novels and many columns, short stories, short sketches, and essays in addition to editing *Best American Essays 1995*.

Jamaica Kincaid receives an honorary degree from Middlebury College President John McCardell, Jr., 1998 (AP/Wide World Photos)

In 1983, several of Kincaid's short stories (seven of which originally appeared in the *New Yorker*) were collected and published in the volume *At the Bottom of the River*. Most of these stories center on her experiences growing up in Antigua, and the collection was recognized with the Morton Dauwen Zabel Award. Though these stories are works of prose, she uses repeated phrases and other lyrical elements reminiscent of poetic styling.

In 1985, Kincaid published her novel *Annie John,* a series of eight interconnected chapters, originally published as discrete short stories in the *New Yorker*. The stories describe a young girl coming of age on a Caribbean island, striving for independence and individuality despite her overbearing, possessive mother. Although the girl deeply loves her mother, she desperately longs to establish her own identity free of her mother's domination. *Library Journal* recognized the book as one of the

best books of the year, and the book was a finalist for the Ritz Paris Hemingway Award. The following year, the Whitney Museum of American Art published Kincaid's *Annie, Gwen, Lilly, Pam and Tulip* (an oversized limited-edition art book with drawings by artist Eric Fischl). Kincaid's text was essentially a conversation among the title characters. (A regular trade edition of the book was published in 1989.)

Kincaid's second novel was *Lucy* (1990), about a Caribbean island girl who moves to the United States as an au pair for a white family (sound familiar?). As in *Annie John,* the turbulence of the mother-daughter relationship looms large in this work. Although physically separated from her mother and from her island home, the daughter still feels tied to them and feels psychologically unconnected to her new environment and to the people in it. *Annie John* is a more continuous narrative than

Lucy, which seemed more like a series of interconnected but discrete short stories.

Kincaid's subsequent novels include *Autobiography of My Mother* (1996), for which she won a National Book Award, and a book about her brother who died of AIDS in Antigua. In addition, Kincaid wrote a nonfiction polemical essay about Antigua, *A Small Place* (1988), after having returned to visit Antigua after a 20-year absence. In it, she describes the social and economic consequences arising as Antigua creeps forward out of British colonial domination. Her furious indictment of colonization and imperialism provoked harsh criticism in the United States and England but was better received in Europe.

Kincaid and her husband, composer and college professor Allen Shawn, have two children, Annie and Harold.

REFERENCES: *BW. EBLG. G-95. LDW. NAAAL. OC20LE. TWT.* Margulis, Jennifer, in *OCAAL.* Yohe, Kristine A., in *OCWW.*

King, "B. B." (Riley B.) (9/16/1925–)
Songs, autobiography

Originally nicknamed "The Blues Boy from Beale Street," King was soon "Blues Boy" and then simply "B. B." His style of blues playing is reminiscent of the *call-and-response* of the African-American **oral tradition**, in which he sings a line of his lyric, then responds with a guitar riff. In his blues lyrics, King highlights the pleasure and pain of true love (e.g., in "The Thrill Is Gone," 1970), rather than glorifying sexual promiscuity or violence. For a lifetime of musical achievement, this five-time Grammy winner was inducted into the Rock and Roll Hall of Fame in 1987. In 1996, he authored *Blues All Around Me: The Autobiography of B.B. King* (with David Ritz).

REFERENCES: *EB-BH-CD.* Bennett, Eric, in *EA-99.* Johns, Robert L., in *BH2C.*

King, Coretta (née) Scott (4/27/1927–)
Memoir, columns

In addition to her nationally syndicated newspaper column (starting in the 1980s), King has written her memoir of her experiences as the wife of **Martin Luther King, Jr.**, *My Life with Martin Luther King, Jr.* (1969). Additionally, in 1969, an award was established in her honor to recognize the contributions to children's literature provided by African-American authors and illustrators, the Coretta Scott King Book Award. Since that time, numerous honorees have been recognized.

REFERENCES: *EB-BH-CD. SEW.* Carson, Clayborne, and Angela D. Brown, in *BWA:AHE.* Edwards, Roanne, in *EA-99.*

King, Martin Luther, Jr.
(1/15/1929–4/4/1968)
Nonfiction—theology, civil rights, history

Martin Luther King, Jr., is the best-known leader of the civil rights movement, which took place in the 1950s and 1960s. Indeed, he was so deeply involved in the movement and so instrumental in its successes that it is often hard to distinguish the story of the civil rights movement from the story of his life and vice versa. In many ways, his upbringing and schooling taught him the philosophy that would make the movement a success, so the conflation of the man and the movement is not altogether unfounded.

Martin Luther King, Jr., was born in Atlanta, Georgia, in 1929, the son of Martin Luther King, Sr., a Baptist minister, and Alberta Christine Williams, a teacher. The senior Reverend King had inherited his ministry at the Ebenezer Baptist Church in Atlanta from his wife's father, Adam Daniel Williams. Young Martin's childhood was spent listening to his father's and his grandfather's thunderous, wall-shaking sermons. From them, he learned the ideals of Christian love that would later permeate his writings and speeches, as well as the African-American Baptist oratory techniques that would make him into one of the best public speakers in the country.

Although Martin Luther King, Sr., hoped that his son would follow in his footsteps and become a copastor of the congregation of Ebenezer Church, as a young man, Martin Luther King, Jr., did not want to become a pastor like his father and his grandfather. Despite the fact that he went to better schools than many African-American children in Atlanta, he had witnessed the evils of segregation firsthand growing up in the South and did not think that becoming a minister would allow him to combat the social evils he saw around him. He entered Morehouse College in 1944, determined to become a doctor or a lawyer, but under the tutelage of his religion professor and the president of the college, he learned of the influence that ministers had had on society, both socially and intellectually, throughout history.

Martin Luther King, Jr., with his wife Coretta, receives the Medal of Honor of the City of New York (Agence France Presse/Archive Photos)

Thus, in 1948, King began studies at the Crozer Theological Seminary, where he was first introduced to the philosophy of passive resistance—nonviolent, direct confrontation. This philosophy was first espoused by Mahatma Gandhi, who led a nonviolent revolution against colonial British rule in India in the 1950s. Through using this method of protest, the people of India had won their independence from British rule without spilling blood. King was so moved by this ideology that he embraced nonviolent resistance as the best, most moral, and most practical way to achieve social reform in the United States. However, he was still not ready to implement these ideas on a social scale, so after finishing his studies at the seminary, he began doing Ph.D. work in theology at Boston University. It was during his time in Boston that he married **Coretta Scott [King],** who would remain his partner throughout his life.

After he completed his Ph.D. coursework, he decided not to join his father in the Ebenezer Baptist Church in Atlanta but instead took a pastorship in Montgomery, Alabama, knowing that

Montgomery was one of the areas in the United States where segregation was most heartily enforced and where he might do the most good combating it. He rose to the head of the civil rights movement rather quickly, brought into the spotlight by his role in the Montgomery bus boycott of 1955–1956. This boycott was initially organized by a number of black activist groups who came together to protest the arrest of Rosa Parks, an African-American woman who had been arrested for refusing to give up her bus seat to a white passenger (as the segregation laws required her to do). These groups all joined together to create the Montgomery Improvement Association (MIA), a group that was supposed to work with city and bus line officers to establish better treatment of blacks in Montgomery. They elected King as MIA's first president.

It was during his time as president of MIA that King delivered his first civil rights address at Holt Street Baptist Church. The speech urged the boycotters to continue their fight for equal rights, which they did for 382 days. During this time,

King helped to organize various means of alternative transportation for the boycotters and kept up the pressure on the city and bus line officials. As a result, he was arrested, received hate mail and verbal insults, and even had his house bombed. Nevertheless, he managed to maintain his adherence to the philosophy of nonviolence, and his teachings and beliefs paved the way for the protesters to win their battle when the Supreme Court declared Montgomery's bus segregation laws to be unconstitutional in 1956.

King's work, however, had only just begun, and in 1957 he gathered with other black leaders to form the Southern Christian Leadership Conference (SCLC), which was created to spread the movement out from Montgomery and through the South as a whole. The movement's first goal was to increase black voter registration in the South, which had been held back by various discriminatory laws that allowed for literacy tests and poll taxes that prevented many African Americans from gaining access to the voting booth. Their ultimate goal, of course, was the complete elimination of segregation.

To achieve this end, King began an extensive tour of the country, giving speeches and sermons attacking segregation, meeting with various public officials, and writing a book, *Stride toward Freedom: The Montgomery Story,* which chronicled the experience of the bus boycott in Montgomery and explained King's philosophy of nonviolence. He also took a trip to Ghana, in sub-Saharan Africa, where he spoke at a ceremony celebrating its independence. The cornerstone of his travels, however, was a trip to India, where he and his wife met with various people who had known Gandhi and visited the major sites where the Indian leader waged his nonviolent struggle against the British. Upon returning, King was infused with an even greater commitment to nonviolence, not only as a philosophy and a way of achieving social change but also as a way of life. He resigned from his position at Dexter Church in Montgomery and joined his father as copastor of Ebenezer Church in Atlanta so he would have more time to devote to his work for civil rights.

His work reached a crucial stage when he decided to focus on fighting segregation in Alabama's capital, Birmingham, which King believed was the most segregated city in the United States. In Birmingham, every place from restaurants to stores was segregated, and African Americans did not have equal opportunities in gaining employment. Local leaders invited King and other SCLC leaders to their city to help them remedy these conditions. They combined forces to march in protest, and in preparation for the march, King and others of the SCLC trained the protesters in nonviolent techniques, exposing them to the kinds of abuse they would receive as they marched and teaching them how to take the physical and verbal abuse and not hit or even talk back.

Volunteers took part in a series of marches that turned out to be some of the most gruesome events in U.S. history. The Birmingham police met the first set of absolutely peaceful demonstrators with attack dogs and clubs. One thousand protesters were arrested and a court order was issued forbidding any more protests. King defied the court order and was arrested and placed in solitary confinement. While in jail, King wrote his famous essay "Letter from Birmingham Jail," in response to the criticism that he was hearing from local white opponents to his work. This letter became one of the classic protest pieces not only of the civil rights movement but also of literary history, and it became a definitive work in laying out the principles of nonviolent protest.

King was released from jail on appeal after being convicted of contempt, and he soon rejoined the protesters. As the enthusiasm of the adult marchers began to falter under the constant opposition of the police and the repeated refusals of the Birmingham business owners to end their segregationist practices, King decided to involve children in the demonstrations. This decision proved to be crucial, as it created one of the most lasting pictures of the evils of segregation ever recorded. The peaceful children were met with the same clubs and attack dogs that the police had turned on the adults; the police also employed tear gas and high-pressure firehoses to turn back the protesters. The millions of viewers who saw this assault on television and the even greater numbers of people who saw pictures of this published in their newspapers were outraged by the brutality being turned against innocent children, and a national and international cry went up to end segregation.

President John F. Kennedy, responding to this public outcry, quickly dispatched a representative from the U.S. Justice Department to negotiate between the protesters and the Birmingham business owners. Fearing the negative publicity, the Birmingham officials agreed to meet King's major demands, resulting in the desegregation of drinking fountains, restrooms, lunch counters, and fitting rooms. They also agreed to implement more equal hiring practices, which allowed African Americans to gain employment in positions that had always been closed to them. While the nation, the Kennedy administration, and the protesters celebrated this victory, white supremacists displayed their anger at the agreement by bombing King's hotel and the home of King's brother. These actions inspired rioting, and the Kennedy administration ordered federal troops into Birmingham to stop the violence so that the agreement would have time to take effect. (EDITOR'S NOTE: King's sermon collection *Strength to Love* [1963] was also published during this time.)

After this victory, King became involved in a massive march on Washington, D.C., which King had planned with leaders of other civil rights groups with the goals of raising national awareness of the civil rights movement and urging Congress to pass a civil rights bill that was coming up for a vote. In front of the Lincoln Memorial, before a crowd of 250,000 people, King delivered his famous "I Have a Dream" speech. This speech, which was largely improvised, has been called "the most eloquent of his career." He mesmerized the crowd with his deep and resounding voice, his rhythmic repetition of the phrase "I Have a Dream," and the picture he painted of a "promised land" where there was racial equality and equal justice for all. He pointed out that although the nation was celebrating the centennial anniversary of Lincoln's Emancipation Proclamation, the children of the freed slaves did not feel emancipated at all but rather were still fighting for equal rights. Early in 1964, King stood by as President Lyndon Johnson signed the Civil Rights Act of 1964, which declared that the federal government was firmly dedicated to ending segregation and discrimination in all public places.

The "I Have a Dream" speech and the signing of the Civil Rights Act marked King's elevation to national and international prominence. In 1964, he became the first black American to be named as *Time* magazine's "Man of the Year." In November of the same year, he was awarded the Nobel Peace Prize, becoming the youngest person ever to win the award. (See also **Ralph Bunche.**)

He continued his efforts on behalf of the civil rights movement, focusing on a campaign for voter's rights in Selma, Alabama. Again, he and fellow protesters were met with violent opposition—the multitude of schoolchildren who had cut school to join King's protest were arrested for juvenile delinquency; adults were arrested for picketing the county courthouse; and nonviolent demonstrators who were marching from Selma to Montgomery to present their demands for voting rights to the governor were beaten by state troopers. In frustration, King asked for help from ministers throughout the nation and was gratified when they joined him in the march, only to feel great sorrow when he learned that two of the white ministers who had joined him were beaten so severely by white supremacists that one of them died.

The death of the minister, however, did gain President Johnson's attention, and within days he appeared on television urging that Congress pass a voting rights bill, which became the Voting Rights Act that was signed into law in 1965. King had finally gained one of his main objectives as a civil rights leader, as the act made literacy tests illegal, gave the U.S. attorney general power to oversee federal elections in seven Southern states, and asked the attorney general to challenge the legality of poll taxes in local and state elections. (EDITOR'S NOTE: The "literacy tests" were actually spurious, in that the testers would ask prospective African-American voters incredibly arcane questions about obscure passages of the law and would judge their answers harshly to prevent them from being able to vote, whereas they would give European-American voters ridiculously easy questions and would judge their answers generously so they could vote.)

Not all of King's protests were successful, however. In 1966, he and others in the SCLC launched a campaign in Chicago, which was designed to expand the civil rights movement into the North and to raise awareness of racial discrimination as manifested in urban areas and in the issues of housing, schools, and employment. The protests broke into violent rioting just two days after they began. This was followed by rioting in Boston, Detroit, Milwaukee, and other Northern cities throughout the United States.

These events marked the beginning of discord in the civil rights movement, as more radical black leaders such as **Malcolm X** and the black power movement refused to accept King's nonviolent ethos, believing that violence could and should be used to achieve political ends. In his book *Where Do We Go from Here: Chaos or Community,* King fought the ideology of the black power group. He re-asserted his unequivocal belief in the philosophy of peaceful protest and pointed out that by resorting to violence, the black community would become self-destructive, pessimistic, and separatist. He also expressed the concern that in resorting to violence, the movement would lose the support of whites by creating fear instead of understanding. More and more, however, he witnessed the nonviolent ideals among his earlier protesters breaking down.

He soon turned his attention to human rights issues as he began to speak against the Vietnam War and on behalf of the poor in urban and rural areas. Many civil rights leaders begged him not to take on the Vietnam War, fearing that in speaking out against it, he would lose the support for the movement from those who believed in the war. However, he felt that his Nobel Peace Prize had given him a commission to work for peace in all areas of the world, even if that meant opposing the actions of his nation.

While voicing his opposition to the Vietnam War, King also turned his attention back to the nation and in 1967 initiated the Poor People's Campaign, designed to recruit the poor of all races and backgrounds, train them in nonviolent techniques, and lead them in a protest designed to fight for greater economic rights. They were supposed to march on Washington, D.C., to begin a series of marches, sit-ins, rallies, and boycotts designed to disrupt the government so that it would pass antipoverty legislation. This movement was never fully realized, however, because on April 4, 1968, while staying in Memphis to plan a demonstration, King was assassinated on a hotel balcony.

News of his death was met with myriad reactions—in 150 cities, furious blacks rioted; world leaders praised him as a great man and a martyr; and close friends and family determined to establish a permanent memorial on his behalf. They succeeded in establishing his birthday as a national holiday—the only national holiday commemorating the birthday of a person from the twentieth century. This holiday, as well as his published and collected speeches, essays, and books and the profound changes he had effected in American society during his 12 years of working toward civil rights ensured that his memory would live on.

—*Diane Masiello*

REFERENCES: *BW:SSCA.* Bigelow, Barbara Carlisle (1992), *Contemporary Black Biography: Profiles from the International Black Community* (Vol. 2) (Detroit: Gale Research). Miller, Keith D., and Emily M. Lewis, in *OCAAL.*

King, Woodie, Jr. (1937–)
Essays, short stories, anthologies, dramas, scripts, criticism

Although some of King's short stories appeared in the anthologies of others (e.g., **Langston Hughes**), he has been well known for editing outstanding anthologies of other writers' works, including *Black Drama Anthology* (1973, with **Ron Milner**), *Black Spirits: A Festival of New Black Poets in America* (1972), *Black Short Story Anthology, the Forerunners: Black Poets in America* (1975), and *Black Poets and Prophets: The Theory, Practice, and Esthetics of the Pan-African Revolution* (with Earl Anthony). King also adapted Hughes's poetry and short stories to the stage in *The Weary Blues* and *Simple's Blues.* As an anthologist, producer, director, and actor, King made major contributions to the **Black Arts movement**, also facilitating the careers of more than a few aspiring writers (e.g., Ronald Milner, **Elaine Jackson**, **Amiri Baraka**).

REFERENCES: Carter, Steven R., in *OCAAL.*

Knight, Etheridge
(4/19/1931–3/10/1991)
Poems, anthology; editor

One of seven children in an impoverished family, Etheridge dropped out of school at age 14 and hung out with older men and other adolescent males in pool halls, bars, and juke joints. Although he learned few or no marketable vocational skills in that environment, he did learn the distinctly African-American craft of *toasting:* long, humorous, rhyming oratory, requiring great verbal competence and skill—as well as a little audience participation. As a youth, his oratorical skills may have earned him the respect of his peers in the juke joints, but they didn't win him any honest means of earning a living. In 1947, when Etheridge was 16 years old, he pursued one of the only legitimate means of livelihood available to him in the segregated South—the deadly career of soldier—and he joined the U.S. Army.

In the juke joints, Knight had learned to use alcohol and other drugs, and his service career didn't teach him to stop that use. At first, he was a medical technician in the Korean War and learned about the appropriate uses for pharmaceuticals.

After he suffered a shrapnel wound, however, he was given narcotics to treat the pain of his wounds, and he eventually became addicted to narcotics.

When he was discharged from the service, he rambled from city to city, often staying in Indianapolis, Indiana, but never for long at a time. His drug addiction, lack of education, and restlessness made steady work virtually impossible for him, and in 1960 he was arrested for robbery and sentenced to prison. While in prison, Knight started educating himself, reading the poetry of **Langston Hughes**, **Gwendolyn Brooks**, and Don L. Lee (**Haki Madhubuti**) as well as the traditional poetry of the Anglo-American tradition and the poetry of Greece, China, ancient Rome, and Japan—especially haiku.

Knight also started to draw on the verbal skills he had developed in his youth. Soon, he was writing poems, and such noteworthy poets as Gwendolyn Brooks, **Dudley Randall**, and **Sonia Sanchez** recognized his talent. Their receptivity to his work may have been aided by the times in which he was imprisoned. The 1960s were a time of tremendous political foment for prison reform, civil rights, and black power. For instance, the flickering flames of **Martin Luther King, Jr.**, and **Malcolm X** came to full brightness—and were extinguished. By the time Knight's sentence was up for parole review, Brooks had visited him in prison and Randall's **Broadside Press** was in the process of publishing his *Poems from Prison*.

In 1968, Knight was released from prison, although he was not freed from his habitual use of alcohol and other drugs. (In fact, for the rest of his life, he intermittently incarcerated himself in Veterans Administration hospitals to undergo treatment attempting to free himself from drugs.) Soon after his release, the high school dropout Etheridge Knight was invited to hold academic positions at a few different universities, and he met and married Sonia Sanchez. Despite his newfound success, Knight was unable to control his drug addiction, and his marriage to Sanchez disintegrated as a result.

About a year after divorcing Sanchez, Knight married Mary Ann McAnally, with whom he had two children. The peripatetic Knight continued moving from city to city (in Minnesota, Missouri, Connecticut, Pennsylvania, Tennessee, and often Indiana). A frequent contributor to magazines, he also served as magazine editor (of *Motive* and of *New Letters*) on occasion. During the 1970s, he also got to know and mutually respect several contemporary white male poets, such as Robert Bly, Galway Kinnell, and James Wright, and he was frequently invited to give poetry recitations (not readings, as he could movingly recite long works without glancing at the text). By 1978, Knight's marriage to McAnally had dissolved, and in December of that year, Knight married Charlene Blackburn, with whom he had a son.

As a leading voice of the **Black Arts movement** of the 1960s and 1970s, Knight rejected the traditional techniques and themes of lyrical verse. In terms of techniques, he used free verse, highly graphic street language, jazzy and bluesy rhythms, and unconventional punctuation in his works. Although he often wrote of love (sexual as well as familial or companionate), his poetic themes frequently centered on the experiences of a black man in a racist society, oppressed by racial segregation but uplifted by a rich African-American cultural heritage. He often talked of imprisonment, particularly focusing on incarceration but also in terms of the constraints of slavery, poverty, and racism. Using the prison as a metaphor, he even acknowledged his own self-imposed imprisonment due to his addiction to drugs. Other common themes in his work included violence and African-American identity.

Knight's writings on imprisonment influenced not only the literary world of the Black Arts movement, but also the very down-to-earth world of the inmates of Attica Penitentiary. Many have said that his writings helped shape the thoughts and actions of the prisoners who staged a revolt in Attica in the 1970s. His great prestige rarely earned him financial rewards, however, and he and his family usually lived in—or very near—poverty. He was, nonetheless, well received among white and black audiences. In 1972 he was given a National Endowment for the Arts grant, and in 1974 he was awarded a Guggenheim fellowship. Although he spoke in a distinctively African-American voice, he clearly acknowledged that much of what he said applied to the experiences and emotions of both blacks and whites.

Knight's first volume of verse, *Poems from Prison* (1968), clearly emerges from his experiences as a toastmaster and is probably his best-known work. His *Belly Song and Other Poems* (1973) diverges from the prison theme and includes many poems on love and ancestry. In his title poem "Belly Song," he speaks of how love's pain and passion is centered in the belly. Often considered his finest work, this collection earned him nominations for both the Pulitzer Prize and the National Book Award. In his 1980 collection *Born of a Woman: New and Selected Poems,* he acknowledges the role women have played in his life, turning him toward life-affirming expressions and away from life-threatening outlets. Perhaps his most outstanding poem in the collection is "The Stretching of the Belly," in which he observes that his wife's scars (stretch marks) appear as evidence of the growing life within her, whereas the scars on black men's bodies show evidence of violence, such as war (and slavery). In 1986, he published *The Essential Etheridge Knight,* which features many of the poems from each of his previous poetry collections, embracing topics from freedom to family.

In addition to his poetry, Knight published the anthology *Black Voices from Prison* (1970), which includes not only his own poems about his prison experiences but also the poetic and prose writings of many other male prisoners. Ironically, given all of Knight's addictions, the addiction that killed him was cigarettes: He died at age 59 from lung cancer.

REFERENCES: *BWA. EB-98. EBLG. G-95. MAAL. MWEL. NAAAL. TtW.* Premo, Cassie, in *OCAAL.*

Komunyakaa, Yusef (4/29/1947–)
Poems

When Komunyakaa won the Pulitzer Prize for Poetry in 1994, he grabbed the attention of the literary world. Decades earlier, when he was a child, his mother had fostered in him a love of reading, buying him a set of encyclopedia. At age 16, he discovered **James Baldwin**'s essay collection *Nobody Knows My Name,* which inspired him to try his own hand at writing. It wasn't until about a decade later, however, that he started to write poetry. Among his many poetry collections are *Dedications and Other Darkhorses* (1977), *Lost in the Bonewheel Factory* (1979), *Copacetic* (1984), *I Apologize for the Eyes in My Head* (1986), *Dien Cai Dau* (1988), *Magic City* (1992), and *Neon Vernacular* (1994, the Pulitzer Prize winner). In addition to the Pulitzer, he has won two fellowships from the National Endowment for the Arts (1981, 1987) and other poetry awards.

REFERENCES: Harris, Trudier, in *OCAAL.*

L

Ladner, Joyce A. (10/12/1943–)
Nonfiction—sociology, edited works

Most notable among Ladner's many important works on teen pregnancy, cultural diversity, the value of higher education, urban issues, public policy, human sexuality, and child welfare is her pioneering sociological study of African-American girls, *Tomorrow's Tomorrow: The Black Woman* (1995, rev. ed.). Ladner also authored *Mixed Families: Adopting across Racial Boundaries* (1977) and *The Ties That Bind: Timeless Values for African-American Families* (1999); and she coauthored *Lives of Promise, Lives of Pain: Young Mothers after New Chance* (1994, with Janet Quint and Judith Musick). In addition, Ladner edited the anthologies *Adolescence and Poverty: Challenge for the 1990s* (1991, with Peter Edelman) and *The Death of White Sociology* (1998). From 1994 to 1995, she was the first woman president of Howard University, and she is currently a senior fellow at the Brookings Institution. Among her numerous awards are doctorates of humane letters from Howard University and from Tougaloo College (where she earned her B.A. in sociology, 1964), and the Distinguished Alumni award from Washington University (where she earned her M.A. in 1966 and her Ph.D. in 1968).

REFERENCES: *33T.* Personal communication, 6/14/1999.

Lane, Pinkie (née Gordon) (1923–)
Poems

Louisiana's first African-American poet laureate and a Pulitzer Prize nominee, Lane has written several noteworthy poetry collections, including *Wind Thoughts* (1972), *The Mystic Female* (1978), *I Never Scream* (1985), and *Girl at the Window* (1991). In addition, she edited the third volume of *Discourses on Poetry and Poems by Blacks*.

REFERENCES: Lowe, John, in *OCAAL*.

Larsen, Nella (née Nellie Walker)
(4/13/1891–3/30/1964)
Novels, short stories

Nellie Walker's African–West Indian father died when she was just two years old. Soon after, her Danish-American mother remarried and had another child. Dark-skinned Nella Larsen felt like an outsider in her all-white, Danish-American family. Raised outside the African-American community, she also felt alienated from African Americans. Rather than being biracial, she felt nonracial—neither white nor black.

An accomplished nursing supervisor, Larsen married Elmer Imes, an African-American research physicist. The couple made a home in the intellectual world of Harlem, becoming friends with the **Du Bois**es, Arthur and **Jessie Fauset**, and other literary luminaries of Harlem. In 1921, Nella quit nursing to work for the New York Public Library, and she began writing (publishing her first two stories in 1926). As the **Harlem Renaissance** blossomed, so did her writing. Eventually, she left the library, finishing her novels *Quicksand* (1928) and *Passing* (1929) in rapid succession.

Quicksand's protagonist Helga—an urban, middle-class, well-educated mulatta—struggles with her racial identity. When her all-white family rejects her for her dark skin, she goes South to teach in an all-black school. There, too, she feels alien. After seeking an identity and a sense of belonging in various locales, she marries a Southern preacher and submerges her identity in mothering their four children. Just when she seems ready to leave them to forge her own identity, she discovers she is pregnant with a fifth child. The novel ends without revealing how she responds to this circumstance. Like other critics, W. E. B. Du Bois praised *Quicksand* as "the best fiction that Negro America has produced since the heyday of **[Charles] Chesnutt**."

Du Bois also praised her *Passing,* calling it "one of the finest novels of the year." Its protagonist Clare easily "passes" in white society, not even telling her white husband of her black ancestry. By chance, she runs into an old acquaintance, Irene, a middle-class African American who knows Clare's heritage. Irene has her own problems, however, as she fears that her husband will be attracted to her light-skinned friend. Neither woman is entirely satisfied with who she is.

Larsen's novels immediately earned her prominence as a visionary novelist, illuminating the inner psyche of the bicultural, urban woman of her time. Just as her literary star was ascending, however, she was dragged into a nasty scandal (falsely accusing her of plagiarism), followed by a humiliatingly sensationalized divorce. Afterward, she left for Europe on a Guggenheim fellowship (the first African-American woman to win one).

In Europe, Larsen started two new novels, but her publisher rejected both of them—and a third novel, too. She then withdrew entirely from the Harlem literary scene, eventually returning to nursing. After her death, her two novels and her short stories have been republished several times.

REFERENCES: *1TESK. AA:PoP. BAAW. BF:2000. EB-98. EBLG. MAAL. NAAAL. OC20LE. RLWWJ. RT.* Davis, Thadious M., in *OCAAL.* Larson, Charles R., in *OCWW.*

Latifah, Queen (née Dana Elaine Owens) (3/18/1970–)
Rap lyrics, memoir

Rita Owens was 18 years old and already the mother of Lance Owens, Jr., when she gave birth to Dana. When Dana was about 8 years old, her parents' troubled marriage fell apart (although she and her brother continued to keep in touch with her father), she was given the name Latifah (meaning "delicate" and "sensitive" in Arabic) by a Muslim cousin, she was identified as intellectually gifted, and she started attending Saint Anne's parochial school. Rita Owens rose to the challenges posed by these changes, working one full-time job and one part-time job to pay for Dana's schooling. While raising her children and working two jobs, Rita also managed to complete a two-year community-college program. When Latifah was 10 years old, Rita started working as an art teacher at Irvington High School—which Latifah later attended.

During high school, Latifah started singing with a rap group, Ladies Fresh, and through contacts with a local D.J., she made a demo, which ended up in the hands of Tommy Boy Music, and in 1988, Tommy Boy released Latifah's first single, "Wrath of My Madness" and "Princess of the Posse," and her second single, "Dance for Me" and "Inside Out." In 1989, she made her first video ("Dance for Me"), her first European tour, her first appearance at the Apollo, and her first rap album, *All Hail the Queen.* Her subsequent albums include *Nature of a Sista'* (1991) and *Black Reign* (1993). In 1993, Latifah was producing her own records and was soon signing other rap artists to produce their records. Latifah has also branched into acting, making appearances in both television and film. In 1994, she and Salt-N-Pepa were the only two rappers to receive a Grammy. Latifah's raps address womanist issues as well as issues of poverty, homelessness, and segregation. In addition to her music, Latifah has published her memoir, *Ladies First: Revelations from a Strong Woman* (1999).

REFERENCES: *BDAA. TAWH.* Johns, Robert L., in *PBW.* Amazon.com, 7/1999.

Latimer, Catherine A. (née Allen) (c. 1895–9/1948)
Bibliography

Soon after the New York Public Library (NYPL) hired Latimer—the first African-American professional librarian hired by the NYPL—she began enthusiastically studying the story of African Americans. At the NYPL Harlem branch library (where she worked 1920–1946), she started collecting clippings on African-American history while carrying out her duties. By the time the library became the home of the Schomburg Collection (in 1926, later named the Schomburg Center for Research in Black Culture), she was the reference librarian in charge of African-American literature and history. In "Where Can I Get Material on the Negro?" an article Latimer wrote for *Crisis* magazine (June, 1934), she described the collection as comprising about 7,000 books, 500 prints and portrait engravings, and 800 "manuscripts, letters, poems, plays, and sermons of writers and prominent citizens." Latimer wrote numerous other articles on bibliography for various publications, and she wrote *The Negro: A Selected Bibliography* (1943). She also guided her protégé Ernest D. Kaiser in continuing to expand and index the clipping collection. He did so, continuing the clippings file until 1985, when the index was first marketed as the *Ernest D. Kaiser Index to Black Resources.*

REFERENCES: *BAAW.* Gubert, Betty K., in *BWA:AHE.*

Latimer, Lewis Howard (9/4/1848–12/11/1928)
Nonfiction—electricity textbook, poems, play

Lewis's mother, abandoned by his father, could not support him and his three siblings, so she sent

Lewis and his brother to a farm "school," which demanded hard labor from its "students." As soon as possible, the boys escaped and Lewis started supporting himself by selling Garrison's *Liberator*. During the Civil War, he joined the Union Navy. After the war, Lewis found a job in a patent attorney's office, where he was inspired to teach himself engineering and drafting so that he too could be an inventor. He ended up making numerous inventions in various fields (e.g., an improvement for bathroom facilities on a train), but his specialty was electric lighting. His *Electric Lighting: A Practical Description of the Edison System* (1890) broke new ground in explaining how such lighting really worked. Also, Latimer's textbook *Incandescent Electric Lighting* (1896) was a key reference for understanding Edison's developments in the field.

Latimer was also socially and politically active in striving for civil rights for all Americans and taught mechanical drawing to immigrants through a social service agency, helping them gain a vocational skill. He also loved reading literature and writing poems. For his seventy-seventh birthday, his friends and his two daughters had his own poems privately printed and bound. In addition to his nonfiction works, Latimer wrote plays and painted and played the flute.

REFERENCES: Bennett, Eric, in *EA-99*.

Lee, Andrea (1953–)
Memoir, fiction

A staff writer for the *New Yorker*, Lee has written *Russian Journal* (1981, based on her 1978–1979 experiences in Russia) and her novel *Sarah Phillips* (1984).

REFERENCES: Smith, Valerie, in *OCAAL*.

Lee, Spike (né Shelton Jackson Lee) (3/20/1957–)
Scripts, memoir, nonfiction—filmmaking

After Lee graduated from his father and grandfather's alma mater, Morehouse College in Atlanta (1979), he interned at Columbia Pictures for the summer and then started at New York University's Institute of Film and Television, where he earned his M.A. (1982). The film he made for his master's degree was *Joe's Bed-Stuy Barbershop: We Cut Heads*, which was awarded the Student Academy Award for best director by the Academy of Motion Pic-

ture Arts and Sciences (i.e., an Oscar). After a false start with a film about a bicycle messenger, Lee's next film was *She's Gotta Have It* (1986), which he produced in just 12 days for $175,000—not much money for a movie. The film grossed more than $7 million and won several awards, most notably the Prix de Jeunesse for the best new film by a newcomer at the Cannes Film Festival.

Columbia Pictures produced his next film, *School Daze* (1988), about his undergraduate experiences and exposing the caste system among lighter- versus darker-skinned blacks. Grossing $15 million, *School Daze* paved the way for Lee's critically acclaimed blockbuster, *Do the Right Thing* (1989), produced by Universal Studios for $6.5 million. Set in the Bedford-Stuyvesant borough of Brooklyn, it highlighted the tensions between Italian Americans (e.g., featuring actor Danny Aiello) and African Americans (featuring actors **Ossie Davis** and **Ruby Dee**) struggling to make a living. Among its many awards and nominations was an Oscar nomination for best original screenplay, and the film grossed $28 million. This film, like many others of his, sparked great controversy. Lee views his writing this way, "All I want to do is tell a story. When writing a script I'm not saying, 'Uh-Oh, I'd better leave that out because I might get into trouble.' I don't operate like that" (quoted in *BH2C*, p. 442).

Lee's subsequent films have included *Mo' Better Blues* (1990), about a musician involved with two women; *Jungle Fever* (1991), about an interracial sexual relationship; *Malcolm X* (1992), a three-hours-plus film about the black nationalist leader; *Crooklyn* (1994), about growing up in Brooklyn; *Clockers* (1995), about a murder investigation involving the relationship between two brothers, one of whom was a low-level worker in the illegal drug trade; *Girl 6* (1996), about a struggling actress who works as a phone-sex operator; *Get on the Bus* (1996), about a journey to the Million Man March; *He Got Game* (1998), about a convict's relationship with his son, a promising basketball player; and *Summer of Sam* (1999), about the terror (white) New Yorkers felt when a (white) serial killer was stalking the city. Lee also produced the documentary *Four Young Girls* (1997), about the four Sunday-school girls whose lives were blown to smithereens in their Birmingham church in 1963. Lee has acted (usually in minor roles) in all his films, and actor Denzel Washington has starred in several of these works.

Film director Spike Lee at a New York Knicks game, 1994 (Reuters/Jeff Christensen/Archive Photos)

Other than the script for *Crooklyn*, which was written by his sister Joie, Lee has written the scripts for all of his films. He has also written companion books for his films—*Spike Lee's Gotta Have It: Guerrilla Filmmaking* (1987), *Uplift the Race: The Construction of School Daze* (1988, with Lisa Jones), *Do the Right Thing: The New Spike Lee Joint* (1989), *Mo' Better Blues* (1990, with Lisa Jones), *By Any Means Necessary: The Trials and Tribulations of Making Malcolm X* (1992), and *The X Factor* (1992)—and he wrote a memoir about his fanatical love of the New York Knicks basketball team, *Best Seat in the House: A Basketball Memoir* (1997, with Ralph Wiley). In addition to his film production company Forty Acres and a Mule (based in his home town of Brooklyn), Lee also has numerous other business and advertising ventures. In 1993, he married attorney Tonya Linnette Lewis, with whom he has a daughter (Satchel Lewis Lee, born in 1994) and a son (Jackson Lee, born in 1997).

REFERENCES: *BDAA. EBLG. G-97. PGAA.* Ashwill, Gary, in *OCAAL.* Sklar, Robert, in *WB-99.* Tuttle, Kate, in *EA-99.* Wise, Flossie E., in *BH2C.*

Lester, Julius (1/27/1939–)

Novels, juvenile fiction, short stories, opinion and commentary, nonfiction (folk songs, history), folktales, poems, autobiography

The son of a Methodist minister, Woodie Daniel Lester, and his wife, Julia B. Smith Lester, Julius Lester converted to Judaism in 1982 (at age 43). Born in St. Louis, Missouri, he grew up in the Midwest (Kansas City, Kansas) and in the segregated South (Nashville, Tennessee). In addition to a semester at San Diego State College, he earned his B.A. from Fisk University (1960). After graduating, Lester worked as an organizer for the Student Nonviolent Coordinating Committee (SNCC), primarily in Mississippi, but he also traveled to Cuba (with **Stokely Carmichael**), North Vietnam, and Korea. He also pursued a career as a folksinger and musician, and he wrote a newspaper column and hosted both television and radio programs. As he noted in an interview for Amazon.com, "I am not sure what led me to become a writer . . . there was a growing certainty . . . that this was what I was supposed to do with my life."

In 1971, Lester earned his M.A. from the University of Massachusetts at Amherst, where he apparently impressed them enough to hire him as a professor. He has written quite a few pieces for adults; in addition to his novel, *Do Lord Remember Me* (1985), he has edited a collection of writings on **W. E. B. Du Bois**, *The Seventh Son: The Thought & Writings of W. E. B. Du Bois* (1971) and has coauthored books of folksongs, *We Shall Overcome! Songs of the Southern Freedom Movement* (1963, with Guy Carawan, Candie Carawan, Ethel Raim, and Joseph Byrd) and *The 12-String Guitar as Played by Leadbelly: An Instructional Manual* (1965/1997 with folksinger Pete Seeger). He has also authored several books of political writings, *The Angry Children of Malcolm X* (1966): *Look Out, Whitey! Black Power's Gon' Get Your Mama!* (1968), his essay collection *Revolutionary Notes* (1969), and his collection of essays on race, religion, and education, *Falling Pieces of the Broken Sky* (1990).

Despite these impressive credits, Lester is probably best known for what he has written for young adults, primarily works intended to instill pride in African-American history and cultural heritage. His first book on black history, a 1969 Newbery Honor Book written for juveniles, was *To Be a Slave* (1968), a collection of six short stories, which incorporated oral histories from former slaves collected by the Federal Writers' Project. Through their stories (and his text), Lester tells the history of slavery from revolutionary times to the end of the Civil War, from the Middle Passage journey (sailing from Africa to the United States) through enslavement on Southern plantations and slave revolts to Civil War and emancipation. Lester followed with *The Long Journey Home: Stories from Black History* (1972), which provided six more stories, also interweaving **slave narratives,** about the post–Civil War Reconstruction era. These stories included accounts of a roaming blues singer ("Satan on My Track") who observes the plight of sharecroppers and of a formerly enslaved cowboy who ponders what he is doing as he rounds up (entraps) a herd of wild (free) mustangs.

Lester has also been captivated by traditional African-American **folktales**, so he has written numerous books based on this lore. Some of these tales originated on African soil, some emerged from the unique African-American experience, and all have been passed down through the generations via the **oral tradition**. In many of the folk stories in *Black Folktales* (1969) and in *The Knee-High Man and Other Tales* (1972), clever beasts and crafty people outwit those who would dominate them through force of greater size and might. In such stories as "People Who Could Fly" and "Stagolee," those who are oppressed escape from and resist their oppressors.

Perhaps the best-known folktales in the United States are the adventures of a wily rabbit and the mighty but foolish animals that he outwits. (See also **trickster tales** and **Joel Chandler Harris**.) Lester has written numerous books about their adventures: *The Tales of Uncle Remus: The Adventures of Brer Rabbit* (1987); *More Tales of Uncle Remus: Further Adventures of Brer Rabbit, His Friends, Enemies, and Others* (1988); *Further Tales of Uncle Remus: The Misadventures of Brer Rabbit, Brer Fox, Brer Wolf, the Doodang, and Other Creatures* (1990); and *The Last Tales of Uncle Remus: As Told by Julius Lester* (1994). In all these adventures, Lester celebrates African-American storytelling with vivid language, delectable humor, and delightful triumphs by the cunning rabbit.

Lester has also written *How Many Spots Does a Leopard Have? and Other Tales* (1989), a collection of a dozen folktales from the African and the Jewish traditions; and *John Henry* (1994), the traditional American story of a hard-working man fighting for his survival against modern technology. More recent picture books by Lester include *Sam and the Tigers: A New Telling of Little Black Sambo* (1996), *Black Cowboy, Wild Horses: A True Story* (1998), and *What a Truly Cool World* (1999). For somewhat older children, he has written *Othello: A Novel* (1995/1999), the nonfiction *From Slave Ship to Freedom Road* (1998), *When the Beginning Began: Stories about God, Creatures, and Us* (1999), *Pharaoh's Daughter: A Novel of Ancient Egypt* (2000), and *Shining* (2000).

Lester has also written a collection of stories about eighteenth-century romances among African Americans, *This Strange New Feeling* (1982); a collection of poems, *Who I Am* (1974); two autobiographies, *All Is Well* (1976) and *Lovesong: Becoming a Jew* (1988/1995); and the books *Search for a New Land: History as Subjective Experience* (1969), *Two Love Stories* (1972), *And All Our Wounds Forgiven* (1994), and *The Man Who Knew Too Much* (1994).

In addition to the Newbery honor, Lester's books have won a National Book Award nomination (1972) and a National Jewish Book Award (1988). Lester has been married twice (Joan Steinem, 1962–1970; Alida Fechner, 1979–present) and has four children.

REFERENCES: *AAL. BDAA. EBLG. WB-99.* Bloom, Karen R., in *OCAAL.* P. D. S., in *CBC.* Amazon.com, 1/2000.

Lewis, Samella Sanders (2/27/1924–)
Nonfiction—art history, documentary films; journal founder

In addition to being an artist (specializing in paintings and serigraphs), an educator, a museum founder, and an art gallery curator, Lewis has written books on art, founded an art journal, and created documentary films on art. Her art books include *Black Artists on Art* (1969, with Elizabeth Waddy, 2 vols.; revised 1976), on contemporary African-American artists; *Art: African American* (1978; rev. ed., 1990), on art history; and *The Art of Elizabeth Catlett* (1984), which appraises the work of this highly acclaimed and innovative artist.

Lewis has been making films on African-American artists, past and present, since the late 1960s. Her films include both short features on individual artists (e.g., *To Follow a Star: The Sculpture of Richmond Barthé* and *Feathers of Wood: The Art of Charles Hutchinson*) and full-length works embracing the work of multiple artists (e.g., *The Black Artists*). In addition, Lewis has extended her celebration of African-American artists through the journal she founded in 1976, *Black Art Quarterly* (since renamed *The International Review of African American Art*). Among the aspects of art the quarterly has featured have been artists from particular times (the twentieth century, the 1930s and 1940s), specific places (e.g., Trinidad and Tobago, the American North and West), special genres (e.g., contemporary folk art), women artists, and even art collectors (e.g., collections at African-American institutions).

—*Tonya Bolden*

REFERENCES: *BAAW.*

Locke, Alain (LeRoy)
(9/13/1886–6/9/1954)
Essays, anthology, nonfiction—philosophy, art, music

The Lockes were well established in Philadelphia's intellectual elite, starting with Ishmael Locke (1820–1852) and his wife, both educators; their son Pliny Locke (1850–1892) and his wife Mary Hawkins Locke (1853–1922), also both educators; and their grandson (Pliny and Mary's only child), Alain, also an educator as well as a writer. Therefore, even though Pliny died when Alain was just six years old, Mary was able to continue ensuring that her son Alain had an excellent education. At first, she hoped that Alain would have a career in

Alain Locke (left), as secretary of Howard University, with Mordecai Johnson (Culver Pictures)

medicine, but a childhood bout of rheumatic fever permanently injured Alain's heart, blocking that career path. Mary quickly shifted gears and provided her son with a broad artistic education, encompassing piano, violin, and literature. By the time Alain graduated from Central High School (second in his class), he was an accomplished musician as well as a gifted student.

After high school, Alain attended the preparatory school where his father had taught, the Philadelphia School of Pedagogy (1902–1904), finishing first in his class. The following fall, he enrolled at Harvard University, where he was named to the prestigious honor society Phi Beta Kappa and earned a B.A. in philosophy (and English), magna cum laude (1907). On graduating, he became the first African American to be awarded a Rhodes Scholarship, which enables a scholar to study at Oxford University in England. (Considered by many to be the highest academic honorary

scholarship in the world, this scholarship was not awarded to any other African American during Locke's lifetime.) Despite the scholarship and his outstanding record as a student, several Oxford colleges denied him admittance because of his race. At last, Hertford College at Oxford admitted him, and Locke spent the next three years there, studying philosophy, Greek, Latin, and literature. In 1910, he was awarded Oxford's B. Litt. degree. Next, Locke went to Germany, where he studied at the University of Berlin (1910–1911), and then he moved to Paris, where he studied under Henri Bergson at the College de France (1911). After that, Locke left Europe to travel through territory that was entirely foreign to him: the American South, where he searched for jobs at various Southern universities and closely observed the distinctive brand of discrimination and racial prejudice practiced there.

At last, in 1912 Howard University (in Washington, D.C.) appointed Locke "Assistant Professor of the Teaching of English and Instructor in Philosophy and Education." In 1915, he proposed establishing a course on race relations at Howard, but the school's trustees (all white at that time) rejected the idea. He then collaborated with Howard's Social Science Club and its National Association for the Advancement of Colored People (NAACP) chapter to develop a lecture series on that subject. During the 1916–1917 school year, Locke took a sabbatical to complete his doctorate at Harvard University. In 1918, Harvard awarded him his Ph.D., making Locke the second African American to receive this degree there. That year, he was named the chair of the philosophy department at Howard. During his tenure at Howard, he also enjoyed occasional stints as a visiting professor elsewhere (e.g., at his alma mater Harvard, in Haiti, at Fisk University, at the University of Wisconsin, at New York's New School for Social Research, at the City College of New York, and at the Salzburg [Austria] Seminar in American Studies), and in 1924 he conducted archeological studies in the Sudan and in Egypt.

In the late 1920s, Locke had a conflict with Howard's president, which led to Locke's dismissal from Howard, to which he didn't return until 1928. During this period of time—the very peak of the **Harlem Renaissance**—he moved to Harlem. There, he was tireless in helping artists, musicians, dramatists, and writers to promote their careers. Among other things, Locke helped writers get their work published; acted as liaison between such writers as **Langston Hughes**, **Zora Neale Hurston**, and **Claude McKay** and wealthy white patrons (e.g., Mrs. Charlotte Osgood Mason) who could support their literary pursuits; paved the way for writers to wend through American cultural institutions; and encouraged writers and other artists to seek inspiration from African culture and artistic expression.

In 1928, Locke returned to Howard, where he remained until his retirement just before he died. The year he retired, Howard University awarded him an honorary degree of doctor of humane letters. Ironically, in 1954, a year after Locke's retirement, Howard honored Locke in a more important way: It established an African studies program, for which Locke had been advocating for many years. He had also encouraged the expansion of Howard University's art collection, urged the establishment of an African-American theater at Howard, and celebrated African-American music as America's most authentic folk music.

In *Callaloo* (February–October, 1981), "Alain Locke: A Comprehensive Bibliography of His Published Writings" listed more than 300 articles, books, and other writings published by Locke between 1904 and 1953 (per *OCAAL*). The topics he addressed include African studies, anthropology, art, culture, education, literature, music, philosophy, political science, race relations, and sociology, among others. A recurrent theme throughout many of his writings was the importance of Africa's influence on American culture, chiefly through African-American culture, but also through having permeated all of the American cultural experience such as visual art, music, folktales, and cuisine.

Other than his doctoral dissertation ("The Problem of Classification in Theory of Value"), Locke's first book-length work was *Race Contacts and Inter-Racial Relations* (1916). Starting in 1923, he began contributing essays to the National Urban League's literary journal *Opportunity*, established by **Charles (Spurgeon) Johnson**. In addition, starting in 1929, Locke wrote an annual critical review of African and African-American literature published in the preceding year. In 1942 or 1943, *Opportunity*'s editorship changed hands, and Locke stopped publishing his annual reviews, but in 1946 he started publishing them again in the social science and literary journal *Phylon* (founded by **W. E. B. Du Bois** in 1940).

Another of the major ways in which Locke contributed to American literature started in March 1925, when he was invited to edit a special issue of the sociology magazine *Survey Graphic*, titled "Harlem, Mecca of the New Negro." Locke wrote the lead essay and organized the issue into sections: "The Greatest Negro Community in the World," "The Negro Expresses Himself," and "Black and White—Studies in Race Contacts." The issue was such a hit that he expanded it into his anthology *The New Negro: An Interpretation* (1925; reprinted 1968). Both the special issue and the anthology included fiction, poetry, drama, music criticism, and essay contributions from such African-American writers as **Countee Cullen**, W. E. B. Du Bois, **Rudolph Fisher**, Langston Hughes, Charles (Spurgeon) Johnson, **James Weldon Johnson**, **Anne Spencer**, **Jean Toomer**, and **Walter White**, as well as various white writers. Writers whose contributions were added in the anthology include **William Stanley Braithwaite, Jessie**

Redmon Fauset, **E. Franklin Frazier**, **Angelina Weld Grimké**, Zora Neale Hurston, Claude McKay, Kelly Miller (see **May Miller**), and J. A. Rogers. In addition to the writings, the special issue and the anthology also included lush African artwork and vivid depictions of the African-American experience by such artists as Miguel Covarrubias, Aaron Douglass, Winold Reiss (a Bavarian artist), and Walter Von Ruckteschell. Many literary critics and scholars have credited the anthology as being the definitive text of the Harlem Renaissance.

In 1934, Locke launched another initiative intended to promote African-American culture, founding the Associates in Negro Folk Education (ANFE). Through ANFE, Locke edited nine volumes in the "Bronze Booklets" series on African-American scholarship and culture, especially art and music. ANFE also published works of criticism by **Sterling A. Brown** and other African-American critics. Locke's volumes included *Negro Art: Past and Present* (1936), *The Negro and His Music* (1936), and *The Negro in Art: A Pictorial Record of the Negro Artist and the Negro Theme in Art* (1940; reprinted 1971), probably Locke's most celebrated work since his 1925 *The New Negro*.

As a champion of African-American culture, he wrote *Four Negro Poets* (1927), celebrating the writings of Claude McKay, Jean Toomer, Countee Cullen, and Langston Hughes; and edited *Plays of Negro Life: A Source-book of Native American Drama* (1927, edited with T. Montgomery Gregory), the first collection of African-American dramatic works. Other works in this vein include *A Decade of Negro Self-expression* (1928), *Frederick Douglass, a Biography of Anti-slavery* (1935), and *The Negro in America* (1933 or 1953). His greatest achievement, however, was to be his final volume, *The Negro in American Culture*, which he worked on for years. In 1954, however, when he realized that his lifelong heart problems would prevent him from completing his work himself, he asked the daughter of a colleague at Howard, Margaret Just Butcher, to complete it for him. In 1956, she published the work, based on his guidelines, notes, and other materials, but the consensus of critical opinion suggests that the work reflects the style and vision of Butcher more than that of Locke.

All aspects of African-American culture were at the forefront of Locke's interests, and he wrote numerous essays on his philosophy of "cultural pluralism." He opposed segregation and favored integration, emphasizing the need for all Americans to respect and appreciate the value of their country's rich cultural diversity within a democratic context. He opposed the notion of the "melting pot" and favored instead what contemporary educators metaphorically call a "stew" or a "salad." Toward this end, from 1940 until his death, he regularly contributed essays about African-American culture for the *Encyclopædia Britannica*'s Book of the Year. In addition, he studied and wrote about race relations, coediting an anthology on global race relations, *When Peoples Meet: A Study in Race and Culture Contacts* (1942, edited with Bernhard J. Stern), which included analytical pieces by prominent anthropologists such as Ruth Benedict and Margaret Mead.

Locke never married and always presented himself as the definition of elegance, culture, and refinement. Although he had several serious conflicts with many writers (often over his rather intrusive and fussy intervention when he edited their works), he was instrumental in promoting the careers of many, and he never hesitated to encourage his students and aspiring writers in their literary pursuits. In addition, his own numerous writings show penetrating insight into African-American culture and helped readers appreciate its distinctive contribution to American (and world) culture.

REFERENCES: *1TESK. AA:PoP. AAW:AAPP. BAL-1-P. BF:2000. BWA. EB-BH-CD. EBLG. G-97. NAAAL. OC20LE. PGAA. WDAA.* Born, Brad S., in *WB-99.* Long, Richard A., in *OCAAL.* Rainey, Cortez, in *BH2C.* Robinson, Lisa Clayton, in *EA-99.*

Logan, Rayford (1/7/1897–11/4/1982)
Nonfiction—African-American history and biography

Among other contributions, Logan helped **W. E. B. Du Bois** with his *Encyclopedia of the Negro* and helped **Carter G. Woodson** found the Association for the Study of Negro Life and History (in 1915). He coedited the *Dictionary of American Negro Biography* and edited *W. E. B. Du Bois: A Profile* (1971). He also wrote *The Betrayal of the Negro from Rutherford B. Hayes to Woodrow Wilson* (1965). For his numerous contributions, he was awarded the National Association for the Advancement of Colored People's prestigious Spingarn Medal (1980).

REFERENCES: Robinson, Alonford James, Jr., in *EA-99.* (See also *BDAA,* articles on Du Bois and on Archibald Grimké.)

Lomax, Louis E. (8/16/1922–7/30/1970)
Nonfiction

In addition to his work as a news reporter (e.g., for *Life, Look,* and the *Saturday Evening Post*), commentator, analyst, director, and broadcaster, Lomax wrote several important books on domestic and global social and political issues: *The Reluctant African* (1960), *The Negro Revolt* (1962), *When the Word Is Given: A Report on Elijah Muhammad, Malcolm X, and the Black Muslim World* (1963), *Thailand: The War That Is, the War That Will Be* (1966), and *To Kill a Black Man* (1968).

REFERENCES: *EBLG.*

Lorde, Audre (née Audrey Geraldine Lorde) (a.k.a. Gamba Adisa)
(2/18/1934–11/17/1992)
Poems, essays, autobiographies

Linda Gertrude Belmar, a native of Grenada, and Frederic Byron Lorde, an African American, had moved to Harlem from Grenada with plans of returning—until the Great Depression dashed their plans of gaining enough money to return. In Harlem, the couple had three daughters, the youngest of which was Audrey. Little Audrey was so nearsighted that she was identified as legally blind, and she didn't learn to speak until she was four or five years old—the same age at which her mother taught her to read and write. From the very start, Audrey started shaping the words she encountered. When she learned to write her own name, she disliked having the tail of the "y" of "Audrey" hanging below the line, so she quickly omitted it altogether.

As Lorde herself later noted,

I was very inarticulate as a youngster. I couldn't speak. I didn't speak until I was five, in fact, not really until I started reading and writing poetry. I used to speak in poetry. I would read poems, and I would memorize them. People would say, 'Well, what do you think, Audre? What happened to you yesterday?' And I would recite a poem and somewhere in that poem there would be a line or a feeling I was sharing. In other words, I literally communicated through poetry. And when I couldn't find the poems to express the things I was feeling, that's when I started writing poetry. That was when I was 12 or 13. (*BWWW,* p. 106)

Lorde also observed, "Words had an energy and power and I came to respect that power early. Pronouns, nouns, and verbs were citizens of different countries, who really got together to make a new world" (*OCWW,* quoting from Karla M. Hammond, *Denver Quarterly,* Spring 1981). When Audre was 15, her first published poem appeared in print. Her school newspaper had refused to print the poem, as it discussed Audre's first love affair with a boy, but *Seventeen* magazine was happy to publish it.

Audre's retreat into literature and poetry helped her escape her parents' strict upbringing and the harsh educational environment of the Catholic schools (St. Mark's and then St. Catherine's schools) she attended while growing up. In addition to its sternness, the schools' racism created an unwelcoming environment for this shy, sensitive girl. Only through words was she able to protect herself. When she hit her teen years, she started embracing her status as an outsider and rebelled against the harshness of her environment. At last, when Audre was in high school, she was enrolled in Hunter College High School, where she became the school arts magazine's literary editor and found a sisterhood of rebellious poets. One of her fellow sister-outsiders was poet Diane Di Prima, with whom she maintained a close friendship after high school.

After high school, Lorde continued her studies part-time at Hunter College while earning a living in various low-paying jobs, such as factory worker, medical clerk, X-ray technician, ghostwriter, social worker, and arts and crafts supervisor. While working in a factory, Lorde had her first lesbian affair. In 1954 she went to Mexico, where she spent a year studying at the National University of Mexico. There, she began speaking in full prose sentences and came into her own, identifying herself as a poet and as a lesbian, enjoying an affair with a woman she knew there.

When she returned to New York, Lorde entered Greenwich Village's mostly white "gay-girl" culture. Back on her home turf, she also decided that she wanted to study librarianship in order to better understand how to organize and analyze information. In March 1955, she got a job at the New York Public Library in Children's Services while studying library sciences at Hunter. She also continued to write poetry and became interested in the Harlem Writers Guild. At the guild, **Langston Hughes** encouraged her writing, but many other guild members were homophobic, and Lorde soon felt alienated from the guild. In 1959, Lorde earned her B.A. in English literature and philosophy from Hunter College.

After graduation, Lorde started working as a librarian at Mount Vernon Public Library and earned her master's degree from Columbia University's School of Library Science (M.L.S., 1961). For the next seven years, she worked as a librarian various places, including a job as the head librarian at the Town School Library in New York (1966–1968). Meanwhile, on March 31, 1962, Lorde married Edward Ashley Rollins, with whom she had two children, Elizabeth (1963) and Jonathan ($1^1/_2$ years younger than Elizabeth). Although the marriage ended in divorce (in 1970), Lorde's role as a mother became central to much of her writing thereafter.

In 1962, Langston Hughes included Lorde's poetry in his anthology *New Negro Poets, USA,* and after that, her poems were published in numerous African-American literary magazines and anthologies. In 1968, Lorde's poetry was recognized with a grant from the National Endowment for the Arts. In the spring of that year, she enjoyed a six-week position as poet-in-residence at historically black Tougaloo College in Mississippi. Lorde's experience at Tougaloo changed her life. During those six short weeks, she discovered that she loved teaching far more than being a librarian; she realized that her poetry was appreciated by a wide community of African Americans; she met Frances Clayton, who was to become her long-term partner in life; and she wrote most of the poems for her second poetry collection, *Cables to Rage* (1970). Lorde later recalled, "[Tougaloo] was pivotal for me. Pivotal. In 1968 my first book had just been published; it was my first trip into the Deep South; it was the first time I had been away from the children; the first time I worked with young black students in a workshop situation. I came to realize that this was my work. That teaching and writing were inextricably combined, and it was there that I knew what I wanted to do for the rest of my life. . . . I realized that writing was central to my life" (*BWWW,* p. 110; see also *BWW,* p. 262).

When Lorde returned to New York, she started offering poetry courses at the City College of New York (1968–1969), and from then on, she taught English, creative writing, and literature at various colleges and universities, including Lehman College (1969–1970), John Jay College of

Justice (1970–1980), and Hunter College (starting in 1980). In addition, during the 1970s, Lorde traveled extensively, touring Africa, the Caribbean, and Europe (including Russia).

In the early 1970s, Lorde gave a public reading of one of her lesbian love poems, thus "outing" herself as a lesbian. (The same poem was later published in *Ms.* magazine.) In 1974, Lorde, **Alice Walker**, and Adrienne Rich were nominated for the National Book Award. When Rich won the award, she announced that she would accept it as a coequal with her two fellow nominees, saying, "We symbolically join here in refusing the terms of patriarchal competition and in declaring that we will share this prize among us, to be used as best we can for women." Seven years later, Rich further championed Lorde's poetry by publishing an interview with her (in *Signs: Journal of Women in Culture and Society,* 1981).

Starting in September 1978, Lorde was diagnosed with breast cancer, launching her 14-year war against cancer. She triumphed in her first battle, although she didn't emerge unscathed: She underwent a radical mastectomy (surgically removing her breasts, lymph nodes, and some muscle tissue) and decided against wearing prostheses (artificial breasts), rebelling against male-centered notions of how females should look. Six years later (February 1984), she was diagnosed with liver cancer, and more than eight years later (November 1992), the liver cancer killed her. Before it did, however, she returned to her mother's birthplace in the Caribbean, and she was given an African name: Gamba Adisa, which means "Warrior: She Who Makes Her Meaning Clear."

Lorde was indeed a warrior, championing the rights of African Americans, women, and homosexuals. Through her poems, essays, and autobiographies, she opposed homophobia, sexism, and racism forthrightly and vociferously. Although she outspokenly denounced oppression and injustice, she wrote often of love (especially motherly love and romantic [lesbian] love), not of hatred. She embraced diversity and urged her readers to work together to use difference as a creative, productive force to heal the wounds caused by conflict and strife and to promote positive change.

Stylistically, Lorde wrote free verse poems rich with figurative imagery. She presented global, political questions and comments through highly personal, specific experiences. Lorde's old pal from high school, Diane Di Prima, edited Lorde's first collection, *The First Cities* (1968), and helped her get the collection published by Poet's Press. Many of Lorde's contemporaries criticized Lorde for writing such personal, introspective poems during a time when most African-American poets were focusing on militantly confrontational political poems. Not everyone shared this view, however. **Dudley Randall**, founder of **Broadside Press**, observed that Lorde "does not wave a black flag, but her blackness is there, implicit in the bone."

Randall's press distributed her next collection, *Cables to Rage* (1970), which explored her feelings about her marriage, her husband's betrayal, her experiences raising her children, and her embrace of her identity as a lesbian. Nonetheless, the tone of this volume was less introspective and more centered on social injustices than was her first volume. That trend continued with Broadside's publication of Lorde's *From a Land Where Other People Live* (1973), which was nominated for a 1974 National Book Award for poetry (which Adrienne Rich shared with her and with Alice Walker). Two more volumes followed: her most politically oriented volume, *New York Head Shop and Museum* (1974), and her chapbook, *Between Ourselves* (1976).

In 1976, major mainstream publisher W. W. Norton published Lorde's *Coal* (1976), thereby introducing Lorde to a much wider audience and offering her a chance for greater critical notice. Many of the poems in *Coal* had been published in her previous collections, but the volume also introduced many previously unpublished poems. Probably Lorde's most highly acclaimed collection, however, was *The Black Unicorn* (1978, also published by Norton), in which she highlighted themes of African ancestry, the diaspora of Africans across other continents, mythology, motherhood, and lesbian relationships and other close ties among women. Both collections included laudatory blurbs by Adrienne Rich on the book jackets.

Lorde's next collection, *Chosen Poems, Old and New* (1982), included poems from each of the preceding volumes as well as new poems. This volume was followed by *Our Dead behind Us* (1986), *Undersong: Chosen Poems Old and New* (1992), and *The Marvelous Arithmetics of Distance, Poems 1987–1992* (1993). In addition, Lorde edited two anthologies: *Lesbian Poetry: An Anthology* (1982) and *Woman Poet—The East* (1984). Lorde's prose was collected in several collections, including *Sis-

ter Outsider: Essays and Speeches* (1984, Crossing Press), which has since been used extensively in women's studies courses. In addition, many of Lorde's essays have been published in numerous anthologies and periodicals.

Lorde's other major contribution to literature is her distinctive approach to autobiography, much of which centers on her war against cancer, starting with *The Cancer Journals* (1980), documenting her personal battle against breast cancer. This book is a pioneering exploration of one woman's battle against this epidemic disease. As she herself noted,

> I couldn't believe that what I was fighting I would fight alone and only for myself. I couldn't believe that there wasn't something there that somebody could use at some other point because I know that I could have used some other woman's words, whatever she had to say. Just to know that someone had been there before me would have been very important, but there was nothing. Writing *The Cancer Journals* gave me the strength and power to examine that experience, to put down into words what I was feeling. It was my belief that if this work were useful to just one woman, it was worth doing. (*BWWW,* p. 116)

Lorde described her further struggles in her autobiographical collection of journal entries and essays, *A Burst of Light* (1988), which won a National Book Award in 1989. In it, she describes her decision to abstain from further invasive medical treatments and to explore alternative treatment modalities. Between her first and her second nonfiction autobiographies, she introduced her experimental "biomythography," which combines autobiography with myth, poetry, and other prose fiction forms, in her book *Zami: A New Spelling of My Name* (1982). *Zami* peers into Lorde's childhood and early adulthood (through 1959), exploring in depth the complexities of the mother-daughter relationship, the difficulties of growing up homosexual in a homophobic society, and the delight in discovering the power of language. Touted for its rich imagery and allegory, the book is considered a landmark in African-American women's autobiography.

Among the many awards Lorde received were a National Endowment for the Arts residency grant (1968), a Creative Artists Public Service award grant (1972, 1980), a Broadside Press Poet's Award (1975), appointment to the Hunter College Hall of Fame (1980), and a Cultural Council Foundation grant for poetry. In addition, in 1991, New York Governor Mario Cuomo named Lorde the Poet Laureate of New York state.

REFERENCES: *AA:PoP. AAW:AAPP. BWW. BWWW. EB-BH-CD. EBLG. MWEL. NAAAL. OC20LE. RLWWJ. RWTC. WDAA. WDAW.* Balfour, Lawrie, in *EA-99*. Homans, Margaret, in *BWA:AHE*. Kulii, Beverly Threatt, in *OCAAL*. Trapasso, Ann, in *OCWW.*

Madgett, Naomi (Cornelia) (née) Long (7/5/1923–)

Poems, anthologies, nonfiction—literature, language, composition; book-press founder and publisher, journalist

Naomi was encouraged to love learning and reading at an early age, and she had a promising start as a poet, with her *Songs to a Phantom Nightingale* (1941), published in her maiden name just a few days after she graduated from high school. After high school, she attended her mother's alma mater, Virginia State College, at which she earned her B.A. (1945). Later, she noted that she felt very isolated from other African-American poets during this time, and many of the poems she wrote during this period were not published until later, in *Phantom Nightingale: Juvenilia (Poems 1934–1943)* (1981).

Although Long started graduate school at New York University, she withdrew after just one semester, when she married Juan F. Witherspoon. The pair then moved to Detroit, where she worked as a reporter and copyreader for the African-American weekly the *Michigan Chronicle* until her daughter Jill was born (in 1947). During this time, a few of her poems were published under her married name, Naomi Long Witherspoon. Within a year or two after Jill was born, Naomi and Juan divorced, and Naomi started working for one of the Bell telephone companies, which she continued until 1954, when she married William H. Madgett.

In 1955, Naomi Madgett started teaching in Detroit-area public schools and attended Wayne State University. In 1956 she earned her master's degree in English education and published her second poetry collection, *One and the Many* (1956). Soon after, she took additional postgraduate courses at the University of Detroit (1961–1962). Throughout her teaching career, she tried to encourage high school and junior high

school students to develop an appreciation of African-American literature. (Among her students was **Pearl Cleage**, who later acknowledged the importance of Madgett's encouragement.) In 1965 she introduced both a course in creative writing and the first African-American literature course ever taught in the Detroit public schools.

During the 1965–1966 school year, Madgett was the first recipient to be granted a $10,000 fellowship from the Mott Foundation to pursue her research interests at Oakland University in Rochester, Michigan. She used this time to write her third poetry collection, *Star by Star* (1965), and an African-American literature textbook for high school students, *Success in Language and Literature/B* (1967, with Ethel Tincher and Henry B. Maloney). In 1968, Madgett was offered a position teaching creative writing and African-American literature in the English language and literature department at Eastern Michigan University in Ypsilanti. She continued to teach there until her retirement in the mid-1980s. As a complement to the textbook she wrote for her high school students, she wrote a college-level textbook, *A Student's Guide to Creative Writing* (1980). That same year, she was awarded a Ph.D. in literature and creative writing from the International Institute for Advanced Studies.

Early in the 1970s, three of Madgett's friends founded Lotus Press, and they asked to publish her fourth poetry collection, *Pink Ladies in the Afternoon* (1972). In 1974, she arranged to take over the press, handling its existing books and using its name. Four years later, Lotus Press published her fifth poetry collection, *Exits and Entrances* (1978), and two years after that, she and her daughter, Jill W. Boyer, and her third husband, Leonard Andrews, incorporated Lotus Press as a nonprofit, tax-exempt corporation. After Madgett's 1984 retirement, she delved into developing this small, independent press. By the early 1990s, the press had published 75 titles, most of which are still in print. The press has been instrumental in keeping African-American poetry in print and was the first to publish the writings of such notables as **Houston A. Baker**, **Lance Jeffers**, **Gayl Jones**, **Pinkie Gordon Lane**, and **Paulette Childress White**.

Madgett's other poetry collections include *Octavia and Other Poems* (1988, published by **Third**

World Press) and *Remembrances of Spring: Collected Early Poems* (1993). She has also edited several anthologies, including *Deep Rivers, a Portfolio: Twenty Contemporary Black American Poets, with Teachers' Guide; A Milestone Sampler: Fifteenth Anniversary Anthology* (1988); and *Adam of Ife: Black Women in Praise of Black Men, Poems* (1992); and her own poems have been widely anthologized. Whether writing in free verse, prose poems, or her own distinctively rhyming, metrical poetry, Madgett pierces to the core of her subject, simply and eloquently voicing its essence.

REFERENCES: *BV. EBLG. TtW.* Deck, Alice A., in *BWA:AHE.* Sedlack, Robert P., in *OCWW.* Amazon.com, 7/1999. Madgett's papers are archived in the Special Collections of Fisk University Library.

Madhubuti, Haki (né Don Luther Lee)
(2/23/1942–)
Poems; cofounder of book press

In Little Rock, Arkansas, Don Lee was born to Jimmy L. and Maxine Graves Lee. The following year, the small family moved to Detroit, Michigan, where Jimmy abandoned the family just before the birth of Lee's sister, during the last half of 1943. Maxine had to support herself and her young children through her earnings as a janitor in the three-story apartment building where they lived. Unbeknownst to Don and his sister, the young and beautiful Maxine also had to perform sexual favors for the landlord—an African-American preacher and undertaker—in exchange for rent. Maxine's mopping, sweeping, hauling of trash, and other janitorial duties put food on the table and clothes on their backs.

In addition to providing a home for her children, Maxine encouraged them to read. Although "poetry in my home was almost as strange as money" (Madhubuti, 1988, p. 295), reading was not at all foreign in the Lee home. When Don was just 13 years old, Maxine urged him to go to the Detroit Public Library and check out a book titled *Black Boy* by **Richard Wright**. Initially, he avoided doing so. As he later recalled, "I refused to go because I didn't want to go anywhere and ask for anything black. The self hatred that occupied my mind, body and soul simply prohibited me from going to a white library in 1955 to request from a white librarian a book by a black author, especially with 'Black' in the title" (Madhubuti,

1994, p. 9). (As Madhubuti has observed since, the U.S. educational system subtly reinforces white supremacy and black self-loathing.) Despite his aversion, Don eventually responded to her repeated requests and read Wright's autobiographical novel. That book changed his life forever, as he felt that his life was very similar to that of Wright. He further realized that by reading Wright, he was beginning to see African Americans in a new light, and he began reading works by other African-American authors.

By the time Don read *Black Boy,* Maxine had changed jobs and was serving drinks in Sonny Wilson's, one of the top bars in Detroit. Sadly, she was heavily imbibing alcohol as well. By the time Don was 15, Maxine had also become addicted to other drugs. At about that time, Don's sister (barely 14 years old) revealed that she was pregnant, and soon after, he picked a fight with the 21-year-old gang leader who had impregnated her. Needless to say, Don was ill prepared for the beating he took, and when he told his mother what had happened, she gave him another licking for having been beaten. Maxine's addiction to alcohol and other drugs continued to deepen, and she turned to prostitution to support her habits. Fifteen-year-old Don ended up spending many a night searching cheap motels looking for Maxine.

Pretty soon, Don's younger sister was pregnant again, and soon after, Maxine took a fatal overdose of drugs. (His younger sister was unwed with six children by the time she was 30 years old.) At age 16, Don Lee was on his own and moved to Chicago, where he stayed with an aunt. There, he sold magazines, worked two newspaper routes, and cleaned a local bar. After a while, he rented a room at the Southside Young Men's Christian Association (YMCA) and finished his high school education at Dunbar High School. Not long after that, he moved to St. Louis, Missouri, where he joined the U.S. Army.

When Don Lee got off the bus at boot camp, he was 1 of 3 African Americans in a group of 200 recruits. In his hand was a copy of *Here I Stand* by **Paul Robeson**. The white drill sergeant grabbed the book from his hand, made a racist remark, tore pages from the book, and handed a page to each recruit, ordering them to use the pages for toilet paper. This did not bode well for Lee's military career. It did, however, teach Lee an important lesson about the power of ideas to incite humans to action. Lee became ever more devoted to reading books by and about African Americans. Throughout the remainder of his two-year military career, Lee read just about a book a day.

By the time Lee left the service in August 1963, he was determined to use words to serve the interests and well-being of African Americans. Four years later, Lee and two fellow poets (**Carolyn M. Rodgers** and **Johari Amini**) bought a mimeograph machine and cofounded **Third World Press** (TWP). By the late 1990s, black-owned TWP was one of the largest African-American publishers in the United States and abroad.

Another of Lee's goals was to uplift and educate fellow African Americans, so in 1969, he started the Institute of Positive Education/New Concept Development Center. He also cofounded the Organization of Black American Culture, which offered writers' workshops. By 1970 Lee had published his collections *Don't Cry, Scream* (1969) and *We Walk the Way of the New World* (1970). He was also a star performer of the **Black Arts movement**, giving about three readings a week throughout the country. Since then, he has been invited to speak throughout the world, including Algiers, Tanzania, Senegal, Nigeria, India, and Brazil. In 1973, Don Lee rejected his birth name (his "slave name") and named himself Haki Madhubuti, which means "strong" and "precise" in Swahili.

Madhubuti writes his poems to be spoken aloud, using a distinctively African-American voice and inviting his listeners to participate with him during his readings. He credits African-American music, lifestyles, churches, and people as the inspiration for his poetry, which expresses both the beauty and the joy of the African-American experience and his outrage at the oppression African Americans endure. As critic Liz Gant said, his "lines rumble like a street gang on the page" (Madhubuti, 1988, p. 295). **Gwendolyn Brooks**, with whom he shared a special mentoring relationship, said of his poetry, "The last thing these people crave is elegance. It is very hard to enchant, with elegant song, the ears of a fellow whose stomach is growling" (Madhubuti, 1969, p. 9). (EDITOR'S NOTE: Madhubuti further illustrated their mentoring relationship in his 1991 book *Say That the River Turns: The Impact of Gwendolyn Brooks.*)

In addition to his poetry, Madhubuti has been a poet–in–residence at Cornell University, the University of Illinois at Chicago, Howard University, and Central State University. He currently teaches English at Chicago State University and directs the university's Gwendolyn Brooks Center. He is also one of the best-selling authors of poetry and nonfiction in the world, with more than 3 million copies of his books in print—one of the few writers of the Black Arts movement who is still widely read today. In addition to his books, his poetry is published in newspapers and in such journals as *Journal of Black Poetry,* **Negro Digest**, *Black Dialogue, Soulbook, Freedomways, Umbra, Liberator,* and many others. In addition to writing these publications, Madhubuti has also appeared on several radio and television programs. According to scholar Steven Henderson, Madhubuti is more widely imitated than any other African-American poet except **Amiri Baraka**.

Madhubuti has also been much honored for his work as a writer, publisher, educator, and social activist. His numerous awards include the American Book Award, the Black Caucus Award of the National Council of Teachers of English, honors from the African American Cultural Center of Los Angeles Foundation, a leadership award from the National Council of Black Studies, a community service award from the African American Heritage Studies Association, and the Paul Robeson Award of the African American Arts Alliance. He was also named 1991 Author of the Year for the state of Illinois and is a founding board member of the National Association of Black Book Publishers and editor of the *Black Books Bulletin.*

In addition to his various publications, Madhubuti's legacy will be his advocacy of a distinctively African-American literature, which celebrates the life experiences and views of African Americans and his belief that African-American literature should positively enhance the living conditions of African Americans. Another of his successes was also self-taught, as he never observed it in his own childhood: He has had a stable marriage and has been an involved father to his children.

—*Michael Strickland*

REFERENCES: Madhubuti, Haki R. (1969), *Don't Cry, Scream* (Chicago: Third World Press). Madhubuti (1988), in *Contemporary Authors* (New Revision Series, Vol. 24) (Detroit: Gale Research). Madhubuti (1994), *Claiming Earth: Race Rage, Rape and Redemption, Blacks Seeking a Culture of Enlightened Empowerment* (Chicago: Third World Press). (See also *BDAA*, "Brooks, Gwendolyn.")

Major, Clarence (12/31/1936–)

Novels, poems, short stories, nonfiction books and essays, anthologies, memoir

Clarence Major's roots extend from the South (both urban Atlanta, where he was born, and the rural South, where he visited his grandparents each summer) to the North (Chicago, where he moved at age ten with his mother after his parents divorced). As a youth in Chicago, Clarence was captivated by an exhibit of modern art, highlighting Vincent Van Gogh and other European artists; these paintings stirred him deeply—particularly the Impressionists—and fostered his lifelong fascination with the visual arts. Another of his fascinations was books, and he read avidly.

When Clarence was 17 years old, he thought he would pursue painting and studied at the Chicago Art Institute. From there, he went on to study at the New School for Social Research (in New York), the State University of New York, and the Union for Experimental Colleges and Universities. During this educational journey, Major also decided to earn his daily bread through literature and to pursue painting as an avocation. He often manages to combine the two, however, as he did in his books *Reflex and Bone Structure* (1975) and *Emergency Exit* (1979), which integrate his paintings and photography into the body of the text. Major has also turned to teaching at various schools, with an extended stay as professor of literature and creative writing in the English Department at the University of California at Davis.

In addition to writing more than 200 published pieces in periodicals such as the *New York Times* and the *Washington Post* and in anthologies, Major has edited an issue of the *Journal of Black Poetry* and has been a member of the Fiction Collective (comprising mostly white authors). Major's published works also include a short-story collection, nine poetry collections, more than half a dozen novels, three nonfiction books, and three anthologies. In virtually all of these works, Majors shows his artistic predilection for experimentation and exploration. In his fiction, he bends, twists, and chops plot structure; toys with the narrative voice; and plays with characters, manipulating identity. Through these devices, he communicates his postmodernist view regarding the difficulty of forming a coherent identity and of finding a clear meaning within our incoherent contemporary society. He has described his own writing process in this way: "I often think that the best writing is done after you've forgotten what you wanted to say, but end up putting something down anyway just as though it were the actual evidence of your original intention" (quoted in *TWL*, p. 48).

In *Fun and Games* (1988/1990), Major collected several of his short experimental fiction works. His nonfiction books include *The Dark and Feeling* (1974), a collection of essays and interviews, and the *Dictionary of Afro-American Slang* (1970), which was revised, expanded, and updated as *Juba to Jive* (1994). Probably his most widely acclaimed nonfiction work is his essay "A Black Criterion," in which he urged African-American poets and other artists to use authentically African-American criteria for writing and judging their own works, rather than using European or European-American standards for their work. Major also encourages all artists to preserve the integrity of their artistic vision and to focus on the quality of their work, rather than on any particular ideological standards—black or white—for their work.

Major applied the standards he proposed in selecting the materials for his anthologies: *The New Black Poetry* (1969/1970), a diverse, eclectic anthology highlighting the work of young male and female poets from across the nation; *Calling the Wind: Twentieth-Century African-American Short Stories* (1993), a collection of both short stories and essays; and *The Garden Thrives: 20th-Century African-American Poetry* (1996).

Major's own poetry volumes include *The Fires That Burn the Heaven* (1954), published when he was just 18 years old; *Swallow the Lake* (1970); *Symptoms and Madness* (1971); *Private Line* (1971); *Cotton Club* (1972); *Inside Diameter: The France Poems* (1985); *Surfaces and Masks* (1988), a book-length poem about links between Europeans and Americans; and *Some Observations of a Stranger at Zuni in the Latter Part of the Century* (1989), focusing on Native Americans.

Major's novels include *All-Night Visitors* (1969), a well-written, often erotic interracial story; *No* (1973), which has been described as a "literary detective story"; *Reflex and Bone Structure* (1975, a murder mystery) and *Emergency Exit* (1979, which incorporates black-and-white reproductions of Major's paintings), in which Major surrealistically explores the relationships among the narrator, the reader, and the story; *My Amputations* (1986), inspired by Cubist paintings; *Such Was the Season* (1987), Major's most conventional, realistic narrative, a memoir about African-American middle-class Atlantans; *Painted Turtle: Woman with Guitar* (1988), about a Native American (Zuni) woman who questions—and seeks—her own cultural identity; and *Dirty Bird Blues* (1996). Major's experimental novels have been called "metafictional," in that they go beyond fiction to include narratives in which the author/narrator reflects on his own narrative stance. Although distinctively African American in his voice, his work clearly shows the influence of European and European-American writers and artists.

REFERENCES: *BAL-1-P. EBLG. G-97. NAAAL. OC20LE. TWL.* Byerman, Keith E., in *OCAAL.*

Malveaux, Julianne (Marie) (9/22/1953–)
Essays, articles, columns, nonfiction—economics

Although Malveaux's first published work was poetry (while she was still in her teens) and a literary review, her primary form of writing has been nonfiction prose—specifically, columns, essays, and articles on scholarly and popular topics. She has also coedited the scholarly book *Slipping through the Cracks: The Status of Black Women* (1986, with Margaret Simms) and collected her popular newspaper columns into *Sex Lies and Stereotypes: Perspectives of a Mad Economist* (1994) and *Wall Street and the Side Street: A Mad Economist Takes a Stroll* (1999).

REFERENCES: Smith, Jessie Carney, in *PBW.* Amazon.com, 8/1999.

Marrant, John (?/1755–1791)
Captivity narrative, spiritual autobiography

In Marrant's first published work (that we know of), *A Narrative of the Lord's Wonderful Dealings with John Marrant, a Black* (1785, London), he describes experiencing a religious conversion and then being captured by Native Americans (Cherokees). His conversion occurs when he overhears an English evangelist. Following that experience, he seeks spiritual guidance while hiking through the forest. Cherokees see him, capture him, and initially appear to threaten him. After a time, however, he wins their favor through his appreciation of their culture, adopting their dress and their manners. He attempts (rather unsuccessfully) to convert them, and they release him, after which he follows a religious lifestyle. During the Revolutionary War, he is captured again—this time by British sailors, who force him into service for six years. Upon his release, Marrant studies for the ministry and devotes himself to missionary work in Canada, which he describes in his *Journal* (1790).

REFERENCES: Costanzo, Angelo, in *OCAAL.*

Marshall, Paule (née Burke) (4/9/1929–)
Novels, novellas, short stories, essays; journalist

Ada and Samuel Burke left their humble home in Barbados at just the right time to reach Brooklyn, New York, during the Great Depression. There, in a "Bajun" (Barbadian) section of the Bedford-Stuyvesant borough, young Paule learned early to savor the sounds, smells, and tastes of her Barbadian mother's kitchen; the rhythms, rhymes, and reasons of African-American culture in her neighborhood; and the European-American culture described in her school.

At home, Paule learned from the "kitchen poets": the womenfolk gathered around her mother's kitchen table, speaking their folk poetry in the rhythmic lyricism of their West Indian homeland. At school, she devoured grandiose novels written by white English men in the nineteenth and twentieth centuries (e.g., Charles Dickens and William Makepeace Thackeray). After high school, Burke attended New York's Hunter College for a time, but an illness soon forced her to drop out. When she returned to college, she majored in English at Brooklyn College, was invited to join Phi Beta Kappa (a prestigious honor society), and graduated cum laude (in 1953).

After graduation, Burke worked briefly at the New York Public Library and then joined the staff of *Our World* magazine—initially as a research assistant and then as a full-time writer. *Our World* sent her to the Caribbean and to Brazil to observe the life experiences of Africa's descendants elsewhere in the Americas. On her own, she continued her literary education. In college, she had read only two African-American writers: **Paul Laurence Dunbar** and **Richard Wright**. In the late 1950s and early 1960s, she read the writings of other African-American men, citing **Ralph Ellison**'s 1964 *Shadow and Act* as her "literary bible" and identifying **James Baldwin**'s essays as powerful influences on her writing and her thinking.

During this time, Burke also started writing her novel *Brown Girl, Brownstones*. She had no reason to believe her book would ever be published, as she had never seen any published novels by

Paule Marshall promotes her book Daughters *in New York, 1991 (Associated Press/AP)*

African-American women. Before the 1960s, books written by African-American women were generally ignored and quickly went out of print. Not until Burke finished her own novel did she discover **Zora Neale Hurston**'s *Their Eyes Were Watching God* (1937), **Dorothy West**'s *The Living Is Easy* (1948), and especially **Gwendolyn Brooks**'s *Maud Martha* (1953), which Burke later called "the finest portrayal of an African American woman in the novel to date." Despite the apparent lack of published African-American women novelists, Burke persisted in writing, figuring that she would at least develop her writing skills and deepen her insights into the human experience.

As Paule Burke extended her literary world, she also expanded her personal world. In 1957 she married Kenneth Marshall, and in 1958 she gave birth to Evan-Keith, her only child. Like other men of the 1950s, Kenneth expected his wife to stay home, contentedly caring for him and for their child. Although he was pleased—and proud—that his wife was intelligent and a gifted writer, he could see no reason why she would take time and energy away from the family in order to write. To make matters more difficult, Paule decided that she needed a private place in which to write, so she found someone to supervise her son and started writing in a friend's apartment. Over Kenneth's objections, she spent the next two years writing *Brown Girl, Brownstones*.

Marshall set her autobiographical novel in a Barbadian community in Brooklyn during and after the Great Depression. Her exquisitely crafted dialogue keenly reveals the coming-of-age experiences of Selina Boyce, the adolescent daughter of Barbadian immigrants. Her pubescent awakening and identity development are complicated by issues of acculturation in a society that devalues her parents' native culture, by the conflicting values and marital difficulties of her parents, and by her own strength and independence within a society that prizes female submissiveness and dependence. Marshall's work was not a superficial survey of these issues, however. Rather, she explores these issues on an intimate level, psychologically probing the emerging sexuality of a young girl, the complexities of forging a mature mother-daughter relationship, and the struggle for personal identity within a family context.

The 1959 publication of Marshall's book presciently heralded the writings of subsequent novelists. In her work, she urged women to recognize their intrinsic power and strength, but her feminist view of gender issues didn't gain prominence for about a decade. She encouraged African Americans to proudly affirm their African heritage, but her distinctively African-American view of race and class issues didn't become popular until a decade later. Marshall also recognized the value of African-American linguistic forms long before the contemporary discussions of Ebonics and Black English. Although Marshall's talent was critically acclaimed and earned her many awards, she suffered the fate of many other artists who are too far ahead of their time: Her novel was virtually ignored when it was first published, although a Feminist Press reprint of it in the early 1980s was popularly acclaimed and at last enjoyed some commercial success.

Next, Marshall turned her attention to *Soul Clap Hands, and Sing,* a Rosenthal Award–winning set of four novellas published in 1961. The novellas, titled to match their settings—*Barbados, Brooklyn, British Guiana,* and *Brazil*—tell the stories of four elderly men who reflect back on their lives and must come to terms with how poorly their materialistic values served them in the end. Afterward, Marshall then turned her attention to short stories for a while. Her 1962 story "Reena" highlighted the experiences of a college-educated activist African-American woman—again, Marshall was ahead of her time, and the work was neglected then but widely anthologized a decade or two later. In the early 1980s, the Feminist Press reprinted it, along with several of Marshall's other stories in *Reena and Other Stories.*

After a time, Marshall turned her hand again to novel writing, and her home life finally fell apart. She and Kenneth divorced while she was writing her second novel, *The Chosen Place, the Timeless People.* This novel takes place on a fictional Caribbean island, where Marshall examines issues of colonialism, neocolonialism, cultural oppression, and economic imperialism. In the novel, West Indian villagers, the descendants of slaves, are confronted by the well-meaning but patronizing staff of an American aid project. Cultural conflicts lead the villagers to rebel against their would-be benefactors.

After her second novel was published (in 1969), Marshall remarried and started to teach creative writing at Yale, Columbia, and various other universities. She also started spending some of her time living in Haiti. Given her many commitments, she did not complete and publish her third novel, *Praisesong for the Widow,* until the early 1980s (1983). This Before Columbus Foundation American Book Award–winning novel centers around Avatara ("Avey") Johnson, a middle-aged, middle-class, well-acculturated African-American suburban New York widow. Avey takes a physical, cultural, and spiritual journey to a Caribbean island, where she reclaims her African heritage. The same year *Praisesong* was published, Marshall published *Merle and Other Novellas* (1983), another step in her literary and spiritual development.

In Marshall's 1991 novel *Daughters,* Ursa, a young African-American New Yorker, confronts a moral dilemma complicated by her relationship with her parents and her mixed cultural heritage. Ursa's mother is African American, and her father is an African–West Indian politician. When her domineering father's reelection campaign gets into trouble, he asks Ursa to help him. She agrees to help but then realizes that the help he needs is not the help he has requested. In order to truly help him, she must resist his powerful influence over her and persuade him to redeem himself, restoring his intrinsic decency and refuting the corrupt political system in which he has become embroiled.

In addition to Marshall's fiction work, she has written numerous essays and articles. Most notably, her "From the Poets in the Kitchen" (*New York Times Book Review,* 1983) acknowledges how profoundly her work was influenced by the **oral tradition** of the women folk poets who gathered in her mother's kitchen years before. Marshall's work is also widely anthologized (e.g., in collections by **Langston Hughes** and **Toni Cade Bambara**) and widely reviewed. **Alice Walker** has been quoted as observing that Paule Marshall is "unequaled in intelligence, vision, [and] craft by anyone of her generation, to put her contributions to our literature modestly." In addition to recognition by her peers, Marshall has been given many awards for her writings, as well as several acknowledging her overall stature as a writer: a prestigious MacArthur fellowship for lifetime achievement (in 1992), a Guggenheim fellowship, a National Endowment for the Arts fellowship, and awards from the Ford Foundation, the National Institute of Arts and Letters, and the Yaddo Corporation.

REFERENCES: *AWAW. BASS. BFC. BI. BV. BW:AA. BWA. BWW. EB-98. EBLG. G-95. MAAL. MWEL. NAAAL. OC20LE. VBA. VOO.* Mitchell, Keith Bernard, in *OCAAL.* Pettis, Joyce, in *OCWW.*

Marshall, Thurgood
(7/2/1908–1/24/1993)
U.S. Supreme Court opinions, legal briefs

Young Thurgood graduated from his all-black high school at age 16. In 1930 Marhsall graduated with highest honors from Pennsylvania's Lincoln University and married Vivien "Buster" Burey. In 1933, he graduated first in his class from Howard University Law School (Washington, D.C.).

After a few years in private practice, Marshall started working as an attorney for the National Association for the Advancement of Colored People (NAACP). A few years later, he became the NAACP chief counsel, helping to develop and implement a plan for using the federal courts to achieve racial equality. He implemented the plan by winning 29 of the 32 cases he argued before the U.S. Supreme Court.

When presenting cases to the Supreme Court, opposing attorneys state why they believe that the justices should decide a case in a particular way. The justices also question the attorneys, probing their reasoning and any constitutional ramifications of the case. The Supreme Court then evaluates how to interpret the relevant laws in light of the U.S. Constitution. For instance, when Marshall won the 1944 *Smith v. Allwright* decision, the justices declared that a Texas law excluding black voters from primary elections was unconstitutional. Other Supreme Court cases that Marshall argued and won during the 1940s and 1950s helped to integrate neighborhoods, public parks, swimming pools, athletic facilities, local bus systems, and university law schools, professional training, and graduate instruction.

Marshall's most outstanding victory was the 1954 *Brown v. Board of Education* case. As a result, the U.S. Supreme Court unanimously ruled that the existing racial segregation in U.S. public schools violated the U.S. Constitution. This decision completely changed the history of segregation in the United States. Marshall's persuasive argument cited the Fourteenth Amendment, which includes an "equal protection clause" requiring that all citizens be treated alike, regardless of race, color, or creed. This groundbreaking decision provided the historical basis for many of the changes brought about by the civil rights movement of the 1950s and 1960s. For his outstanding achievements, the NAACP awarded Marshall its prestigious Spingarn Medal.

Sadly, in 1955 Marshall's wife "Buster" died. Later, Marshall married Cecilia Suyat, with whom he had two sons. In September 1961, Marshall was nominated to the U.S. Court of Appeals, where he wrote nearly 100 judicial opinions, none of which was overturned by the Supreme Court. Many of his opinions defended civil liberties, such as academic freedom and the right to a fair trial, as well as civil rights. In 1965, Marshall was named U.S. solicitor general, arguing on behalf of the federal government before the Supreme Court. Two years later, he became the first African American to serve on the Supreme Court, where he wrote countless judicial opinions. The Center for the Study of Democratic Institutions later published his writings as *Racial Equality: Criminal Proceedings and the Courts.*

REFERENCES: *1TESK. AA:PoP. BaD. BDAA. BF:2000. E-97. EB-98. G-95. MW-10. WB-98.*

Matheus, John F. (Frederick)
(9/10/1887–1983)
Short stories, plays, book reviews

Among Matheus's more than 20 short stories are "Fog" (**Opportunity**, 1925), "Clay" (*Opportunity*, 1926), and "Sallicoco" (*Opportunity*, 1937); many of his stories were privately published in a collection edited by Leonard A. Slade, Jr. (1974). His 6 plays, most of which highlight the oppression of African Americans, include *Black Damp, 'Cruiter, Guitar, Ouanga!, Tambour,* and *Ti Yette.* Earlier, while he was teaching modern languages (1910–1922), he also published numerous articles and book reviews in scholarly journals related to his work.

REFERENCES: Dandridge, Rita B., in *OCAAL*.

Mathis, Sharon Bell (1937–)
Juvenile fiction and biography, columns, poems

Mathis's books include her juvenile storybooks *Brooklyn Story* (1970), *Sidewalk Story* (1971), her award-winning *Teacup Full of Roses* (1972), her *Listen for the Fig Tree* (1974), *The Hundred Penny Box* (1975), *Cartwheels* (1977), and *Red Dog Blue Fly* (1991); and her juvenile biography *Ray Charles* (1973). In addition, starting in 1972, she began writing a monthly column, "Ebony Juniors Speak!" (in *Ebony Jr.!*), and a biweekly column, "Society and Youth" (in *Liteside: D.C. Buyers Guide*). Mathis has also worked as a librarian, a teacher, and a writer-in-residence.

REFERENCES: Liggins, Saundra, in *OCAAL*.

Matthews, Victoria (née) Earle
(5/27/1861–3/10/1907)
Novella, edited work, children's stories, articles, essays, speeches

Born a slave, Victoria had to spend many of her early years supporting her family through domestic service while trying to educate herself on her own. In 1879, she married William Matthews and soon after started having her essays and short stories appear in various periodicals (e.g., *New York Weekly* and *Waverly*). She also wrote a novella (*Aunt Lindy*, 1893, penned by "Victoria Earle") and quite a few children's stories. While working on the staff of **T. Thomas Fortune**'s *New York Age*, she compiled and edited the collection *Black Belt Diamonds: Speeches, Addresses and Talks of Booker T. Washington* (1898).

In the late 1890s and early 1900s, after her son died (at age 16), Matthews devoted her attention more fully to social and political activism, helping to organize a women's group, establish a travelers' aid society for young women from the South, and raise funds for **Ida B. Wells** (later, Wells-Barnett), after Wells's newspaper offices had been destroyed by Southerners who wished to stop her from publishing her antilynching articles. (Shortly afterward, Wells joined Matthews at the *New York Age*.)

Matthews also founded a nonsectarian Christian home for homeless African-American women and children. There, she set up a library of books by and about African Americans, which she used for her own research in preparing lectures and addresses on African-American history. Perhaps her most famous address, given in 1895 to the first national conference of African-American women, was "The Value of Race Literature," in which she urged the conferees to recognize and preserve the works of African Americans. Two years later, she addressed the Society of Christian Endeavor with her speech, "The Awakening of the Afro-American Woman." Surely, she had contributed to that awakening.

—*Tonya Bolden*

REFERENCES: *BAAW. EA-99.* Cash, Floris Barnett, in *BWA:AHE*.

Mayfield, Curtis (6/3/1942–12/26/1999)
Songs

Among Mayfield's numerous hit songs are "For Your Precious Love" (1958), "People Get Ready" (1965), "We're a Winner," and the songs for movies such as *Superfly* (1972) and *Let's Do It Again* (1975). In 1990, Mayfield was injured when a lighting rig fell on him, causing him to be paralyzed from the neck down. Since then, in 1994, he was recognized with a Grammy Legend Award. On hearing of his death, myriad writers, musicians, and other celebrities mourned the loss of this outstanding talent.

REFERENCES: *EA-99.* Gross, Terry, *Fresh Air,* National Public Radio, 12/27/1999. *NewsHour with Jim Lehrer,* 12/27/1999.

Mayfield, Julian (6/6/1928–1985)
Novels, plays, scripts, critical essays, anthology; broadcast journalist, journal founding editor

After marrying a Mexican physician, Ana Livia Cordero, Mayfield moved to Mexico (in 1954), where he cofounded Mexico's first English-language radio station, for which he also served as newscaster. During this time, he also started editing and writing theater reviews for Puerto Rico's *World Journal,* and he began writing fiction. Mayfield has since written the novels *The Hit* (1957, based on a one-act play, *417,* which he had written previously), *The Long Night* (1958), and *Grand Parade* (1961), and edited the short-story collection *Ten Times Black* (1972). From 1961 to 1966, Mayfield lived in Ghana, where he was the founding editor of *African Review* while advising Ghana's President Kwame Nkrumah. From 1966 to 1971, he returned to the United States, then from 1971 to 1973 he lived in Guyana and advised Guyana's Prime Minister Burnham Forbes. After that, he returned to live in the United States, writing dozens of critical essays and articles for various periodicals.

REFERENCES: Rodney, Ruby V., in *OCAAL*.

McElroy, Colleen (née Johnson) (1935–)
Poems, short stories, plays, novel, nonfiction

McElroy's nine or more poetry books include *Queen of the Ebony Islands* (1984) and *What Madness Brought Me Here: New and Selected Poems, 1968–1988* (1990); her short-story collections include *Jesus and Fat Tuesday* (1988) and *Driving under the Cardboard Pines* (1991); and she has written two plays, a novel, and a nonfiction volume. In addition, McElroy's short stories are widely anthologized. Among other honors, she has been awarded two National Endowment for the Arts fellowships, a Fulbright fellowship, and a Rockefeller fellowship. In addition to her prodigious writing output, she has been a college professor and a speech therapist, not even beginning to publish her writing until she reached her mid-thirties.

REFERENCES: Margulis, Jennifer, in *OCAAL*.

McGhee, "Brownie" (Walter Brown)
(11/30/1915–2/16/1996)
Blues songs

Widely known for his collaboration with blues harmonica player Sonny Terry, McGhee wrote numerous blues songs, many of which have been performed with and by other folk singers, both white (Woody Guthrie, Pete Seeger, etc.) and black (e.g., his and Terry's former roommate, Huddie Ledbetter, a.k.a. Leadbelly).

REFERENCES: "Obituary: McGhee, Walter Brown," 1997 Book of the Year, *Encyclopedia Britannica*. *EB-BH-CD*.

McKay, Claude (né Festus Claudius McKay) (9/15/1889 [or 1890]–5/22/1948)
Poems, commentary, novels

Although many critics have disagreed as to the merit of Claude McKay's literary works, his historical importance in the field of African-American literature in the twentieth century is indisputable. He was a key figure in, if not the first major poet of, the **Harlem Renaissance**, and many of his works paved the way for the 1920s literary movement and defined the trends that would characterize it. His political activism, as well as his literary achievements, garnered both praise and condemnation, making him one of the more controversial figures of the time.

Born in Sunny Ville, Jamaica, McKay was raised by his father and mother, who were relatively prosperous members of the peasant class. He was educated as a subject of the British colonial empire, learning British poetry and conventional verse forms such as the sonnet. However, he received an alternative education from his father, whose own father was brought over from West Africa as a slave: McKay's father attempted to teach him the customs and traditions of the Ashanti, his native people, and repeatedly told him the story of how his father was enslaved. This story instilled in McKay a distrust of whites.

This distrust only deepened when, in 1911, he moved away from rural Sunny Ville to the Jamaican capital of Kingston. It was in Kingston that he first encountered racism and bigotry. The town of Sunny Ville was populated mostly by blacks, so while growing up he had encountered relatively little racism there. However, Kingston's predominantly white and mulatto population held dark-skinned blacks in contempt and often exploited them, allowing them access to only the most menial of jobs—and this troubled McKay to no end. In Kingston at age 19, he became a constable but left in less than a year because he felt that he was oppressing his people by enforcing laws unjustly slanted against the black residents of the city.

The contrast between life in Sunny Ville and life in Kingston struck a deep chord in McKay, and in 1912 he published his first two books of poetry, *Songs of Jamaica* and *Constab Ballads*. These books were published by Walter Jekyll, a British man who came to Jamaica to study folklore. He had, earlier in McKay's career, encouraged McKay to stop writing conventional poetry and instead to write poetry rooted in Jamaican folk culture and using the Jamaican dialect. Jekyll's influence can be seen in these books, which, though published separately, when read together clearly illustrate the differences McKay found in both lifestyle and sentiment when he compared the lives of rural citizens and city dwellers in Jamaica.

Songs of Jamaica focuses largely on presenting the peasant life as idyllic—tied to nature and the land, free from bigotry and oppression, and ultimately peaceful. *Constab Ballads,* based on McKay's experiences as a constable, centers on life in the city, which is shown to be dark, bleak, and full of bigotry, exploitation, and contempt for blacks. These works were well received by the public, and McKay became the first black writer to receive the medal from the Jamaican Institute of Arts and Sciences. The frankness, realism, and honesty of these works differed greatly from the work that African Americans were producing in the United States, which focused less on issues of racism and equality and more on conventional poetic topics such as death, life, love, and beauty.

The award McKay received from the Jamaican Institute came with a stipend, and in 1912 McKay used this money to transport himself to the United States, where he began to pursue a degree in agriculture at Alabama's Tuskegee Institute. In two months, he transferred to Kansas State College but by 1914 had decided to abandon his course of study and return to writing. He worked at various jobs to finance his move to Harlem in New York City, where he continued to work at menial jobs to support himself. The racism he encountered on the trip and in the city made him more determined to pursue his career as a poet.

After arriving in New York, he made contacts with various publishers, sending his works not only to black magazines but also to white publications, particularly leftist political magazines. Once a part of these literary circles, McKay became involved with various radical liberals such as Max Eastman, who was a major leader of leftists in the literary field. In addition to having his poetry and essays published in these magazines, McKay worked on the editorial staff of Eastman's magazine *The Liberator* and wrote various reviews.

It was in *The Liberator* that McKay first published what may be his most famous poem, "If We Must Die." This poem was inspired by the "Red Summer" of 1919, when racial violence directed against blacks broke out throughout the United States, but particularly in Chicago. It asserts and defends the rights of blacks to fight back against such abuse and is a rallying cry to battle, saying that blacks will not "die like hogs" but will instead "face the murderous, cowardly pack / Pressed to the wall, dying, but fighting back!" The poem brought him instant fame when it was published

and endured as a poem that Jean Wagner notes "voices the will of oppressed people of every age who, whatever their race and wherever their region, are fighting with their backs against the wall to win their freedom." It became so famous that it was still remembered in the late 1930s when Winston Churchill used it in a speech against the Nazis, and it became an unofficial battle cry of the Allied Forces in World War II.

McKay was not affected by the fame the poem brought him but instead traveled to England, where he became even more politically active. He began writing for a British socialist named Sylvia Pankhurst, who published a communist magazine called *Worker's Dreadnaught*. In these writings, he urges the communist leadership in Europe and the United States to accept blacks as equals and to oppose European imperialism in other countries. He claims that only after the leadership does this will the black workers in Europe and the United States join the movement, and he points out that without them, the communist revolution will never succeed.

McKay continued to write poetry during his time in England, and in 1920 he published his third book of poetry, *Spring in New Hampshire*. The book was deeply admired by both **Countee Cullen** and **Langston Hughes** and was praised by I. A. Richards, a highly respected literary critic of the time, as "the best work that the present generation is producing" in England. Although it included poems that dealt with both island life and race relations in the United States, it also reflected McKay's conscious effort to avoid publishing very many poems focusing on racial themes.

A year later, after returning to New York, McKay published *Harlem Shadows,* which contained many works from his previous books and magazine publications. The masterful treatment of racial issues in this book ensured his position as a leading member of the Harlem Renaissance. Before, poems about matters of race were only occasionally used as subjects for poetry. This pioneering book proved to other writers of the Harlem literary circle that a black writer's insights on racial issues could succeed as the focus of an entire collection of literary works.

By this time, McKay had become dissatisfied with the efforts he saw being made toward confronting racism in the United States and abroad, so he used his fame to redouble efforts toward that end. He traveled to the Soviet Union and attended the Fourth Congress of the Third Communist

International as a special delegate-observer. The Moscow crowds loved him so much that the Soviet leaders sent him on a six-month tour of the Soviet Union, during which he lectured on art and politics. He also wrote for Soviet journals and magazines, analyzing the history of African Americans in the United States from a Marxist perspective. These works were published under the title *Negroes in America* in 1923.

McKay soon tired of acting as a politician rather than as a poet and also tired of being seen as a novelty, so he left the Soviet Union to embark on what he did not know would be ten years of travel throughout Western Europe and North Africa. Although his health began to fail him, he still continued to write, producing his first novel, *Home to Harlem,* during the time he spent in Paris. Published in 1928, it became the first best-seller written by a black author. The book focuses on a black soldier who leaves the army to return to Harlem and who falls in love and finds happiness with a former prostitute. The characters the soldier encounters along the way and upon his arrival in Harlem are not necessarily positive—they are rough, hard, and not fully respectable figures who often cross lines of morality and legality in their daily lives.

Home to Harlem differed from much of the writing produced by African-American writers of the time. Many black authors had decided to assert only the positive aspects of blacks in both the cities and the countryside. McKay's decision to realistically portray the negative elements of black society, which he had encountered during his travels as a young man, earned him scathing criticism from various figures. **W. E. B. Du Bois** claimed that the book was disgusting; other critics stated that it was written to appeal to whites' stereotypes of blacks for commercial success. Others, however, defended the book as celebrating lives of the most marginal black figures of the ghettos and showing their strength and staying power.

Undeterred by critics, McKay continued his efforts at realism in his later books, *Banjo* and *Banana Bottom,* published in 1929 and 1933, respectively. *Banana Bottom* is considered to be his best work by far. Set in Jamaica, it initially appealed to audiences because of its realistic depictions of the lush tropical landscape. Today, however, it is praised for its affirmation of black culture. In the book, the heroine, Bita—a peasant girl who is adopted by white missionaries after being raped—discovers the dangers that Western imperialists pose to African

Americans and learns that her healing can only commence when she escapes from her white guardians and returns to her native people. This book asserts McKay's belief that African Americans needed to derive their basic values from their racial heritage, cultural traditions, and experiences, rather than Western traditions that actually put black life and culture into danger. He felt that the only way African Americans had resisted the deadly effects of slavery, racism, and segregation was by rooting themselves in such tradition. He also believed that the only way they would acquire equal rights would be to unite and build their own labor, business, and social institutions within their own communities so that they could integrate into American life as a whole.

Claude McKay's ideas and politics did not always make him popular, but they did make him a pioneer in the African-American community. His novels inspired the founders of the Negritude movements in West India and French West Africa, and he helped initiate the New Negro movement. A touchstone for those who defend the idea of black cultural autonomy, he became an important reference for black nationalism during the civil rights era. He achieved new heights in racial poetic achievement, refusing to hide his impatience with racism behind traditional poetic forms despite the fact that other writers felt he should do just that. When he died of heart failure after years of illness, he left behind a life that had been devoted to art and social protest—and whether or not critics consider him to be a figure of great literary merit, he is most certainly a figure of great historical importance: He is the man who began an era of Renaissance in Harlem.

—*Diane Masiello*

REFERENCES: *AAW. BW:SSCA. NAAAL.* Hathaway, Heather, in *OCAAL.*

McKissack, Pat (née Patricia L'Ann Carwell) (8/9/1944–)

Juvenile fiction, biography, history, scripts

Each day after school, Pat and her siblings stayed with her mother's parents: Her "Mama Frances" told them family stories, and her "Daddy James" spun **trickster tales** featuring his grandchildren. In addition, her father's mother, "Mama Sarah told creepy, scary stories at twilight."

Pat grew up loving the public library, a refuge from Jim Crow segregation. An avid reader, she particularly enjoyed "world myths, legends, and fairytales." She also made up her own stories: "I was forever scribbling a poem, a play, or a story" (*CYI,* p. 13).

At Tennessee State University, Pat rediscovered her childhood acquaintance Fredrick McKissack. In 1964, she got her B.A. in English and education—and married Fredrick. The couple has since coauthored many books, managed a business partnership, and raised Fredrick Jr., Robert, and John.

When her sons were young, Patricia spent a lot of time with them in the library. At that time, her lifelong journal writing was her main literary output. In 1969, she started teaching eighth graders and noticed the need for biographies of noteworthy African Americans. She particularly wanted a juvenile biography of **Paul Laurence Dunbar**. When she could find none, she spent the summer of 1971 gathering information and writing one. That fall, she invited her students to respond honestly to her manuscript: They said it was boring. Several revisions later, they responded more enthusiastically. As she later said, "My students taught me [to] keep the material interesting, fast-moving, and up-beat."

In 1975, Pat earned her master's degree in early childhood literature and media programming. The next year, she started teaching a college course on "Writing for Children" (1976–1982) and working as a children's book editor (1976–1981). Later on, with Fred's encouragement, she quit these jobs and started writing full-time. Soon after, the couple founded All-Writing Services, conducting educational workshops, book talks, and lectures.

The McKissacks often cowrite books: Fred does most of the research, and Pat does most of the writing. Their sons and other family members often help, too. Pat and Fredrick, Jr. (a journalist), also cowrote an award-winning children's book, and Robert wrote his own children's book as well.

Pat has written numerous children's picture books that echo Daddy James's rural Southern dialect (e.g., *Flossie and the Fox,* 1986). Alone or with Fred, Pat has also written dozens of books on such topics as African-American **folktales** (e.g., *The Dark-Thirty: Southern Tales of the Supernatural*), biographies (e.g., **Carter G. Woodson, Mary Church Terrell**), diverse cultures (e.g., Incas), history (e.g., *The Civil Rights Movement in America from 1865 to the Present,* 1987), and religious stories. In addition to writing more than 100 books, Pat has written radio and television scripts and collaborated on an award-winning movie script.

For her books, Pat has won numerous book awards, including Caldecott, Newbery, Coretta Scott King, and Jane Addams Children's Book honors. Also, the McKissacks won the National Association for the Advancement of Colored People's Image Award for their work in children's literature, and in 1994, the McKissacks were awarded honorary doctorate degrees.

REFERENCES: *CBC. CYI. EBLG. WB-98.* MacCann, Donnarae, in *OCAAL.* Smith, Jessie Carney, and Phyllis Wood, in *PBW.*

McMillan, Terry (10/18/1951–)
Novels, anthologies

Port Huron, Michigan, is just 60 or so miles northeast of Detroit. In that economically depressed community, Madeline Washington Tillman and Edward Lewis McMillan struggled to raise their five children—Madeline working as a domestic servant and a factory worker and Edward working intermittently as a sanitation worker and a factory worker. When Terry, their oldest child, had just entered her teen years, Madeline decided she had had enough of Edward's alcoholism and abuse, and she divorced him, taking charge of raising her five children alone. Edward died three years later. Terry later recalled that her mother's example taught her and her siblings "how to be strong and resilient. She taught us about taking risks" (quoted in *BWA:AHE*).

The only contact that Terry had with books during her childhood were with the Bible and her required textbooks for school. Her parents never read to her or her siblings. When she was 16, however, Terry got a job (paying $1.25/hour) shelving books for the local public library to help support her family. As she wrote in her introduction to her anthology *Breaking Ice* (1990, p. xv), "As a child, . . . I did not read for pleasure, and it wasn't until I was sixteen . . . that I got lost in a book. It was a biography of Louisa May Alcott. I was excited because I had not really read about poor white folks before; . . . I related to Louisa because she had to help support her family at a young age, which was what I was doing at the library."

Up to that time, she had never read—or even heard of—any African-American writers. "Then one day I went to put a book away, and saw **James Baldwin**'s face staring up at me. 'Who in the world is this?' I wondered . . . not only had there not been any African-American authors included

Best-selling author Terry McMillan, 1993 (Frank Capri/SAGA/Archive Photos)

in any of [my] textbooks, but I'd never been given a clue that if we did have anything important to say that somebody would actually publish it. Needless to say, I was not just naïve, but had not yet acquired an ounce of black pride. I never once questioned why there were no representative works by us in any of those textbooks. After all, I had never heard of any African-American writers, and no one I knew hardly read *any* books."

Later on, however, she said "I read **Alex Haley**'s biography of [**Malcolm X**] and it literally changed my life. First and foremost, I realized that there was no reason to be ashamed of being black, that it was ridiculous. That we had a history, and much to be proud of. I began to notice how we had actually been treated as less than human; began to see our strength as a people. . . . I started *thinking*. Thinking about things I'd never thought about before, and the thinking turned into questions. But I had more questions than answers. . . . So I went to college" (pp. xv–xvi).

After finishing high school in Port Huron, she enrolled in Afro-American literature at Los Angeles City College. Again, as McMillan herself ob-

served, "I remember the textbook was called *Dark Symphony: Negro Literature in America* because I still have it. I couldn't believe the rush I felt over and over once I discovered **Countee Cullen**, **Langston Hughes**, **Ann Petry**, **Zora Neale Hurston**, **Ralph Ellison**, **Jean Toomer**, **Richard Wright**, and rediscovered and read **James Baldwin**, to name just a few. I'm surprised I didn't need glasses by the end of the semester. My world opened up. . . . Not only had we lived diverse, interesting, provocative, and relentless lives, but during, through, and as a result of all these painful experiences, some folks had taken the time to write it down" (*BI,* p. xvi).

During this time, McMillan also had a love affair that broke her heart. As she recalled, "I was so devastated and felt so helpless that my reaction manifested itself in a poem. I did not sit down and say, 'I'm going to write a poem about this.' It was more like magic. I didn't even know I was writing a poem until I had written it. Afterward, I felt lighter, as if something had happened to lessen the pain. And when I read this 'thing,' I was shocked because I didn't know where the words came from" (pp. xvi–xvii). She continued, "I read that poem over and over in disbelief because *I* had written it. One day, a colleague saw it lying on the kitchen table and read it . . . he liked it, then went on to tell me that he . . . wanted to publish it. Publish it? He was serious and it found its way onto a typeset page" (p. xvii). "Seeing my name in print excited me. And from that point on, [almost everything inspired me to write poems.] . . . Years passed. . . . Those poems started turning into sentences. . . . Writing became an outlet for my dissatisfactions, distaste, and my way of trying to make sense of what I saw happening around me" (p. xvii).

By the time McMillan transferred to the University of California at Berkeley (1973), writing had become easy for her, and she majored in journalism. In 1976, she published her first short story—"The End" was her beginning—in a campus literary magazine, and by the time she graduated (B.S., 1979), she had realized that writing news stories was not the kind of writing she enjoyed. She had already submitted a collection of her short stories to major mainstream publisher Houghton Mifflin. The editor there rejected her stories but told her the writing was good enough that if she submitted a novel, the editor might be interested in seeing it.

With Berkeley behind her, McMillan left California to go to New York City. There, she entered Columbia University to study screenwriting. She didn't complete the master's program there, however, because she had already realized that this type of writing was not her main interest. She left Columbia, got a job doing word processing, became involved with Leonard Welch, and continued to write fiction. When Welch lost his job, he started selling cocaine, and he and she got involved in using cocaine and alcohol. In 1984, McMillan and Welch had a son, Solomon Welch, and soon after, McMillan was raising Solomon on her own. By this time, she had overcome her addiction, and she has stayed away from alcohol and other drugs ever since.

Meanwhile, McMillan had enrolled in a writing workshop at the Harlem Writers Guild. Fellow writers there had encouraged her to turn her short story "Mama" into a full-length novel. In 1983, while at the prestigious MacDowell Colony, she started writing the first draft of *Mama*. Once she completed it, she sent it to Houghton Mifflin, which accepted it. Even before the book's 1987 publication, however, McMillan decided that she would do whatever she could to promote it. Through her contacts with other writers, she knew that publishers make very little effort to promote the work of most authors, particularly first-time novelists. Hence, she wrote (thanks to her word-processing skills) and sent out (thanks to her friendly contacts with the guys in her firm's mail room) more than 3,000 letters to bookstores, college campuses, and African-American organizations.

As she later recalled, "I did it all summer long: my friends were hanging out at the beach, and I was licking envelopes" (*WYL2*, p. 140). In her letters, she encouraged recipients to promote her book and offered to give talks or readings. She launched her own publicity tour, going wherever she was invited to speak. *Mama* had sold out its first printing before it was published, and it was in its third printing by the time it was two months old. Even her editors at Houghton Mifflin acknowledged, "Terry, we don't think this would have happened if you had not done all this" (*BI*). A trade paperback edition was published by Washington Square Press in 1991, and a mass-market paperback (Pocket Books) appeared in 1994.

In *Mama*, 27-year-old protagonist Mildred Peacock struggles to raise her five children in Port Haven, Michigan, an economically depressed town with few job opportunities for African Americans. After getting herself and her children away from her alcoholic, abusive husband, she works at whatever jobs she can find, draws on her inner strength, and somehow manages to create a decent—though very difficult—life for herself and her children. (Wonder where she got that story idea?) Mildred is definitely no saint, but she teaches her children how to rely on themselves and their family to get through hard times. In the *New York Times Book Review*, critic Valerie Wayers called *Mama* "original in concept and style, a runaway narrative pulling a crowded cast of funny, earthy characters" (quoted in *PBW*), and the book won an American Book Award in 1988.

The year *Mama* was published, McMillan was invited to be a visiting writer at the University of Wyoming at Laramie (1987–1988), and the following year (1988) she was named an associate professor in creative writing at the University of Arizona at Tucson. In 1988, she was also awarded a literary fellowship by the National Endowment for the Arts. The next year, she published her second novel, *Disappearing Acts* (1989), which sold even more copies than her first novel. Houghton Mifflin didn't receive the benefit of those sales, however, as the publisher and McMillan had parted company because of disputes regarding how McMillan was approaching the work. While Houghton Mifflin was still dickering about making an offer, Viking Penguin bought the manuscript within a couple of days of hearing about it. Washington Square Press sold more than 100,000 copies in paperback (1990), and Pocket Books sold additional copies (1993).

Disappearing Acts comprises alternating first-person narrations by Zora Banks, a college-educated aspiring songwriter, and by Franklin Swift, a poorly educated and often unemployed laborer. Although their relationship is troubled and unhappy, the story is not, as McMillan's humor and compassion sizzle throughout the book. Leonard Welch apparently thought the story too closely resembled his experiences with McMillan, and in 1990 he sued her for defamation of his character. Eventually, McMillan prevailed in their legal battles, winning both the case and a later appeal, just as she had emerged triumphant (i.e., drug free and with her beloved son) from the earlier battles of their previous relationship. Meanwhile, MGM purchased the movie rights to the book, optioned by Tri-Star, and McMillan was commissioned to write the screenplay herself, which she did while on sabbatical from the University of Arizona.

While McMillan was still teaching in Arizona, she made it her mission to find an anthology of U.S. literature reflecting the cultural diversity of U.S. culture. She looked through all her own books and all the books in the library, but she found none. She then decided just to augment a European-American–centered anthology with an African-American–centered one. Every anthology in her own library—and in her college's—included works from the 1960s or before. She called friends and colleagues around the country, asking them for recommendations of anthologies of contemporary African-American fiction. No one knew of anything worthwhile.

Once she was satisfied that nothing existed to meet her specifications, she decided to create her own anthology—and thus was born the manuscript for *Breaking Ice: An Anthology of Contemporary African-American Fiction* (1990). All 57 of the works are by post-1960s authors, which she categorized as "seasoned, emerging, and unpublished." The works represent diverse topics, perspectives, and orientations, few of which focus on race as a central theme. McMillan chose these pieces from nearly 300 submissions she received, and she ended up choosing quite a few excerpts from novels, as she wasn't satisfied with the selection of superb short stories available. (In thinking about this dearth of fine short stories, she observed that publishers frequently encourage talented writers to abandon short stories in favor of novels, which they believe will sell better and will be more deserving of critical attention.) As if the 300 submissions weren't enough fiction reading to satisfy anyone, McMillan also served as a judge for the National Book Award for fiction the year that *Breaking Ice* was published.

While retaining her tenured position in Arizona, McMillan and her son moved from Tucson to Danville, California, in the San Francisco Bay area. She was still working on completing her third novel, *Waiting to Exhale* (1992), while the movers were loading—and then unloading—her desk. Viking, McMillan's publisher, set a $700,000 bidding minimum each for the movie rights and for the paperback rights. Not to worry: The paperback rights were sold to Pocket Books (paperback, 1993) for $2.64 million. Viking then paid for a 20-city, 6-week, nearly 30-bookstore tour—quite a change from McMillan's industrious self-promotion of her first novel.

Viking's investment paid off big-time, too: *Waiting to Exhale* had sold more than 700,000 hardcover copies by the end of 1992. In its first week of publication, it went on the *New York Times* bestseller list, where it stayed for months. That same year, award-winning novelist **Alice Walker**'s *Possessing the Secret of Joy* and Nobel laureate **Toni Morrison**'s *Jazz* had been released, but McMillan's *Waiting* outsold both books by three to one (eventually selling more than 3 million copies). The 1995 film made from the book was also a smash hit. McMillan hadn't exactly predicted this great success herself, however. She later recalled, "After about 90 pages [of writing the *Waiting* manuscript], I'm saying to myself, 'Are they going to think this is as good as *Disappearing Acts*? Are they going to be disappointed?' Eventually, I just had to say, 'I cannot think about my audience; I can't guess what people are going to like'" (*WYL2*, p. 142). Regarding the book's tremendous success, she noted, "It's like having a baby and praying that people think it's cute" (*OCAAL*).

Waiting to Exhale is about four smart, funny, sexy African-American professional women and the ups and downs of their relationships with men (lovers, husbands, ex-lovers, friends, sons), with one another, and with their careers. As with all McMillan's previous novels, her writing style is warm and conversational. Although some critics have scorned her work for treating African-American men too negatively, critic **Charles (Richard) Johnson** called it "a tough love letter to black males everywhere." Other critics have whined that *Waiting* (and McMillan's other novels) uses too much profanity and vulgarity, but McMillan has rebutted, "basically, the language that I use is accurate. . . . That's the way we talk. And I want to know why I've never read a review where they complain about the language that male writers use!" (*WYL2*, p. 142).

The tremendous success of *Waiting* helped McMillan gain a $6 million publishing deal for her fourth novel, *How Stella Got Her Groove Back* (1996), which was also made into a film (1998). The protagonist of the novel, 42-year-old Stella, has been highly successful in her corporate career as well as in raising her child single-handedly, but she still feels dissatisfied, discontent. Her fun-spirited—and outrageously outspoken—friend gets her to take a vacation in Jamaica. There, Stella meets a handsome 20-year-old Jamaican cook, who seduces her, falls in love with her, and charms her into loving him in turn. Complicating the situation are the young man's parents—who at first seem horrified at their son's relationship—and Stella's two sisters, Vanessa (a single parent) and Angela (married and pregnant). Vanessa is highly impulsive herself, so she encourages Stella to go for it, but Angela is unable to appreciate anything outside the traditional family she prizes.

In all her works to date, McMillan speaks to the heart of her readers, tying the experiences of her characters to their own. Through candor and humor, she depicts spirited, independent African-American women who care deeply about their relationships with loved ones and who seek to form meaningful relationships with men without losing their own identities or their independence. Because her writing is so forthright, she appeals to a far wider audience than just African-American readers (or film viewers). McMillan also hopes her own example will encourage other African Americans to become writers. In her introduction to *Breaking Ice,* she wrote, "I've been teaching writing on the university level now for 3 years, and much to my dismay, rarely have I ever had an African-American student. I wish there were more ways to encourage young people to give writing a shot" (p. xxii).

Regarding her own advice to writers, McMillan noted, "It took [a long time] to realize that writing was not something you aspired to, it was something you did because you had to" (*BI,* p. xviii). "Persist. Acknowledge your bewilderment. Remember. Writing is personal. Try to write the kind of stories you'd like to read. Do not write to impress. Do not write to prove to a reader how much you know, but instead write in order *to know.* At the same time, you want to snatch readers' attention, pull them away from what they're doing and keep them right next to your characters. You want them to feel what your characters feel, experience it with them so the readers are just as concerned about their outcome as the character is. Perhaps, if you do your job well and you're lucky, readers may recognize something until it clicks" (*BI,* p. xxiii).

REFERENCES: *AA:PoP. BI. EB-BH-CD. EBLG. MWEL. NAAAL. WDAA.* Mason, Wanda, in *OCAAL.* Robinson, Lisa Clayton, in *EA-99.* Shaw, Brenda Robinson, in *PBW.* Smith, Wendy, in *WYL2.* Thompson, Kathleen, in *BWA:AHE.* Woodard, Helena, in *OCWW.*

McPherson, James Alan (9/16/1943–)
Short stories

Little James's father, also named James, shared his love of comic books with his two sons. The three McPherson males would leave Mable (Smalls) McPherson behind and go to a comic-book wholesale house in Savannah, where they would luxuriate in bins of remaindered comic books. The white man who ran the operation was a pal of big James, and he would let the boys take home as many leftover comic books as their arms could hold.

When young James was a little older, he found his way to the Colored Branch of the Carnegie Public Library, within a block of their home. (While James was growing up, Jim Crow segregation was the rule in schools, libraries, and other public places.) As he later recalled, "I liked going there to read all day. At first the words, without pictures, were a mystery. But then, suddenly, they all began to march across the page. They gave up their secret meanings, spoke of other worlds, made me know that pain was a part of other people's lives. After a while, I could read faster and faster and faster and faster. After a while, I no longer believed in the world in which I lived. I loved the Colored Branch of the Carnegie Public Library" (*TWL*).

After finishing public school, McPherson worked as a Pullman waiter aboard the Great Northern Railroad while attending college at Morgan State University (in Baltimore, 1963–1964) and then at Morris Brown College (in Atlanta, where he earned his B.A., 1965). After graduating, he was recruited by Harvard University Law School, and in 1968, he earned his L.L.B. degree there. After Harvard, he went to the University of Iowa Writers' Workshop, where he earned a master's degree (M.F.A., 1969). After all that schooling, McPherson was ready to go out into the world—and teach English at several universities, including the University of Iowa Law School; the University of California at Santa Cruz; Morgan State University; and the University of Virginia at Charlottesville. In 1981, he became an English professor at the University of Iowa Writers' Workshop.

Meanwhile, in the late 1960s, McPherson entered his short story "Gold Coast" in a fiction contest sponsored by the editors of *Atlantic Monthly* magazine. "Gold Coast" won first prize, and McPherson gained a prestigious start to his literary career. By the end of the decade, *Atlantic* had awarded McPherson a writer's grant and had invited him to become a contributing editor for the magazine. More of his short stories started being published in other periodicals as well. Rarely does a writer earn a distinguished literary reputation based on short stories, but McPherson has done so based chiefly on two collections of his stories: *Hue and Cry: Short Stories* (1969) and *Elbow Room* (1977).

The stories in *Hue and Cry* were written while McPherson was still a student, yet they were praised by such luminaries as **Ralph Ellison** for his mastery of the writing craft. Although race is not central to McPherson's stories, they nonetheless indict social injustice and discrimination based on race, class, and sex. Two of the stories—"On Trains" and "A Solo Song: For Doc"—offer readers a glimpse into the lives of the legendary Pullman porters with whom McPherson worked on the Great Northern Railroad; two of the stories—"Hue and Cry" and "Cabbages and Kings"—tell of the travails of interracial relationships; "Gold Coast" explores race, class, and age differences between two men; and "An Act of Prostitution" reveals some of the injustices of legal justice. In these stories, McPherson withholds judgment, permitting his readers to form their own opinions about the characters and their situations. In recognition of his work, McPherson was awarded a National Institute of Arts and Letters grant (1970), a Rockefeller grant (1970), and a Guggenheim fellowship (1972–1973).

McPherson's next collection, *Elbow Room* (1977), was awarded a Pulitzer Prize in 1978 and again was given laudatory praise from Ralph Ellison. The stories in this book range from reminiscence ("Why I Like Country Music," in which a New Yorker recalls a partner at a country dance during his Southern boyhood) to tall tale ("The Story of a Dead Man," about a mythical African-American folk figure) to travel ("I Am an American," about a young African-American couple in London). As with *Hue and Cry,* most of his characters are still confronting social constraints and limitations, but they seem better equipped to face their challenges. All of his stories are realistic and centered around his richly detailed characters.

Since 1977, most of McPherson's writing has involved essays, including both personal ones and political ones addressing his vision of a cultural synthesis among America's diverse people. In 1981, McPherson was one of three African-American writers to be awarded a five-year "genius" grant by the MacArthur Foundation for his exceptional writing talent.

REFERENCES: *AA:PoP. E-98. EB-BH-CD. NAAAL. OC20LE. TWL. WDAA.* Wallace, Jon, in *OCAAL.*

Meriwether, Louise (née Jenkins)
(5/8/1923–)
Novels, short stories, biographies, juvenile fiction and nonfiction, articles; journalist

When Julia and Marion Lloyd Jenkins left South Carolina, they surely didn't expect to arrive in the North on the brink of an economic depression. By the time Louise came along (their only daughter and their third child), they were living in Haverstraw, New York, where Julia was busy caring for a houseful of children while Marion worked as a bricklayer. When the Great Depression hit, there were five Jenkins children, and Marion had lost his job. To make ends meet, Marion worked as a "numbers runner" (small-time helper in an illegal gambling operation), and Julia collected welfare checks. In those days, the Jenkins family was not alone in their poverty—or in their various ways of trying to get by.

After Louise finished P.S. (public school) 81 and then graduated from Central Commercial High School (in downtown Manhattan), she went on to study English at New York University, where she earned her B.A. By the 1960s, she had married Angelo Meriwether and had moved with him to Los Angeles, where she worked as a freelance reporter for the *Los Angeles Sentinel* (1961–1964). Her book reviews, biographical sketches of local African-American heroes and of Arctic explorer **Matthew Henson**, and other writings started appearing in the *Los Angeles Times* and the *Sentinel*. During the mid-1960s, she had become a dedicated social activist, fighting for better working conditions for African-American laborers; working with the Congress of Racial Equality (CORE) for civil rights; and collaborating with the Deacons, a self-defense coalition that maintained an all-day, all-night patrol to protect the African-American community from Ku Klux Klan attacks.

In 1965, Meriwether earned an M.A. in journalism from the University of California at Los Angeles, and she got a job as a story analyst for Universal Studios (1965–1967). In 1967, William Styron's white-male account of *The Confessions of Nat Turner* sparked fury among many African Americans, including Meriwether, who helped prevent the prize-winning book from being made into a movie. In the late 1960s, she joined the Watts

Writers' Workshop and started writing short stories (e.g., "Daddy Was a Number Runner," 1967; "A Happening in Barbadoes," 1968; and "The Thick End Is for Whipping," *Negro Digest*, 1969).

While protesting Styron's work, Meriwether had temporarily set aside work on her young adult novel, *Daddy Was a Number Runner* (1970), which she had started writing as a short story in the mid-1960s. Her five years of labor paid off, however, in terms of critical acclaim, including high praise from such noted authors as **James Baldwin** and the monetary rewards of writing, including a grant from the National Endowment for the Arts (1973) and a grant from the Creative Arts Service Program, an auxiliary of the New York State Council on the Arts (1973). The semiautobiographical novel views the Great Depression through the eyes of 12-year-old Francie Coffin. Despite the youth of the narrator, the story is no fairy tale. Pubescent Francie watches her father abandon his family to run off with a young woman, her mother beg welfare workers to help her feed her family, and her brother become a pimp. (Meriwether's own life had no fairy tale ending, either, as she was twice divorced—from Angelo and from her second husband, Earl Howe.)

After finishing *Daddy*, Meriwether wrote three biographies of notable African Americans intended for young adult (teenage) readers: *The Freedom Ship of Robert Smalls* (1971), about a former slave who became a national politician; *The Heart Man: Dr. Daniel Hale Williams* (1972), about the first doctor to perform open-heart surgery; and *Don't Ride the Bus on Monday: The Rosa Parks Story* (1973), about the Alabama seamstress and civil rights activist who initiated a major protest action for social change. Meriwether later noted, "I have been deeply concerned for many years by the way African Americans fell through the cracks of history, and I reacted by attempting to set the record straight" (*BWA:AHE*, quoting a 1981 letter from Meriwether to article author Rita Dandridge). Thus, her writing may be viewed as an extension of her devotion to social activism.

By the late 1970s, Meriwether had left California, returning to the East Coast, where she served on the faculty of Sarah Lawrence College in Bronxville, New York (with a little time out for teaching creative writing at the University of Houston, Texas). In 1994, Meriwether's second novel for young adults, *Fragments of the Ark*, was published. This Civil War–era historical novel fictionally re-creates the story of Robert Smalls in the character of Peter Mango, a fugitive slave from Charleston, North Carolina, who runs away to aid the Union army and gain his freedom. A 1980s grant from the Mellon Foundation helped fund her research for the novel, so that she could make several trips to the Sea Islands off the coast of Charleston in South Carolina.

REFERENCES: *EBLG*. Brown-Guillory, Elizabeth, in *OCWW*. Dandridge, Rita, in *BWA:AHE* and in *OCAAL*.

Merrick, Lyda (née) Moore
(11/19/1890–2/14/1987)
Founder and editor of periodical for the blind

While raising her two daughters, Merrick worked in the library her father had founded for his community. (Her father, a physician, had also cofounded a hospital and a life-insurance company.) While working with members of the library's club, Library Corner for the Blind, she discovered the need for a periodical that would appeal to blind African-American readers. In June 1951, she established the journal *Negro Braille Magazine*, serving as its editor until 1969. Even after she had stepped down as editor, she continued to be involved with the journal for another ten years. As the journal gradually addressed a wider audience and no longer focused exclusively on blind African-American readers, it was renamed *Merrick-Washington Magazine for the Blind* (in 1981).

—*Tonya Bolden*

REFERENCES: *BAAW*.

Micheaux, Oscar (1/2/1884–3/25/1951)
Screenplays, novels; book publisher

Of the 50 or more films Micheaux made, only about a dozen are still available for viewing today. Before he started writing screenplays, though, he wrote a string of novels, starting with his highly autobiographical *The Conquest: The Story of a Negro Pioneer* (1913). Who would publish the first novel of an African-American Midwestern homesteading farmer named "Oscar Devereaux," who gets romantically involved with a white woman? Western Book Supply Company—owned and operated by Micheaux. Surprisingly, the stockholders and even the first purchasers of his books were mostly European-American Midwestern farmers. His next two novels were just as obviously autobiographical: *The*

Forged Note: A Romance of the Darker Races (1915) and *The Homesteader* (1917).

When the owners of Lincoln Film Motion Picture Company, one of the first African-American movie companies ever, offered to turn *The Homesteader* into a film, Micheaux agreed to let them do so—as long as they let him direct the film. They refused, so Micheaux—ever the intrepid entrepreneur—started the Micheaux Book and Film Company. Without any prior experience as a film producer, director, publicity agent, and so on, Micheaux managed to complete his film by 1919 and personally sold it, traveling from movie house to movie house and town to town.

Pretty soon, Micheaux's productions included *Within Our Gates* (1919) and *The Brute* (starring the prizefighter Sam Langford), *Son of Satan, The Millionaire,* and *Wages of Sin* (all produced in the 1920s). Micheaux could sell anyone two nickels for a quarter, and his ability to sell his films—in the North and the South—was legendary. For that reason, African-American actors jumped at the chance to launch their careers through his films. The acting titan **Paul Robeson** made his moving-picture debut in Micheaux's *Body and Soul* (1924).

It must be acknowledged that Micheaux's films may have starred some acting geniuses, but Micheaux himself was no writing genius. His hastily produced films were melodramatic, technically flawed, and far from exalting African-American virtues. In fact, many intellectuals carped that in his films, skin hue correlated very strongly with virtue—and definitely not the blacker the berry, the sweeter the juice. Nonetheless, at least he gave work to African-American actors and film workers, and he gave African-American theater audiences something to see on a Saturday afternoon without having all-white faces on the screen. Given what was available at the time—and the prevailing sentiments of his era—he contributed a great deal. The mere fact that his film company survived the Great Depression says something about the man. His films from this era include *The Exile* (the first all-black-cast talkie, 1931), *Harlem after Midnight* (1934), *Underworld* (1937), *Lying Lips* (1939, coproduced by black star aviator Hubert Julian), and *The Notorious Elinor Lee* (1940).

In the 1940s, Micheaux returned to novel writing; what he lacked in creativity, he definitely compensated for with stamina and selling skill. His 1940s-era books include *The Wind from Nowhere* (1941), another autobiographical novel, reworking

the material in his first novel and his first film, *The Case of Mrs. Wingate* (1944, a detective novel), *The Story of Dorothy Stanfield* (1946, about an insurance con), and *The Masquerade* (1947, which owes much to **Charles Chesnutt**'s *The House Behind the Cedars*). One last film was made from Micheaux's work: In 1948, *The Betrayal* (adapted from *The Wind from Nowhere*), essentially the story from his first novel and his first film, was a fitting last work. The final tributes to Micheaux came in 1974, when the Oscar Micheaux Award was created by the Black Filmmaker's Hall of Fame, and in 1987, when the Oscar Micheaux star was placed on Hollywood's Walk of Fame.

—*Tonya Bolden*

REFERENCES: *EAACH. SMKC.*

Miller, E. (Eugene) Ethelbert (1950–)
Poems, essays, literary criticism, anthologies; editor

Miller's publications include his edited poetry anthologies *Synergy D. C. Anthology* (1975), *Women Surviving Massacres and Men* (1977), and his highly acclaimed anthology *In Search of Color Everywhere* (1994); and his collections *The Land of Smiles and the Land of No Smiles* (1974), *Andromeda* (1974), *The Migrant Worker* (1978), *Season of Hunger/Cry of Rain: Poems 1975–1980* (1982), *Where Are the Love Poems for Dictators?* (1986), *First Light: New and Selected Poems* (1993), and *How We Sleep on the Nights We Don't Make Love* (1996). Perhaps at least as important, however, is Miller's literary contribution as an archivist of rare African-American literature and history, which he has collected as director of the African American Studies Resource Center at Howard University. Miller also champions up-and-coming African-American writers and guides them through a series of readings and professional workshops through the Ascension Poetry Series he founded and directs. He also serves as senior editor of *African American Review* (see **Black American Literature Forum**) and of *Washington Review.*

REFERENCES: *MAAL.* Haywood, Elanna N., in *OCAAL.*

Miller (married name: Sullivan), May
(1/26/1899–2/8/1995)
Plays, poems

Kelly Miller was a prominent sociology professor and dean at Howard University (in Washington, D.C.), as well as a published poet, but to May, he was best known as her (and her four siblings') dad and the husband of her mother, Annie May (Butler) Miller. At their home, **W. E. B. Du Bois** and **Booker T. Washington** were frequent guests. At M Street School (later Paul Dunbar High School), her instructors included playwrights **Angelina Weld Grimké** and Mary Burrill. Burrill encouraged May to write her first play, *Pandora's Box,* published in 1914.

In 1916, May graduated from Dunbar and entered her daddy's university, where she once again studied drama, while acting, directing, and producing plays. She collaborated with Howard University professor **Alain Locke** and others to found an African-American drama movement on campus. She also earned an award for best play for her one-act play *Within the Shadows,* thereby becoming the first student from Howard University to receive this award. Four years after she entered Howard, she graduated at the academic head of her class (B.A., 1920).

After graduation, Miller taught drama, speech, and dance at Frederick Douglass High School in Baltimore. While school was out during the summer, she studied playwriting at Columbia University, and she continued to write her own plays. Miller's timing could not have been better. While the **Harlem Renaissance** was blooming in New York, poet and playwright **Georgia Douglas Johnson** was hosting her weekly literary salon, so Washington, D.C., was also a major gathering place for writers to share their works and to give one another support and encouragement. Each weekend, Miller commuted to 1461 S Street, N.W., Johnson's home, where she joined such celebrated writers as **Langston Hughes**, **Zora Neale Hurston**, **Willis Richardson**, and **Carter G. Woodson** in the warm, nurturing ambience of Johnson's salon. Soon, Miller was probably the most widely published and produced woman playwright of that highly productive era.

Miller's plays included *The Bog Guide* (1925), her humorous but provocative *Riding the Goat* (1925), her prize-winning *The Cuss'd Thing* (1926), and *Moving Caravans* (193?). Several of her plays clearly addressed racial issues, such as *Scratches* (1929), highlighting the biases within the African-American community (e.g., color distinctions and class differences); *Stragglers in the Dust* (1930), about African Americans in the military; and her anti-lynching play *Nails and Thorns* (1933). Less success-

ful were her plays *Christophe's Daughters* (1935), set in Haiti, and *Samory* (1935), set in the African Sudan. She also wrote many historical plays, four of which (including plays on **Harriet Tubman** and **Sojourner Truth**) were anthologized in *Negro History in Thirteen Plays* (1935), which she and playwright Willis Richardson edited. The last play she wrote, *Freedom's Children on the March* (1943), was also a historical play. Like other African-American women writers of her era, Miller focused on social and political issues in her works. Unlike most others, however, her work strayed from the home and family; in addition, she was innovative in including both African-American and European-American characters in many of her works, so that she could more fully explore issues of race from multiple perspectives.

In 1943 (the year her last play was published), Miller retired from teaching in the Baltimore public school system, and she and her husband, John Sullivan (a high school principal whom she had married in 1940), moved to Washington, D.C. In addition to teaching public school students, Miller taught college students as a visiting lecturer and poet at Monmouth College and the University of Wisconsin at Milwaukee, and taught high school students at Philips Exeter Academy.

Miller did not, however, retire from writing. To the contrary, she turned her attention from plays to poetry, and she was at least as prolific in her new genre as she had been in her old one. Her poetry was well received, too, earning praise from poets **Gwendolyn Brooks** and **Robert Hayden**. Although her poems were rather conventional in form and language, they inspired readers to question social conventions. Just as she had posed ethical and spiritual questions in her plays, her poems raised issues of humanistic values. Soon, her poems were widely published in such periodicals as *Phylon, Antioch Review, Crisis, Nation, New York Times,* and *Poetry.* Miller's poetry collections include *Into the Clearing* (1959), *Poems* (1962), *Lyrics of Three Women: Katie Lyle, Maude Rubin, and May Miller* (1964), *Not That Far* (1973), *The Clearing and Beyond* (1974), *Dust of Uncertain Journey* (1975), *The Ransomed Wait* (1983), and *Collected Poems* (1989) as well as her collection of poems for children, *Halfway to the Sun* (1981).

REFERENCES: *EB-BH-CD. WDAA.* Koolish, Lynda, in *OCAAL.* Perkins, Kathy A., in *BWA:AHE.*

Millican, Arthenia (Bernetta) J. (née Jackson) Bates (6/1/1920–)

Poems, short fiction

Millican's publications include the highly acclaimed short-story collection *Seeds beneath the Snow: Vignettes from the South* (1969) as well as her *The Deity Nodded* (1973) and her *Such Things from the Valley* (1977). She also wrote numerous scholarly and critical articles, short stories, and poems. Millican's work reveals her warm appreciation of the folks she has known in the American South.

REFERENCES: Gill, Glenda E., in *OCAAL*.

Milner, Ronald (5/29/1938–)

Plays, screenplays, anthology, criticism, short stories, novel

Although Milner's first published book was a novel (*The Life of the Brothers Brown,* 1965), he is chiefly known for his plays, which include *Who's Got His Own* (1967), *The Warning: A Theme for Linda* (1969), *The Monster* (1968), *(M)Ego and the Green Ball of Freedom* (1968), *What the Wine-Sellers Buy* (1973/1974), *Jazz Set* (1980), *Roads of the Mountaintops* (1986), *Checkmates* (1987), and *Don't Get God Started* (1988). He has also published several short stories and articles of literary criticism, and he has been writing film and television scripts while continuing to teach creative writing, particularly playwriting. Perhaps his most notable achievements have been with **Woodie King**, **Jr.**, with whom he coedited *Black Drama Anthology* (1971) and cofounded the Concept-East Theatre company (1962).

REFERENCES: Aguilar, Marian, in *EA-99*. Williams, Derek A., in *OCAAL*.

Mitchell, Loften (4/15/1919–)

Plays, novel, nonfiction—drama history

After completing his A.B. (Talladega College in Alabama, 1943) and a tour in the navy (1944–1945), Mitchell went to Columbia University, where he studied playwriting with John Glassner (M.A., 1951). Mitchell's first three plays—*Shattered Dreams* (1938), *The Bancroft Dynasty* (1948), and *The Cellars* (1952)—received little notice, but his *A Land Beyond the River* (1957) was both popularly and critically acclaimed. It probably helped that the play appeared just three years after the landmark *Brown v. Board of Education* decision and dramatized a court case ending school segregation.

His many other plays include *The Photographer* (1962), *Ballad of [or for] Bimshire* (1963), *Ballad for [or of] the Winter Soldiers* (1964), *Star of the Morning* (1965), *Tell Pharaoh* (1967), *The Phonograph* (1969), *Sojourn to the South of the Wall* (1973, a one-act play; expanded to the full-length *The Walls Came Tumbling Down,* 1976), and *Bubbling Brown Sugar* (1975, with Rosetta LeNoire), a popular musical that won a 1976 Tony Award nomination and was named the best musical of the year in 1977 in London. In addition, paperbacks have been published about his musical (*Bubbling Brown Sugar: A Musical Revue,* 1985) and his play *Tell Pharaoh* (1987). Mitchell has also published two histories of drama, *Black Drama: The Story of the American Negro in the Theatre* (1967) and *Voices of the Black Theatre* (1975). He also tackled the novel form in his *The Stubborn Old Lady Who Resisted Change* (1973). From 1971 through 1985, Mitchell taught drama at the State University of New York at Binghamton.

REFERENCES: Aguiar, Marian, in *EA-99*. Walker, Robbie Jean, in *OCAAL*. Amazon.com, 7/1999.

Moody, Anne (9/15/1940–)

Short stories, autobiography, essays

Mississippi sharecroppers Fred and Elmire Moody had six children, the oldest of whom was Anne. Eventually, Fred got tired of harsh fieldwork and impoverished living conditions, and he left Elmire to raise the children as best she could. Although the segregated schools of rural Mississippi could not be said to have offered an outstanding education, Anne drew every bit of learning she could from the limited opportunities available. A couple of weeks before Anne turned 15 years old, the week before high school started, 14-year-old Chicagoan Emmett Till was lynched and murdered in Mississippi for being black in the wrong place. In addition to the 100,000 people who went to Mississippi to pay him a final tribute, the nation—and the world—was outraged by this egregious wrong. While Anne was in high school, an all-male, all-white jury acquitted the men who had been positively identified as involved in the lynching. These events stirred Anne's emotions; they probably would have affected her anyway, but Emmett's physical proximity and his age deepened and intensified their impact. Nonetheless, Anne continued her academic achievements and added to them athletic success as a basketball player.

After high school, Moody went on to spend two years at Natchez Junior College on a basketball scholarship. From there, she transferred to Tougaloo College, in Jackson, Mississippi, on a full academic scholarship. Meanwhile, however, she was becoming deeply committed to and involved in the civil rights movement, raising funds and organizing people and activities for the Congress of Racial Equality (CORE) in the state noted for its most violent opposition to civil rights: Mississippi. When sit-in demonstrations were held to integrate a Woolworth's lunch counter in Jackson, Mississippi, Moody sat in. She also became involved in other civil rights organizations, including the National Association for the Advancement of Colored People (NAACP) and the Student Nonviolent Coordinating Committee (SNCC). After graduating from Tougaloo (B.S., 1964), she continued her civil rights activities, working for Cornell University as a civil rights project coordinator. Eventually, however, she grew disenchanted with the movement, feeling that it had become too narrowly focused on black nationalism and too factional, hoping instead that African Americans would see themselves as part of a global struggle for civil rights and freedom from oppression.

Moody has written numerous short stories and essays, which have appeared in national magazines such as *Ms.* and *Mademoiselle;* in 1970, *Mademoiselle* awarded her its silver medal for her article "New Hopes for the Seventies." A few of her short stories have also appeared in her collection *Mr. Death* (1975). Her best-known literary work, however, is her autobiography *Coming of Age in Mississippi* (1968), which was favorably reviewed by critics and was lauded with the Best Book of the Year Award from the American Library Association (1969) and the Brotherhood Award from the National Council of Christians and Jews. The book traces her childhood of desperate poverty, segregation, and discrimination in rural Mississippi and her efforts to win civil rights for the African Americans of Mississippi—and the nation. Through her very personal one-woman account, she revealed the travails and troubles of many people, both in Mississippi and anywhere else people have faced cruel poverty and oppressive racism.

REFERENCES: *EBLG. OC20LE. SMKC.* Beavers, Gina, in *BWA:AHE.* Eckard, Paula Gallant, in *OCAAL.* Fay, Robert, in *EA-99.*

Moore, Alice Ruth
See **Dunbar Nelson, Alice Ruth**

Moore, Opal (1953–)
Poems, short stories, essays, literary criticism—children's literature

In 1970, Moore started writing journal entries and poems in an effort to cope with the racism she was encountering in art school. Among the writers who have shaped Moore's work have been her teachers **Paule Marshall** and **James Alan McPherson**, her first idol **Gwendolyn Brooks**, and **Toni Morrison**. Among her publications are numerous short stories, poems, and critical essays focusing on children's literature.

REFERENCES: Dance, Daryl Cumber, in *OCAAL.*

Morgan, Garrett A. (Augustus) (3/4/1875–7/27/1963)
Newspaper publisher

Best known as an inventor (the gas mask, the three-way traffic signal, a hair-straightening process, among other things), Morgan founded and published the *Cleveland Call* newspaper (1920–1923).

REFERENCES: *BDAA. E-99. EA-99.*

Morrison, Toni (née Chloe Anthony Wofford) (2/18/1931–)
Novels, criticism; editor

In 1993, Toni Morrison became the first black woman to receive the Nobel Prize for literature. Her works are noted for their powerful storytelling, provocative themes, and poetic language. Morrison's novels explore racial and gender conflicts and the various ways that people express their identities. She writes about familiar subjects and themes, but her approaches to them distinctly differ from those of any other American author. For example, in her novel *The Bluest Eye* (1970), Morrison uses the unique style and motifs of fairy tales. In *Song of Solomon* (1977), she uses Greek tragedy motifs; and in *Tar Baby* (1981), she uses garden metaphors and Christian symbolism. Her troubled characters seek to find themselves and their cultural riches in a society that impedes and warps such crucial growth.

Chloe Anthony Wofford was born in Lorain, Ohio. Her parents had moved to Ohio from the

Toni Morrison won a Pulitzer Prize for Beloved, *1988 (Bernard Gotfryd / Archive Photos)*

South to escape racism and to find better opportunities. She was the second of four children of George Wofford, a shipyard welder, and Ramah Willis Wofford. While the children were growing up, George worked three jobs at the same time for almost 17 years. He took a great deal of pride in the quality of his work, so that each time he welded a perfect seam, he'd also weld his name onto the side of the ship. He also made sure to be well-dressed, even during the Depression. Chloe's mother was a churchgoing woman who sang in the choir.

At home, Chloe heard many songs and tales of Southern African-American folklore. The Woffords were proud of their heritage. Lorain was a small industrial town populated with immigrant Europeans, Mexicans, and Southern blacks who lived side by side, and Chloe attended an integrated school. She was the only African-American student in her first-grade class and the only child who could already read. She was friends with many of her white schoolmates and did not face racism until she started dating.

Chloe hoped to one day become a dancer like her favorite ballerina, Maria Tallchief. She also loved to read. Her early favorites were the Russian writers Leo Tolstoy and Fyodor Dostoyevsky, French author Gustave Flaubert, and English novelist Jane Austen. She graduated with honors from Lorain High School in 1949.

The sense of community that Wofford acquired from her youth in Lorain is very important to her life. Underlying themes of family and community are present throughout all of her later work. Her father, a dignified man, impressed a positive self-image on his daughter. Biographers Clenora Hudson and Wilfred Samuels suggest that although Wofford's father died before she began her third novel, she continues to hold up her accomplishments for his approval. The resonance of such authority resides in all of her books.

The Bluest Eye (1970) is set in Lorain. Its explicit portrayal of an interwoven African-American community can be seen as a partially autobiographical picture of her childhood home. The sense of community expands and diversifies with her later novels, but the essence of that community remains. Even in her novel *Jazz* (1992), in which she depicts the complex social structure of New York City in the 1920s, the author suggests that the same principles of community that existed in the small town of Lorain, Ohio, can be found in the great metropolis.

After high school, Wofford attended Howard University, where she majored in English with a minor in classics. It was there that she changed her name to Toni because many people couldn't pronounce Chloe correctly. Toni Wofford joined a repertory company, the Howard University Players, with whom she made several tours of the South. She experienced firsthand the life of the African Americans there, the life her parents had escaped by moving North.

Wofford graduated from Howard in 1953 with a B.A. in English. She then attended Cornell University and earned a master's degree in 1955. After graduating, she was offered a job at Texas Southern University in Houston, where she taught introductory English. Negro History Week was a regular event at Texas Southern. There, she was introduced to the idea of black culture as a discipline, rather than just personal family reminiscences.

In 1957, Wofford returned to Howard University as a member of the faculty. The civil rights movement was gaining momentum, and she met several people who were later active in the struggle. She met the young poet **Amiri Baraka** (at that time called LeRoi Jones) and Andrew Young, who later became mayor of Atlanta. Her students included **Stokely Carmichael** and **Claude Brown**.

At Howard, Wofford met and fell in love with a young Jamaican architect, Harold Morrison. They married in 1958, and their first son, Harold Ford, was born in 1961. She continued teaching after her marriage while helping take care of the family. Her married life was unhappy, however, so she joined a small writer's group as temporary escape, filling her need for companionship with other lovers of literature. Members of the writer's circle were required to bring a story or poem for discussion each week. One day, having nothing to bring, Morrison quickly wrote a story, loosely based on a girl she knew in childhood, who had prayed to God for blue eyes. The group received the story well, and feeling satisfied, Morrison put it away.

Meanwhile, Morrison's marriage continued to deteriorate. While pregnant with their second child, Toni left her husband and her job at the university. She divorced Harold and returned to her parents' house in Lorain with her two sons.

In the fall of 1964, Morrison began work with a textbook subsidiary of Random House as an associate editor in Syracuse, hoping to be transferred to New York City. She found writing exciting and challenging, working on her own pieces while the children were asleep. With the exception of parenting, Morrison found everything else boring in comparison to writing. She went back to the story she had composed for the writer's group and decided to make it into a novel. She utilized her childhood memories, expanding the facts with her imagination. This made the characters develop a life of their own.

In 1967, she was transferred to New York and became a senior editor at Random House. While editing books by prominent black Americans such as Muhammad Ali, Andrew Young, and **Angela Davis**, she was busy sending her own novel to various publishers. *The Bluest Eye* was eventually published in 1970 to much critical acclaim, although it was not commercially successful.

From 1971 to 1972, Morrison was an associate professor of English at the State University of New York at Purchase while she continued working at Random House. In addition, she soon started writing her second novel, *Sula* (1973). *Sula* examines (among other issues) the dynamics of friendship between two adult black women and the expectations for conformity within the community.

Sula became an alternate selection of the Book-of-the-Month Club, excerpts were published in *Redbook* magazine, and it was nominated for the 1975 National Book Award in fiction.

From 1976 to 1977, Morrison was a visiting lecturer at Yale University and was writing her third novel. In this work, she focused on strong black male characters, with insight gained from watching her sons. *Song of Solomon* (1977) brought her national attention, winning the National Book Critics Circle Award and the American Academy and Institute of Arts and Letters Award. In 1980, President Jimmy Carter appointed her to the National Council on the Arts. The next year, she published her fourth novel, *Tar Baby* (1981). For the first time, she described the interaction between black and white characters, exploring conflicts of race, class, and gender.

Morrison continued to forge her place in American literary history. Her picture appeared on the cover of the March 30, 1981, issue of *Newsweek* magazine. In 1983, she left her position at Random House, having worked there for almost 20 years. In 1984, she was named the Albert Schweitzer Professor of the Humanities at the State University of New York in Albany. While living in Albany, she started writing her first play, *Dreaming Emmett*. It was based on the true story of Emmett Till, a black teenager killed by racist whites in 1955 after being accused of making a snide remark to (or perhaps of whistling or catcalling at) a white woman. The play premiered January 4, 1986, at the Marketplace Theater in Albany.

Morrison's next novel, *Beloved* (1987), was influenced by a published story about a slave, Margaret Garner, who in 1851 escaped with her children, fleeing to Ohio and leaving behind her master in Kentucky. When she was about to be recaptured, she tried to kill her children rather than return them to a life of slavery. Only her infant daughter died, and Margaret was imprisoned for her deed. She refused to show remorse, saying she was unwilling to have her children suffer slavery as she had. *Beloved* became a best-seller, winning a 1988 Pulitzer Prize for fiction.

In 1987, Morrison was named the Robert F. Goheen Professor in the Council of Humanities at Princeton University. She became the first black woman writer to sit in an endowed chair at an Ivy League university. She taught creative writing and also took part in the African-American studies, American studies, and women's studies programs.

In 1993, Toni Morrison received the Nobel Prize for literature. She was the eighth woman and the first black woman to do so. A work of criticism, *Playing in the Dark, Whiteness and the Literary Imagination,* was published in 1992.

(EDITOR'S NOTE: Morrison's *Jazz* was also published in 1992. In 1999 she and her son Slade published their rhyming picture book, the inspiration for which arose when Slade was just nine years old. Morrison has also edited several other volumes, including a posthumous collection of **Toni Cade Bambara**'s work, *Deep Sightings and Rescue Missions: Fiction, Essays, and Conversations* [1996/1999]. When accepting the Nobel Prize, Morrison noted, "Winning as an American is very special—but winning as a black American is a knockout." References: *BDAA*. Amazon.com, 1/2000.)

—*Michael Strickland and Lisa Bahlinger*

REFERENCES: Bauer, Eric Jerome (1997), "Biographical Information on Toni Morrison," http://www.viconet.com/~ejb/bio.htm. Bauer (1997), "Toni Morrison: Women of Hope, African Americans Who Made a Difference," http://www.mvhs.srvusd.k12.ca.us/~jaymeyer/toni.html. Century, Douglas (1994), *Toni Morrison* (Chelsea House Publishers). Lifetime Online (1997), "Connections: Toni Morrison," http://www.lifetimetv.com/Connections/toni.htm. Morrison, Toni (1970), *The Bluest Eye* (New York: Knopf). Samuels, Wilfred D., and Hudson-Weems, Clenora (1990), *Twayne's United States Authors Series: Toni Morrison* (Boston: Twayne).

Mosley, Walter (Ellis) (1/12/1952–)
Novels, especially mysteries

Walter Mosley's parents Leroy (an African-American school custodian) and Ella (a Jewish-American schoolteacher and school administrator) raised him in South Central Los Angeles, where he attended public schools. Leroy plays a central role in many of Walter's novels, in that Walter's Easy Rawlins character bears a striking resemblance to Leroy: Both of them grew up in a ghetto in Houston, Texas; both were involved in combat during World War II; and both knew how to tell a captivating story. In appreciation for his father's literary gifts—his love of language, storytelling skills, and specific tales of Leroy's experiences—Walter dedicated three of his novels to his father.

After high school, Mosley went on to college, eventually earning a political science degree from Vermont's Johnson State College in 1977. After college, he flitted through a few different jobs, working as a potter and a caterer before settling into work as a computer programmer. After a while, he enrolled in a creative writing program at the City College of New York, where he pursued an interest in poetry and then in fiction. By the end of the 1980s, Mosley had quit his job writing computer programs and had written his first novel.

Mosley's first novel, *Devil in a Blue Dress* (1990), is set in the Watts section of Los Angeles in 1948 and is narrated by Mosley's Easy (Ezekiel) Rawlins character. In this novel, World War II veteran Easy loses his aircraft industry job. He has an upcoming mortgage payment and other bills to pay, so he somewhat reluctantly takes a job as a private detective, searching for Daphne Monet, a missing white woman known to hang out in jazz clubs in black parts of town. The case ends up embroiling Easy in an organized crime ring, and issues of race relations and sexual mores during that era further complicate the situation. The novel earned Mosley the John Creasey Award for the year's best first crime novel, the Private Eye Writers of America's Shamus Award, a nomination for the Mystery Writers of America's Edgar Award, and that most lucrative award of all: a 1995 film starring Denzel Washington. (Mosley has also been named President Bill Clinton's favorite writer.)

Mosley's next Easy Rawlins novel was set in 1953: *A Red Death* (1991). In it, Easy is working as a janitor but secretly buys some apartments, thereby getting into some trouble with the Internal Revenue Service (IRS). To wiggle out of this problem (and avoid prosecution), he's asked to do a dirty job for the Federal Bureau of Investigation (FBI): He is supposed to spy on a labor-union organizer. This McCarthy-era dirty deed leads Easy into an investigation for murder.

The next Easy Rawlins sequel, *White Butterfly* (1992), takes place in 1956. Easy has married, and he and his wife have a new baby girl. Three young African-American women are viciously slaughtered, but the police show only lackluster interest in solving the crimes. However, when the serial killer murders Cyndi Starr, a white college coed and stripper known as the "White Butterfly," the police decide that they need outside help to solve the crime, so they call on Easy to help them find the murderer.

The events in Mosley's fourth Easy Rawlins novel, *Black Betty* (1994), occur in 1961. By this time, Rawlins has separated from his wife and child, and he has two children living with him. His adopted Mexican son Jesus was made mute by traumatic early experiences as a child prostitute, and his adopted daughter Feather was orphaned when her white grandfather killed her mother after finding out that Feather's father was black. A wealthy Beverly Hills family hires Easy for another missing-persons case. It turns out that the missing housekeeper is Elizabeth Eady, with whom Easy was infatuated when he was a young boy.

Mosley's model for Easy, his father Leroy, died of cancer in 1993. In 1995, Mosley published a different kind of novel, *RL's Dream* (1995), about a dying elderly blues guitarist who reflects back on blues musician Robert Johnson. Since then, Mosley has written additional Rawlins novels: a sequel, *A Little Yellow Dog* (1996), and a prequel, *Gone Fishin'* (1997), which Rawlins decided to publish with Black Classic Press, a small, independent African-American publisher. Other Mosley novels center around his character "Socrates," a streetwise philosopher of sorts.

Mosley has been quoted as saying that Easy Rawlins novels will continue until Easy reaches his seventies (some time in the historical setting of the 1980s). Easy's character appeals to readers because this working-class hero is imperfect, flawed. He has trouble with his personal relationships, financial woes, and anger-control issues. Although he's streetwise and crafty, he often makes mistakes in his sleuthing. He tries to stick to his principles, but practical concerns sometimes make him stray a little from time to time. Mosley's character never whines, but he does candidly tell of his interactions with racist police officers and other situations involving racial discrimination and prejudice. Also, Easy sometimes gets help from his sidekick and best friend, Raymond "Mouse" Alexander, who frequently explodes into violence with little provocation. Overall, Mosley's characters have added to the American literary canon some distinctive twentieth-century African-American perspectives, experiences, and language.

REFERENCES: *AA:PoP. EB-98. EBLG. MAAL. MWEL. NAAAL. OC20LE.* Foster, Frances Smith, in *OCAAL.*

Mossell, Gertrude (née) Bustill
(7/3/1855–1/21/1948)
Poems, essays

The most memorable work by Mossell is her book *The Work of the Afro-American Woman* (pub-

lished under her married name, Mrs. N. F. Mossell, 1894; reprinted 1988, with an introduction by **Joanne Braxton**). In it, she offers 17 poems and 8 essays celebrating the achievements of African-American women in almost every field of endeavor. She also wrote *Little Danisie's One Day at Sabbath School* (1902, a book for children) and myriad articles for both white and black periodicals. Mossell shared her beliefs in the value of her race and her sex with her family. Her great-aunt was abolitionist and educator Grace Bustill Douglass (whose daughter was **Sarah Mapps Douglass**), and her nephew was **Paul Robeson**.

—*Tonya Bolden*

REFERENCES: *BAAW.* Ashe, Bertram D., in *OCAAL.*

Motley, Willard (1909–1965)
Novels, diaries, essays; journal cofounder

When Willard was only 13 years old, the *Chicago Defender* (see **Robert Abbott**) published his first short story. Because the Great Depression prevented his going to college, Motley plunged into writing full time with help from the Federal Writers' Project (in 1940) and a couple of fellowships. He also cofounded a literary journal during this time. Motley's novels include his best-seller *Knock on Any Door* (1947), *Let No Man Write My Epitaph* (1958), *We Fished All Night* (1951), and *Let Noon Be Fair* (1966). His first two novels were made into movies. Although his novels addressed issues of social class and poverty, they were not strongly identified with his race at a time when race consciousness was emerging, so his reputation and popularity declined. He died in relative poverty and near obscurity in Mexico, where this lifelong bachelor had adopted a son. Since his death, however, his diaries have been published (*The Diaries of Willard Motley,* 1979, Jerome Klinkowitz, Ed.).

REFERENCES: Fikes, Robert, Jr., in *OCAAL.*

Moutoussamy-Ashe, Jeanne (1951–)
Nonfiction—photograph books

Among Moutoussamy-Ashe's photo essays are *Daufauskie Island: A Photographic Essay* (1982), about the cultural heritage evident in the Gullah-speaking residents of a South Carolina sea island; *Viewfinders: Black Women Photographers* (1986, including photographers as early as the 1860s); and

Daddy and Me (a photo essay of everyday experiences observing her husband, tennis player **Arthur Ashe,** with their daughter, Camera, with text authored by Camera). Moutoussamy-Ashe also provided the photographs for her husband's book *Getting Started in Tennis* (1977). Since her husband died of AIDS-related complications (in 1993), she has continued her photojournalism work for such periodicals as *Life, Smithsonian, Sports Illustrated, Ebony, Essence,* and *Black Enterprise.*

REFERENCES: *33T.* Alexander, Adele Logan, in *BWA:AHE.* McDaniel, Karen Cotton, in *PBW.*

Murphy, Beatrice M. (1908–1992)
Poems, columns, anthologies, reviews; editor

In addition to her own poetry collections—*Love Is a Terrible Thing* (1945) and *The Rocks Cry Out* (1969)—Murphy edited the poetry anthologies *Negro Voices* (1938), *Ebony Rhythm* (1948), and *New Negro Voices* (1970), which brought to prominence the work of young and previously unknown poets. She also published numerous poems and critical reviews in various periodicals while working as a columnist (e.g., for the Associated Negro Press), a book review editor (e.g., for the *Afro-American*), and a journal editor (*Bibliographic Survey: The Negro in Print,* 1965–1972). Even so, perhaps her most significant contribution to literature was to found the Negro Bibliographic and Research Center in the 1960s.

REFERENCES: Andrews, Larry R., in *OCAAL.*

Murphy, Carl (1/17/1889–2/26/1967)
Newspaper publisher

Carl's father, John Henry Murphy, had bought the weekly ***Baltimore Afro-American*** before Carl graduated from Howard and Harvard universities. In 1918, John Henry's health began to fail, so Carl Murphy took the reins as editor of his father's paper. When John Henry died four years later, Carl became the paper's publisher, overseeing a circulation of about 14,000. Carl's vision extended beyond Baltimore, and he expanded the paper's reach to Washington, D.C.; Richmond, Virginia; Philadelphia, Pennsylvania; and Newark, New Jersey. He also expanded the paper's coverage to include national and international events as well as local news. Under his stewardship, the paper had a circulation of more than 200,000, with semiweekly editions. The paper, still in publication, is the sec-

ond-oldest continuously published African-American newspaper (founded in 1892). For his (and his paper's) contributions to numerous civil rights endeavors (e.g., providing funding for court cases opposing Jim Crow laws), Murphy was awarded the National Association for the Advancement of Colored People's prestigious Spingarn Medal in 1955.

—*Tonya Bolden*

REFERENCES: *SMKC.*

Murray, Albert L. (5/12/1916–)
Essays, novels, criticism, memoir, nonfiction

Mattie (James) Murray, a homemaker, and her husband, a manual laborer (named either Hugh or Albert Lee), adopted little Albert and raised him in Magazine Point, a little town outside of Mobile, Alabama. Early on, Albert developed a passionate interest in literature and music. With the guidance of Mobile County Training School principal Benjamin Francis Baker, Albert excelled academically and became a talented athlete.

In 1935, he won a scholarship to the Tuskegee Institute, where he delved deeply into studying literature, reading both the assigned texts and numerous other works, including those by scholars championing modern literature. (He was there at the same time **Ralph Ellison** was, but at that time Ellison was a music major, so the two did not become close friends until later on. Nonetheless, Murray shared Ellison's interest in America's cultural complexity, especially the influence of African Americans, and he highlighted Ellison's literary influence in a series of lectures Murray gave in the 1970s.) After earning his bachelor's degree at Tuskegee (1939), he went on to graduate study at the University of Michigan. He returned to Tuskegee for a while to teach English and theater there, and then in 1943 he enlisted in the U.S. Air Force, where he stayed for the next two decades. While in the service, he earned a master's degree at New York University (1948).

In 1962, Murray retired from the Air Force as a major. Since then, he has lived on the East Coast (mostly in New York City) and has been a visiting professor, writer-in-residence, and special lecturer in various schools, including Barnard (New York City), Colgate University (Hamilton, New York), Columbia University School of Journalism (New York City), Emory University (Atlanta), the University of Massachusetts at Boston, and Washington and Lee (Lexington, Virginia).

Through his essays, literary criticism, memoirs, and even his fiction, Murray has made clear his belief in the powerful influence of African Americans on American culture. He particularly values the blues idiom and touts its importance to American culture, not just in music but also in literature and other aspects of artistic expression. He expresses similar sentiments for jazz as well.

Murray's first published volume was his collection of essays and reviews *The Omni-Americans* (1970), in which he criticized what he called "social science fiction," which emphasizes the subordination of African Americans in American culture. Instead, Murray contends that African Americans have always played a vital role in the cultural development of this country, and he supports this contention with examples from history, music, and literature. As he observed, "The background experience of U.S. Negroes includes all of the negative things that go with racism and segregation; but it also includes all of the challenging things that make for ambition, integrity, and transcendent achievement" (quoted in *AAW:AAPP*). In Murray's view, African Americans, far from being marginalized victims of the dominant culture, are the quintessential Americans, *Omni-Americans* who embrace the riches of America's diverse cultural heritages.

After showing the national—and perhaps global—impact of African Americans, Murray took his readers on a very personal journey into his own experiences in his memoir *South to a Very Old Place* (1971). In the narrative, Murray takes his readers along a geographical journey from New York to Alabama and a chronological journey from the present to the days of his boyhood. Along the way, he visits with and interviews a wide array of Southerners, white and black, humble and high ranking. His work is an intriguing blend of the **oral tradition** and the new journalism, chronicling the changes from the rule of Jim Crow through the heyday of the civil rights movement to the end of the 1960s.

Murray's next major publication was a collection from the Paul Anthony Brick lectures he gave at the University of Missouri, *The Hero and the Blues* (1973). The theme of these lectures centers on the importance of the blues (and jazz) idiom to contemporary literature, illustrated by the works of Ralph Ellison and **Richard Wright**, as well as those of James Joyce, Ernest Hemingway, and Thomas Mann. In this collection of lectures, Murray also offers this sound advice to aspiring artists of all kinds: "Such is the nature of art that the only thing the creative person is justified in straining for is his personal point of view, and paradoxically this probably has much to do not with straining but with learning to relax so as to discover how one actually feels about things" (quoted in *AAW:AAPP*).

In Stomping the Blues (1976) continued Murray's emphasis on the blues (and jazz) idiom, highlighting its value as a life-affirming, constructive response to deprivation and misery. Touted as one of the best—if not the best—books on the aesthetics of jazz, it won the Deems Taylor Award for music criticism in 1977. Murray's next major project was to cowrite jazz pianist, bandleader, and composer Count Basie's autobiography *Good Morning Blues* (1985). Through this work, he was able to personalize the aesthetic theory he had described in previous works. Murray's most recent essay collection is *The Blue Devils of Nada* (1996), in which he describes the process of writing Basie's autobiography, and he analyzes the artistry of Romare Bearden, Duke Ellington, and Ernest Hemingway, showing—once again—the influence of the blues idiom. In Murray's view, the best way to triumph over "the blue devils of nada" (the meaninglessness and randomness of the forces of decay) is through embracing the blues.

In addition to his nonfiction, Murray has written a few novels tracing the life of a charming, clever fellow named "Scooter," whose life experiences often resemble Murray's own. Murray started working on his first novel after retiring from the military, and he continued to work on it intermittently for the next three decades. At last, in 1974, *Train Whistle Guitar* appeared in print and won the Lillian Smith Award for Southern Fiction. The novel starts in the 1920s, during Scooter's boyhood in Alabama. There, Scooter learns not just from his school textbooks but also from the adults in his community and his home. The next part of Scooter's story appears in *The Spyglass Tree* (1991), in which he goes to college (a very Tuskegee-like institution), and his worldview grows ever wider. In *Seven League Boots* (1996), Scooter has graduated from college and gets a job as a bass player with a Duke Ellington–like band. As you would expect, in all these works Murray pays careful attention to rhythm in his storytelling, and his stories have a jazzy, bluesy feel to them.

REFERENCES: *AAW:AAPP. EB-BH-CD. EBLG. NAAAL. WDAA.* Brown, Eva Stahl, in *EA-99.* Shank, Barry, in *OCAAL.*

Murray, (Anna) "Pauli" (Pauline)
(11/20/1910–7/1/1985)
Autobiographies, poems, nonfiction—law

Before she died, Agnes Georgianna Fitzgerald Murray gave birth to six children, the fourth of which was Pauli. Both Agnes and her husband, William Henry Murray, were of racially mixed ancestry and middle-class status. Sadly, however, Agnes died in March of 1914, before little Pauli was four years old. William was overwhelmed with grief and with the care for his many children, so Pauline Fitzgerald Dame, Agnes's oldest sister, adopted her namesake and moved her from Baltimore to her home in Durham, North Carolina, near the Fitzgeralds, Agnes and Pauline's parents. In 1917, William was committed to a mental institution, and in 1923 he died there.

Pauline was a schoolteacher, and she taught little Pauli to read and write when Pauli was quite young. Pauli attended Durham's segregated public schools, graduating from Hillside High School in 1926. After that, she moved to New York City, where she hoped to enter Hunter College, but before she could do that, she had to attend Richmond Hill High School for one year because of rigorous college entrance requirements. At Hunter, she majored in English and minored in history, and she immersed herself in the world of literature. She had entered Hunter just as the Great Depression was forcing an end to the **Harlem Renaissance**. Nonetheless, while there, she met **Sterling A. Brown**, **Countee Cullen**, **Robert Hayden**, **Langston Hughes**, and **Dorothy West**, and she was stirred profoundly by Stephen Vincent Benét's poetry, especially his "John Brown's Body." Although a brief marriage temporarily interrupted her studies, she graduated from Hunter College in 1933, among the 4 African-American students in the class of 247 women. Later on, Hughes and Benét were important mentors for Murray, encouraging her and helping her get her works published.

After college, she worked for a while as a schoolteacher. After unsuccessfully trying to be the first African American to enroll at the University of North Carolina at Chapel Hill (which later awarded her an honorary degree and honored her with a scholarship in her name), she was accepted to Howard University Law School in Washington, D.C. There she was the top student in her class and the only female when she earned her LL.B. degree in 1944. As if this weren't enough, she was also actively participating in nonviolent civil rights demonstrations, such as by taking freedom rides and leading student sit-ins at Washington-area restaurants. The next obstacle she faced was on trying to enter Harvard Law School, where her race posed no problem; rather, she was denied entry to the all-male graduate law program at Harvard University because she was a woman. Once again, Murray found another way, completing an L.L.M. degree at Boalt Hall of Law at the University of California at Berkeley in 1945.

In the mid-1940s, Pauli Murray was clearly an up-and-comer, named one of the twelve outstanding women in Negro life (1945) by the National Council of Negro Women, deputy attorney general of California (the first woman to hold that post, 1946), and Woman of the Year by *Mademoiselle* magazine (1947). Her law practice included being a member of the California, New York, and Supreme Court bars, serving on a presidential (Kennedy's) commission (1962–1963), and championing victims' rights in numerous sex discrimination cases. In 1966, she, Betty Friedan, and others helped found the National Organization for Women (NOW). The previous year, she had become the first African American (man or woman) to be awarded Yale University Law School's doctor of juridical science degree (1965), with her dissertation "Roots of the Racial Crisis: Prologue to Policy." Starting in 1968, she taught law and constitutional history at Brandeis University, as well as at Yale and in Ghana.

During this time, she wrote and published several books on law and jurisprudence. These included *Human Rights U.S.A., 1948–1966* (1967) and *States' Law on Race and Color* (1951), which **Thurgood Marshall** touted as the best available reference book for lawyers who advocated civil rights and fought segregation in the courts. She also coauthored (with Leslie Rubin) *The Constitution and Government of Ghana* (1961), held to be the first textbook on law there. Murray received numerous honorary degrees in recognition of her scholarship and her legal work on behalf of civil rights.

After a lifetime of achievement, when many others would have happily retired and savored their successes, in 1972 Murray "heard (and heeded) the call" to the ministry. Four years later, she had earned her master's degree in divinity from General Theological Seminary, and in January 1977 she was consecrated as a minister, the first African-American female priest to be ordained in the 200-year-old Episcopal Church.

Murray's law books were not the only—or even the first—publications she wrote. Her interest in writing had started in early adolescence, and in the early 1950s she had been a resident at the prestigious MacDowell Colony for writers, with **James Baldwin**. In 1956, after years of research, she published *Proud Shoes: The Story of an American Family* (1956; revised 1978), a memoir of the interracial Fitzgerald family. Through her family's personal history, Murray offers readers greater insight into the wider historical context of racism, interracial relationships, and sexism. Three decades later, Murray finished her own autobiography, *Song in a Weary Throat: An American Pilgrimage* (1987), which chronicles her commitment to political and social activism and her spiritual quest leading to her ordination. The book, not published until after her death, was honored with the Robert F. Kennedy Book Award and the Christopher Award, and it was reprinted in 1989 as *Pauli Murray: The Autobiography of a Black Activist*. As with her family memoir, her personal memoir illuminates the broader historical context in which she lived and to which she contributed greatly.

Starting in the 1930s, while Murray was first opening herself to the world of literature, she began writing poems, and she continued to do so over the next four decades. In 1970, her poems were collected in *Dark Testament and Other Poems.* As with her other works, these poems include insights into both her personal experiences and her political and social concerns. Because the poems were written in such a historically and politically dynamic time, they aptly reflect the historical changes that occurred during their writing.

REFERENCES: *EA-99. EBLG. G-97. OC20LE.* Jacobs, Sylvia M., in *BWA:AHE.* Hughes, Sheila Hassell, in *OCAAL.*

Myers, Walter Dean (8/12/1937–)

Juvenile novels and nonfiction, picture books, poems; editor

When Walter was just three years old, Herbert and Florence Dean adopted him and moved him from Martinsburg, West Virginia, to New York City's Harlem neighborhood. For Myers, Harlem was an engaging community, rich with opportunities for playing games with his pals on the street, for daydreaming about being a cowboy or a famous athlete, for listening to his grandfather's biblical stories or his adoptive father's scary stories,

and for delving into the world of books. As a young boy, he especially enjoyed *The Three Musketeers* and *Little Men,* but as a teenager, he started longing for books that more realistically related to his own experiences. Unfortunately, on those all-too-rare occasions when he could find *anything* written about African Americans, they were depicted as criminals or as victims and, in any case, people who didn't make positive contributions to the world.

Later, as Myers recalled, "After leaving school and a stint in the army, I bounced around in a series of jobs, none very satisfying, until I finally reached a point where I was writing full time. I was writing fiction primarily, putting my world on paper, exploring the real and imagined lives that comprise my existence. I had found that my real life, the life in which I found my truest self, was the life of the mind. And this life is the one I would use to write my books" (Myers, "Voices of the Creators," in *CBC*). When he was first learning his craft, he joined **John Killens**'s writers workshop, where he got to know fellow writers such as **Askia Touré**. In 1970, he became an acquisitions editor for the publisher Bobbs-Merrill. In this role, he was able to help **Nikki Giovanni**, **Ann Shockley**, and other writers get their work published—and he figured out quite a lot about writing and publishing in the process.

In addition to having written and published more than 40 books himself, Myers had his writing widely published in numerous periodicals. Among the many awards he has been given for his writing are such prestigious citations as the American Library Association Best Book for Young Adults, the Newbery Honor Book, the *Boston Globe*/Horn Book Honor Book, and the Coretta Scott King Award. One of the earliest and most important honors he received, however, was the appreciation of his son, to whom he told his stories and who offered him excellent critical feedback regarding how to tell a captivating story.

In addition to being prolific, Myers is the master of diverse kinds of fiction and nonfiction for young readers. Just a sampling: *The Righteous Revenge of Artemis Bonner* (1992), a humorous, fanciful Wild West tale; *The Golden Serpent* (1980), an Indian (Asian) fairy tale; *The Black Pearl and the Ghost* (1980) and *Mr. Monkey and the Gotcha Bird* (1984), ghost stories and legends he heard when he was young; *The Nicholas Factor* (1983) and *The Hidden Shrine* (1985), adventure tales set in foreign lands

(Peru and Hong Kong, respectively); and *The Mouse Rap* (1990), droll play with words. His first children's picture book, *Where Does the Day Go?* (1969), won a picture-book competition sponsored by the Council on Interracial Books for Children and was published by *Parent's Magazine* Press. As he later recalled, he entered the contest "more because I wanted to write *anything* than because I wanted to write a picture book" (quoted in *CBC*).

Myers has also written numerous nonfiction works, including *Sweet Illusions* (1987), which explores teen pregnancy from the perspective of 14 different people intimately aware of the issue—and of the experience; *Now Is Your Time! The African-American Struggle for Freedom* (1991), a Coretta Scott King Award–winning history; *Brown Angels: An Album of Pictures and Verse* (1993), in which Myers interweaves his own poems with turn-of-the-twentieth-century photos of African-American children; and *The Great Migration* (1994), in which Myers intersperses his own poems with the artwork of noted artist Jacob Lawrence. In *Malcolm X: By Any Means Necessary* (1993), Myers incorporated photographs, newspaper clippings, interviews, and magazine snippets. His own description of how he approached the writing of this book offers an insight into how a master artisan executes his craft:

> To write *Malcolm X: By Any Means Necessary,* a biography of the fiery black leader, I played his taped voice constantly, surrounded myself with pictures of him as a boy and as a young man, walked down the same Harlem streets that he walked down, and tried to put myself in his classroom when a teacher said that it wasn't practical for him to be an attorney because of his race. In seeing what Malcolm saw, in allowing his voice to fill my imagination, by touching upon those instances of racism that touched my life and mirrored his, I re-created Malcolm as surely as I have created fictional characters. As I wrote, I felt him looking over my shoulder, and so I could write with a sureness of voice, with an authority that went beyond the factual material. (Myers, "Voices of the Creators," in *CBC*)

Needless to say, Myers is a highly innovative, creative, and careful writer. The works for which he is best known are his young adult novels, most of which revolve around youngsters growing up in

Harlem. Although Myers never glosses over issues such as gang violence, street crime, drug use and abuse, economic and racial oppression, and sexuality, his novels are neither heavy nor disheartening. Humor and optimism prevail among his quirky but very likeable characters. Although most of his characters are males, and he focuses mostly on male–male relationships, the female protagonists in his works are depicted as realistic and nonstereotypical. A selection of his many young adult novels include *Fast Sam, Cool Clyde, and Stuff* (1975); *Mojo and the Russians* (1977); *It Ain't All for Nothin'* (1978), which addresses problems of the elderly and of family members involved in criminal activities; *The Young Landlords* (1979), a Coretta Scott King Award–winner; *Won't Know Till I Get There* (1982), about peer loyalties, friendships, and youth crime; and *The Outside Shot* (1984), about the racial prejudice at a Midwestern college confronting an athletic scholarship student from Harlem.

Both *Motown and Didi: A Love Story* (1984) and *Crystal* (1987) include female protagonists; in the former, family troubles pose obstacles to a young woman's success, and in the latter, a highly successful young woman feels unsatisfied with her fame and fortune. Probably one of Myers's best-known novels is *Scorpions* (1988), a Newbery Honor Book about a seventh-grader who longs to feel he's important and that he belongs, so he ends up in a world of trouble by agreeing to hold onto a gun for an older teen who belongs to a gang. *Fallen Angels* (1988) follows a Harlem youth to Vietnam, where he must literally battle to survive as well as to keep from losing his heart and his soul. In *Me, the Mop, and the Moondance Kid* (1988) and *Mop, Moondance, and the Nagasaki Knights* (1992), Mop is a white girl who pals around with two adopted brothers and their softball team.

Like many of Myers's other books, *Somewhere in the Darkness* (1992) explores a troubled father-son relationship. In *Somewhere,* Lonnie's father gets out of prison and decides to get close to his son by having Lonnie go with him to his native Arkansas. Myers ("Voices of the Creators," *CBC*) later reflected, "A book like *Somewhere in the Darkness* deals more with imagined feelings and encounters that might have been. Although I did meet my real father, I had never had an intimate moment with him, had never seen him in that wholeness of being with which we get to know people."

The writers whose works Myers has admired

include **Frank Yerby** and **Langston Hughes**. His most important model, however, comes from his own imagination. For instance, "My son ... finds it amusing to walk into a room to discover me in conversation with imaginary companions, or to see in my face the reflection of some inner dialogue, some adventure of the mind" ("Voices of the Creators," *CBC*). Myers's son Christopher has also delved into Walter Dean's fanciful world, creating the rhythmic rap and the illustrations for his own Coretta Scott King Honor picture book *Black Cat* (1999) and creatively illustrating his father's books *Shadow of the Red Moon* (1995), *Harlem: A Poem* (1997, Caldecott Honor), and *Monster* (1999).

In Myers's young-adult novel *Monster* (1999), 16-year-old Steve is on trial for participating in a crime that led to a murder. An amateur filmmaker, Steve decides to write a movie script of the trial, and he records in a journal his most private thoughts about how his past experiences and choices led to his present situation. Myers thus tells the story by interweaving scenes from the movie script with passages from the journal. In January, 2000, the American Library Association awarded Myers the first Michael L. Printz Award, as well as a Coretta Scott King Honor for the book. The Printz selection committee chair noted, "The detached style of the screen play, juxtaposed with the anguished journal entries, reveals the struggle within Steve's conscience. . . . [Myers's] distinctive format creates narrative and moral suspense that will leave readers with questions that have no real answers" (http://www.ala.org/news/printzaward. html). In this book and others, Myers, "[creates] windows to my world that all may peer into. I share the images, the feelings and thoughts, and, I hope, the delight" ("Voices of the Creator," *CBC*).

REFERENCES: *EBLG*. *WB-99*. Foster, Frances Smith, in *OCAAL*. M. F. S., in *CBC*. Myers, Walter Dean, "Voices of the Creators," in *CBC*. *LLBL*. *About Books,* Aired 4/17/99. http://teacher.scholastic. com/authorsandbooks/authors/myers/bio.html. http://www. ala.org/news/printzaward.html. http://www.ala.org/yalsa/index.html. http://www. ala/org/yalsa/printz/2000winnerpr.html. http://www.ala.org/news/kingawards2000.html. Amazon. Com.

Naylor, Gloria (1/25/1950–)
Novels, screenplays

Best known for her first novel, *The Women of Brewster Place* (1982), which received the American Book Award for best first novel in 1983, Gloria Naylor has become a prominent voice in modern African-American fiction. Her works, which also include *Linden Hills* (1985), *Mama Day* (1988), and *Bailey's Café* (1992), all focus sharply, as Donna Perry has put it, on women's friendships and inter-relationships, "love, tragedy, self-sacrifice and the enduring strength of women."

The Women of Brewster Place comprises the interrelated tales of seven African-American women living on a dead-end street in a Northern ghetto. Besieged and betrayed by men—one character has been stripped of her home and money; one completely deprived of the ability to form her own identity because of her reliance on men; one forced into an abortion that makes her neglect her living child, who then dies of electrocution; and one gang-raped by a group of men who are threatened by her lesbian relationship and feel the need to teach her a lesson—these women, who range in age from their twenties to their fifties, rely on each other for the support they need to get through their devastating experiences.

The novel has been attacked by various critics for creating extremely negative and violent portraits of black men. Naylor claims that her focus, however, comes less out of any dislike she holds for black males and more out of her desire to concentrate intently on black females. She believes that any good story needs to have some type of conflict and turns to male characters as a source for much of it. Her desire to hone in on portraits and issues of women comes out of her belief that society has been taught to value men's stories over women's. She wants her readers to question their own resistance to reading stories solely about women so as to fight this subconscious discrimination.

Naylor's intention to move her readers to a greater awareness of women's issues stems largely from the fact that she had little to no exposure to African-American literature during her younger years. Although she was born in New York City, she was nevertheless born before the height of the civil rights movement and the end of legally sanctioned segregation in the South. Thus, Naylor grew up in a society that had not yet acknowledged the place of African-American writers in the English curriculum. Growing up in New York City as a shy, introverted child who wrote poetry and short science fiction stories and who kept a vast array of journals, she thought that her penchant for writing was freakish because she honestly believed that black women did not write books. Her high school education did little to disabuse her of this notion, as it focused on English and white male U.S. writers but never exposed her to the vast array of African-American literature that was beginning to gain critical attention during those years.

It took a while for Naylor to gain exposure to that literature because after high school she became a Jehovah's Witness missionary for seven years. Her decision to join the fundamentalist group came as a result of her disillusionment with the current system of government. Influenced largely by the presence of the Vietnam War throughout her years in high school and the assassination of **Martin Luther King, Jr.**, in her senior year, she came to believe things could only get better if the current system of government was overthrown by a theocracy. After seven years, she left the missionary life because despite her belief and hard work, things had not gotten any better. She decided to try to make a difference by operating from within the system rather than hoping that the system would somehow just go away.

Naylor began to study nursing at Medgar Evers College but found herself less interested in nursing and much more interested in English literature, so she decided to pursue her B.A. in English at Brooklyn College. It was while at Brooklyn College that she took a class with poet Joan Larkin, who exposed her to books by **Toni Morrison**, **Alice Walker**, and **Paule Marshall**. These books inspired her to study African-American literature and also to begin writing the short stories that would become *The Women of Brewster Place.* She has claimed, in an interview with Donna Perry, that "*Brewster Place* really got written as a result of my discovering these writers." She continues on to point out that her focus on women in her novels came out of her realization that "women were despised to the point that [students] weren't even taught that they did such wonderful things for the country and the arts" and that her "presence as a black woman and [her] perspective as a woman in general had been underrepresented in American literature."

Spurred on by these beliefs, Naylor decided to pursue a master's degree in African-American studies at Yale. *Linden Hills,* her second book, was her master's thesis. Unlike *Brewster Place,* which she describes as "a gush of raw emotion," *Linden Hills* is structured like, and loosely based on, Dante's *Inferno,* with hell being a black middle-class neighborhood. It is a scathing judgment against black middle-class life, which strives more toward assimilation into white culture than attempting to rise up in society by maintaining black identity.

The figures in *Linden Hills,* particularly the men, are again extremely negative characters. The main character, Luther Nedeed, is a Satanic figure, a descendent of several generations of Nedeeds, all of whom presided over the community and its descent into hollowness by encouraging its members to turn away from their past and who they are. The wives of the Nedeed men have all been "despised" figures stripped of their identity, and the wife of the latest one, Willa, is left the task of reclaiming their identities by finding the ways that the women of the household had left their mark—in Bible scribblings, photos, and recipes. In reviews of this book, Naylor was harshly criticized for creating such negative images of blacks, particularly by those critics who believe that there are enough images of destructive blacks in literature and that black writers should portray positive images.

This criticism has led Naylor to enunciate some of her ideas about the separation of her personal self from her writerly self, as well as leading her to explain the role she believes she plays in the writing of her novels. Naylor feels that her books are "something separate and apart from the way I live my life and try to help my community." Her books seem to have a life of their own and develop organically, almost out of her control. She sees herself as a filter for stories that come to her, stories that begin as images in her mind; these images do not go away and

instead develop as she writes to try to figure out what the images mean. Sometimes she is sad at what she finds, as the writing leads her to report the deaths of characters that she hopes will live or to describe the suffering of characters she hopes will find peace. She allows these developments just to happen rather than altering them to make herself or anyone else happy because she feels she is entrusted with the story and must tell it as it comes. She makes conscious decisions not to censor her characters because she does not believe her art should serve a particular political end—she saves that for her private life. Yet just because she does not skew her art to conform to political ideas does not mean that her work does not have a particular ideology. She feels that every writer has an ideology and that she may be more political than other writers because she feels that her "existence [as an African-American woman] in this country was an act of politics."

Although still ideological, her later novels, *Mama Day* and *Bailey's Café,* seem much more subdued than her earlier ones, with many more positive male characters and strong female ones. These works focus much more on the supernatural but hearken back to her earlier works, if only because all of her novels are linked by carrying over characters from one novel to another. Yet they are also linked by her inimitable writerly style, which is characterized by naturalism and a poetic prose that has the spiritual rhythms of gospel riffs. They are also connected by her move toward constant experimentation, which leads her to draw on both European and American traditions. For instance, *Mama Day* has been seen as being loosely based on both Shakespeare's *The Tempest* and **Toni Morrison**'s *The Song of Solomon,* and *Bailey's Café* has been seen both as a continuation of the experimental narrative work of William Faulkner and as bearing a strong resemblance to Morrison's *Jazz.* Naylor continues to write, working to produce screenplays of her books as well as writing plays. She says that she hopes to continue writing, to have something to say in the twenty-first century, whether in the medium of the novel, the screenplay, the dramatic play, or in producing movies of her earlier works.

—*Diane Masiello*

REFERENCES: *AAW. BW:SSCA.* Gates, Henry Louis, Jr., and K. A. Appiah (1993), *Gloria Naylor: Critical Perspectives Past and Present* (New York: Amistad Press). Perry, Donna (1993), *Backtalk: Women Writers Speak Out* (New Brunswick, NJ: Rutgers University Press), pp. 216–244. Yohe, Kristine A., in *OCAAL.*

Neal, "Larry" (Lawrence Paul) (9/5/1937–1/6/1981)

Poems, essays, plays, criticism, anthology; journal founder and editor

Neal wrote two plays (*The Glorious Monster in the Bell of the Horn,* 1976; and *In an Upstate Motel: A Morality Play,* 1980), numerous literary reviews (published in various periodicals), and many poems (collected in the books *Black Boogaloo: Notes on Black Liberation,* 1969; and *Hoodoo Hollerin' Bebop Ghosts,* 1971/1974). In addition, some of his writings have been published in the posthumous collection *Visions of a Liberated Future: Black Arts Movement Writings* (1989). His importance to the **Black Arts movement**, however, may be more closely related to his work in cofounding a repertory theater (with **Amiri Baraka**), founding and editing several literary journals of that movement (e.g., *Journal of Black Poetry, Cricket, Liberator Magazine*), and coediting the anthology *Black Fire: An Anthology of Afro-American Writing* (1968, also with Baraka). His essays in *Black Fire* are considered some of the clearest statements of the **Black Aesthetic**.

REFERENCES: Engelhardt, Elizabeth Sanders Delwiche, in *OCAAL.* Hudson, Peter, in *EA-99.*

Neely, Barbara (1941–)

Short stories, novels

Although Neely's two novels, *Blanche on the Lam* (1992) and *Blanch among the Talented Tenth* (1994), have been well received, her passion for writing focuses on the short-story form, and her stories are widely anthologized and published in journals such as *Essence.* In all her stories—long and short—Neely considers issues of race, gender, and class, reflecting her life's work as a feminist social activist.

REFERENCES: Govan, Sandra Y., in *OCAAL.*

Negro American Literature Forum
See Black American Literature Forum

Negro Digest (also known as Black World and First World) (1942–1951, 1961–1976, 1977–1983)

In 1942, publisher **John H. Johnson**, who also published *Ebony, Tan Confessions,* and *Jet* magazines, created *Negro Digest,* originally a monthly, published from 1942 to 1951. Its style imitated *Reader's Digest,* and it contained articles of general interest to African Americans, with an emphasis on racial progress and occasional reprints from mainstream white publications. *Negro Digest* ceased publication in 1951 and then reappeared ten years later with the same basic mission but a greater emphasis on African-American literature, history, and culture.

Hoyt Fuller, the digest's managing editor, became the most influential editor among African-American journal editors at that time. When Fuller's ideology became more focused on black power and black arts, the change was reflected in the magazine, with an increasing emphasis on what Fuller perceived as the responsibility of black writers to be politically and publicly committed to black causes. By 1970, the name of the magazine changed to *Black World* to more accurately reflect the new direction.

The final issue appeared in 1976, but it later reappeared as *First World,* a relatively more polished journal, from 1977 to 1983, published by the First World Foundation of Atlanta, Georgia, edited by **Hoyt Fuller** and Carole A. Parks. *First World* featured fiction, poetry, journalism, and scholarly pieces addressing a broad range of issues, including apartheid, environmental issues, and desegregation. Many well-known writers were published in this journal, including **John Henrik Clarke**, **June Jordan**, and Sterling Stuckey.

—*Lisa Bahlinger*

REFERENCES: *EAACH* (Vol. 1). Sale, Maggie, "*First World,*" in *OCAAL.*

Negro World (1918–1933)

The literary journal of **Marcus Garvey**'s Universal Negro Improvement Association (UNIA), *Negro World* was published from 1918 to 1933. This journal may have been the most widely read black periodical of its time. Marcus Garvey was a journalist and activist, and *Negro World* promoted art and writing that supported racial equality and freedom, especially among new and emerging writers. If Garvey had not been arrested and deported, *Negro World* would probably have rivaled the currently better known and more politically moderate journals *Crisis, Opportunity,* and *Messenger.*

—*Lisa Bahlinger*

REFERENCES: Sale, Maggie, in *OCAAL.*

Nell, William C. (Cooper)
(12/20/1816–5/25/1874)
Nonfiction—history; newspaper printer

As a young man, Nell apprenticed himself as a printer for William Lloyd Garrison's *Liberator* newspaper. A little later, he switched to working with **Frederick Douglass**, publishing his *North Star,* also an abolitionist newspaper. Meanwhile, Nell was doing research, making notes, interviewing those with first- or second-hand information, checking cemeteries for facts and figures, gathering honorable discharge papers and war memorabilia (e.g., flags or banners), and investigating whatever he could find out about African-American soldiers who had fought in the American Revolutionary War and the War of 1812. In 1851, he published his 23-page pamphlet, *Services of Colored Americans in the Wars of 1776 and 1812,* which he revised and published again in 1852. By 1855, he had expanded his pamphlet to a full-length book—nearly 400 pages—published as *The Colored Patriots of the American Revolution, with Sketches of Several Distinguished Colored Persons: To Which Is Added a Brief Survey of the Condition and Prospects of Colored Americans.* In addition to this historic—and historical—writing, Nell continued as an abolitionist orator and journalist, and he is reputed to have helped **Harriet Ann Jacobs** publish her autobiography.
— *Tonya Bolden*

REFERENCES: *SMKC.* Eiselein, Gregory, in *OCAAL.* Quarles, Benjamin (1988), in *BM:EAAHH.*

Nelson, Marilyn
See **Waniek, Marilyn Nelson**

Newsome, (Mary) Effie (née) Lee
(?/?/1885–1979)
Children's literature, poems; editor

Newsome's primary contribution to literature was her work as *Crisis* magazine's editor of a literary column for children (1925–1929), filling the column with delicious verses and short stories (e.g., fables and parables). Some of her poems for children also appear in her anthology *Gladiola Garden* (1940), and her poems for adults have been anthologized by **Langston Hughes** and **Arna Bontemps**. She was also an outspoken advocate for increasing the amount of children's literature by and about Africans and African Americans.

REFERENCES: MacCann, Donnarae, in *OCAAL.*

Nugent, Richard Bruce (a.k.a. Richard Bruce, Bruce Nugent)
(7/2/1906–5/27/1987)
Poems, short stories, plays; journal cofounder, coeditor

Nugent securely ensconced himself in the center of the flame of the **Harlem Renaissance** when he cofounded the short-lived literary journal *Fire!!* with **Wallace Thurman** (the journal's editor), **Langston Hughes** (the driving force behind it), **Zora Neale Hurston**, and Aaron Douglas. The solitary issue of *Fire!!* included two of his brush-and-ink drawings and his "Smoke, Lilies and Jade," which was probably the first published short story written by an African American explicitly depicting a homosexual encounter. (Nugent had been openly gay since his late teens, but he often used pseudonyms to protect his mother from being denigrated or embarrassed because of his homosexuality.) Although some certainly shunned him for his gay identity, he had numerous gay or bisexual contemporaries with whom to associate, including E. M. Forster, **Langston Hughes**, **Alain Locke**, and **Carl Van Vechten**.

After *Fire!!* flickered out, Nugent coedited (with Thurman) and boldly illustrated *Harlem* (1928). Both his artwork and his poems were published in ***Opportunity*** and ***Crisis*** magazines, as well as *Ebony* and other periodicals, and many were anthologized (e.g., his first poem, "Shadows," which was anthologized by **Countee Cullen** in 1927), although they haven't been collected into a single volume. His short story "Sahdji," which includes themes of homosexuality and biblical imagery, served as the starting point for his one-act musical *Sahdji: An African Ballet* (with music by William Grant Still). The play was later anthologized in Alain Locke's *Plays of Negro Life: A Sourcebook of Native American Drama* (1927) and was produced in 1932. In addition to his writing and his artwork, Nugent acted.

REFERENCES: *EA-99. EB-BH-CD. WDAA.* Grant, Nathan L., in *OCAAL.*

Oliver, Diane Alene
(7/28/1943–5/21/1966)
Short stories

While at the University of North Carolina at Greensboro, Oliver was managing editor of her campus newspaper, started writing short stories, studied poetry under Randall Jarrell, and served as guest editor of the June 1964 issue of *Mademoiselle* magazine. Just days before she graduated from college, she was killed in an auto/motorcycle accident, thus cutting short her promising literary career. Several of her short stories were published, but we can only imagine what works she might have produced had she lingered a little longer.

REFERENCES: Smith, Virginia Whatley, in *OCAAL*.

Opportunity: A Journal of Negro Life
(1923–1949)

Opportunity, the official publication of the National Urban League, was originally intended as a scientific journal with a sociological point of view of African-American life. During the 1920s, however, the magazine was instrumental in encouraging young writers and artists of the **Harlem Renaissance**, including **Langston Hughes**, **Countee Cullen**, **James Weldon Johnson**, **Claude McKay**, **Gwendolyn Bennett**, and **Sterling A. Brown**. The 1930s brought some dissension on the editorial board as to the vision of the journal, and the Great Depression brought financial difficulties. In the 1940s, despite a lack of funds, the journal was an important voice for wartime discussions of racial equality. *Opportunity* journal was an early champion of integration.

EDITOR'S NOTE: Sociologist **Charles [Spurgeon] Johnson** founded the journal while directing research for the league during the 1920s.

—*Lisa Bahlinger*

REFERENCES: *EAACH* (Vol. 4).

Oral Tradition (including *griot, storytelling*)

The oral tradition is the custom of preserving and transmitting a culture's body of beliefs, knowledge, and literature through word of mouth, from person to person, across generations. Since the first human grunted, wailed, or chortled to a fellow human, the oral tradition was the primary means of communicating and preserving the shared knowledge of a culture. Such knowledge, known as folklore, included ancestry, lineage, and history, as well as myths, legends, religious beliefs, and the oral equivalent of how-to books. Other aspects of folklore may be aided by the oral tradition but rely more on shared observance than on speaking and listening; these aspects include festivals, ritual celebrations (e.g., harvest, planting), rites (e.g., birth, coming-of-age, marriage, death), dances, music and rhythms, costumes, games, foods, arts and crafts, and other customs.

When specialized knowledge must be preserved orally across generations, particular individuals often assume responsibility for memorizing and transmitting that information. For instance, tribal *shamans* take charge of the extensive spiritual, religious, and healing beliefs and practices of a culture. In addition to knowing how to use folk medicines, shamans must know words of healing and power: charms, remedies, superstitions, omens, divination rituals, spells, religious beliefs, and perhaps communications with deceased ancestors, spirit guides, or deities. Village *griots* memorize the lineage and folk history of families within their communities; traveling troubadours learn and perform the folk songs of a given region; chiefs and other leaders master the laws, codes, and mores of the groups they lead; elders transmit **folktales** from one generation to the next; and eyewitnesses to important events tell family and friends about what they saw.

By definition, the knowledge preserved through the oral tradition must be memorized. Hence, oral folklore usually has distinctive features that aid memorization. For instance, folk songs usually include repetitive refrains and predictable rhythms and rhymes; they may use the same familiar tunes with various lyrics. Folk stories usually include a familiar set of phrases (e.g., "Once upon a time") and actions (e.g., the antagonist challenges the protagonist, then the protagonist defeats the challenger). These stories follow predictable plot lines with recurring themes. Folk stories also evoke vivid imagery and intense emotions, which help the storyteller (and the listeners) envision the characters and events. The stories center on plot, as the setting is either ambiguous (e.g., "Long ago and far away") or unvarying. These stories usually rely on a set of somewhat stereotyped characters with relatively predictable behavior. Whatever the form of folk information, however, it must be exciting—or at least attention getting—or listeners will not learn and retain the folklore. The information must be as simple and concise as possible. As **Zora Neale Hurston** said, "Folklore is the boiled-down juice, or pot-likker, of human living."

Within the oral tradition, oral literature serves important functions: communal sharing of an experience, entertainment and diversion, shared understandings of communal history and religious beliefs, moral and social education, and safe opportunities to flout social conventions and cultural taboos. Oral literature takes a wide variety of forms: very brief forms (e.g., **proverbs**, riddles, and jokes), poems (e.g., rhymes, verse narratives), chants and songs (e.g., lullabies, ballads, work songs), realistic short stories and anecdotes, and various folktales.

There are many variations within each type of folktale, and the various forms of folktales often overlap. In myths, deities and demigods use superhuman powers to create the universe and all the habitants of it. In *folk epics, legends,* and *tall tales,* a hero (e.g., John Henry, Odysseus, Robin Hood) who lacks superhuman powers still manages to accomplish seemingly impossible feats. *Fairy tales* and *märchen* are unbelievable fantasies involving magical assistance, such as from fairy godmothers, golden-egg-laying geese, or Jack's amazing beans. The most common animal tales are **trickster tales** and fables. *Fables* are brief moralistic or cautionary stories in which animal characters speak and act like humans. *Formula tales* follow a predictable pattern. These include *cumulative tales,* in which the storyteller continually adds new elements to a base statement or phrase (e.g., "The House That Jack Built"); *endless stories,* in which the story action is repeated—endlessly; *catch stories,* in which the story seems to be proceeding down one predictable path, when suddenly the story ends in a surprising—and usually humorous—way; and *dilemma tales,* in which the storyteller sets up a tricky situation or problem and invites the listeners to supply the ending or solution.

Africa has a particularly rich oral literature, at least in part because there was no written language in most of sub-Saharan Africa until the nineteenth century. Exceptions include Ge'ez (Ethiopia), Arabic (Saharan Africa), Swahili (East African coast), and Arabic-influenced Hausa writing (parts of Nigeria, Niger, and Chad). Christian missionaries spread the written word in the rest of Africa during the nineteenth century, chiefly using the Latin alphabet and European languages (e.g., English, French). For the most part, distinctive written literature didn't emerge in sub-Saharan Africa until after World War II. Even now, African illiteracy rates are still extremely high, so the power of the oral tradition remains great.

Many African peoples use *praise names* (elaborate descriptions of revered personages), myths, trickster tales, legends, songs, proverbs, and riddles. Other oral literature includes dance-stories, chants, magical spells, incantations, and divinations. Throughout Africa, oral literature is closely linked to music and rhythm (e.g., the "talking drum"). Storytelling and singing also often involve a *call-and-response* form, in which the narrator frequently elicits the participation of the listeners in a back-and-forth interaction.

Starting in the 1500s and continuing into the 1800s, West Africans were captured, enslaved, and brought to the Americas. The captives were forced to leave behind their belongings, their names, and even their identities. Their only remaining possession was their folklore. As **Ralph Ellison** observed, they had rites, not rights. Over time, the early African Americans adapted their traditional lore to suit their new environment and their new life circumstances. Myths about how the giraffe got its long neck disappeared, and tales about tricksters undermining cruel oppressors gained popularity. In America, various African cultures blended and interacted with Native American and European-American cultures. As Christianity spread among the slaves, they adapted biblical stories to their circumstances, particularly finding solace in the stories of Moses leading his people—Jews enslaved in Egypt—to the promised land in Israel.

African story types, plots, characters, themes, and storytelling styles mutated and changed, and new stories and story forms emerged. Whatever their modifications and variants, however, these stories retained a distinctively African-American flavor. For one thing, these stories have a definite oral character, with distinctive story sounds, vocal inflections, pauses, whispers, and roars. They highlight rhythm and often feature ear-pleasing music and rhyme. Vivid metaphors and similes help listeners picture the stories being told. Many stories also retain the call-and-response interaction of narrator and listeners. Through frequent call-and-response interactions of storytellers and listeners, improvisation has emerged, and spontaneous verbal cleverness has been prized.

Through their oral literature, slaves were able to preserve their own cultures and beliefs, affirm their own perceptions and experiences, and create their own identities and self-definitions, separate from their oppressors. African-American literature has included proverbs, trickster tales, jokes, folk epics, folk sermons and testimonials, ghost stories, story-songs such as blues ballads, and legends, myths, and tall tales of heroes (e.g., John Henry) and scoundrels (e.g., Stagolee), some realistic (e.g., Harriet Tubman) and some mythical (e.g., High John the Conqueror).

A distinctively African-American oral form is the *toast,* traditionally a male form of literature. Toasts are highly stylized dramatic narratives comprising a long series of rhyming couplets, with a definite rhythm and meter—usually four stressed syllables per line in each couplet. Toasters gain prestige by being entertaining and establishing dominance in verbal skill. They use active verbs and vivid imagery to regale their listeners with stories of bad characters (e.g., Stagolee and the Signifying Monkey) who exhibit tremendous sexual prowess, great physical strength, brutal aggression, and sneaky treachery, using any means to get whatever they want.

Related to toasts are *boasts,* in which the narrator brags of his own sexual prowess, physical strength, aggressive ability and readiness, and other masculine characteristics, offering autobiographical evidence of these traits. When competing narrators add insulting put-downs and challenges to their boasts, they are *sounding.* Typical put-downs may be mild challenges (e.g., "Let the door hit you where the good Lord split you"), direct insults (e.g., "You so stupid you don't believe fat meat is greasy"), or metaphorical threats (e.g., "Your ass is grass, and I'm the lawnmower").

To escalate the competition, however, speakers *play the dozens,* derogating one another's family members. As **Maya Angelou** said in her *All God's Children Need Traveling Shoes* (1986), "Blacks concede that hurrawing, jibing, jiving, signifying, dis-

respecting, cursing, even outright insults might be acceptable under particular conditions, but aspersions cast against one's family call for immediate attack." For instance, a player might say, "Yo' mama so short she can sit on a sheet of paper and swing her legs." More aggressive insults refer to sexual acts with the listener's mother. Typically, adolescent males boast, sound, and play the dozens, but girls, women, and men may also do so.

Men and women, boys and girls may engage in *signifying,* which communicates indirectly, usually signaling insults and criticism without explicitly stating them. Signifying exalts verbal power over economic and physical power. Humor is important in signifying, as signifiers communicate not only the insult but also a sense of shared understanding among a community of listeners. Variations of signifying include *loud-talking* (in which the speaker talks so loudly to a primary listener that others can overhear, thereby embarrassing the primary listener), *jiving* (playful conversations using distinctively African-American vernacular foreign to European Americans), *rapping* (lively, highly stylized conversation, usually intended to persuade listeners), and *marking* (mocking someone's words or mannerisms).

Related to signifying is *masking,* in which a speaker hides his or her true intentions, attitudes, feelings, thoughts, beliefs, and abilities from listeners. Masking provides an excellent complement to signifying, in that the speaker can mask the truth from one listener (such as a slave owner or other person in authority), while signifying to other listeners who overhear the communication (e.g., fellow slaves or other African Americans). Masking and signifying have been vital means of hiding and revealing messages in oppressive circumstances. Literary examples of masking include Ralph Ellison's grandfather character in *Invisible Man* (1952), who advises his grandson to "overcome 'em with yeses"; **Paul Laurence Dunbar**'s poem "We Wear the Mask," in which the masker "grins, lies, hides our cheeks, and shades our eyes"; and **Charles Waddell Chesnutt**'s passing and conjuring stories, **Langston Hughes**'s *Not without Laughter,* and **Richard Wright**'s *Uncle Tom's Children.*

Because African-American slaves were barred from learning to read and write, they continued to prize the oral tradition despite being immersed in a culture that prized written language. They preserved their histories and their literature through word of mouth. Distinctively African-American music and oral literature emerged. By the dawn of the twentieth century, a distinctive African-American written literature also emerged. Paul Laurence Dunbar's poems (e.g., *Oak and Ivy,* 1893) and Charles Waddell Chesnutt's short stories (e.g., *The Conjure Woman,* 1899) were steeped in African-American folklore.

Decades later, Zora Neale Hurston (*Mules and Men,* 1935) studied and described African-American folklore of the South. Hurston illustrated what she had learned in her novel *Their Eyes Were Watching God* (1937), which she filled with proverbs, signifying, playing the dozens, trickster tales, folk wisdom and wit, and folksy patterns and styles of speech (e.g., mock call-and-response among multiple narrators). (Her 1934 *Jonah's Gourd Vine* similarly highlights African-American folklore.) Other writers of the **Harlem Renaissance** shared her appreciation of African-American oral literature as fundamental elements in their own works (e.g., Langston Hughes, *The Weary Blues,* 1926; **James Weldon Johnson**, *God's Trombones,* 1927; **Jean Toomer**, *Cane,* 1923; Richard Wright, *Native Son,* 1940).

Subsequently, many other writers have drawn on the wealth of African-American oral tradition in their written literature: **James Baldwin** (*Go Tell It On the Mountain,* 1953), **Toni Cade Bambara** (*The Salt Eaters,* 1980), Ralph Ellison (*Invisible Man,* 1952), **Ernest Gaines** (*The Autobiography of Miss Jane Pittman,* 1971), **Paule Marshall** (*Praisesong for the Widow,* 1983), **Toni Morrison** (*Song of Solomon,* 1977; *Tar Baby,* 1981; *Jazz,* 1992), **Gloria Naylor** (*Mama Day,* 1988), **Ntozake Shange** (*Sassafras, Cypress & Indigo,* 1982), **Alice Walker** (*The Temple of My Familiar,* 1989; *Possessing the Secret of Joy,* 1992), **Sherley Anne Williams** (*Dessa Rose,* 1986), and others. Children's works also frequently reflect the oral foundation of written literature, such as Verna Aardema's *Why Mosquitoes Buzz in People's Ears* (1975); Phillis Gershator's *The Iroko-Man: A Yoruba Folktale* (1994); **Virginia Hamilton**'s *The People Could Fly: American Black Folktales* (1985); and many works by **Julius Lester.**

Increasingly, written records accompany—or even replace—the oral tradition as a means of communicating and preserving important information. Nonetheless, in the workplace, within the family, and in neighborhoods, gossip, stories, sayings, anecdotes, and lore continue to be *told:* "Did I tell you what Johnnetta did?" "You'll never guess what happened to me today!" Some things simply don't translate easily from spoken to written language.

For instance, how can an author write down distinctive sounds such as the "tst, tst, tst" of the tongue tip swiftly sucked away from the back of the teeth? Would a standup comic's joke be funny without the comic's vocal expression and facial gestures? Would playgoers pay big bucks to see a play if reading the script had the same emotional impact? Increasingly, new communications technologies are being added to written ones, but it's probably not time yet to predict the end of the oral tradition.

REFERENCES: *AP. AP&W. EBLG. MSD-CD (AHD-3). NAAAL.* "Folklore," "Folktale," "Oral Transmission," in *AHL.* "Folklore," in *BRE.* "Folklore," "Mythology," and "Native American Religions," in *E-98.* "African Arts" and "Folk Arts," in *EB-98.* "African Literature," "African Religion," and "Folklore," in *G-96.* "African Literature" and "Tutuola, Amos," in *MSE-CD.* "Folk Literature" and "Folklore," in *MWEL.* "Folklore," in *OCWW.* "Aesop," "Fables," and "Folklore," in *WB-98.* "African Literature," in *WCE-CD.* Lowe, John, "Humor," in *OCAAL.* Mason, Theodore O., Jr., "Signifying," in *OCAAL.* Olson, Ted, "Folklore," in *OCAAL.* Peters, Pearlie, "Masking," in *OCAAL.*

Ormes, "Jackie" (née Zelda Jackson)
(1917–1/2/1986)
Comic strip; journalist

On May 1, 1937, "Torchy Brown in Dixie to Harlem" first appeared as a comic strip in the *Pittsburgh Courier.* Although this was the first comic strip to feature an African-American female, it was not the first work of Jackie Ormes to appear in that newspaper. Ormes had started on the paper's staff about a year earlier, contributing feature articles and pieces of art. Unlike her creator, Torchy was born and raised on a farm in Dixie and migrated to New York to make it big in show business. In later strips, however, Torchy decided to become a newspaper reporter, rather emulating her creator. In any case, Torchy may have been naïve, but she sure wasn't helpless or stupid. With wit and plucky independence, she made her way in the world (despite frequent encounters with male chauvinism and white racism).

While in Pittsburgh, Ormes had started art school, and when she and her husband Earl made a new home in Chicago in the early 1940s, she continued her schooling at the Art Institute of Chicago and got a job reporting for the *Chicago Defender.* Pretty soon, she had developed a new strip for her new locale: "Patty Jo 'n' Ginger," about a pair of sisters, featuring their experiences with educational segregation and inequality, with sexism and gender issues, and with political issues of the day (e.g., the unprovoked murder of Emmett Till). The sisters were soon appearing in African-American newspapers across the land, making Ormes the first African-American woman cartoonist to be nationally syndicated. (EDITOR'S NOTE: See also **Barbara Brandon,** the first African-American woman to have her cartoon nationally syndicated in mainstream, white-owned papers.) After a while, the popularity of Ormes's strip was so great that she even made a few bucks on some dolls based on the two sisters. In the late 1960s, rheumatoid arthritis forced Ormes to stop drawing her popular strip, but she still remained active in Chicago community activities.

—*Tonya Bolden*

REFERENCES: *BAAW.* Brown, Elsa Barkley, in *BWA:AHE.*

Osbey, Brenda Marie (1957–)
Poems

Osbey's poetry collections include *Ceremony for Minneconjoux* (1983), *In These Houses* (1988), and *Desperate Circumstance, Dangerous Woman: A Narrative Poem* (1991) as well as *All Saints* (about her native New Orleans).

REFERENCES: Lowe, John, in *OCAAL.*

Owen, Chandler (4/5/1889–1967?)
Commentary, editorials, speeches; periodical founder and editor

In 1917, Owen cofounded and coedited (with **A. Philip Randolph**) *The Messenger,* a socialist pro-union magazine, which he continued to coedit until 1923. After leaving, he worked as managing editor of the *Chicago Bee,* a less radical African-American newspaper. He also wrote a pamphlet encouraging African Americans to fight in World War II (*Negroes and the War*), distributed in the millions by Democrat Franklin D. Roosevelt's Department of War, and he wrote numerous speeches for Republican Party politicians (including presidential candidates such as Dwight Eisenhower).

REFERENCES: *AAL. EA-99.*

Park, Robert E. (Ezra)

(2/14/1864–2/7/1944)

Nonfiction—urban sociology, biography; journalist, newspaper founder

After graduating from the University of Michigan (1887), Park went to work as a newspaper reporter in Detroit, New York City, and some other big cities, spending the next 11 years closely scrutinizing how people behave in urban environments. With philosopher and educator John Dewey and others, he later founded the short-lived newspaper *Thought News,* dedicated to providing in-depth coverage and analysis of serious contemporary social issues. In the late 1890s, Park took graduate coursework from Dewey (at the University of Michigan), from psychologist and philosopher William James (at Harvard University, from which he earned a master's degree in 1899), and from sociologist Georg Simmel (in Heidelberg, Germany, where he earned a Ph.D.). With his doctorate in hand, he returned to the United States and taught at Harvard (1904–1905), at the University of Chicago (1914–1933), and at Fisk University in Nashville (1936–1943). In the interim between teaching at Harvard and at the University of Chicago, he became secretary of the Congo Reform Association and wrote two articles about Belgian colonial oppression of the Congolese. Through that association, he got to know **Booker T. Washington**. When he turned his attention to Americans of African descent, he became Washington's secretary and is believed to have ghostwritten most of Washington's *The Man Farthest Down* (1912).

At the University of Chicago, Park led the prestigious Chicago school of sociology, where he shaped the field and guided the research in that discipline. In that role, he and Ernest E. Burgess wrote their landmark textbook, *Introduction to the Science of Sociology* (1921), which was later updated and revised. He also guided the thinking of many of his students, such as **Charles (Spurgeon) Johnson**. With his background in psychology and philosophy, he fostered a multidisciplinary approach to sociology and popularized (and perhaps even coined) the terms *human ecology,* referring to both the physical and the moral and social environment in which humans live; and *collective behavior,* referring to the actions of people in groups, which often differ from their behavior as individuals. Park also wrote numerous journal and magazine articles and essays, many of which were collected and published posthumously in three volumes: *Race and Culture, Human Communities,* and *Society* (1950–1955, edited by Everett C. Hughes et al.). Park's other books include *The Principles of Human Behavior* (1915) and *The Immigrant Press and Its Control* (1922).

REFERENCES: *EB-98. G-97.* Marx, Gary T., in *WB-99.*

Parks, Gordon (Roger), Sr.

(11/30/1912–)

Novels, autobiographies, screenplays, documentary scripts, nonfiction books—photography

For most people, Parks's accomplishments as a photographer would be sufficient to merit claiming a lifetime of satisfying achievement. The same could be said about his writing, his filmmaking, his painting, and even his composing. Parks's writings include his books on photography (*Flash Photography,* 1947; *Camera Portraits: Techniques and Principles of Documentary Portraiture,* 1948); his best-selling autobiographical novel (*The Learning Tree,* 1963); his collection of essays and photographs (*Born Black,* 1971); four collections of poetry and photographs (*Gordon Parks: A Poet and His Camera,* 1968; *Gordon Parks: Whispers of Intimate Things,* 1971; *In Love,* 1971; and *Moments without Proper Names,* 1975); his collection of his photographs, his poems, *and* his paintings (*Glimpses toward Infinity,* 1996); his second (nonautobiographical) novel (*Shannon,* 1981); and three—in his case, three might be too few—autobiographies (*A Choice of Weapons,* 1966; *To Smile in Autumn, A Memoir,* 1979; and *Voices in the Mirror, An Autobiography,* 1990).

In addition to the photographs featured in his books, his photographs have appeared in nearly every prestigious magazine, including fashion maga-

Director and photographer Gordon Parks, Sr., 1970s (Archive Photos)

zines such as *Vogue* and *Glamour* as well as the ultimate lifestyles magazine *Life*. His musical compositions include a libretto and music for a five-act ballet titled *Martin,* which aired on national TV on **Martin Luther King, Jr.**'s birthday, as well as several pieces performed by symphony orchestras around the country and many musical scores for his films. Some of his films have been documentaries: *Diary of a Harlem Family* and *Mean Streets,* both made in the 1960s; and biographies, *Leadbelly* (1976, on the folk-music legend), *Flavio* (1978, on impoverished Brazilian boy Flavio da Silvia), *The Odyssey of Solomon Northrup* (1984, about a freeborn man who was kidnapped in 1841 and enslaved for 12 years), and of course, *Gordon Parks: Moments without Proper Names* (1988). Parks's first nondocumentary film was *The Learning Tree* (1968, Warner Brothers), adapted from his autobiographical novel of the same name. This film made him the first African American to produce, direct, and script a major Hollywood movie, and in 1989 the National Film Registry of the Library of Congress named it among the 25 most significant films in the United States. Parks also knew how to make commercially successful films: *Shaft* (1971, featur-

ing Richard Roundtree), *Shaft's Big Score* (1972), and *The Super Cops* (1974).

On December 7, 1934, Gordon Parks, Jr., entered the lives of Parks and his wife, Sally Alvis. Junior worked as a camera operator on several of Senior's films, and as an adult, Junior started making his own films, virtually creating the blaxploitation genre with his film *Superfly* (1972), which grossed more than $24.8 million at the box office. After producing three more feature films in this country, he moved to Kenya, where he tragically died in a plane crash April 3, 1979.

EDITOR'S NOTE: Parks and his wife also have a daughter and another son. Parks's books also include *Arias in Silence* (1994) and *Half Past Autumn: A Retrospective* (with Philip Brookman, 1997).

—*Tonya Bolden*

REFERENCES: *BDAA. SMKC.* Aguiar, Marian, "Parks, Sr., Gordon" and "Parks, Jr., Gordon," in *EA-99.* Houston, Helen R., in *BH2C.* Schultz, Elizabeth, in *OCAAL.*

Parks, Suzan-Lori (1963–)
Plays

Parks's plays include *Imperceptible Mutabilities in the Third Kingdom* (1989), *Devotees in the Garden of Love* (1991), *The America Play* (1992), and *The Death of the Last Black Man in the Whole Entire World* (1992).

REFERENCES: *NYPL-AADR.*

Parsons, Lucy Gonzalez
(3/?/1853–3/7/1942)
Journalist, periodical publisher and editor

Parsons's heritage included African, Mexican, and Native American (Creek) ancestry, and she felt a deep sympathy for all peoples who suffered oppression of any kind, particularly economic oppression. She wrote articles against lynchings and other racist violence several years before **Ida B. Wells** did so. In addition to writing articles for several leftist periodicals, she edited and published *Freedom: A Revolutionary and Anarchist-Communist Monthly.*

REFERENCES: *EA-99.* Kelley, Robin D. G., in *BWA:AHE.*

Patterson, Lillie (1920–)
Biographies, juvenile fiction and nonfiction

Patterson has published more than two dozen books, most of them for juveniles (chiefly readers in grades four to six). Her biographies include *Francis Scott Key* (1963), *Sequoyah: The Cherokee Who Captured Words* (1975), and *David, the Story of a King* (1985) as well as biographies of African Americans, including *Booker T. Washington* (1962), *Frederick Douglass: Freedom Fighter* (1965), her Coretta Scott King Award–winning *Martin Luther King, Jr.: Man of Peace* (1969), *Coretta Scott King* (1977), *Benjamin Banneker: Genius of Early America* (1978), *Sure Hands, Strong Heart: The Life of Daniel Hale Williams* (1981), *Martin Luther King, Jr. and the Freedom Movement* (1989), and *Oprah Winfrey: Talk Show Host and Actress* (1990). Her general nonfiction includes *Meet Miss Liberty* (1962), *Halloween* (1963), *Birthdays* (1965), *Easter* (1966), *Lumberjacks of the North Woods* (1967), *Christmas Feasts and Festivals* (1968), *Christmas in America* (1969), and *Christmas in Britain and Scandinavia* (1970). Her fiction includes *The Grouchy Santa* (1979), *Haunted Houses on Halloween* (1979), *The Jack-o'Lantern Trick* (1979), *Janey, the Halloween Spy* (1979), and *Christmas Trick or Treat* (1979).

REFERENCES: Smith, Karen Patricia, in *OCAAL.*

Patterson, Orlando (1940–)
Novels, nonfiction—history

Educated at Kingston University and at the London School of Economics, in 1971 Patterson was awarded an honorary degree from Harvard University, where he also teaches. Patterson's novels include *The Children of Sisyphus* (1964, "now required reading in Jamaica," Amazon.com review, May 5, 1998), *An Absence of Ruins* (1967), and *Die the Long Day* (1972). His scholarly works include *The Sociology of Slavery: An Analysis of the Origins, Development, and Structure of Negro Slave Society in Jamaica* (1967), *Slavery and Social Death: A Comparative Study* (1982; 1985, paperback), *Freedom* (Vol. 1: *Freedom in the Making of Western Culture,* 1991, National Book Award; Vol. 2: *Freedom in the Modern World,* 1999), *The Ordeal of Integration: Progress and Resentment in America's "Racial" Crisis* (1998, paperback), *Chronology of World Slavery* (1999, with Junius Rodriguez), and *Rituals of Blood: Consequences of Slavery in Two American Centuries* (1999).

REFERENCES: *OC20LE.* Amazon.com, 7/1999.

Patterson, William (8/27/1891–3/5/1980)
Political commentary, autobiography; editor

An attorney and political activist, Patterson wrote articles and edited such communist newspapers as the *Daily Record* and the *Daily Worker.* In 1951, he and **Paul Robeson** petitioned the United Nations, accusing the United States of genocide, and the same year, he edited the book *We Charge Genocide: The Crime of Government against the Negro People.* Two decades later, he published his autobiography, *The Man Who Cried Genocide* (1971).

REFERENCES: Schmidt, Jalane, in *EA-99.*

Payne, Daniel A. (Alexander) (2/24/1811–1893)
Poems, autobiography, nonfiction—history

A lifelong learner who pursued a self-directed program of study, Payne opened his first school in 1929 in South Carolina when he was just a teenager himself, teaching youths during the day and adults during the evenings. He continued teaching until the mid-1830s, when the state legislature passed a law prohibiting anyone from teaching slaves to read or write. With his school outlawed, in effect, Payne moved to Gettysburg, Pennsylvania, where he studied at the Lutheran Seminary. By 1837, however, his failing eyesight forced him to leave school. Despite the abbreviation of his education, he was licensed to preach, and in 1839 a synod of the Lutheran Church ordained him as its first African-American minister. Unable to find a Lutheran parish that would hire him, Payne briefly ministered to a Presbyterian Church in New York, and then he returned to Pennsylvania and opened a church in Philadelphia in 1940. When he was still unable to find a Lutheran parish to shepherd, he became a minister (and later a bishop) of the African Methodist Episcopal (AME) Church in 1841, although he did not readily warm to the less intellectual and more emotional style of most AME services. For years, Payne traveled from place to place, establishing churches and schools. During those years, he published his poetry collection, *The Pleasures and Other Miscellaneous Poems* (1850), most of which focused on the need for "moral purity" and "holy virtue." Among his most affecting poems were tributes to his first wife and his daughter, both of whom had died in the late 1840s, and a poem celebrating emancipation in the West Indies in 1838. (Payne remarried in 1853, wedding Eliza Clark.)

In 1863, Payne had raised enough money to purchase Wilberforce University, in Xenia Ohio, from the Methodist Episcopal Church and to establish it as an AME institution. That done, Wilberforce became the first U.S. college governed by African Americans, and Payne became the first African American to preside over the college. Raising funds and attracting faculty and students dominated his early years there. By 1876, the school was established academically and financially, and he resigned as president but stayed on as chancellor.

In his later years, Payne wrote *Treatise on Domestic Education* (1885), on his experiences as an educator, and his massive *History of the African Methodist Episcopal Church* (1891, two vols.), which he had started more than four decades earlier. Even his autobiography, *Recollections of Seventy Years* (1888), was largely theological and historical, including detailed descriptions of the AME Church, the abolition movement among African Americans, and the civil and social activism of African Americans during the Reconstruction era (to 1888). Also, about eight decades after his death, his sermons and other addresses were gathered in *Sermons and Addresses, 1853–1891* (1972).

REFERENCES: *BDAA. EA-99.* Carson, Sharon, in *OCAAL.*

Payne, Ethel L. (Lois)
(8/14/1911–5/28/1991)
Journalist

As the Washington, D.C., correspondent for the *Chicago Defender* during the 1950s, Payne covered many historic events from our nation's capital. She considered herself an "advocacy journalist" rather than an objective reporter, never hesitating to press the high and the mighty for social and political progress. She also sojourned to the deep South whenever she needed to cover critical civil rights events, such as the Montgomery bus boycott (1955–1956); the desegregation of Central High School in Little Rock, Arkansas (1957); and demonstrations in Birmingham, Alabama (1963). Although her advocacy had prompted President Dwight Eisenhower to avoid her questions in Washington press conferences, they led President Lyndon Johnson to invite her to attend his signing of the 1964 Civil Rights Act and the 1965 Voting Rights Act. In the late 1960s and the 1970s, Payne reported on her travels to Vietnam; Nigeria, Zaire, and many other African nations; the People's Re-

public of China; and Mexico. In addition to her work for the *Defender,* she was a commentator for a thrice-a-week network news broadcast (1972–1982) and wrote a nationally syndicated column.

REFERENCES: Streitmatter, Rodger, in *BWA:AHE.*

Paynter, John H. (?/1862–1947)
Memoirs, travelogue, fiction

Paynter's memoirs serve as bookends to his life experiences and his change in perspective: In his first memoir, *Joining the Navy, or Abroad with Uncle Sam* (1895), he seldom says much about the racial discrimination he experienced in the navy, but in his final memoir, *Horse and Buggy Days with Uncle Sam* (1943), he angrily deplores the racial persecution he endured during his nearly 40 years in the Treasury Department. Paynter also wrote a travel book, *Fifty Years After* (1940, about his travels abroad and his experiences in Washington, D.C.), and a historical novel, *Fugitives of the Pearl* (1930).

REFERENCES: Carson, Sharon, in *OCAAL.*

Pennington, James W. (William) C. (Charles) (?/1807–1870)
Slave narrative, textbook, speeches

In 1828, Pennington fled from slavery, and soon after, he settled in Long Island, New York, a free state, where he attended night school. Pennington also constantly sought ways to help fellow African Americans through aid societies and through teaching and preaching. In fact, it was Pennington who performed the wedding ceremony for Anna Murray and **Frederick Douglass** on September 15, 1838, a dozen days after Douglass had escaped from slavery.

Although Pennington's best-known literary work is his **slave narrative,** *The Fugitive Blacksmith, or Events in the History of James W. C. Pennington* (1849), that was not his only work—or even his first publication. His first book, *A Text Book of the Origin and History . . . of Colored People* (1841), was intended to be used as a guide for teachers, to help them to enlighten, inform, and uplift their students with knowledge of their distinctive history. In addition, several of his sermons, abolitionist lectures, and other addresses were published as pamphlets.

REFERENCES: Wilson, Charles E., Jr., in *OCAAL.*

Perkins, Eugene (9/13/1932–)

Poems, plays, anthologies, political commentary, nonfiction

At age 10, on seeing **Paul Robeson** portray the title character in Shakespeare's *Othello*, Perkins decided he wanted to become a writer, and at age 11, he published his first poem (in the *Chicago Tribune*). During high school, he edited his school's newspaper, in which he published his own poems, essays, and short plays. Even after he began his career as a social worker, he continued to write poems and other works. His poetry collections include *An Apology to My African Brother* (1965), *Black Is Beautiful* (1968), *West Wall* (1969), *Silhouette* (1970), *When You Grow Up: Poems for Children* (1982), and *Midnight Blues in the Afternoon and Other Poems* (1984). He has also edited the poetry anthologies *Black Expressions: An Anthology of New Black Poets* (1967) and *Poetry of Prison: Poems by Black Prisoners* (1972). His other work includes his nonfiction book *The Social Oppression of Black Children* (1975), his musical *The Black Fairy* (1976), and several stage plays: *Nothing but a Nigger* (1969), *Cry of the Ghetto* (1970), *Black Is So Beautiful* (1970), *Fred Hampton* (1970), *Professor J. B.* (1974), and *Pride of Race* (1984).

REFERENCES: Toombs, Charles P., in *OCAAL*.

Peterson, Louis (Stamford) (6/17/1922–)

Screenplays, plays

Peterson's plays include *A Young American* (1940s), *Our Lan'* (1947), his highly celebrated *Take a Giant Step* (1953, which had 264 off-Broadway performances), *Entertain a Ghost* (1962), *Crazy Horse* (1979), *Another Show* (1983), and *Numbers* (mid-1990s). In addition, he did some screenwriting in Hollywood during the late 1950s and early 1960s.

REFERENCES: Smith, Virginia Whatley, in *OCAAL*.

Petry, Ann (née Lane)
(10/12/1908–4/28/1997)

Novels, short stories, children's books, poems, essays, articles, columns; editor

Ann's childhood home rested atop her father's drugstore in Old Saybrook, Connecticut, an almost-all-white New England town. Ann longed to be a writer, but instead she dutifully earned her pharmacology degree in 1931 and spent several years working in her family's drugstores, writing unpublished short stories in her spare time. Her life changed, however, when she met and married George Petry, who whisked her away to Harlem in 1938.

In Harlem, Ann focused on writing. She started out reporting for the *Amsterdam News* and then switched to the *People's Voice*. There, she also edited the women's page and then wrote a weekly column, "The Lighter Side," about the goings-on of Harlem's upper middle class.

Meanwhile, Petry studied creative writing at Columbia University and started submitting her stories to magazines. Though she frequently faced rejection, with persistence, some of her stories were eventually published in *Phylon* and *Crisis*. One of her *Crisis* stories earned her a chance to compete for a Houghton Mifflin Literary Fellowship Award. The first five chapters of her first novel, *The Street*, won her the 1945 $2,400 fellowship.

When Houghton Mifflin published *The Street*, the critically acclaimed 1946 novel quickly made Petry the first African-American woman to write a book selling more than a million copies. Petry's vividly crafted main character, Lutie Johnson, a working-class African-American mother of an eight-year-old son, dreams of escaping Harlem's violence, street crime, economic exploitation, and psychological despair. Unfortunately, poverty, sexism, and racism prevent her escape. Although Lutie's story ended tragically, it transformed Petry's career felicitously. Reissued at least twice, the novel has sold close to 2 million copies to date and is still considered Petry's best-known novel and an American literary classic.

Petry's second novel, *The Country Place* (1947), turns away from urban, mostly black Harlem and returns to white-dominated small-town New England. Petry's novella *Darkness and Confusion* was also published that year, and the following year, the Petrys returned to Old Saybrook, where they raised their only daughter. For the next several years, Petry wrote short stories, as well as her third novel, *The Narrows* (published in 1953).

Petry also wrote children's books, including *The Drugstore Cat* (1949); *Harriet Tubman, Conductor on the Underground Railroad* (1955); *Tituba of Salem Village* (1964); and *Legends of the Saints* (1970); as well as her short-story collection *Miss Muriel and Other Stories* (1971). Her novels and juvenile works have been widely translated, and her poems, short stories, and essays have been widely anthologized. Petry's short stories and essays have appeared in national magazines such as the *New Yorker, Redbook*, and the *Horn Book*.

Ann Petry, first African-American woman to write a book that sold more than 1 million copies, 1946 (Associated Press/AP)

Petry's work and talent have been recognized in various ways, including honorariums, lectureships, and honorary doctorates at several universities, as well as placement in various *Who's Who* guides since the 1970s.

REFERENCES: *1TESK. AA:PoP. BASS. BFC. BV. BWA. EB-98. EBLG. LDW. MAAL. MWEL. NAAAL. OC20LE. RT.* Ervin, Hazel Arnett, in *OCAAL.* Holladay, Hilary, in *OCWW.*

Phylon (1940–)

This scholarly review was founded in 1940 by **W. E. B. Du Bois**, who served as its editor until 1944. The fundamental principle of *Phylon,* which primarily focuses on the social sciences, is that the idea of "race" is a social, cultural, and historical construct with no basis in actual biological or psychological differences among people. *Phylon* broadened its readership through the inclusion of poetry, fiction, and book reviews, and it still continues to make an important contribution to African–American cultural studies.

—*Lisa Bahlinger*

REFERENCES: *OCAAL.*

Pickens, William (1/15/1881–4/6/1954)
Essays, articles, autobiographies

In addition to writing numerous provocative and outspoken articles for *Voice of the Negro* (starting in 1904), Pickens wrote two autobiographies (*Heir of Slaves,* 1911; greatly expanded to create the much more strident *Bursting Bonds,* 1923), a collection of essays (*The New Negro: His Political, Civil and Mental Status,* 1916), and a somewhat preachy fiction work (*The Vengeance of Gods and Three Other Stories of the Real American Color Line,* 1922).

REFERENCES: Andrews, William L., in *OCAAL.*

Pickett, Wilson (3/18/1941–)
Songs

Starting at age 15, Pickett wrote some of the songs his band made popular, such as "I Found a Love" (1962). In 1991, he was elected to the Rock and Roll Hall of Fame.

REFERENCES: Tuttle, Kate, in *EA-99.*

Pietri, Pedro Juan (3/21/1943–)
Poems, plays

A U.S. resident since 1947, Afro–Puerto Rican poet and playwright Pietri has published several poetry collections, including his celebrated *Puerto Rican Obituary* (1971, a response to his experiences during the Vietnam War) and his *Traffic Violation* (1973), *Invisible Poetry* (1979), *Out of Order* (1980), and *Uptown Train* (1980); and his narrative *Lost in the Museum of Natural History* (1981). Pietri was also instrumental in founding the U.S. Afro–Puerto Rican poetry movement known as "Nuyorican poetry," affirming both African and Hispanic heritage within a U.S. context—often with verse rich with puns in both English and Spanish. (Other Nuyorican poets include Miguel Algarín, Sandra María Esteves, Felipe Luciano, and Victor Hernández Cruz.) His plays include *The Livingroom* (1975), *The Masses Are Asses* (1983), and *Mondo Mambo/A Mambo Rap Sodi* (1990). Pietri has also taught creative writing to college students and offered poetry workshops to children, and his poems have been widely anthologized.

REFERENCES: *EA-99.*

Plato, Ann (fl. 1800s)
Essays, poems

The only published book of Plato's work that has survived to this day is *Essays: Including Biographies and Miscellaneous Pieces of Prose and Poetry* (1841/1988), which includes 4 biographies (of deceased personal acquaintances), 16 brief essays, and 20 poems. Her preacher's very brief introduction to the book mentions that she is young but does not tell how young. Little else is known about her, as she reveals little about herself in her work.

REFERENCES: Williams, Kenny Jackson, in *OCAAL.*

Plumpp, Sterling (1/30/1940–)
Poems, anthology

Emmett Till's murder for having supposedly flirted with a white woman traumatized Plumpp, who soon after underwent a deep religious conversion to Catholicism and sought means of escaping Mississippi (and the deep South altogether). While attending St. Benedict's College in Kansas (on an academic scholarship), he read **James Baldwin**'s writing and ancient Greek literature and decided to become a writer, leaving college after two years. He then moved to Chicago, finished college there, and continued to write. His poetry collections include *Portable Soul* (1969); *Half Black, Half Blacker* (1970); *Black Rituals* (1972); *The Mojo Hands Call/I Must Go* (1982); *Blues:The Story Always Untold* (1989); *Johannesburg and Other Poems* (1993, following a 1991 trip to South Africa); and *Hornman* (1995). Plumpp also edited an anthology of poetry from South Africa, *Somehow We Survive* (1982).

REFERENCES: Collins, Michael, in *OCAAL*.

Polite, Carlene (née) Hatcher
(8/28/1932–)
Novels, essays, commentary

Polite has published two novels, which have been labeled by some as "experimental" and by others as "innovative": *The Flagellants* (1966 in French, 1967 in English) and *Sister X and the Victims of Foul Play* (1975). In addition, her 1968 article in *Mademoiselle* magazine offered four distinctive views of black power presented through four distinct voices. Polite is perhaps better known, however, as a dancer and a civil rights activist.

REFERENCES: Dubey, Madhu, in *BWA:AHE*. Johnson, Ronna C., in *OCAAL*.

Porter, James Amos
(12/22/1905–2/28/1970)
Art history

An artist (chiefly a portrait painter) himself, Porter wrote an outstanding text on art history, *Modern Negro Art* (1943), which is still studied. His wife, **Dorothy Burnett Porter** (later Wesley), was the curator of the library that was to become the Moorland-Spingarn Research Center at Howard University.

REFERENCES: *EA-99*.

Porter Wesley, Dorothy (Louise) (née) Burnett (5/25/1905–12/17/1995)
Bibliographies, anthologies; librarian and curator

The eldest of the Burnetts' four children, Dorothy Louise—like her siblings—was expected to get a college education. Boy, did she. She graduated from a teacher's college, then earned her A.B. from Howard University (1928), and then she earned another bachelor's degree and a master's degree at Columbia University's School of Library Science—and then she was awarded a few hon-

orary doctorates for good measure.

A year after Dorothy graduated from Howard, she married **James Porter**—art historian, painter, Howard grad, and Howard faculty member—with whom she had a daughter, Constance Burnett Porter (later Uzelac), on August 22, 1939. Starting even before she graduated, however, Dorothy had been working in the university's library, cataloging materials. In 1930 newlywed Mrs. Porter and her boss realized that a wealth of African-American literature was in danger of being lost to history unless special care was taken to preserve it. They agreed that Porter was just the person to take charge of that task. Porter spent the next 40-plus years doing just that.

First, she cataloged about 3,000 items donated to Howard by Jesse Moorland, Lewis Tappan, and a few other donors. Next, she set about collecting additional materials by asking everyone she could find (including bibliophile and enthusiastic book collector **Arthur Spingarn**) to donate them. She also searched through discard heaps, book sales, and even the estates of deceased African Americans. By the time Porter retired in 1973, the Moorland-Spingarn Collection comprised 180,000 items, including documents, microfilms, books, and periodicals. After she retired, Howard expanded the collection to embrace other parts of the library, founding the Moorland-Spingarn Research Center and naming Porter its curator emerita. In that role, Porter continued to consult and do research for the center until about a month before she died. Three years before she retired, Porter was widowed, and in 1979, she married noted Howard historian **Charles Wesley**.

Throughout her career, Porter (Wesley) had published hundreds of articles, including biographies, bibliographies, and histories of books and libraries. Probably her best-known book is *Early Negro Writing, 1760–1837* (1971; reprint Baltimore: Black Classic Press, 1995), based on her master's thesis. She also wrote several bibliographies: *A Selected List of Books by and about Negroes* (1936); *North American Negro Poets: A Bibliographical Checklist of Their Writings 1760–1944* (1945), with annotations on poetry anthologies as well as pamphlets and books by individual poets; *Catalogue of the African Collection at Howard University* (1958); *The Negro in American Cities: A Selected and Annotated Bibliography* (1967); *A Working Bibliography on the Negro in the United States* (1969); *Negro Protest Pamphlets: A Compendium* (1969, editor); *The Negro in the United*

States: A Selected Bibliography (1970/1978); Howard University: A Selected List of References (1965); Documentation on the Afro-American: Familiar and Less-Familiar Sources (1969); and Afro-Braziliana: A Working Bibliography (1978).

Porter Wesley was given numerous awards for her outstanding achievements, including the Charles Frankel Award, given to her in 1994 by President Bill Clinton and Hillary Clinton in a White House ceremony.

REFERENCES: EA-99. Barnes, Bart, "Obituaries, Librarian Dorothy Wesley Dies: Black History Curator at Howard," Washington Post (December 19, 1995), p. E05. Bhan, Esme, "Legacy of a Job Well Done," Washington Post (December 31, 1995), p. C08. Ferguson, Sally Ann H., in OCAAL. Gunn, Arthur C., in BWA:AHE. Weeks, Linton, "The Undimmed Light of Black History Dorothy Porter, Collecting Forgotten Memories," Washington Post (November 15, 1995), p. C01. http://www.artnoir.com.

Poussaint, Alvin Francis (5/15/1934–)
Nonfiction—education, psychology, psychiatry

In addition to serving as educational consultant to **Bill Cosby**'s TV shows, Poussaint (professor of psychiatry and associate dean of Harvard's Medical School) has written numerous scholarly and popular articles on how racism affects the psychological development of African-American children and about the development and experiences of children of interracial marriages. His books include Why Blacks Kill Blacks (1972) and Raising Black Children (1992, with James Comer; originally Black Child Care, 1975).

REFERENCES: Goodson, Martia Graham, in BH2C. Myers, Aaron, in EA-99.

Powell, Adam Clayton, Jr.
(11/29/1908–4/4/1972)
News articles and columns; newspaper founder

In the mid-1930s, Powell wrote many political pieces for the New York Post, followed by a popular column (aptly titled "Soap Box") for the Amsterdam News of Harlem. From 1942 to 1946, he published the weekly newspaper People's Voice, which he founded. More often, however, his words could be heard from the pulpit (after taking over the ministry of a Baptist church from his father, **Adam Clayton Powell, Sr.**, in 1937) and in the chambers of the U.S. Congress (representing his New York City district from 1945 to 1970). Legendary for his civil rights activism, he was also notorious for his financial indiscretions.

REFERENCES: BDAA. EA-99. EB-BH-CD. PGAA. Stone, Les, in BH2C.

Powell, Adam Clayton, Sr.
(5/5/1865–6/12/1953)
Sermons, books

Perhaps best known as the Baptist minister who fathered **Adam Clayton Powell, Jr.**, Powell, Sr. wrote three books and countless sermons.

REFERENCES: Balfour, Lawrie, in EA-99.

Prince, Mary (c. 1788–after 1833)
Slave narrative

Mary Prince's The History of Mary Prince, a West Indian Slave, Related by Herself, published in London in 1831, was the first published **slave narrative** written by a woman of African descent living in the Americas. (**Harriet Jacobs** wrote the first U.S.-published slave narrative [in 1861], authored by an African-American woman.) Slave narratives written by African-American men had been published previously (e.g., **Olaudah Equiano**'s [1789, England; 1791, United States], Charles Ball's [1836], and **Moses Roper**'s [1838, United States; 1837, England]), and some of these accounts described some of the sexual abuse and violently cruel treatment of women. Nonetheless, Prince's vivid description of her slave experiences awakened many Americans to the brutality of slavery that women were forced to endure in the Americas (she was enslaved in Bermuda, Antigua, and other islands in the West Indies).

Previously, many whites had unquestioningly asserted that slaves really didn't mind being enslaved and didn't really seek to escape bondage. This assertion was rather unconvincing after Prince's highly popular and controversial book came to light, including this observation: "They [whites] put a cloak about the truth. It is not so. All slaves want to be free. . . . I have been a slave myself—and I know what slaves feel—I can tell by myself what other slaves feel, and by what they have told me. The man that says slaves be quite happy in slavery—that they don't want to be free—that man is either ignorant or a lying person" (quoted in CSN, p. xvi). She gave first-person testimony to the emotionally scarring sexual exploitation and physically scarring savage beatings she suffered, as well as her long hours of labor spent working in harsh chemicals that deformed her feet.

While in Bermuda in 1826, she had married a free black man. In 1828, she left her husband in Bermuda to travel with her barbarous "owners," the Woods, in England. While there, Prince escaped from them and fled to the Moravian Church in London, seeking sanctuary. There, the British Anti-Slavery Society offered her legal and financial aid. Through the society, British abolitionist poet Susan Strickland recorded Prince's firsthand telling of her experiences, and society secretary Thomas Pringle edited the work (with Prince's approval of the final wording), added some supporting documentation, and published it as an abolitionist tract. Pringle also hired Prince as his paid employee and offered to purchase her freedom from the Woods. They refused, insisting that she return with them to Bermuda. Prince refused to return with them (realizing that she would never again see her husband), remaining in England to fight in the courts, in the press, and in the British Parliament. Ultimately, in 1833, she won her battle through Parliament when it abolished slavery in Britain and its colonies (including those in the West Indies). Almost nothing is known about Prince after she gained her freedom. Perhaps she managed to return to her husband on a slavery-free Caribbean island; perhaps she started a new life in England; perhaps. . . . During the twentieth century, Prince's work was rediscovered and republished (1987, in *CSN*).

REFERENCES: *CSN*. Keough, Leyla, in *EA-99*. Paquet, Sandra Pouchet, in *OCAAL*.

Prince, Nancy (née) Gardner
(9/15/1799–1856 or after)
Autobiography, travel chronicles

Nancy Prince's major literary contribution is her *Narrative of the Life and Travels of Mrs. Nancy Prince, Written by Herself* (1850), in which she describes some family history, her own experiences and living conditions as a free black in New England before the Civil War, and her travels through Europe and the Caribbean. In describing her family history, she shows her outrage that Africans were abducted from their homeland, subjected to bondage and inhumane cruelty in a foreign land, and then forced to live in abject poverty if they managed to gain their freedom. Her account also imparts the pride she feels for her racial heritage and her forebears, including her mother's father, an African brought to this country as a slave who fought at Bunker Hill during the Revolutionary War; her mother's mother, a Native American who had been captured and enslaved by the British; and her African-born stepfather, who literally leaped to freedom when he jumped off a slave ship. Nancy's mother was widowed twice: first by Nancy's father, when Nancy was just three years old, and then by Nancy's stepfather. After he died, Nancy's mother was overwrought, and Nancy had to take charge of parenting her six siblings, including her oldest sister, whom she and a cane-wielding friend abducted from a brothel and returned home.

In 1824, Nancy married Nero Prince (a former sailor and a servant to a Russian princess). With him, she traveled through Europe to Russia, where she spent nearly a decade working as a seamstress, directing an orphanage, and doing various other jobs—as well as learning several languages and observing world events from this distinctive vantage point. In 1833, the Princes returned to the United States, and Nancy was widowed soon after. Soon, she was working for the American Anti-Slavery Society in Boston, where she established an orphanage for "colored children." A deeply religious woman, in 1840–1841 and 1842 Prince made two evangelistic trips to Jamaica, hoping to ignite Christian zeal in the newly freed former slaves she met there. Back in Boston in 1843, she wrote her autobiography in the hope that she might gain enough from its sale to support herself. Her preface to the 1856 third edition of her book noted that she was gravely ill, and nothing more has been uncovered about her life or her death.

REFERENCES: *EA-99*. Henderson, Australia Tarver, in *BWA:AHE*. Winter, Kari J., in *OCAAL*.

Proverbs

A *proverb* is a short, highly meaningful folk saying, originating in and preserved by word of mouth, which memorably expresses a widely recognized truism about human experience and the ways of the world. Proverbs generally have no known author, or at least they are customarily quoted without identifying an author. In contrast, *aphorisms* are widely quoted pithy sayings for which the author is known. Thus, some expressions may originate as quotations, gain such popularity that they become aphorisms, and then lose their association with their distinctive authors to become proverbs. For instance, even within the past few decades, many people don't recall that it was **Eldridge Cleaver** who said, "You're either part of the solution or part of the problem." By the middle of the next century, this may slip from being an aphorism to being a proverb.

Proverbs are a form of *folklore,* a particular culture's large body of commonly recognized knowledge, which people transmit across generations through the **oral tradition**. Often, proverbs are *maxims,* basic propositions or widely accepted rules about how the world works, how to behave, or how to handle various situations (e.g., "Never say never"). Maxims give advice or make observations about common situations (e.g., "Feed a cold, starve a fever"), practical matters of everyday living (e.g., "Don't put all your eggs in one basket"), moral conduct (e.g., "Waste not, want not"), or the ways of the world (e.g., "Nature abhors a vacuum"). Some proverbs are *admonitions,* giving warnings (e.g., "Don't throw the baby out with the bathwater"). Some proverbs are epigrams, although the authors of epigrams are often identifiable. *Epigrams* are concise, ingeniously clever or satirical poems (e.g., Ogden Nash's "'Neath tile or thatch / That man is rich / Who has a scratch / For every itch") or witty prose statements (e.g., Oscar Wilde's "Experience is the name everyone gives to his mistakes").

In addition to losing their connection to a known author, proverbs change in other ways as they pass from generation to generation. For one thing, as a spoken language changes, some of the words, idioms, or word meanings within proverbs drop out from common use in the language. For instance, in the proverb "tide and time wait for no man," the word *tide* means "season," but that meaning of the word is archaic now. In addition, the original meanings of the proverbs themselves sometimes get lost along the way. For example, in the proverb "The exception *proves* the rule," the original meaning of "proves" was "tests." Nowadays, however, we commonly infer that "proves" means "shows a known truth," which is almost the opposite of the original meaning.

Because human experience is so complex and often paradoxical, many proverbs have conflicting counterparts. For instance, "Nobody tells all he knows" (Senegal) seems to contradict "Wisdom is not like money to be tied up and hidden" (Akan); "Too many cooks spoil the broth" goes against "Many hands make light work"; "Birds of a feather flock together" contrasts with "Opposites attract"; and "Look before you leap" challenges "He who hesitates is lost."

Given the problems associated with proverbs—changes in meanings, archaic terms and idioms, contradictions—why do we so often use them and cherish them across countless generations? Because these little truisms offer sound advice, comfort in times of trouble, and brief summaries of shared knowledge. What helps us to remember these folk sayings? In addition to their brevity, proverbs often use several memorable features:

- metaphors with vivid imagery ("If you bring your firebrand into your hut then do not complain of the smoke," West Africa)
- repetition ("An eye for an eye, a tooth for a tooth," Jewish)
- rhyme ("If I'm lying, I'm flying," African American)
- alliteration and consonance (e.g., "Strategy is better than strength," Hausa)
- parallelism ("Pretty is as pretty does," African American) or comparison ("The blacker the berry, the sweeter the juice," African American)
- antithesis ("Do as I say, not as I do," British) or contrast ("A healthy ear can stand hearing sick words," Senegal)
- irony ("Before healing others, heal thyself," Nigeria)

Proverbs, as expressions of common human experiences, may be found across cultures and across time. Because they often express universal truths, differing cultures frequently express the same ideas through distinctive proverbs. For instance, the Nigerian proverb "Some birds avoid the water; ducks seek it" conveys the same sentiment as the Roman proverb "One man's meat is another man's poison." The African-American proverb "What goes around comes around" expresses the same idea as the Jewish proverb "You reap what you sow."

Unfortunately, the only way of being sure when a particular proverb came into use is to search for written records showing where and when the proverb emerged. For instance, written records show ancient Egyptian collections of proverbs dating from 2500 B.C., and one of the earliest sources of proverbs in the Western tradition is the book of Proverbs in the Old Testament (ca. 400s–300s B.C.). Because most of sub-Saharan Africa had no written language before the nineteenth century, there is no way to be sure of when or where most African proverbs emerged.

Nonetheless, proverbs play a vital role in African culture and in the African oral tradition. In fact, Africans highly revere the ability to cite proverbs in conversations, arguments, and speeches. Elders and other leaders generally have a great command of pithy proverbs, by which they guide people's behavior. One illustration of proverbs' importance can be seen in various proverbs about proverbs, such as "Proverbs are the palm oil with which words are eaten" (Ibo); "One who applies proverbs gets what he wants" (Shona, Zimbabwe); and "A wise man who knows proverbs reconciles difficulties" (Yoruba, Nigeria).

In addition to African proverbs, other sources of African-American proverbs are the Old and New Testaments of the Bible and various British authors (e.g., George Herbert's "He that makes his bed ill, lies there" paved the way for "If you make your bed hard, you're gonna have to lie in it"). Many other African-American proverbs have originated in songs, such as **spirituals** (e.g., "If you cain't bear no crosses, / You cain't wear no crown"), blues songs (e.g., "You never miss your water 'til the well runs dry"), civil rights songs (e.g., "Keep your eyes on the prize"), and soul songs (e.g., "Different strokes for different folks"). Several Americanisms have also become common African-American folk sayings, such as "If you can't stand the heat, get out of the kitchen" and "You can lead a horse to water, but you can't make him drink."

In addition, the struggles for abolition and for civil rights have led to folk sayings, such as "We ain't what we wanna be; we ain't what we gonna be; but thank God we ain't what we was" and "In the South they don't care how close you get, as long as you don't get too high. In the North they don't care how high you get, as long as you don't get too close." In addition, several contemporary aphorisms are headed toward becoming proverbs: **Frederick Douglass**'s "If there is no struggle, there is no progress"; Fannie Lou Hamer's "I'm sick and tired of being sick and tired"; **Jesse Jackson**'s "We must turn to each other and not on each other" and "Your children need your presence more than your presents"; and **Martin Luther King, Jr.**'s "Injustice anywhere is a threat to justice everywhere."

REFERENCES: *AHL. AP&W. BRE. E-98. G-96. MSC-CD. MSE-CD. MWEL. WB-98.* Beilenson, John, and Heidi Jackson (1992), *Voices of Struggle, Voices of Pride* (White Plains, NY: Peter Pauper Press). Bell, Janet Cheatham (1986/1995), *Famous Black Quotations* (New York: Warner Books, Time Warner). Diggs, Anita Doreen (1995), *Talking Drums: An African-American Quote Collection* (New York: St. Martin's Griffin). Hudson, Cheryl and Wade (1996), *Kids' Book of Wisdom: Quotes from the African-American Tradition* (East Orange, NJ: Just Us Books). Leslau, Charlotte, and Wolf Leslau (1962, 1985), *African Proverbs* (White Plains, NY: Peter Pauper Press). Scheffler, Axel (1997), *Let Sleeping Dogs Lie and Other Proverbs from Around the World* (Hauppage, NY: Barron's Educational Series). Simpson, John (1982), *The Concise Oxford Dictionary of Proverbs* (New York: Oxford University Press).

Purvis, Robert
See **Fortens, Grimkés, and Purvises**

Purvis, Sarah (Louisa) (née) Forten
See **Fortens, Grimkés, and Purvises**

Quarles, Benjamin
(1/23/1904–11/17/1996)
Histories, essays, textbooks; editor

The son of a subway porter, Benjamin Quarles dedicated his adult life to learning and teaching others about African-American history, particularly the people and events emerging before the start of the twentieth century. Toward this end, Quarles earned a B.A. (1931) from Shaw University and both an M.A. (1933) and a Ph.D. (1940) from the University of Wisconsin. After earning his degrees, he taught briefly at Shaw University, then was dean at Dillard University (New Orleans), and then history department chair at Morgan State University (Baltimore).

Starting with his first published journal article ("The Breach between Douglass and Garrison," 1938, *Journal of Negro History*) and his first book (*Frederick Douglass,* 1948), Quarles probed race relations throughout U.S. history, and he told true, well-researched stories that inspired an appreciation of African-American contributions to American life and history. Quarles went on to publish numerous other scholarly articles, contribute to the journal **Phylon**, and serve as an associate editor of the *Journal of Negro History.*

Among Quarles's scholarly books are *The Negro in the Civil War* (1953; reprint 1989), *The Negro in the American Revolution* (1961; reprint 1996), *Lincoln and the Negro* (1962; reprint 1991), *Black Abolitionists* (1969; reprint 1991), and *Black Mosaic: Essays in Afro-American History and Historiography* (1988). Quarles also wrote two textbooks to inform a wider readership of what he and other scholars had learned: *The Negro in the Making of America* (1969; 3rd ed., 1996) and *The Negro American: A Documentary History* (1967; later rev. ed. retitled *The Black American: A Documentary History,* 1970). He also edited the volumes *Blacks on John Brown* and *Narrative of the Life of Frederick Douglass: American Slave.*

REFERENCES: *EBLG. G-97.* Fay, Robert, in *EA-99.* Toppin, Edgar Allan, in *WB-99.* Amazon.com, 7/1999.

R

eminent authorities on these two outstanding African Americans. Rampersad also authored *Melville's Israel Potter: A Pilgrimage and Progress* (1969) and coauthored **Arthur Ashe**'s autobiography *Days of Grace* (1993). For his scholarship, Rampersad has been recognized with a MacArthur fellowship and an American Book Award.

REFERENCES: Mason, Theodore O., Jr., in *OCAAL*.

Rahman, Aishah (1936–)
Plays, libretto

Rahman's surrealistic, avant-garde plays include *Lady Day: A Musical Tragedy* (1972, about the life and times of **Billie Holiday**), *Unfinished Women Cry in No Man's Land While a Bird Dies in a Gilded Cage* (1977, which takes place on the day jazz saxophonist Charlie Parker dies), *The Tale of Madame Zora* (1986, based on the life of **Zora Neale Hurston**), *The Mojo and the Sayso* (1987), and *Only in America* (1993). In addition, she wrote the libretto for *The Opera of Marie Laveau* (1989, later renamed *Anybody Seen Marie Laveau?*). Three of her plays have been published in *Three Plays by Aishah Rahman,* and she was known to be working on a novel in the mid-1990s.

REFERENCES: Margulis, Jennifer, in *OCAAL*.

Rainey, "Ma" (née Gertrude Pridgett) (4/26/1886–12/22/1939)
Songs

Among the ninety-three or so songs she performed and recorded, she wrote more than a third of them. She also inspired playwright **August Wilson** to write his *Ma Rainey's Black Bottom* (1984) and poet **Sterling Brown** to write "Ma Rainey."

REFERENCES: *BDAA. EA-99. EB-BH-CD. SEW.* Griffin, Farah Jasmine, in *OCAAL*. Lieb, Sandra, in *BWA:AHE*.

Rampersad, Arnold (11/13/1941–)
Literary and cultural criticism, biography

Rampersad is perhaps best known for his thorough accounts of the lives of two other literary figures: *The Art and Imagination of W. E. B. Du Bois* (1976) and *The Life of Langston Hughes* (2 vols., 1986–1988). Both works are considered the pre-

Randall, Dudley (Felker) (1/14/1914–)
Poems, memoir, anthology; publisher, editor

The son of a teacher (Ada Viola Bradley Randall) and a preacher (Arthur George Clyde Randall), Dudley had his first published poem appear in the *Detroit Free Press* when he was just 13 years old, and thus began his literary career. Like many other African Americans of his era, his early work was influenced mostly by his reading of English poets; only later was he awakened to the works of African-American writers such as **Countee Cullen** and **Jean Toomer**. Randall was highly influential in changing that situation, so that subsequent generations of budding African-American writers were reading and learning about African-American poets early on.

After high school, Randall worked in a foundry for the Ford Motor Company and he served in the Army during World War II before returning to his education when he was in his early thirties. While earning his bachelor's degree ·in English (1949, Wayne [State] University) and his master's degree in library science (1951, University of Michigan), Randall worked in the post office. Later, after working as a reference librarian at Morgan State University and Lincoln University (Missouri) for a few years, he returned to Detroit to take a job with the Wayne County Federated Library System. In 1969, he briefly tried teaching poetry at the University of Michigan before becoming a librarian and poet-in-residence at the University of Detroit, from which he retired in the mid-1970s.

In 1965, Randall published a *broadside* (a publication printed on a single sheet of paper) of his poem "Ballad of Birmingham," about the 1963 racially motivated bombing of a Birmingham church, in which four little girls were killed while attending Sunday school. With that initial publication, he founded **Broadside Press**. The first poetry collection the press published was *Poem Counterpoem* (1966), which included 10 poems by Randall and 10 poems by **Margaret Danner**, with each poet addressing the same theme in poems printed on facing pages. One of his most intriguing poems in this collection was "Booker T. and W. E. B.," which concisely articulates the philosophical differences that separated **Booker T. Washington** and **W. E. B. Du Bois**. In the following years, his press published several of Randall's poetry collections, including *Cities Burning* (1968), in response to a riot in Detroit; *Love You* (1970), with 14 love poems; *More to Remember: Poems of Four Decades* (1971), with 50 poems on diverse subjects; *After the Killing* (1973), addressing issues of racial pride and black nationalism; and *A Litany of Friends: New and Selected Poems* (1981), dozens of poems on a variety of topics. Across his body of work, Randall has explored various poetry structures (haiku, triolet, sonnet, dramatic monologue, and so on), poetry techniques (slant rhyme, blues stylings, typographical arrangements on the page, and so on), and even poetry styles (e.g., trying on the styles of fellow poets).

Broadside Press did far more than publish and promote the works of Dudley Randall, however. It also played a crucial role in the development of the **Black Arts movement** of the late 1960s and early 1970s, publishing the works of other poets, including **Gwendolyn Brooks**, **Nikki Giovanni**, **Etheridge Knight**, **Audre Lorde**, Don L. Lee (**Haki Madhubuti**), and **Sonia Sanchez**. These works included an anthology (*For Malcolm: Poems on the Life and Death of Malcolm X,* 1967, which Randall edited with **Margaret Burroughs**), some broadsides, quite a few chapbooks, and a series of essays of literary criticism. Through Broadside's affordable paperbacks, these writers were able to reach an audience eagerly waiting to read their works. Randall reflected on his experiences with the press in his memoir *Broadside Memories: Poets I Have Known* (1975). He sold the press in 1977 but has remained on the press's staff as a consultant. Two other works by Randall are currently in print: *Black Poets* (reissued in 1985), an anthology he edited; and *Homage to Hoyt Fuller* (1984).

REFERENCES: *EA-99. EBLG. TtW.* Madgett, Naomi Long, in *OCAAL.* Amazon.com, 7/1999.

Randolph, A. (Asa) Philip
(4/15/1889–5/16/1979)
Essays, articles, commentaries; periodical cofounder

By the time Randolph was in his twenties, he was well versed in progressive politics and a self-proclaimed socialist. In 1914, he married Lucille Green, whose unflagging support for Randolph and his beliefs was more than emotional and moral: Her highly successful beauty parlor business provided the sole means by which the Randolphs stayed financially afloat.

In 1917, Randolph cofounded the outspokenly radical monthly magazine *The Messenger* (with **Chandler Owen,** who left *The Messenger* in 1923). *The Messenger* unflinchingly denounced leaders in the African-American community (e.g., **Booker T. Washington**, for his accommodationism; **Marcus Garvey,** for his separatism; and **W. E. B. Du Bois**, for his failure to recognize the importance of class struggle). Randolph also attacked job and housing discrimination, railed against lynching, condemned African-American participation in World War I, and generally provoked the U.S. Justice Department into calling him "the most dangerous Negro in America" in 1919, holding *The Messenger* to be "the most able and the most dangerous of all Negro publications." Despite the best efforts of the government, however, Randolph continued delivering his message month after month, year after year.

Randolph also took up the cause of the Pullman porters who worked for the railroads, leading them to found the Brotherhood of Sleeping Car Porters in 1925. Through the 1930s, the 1940s, the 1950s, and the 1960s, A. Philip Randolph was always in the lead, championing the rights of hard-working folks to earn a decent wage, without suffering discrimination, and with full civil rights.

EDITOR'S NOTE: The 1963 March on Washington signaled a change in Randolph's politics, and he worked more closely with liberals for civil rights reform, publishing his writing in ***Opportunity*** and other liberal periodicals instead of radical socialist ones.

—*Tonya Bolden*

REFERENCES: *EAACH. SMKC.* Anderson, Jervis (1986, reprint), *A. Philip Randolph: A Biographical Portrait* (originally published 1973) (Berkeley: University of California Press). Johns, Robert L., in *BH2C.* Pfeffer, Paula F. (1996, reprint), *A. Philip Randolph: A Pioneer of the Civil Rights Movement* (originally published 1990) (Baton Rouge: Louisiana State University Press).

Raspberry, William (James)
(10/12/1935–)
Editorials

Raspberry has been writing three politically conservative opinion columns each week for the *Washington Post* since 1966. In 1991, 50 of his columns were collected in the book *Looking Backward at Us*.

REFERENCES: *EBLG*.

Ray, Henrietta Cordelia (c. 1849–1916)
Poems

In her collections *Sonnets* (1893) and *Poems* (1910), Ray's lyrical sonnets, ballads, and quatrains explore traditional poetic themes (nature, platonic love, religious ideals) and pay homage to members of her family, as well as to other heroic figures of her era (e.g., **Frederick Douglass**, **Paul Laurence Dunbar**, Harriet Beecher Stowe). Her poetry also reflects her superb formal education, including her master's degree in pedagogy from the University of the City of New York (1891), and her mastery of the Greek, Latin, French, and German languages. (Before Ray started earning money for her poetry, she taught at the Colored Grammar School Number One.) Many of her poems were published in the *A.M.E. Review* before they were gathered into her collections.

Ray's poem "Verses to My Heart's-Sister" (published in her *Poems*) reveals her passionately profound affection and loyalty toward her older sister Florence, who was her lifelong companion. She and Florence also wrote *Sketches of the Life of Rev. Charles E. Ray* (1887), a brief biography of their father, an abolitionist and editor of a periodical. Another of Ray's poems, "Commemoration Ode" or "Lincoln/Written for the Occasion of the Unveiling of the Freedman's Monument in Memory of Abraham Lincoln/April 14, 1876" was read at the unveiling in Washington, D.C. (printed in her *Sonnets*).

REFERENCES: Sanders, Kimberly Wallace, in *OCAAL*.

Razaf, Andy (12/15/1895–2/3/1973)
Song lyrics

The second lyricist (after **Noble Sissle**) to have a long-standing collaboration with noted composer Eubie Blake, Razaf wrote the lyrics for the musical *Blackbirds of 1930,* including "Memories of You," a popular song of the day. He also collaborated with Thomas ("Fats") Waller, producing such hit songs as "Honeysuckle Rose," "Ain't Misbehavin'," and "The Joint Is Jumpin'." Among his four wives was the Schomburg Collection curator and librarian **Jean Blackwell** (later **Hutson**).

REFERENCES: "Eubie Blake," in *EB-98*. Fay, Robert, "Andy Razaf," in *EA-99*.

Reagon, Bernice (née) Johnson
(10/4/1942–)
Music history, songs, memoir

Reagon has always interwoven her commitments to family, music, civil rights, and education. In the early 1960s, while she was studying music at Spelman College, she joined the Student Nonviolent Coordinating Committee's (SNCC's) Freedom Singers and married fellow Freedom Singer Cordell Reagon. In 1964, her daughter Toshi was born, and she became pregnant with her son, Kwan. Before Kwan was born, she and Cordell separated and eventually divorced. In 1966 and 1967, Reagon released her first and second solo song albums while raising her children and conducting her own research on traditional African-American songs and stories. Her research eventually led to her earning a Ph.D. from Howard University (in the 1970s) in American history, with a concentration in African-American history, cultural and oral history methodologies.

In 1973, Reagon founded the group Sweet Honey In The Rock, the dynamic all-woman a cappella ensemble, with whom she has produced various albums and performed numerous concerts. The group's repertoire includes songs from musical styles as varied as gospel, the blues, reggae, folk songs, rap, and West African chants. Their songs speak of the cultural riches of African-American heritage and of the struggles of Africa's descendants in the United States, past and present. These powerful women sing out against racism, sexism, and oppression of all kinds. The group has won numerous Grammies and other awards and has a wealth of recordings, including such items as a CD accompanying a life- and love-affirming children's book (Ysaye M. Barnwell, 1998, *No Mirrors in My Nana's House*). Reagon's work with her group also led her to write *We Who Believe in Freedom: Sweet Honey In The Rock . . . Still on the Journey* (1993).

Reagon has also worked for the Smithsonian Institution in various capacities (as cultural historian of the African Diaspora Project in the Division of Performing Arts Festival of American Folklore,

1974–1976; for the National Museum of American History as cultural historian of the Program in Black Culture, 1976–1988; and as curator of the Division of Community Life, 1988–1993). During her tenure there, she wrote various articles, including "African Diaspora Women: The Making of Cultural Workers," "The Albany Georgia Movement," "Women as Culture Carriers in the Civil Rights Movement," and "The Power of Communal Song." She has also spearheaded several projects: *Voices of the Civil Rights Movement: Black American Freedom Songs 1960–66,* a three-record collection, and *Voices of the Civil Rights Movement, 1960–1965,* a remastered two-CD collection with booklet anthology. She also edited *"We'll Understand It Better By and By": Pioneering African-American Gospel Composers* (1992). That served as the start of her Smithsonian Institution/National Public Radio series *Wade in the Water: African-American Sacred Music Traditions,* for which she was conceptual producer and host narrator. The Peabody Award–winning 26-hour-long radio programs started airing in January 1994. Other prize-winning projects with which she has been associated are the television documentary series *Eyes on the Prize,* for which she was music consultant, performer, and music producer; and the PBS *American Experience* series film on the Underground Railroad, "Roots of Resistance," for which she was music consultant, composer, and music producer.

Meanwhile, Reagon has raised her children, and her daughter Toshi has become an accomplished musician, composer, band leader, and recording producer in her own right as well as an outspoken champion of gay rights and other civil rights. Reagon has also managed to hold visiting fellow posts and to lecture at various colleges around the country, and in 1993 the College of Arts and Sciences at American University appointed her its Distinguished Professor of History. She was also awarded a 1989 John D. and Catherine T. MacArthur Foundation grant (often called a "genius award"); a Trumpet of Conscience Award from the Martin Luther King, Jr., Center for Nonviolent Social Change; and a National Endowment for the Humanities 1995 Charles Frankel Prize for outstanding contribution to public understanding of the humanities.

—*Tonya Bolden*

REFERENCES: *BAAW. WDAW.* Reagon, Bernice Johnson, and Toshi Reagon, "Remember . . . Believe . . . Act," in *33T.*

Reason, Charles L. (1818–1893)
Essays, poems

A friend of abolitionists and social activists Charles Ray (father of **Henrietta Cordelia Ray**), **Frederick Douglass**, and **Robert Purvis** (husband of **Harriet Forten**), Reason devoted his life to issues of social justice, civil rights, and suffrage. A college graduate, he also firmly believed in the value of education, working as a teacher and a principal in various schools and colleges in New York City and in Philadelphia, Pennsylvania. His essays and poems, which have yet to be collected, were also focused on the issues of importance to him and reflected his broad, deep knowledge of many subjects. His poems include his 86-line ode "The Spirit Voice" (1841) and his 48-stanza poem "Freedom" (1846); both eloquently express his fervor for freedom for African Americans.

REFERENCES: Sherman, Joan R., in *OCAAL.*

Redding, Jay Saunders
(10/13/1906–3/2/1988)
History, social and literary criticism, anthology, novel

In high school, one of Redding's teachers was **Alice Ruth (Moore) Dunbar Nelson**. After high school, Redding spent most of his life in academia, earning his bachelor's degree (Ph.B., 1928) and master's degree (M.A., 1932) from Brown University and teaching English at several colleges and universities (Morehouse College, 1928–1931; Louisville Municipal College, 1934–1936; Southern University in Baton Rouge, Louisiana, 1936–1938, where he chaired the English department; Hampton Institute, 1943–1966; visiting professor at Brown University, becoming the first African American to be on the faculty at an Ivy League school; George Washington University, 1968–1970; and Cornell University, 1975– 1988).

An ardent integrationist, Redding lost his job at Morehouse for denouncing the views of **Booker T. Washington**, favoring those of **W. E. B. Du Bois** instead. In the 1960s, his views cost him the favor of **Amiri Baraka** and other black nationalists who called for cultural separatism. Through his teaching and his writing, Redding challenged his peers, students, and readers to rethink their existing views of literature and history. In his first book, *To Make a Poet Black* (1939), he critically surveyed and analyzed African-American literature, suggesting the development of a **Black Aesthetic** and showing how individual poets (e.g., **Paul Laurence Dunbar**) and novelists (e.g., **Zora Neale Hurston**) participated in that development. Impressed with his scholarship in this work, the Rockefeller Foundation awarded him a fellowship to study African Americans in the South. This study yielded his *No Day of Triumph* (1942), which includes a chapter on his own family. That book further enhanced his scholarly reputation, as did his subsequent works, including *They Came in Chains: Americans from Africa* (1950), *The Lonesome Road: The Story of the Negro's Part in America* (1958), and *The Negro* (1967). These works combine biographical vignettes with information from primary sources to tell the story of race relations in the United States and to chronicle African-American history. With Arthur P. Davis, Redding edited the anthology *The Cavalcade: African-American Writing from 1760 to the Present* (1971; revised as *The New Cavalcade,* 1991). Redding also popularized some of his own scholarly work, writing articles for *Atlantic Monthly, Saturday Review,* and other national magazines.

A Guggenheim fellowship made it possible for Redding to take time out to write his only novel, *Stranger and Alone* (1950; reprinted 1989), about the son of a black mother and a white father, set in the segregated South in the 1920s and 1930s. In addition to Rockefeller and Guggenheim fellowships, Redding was awarded a Ford Foundation fellowship and numerous honorary degrees.

REFERENCES: *EA-99. EBLG.* Ashwill, Gary, in *OCAAL.* Amazon.com, 7/1999

Redding, Otis (9/9/1941–12/10/1967)
Songs

Redding's love of playing and singing music began at an early age, and when he had to drop out of school, to take menial jobs to help support his family, he still managed to squeeze in time for his music. In the mid-1950s, he played the drums for gospel performers on a local radio station, and by the late 1950s, he was singing in local amateur contests. In 1961, he made his first record, on a small local label in Georgia. In 1963, Redding's rhythm-and-blues (R&B) ballad "These Arms of Mine" earned him a recording contract with Stax Records in Memphis. His sonorous, gravelly voice and original songs were soon strongly identified with the Memphis Soul sound. Among Redding's hits in 1965 and 1966 were "Mr. Pitiful," "I've Been Loving You Too Long," and "Try a Little Ten-

derness." In 1967, Aretha Franklin popularized his song "Respect," and other singers (e.g., the Rolling Stones) started showing interest in his songs. When Redding appeared at the 1967 Monterey Pop Festival, his career seemed destined for meteoric heights. By the end of that year, a plane crash had ended his life, but ironically, it didn't end his fame. Redding's first number-one pop single was his song "Sittin' on the Dock of the Bay," recorded three days before he died, and released in 1968.

REFERENCES: *EA-99. G-97.*

Redmond, Eugene (12/1/1937–)
Poems, plays, criticism; newspaper cofounder and editor, book publisher and cofounder

Starting in high school, Redmond was involved with journalism, working on his high school (and later his college) newspapers (and yearbooks), then becoming associate editor of the *East St. Louis Beacon,* and then cofounding and editing the *East St. Louis Monitor.* In college, he shifted his focus to literary writing and he soon published numerous volumes of poetry, including *A Tale of Two Toms, or Tom-Tom (Uncle Toms of East St. Louis and St. Louis)* (1968), *A Tale of Time & Toilet Tissue* (1969), *Sentry of the Golden Pillars* (1970), *River of Bones and Flesh and Blood* (1971), *Songs from an Afro/Phone* (1972), *Consider Loneliness as These Things* (1973), *In a Time of Rain & Desire* (1973), and *Eye on the Ceiling* (1991). A poet of the **Black Arts movement**, he also helped shape the movement through the company he cofounded (with **Henry Dumas** and Sherman Fowler), Black Writers Press, which published three of his collections. After Dumas's life was tragically cut short, Redmond was instrumental in preserving and promoting Dumas's remaining literary works.

REFERENCES: Burton, Jennifer, in *OCAAL.*

Reed, Ishmael (2/22/1938–)
Novels, essays, poems, songs, plays, edited works; newspaper cofounder, book press cofounder

Perhaps the most widely reviewed African-American literary figure since **Ralph Ellison,** Ishmael Reed has created a distinct niche in American letters. His experimental works often parody both the white and the black establishment. In addition to being a novelist, poet, teacher, and essayist, he is a songwriter, television producer, publisher, maga-

Ishmael Reed, who savors the controversies his parodies provoke, 1975 (Archive Photos)

zine editor, playwright, and founder of the Before Columbus Foundation and There City Cinema, both of which are located in northern California.

Reed and **Amiri Baraka** are probably the most controversial African-American literary figures alive today. An innovative poet, Reed uses phonetic spellings and wordplay blended with what he calls neo-Hoodooism, offering an alternative cultural tradition for African Americans. Despite criticism from other African-American writers and from feminists, he remains committed to his satiric commentaries.

Two of Reed's books have been nominated for National Book Awards, and he has received numerous honors, fellowships, and prizes, including the Lewis H. Michaux Literary Prize, awarded to him in 1978 by the Studio Museum in Harlem. He has taught at Harvard, Yale, and Dartmouth, and for more than 20 years he has been a lecturer at the University of California at Berkeley.

Reed was born in Chattanooga, Tennessee. In 1942 he moved to Buffalo, New York, and grew up in the city's working-class neighborhoods, attending Buffalo public schools. Later, he graduated from the State University of New York at Buffalo. In 1960, he married Priscilla Rose, but they di-

vorced a few years later, after which Reed settled in New York City. There, he helped found an underground newspaper, *East Village Other*, and participated in several cultural organizations, experiences that helped shape his artistic development.

By the late 1960s Reed had published and won critical acclaim for his first novel, *The Free Lance Pallbearers* (1967), a parody of the African-American confessional narrative. His second novel is a parody as well: *Yellow Black Radio Broke Down* (1969) targets Western pulp fiction and what Reed sees as the repressiveness of American society. In the work, Reed also introduces his theory of neo-Hoodooism, a blend of voodoo, West African religious practices, and nonlinear time.

During this time, Reed had begun teaching at the University of California at Berkeley, and in 1970 he married Carla Blank. In the ensuing decade he helped establish the Before Columbus Foundation and cofounded both Yardbird Publishing and Reed, Cannon & Johnson Communications. He also published his first major work of poetry, *Conjure: Selected Poems 1963–1970* (1972), which garnered him a Pulitzer Prize nomination. In addition, he produced the mystery parodies *Mumbo Jumbo* (1972), set during the **Harlem Renaissance**, and *The Last Days* *of Louisiana Red* (1974), featuring voodoo trickster detective PaPa LaBas.

Mumbo Jumbo was the work that first achieved wide celebrity for the author, and it is considered by several scholars to be his best, along with *Flight to Canada* (1976), in which Reed parodies the **slave narrative** form. *Mumbo Jumbo* is a mythic/ magic epic centered in such places as New Orleans and Harlem during the Jazz Age and the Harlem Renaissance of the 1920s. The story depicts the struggle among Jes Grew, purveyors of the black cultural impulse, and supporters of the Western monotheistic tradition, whom Reed calls the Atonists. Reed incorporates illustrations, foot-notes, and bibliographies in parody of the documentary conventions of black realism.

Throughout the 1980s, Reed won critical respect more for his poetry and his essays than for his novels. His 1980s poetry was collected in *Such as New and Collected Poems* (c. 1988), which blends black dialect with mythic elements. His essays were collected in *God Made Alaska for the Indians* (1982) and *Writin' Is Fightin': Thirty Seven Years of Boxing on Paper* (1988). Among his novels are *The Terrible Twos* (1982), a satire of the Reagan years; its 1989 sequel, *The Terrible Threes;* and *Reckless Eyeballing* (1986), an attack on literary politics.

Under the pseudonym of Emmett Coleman, Reed edited *The Rise, Fall, and . . . ? of Adam Clayton Powell.* In 1993 he published both a novel, *Japanese by Spring,* a parody of academia, and a nonfiction collection, *Airing Dirty Laundry,* a compilation of writings addressing such subjects as the news media and black anti-Semitism.

Reed's literary style is best known for its use of parody and satire in attempts to create new myths and to challenge the formal conventions of literary tradition. His works have been criticized as incoherent, muddled, and abstruse. Other critics have praised him as multicultural, revolutionary, vivid, and profoundly aware of mythic archetypes. He writes his fiction in a tone that is irreverent and harsh and mixes standard English with a vernacular from the street, television, and popular music.

Reed constructs a resistance to the dominant Western conceptions of literature in his mixing of multimedia into the text. His novel *Mumbo Jumbo* establishes him as a multimedia enthusiast much in the same vein as Kathy Acker, a notoriously controversial author who clearly rejects the constraints of pure text. On one page of *Mumbo Jumbo* is a pic-ture of a Black Panther demonstration, obviously relevant to the plot of African-American resistance to Anglo traditions, but extremely anachronistic in a book about the 1920–1930s. Reed makes deliberate use of this apparent absurdity.

In *Japanese by Spring,* Reed mixes literary forms constantly, shuffling back and forth from fiction to nonfiction to narrative to essay to description to commentary, and so on. Placing himself as a character in *Japanese by Spring,* he wrote, "Historically, when whites moved among yellows, blacks and reds, death always resulted. . . . Reed believed that racism was learned. That racism was the result of white leaders of western nations placing little value on nonwhite life, or indeed, projecting violent impulses upon those who lived under constant fear of white terror." Reed's books possess a common theme of resistance to cultural and racial oppression, tied in with the repulsion of dominant ideologies and formats.

Two albums of Reed's songs, *Conjure I: Music for the Texts of Ishmael Reed* and *Conjure II: Cab Calloway Stands in for the Moon,* have been released by Pangaea Records. Reed lives in Oakland, California.

—*Michael Strickland*

REFERENCES: *EBLG.* Dougherty, Brian Fox (1995), "Metalanguages and Contemporary Authors, Page: Ishmael Reed, *Mumbo Jumbo,*" http://www.uiowa. edu/~english/litcult20/bdougherty/reed.html. Medgar Evers College (1995), Website produced by Arts Wire, a program of the New York Foundation for the Arts; Panel entitled "Politically Correct in a Politically Incorrect World" at the Fourth National Black Writers Conference, http://www.tmn.com/ CGI/Artswire/black/reed.htm. Reed, Ishmael (1996), *Japanese by Spring* (New York: Penguin). Reed (1972), *Mumbo Jumbo* (Garden City, NY: Doubleday). University of Delaware Library (1996), "Treasures of the University of Delaware Library," http://www.lib.udel.edu/ud/spec/exhibits/ treasures/american/reed.html.

Remond, Sarah Parker
(6/6/1826–12/13/1894)
Nonfiction—abolitionist lectures

Starting in July 1842, Sarah Parker Remond joined her brother Charles Lenox Remond in delivering more than 50 abolitionist lectures across this country and in England. A letter of hers was published in London's *Daily News* (1865), and a lecture was published in London's *The Freedman* (1867). In 1866, she moved to Europe, studied medicine in Florence, and received her diploma for professional medical practice in 1868, and she practiced medicine there for more than two decades. In 1877, she married Italian Lorenzo Pintor and remained in Italy thereafter.

Sarah and Charles were also friends of the Fortens and the Grimkés, and they offered their home to Charlotte Forten while she attended school in Salem, Massachusetts. Forten met abolitionists poet John Greenleaf Whittier and *Liberator* publisher William Lloyd Garrison in their home. (See also "Forten, Charlotte L." in *BDAA*.)

REFERENCES: *EA-99*. Wesley, Dorothy Porter, in *BWA:AHE*.

Richardson, Willis (1889–1977)
Plays, anthologies

Richardson is best known as the first African American to have a nonmusical play produced on Broadway (his *The Chip Woman's Fortune,* 1923). Prior to that landmark event, however, he wrote several one-act plays, which were published in the **Brownies' Book**. Also a director, Richardson wrote many other plays for adults, including *The Deacon's Awakening* (1920, published in **Crisis**); *Mortgaged* (1924); *Broken Banjo, a Folk Tragedy* (1925, which won *Crisis's* first drama contest, established by **W. E. B. Du Bois**); and *The Bootblack Lover* (1926, also a *Crisis* drama contest winner). Richardson also published three important anthologies of African-American dramas: *Plays and Pageants from the Life of the Negro* (1930), *Negro History in Thirteen Plays* (1935, coedited with **May Miller**, including 5 of his own plays), and *The King's Dilemma and Other Plays for Children* (1956, including 6 of his own plays). In addition to his more than 30 published plays, Richardson wrote numerous other unpublished plays, which may be found in collections at the Schomburg Center and at the Howard University library. A playwright of the **Harlem Renaissance**, Richardson anticipated the **Black Arts movement**, lobbying for the development of an African-American theater, which would promote plays written and performed by and about African Americans.

REFERENCES: *NYPL-AADR*. Houston, Helen A., in *OCAAL*.

Riggs, Marion Troy (2/3/1957–4/5/1994)
Films

Riggs independently wrote, directed, and produced numerous antihomophobic and antiracist films, including his 1988 Oscar-winning *Ethnic Notions* (produced in 1986). His other films include *Tongues Untied* (1989, made famous by the attacks from right-wing Senator Jesse Helms and political columnist Patrick Buchanan), *Anthem* (1990), *Non Je Regrette Rien/No Regret* (1991), *Color Adjustment* (1991, Peabody Award–winning documentary), and his final film, *Black Is . . . Black Ain't* (1995, completed by his collaborators after his death).

REFERENCES: Balfour, Lawrie, in *EA-99*.

Ringgold, Faith (Willi) (née Jones) (10/8/1930–)
Children's books, memoirs

Faith Jones was born in Harlem Hospital in New York City and has lived in or near Harlem ever since. (In recent years, Ringgold has been living in Englewood, New Jersey, but she still keeps her art studio in Harlem; she also spends almost half the year in La Jolla, California, where she teaches at the University of California at San Diego.) Because young Faith had asthma (which makes breathing difficult), she was frequently kept home from school. At home, in addition to doing her schoolwork, she was allowed to draw with crayons and to create clothes and other items from the fabric, thread, and needles her mother gave her. (Faith's mother earned a living by designing fashions and making dresses.) Her family also included her brother Andrew (the oldest) and her older sister Barbara. During her early years, Faith's father, a sanitation department truck driver, also lived with them.

When Faith was still in high school, she came to realize that she wanted to be an artist, and in 1948 she enrolled in the City College of New York to study art. During that time, women weren't allowed to enroll in the liberal arts program, so she had to attend the School of Education. While still attending college, she married; her marriage (and later divorce) slowed her down a little in completing her degree, but she nonetheless earned her B.A. in art (her major) and education (her minor) in 1955. Four years later, she had earned an M.F.A. (master's in fine arts, 1959) there as well. By 1960, she started teaching art in the public schools while continuing to paint. That year, she remarried (to

Burdette Ringgold), and within a few years, Faith had started painting professionally. She and Burdette had two daughters, Barbara and Michelle, who have since completed the family with three granddaughters: Martha, Teddy, and Faith.

During the 1960s and 1970s, Ringgold expanded her art to include sculpture and performance art, and the subject of her art has often centered on the experiences of African-American women (and men and children). To gain a deeper understanding of African-American culture and history, Ringgold began reading extensively, such as the works of **James Baldwin** and **Amiri Baraka**, and studying African art traditions, having learned about European art traditions almost exclusively during her schooling. Both her paintings and her sculpture often depict her family members and important African Americans such as **Martin Luther King, Jr.**

Ringgold's sculptures draw on a lifetime of experience in creating artwork with fabric, as she creates soft sculptures with fabric that she stuffs and paints. As she said in her pictorial autobiography, *Talking with Faith Ringgold* (1996; with Linda Freeman and Nancy Roucher, p. 14), "My soft sculptures began as dolls, then masks, then hanging figures, then free-standing sculptures." Interestingly, one of the next steps in Ringgold's artistic evolution arose out of a practical concern:

When I was starting out, there were hardly any galleries that showed the work of black women or women in general. . . . I had an opportunity to show my work provided I could ship it easily. Framed paintings have to be packed in crates, which are heavy and expensive to ship. In Amsterdam, Holland, I saw several examples of Tibetan *tankas,* which are paintings that are framed in cloth. I thought this was an excellent alternative to framing paintings in wood, because the painting could be rolled up and placed in a trunk and shipped rather inexpensively. So when I got home I shared the idea with my mother and she started making cloth frames. And it worked. I got a lot of exhibitions and lectures for which I was paid. Then I decided to write stories and put them on my paintings. (*Talking,* pp. 16–17)

This development led to Ringgold's creation of her "story quilts": huge fabric quilts onto which she paints important scenes from African-American culture and history and onto which she writes out a story about the scene and the characters depicted there. As Ringgold observed, the process of making quilts reflects not only her own childhood experiences but also the experiences of African-American women through the centuries. In her own family, Ringgold's great-great grandmother had made quilts for the plantation owners who enslaved her, and she had taught the skill to Ringgold's mother's grandmother, and so on down the generations. Further, Africans have a long-standing tradition of making useful objects beautiful, and much of African art reflects this tradition.

In 1980, Faith Ringgold and her mother, Willi Posey, worked together to create Ringgold's first vividly painted quilt, *Echoes of Harlem.* Within three or four years, she started including in her quilts fabric swatches onto which she wrote story text, beginning with *Who's Afraid of Aunt Jemima?* and continuing for at least 75 more story quilts. Subsequent quilts include *Sonny's Quilt* (1986; showing Sonny Rollins playing the jazz saxophone on the Brooklyn Bridge) and *Tar Beach* (1988; showing a scene from Ringgold's childhood).

Tar Beach led to yet another progression in Ringgold's evolution as an artist: She adapted the story quilt into a children's book (1991), which was named a Caldecott Honor Book (1992), a *New York Times* Best Illustrated Book, and an American Library Association Notable Book; it was also featured as a Reading Rainbow selection and given a Coretta Scott King Award for illustration, a Parents Choice Gold Award, and numerous other honors. In *Talking* (p. 7), Ringgold noted,

If you look closely at *Tar Beach,* you may learn more about me. It's really about going up to the roof, which has a tar floor, in the summertime when I was a child. My father would take the mattress up and my mother would place a sheet on it and some pillows and we kids would lie on the mattress. It was very hot and we could have food up there— watermelon and fried chicken and all kinds of goodies. The adults would play cards and the children would lie there and listen to them talking and it was cool. I wrote about this little girl [eight-year-old Cassie Louise Lightfoot] in the picture who is dreaming that she owns all the skyscraper buildings that she can see from the roof and the

George Washington Bridge. She imagines that she can fly and that she can make life better for her family.

Since its publication in hardcover in 1991, *Tar Beach* has been published in library binding (1992), as a puzzle and paperback (1992), as a (13-inch) doll and paperback (1992), as a paperback (1995), and as a "Turtleback" (1996).

Since the publication of *Tar Beach,* Ringgold has published several other books for children, including *Aunt Harriet's Underground Railroad in the Sky* (1992), in which Cassie and her brother journey across time and space to find out how African Americans escaped from slavery through the Underground Railroad; *Dinner at Aunt Connie's House* (1993), which introduces a dozen famous African-American women who have made substantial contributions to American history (and is adapted from Ringgold's 1986 story quilt, *The Dinner Quilt*); *My Dream of Martin Luther King* (1995), a whimsical yet powerful biography of the great man; *Bonjour, Lonnie* (1996), which explores African-American history and mixed cultural ancestry with Lonnie, an orphan, who travels back in time to World War I Paris, where he meets his African-American grandfather and French grandmother, and then forward to World War II, where he meets his father and his Jewish mother, who ensured his safekeeping before she was discovered by Nazis; *The Invisible Princess* (1998), a rather frightening fairytale in which a charming princess saves her parents and others from slavery through her own courage; *If a Bus Could Talk: The Story of Rosa Parks* (1999); and *My Grandmother's Story Quilt* (1999). Many of these books have been praised in such noteworthy review publications as *Horn Book, School Library Journal, Publishers Weekly, Booklist,* and *Kirkus Reviews,* among others.

In addition to these works, Ringgold has written *Dancing at the Louvre: Faith Ringgold's French Collection and Other Story Quilts,* a companion book to a solo traveling art exhibition of her story quilts (1998); her memoirs, *We Flew over the Bridge: The Memoirs of Faith Ringgold* (1995), glowingly reviewed in the American Library Association's *Booklist;* and her autobiography for young readers, *Talking with Faith Ringgold,* mentioned previously. In addition, a few videos have been produced by or about Ringgold: *Faith Ringgold: The Last Story Quilt* and *Faith Ringgold Paints Crown Heights* (both produced by Linda Freeman), *Crown Heights Children's*

History Story Quilt (1994), and *Tar Beach, with Faith Ringgold* (produced by Rosemary Keller). In addition to the awards she has received for her literary works, Ringgold has received quite a few awards honoring her artistic achievements, including a grant from the National Endowment for the Arts (for her sculpture), a Creative Artistic Public Service Award Grant, and a Guggenheim fellowship.

REFERENCES: *33T. AA:PoP. EA-99. EB-BH-CD. SEW. WDAW.* Cousins, Emily, in *BWA:AHE.* Ringgold, Faith, Linda Freeman, and Nancy Roucher (1996), *Talking with Faith Ringgold* (New York: Crown Publishers). http://www.artnoir.com, 7/1999. Amazon.com, 8/1999.

Rivers, Conrad Kent (1933–1968)
Poems, short stories, and a play

While still a college student, Rivers had his first poetry collection, *Perchance to Dream, Othello* (1959), published. His subsequent collections include *These Black Bodies and This Sunburnt Face* (1962), *Dusk at Selma* (1965), *The Still Voice of Harlem* (1968, which appeared a few weeks after his death), and *The Wright Poems* (1972, a posthumous collection in homage to **Richard Wright**, edited by Paul Breman); Rivers's poems have also been published widely in journals and anthologies. His play and his short stories remain unpublished.

REFERENCES: Foster, Frances Smith, in *OCAAL.*

Robeson, Eslanda ("Essie") Cardozo (née) Goode (12/12?/ or 12/15?/1896–12/13/1965)
Biography, memoir

Although Robeson is best known for managing the career of her famous husband, **Paul Robeson**, she was quite a shining intellect in her own right. After marrying him in 1921, she earned a B.S. in chemistry (1923, Columbia University) and a Ph.D. in anthropology (1945, Hartford [CT] Seminary). Both she and he well deserved their reputations as fervent leftist social activists and outspoken advocates of social justice. The couple had a son, Paul, Jr., in 1927, and although they separated for a time (following an adulterous affair of Paul's), they later reunited, staying together until her death separated them. She wrote a biography of him, *Paul Robeson, Negro* (1930), relatively early in his career.

Starting in the 1930s, Eslanda Robeson worked ardently to champion the cause of colonized people in Africa and other places in the world. In 1936, she and her young son traveled to Africa, and she later published her diary of the experience in *African Journey* (1945). A more political analysis of her experiences appeared in *What Do the People of Africa Want?* (1945). Over the next three decades, the Robesons—as a couple and as individuals—traveled all over the globe, going wherever they thought their voices would help the causes they believed in: supporting anti-Fascist forces in Franco's Spain, attending pan-African conferences in Ghana, and living in the Soviet Union for a time. Because of their outspoken dissent, they were caught up in the anticommunist fervor of the 1940s and 1950s, and when Eslanda refused to cooperate with the witch hunts being staged by Senator Joseph McCarthy and by the House Un-American Activities Committee, Paul was prevented from getting work in this country.

REFERENCES: *BDAA*. Myers, Aaron, in *EA-99*. Ransby, Barbara, in *BWA:AHE*.

Robeson, Paul (Bustill)
(4/9/1898–1/23/1976)
Autobiography; periodical cofounder

The story of Paul Robeson has been called an "American Tragedy," and this appellation does not seem to be an exaggeration at all. He was a man who rose to great heights because of his brilliance and talent—but that meteoric rise made his eventual fall all the more tragic. During the course of his life, he was a scholar, an all-American football player, a lawyer, a singer, an actor, and an author. He mastered all of these roles with tremendous grace and skill, but it was his acting that earned him international fame. He was cut down at the height of his career because he chose to defend the principles of communism (which he thought would eventually bring racial equality to the world) during the beginning of the Cold War. It was a fall from which he never recovered.

Paul was born in Princeton, New Jersey, in 1898 to William Drew and Maria Louisa Robeson. His father was a runaway slave who became a cleric and raised Paul alone after Paul's mother died when Paul was only six years old. Despite this early loss, he grew up to be immensely successful—he was admitted to Rutger's College (now a university) on a full scholarship, elected to the Phi Beta Kappa honor society in his junior year, and

graduated as valedictorian of his college class. On top of his academic honors, he also excelled in athletics. He chose academics over sports in the end, earning a law degree from Columbia Law School in 1923.

During his first job at a law firm, however, he realized that the legal profession in 1923 would never allow a black American to reach his fullest potential. After facing a great deal of discrimination from employees who refused to work under an African American, he concluded that, as Martin Duberman states in his biography of Robeson, law was a profession "where the highest prizes from the start were denied to me." He decided to leave the law firm less than a year after starting work there.

While in law school, Robeson had acted in a few small theater productions; after deciding to leave law, he returned to the theater. In 1924 he joined an acting group called the Provincetown Players, which was associated with and put on plays written by famous playwright Eugene O'Neill. Robeson played the lead in two O'Neill plays— *The Emperor Jones* and *All God's Chillun Got Wings* (a controversial play about interracial marriage)— and a star was born. He achieved tremendous critical acclaim and before long became an internationally celebrated figure in both dramatic and musical theater. Unlike many of his fellow African-American singers and actors, whose opportunities on stage were usually limited to playing comic characters or characters with racist stereotypes, Robeson became a prominent actor who performed in serious roles.

While touring in Europe, he was introduced to leftist views, and their emphasis on justice and racial and economic equality immediately appealed to him. Over the following years, he became increasingly outspoken about his views. His political opinions made him one of many prominent Americans dragged into the McCarthy hearings, a witch hunt in which Americans who were suspected of having any communist leanings were browbeaten with questions as U.S. senators tried to insinuate that they posed a threat to the country's national security. Finding that Robeson was even then unwilling to renounce his beliefs in the rectitude of communism, a senator asked him why he didn't stay in the Soviet Union. He paid dearly for his response: "Because my father was a slave, and my people died to build this country, and I am going to stay right here and have a part of it just like

Paul Robeson sings a ballad on the radio, 1940 (Culver Pictures)

you. And no fascist-minded people will drive me from it. Is that clear?"

So clear was his statement that, in essence, it heralded the end of his career. His popularity fell drastically. A riot erupted outside of a building in Peekskill, New York, where he was to hold a concert, when people who opposed his political views began to harass and assault his audience. Thereafter, he was never able to put on concerts and found few opportunities to perform. His income plummeted as concert managers blacklisted him, falling from $104,000 in 1947 to $2,000 afterward. In 1950, because Robeson would not sign an anti-communist oath of loyalty, the U.S. government revoked his passport, which cut off his access to Europe and his audiences there. When he published his autobiography, *Here I Stand* (1958), the *New York Times* and prominent literary journals not only refused to review it but even refused to put its title on their lists of new books. (EDITOR'S NOTE: During the 1940s and 1950s, Robeson made his views known by publishing his newspaper *Freedom,* and in the late 1950s or early 1960s, he and his wife **Eslanda Robeson, W. E. B. Du Bois** and his wife **Shirley Graham Du Bois,** and others cofounded the journal *Freedomways: A Quarterly Review of the Negro Freedom Movement.*)

Robeson, who was described in the journal *American Heritage* in 1943 as a man "being hailed as America's leading Negro," had been transformed into, as Sterling Stuckey pointed out in the *New York Times Book Review,* a man whose name had become "a great whisper and a greater silence in black America." Although his passport was restored in 1958 after a Supreme Court ruling on a similar case agreed with Robeson's complaint that Americans cannot be prohibited from traveling because of their political views, the ruling came too late. Robeson made one more trip to the Soviet Union, but he soon fell ill. As his health failed, he remained in the United States, cut off from audiences and friends, and he refused even to attend tributes organized in his honor. He died in 1976 after suffering a stroke.

Although some condemn Robeson's adherence to communism despite his knowledge that doing so would bring about his own downfall, others praise him, saying that his story is, as Jim Miller said in a *Newsweek* article, "a pathetic tale of talent sacrificed, loyalty misplaced and idealism betrayed." **Coretta Scott King**, wife of **Martin Luther King, Jr.**, told the people who gathered at a gala celebration of Robeson's seventy-fifth birthday (which he refused to attend) that Robeson "had been buried alive . . . [because he had] tapped the same wells of latent militancy" among African Americans that her husband had.

Whatever one chooses to believe, it is irrefutable that Paul Robeson must be seen as one of the great, if tragic, figures in African-American history—he was a man who achieved much, rose to great heights, and fell to great depths, but all the while kept the goal of the advancement of African Americans and the fight against racism uppermost in his heart.

EDITOR'S NOTE: For more information on Paul and Eslanda Robeson, see *BDAA* as well as Eslanda's book *Paul Robeson, Negro* (1930); his daughter Susan Robeson's book, *The Whole World in His Hands: Paul Robeson, a Family Memoir in Words and Pictures* (1998); and his son Paul Robeson, Jr.'s book of provocative essays, *Paul Robeson, Jr. Speaks to America* (1993).

—*Diane Masiello*

REFERENCES: *BW:SSCA. EB-BH-CD. EBLG.* Bigelow, Barbara Carlisle (1992), *Contemporary Black Biography: Profiles from the International Black Community* (Vol. 2) (Detroit: Gale Research). Mason, Theodore O., Jr., in *OCAAL.*

Rodgers, Carolyn (Marie) (12/14/1945?–)
Poems, literary criticism and theory, fiction, lectures; press cofounder

At age nine, Carolyn started writing a journal. By the time she reached adolescence, she was reciting poems and had started writing her own poems. In college, she met **Gwendolyn Brooks**. With Brooks's encouragement, Rodgers submitted some of her poems to **Hoyt Fuller**, editor of *Negro Digest*.

After several of her poems had been published, Rodgers self-published her first volume of verses, *Paper Soul,* in 1968. The volume was reviewed favorably, and she was soon active in the **Black Arts movement**. During the late 1960s and early 1970s, Rodgers traveled widely giving readings and lectures. Often, she gained appointments as lecturer or writer-in-residence at various colleges across the country. Wherever she went, she read of cultural revolution and African-American traditions, advocating a **Black Aesthetic** through street dialect and free verse, while voicing feminist objections to "The Movement."

During this time, Rodgers cofounded **Third World Press** in Chicago, which published several of her poetry collections (e.g., *Songs of a Black Bird, 2 Love Raps,* and *Now Ain't That Love*). Her written poems used unconventional capitalization, punctuation, spacings, and spellings, thereby reinforcing her distinctive free verse, nonmetrical, nonrhyming style. Her themes often focused on racial issues, as well as relationships between men and women or between mothers and daughters.

In the mid-1970s, Rodgers's poetry shifted away from militant nationalist politics and toward more personal and introspective themes, such as loneliness and love and even some religious themes. Her *how i got ovah: New and Selected Poems* was published by mainstream publisher Anchor/Doubleday in 1975 and was nominated for the National Book Award in 1976. In 1978, Anchor/Doubleday published her *The Heart as Ever Green: Poems*. In both collections, Rodgers viewed politics from a feminist perspective and revealed the spiritual and personal guidance she receives from her church and from her mother. Her subsequent poetry volumes include *Translation* (1980), *Eden and Other Poems* (1983), *Finite Forms: Poems* (1985), and *Morning Glory: Poems* (1989). Many of her poems have been published in periodicals such as *Ebony* and *Essence* and in more than a dozen anthologies.

In addition to her poetry, Rodgers often publishes literary criticism, noting that literature "speaks not only to the political sensibility but to the heart, the mind, the spirit, and the soul of every man, woman, and child." Rodgers also published a novel, *A Little Lower Than Angels* (1984). Rodgers has received numerous awards, such as a National Endowment for the Arts award and PEN Awards. Even after receiving such praise and recognition, however, she "continued writing and publishing and practically starving to death" (*MAAL*, p. 435). Apparently, in this country, poetry writing is not a lucrative career for an African-American woman—even a highly talented one.

REFERENCES: *BWW. EBLG. MAAL. NAAAL.* Vick, Marsha C., in *OCAAL*. Woodson, Jon, in *OCWW.*

Rollin Whipper (married name), Frances A.
See **Whipper, Frances A.**

Rollins, Charlemae (née) Hill
(6/20/1897–2/3/1979)
Biography, anthology, bibliography, children's books; librarian

We rarely think of children's librarians as crusaders, but Charlemae Hill Rollins was indeed a crusader on behalf of promoting worthwhile books for children. She strived to make available to children books that clearly portrayed the valuable contributions African Americans have made to American history and contemporary experience. The only thing worse than the total absence of African Americans from most of American literature was the distorted caricatures and stereotypes she saw in many books written for children and adolescents. To spread the word of her crusade, she lectured widely; taught workshops on storytelling; wrote numerous articles for professional journals; wrote bibliographies, anthologies, and biographies; and led by example in her own work as a librarian and storyteller.

After graduating from Western University in 1915, Charlemae Hill went on to study library sciences at Columbia University and the University of Chicago. In 1918, she married Joseph Walker Rollins, with whom she had a son, Joseph, Jr. At home with her son, she gained lots of practice in reading and telling stories, perfecting the most artful ways of charming and delighting a child through words. In 1926, Rollins started working for the Chicago Public Library (CPL), which was to be her professional home for the next 36 years. In 1932, the CPL opened its George C. Hall Branch and appointed her its children's librarian. From 1949 until 1960, she also found another avenue for her crusade: teaching students about outstanding African-American literature at Roosevelt University.

When Rollins wasn't captivating children with her storytelling skills or lecturing to adults, she was writing. Her first book, *We Build Together: A Reader's Guide to Negro Life and Literature for Elementary and High School Use* (1941), listed nonfiction and fiction books suitable for children, which portrayed African Americans through authentic characters, realistic events, and interesting narratives. This bibliography was published by the National Council of Teachers of English and was revised in 1948 and again in 1967. In 1963, she offered a selection of works in *Christmas Gif': An Anthology of Christmas Poems, Songs, and Stories, Written by and about Negroes* (1963; reprinted 1993).

Rollins also wrote quite a few children's books of her own, including *Magic World of Books* (1952) and *Call of Adventure* (1962). Most of her books were biography collections, such as *They Showed the Way: Forty American Negro Leaders* (1964), *Famous American Negro Poets for Children* (1965), *Great Negro Poets for Children* (1965), and *Famous American Negro Entertainers of Stage, Screen, and TV* (1965). In addition, as an outgrowth of her personal friendship with poet **Langston Hughes**, she wrote *Black Troubadour: Langston Hughes* (1970), which won a Coretta Scott King Award (1971). Rollins also received numerous other awards from the American Library Association and from various book associations and women's groups, and she was awarded an honorary doctorate from Columbia College in Chicago.

REFERENCES: *EBLG.* Jenkins, Betty L., in *BWA:AHE.*

Roper, Moses (1816–after 1856?)
Slave narrative

A Narrative of the Adventures and Escape of Moses Roper, from American Slavery (1837, London; 1838, United States; later editions, 1838–1840, London and Philadelphia; 10th ed., 1856) was one of the first such narratives by an African American to appear in print. Roper's chronicle vividly documents the brutal treatment of slaves across the American Southeast before he escaped North to New England and then to England in 1835 (where slavery had been abolished in 1833), with the aid of American abolitionists. (See the editorial note for **slave narratives** for more on other narrators.)

REFERENCES: Wilson, Charles E., Jr., in *OCAAL.*

Ross-Barnett, Marguerite
(5/21/1942–2/26/1992)
Nonfiction—political science, Indian and African-American studies

In addition to writing 40 articles, University of Houston president (1990–1992) Ross-Barnett wrote and edited 5 books, including *The Politics of Cultural Nationalism in South India* (1976) and *Images of Blacks in Popular Culture: 1865–1955* (1985), as well as *Public Policy for the Black Community: Strategies and Perspectives* (1976, coedited with James Hefner) and *Educational Policy in an Era of Conservative Reform* (1986, coedited with Charles Harrington and Philip White).

REFERENCES: Aguilar, Marian, in *EA-99.* Williams-Andoh, Ife, in *BWA:AHE.*

Rowan, Carl T. (Thomas) (8/11/1925–)
Biographies, history, political commentary, autobiography; journalist

Although Carl was born in Ravenscroft, Tennessee, his family had moved to McMinnville, Tennessee, a small lumber mill town, when he was still an infant. During Carl's childhood, the entire country was suffering an economic depression, and the Rowan family suffered particularly. Thomas David Rowan, Carl's father, stacked lumber for 25 cents an hour, and his mother, Johnnie Rowan, earned a little by doing laundry for other folks. Johnnie also taught young Carl how to find various wild plants to add to the family meals. Nonetheless, Carl, his brother Charles, and his sister Ella never had electricity in their home, they marked the time by the trains that rattled past their house, and they lived in terror of the rats that infested their home and stalked them in their nightmares.

From an early age, Carl started working at various menial jobs to help out his family, but he managed always to have hope of using education to lift himself out of his desperate poverty. Fortunately, while he was still at McMinnville's segregated Bernard High School, Miss Bessie Taylor Gwynn encouraged his belief in himself and in the value of education. As he later wrote in his autobiography *Breaking Barriers,* Miss Bessie used to say, "If you don't read, you can't write, and if you can't write, you stop dreaming." She inspired him to want to pursue journalism, and she helped him more directly by smuggling books to him from the whites-only library in town.

After Carl graduated as valedictorian of his high school class, he left McMinnville with 77 cents in his pocket, wearing his best clothes, carrying a cardboard box of his other belongings, and hoping to go to college. His grandparents lived in Nashville, and he planned to stay with them while studying journalism at Fisk University. Originally, he had hoped to get a football scholarship, as he had played football in high school. When Fisk turned him down, he went to work mopping floors and delivering food (for $30 per month) in a local hospital where his grandfather worked. By the fall (1942), he had saved up enough money to enroll in Tennessee A&I (agricultural and industrial) College (now Tennessee State University).

In 1943, while Rowan was still in college, a professor recommended him for taking a written examination to enter the U.S. Navy's V-12 officer-training program. Rowan passed the test and became one of the first 15 African Americans to train to become a commissioned officer in the U.S. Navy. At first, he trained at Washburn University in Topeka, Kansas, and then later he attended Oberlin College in Ohio and then the Naval Reserve Midshipmen School in Fort Schuyler, in the Bronx, New York. After his training, he was commissioned as an officer and assigned to sea duty, serving as a deputy commander of communications aboard the USS *Chemung* during World War

Carl T. Rowan with President Lyndon B. Johnson, 1964 (UPI/Corbis-Bettmann)

II. In the Navy, even white Southerners had to listen to Rowan and follow his orders in regard to communications.

After being discharged, Rowan returned to McMinnville. While riding the train home, he read numerous African-American newspapers of that era—the *Pittsburgh Courier,* **Baltimore Afro-American,** *Chicago Defender,* and so on—and became even more determined to pursue a career in journalism. After a very brief stay in McMinnville, Rowan headed back to Oberlin to complete his college degree in journalism. While finishing his bachelor's degree (1947), he worked as a freelance writer for the *Baltimore Afro-American.* During graduate school (University of Minnesota; M.A., journalism, 1948), he continued working for the *Afro-American* as a Northern correspondent, and he started working for the *Minneapolis Spokesman* and the *St. Paul Recorder.*

Once Rowan had his M.A. in hand, the formerly all-white *Minneapolis Tribune* hired him as a copywriter, and two years later he was made a general assignment reporter, thereby becoming one of the first few African-American reporters to be employed by a major urban daily newspaper. In 1951, Rowan wrote a series of 18 articles titled "How Far from Slavery?" while he took a 6,000-mile sojourn through 13 Southern states. Actually, the idea for the articles emerged much earlier, from a discussion with a white Texan when Rowan was still in the Navy. This seaman had encouraged Rowan to write about "all the little things it means being a Negro in the South, or anyplace where being a Negro makes a difference." Rowan's articles opened the eyes of Northern readers about the realities of the Jim Crow South, as he described his own experiences and those of others in Southern hotels, restaurants, buses, trains, and other public places. The series earned Rowan a 1952 Sidney Hillman Award for the best newspaper reporting in the nation and a check for $500 (the equivalent of six of Rowan's weekly paychecks at the time). The articles also became the basis of Rowan's first book, *South of Freedom* (1952).

For another of Rowan's series, "Jim Crow's Last Stand," Rowan returned to the South again, this time to document the various court cases leading to the historic 1954 Supreme Court decision, *Brown v. Board of Education of Topeka, Kansas.* This series gained Rowan a 1954 Sigma Delta Chi Journalism Award from the Society of Professional Journalists for the best general reporting of 1953, and it played a role in his being named among the ten most outstanding men of 1953 by the U.S. Junior Chamber of Commerce. Another of his series, "'Dixie Divided," probed the South's efforts to resist the Supreme Court's desegregation orders following the *Brown* decision. During the 1955–1956 Montgomery bus boycott led by **Martin Luther King, Jr.**, Rowan was the only African-American reporter covering the story for a national newspaper.

In the mid-1950s, Rowan was also asked to cover international affairs, such as the United Nations, the Suez Canal crisis (in Egypt, when England, France, and Israel tried to seize the canal) and the Hungarian uprising (in which the Union of Soviet Socialist Republics [USSR] brutally suppressed a Hungarian attempt to break free from the Soviet bloc). In 1954, the U.S. State Department invited Rowan to travel to India and to Southeast Asia to lecture on the importance of a free press. While in India, he also wrote a series of articles for the *Tribune,* and in Southeast Asia, he wrote about the political tensions of that region, as well as about the 1955 Bandung Conference, attended by representatives from 23 less developed nations. In recognition of his journalistic skills, Rowan won two more Sigma Delta Chi awards (for foreign correspondence) and was invited to become the first African-American member of the Gridiron Club, an organization of Washington, D.C., journalists (founded in 1885).

In 1961 Rowan left the *Minneapolis Tribune* and accepted appointments in the Kennedy and then the Johnson administrations. From 1961 to 1963, he served as Kennedy's deputy assistant secretary of state for public affairs, handling press relations for the State Department. In that role, he made top-secret negotiations with the USSR to free U.S. pilot Francis Gary Powers, whose U2 spy plane had been shot down over the USSR. He also became not only the first African American to serve on the National Security Council (NSC) but also the first ever to attend an NSC meeting. Rowan also toured Southeast Asia, India, and Europe with then–Vice President Lyndon Johnson. In 1963, Rowan was appointed ambassador to Finland, thereby becoming the youngest ambassador and only the fifth African American ever to serve as an envoy.

In 1964 President Johnson asked Rowan to leave his ambassadorship to become the director of the United States Information Agency (USIA). The USIA operates an assortment of educational and cultural programs abroad, including the worldwide radio broadcasts of the "Voice of America." Again, Rowan broke ground as the first African American to hold this important post and was then the highest-ranking African American ever to serve in the State Department and the highest-ranking African American in the federal government at that time.

In 1965 Rowan left his USIA position to return to journalism. From 1965 to 1978 he wrote a column for the *Chicago Daily News,* and in 1978 he started writing a column for the *Chicago Sun-Times.* Since then, he has written a nationally syndicated column for the *Chicago Tribune.* In addition to his columns, Rowan has made regular appearances as a broadcaster on radio (his five-day-a-week *The Rowan Report*) and television (frequently appearing on *Meet the Press, Inside Washington,* and other programs).

Rowan has also written several books, including the previously mentioned *South of Freedom* (1952; reprinted in 1997). Rowan's other books include *The Pitiful and the Proud* (1956), about his experiences in Asia; *Go South to Sorrow* (1957), a provocative book about the need for immediate action in civil rights; *Wait Till Next Year: The Life Story of Jackie Robinson* (1960); *Just between Us Blacks* (1974); his nationally best-selling *Breaking Barriers: A Memoir* (1991); *Dream Makers, Dream Breakers: The World of Justice Thurgood Marshall* (1993/1994), about the memorable Supreme Court justice and their 40-year friendship; and *The Coming Race War in America: A Wake-Up Call* (1996), about the country's highly charged racial relations following the O.J. Simpson case, exacerbated by increasing disparities between rich and poor, the rising number of right-wing militias and other hate groups, the growing opposition to affirmative action and to welfare support of the underclass, and burgeoning prison populations.

In addition to his numerous awards for his reporting, in 1997 Rowan won the National Association for the Advancement of Colored People's Spingarn Medal for his outstanding achievements and contributions. Rowan also established "Project Excellence," a million-dollar scholarship fund for Washington, D.C., high school students who wish to become journalists. Rowan and his wife Vivien have three children.

REFERENCES: *AA:PoP. AAB. BF:2000. EBLG. G-99.* Aguiar, Marian, in *EA-99.* Emery, Michael, in *WB-99.* Mueller, Michael E., and Michelle Banks, in *BH2C.* Amazon.com, 8/1999.

Ruggles, David (3/15/1810–1849)
Abolitionist pamphlets, lectures; publisher, journalist, bookseller

David Ruggles wasn't shy about his beliefs. Although he was born free, of free parents, in a free state (Connecticut), he had passionate feelings against slavery. When he was just 20 years old, he wrote a letter to the French Marquis de Lafayette, asking him to help abolish slavery. As Ruggles said, "The pleas of crying soft and sparing never answered the purpose of a reform, and never will." A self-educated man, he worked in a temperance (anti-alcohol) grocery, bookstore, reading room, and printing business.

Ruggles was a regular contributor to the *Emancipator* and the *Liberator,* and in 1833 he worked as an agent lecturing for the *Emancipator,* drumming up business for the abolitionist newspaper and stirring his listeners to oppose slavery. The next year (1834), in New York City, he opened the first known African-American bookshop, where he sold abolitionist pamphlets (some of which he authored) and other materials. He also founded the New York Committee for Vigilance, putting his beliefs into action. The committee worked with the Underground Railroad, interposing its members between slave catchers and fugitive slaves. In this way, Ruggles risked his own life and wellbeing to protect more than 1,000 fugitive slaves, including **Frederick Douglass**. In 1838, Ruggles started publishing the committee's *Mirror of Liberty,* perhaps the nation's first African-American weekly magazine. Ruggles also published a *New York Slaveholders Directory* (1839), unmasking whites who were thought to have captured and enslaved free men and women.

In 1842, the Vigilance Society folded, leaving a nearly blind Ruggles financially devastated. Fortunately, his friend, fellow abolitionist **Lydia Maria Child**, suggested that he move to Massachusetts and join her in starting a hydropathy ("water cure") business, which proved quite successful.

REFERENCES: Aguiar, Marian, in *EA-99.* Carruth, Mary C., in *OCAAL.*

Rush, Gertrude E. (née) Durden
(8/5/1880–9/8/1918)
Songs, plays

Rush's plays include *Satan's Revenge* (a staging of Milton's *Paradise Lost*), *Sermon on the Mount* (1907), *Uncrowned Heroines* (1912), and *Black Girls*

Burden (1913). Her songs include "Jesus Loves the Little Children."

REFERENCES: Warwick, Judy, in *BWA:AHE.*

Russwurm, John (né) Brown
(10/1/1799–6/9/1851)
Journalist, editor, newspaper founder

John Brown's mother was a Jamaican slave impregnated by a white American merchant. On the insistence of his father's wife (and John's stepmother), Mr. Russwurm acknowledged his paternity and gave his son his surname. In 1807 Russwurm sent his son to Quebec for his early schooling. When John was a teenager, his father brought him home to Portland, Maine, and young John Russwurm attended the Hebron Academy starting in 1812. After completing his studies at the academy in Hebron, Russwurm went to Bowdoin College in Brunswick, from which he graduated in 1826, one the first African Americans to earn a bachelor's degree from a U.S. college. An early advocate of emigration, in the speech he gave on graduation, he urged African Americans to leave the United States and resettle in Haiti.

The following year, Russwurm moved to New York City, and on March 16, 1827, he and **Samuel E. Cornish** (an African-American Presbyterian minister) published the first issue of **Freedom's Journal,** the first African-American weekly published in this country. Cofounders Russwurm and Cornish coedited the paper and employed itinerant African-American abolitionists to print and operate the paper, thereby affirming the paper's motto, "We Wish to Plead Our Own Cause." Their cause, of course, was the abolition of slavery in the South and of inequality in the North. (One of the most powerful arguments for this cause was **David Walker**'s *Appeal,* which was first printed in the pages of this paper in December of 1828.) While Cornish was involved in editing the paper, the official editorial policy of the paper was to oppose the emigration of African Americans, holding that African Americans had built this nation and had every right to enjoy the full benefits of their labor within it. In September of 1827, however, Cornish resigned from his editorial duties in order to give more time to his ministry.

Russwurm was less firmly committed to opposing emigration. About the time of the paper's two-year anniversary, he had despaired of achieving any reforms in the United States and joined the American Colonization Society, embracing its aims of having all African Americans be free to leave the country and resettle in Africa. He turned the newspaper back to Cornish and moved to Liberia, which had been established as an independent nation in 1822, offering a homeland in which freed African-American slaves could resettle. There, Russwurm joined the American Colonization Society's settlement and accepted a job as the superintendent of education. He also edited the *Liberia Herald* and continued to advocate the emigration of African Americans to Liberia. In 1836 he was elected the first African-descended governor of his colony in Liberia, and in that position, he continued striving to improve Liberia's economic conditions and diplomatic status. When he died, he left his widow, Sarah McGill Russwurm, and four children as well as his landmark contribution to journalism.

Meanwhile, back in the States, Cornish tried to revive the paper as the *Rights of All,* but after a year, he found it impossible to keep the paper afloat financially and folded its operation. The end of the paper was not, however, the end of Russwurm's legacy. The Black Press celebrated its 170th anniversary in 1997, and each year the National Newspaper Publisher's Association, an African-American newspaper syndicate (with a cumulative circulation of 10 million) honors recipients with the John Russwurm Trophy and Merit Award.

REFERENCES: *BDAA. EA-99. G-97. PGAA. SMKC.* Andrews, William L., in *OCAAL.* Bardolph, Richard, in *WB-99.*

Rustin, Bayard (3/17/1910–8/24/1987)
Nonfiction essays and book

Born into a Quaker family, Rustin learned early the importance of nonviolent struggle for civil rights, and he perfected his political strategies as a protégé of **A. Philip Randolph**. In addition to his numerous essays (many of which were collected in *Down the Line: The Collected Writings of Bayard Rustin,* 1971), Rustin published *Strategies for Freedom: The Changing Patterns of Black Protest* (1976). He also ghostwrote many of the civil rights writings and speeches by and about **Martin Luther King, Jr.**, and he kept a journal of his thoughts and experiences.

REFERENCES: *E-98. EA-99. EB-98. EB-BH-CD. EBLG. G-95.* Szymczak, Jerome, in *BH2C.*

Salaam, Kalamu ya (né Vallery Ferdinand III) (3/24/1947–)

Plays, poems, essays, literary and cultural criticism, short stories

Salaam's plays, reflective of the **Black Arts movement**, include *The Picket* (1968), *Mama* (1969), *Happy Birthday Jesus* (1969), *Black Liberation Army* (1969), *Homecoming* (1970), and *Black Love Song* (1971). His poetry collections include *The Blues Merchant* (1969), *Hofu Ni Kwenu* (1973), *Pamoja Tutashinda* (1974), and his best-known volume, *Revolutionary Love* (1978). Salaam's other works (primarily literary or scholarly) include *Ibura* (1976), *Tearing the Roof off the Sucker* (1977), *South African Showdown* (1978), *Who Will Speak for Us? New Afrikan Folktales* (1978, coauthored by his wife, Tayari kwa Salaam), *Herufi: An Alphabet Reader* (1978), *Iron Flowers: A Poetic Report on a Visit to Haiti* (1979), and *Our Women Keep Our Skies from Falling* (1980). In addition, many of Salaam's stories, essays, and poems have been published in various scholarly and literary journals and anthologies.

REFERENCES: Toombs, Charles P., in *OCAAL*.

Sanchez, Sonia (née Wilsonia Driver) (9/9/1934–)

Poems

Sonia Sanchez's work has an impact on readers like that of few other writers. A prolific writer, she sometimes functions as a prophet when she calls for justice and equality for all peoples of the world. At other times, she writes passionately of love and intimate relationships. Her honesty can be loving and sensual, angry and biting, or hopeful and humorous. Sanchez grew up listening to jazz and blues music, and consequently much of her work is imbued with a distinctive lyrical quality. Ultimately, her powerful language and her universal messages make her one of the most significant African-American writers to emerge from the **Black Arts movement**.

Wilsonia Driver was born in Birmingham, Alabama, one of the two daughters of Lena and Wilson L. Driver. When Sonia was one year old, her mother died, and she and her older sister, Patricia, lived with extended family until Sonia was nine years old. For most of her childhood and youth, Sonia stuttered. When she was nine, her musician father took her and Patricia to live with him in Harlem, New York, leaving Sonia's half-brother in the South. (Her half-brother later moved to New York, where he died from AIDS in 1981. Sanchez's *Does your house have lions?* reflects on this family tragedy.)

Sanchez graduated from Hunter College in New York in 1955 with a B.A. in political science. She spent the next year at New York University studying poetry with Louise Bogan, who encouraged Sanchez to publish her work.

Twice divorced, Sanchez has one daughter (1957) and twin sons (1968). One of her marriages was to fellow writer and political activist **Etheridge Knight**.

Sanchez began her academic career in 1965 at the Downtown Community School in San Francisco. She then taught at San Francisco State College (1967–1969), where she helped establish the first black studies program in the United States. During these years, Sanchez became politically active in the Congress of Racial Equality (CORE) and the Nation of Islam (1972–1975). After holding several posts at various colleges and universities, she settled in Philadelphia at Temple University in 1977. She remains on the faculty there, teaching and maintaining a schedule of national and international readings of her work. Her travels include trips to China, Africa, and the Caribbean.

Sanchez has published more than ten books of poetry: *home coming* (1969); *We a BaddDDD People* (1970); *Love Poems* (1973); *Blues Book for Blue Black Magical Women* (1974); *Selected Poems* (1974, 1975); *homegirls & handgrenades* (1984); *I've Been a Woman: New and Selected Poems* (1985); *Generations: poetry, 1969–1985* (1986); *Under a Soprano Sky* (1987); *Wounded in the House of a Friend* (1995); *Does your house have lions?* (1997); and *Like the Singing Coming off the Drums* (1998). She has also published six plays and three children's books: *It's a New Day: Poems for Young Brothas and Sistuhs* (1971); *The Adventures of*

Flathead, Smallhead, and Squarehead (1973); and *A Sound Investment: Short Stories for Young Readers* (1980). Sanchez also edited two books, and her work has been anthologized in numerous books and published in many journals and magazines. She has garnered several important academic distinctions and literary awards as well, notably including the 1985 American Book Award for *homegirls & handgrenades.*

During the early years of her writing career, Sanchez played a prominent role in the Black Arts movement, and her poetry reflects the political turmoil present in the United States at that time. In the 1960s, African Americans sought to publish and promote their own creative work for a general audience. Alternative publishing houses and periodicals were established, and they served as wellsprings of innovative works. This aggressive business and political venture was later named the Black Arts movement and included other celebrated African-American writers, such as **Mari Evans** and **Nikki Giovanni**. These and other writers realistically focused on the minority-black experience in a majority-white United States during the civil rights movement and prior to affirmative action.

Sanchez's work has evolved as she has grown as an artist. Her first published book of poetry, *home coming,* is hard-hitting and controversial, with its cries for social justice and black pride and its condemnation of the established white power structure. Poems such as "the final solution" and "definition for blk/children" use a form and vocabulary so distinctive and powerful that Sanchez's words crush the printed page. Here Sanchez is her most angry and militant, cursing and rejecting white culture and encouraging blacks to embrace their own blackness as a positive image. She has said of that time and her work that "you have to really understand the time and what the politics were about."

In contrast, Sanchez's more recent work, *Like the Singing Coming off the Drums: Love Poems,* follows a more traditional form, vocabulary, and subject matter. In this book, Sanchez uses haiku extensively and writes with sensuality, wisdom, and humor. One selection, simply titled "Haiku," says, "is there a fo rent /sign on my butt? / you got no / territorial rights here." In another, Sanchez writes, "i am who i am. / nothing hidden just black silk / above two knees."

Throughout all of her work, Sanchez has continued to lobby for a more humane society for all peoples of the world. In "Poem for July 4, 1994," Sanchez says, "All of us must finally bury / the elitism of race . . . sexual . . . economic . . . [and] religious superiority." A speech she gave to Temple University's 1998 graduation class reads not like a speech but like poetry, and it, too, calls for a just world. Sanchez writes, "How can I bind you together . . . Away from Racism. Sexism. Homophobia. Exploitation. Militarism. Extreme materialism. Towards Unity. . . . Inaugurate a new way of breathing for the world, . . . and it will get better."

These short excerpts give only a small taste of the feast of words that Sanchez spreads before her readers. She has shown that a poet can be an activist, a loving sister, and a creative commentator on the U.S. political scene. Whether structured or unstructured, loud or serene, Sanchez's work always retains its impact.

—Janet Hoover

REFERENCES: *BWW.* Madhubuti, Haki, "Sonia Sanchez: The Bringer of Memories," in *BWW.* Melhelm, D. H. (1990), "Sonia Sanchez: The Will and the Spirit," *Heroism in the New Black Poetry: Introductions & Interviews* (Lexington: University Press of Kentucky). Salaam, Kalamu ya, "Black Arts Movement," in *OCAAL.* "Selected Bibliographies" and "Sonia Sanchez," in *NAAAL.* Sitter, Deborah Ayer, in *OCAAL.* Williams, David, "The Poetry of Sonia Sanchez," in *BWW.* http://english.cla.umn.edu/LKD/VFG/Authors/SoniaSanchez.

Scarborough, William Sanders
(2/16/1852–1926)
Scholarly works, textbook, translations, commentary

William's father was believed to be the great-grandson of an African chief, and his mother was of Spanish, Native American, and African-American ancestry; his father was freed by the time William was born, and his mother was a slave in name only, as her "owners" allowed her to live with her husband and children. Because the children of slave mothers were legally considered slaves, William was born into slavery and was not freed until the Civil War. Nonetheless, despite the strictures against slaves learning to read and write, both of William's parents were literate, and William, too, learned to read and write while still considered a slave.

After emancipation, William was able to gain an education, eventually attending Atlanta University and graduating from Oberlin College (in Ohio) in 1875. After brief attempts to teach school in the

South, where angry whites fought the reforms of Reconstruction, Scarborough returned North to Ohio, earning an M.A. at Oberlin and then becoming a professor of Latin and Greek at Wilberforce University (also in Ohio). (In 1881, Scarborough married Sarah Bierce, a white woman on the Wilberforce faculty, 1877–1914.) From 1892 to 1897, he had a hiatus from Wilberforce, as the demand for instruction in the classic languages was slight. (During this hiatus, he taught at Payne Seminary in South Carolina.) When he returned to Wilberforce, he was made vice president, then in 1908, he was named president of the university.

While maintaining his administrative duties, Scarborough continued to write scholarly works on language (specifically, linguistics and philology), as well as translations (e.g., of Greek playwright Aristophanes's *The Birds,* 1886). In addition to Greek and Latin, Scarborough knew Sanskrit and Hebrew as well as Slavonic languages. In recognition of his scholarship on language, he was elected to the American Philological Association (the third African American to be so honored). His most acclaimed work was his *First Lessons in Greek* (1886), which was used on campuses across the United States; in 1897, he published a highly esteemed paper on black folklore and dialect. In addition, he advocated for civil rights and wrote articles and other works championing that cause. His *The Educated Negro and His Mission* (1903) was well regarded enough to be reprinted and published again in 1969.

REFERENCES: *BDAA.*

Schomburg, Arthur A. (né Arturo Alfonso Schomburg) (occasional pseudonym: Guarionex)

(1/24/1874–6/10/1938)

Bibliography, essays, articles, nonfiction—history; bibliophile, curator

Arturo's mother, West Indian laundress Maria Josepha (Mary Joseph), was not married to his father, German-born merchant Carlos Federico Schomburg, when she gave birth to Arturo. Although Arturo adopted his father's surname, it appears that his father failed to support or even to acknowledge his son. Born in Saint Thomas, in the U.S. Virgin Islands, young Arturo was raised by his mother's family in Puerto Rico. Later in life, Arthur Schomburg provided very little information about his childhood experiences, and biographers have not been able to dig up much more information. Apparently, he had an older sister, Dolores María (called "Lola"), and his mother's parents were born free in St. Croix.

Accounts of his schooling vary, including suggestions that he attended school in San Juan, Puerto Rico, at a Jesuit school, the Instituto de Párvulos, or at the Institute of Popular Teaching (or of Instruction); that he attended school in the Virgin Islands; or that he was entirely self-educated, never having attended school. At one point, Schomburg reported that he attended St. Thomas College in the Virgin Islands, but no documentation supports that claim. Accounts also vary as to whether his mother lived with him and her parents in Puerto Rico or she remained in the Virgin Islands, sending him to Puerto Rico alone to live with her parents.

At some time during his adolescence, someone (reportedly a teacher of his) told young Arturo that Africans in the Americas had no history. (In Puerto Rico and in other Latin American countries, many persons of Spanish heritage have celebrated the splendid achievements of their Spanish ancestors, neglecting to appreciate the heritage of the pre-Columbian native civilizations in the Americas and discounting altogether the fact that Africans ruled Spain for three centuries until very shortly before Ferdinand and Isabella sent Columbus across the Atlantic.) Apparently, this person's offhand remark moved Schomburg to prove otherwise. Essentially, Schomburg dedicated the rest of his life to demonstrating the long, rich history of Africans, both in Africa and in the Americas, and to showing the countless profoundly important contributions of persons of African descent across the world.

Whatever his educational background, there can be no doubt that Schomburg was a well-educated man who continually sought to enrich his knowledge of his own cultural heritage and that of other persons of African descent in the Americas. While still in Puerto Rico, he joined a literary club, frequently participating in intellectual discussions, and he read widely in both Spanish and English. He particularly loved studying the history of the Caribbean and elsewhere in the Americas. Eventually, he realized that he would have greater opportunities for educating himself if he moved to the United States. Some reports suggest that he worked as a printer (typesetter) to earn money to move, and in 1891, at age 17, Arturo Schomburg left Puerto Rico.

Bibliophile Arthur A. Schomburg, undated (Corbis)

Friday, April 17, 1891, Arthur Schomburg arrived in New York City, where he settled in the Puerto Rican and Cuban section of the east side of Manhattan borough. He had brought with him some letters of introduction confirming his experience as a typographer, and he found work right away as a printer, as well as doing various service jobs (bellhop, porter, elevator operator, and so on). In addition, he attended night school at Manhattan's Central High School. Meanwhile, he continued to use his excellent memory to plumb the depths of history about Africans around the world, especially in the Americas. He also became active in political organizations involved with the Cuban and Puerto Rican independence movements.

By the time Schomburg had been in New York City a decade, he had gained work as a researcher clerking in a law office. For a time, he also studied law and had aspirations of becoming an attorney. When the state of New York barred him from taking the New York State Regents Examination to qualify for a "law certificate," however, he abandoned that goal and left the law firm in 1906. That year, he began working for the Bankers Trust Company (BTC) in the Latin American section of its mailroom. After a while, he was promoted to supervisor of the department, and he remained in

that position until he retired in 1929, with a medical disability. On his modest salary from BTC, he managed to support himself and his very large family as well as his chief true love: books and other materials about the history of Africa's descendants.

Actually, Schomburg had already been married twice by the time he started working at BTC. First, Schomburg had married Elizabeth ("Bessie") Hatcher June 30, 1895, and she and he had three sons: Maximo Gomez, Arthur Alfonso Jr., and Kingsley Guarionex. Bessie died in 1900, and two years later (March 17, 1902), Schomburg married Elizabeth Morrow Taylor, with whom he had two more sons: Reginald Stanfield and Nathaniel José. She too died young, and both sets of children were sent to live with their respective maternal relatives out of state. Undaunted, Schomburg married a third Elizabeth—Elizabeth Green—with whom he had three more children: Fernando, Dolores Marie (his only daughter, named after his older sister), and Plácido Carlos.

In addition to his family ties, he had important ties to his community. For instance, he was an active member of the Prince Hall Masons, serving as the grand secretary of the Grand Lodge of New York from 1918 to 1926. Despite these diversions, Schomburg's primary energies and efforts were always focused on his main love—African-American culture and history. In 1911, he joined John Edward Bruce's Men's Sunday Club, dedicated to discussing race-related issues and books. The club had an extensive library of materials on African-American history, and club members had been raising funds to buy additional materials for it. Bruce's club served as a springboard for the Negro Society for Historical Research, which Schomburg and Bruce cofounded that year. The society (of which Schomburg was secretary-treasurer and librarian for many years) was dedicated to publishing articles on African-American history, based on research conducted by society members. Participation in these groups encouraged Schomburg to be more rigorous and systematic in his own collection of books and other artifacts.

In 1914, Schomburg was invited to join the American Negro Academy (ANA), which **Alexander Crummell** had founded in 1879. Fellow members included **W. E. B. Du Bois**, **Alain Locke**, Kelly Miller (see **May Miller**), **Carter G. Woodson**, and numerous other scholars. This association helped Schomburg further refine his bibliophilic research skills and encouraged his abiding dedication to research in African-American culture and history. In 1922, he was elected the ANA's fifth (and last) president, although he was chiefly an absentee executive for the Washington, D.C.–based academy. In 1929, when the academy ceased operation, he had already become rather disillusioned with it. Schomburg also had rocky relationships with many other organizations (including the National Association for the Advancement of Colored People, the National Urban League, the Negro Writers' Guild, and about 25 or more others). Often he resigned from these organizations over a disagreement, particularly if he felt that his opinion was unappreciated or he felt slighted or overlooked. Perhaps because of his lack of formal educational credentials, we may speculate that he was overly sensitive to criticism or neglect from African-American intellectuals, but we can only guess as to the reason.

Over time, Schomburg amassed a wealth of literary works and visual artwork by persons of African descent. By the time he had been in New York for a couple of decades, he had accumulated a broad, well-organized, prodigious collection. He had also become well known for his sophisticated ability to recognize choice items and to find rare or missing materials. In 1926, the New York Public Library (NYPL) opened its Division of Negro Literature, History, and Prints at its 135th Street branch (off Lenox Avenue in Harlem), based largely on the purchase of Schomburg's private collection. That year, the Carnegie Corporation had paid Schomburg $10,000 for his collection, which it donated to the NYPL. At the time of the purchase, his collection included more than 10,000 items (about 5,000 books, 3,000 manuscripts, numerous pamphlets and prints, 2,000 etchings and drawings, and countless other artifacts). (Sadly, the original inventory of his contribution has been lost, so these numbers are just estimates.)

What did Schomburg do with all that money? (To give you an idea of what he could have done, at that time a Sears, Roebuck and Co. catalogue sold kits for building a five-room home for about $2,000.) Instead of squandering his money on real estate, Schomburg crossed the country and the globe (contacting booksellers in Europe, Latin America, and elsewhere) to gather still more materials, which he continued to contribute to the NYPL. Fortunately, during the era of the **Harlem Renaissance**, many writers and scholars came to recognize Schomburg for his dedication to

African-American scholarship and research, as well as for his collection. He was frequently invited to lecture across the country, and he inspired **James Weldon Johnson**, **Kenneth Clark**, **Claude McKay** (probably his closest friend), **Walter White**, and others in their literary and scholarly pursuits. Schomburg also admired **Marcus Garvey** and valued Garvey's goals of fostering African-American pride, independence, and self-sufficiency. Schomburg's collection itself also offered a tremendous resource to writers and other artists of the Harlem Renaissance and of every era since.

Another of Schomburg's close associates was historian **Charles (Spurgeon) Johnson**. Through his contact with Johnson, in 1929 or 1930, Schomburg was invited to establish and curate a collection of resources on African-American history and culture for the library of Fisk University (in Nashville, Tennessee). There, he not only established a highly respected collection but also mapped out a plan for the library to continue to add to its collection through future acquisitions.

In 1932, Schomburg received another job offer, which he found irresistible: An additional Carnegie Corporation grant funded the NYPL's appointment of Schomburg as the curator of his own collection at the Harlem branch. There, he remained for the next several years until his death (in 1938). During his final years, in addition to his own travels and contacts, he asked other scholars and writers (e.g., **Langston Hughes**) to help him find further materials for the collection. Frequently, if he was unable to get the library to purchase materials he deemed important, he purchased them out of his own funds. He also managed to persuade composers, visual artists, scholars, writers, and others to contribute their manuscripts and other materials to the collection. At some point, the collection was renamed the Schomburg Collection of Negro Literature and History (in 1934 or 1940) and still later was renamed the Schomburg Center for Research in Black Culture (in 1973). (See also **Jean Blackwell Hutson** and **Catherine A. Latimer**.) Many researchers acknowledge the center as the world's largest and most important repository of materials on African and African-American history and culture, now including more than 5 million items. (The five divisions of the center are art and artifacts; general research and reference; manuscripts, archives, and rare books; moving image and recorded sound; and photographs and prints.)

Schomburg's own publications include a bibliography (*A Bibliographical Checklist of American Negro Poetry*, 1916), an exhibition catalogue, and various articles published in the *A.M.E. Review*, **Crisis**, *The Messenger*, **Negro Digest**, **Negro World**, *New Century*, **Opportunity**, and *Survey Graphic*. Among his best-known articles are "Economic Contribution by the Negro to America" (1916), published by the ANA, and "The Negro Digs Up His Past" (1925), published in *Survey Graphic* and reprinted in Alain Locke's anthology *The New Negro*. Given that English was Schomburg's second language and that he lacked much formal education, his writing served him well. Nonetheless, he profited from having skilled editors such as W. E. B. Du Bois, Charles (Spurgeon) Johnson, and Alain Locke edit his work for readability. With their help, he was able to show his great analytical skills, keen insight into African-American culture and history, and tremendous scholarship in the field.

REFERENCES: *AA:PoP. BDAA. EA-99. NAAAL.* Barnes, Deborah H., in *OCAAL.* Fay, Robert, "Schomburg Library," in *EA-99.* Smith, Jessie Carney, in *BH2C.*

Schuyler, George Samuel
(2/25/1895–8/31/1977)
Satire, novels, political commentary, autobiography; editor, journalist

As a young adult, Schuyler was a socialist associated with **A. Philip Randolph**, but he is better known for his anticommunist, conservative political views in his later years. For about a decade, starting in 1923, his writing centered on articles and columns (e.g., "Shafts and Darts: A Page of Calumny and Satire") appearing in several newspapers. While working for Randolph's *The Messenger* (1923–1928), he started out as a staff writer and then became an assistant editor and then managing editor. From 1924 until the mid-1960s, he was also the New York correspondent for the *Pittsburgh Courier*. Nine of his essays were published in H. L. Mencken's *American Mercury* magazine (1927–1933), and many other articles and columns of his were published in other white-owned publications, such as *Nation, Plain Talk,* and *Common Ground*. Schuyler also wrote nonfiction books, including *Racial Intermarriage in the United States* (presaged by his own marriage to a white woman, Josephine Cogdell, in 1928), *Slaves Today: A Story of Liberia* (1931, an account of the slavelike working conditions of laborers in Liberia), and *Black and Conservative: The Autobiography of George S. Schuyler* (1966).

In the 1930s, Schuyler turned his attention to fiction. His best-known novel is his satire *Black No More, Being an Account of the Strange and Wonderful Workings of Science in the Land of the Free* (1931), which satirically addresses the issue of race in the United States. In addition, between 1933 and 1939, he wrote 54 short stories and 20 serialized novels or novellas, which were published under pen names. In the 1990s, 4 of these serialized novels were printed in 2 volumes: *Black Empire* (1991) and *Ethiopian Stories* (1995). Perhaps Schuyler's most distinguished production, however, was his daughter—musician, composer, and writer **Philippa Duke Schuyler** (b. 1931)—the fruit of his marriage to Cogdell.

REFERENCES: *BAAW. EBLG.* Davidson, Adenike Marie, in *OCAAL.* Fay, Robert, in *EA-99.*

Schuyler, Philippa Duke
(8/2/1931–5/9/1967)
Autobiography, articles, political commentary, biography, nonfiction—politics, dream interpretation, war observations; journalist

Schuyler's parents certainly knew how to provoke controversy. Josephine "Jody" Cogdell, a wealthy European-American journalist from Texas, firmly believed that the ultimate solution to U.S. race problems was interracial marriage. What's more, she believed that the offspring of such marriages would be extraordinary as a result of "hybrid vigor." When she met **George Schuyler**, novelist and journalist, she found a soulmate to share her theory and her life. To their delight, their daughter Philippa (named after both Philip of Macedon and Revolutionary War hero Philip Schuyler) turned out to be exceptional in many ways.

Of course, Philippa's parents provided her with private tutoring and almost every other cultural and educational advantage they could offer. Still, she certainly flourished in this environment, reading at age $2^1/_2$, playing the piano at age 3, and composing at age 4. By the time she was 13 years old, she had already composed more than 100 pieces, including *Manhattan Nocturne,* which won the Grinnell Foundation's young composers contest for both originality and skill (including parts for 100 instruments), and which has since been performed by the New York Philharmonic and several other major symphony orchestras in this country. At age 15, she herself debuted for the New York Philharmonic in Lewisohn Stadium with an audience of about 12,000 listeners.

Despite her early promise, however, her career as a concert pianist didn't take her to the stratosphere, so she shifted from music to writing. As her parents' daughter, she felt right at home lecturing on "The Red Menace in Africa" for the John Birch Society and other right-wing organizations. Her book *Who Killed the Congo?* (1962) elaborated on that theme. Her other published books include an autobiography, *Adventures in Black and White* (1960); *Jungle Saints: Africa's Heroic Catholic Missionaries* (1963); a book on dream interpretation, *Kingdom of Dreams* (1966, coauthored with her mother); and her eyewitness view of the Vietnam War, *Good Men Die* (1969, published posthumously).

Schuyler wrote her final published book while covering the war as a journalist. (She had been working as a journalist for various American and European publications, often corresponding in French and German, as well as English.) While in Vietnam, she was helping to rescue children from a battle site in Hue to a school in Da Nang when the helicopter in which she was riding crashed.

Schuyler also left behind some unpublished fiction, which she hadn't completed: *Sophie Daw,* a novel about the oppression of women; and *Dau Tranh,* about a tragic American mulatto. Ironic.

—*Tonya Bolden*

REFERENCES: *BAAW. EA-99.* Richardson, Deborra A., in *BWA:AHE.* Talalay, Kathryn (1995), *Composition in Black and White: The Life of Philippa Schuyler* (New York: Oxford University Press).

Shadd Cary (married name), Mary Ann
See **Cary, Mary Ann (née) Shadd**

Shakur, Assata Olugbala (née JoAnne Deborah Byron; married name: Chesimard) (7/16/1947–)
Autobiography

In Shakur's book, *Assata: An Autobiography* (1987), she candidly (and often with good humor) describes her formative years as well as her experiences as an activist in the Black Panther Party (early and mid-1970s), a questionably convicted accomplice to the murder of a white state trooper (1977), a prisoner, and an escaped pris-

oner who was granted political asylum in Cuba (since 1979).

—*Tonya Bolden*

REFERENCES: *BAAW.*

Shakur, Tupac ("2Pac")
(6/16/1971–9/13/1996)
Rap songs

One of Shakur's first rap hits was "Brenda's Got a Baby," which depicted the hardships faced by single African-American mothers, much like his own mother, Black Panther Party activist Afeni Shakur. Sadly, the drugs and violence Shakur described in his songs (e.g., "If I Die 2Nite" and "Death Around the Corner") also mimicked his own life experiences: He was shot multiple times, jailed and imprisoned, and eventually died as a result of a shooting. His career had been promising before his demise, as his records had sold millions of copies, and he was nominated for two Grammy Awards.

REFERENCES: Robinson, Alonford James, Jr., in *EA-99.*

Shange, Ntozake (née Paulette Williams) (10/18/1948–)
Plays, poems, novels, essays

The Williams family—Eloise, a psychiatric social worker; Paul T., a surgeon; and their four children—regularly enjoyed a broad array of cultural experiences, including jazz, blues, soul, Latin, and classical music; selected readings from William Shakespeare, **Paul Laurence Dunbar**, and **Langston Hughes**; attendance at ballets and concerts; and Sunday afternoon family variety shows, with Paul T. playing the congas and the children dancing or playing an assortment of instruments. These family events were often highlighted with visits from such outstanding entertainers as Josephine Baker, Chuck Berry, Dizzy Gillespie, and Charlie Parker. On at least one occasion, **W. E. B. Du Bois** illumined her family's home, and guests from "virtually all of the colonized French-, Spanish-, and English-speaking countries" were welcome in the Williams home. Paulette and her younger siblings felt very much connected to Africa's descendants around the world as well as to the breadth of Third World cultures.

After Paulette's birth, the Williamses spent eight years in Trenton, New Jersey, and then five years in St. Louis, Missouri, before returning again to Tren-

Ntozake Shange (right) in a scene from "for colored girls who have considered suicide/when the rainbow is enuf," 1976 (UPI/Corbis-Bettmann)

ton. During their years in St. Louis, Paulette was among the first African-American children to integrate the public school system, and she experienced firsthand the poignant cruelty of racism. While her parents took pride in their courageous, independent young racial pioneers, Paulette was developing a belly-deep rage toward racism. Although she had been writing stories since her early years, when she heard in school that Negroes don't write, she stopped writing.

When the family returned to Trenton, Paulette started reading all the literature she could put her hands on: Carson McCullers and Simone de Beauvoir, Fyodor Dostoyevsky and Herman Melville. In high school, she even started writing again. After some of her poetry was published in her high school magazine, she felt encouraged to write more. In her English class, she wrote essays about African Americans. After writing numerous essays, however, she was told that she should start writing

about other topics, and she again stopped writing until after she finished high school.

After high school, Paulette entered Barnard College (in 1966) and soon married a law student. After she and her husband went through an agonizing separation, she made a series of suicide attempts. Compounding her emotional distress was her intensifying awareness that the society in which she lived—unlike her supportive family—devalued intelligent African-American women. Despite this emotional turmoil, she managed to graduate cum laude with a B.A. in American studies in 1970.

After Barnard, Paulette moved to Los Angeles, where she lived communally with several other performance artists and writers. During this time (in 1971), she adopted her name Ntozake Shange. *Ntozake* is a Zulu name for "she who comes with her own things," and *Shange* means "she who walks like a lion." By the time she earned her master's degree (in 1973), she signed all of her work with her self-chosen name.

With her master's degree in hand, Shange moved to the San Francisco Bay area, where she taught at various colleges until 1975. During this period, she also made numerous public appearances as a performance artist, dancing and reciting her own original poetry. Even after her literary career took off, Shange has continued to teach (e.g., at Yale University, Howard University, and the University of Houston).

Through Shange's numerous performances, she developed a distinctive form that she calls a "choreopoem"—verse narratives that are presented onstage, accompanied by music and dance. Her first finished choreopoem was *for colored girls who have considered suicide / when the rainbow is enuf* (published in 1976). In this choreopoem, seven African-American women act, sing, dance, and recite 20 poems. Their characters are identified as the Lady in Brown, the Lady in Yellow, in Red, Green, Purple, Blue, and Orange. Each woman takes a turn reciting her story as a poetic monologue. Each story highlights an aspect of African-American women's experiences across the life span (e.g., a childhood crush, a first sexual experience, an abusive relationship with a violent Vietnam veteran).

Although many critics praised the play for its freshness and wit and for highlighting the experiences of courageous, outspoken women who triumph over despair, some critics condemned it for its lack of winsome men and its superficial characterizations. Apparently, the praises outweighed the detractions, as her choreopoem was performed on Broadway (only the second play by an African-American woman to reach Broadway; see **Lorraine Hansberry**) for two years in the mid-1970s, winning an Obie Award as well as Emmy, Tony (for best play), and Grammy Award nominations. The play also earned Outer Critics Circle, Audelco, and *Mademoiselle* awards and was chosen for international performances. Shange's peers recognize her achievement, too. For instance, **Nikki Giovanni** (*BWWW,* p. 67) said of her, "I loved *For Colored Girls.* First of all Ntozake is an extremely bright, sensitive, *good poet.* She writes exceptionally well. . . . *For Colored Girls* is . . . one of my favorite poems."

Additional plays by Shange include her 1981 Obie Award–winning *Mother Courage and Her Children* (1980), a Civil War–era adaptation of Bertolt Brecht's play *Mother Courage;* her 1981 *Los Angeles Times Book Review* Award–winning *Three Pieces: Spell #7: A Photograph: Lover in Motion: Boogie Woogie;* her choreopoem *From Okra to Greens! A Different Kinda Love Story: A Play! With Music and Dance* (1985); *Betsey Brown* (1989), based on her 1985 novel; *Daddy Says* (1989), a somewhat conventional one-act play; *The Love Space Demands: A Continuing Saga* (1991), a choreopoem performance piece; and *Where the Mississippi Meets the Amazon* (coauthored with Jessica Hegedorn and Thulani Nkabinda).

In addition to her plays, Shange has written several novels. As with her plays, Shange has developed her novels in her own distinctive way. Often, she has taken work from one medium (e.g., a play) and adapted it to another medium (e.g., a novel), or she has taken a smaller work (e.g., a novella) and amplified it to create a much broader work (e.g., a novel). For instance, she transformed her dance-drama *Sassafras,* presented in 1976, into a novella, *Sassafras: A Novella,* published in 1977; then she developed that work further and expanded it to create *Sassafras, Cypress & Indigo: A Novel,* published in 1982. Her novel tells the story of three sisters: Sassafras, a weaver; Cypress, a dancer; and Indigo, a midwife. Each sister is struggling with her own identity and her need for creative freedom and purpose. Also, in Shange's initial novella, she minimally punctuated the book, "because I didn't want the reader to be able to put the book down" (*BWWW,* p. 156); the novel, however, follows standardized punctuation conventions. Additional novels by Shange include *Some Men* (1981); *Betsey Brown* (1985), a semiautobiographical novel set in the late 1950s, when the author and the civil rights movement were coming of age; *Melissa and Smith: A Story* (1985), a novella; and *Liliane: Resurrection of the Daughter* (1994), about the psychological development of a wealthy African-American woman living in the South.

In addition to her plays and her fiction, Shange has written several free verse poetry collections, which also flout conventional language forms: *Nappy Edges* (1978), exulting in outspoken independent women's voices; *A Daughter's Geography* (1983); *From Okra to Greens: Poems by Ntozake Shange* (1984); *Ridin' the Moon in Texas: Word Paintings* (1987), which highlights the African-American **oral tradition** through nonconformist syntax, capitalization, spelling, and idiomatic vocabulary and language structure; and *I Live in Music* (1994). Regarding her distinctive spellings,

Shange has said, "The spellings result from the way I talk or the way the character talks or the way I heard something said. Basically, the spellings reflect language as I hear it" (*BWWW,* p. 163). Bridging the gap between prose and poetry is Shange's collection *Natural Disasters and Other Festive Occasions* (1977). Her nonfiction writings have been gathered in *See No Evil: Prefaces, Essays and Accounts 1976–1983* (1984).

Among the many honors and awards Shange has earned are the 1991 World Heavyweight Champion at the Taos Poetry Circus, a Guggenheim fellowship, a Columbia University Medal of Excellence, and appointment to the New York State Council of the Arts. Perhaps more astonishingly, Shange has managed to achieve such success while raising her daughter Savannah as a single working mother.

REFERENCES: *1TESK. AA:PoP. BWWW. EBLG. MAAL. MWEL. NAAAL. OC20LE.* Lester, Neal, in *OCWW.* Taylor-Thompson, Betty, in *OCAAL.*

Shockley, Ann (née Allen) (6/21/1927–)
Criticism, novels, short stories, bibliographies, biographies, essays, compilations; journalist, archivist

Henry and Bessie Lucas Allen, both social workers, raised Ann, their only daughter, to savor reading and writing. In junior high school, Ann edited her school newspaper, and she was soon writing short articles for the local *Louisville* [Kentucky] *Defender.*

While working toward her B.A. at Fisk University, Ann wrote essays and short stories for the *Fisk Herald*. She earned her B.A. in 1948, and in 1949 she married William Shockley, with whom she had a son and a daughter. (The Shockleys subsequently divorced.) Between 1949 and 1959, Ann wrote weekly newspaper columns focusing on African-American political, cultural, social, community, family, and women's issues. She also worked as a public school teacher and then a librarian. By 1959 she had earned an M.S. in library science, and for years she curated various African-American collections at nearby colleges. At last, by 1969 she had earned her way home to Fisk, where she has since been recognized as one of the leading university archivists of African-American women's writing.

Shockley's first book-length projects were outstanding reference works used by fellow archivists: Her "History of Public Library Services to Ne-

groes in the South, 1900–1955" (unpublished) thoroughly describes the inadequacies of segregated public library services in the Jim Crow South; her *Living Black Authors: A Biographical Directory* (1973) describes numerous African-American writers; and her *A Handbook for Black Librarianship* (1977) specifically tells how to gather and protect materials on African-American history. In addition, Shockley has written articles and has edited volumes about various issues of interest to professionals (e.g., oral history, literacy, racism in children's literature). Her most recent nonfiction work has wide appeal: *Afro-American Women Writers (1746–1933): An Anthology and Critical Guide* (1988), which places more than 40 writers in their historical and cultural context.

Shockley has also written fiction. Her 1974 novel *Loving Her* focuses on an interracial lesbian love affair, and her second novel, *Say Jesus and Come to Me* (1982), addresses the issue of homophobia in the African-American church. Her other fiction book, *The Black and White of It* (1980), is a collection of short stories centering on lesbian love and issues of race. In it, "A Meeting of the Sapphic Daughters" reveals racism in the women's movement. In this collection and elsewhere, Shockley's short stories address a wide range of issues (homophobia in the African-American community, de facto public school segregation, interracial dating, and so on).

Despite the triple jeopardy she has faced—being black, female, and homosexual in a racist, sexist, and homophobic society—Shockley has been honored for her work, including a 1962 National Short Story Award from the American Association of University Women and a 1982 Martin Luther King Award for literature.

REFERENCES: *EBLG.* Dandridge, Rita B., in *OCAAL.* Schulz, Elizabeth, in *OCWW.*

Simmons, Herbert Alfred (1930–)
Novels, play, poems

Simmons has written some poetry, the award-winning play *The Stranger* (1956), and the novels *Corner Boy* (1957) and *Man Walking on Eggshells* (1962), which have an improvisational, jazzlike quality.

REFERENCES: Margulis, Jennifer, in *OCAAL.*

Simmons, William J.

(6/26/1849–10/30/1890)

Biographies; magazine editor

Despite being born into slavery and spending his childhood as a fugitive from slavery, Simmons ended up gaining a good education and became an educator himself. In 1880, he was appointed the president of the Normal and Theological Institution, run by Baptists, which later became the State University of Kentucky at Louisville under his leadership. In 1881, he earned his M.A. from Howard University, and the following year (1882), he was named editor of the *American Baptist* magazine. Five years later, Simmons published his landmark biographical dictionary of important African-American men: *Men of Mark: Eminent, Progressive, and Rising* (1887; reprinted 1968 but now out of print). When Simmons died, at age 41, he left behind his wife, Josephine Silence Simmons, and their seven children.

References: *BDAA.*

Sissle, Noble (7/10/1889–12/17/1975)

Songs

Sissle was the primary lyricist to collaborate with noted pianist and composer Eubie Blake, such as in their ground-breaking 1921 show, *Shuffle Along,* one of the first musicals to be written, directed, and produced by African Americans, as well as performed by blacks. This show was so successful that three companies of the show were touring the country at the same time, and their "I'm Just Wild about Harry" was popular for many years.

References: "Blake, James Hubert ('Eubie')," in *BDAA. EA-99.*

Slave Narratives

Slave narratives are the recordings and recollections of slaves and former slaves. Slave narratives give voice to history, enabling us to trace more than 300 years of history in which millions of people were brought to the United States, literally in chains. The narratives provide distinctive insight into the everyday experiences of slaves and former slaves, from the earliest days of fifteenth and sixteenth-century slave trading in Africa through the postemancipation period. Without such narratives, these experiences are otherwise invisible to most readers of traditional history books. Across the history of slavery, slave narratives help us to piece together a genuine understanding of the lives, experiences, and humanity of those who have been enslaved in our country. As Thomas Frazier (1970) said, "Much of the writing and teaching of American history, when it has considered the black man at all, has considered him as a slave up to 1863 and as a problem after that." Slave narratives may shed light on the value of the men and women whom this country enslaved and whose unpaid arduous labor helped create a nation of great wealth.

The narratives also offer distinctive insight into particular aspects of U.S. history. For instance, many of these narratives show how Southern plantations underwent historical changes. In the early years, most of these plantations were relatively small, independent farms with a few slaves, located mainly in the coastal colonies of Virginia and the Carolinas. Over time, however, the plantations grew to large, complex slave-holding plantations, which spread west from the coastal colonies through the southern colonies and states to Texas.

Slave narratives may be sorted into three types, based on the origin of the account: (1) authentic narratives, written directly by slaves in their own words, during or soon after their enslavement; (2) narratives recorded by *amanuenses* (people who wrote down what others dictated) during or soon after the narrator's enslavement, which were often heavily edited by the amanuenses; or (3) narratives recorded after slavery had officially ended (in 1863), based on interviews between former slaves and government workers. Clearly, the credibility and reliability of the account varies across these three basic forms. Therefore, readers need to know which type of account they are reading in order to know how readily to believe the account.

Often, scholars disagree about how to categorize particular narratives, with some giving evidence that an account was authentic, while others firmly assert that the same account was recorded and edited by an amanuensis. The age, gender, and literacy of the slave or former slave and of the possible amanuensis are closely analyzed in trying to assess the true origin of accounts in question. For instance, if an account seems to be written by a well-educated 50-year-old man, but its author is identified as a poorly educated 20-year-old woman, questions will emerge.

Authentic, unedited narratives written directly by the slaves themselves were more likely to emerge during the early slavery period, when slaves were still being captured and brought to this

A group of slaves in front of their cabin before emancipation, 1861 (Archive Photos/American Stock)

country. Because some of the enslaved were already literate when they were captured, they were able to record their narratives in their native languages. If they then mastered English (or French or another European language), they could easily write their narratives themselves. On the other hand, if they didn't arrive in this country knowing how to read and write, they were unlikely to learn that skill here.

A rare example of a slave narrative written during the time of his enslavement was that of Omar ibn Sied (born in 1770). Ibn Sied, a literate Muslim abducted from what is now Senegal, wrote his life story on the walls of his cell in North Carolina. After learning English, he then transcribed his autobiography into English. More commonly, these narratives were by former slaves, such as Ukawsaw Gronniosaw and **Olaudah Equiano** (also called "Gustavus Vassa"), both of whom gained their freedom in the United States. Gronniosaw wrote his narratives in the United States, and Equiano wrote his in England. According to Frazier (1970), both men's writings were "highly emotional and introspective autobiographies," which gave lie to the slave owners' pretense at jus-

tifying slavery on the basis of the intellectual inferiority of the slaves.

Equiano's narrative is one of the most widely referenced narratives describing enslavement in West Africa. Equiano was born into the family of an Ibo tribal elder in 1745 in what is now Nigeria (the Benin Empire at that time). Kidnapped at age 11, he described the white men on the slave ship as having "horrible looks, red faces and long hair," and the journey through the Middle Passage (the trip from Africa to America) as "a scene of horror almost inconceivable." He recorded that, on landing in Barbados, he and others feared that the whites were cannibalistic, remembering that "there was much dread and trembling among us, and nothing but bitter cries" (Blassingame, 1979). The narratives written during the early period of slavery help to dispel the myth that slaves, as a whole, were nonliterate.

Once the majority of slaves were born in this country (rather than being kidnapped and shipped here), it became less and less likely that a narrative would be authored by a slave during her or his time of captivity. Customarily, slave owners tried to ensure that their slaves were *prevented* from learning to read and write. In fact, toward the end of the slavery period, slave owners imposed harsh penalties on any slave who could read or write and on anyone who was caught teaching a slave to read or write. This made it highly unlikely for a narrative to be written by a slave during his or her time of enslavement. Therefore, during this later period, authentic slave narratives were chiefly written by former slaves who had escaped, had bought their freedom, or had been proclaimed emancipated (after 1863).

The degree to which former slaves were able to master reading and writing varied widely. Most of these former slaves had only rudimentary writing skills, and their narratives reflected the speech patterns they had acquired during their time of enslavement, rather than the patterns of educated Northerners. Some former slaves, however, had illicitly learned to read and write before their escape, and some escaped at a young enough age to master the new skill. For instance, **Frederick Douglass**, born in slavery about 1818, was taught the rudiments of English from his second owner, and young white boys had helped him learn to read. His later mastery of reading and writing are without question.

To summarize, the authors of authentic narratives included fully literate people who wrote their narratives during or soon after their enslavement, former slaves who had rudimentary literacy skills, or former slaves who were educated after their emancipation and recollected their earlier experiences of enslavement. In all cases, these narratives were written in the authentic words of the slave or former slave. In reflecting on the slave writings of the nineteenth century, William L. Andrews and **Henry Louis Gates, Jr.** (1999), noted that "the slave wrote not only to demonstrate humane letters, but also to demonstrate his or her own membership in the human community."

As you may have guessed, there are very few authentic slave narratives based on firsthand experiences of the author recorded after the early period of American slavery. After 1800, the most prevalent slave narratives were the second type of slave narrative: the account of an amanuensis who purportedly recorded the words dictated by the narrator. In these accounts, only through the record of the amanuensis does the reader discover the horrors of the Middle Passage, life and work on the plantations, and the period following emancipation.

The amanuensis could have been a fellow slave, a freed slave, a white plantation worker or owner, or a white abolitionist. The amanuensis may have been writing a letter, a report to a Freedmen's Bureau, or an antislavery tract. Whatever the source, their writings remain few when compared to the large number of slaves, but as Herbert Gutman (1976) says, "These few letters are quite unusual historical documents . . . the letters' importance does not rest upon whether they were a common form of expression. They were not. What is important is their relationship to the beliefs and behaviors of other slaves who left no such historical record."

Although many amanuenses took pains to record the narratives as faithfully as possible, many others heavily edited the narratives. The prevalence of editing and other distortions is in little doubt. Andrews and Gates (1999) observed that "the great nineteenth-century slave narratives typically carry a black message in a white envelope." Editing ranged from modest changes in wording or emphasis to entirely ghostwritten text as well as recollections edited much later, far from the narrator. Abolitionists played an important role in these writings. They often imposed their own biases on the narratives, whether or not they acknowledged doing so. Nonetheless, there is reason to believe that many amanuenses recorded the actual words of the former slaves with great care.

One such narrator who relied on the help of an amanuensis was **Venture Smith**. Smith dictated his *A Narrative of the Life and Adventures of Venture Smith* (1789) to an amanuensis, probably Elisha Niles, a schoolmaster in Connecticut. The narrative described Smith's life in Guinea after he had been given his freedom by his third owner (Frazier, 1970). In it, Smith remembered his father, a wealthy prince, as "a man of remarkable strength and resolution, affable, kind and gentle, ruling with equity and moderation" (Blassingame, 1979). It seems likely that the recollections are genuine, but the wording may be influenced by the amanuensis.

Even when narratives were from the author's own pen, white abolitionists or others often added prefatory or appended writings intended to legitimize the works. This was true even for Frederick Douglass's narrative (1845/1963). Wendell Phillips, in a letter included as part of the introduction to Douglass's moving narrative, wrote, "I am glad the time has come when the 'lions write history.' We have been left long enough to gather the character of slavery from the involuntary evidence of the masters."

The third type of slave narratives appeared after the proclamation of emancipation in 1863. These were gained through interviews of former slaves, conducted by volunteer or paid employees of the federal government. These were funded by two different federal programs, implemented decades apart. Immediately following the Civil War (starting in the late 1860s), many states' Freedmen's Bureaus conducted interviews of former slaves. During the 1930s, interviews were conducted as part of the Federal Writers' Project (FWP) for the Works Progress Administration (WPA; part of President Franklin D. Roosevelt's New Deal).

Narratives submitted to the Freedmen's Bureaus highlighted the variety of work relationships that emerged through slavery. In states from Alabama to Texas, owners of many large plantations had impersonal relations with their slaves, with a white overseer supervising huge gangs of field workers. On plantations in the eastern states, from the Carolinas to Georgia, owners had more personal relationships with the slaves who worked for them, identifying them by face and knowing them by name. The narratives gathered during this early postslavery period also served as records of slave families, documenting that some family members resided together while others were separated from the main family, often because of having been sold (Tyler and Murphy, 1974).

Regarding the second main federal program for recording slave narratives, John Cade, a Southern professor, was one of the first to conceive of interviewing former slaves in the 1930s. His initial work was published in 1935. Lawrence Reddick is credited with suggesting to New Deal leaders what came to be known as the Federal Writers' Project.

The accuracy and authenticity of the interviews gathered through this program have been questioned. For one thing, it had been almost 70 years since emancipation, so the informants (former slaves or children of slaves) had had a *long* time to forget their experiences and the stories they had heard about slavery. Also, most of them were very old, so age may also have impaired their memories. In addition, most of the WPA workers were white and lacked personal knowledge of the history of slavery, and very few had any training in techniques for conducting oral history interviews. What's more, the interviewers rarely used recording devices for conducting the interviews, so whatever they didn't write down at the time or recall later on was left out. This project depended heavily on the memories of the interviewers as well as of the interviewees. Finally, the interviews

were edited by government workers in Washington, D.C., or some other locale.

Even with these limitations, however, these narratives contain many truths. Much of the information and many of the events revealed in the FWP interviews were corroborated by earlier interviews and other evidence (Elkins, 1963). In addition, these narratives aptly chronicled daily experiences. For instance, former slaves such as Hannah Davidson described her hard daily life in interviews with an FWP worker. She recalled working six days a week from dawn to midnight, with Sunday being used for home chores: "Work, work, work, . . . I been so exhausted working, I was like an inchworm crawling along a roof. I worked till I thought another lick would kill me" (Jones, 1985).

In combination, the various types of narratives are important in countering the perspectives of white owners and historians who had depicted the slave as being well cared for, well fed, and rarely mistreated, or slave life as being more bearable in one part of the South than another (Tyler and Murphy, 1974). In fact, these diverse narratives chronicle the full range of interactions with owners and other whites. The records range from brutal treatment for minor infractions to slaves' recollections of getting sick when working in the hot sun and having their owners insist they sit in the shade until they had recovered (Genovese, 1974). These narratives provide a voice to the story, correcting distortions in much of recorded history and documenting the participation of slaves and former slaves in the human community, as evidenced by Frederick Douglass in the closing paragraph of his narrative:

> Sincerely and earnestly hoping that this little book may do something toward throwing light on the American slave system, and hastening the glad day of deliverance to the millions of my brethren in bonds—faithfully relying upon the power of truth, love, and justice, for success in my humble efforts— and solemnly pledging my self anew to the sacred cause,—I subscribe myself,
> Frederick Douglass, Lynn, Mass.,
> April 28, 1845

EDITOR'S NOTE: Some of the better-known slave narratives include *The Interesting Narrative of the Life of Olaudah Equiano, or Gustavus Vassa, the African* (1789, England; 1791, United States); *The History of Mary Prince, a West Indian Slave, Related by*

Herself (1831, published in London); *Slavery in the United States: A Narrative of the Life and Adventures of Charles Ball, a Black Man* (1836, written with abolitionist Isaac Fisher; reprinted 1970); *A Narrative of the Adventures and Escape of Moses Roper, from American Slavery* (1837, London; 1838, United States); *Narrative of the Life of Frederick Douglass, an American Slave, Written by Himself* (1845); and **Harriet Jacobs**'s *Incidents in the Life of a Slave Girl: Written by Herself* (1861), regarding her escape in 1835, edited and promoted by **Lydia Maria Child**, the first slave narrative written by a woman and published in the United States. Perhaps the earliest narrative written by a slave—but hardly a characteristic slave narrative—was *A Narrative of the Uncommon Sufferings, and Surprising Deliverance of Briton Hammon, a Negro Man—Servant to General Winslow* (1760, published in Boston), a 14-page memoir of his experiences as a sailor and as a captive of Floridian Cherokees and then of a press-gang in Cuba, and his joy and gratitude that "Providence" returned him to his master.—REFERENCES: *AA:AJS,* pp. 270–273, notes pp. 461–462. Andrews, William L., "Slave Narrative," in *OCAAL.*

—*Randall Lindsey*

REFERENCES: Andrews, William L., and Henry Louis Gates, Jr. (1999), *The Civitas Anthology of African American Slave Narratives* (Washington, DC: Civitas/Counterpoint). Bennett, Lerone, Jr. (1964), *Before the Mayflower: A History of the Negro in America* (New York: Penguin Books). Berlin, Ira (1974), *Slaves without Masters: The Free Negro in the Antebellum South* (New York: Vintage Books). Blassingame, John W. (1979), *The Slave Community: Plantation Life in the Antebellum South* (New York: Oxford University Press). Douglass, Frederick (1963), *Narrative of the Life of Frederick Douglass: An American Slave* (originally published 1845; Garden City, NY: Dolphin Books of Doubleday). Elkins, Stanley M. (1963), *Slavery: A Problem in American Institutional and Intellectual Life* (New York: Universal Library). Franklin, John Hope, and Alfred A. Moss, Jr. (1988), *From Slavery to Freedom* (New York: McGraw-Hill). Frazier, Thomas R. (Ed.) (1970), *Afro-American History: Primary Sources* (New York: Harcourt Brace and World). Genovese, Eugene D. (1974), *Roll Jordan Roll: The World the Slaves Made* (New York: Vintage Books). Gutman, Herbert G. (1976), *The Black Family in Slavery and Freedom, 1750–1925* (New York: Pantheon Books). Herskovits, Melville J. (1958), *The Myth of the Negro Past* (Boston: Beacon Press). Jones, Jacqueline (1985), *Labor of Love, Labor of Sorrow: Black Women, Work, and the Family, from Slavery to the Present* (New York: Vintage Press). Lerner, Gerda (Ed.) (1972), *Black Women in White America: A Documentary History* (New York: Vintage Books). Myrdal, Gunnar (1972), *An American Dilemma: The Negro Problem and Modern Democracy* (Vol. 2), (New York: Pantheon Books). Shields, John, "Literary History: Colonial and Early National Eras," and "Smith, Venture," in *OCAAL.* Tyler, Ronnie C., and Lawrence R. Murphy (Eds.) (1974), *The Slave Narratives of Texas* (Austin: Encino Press). Weinstein, Allen, and Frank Otto Gatell (Eds.) (1968), *American Negro Slavery: A Modern Reader* (New York: Oxford University Press).

Slim, Iceberg
See **Iceberg Slim**

Smith, Amanda (née) Berry
(1/23/1837–1915)
Autobiography

To raise funds for an orphanage and industrial school she wanted to establish for African-American children, Smith wrote a monthly newspaper, the *Helper,* and she wrote her autobiography, *An Autobiography: The Story of the Lord's Dealings with Mrs. Amanda Smith, the Colored Evangelist* (1893). Her autobiography describes her own spiritual quest, her pursuit of an education, and her struggles with sexism in the African Methodist Episcopal Church, which led to her becoming an independent evangelist.

REFERENCES: Carruth, Mary C., in *OCAAL.* Israel, Adrienne, in *BWA:AHE.*

Smith, Anna Deveare (9/18/1950–)
Plays, documentaries

After her experiences as an actor, director, and drama teacher, Smith initiated a series of one-woman shows, starting with *On the Road: A Search for American Character* (1983). Each of her performances comprises multiple characters with differing voices and identities. Her *Fires in the Mirror* (1992, comprising 26 characters, based on a series of riots that erupted in Crown Heights, Brooklyn, following a tragic accident) won her an Obie Award, a Drama Desk Award, a Pulitzer Prize nomination, a Kesselring Prize (for $10,000), and other awards. She was then commissioned to write *Twilight: Los Angeles 1992* (1993), about the riots that erupted following the acquittal of the police officers who had severely beaten motorist Rodney

King. After a Los Angeles run, *Twilight* opened on Broadway in New York, the first play by an African-American woman to do so since 1983, and it won two Tony nominations, an Obie, a Drama Desk, and an Outer Critics Circle Special Achievement Award. (Because the play was based on the actual testimony of participants and observers, Smith was denied a Pulitzer nomination for *Twilight*.) Smith's other plays include *A Birthday Card and Aunt Julia's Shoes* (1983) and *Aye, Aye, Aye, I'm Integrated* (1984). Smith is now a tenured professor at Stanford University in Palo Alto, California.

REFERENCES: *EA-99.*

Smith, Barbara (1946–)
Nonfiction, anthologies, criticism; book press cofounder

Little has been written about Barbara Smith, but she has written a great deal to deepen our understanding of other important African-American women writers. For instance, in 1977 she wrote *Toward a Black Feminist Criticism,* and five years later Gloria T. Hull, Patricia Bell Scott, and she published their groundbreaking anthology *All the Women Are White, All the Blacks Are Men, But Some of Us Are Brave: Black Women's Studies* (1981; paperback, 1986). Smith herself is brave indeed: To the double jeopardy of being African American and female, Smith adds her identification as an openly gay woman—triple jeopardy! Undaunted by these challenges, in 1981 Smith cofounded (with Myrna Bain, Cherríe Moraga, and Mariana Romo-Carmona) Kitchen Table: Women of Color Press, the first U.S. publisher dedicated to publishing the writings of women of color (including Third World women). The press has chiefly published poetry, fiction, and literary and social criticism (e.g., Cherríe Moraga and Gloria Anzaldúa's landmark *This Bridge Called My Back: Writings by Radical Women of Color,* 1981).

Smith also continues to write and edit other publications, such as her essay collection *The Truth That Never Hurts: Writings on Race, Gender, and Freedom* (1998, published by Rutgers University Press), her opinion piece *Yours in Struggle: Three Feminist Perspectives on Anti-Semitism and Racism* (1991, with Elly Bulkin and Minne Bruce Pratt), and her anthology *Neither Separate nor Equal: Women, Race, and Class in the South* (1999, in the Women in the Political Economy series published by Temple University Press). Smith's other anthologies include *Conditions: Five, the Black Women's Issue* (1979) and *Home Girls: A Black Feminist Anthology* (1983).

REFERENCES: *AA:PoP. TWT.* Amazon.com, 7/1999.

Smith, Effie Waller (1/6/1879–1/2/1960)
Poems, short stories

Smith's published poetry collections include *Songs of the Months* (1904), *Rhymes from the Cumberland* (1909), and *Rosemary and Pansies* (1909), but she also wrote many more poems and several short stories, continuing to write poems until she died. Her works may be found in *The Collected Works of Effie Waller Smith* (1991).

REFERENCES: Barnes, Paula C., in *OCAAL.*

Smith, Jessie Carney (9/24/1930–)
Nonfiction—African-American history and biography, bibliography

What readers need is to have an outstanding scholar of African-American history and biography write a definitive essay on the life experiences and contributions of Jessie Carney Smith. Ironically, one of the persons best known for writing such biographies about talented, interesting African-American women is Smith herself. We do know that Smith earned several degrees from several universities: North Carolina A&T State University (B.S.), Michigan State University (M.A.), Peabody College of Vanderbilt University (M.A. in library sciences), and the University of Illinois (Ph.D., 1964). Thereafter, she began her tenure as a librarian and professor of library science at Fisk University in Nashville, Tennessee. She has since been named the William and Camille Cosby Professor at Fisk.

Among the many books Smith has edited on African-American history and biography are these: *Images of Blacks in American Culture* (1988); *Notable Black American Women* (1991); *Epic Lives: 100 Black Women Who Made a Difference* (1993); *Black Firsts: 2,000 Years of Extraordinary Achievement* (1994, with Robert Johns and Casper L. Jordan); *Historical Statistics of Black America: Agriculture to Labor and Employment* (1994, with Carrell Peterson Horton); *Statistical Record of Black America* (1994, with Robert L. Johns; 4th ed., 1996, with Carrell P. Horton); *Notable Black American Women, Book II* (1996); *Powerful Black Women* (1996); *Black Heroes of the 20th Century* (1998); and *Notable Black American Men* (1998). Jay P. Pederson and she also edited a work for middle-school-age students, drawing on her *Black Firsts,* titled *African American Break-throughs: 500 Years of Black Firsts* (1994).

Smith has also written several books intended to facilitate the work of fellow librarians, including her first book, *Bibliography for Black Studies Programs* (1969), as well as *Minorities in the United States: Guide to Resources* (1973), *Black Academic Libraries and Research Collections: An Historical Survey* (1977), and *Ethnic Genealogy: A Research Guide* (1983).

Smith's numerous honors include the 1982 Martin Luther King, Jr., Black Author's Award, the United Negro College Fund's 1986 Distinguished Scholars Award, the 1992 Women's National Book Association Award, the National Coalition of 100 Black Women's Candace Award for excellence in education, and *Sage* magazine's Anna J. Cooper Award (for *Epic Lives*).

REFERENCES: *EBLG.* Amazon.com, 7/1999. (See also *BH2C* and *BWA:AHE.*)

Smith, Lillian Eugenia
(12/12/1897–1966)
Novels, commentary, essays; journal founder, editor, publisher

A lifelong resident of the American South, this European-American woman's most important literary contributions were her books confronting issues of race in the middle of the twentieth century. Although Smith had attended Piedmont College and a college in Maryland, she had to leave school early to take over managing her parents' summer camp when their health failed. In 1936, Smith started her own magazine, eventually titled *The North Georgia Review,* the first journal published by a white Southerner, which regularly printed literary and scholarly writings by blacks.

As if that wasn't stirring up enough trouble, Smith's very first novel, *Strange Fruit* (1944), told the story of how an interracial love relationship within a racist environment could lead to murder and a public lynching. Not only was the book banned in the South, but it was also banned in the North (Massachusetts), supposedly for "obscenity," and even the U.S. Post Office barred it from being sent through the U.S. mail until First Lady Eleanor Roosevelt intervened on behalf of Smith (and the U.S. Constitution). Much to the chagrin of the racists who opposed her, these actions stirred up tremendous publicity for her book, which ended up selling quite well. The novel was later (1945) made into a play, produced by José Ferrer.

Smith's subsequent works include *Killers of the Dream* (1949), which openly and unhesitatingly attacked segregation; *One Hour* (1959), a novel covertly assailing McCarthyism; and several other books, none of which engendered as much public attention as did *Strange Fruit.* She still, however, managed to irk white Southern racists, and mysteriously lit arson fires destroyed her manuscripts and other materials twice in 1955 and once in 1958. Among the documents that went up in flames were about 9,000 letters she had written during the 1940s and 1950s, which the U.S. Library of Congress had requested for the nation's archives. Smith was also active in the nonviolent struggle for civil rights during the 1950s and 1960s. She was in the process of writing her autobiography when cancer took her life.

REFERENCES: *BC. RLWWJ.* NPR, *Writer's Almanac,* 12/12/1998. (See also *BWA:AHE* and *OCWW.*)

Smith, Venture (c. 1729–9/19/1805)
Slave narrative

A native of Guinea, West Africa, Venture was captured, enslaved, and shipped to a colonial port in Rhode Island when he was about eight years old. By his own account, he spent the next 28 years of his life seeking his own freedom and then spent the rest of his life earning enough money to purchase the freedom of his wife Meg, his daughter Hannah, his sons Solomon and Cuff, and three enslaved men of African descent. In 1798, he dictated his life story to an *amanuensis* (someone who writes down the words spoken by another), probably Elisha Niles, a white schoolmaster in Connecticut, who clearly never believed Smith to be his intellectual equal—or perhaps his equal in other terms, as well. Smith's autobiographical story, *A Narrative of the Life and Adventures of Venture Smith, A Native of Africa: But resident above sixty years in the United States of America, Related by Himself* (1789), describes the three phases of Smith's life in three discrete chapters: his youth in Africa, his decades-long struggle to free himself, and his dedicated efforts to free his family and acquaintances. Despite having a less than sympathetic amanuensis, Smith's **slave narrative** makes clear that he resents the treatment he received as a black man of African descent, even after his liberation from bondage.

REFERENCES: *NYPL-AADR.* Shields, John C., in *OCAAL.*

Smith, William Gardner
(2/6/1927–11/6/1974)
Novels; journalist, English language editor

Smith's novels include *Last of the Conquerors* (1948), *Anger at Innocence* (1950), *South Street* (1954), *The Stone Face* (1963), and *Return to Black America* (1970). His novels reflect his own turmoil about the situation of blacks in white America. Smith once observed that African-American writers "write only about the here and now. Thus their novels come and they go: in ten years they are forgotten." We hope that this book and other works ensure that his observation proves untrue.

REFERENCES: Dawson, Emma Waters, in *OCAAL*. Fay, Robert, in *EA-99*.

Snellings, Rolland
See **Touré, Askia M.**

Southerland, Ellease (6/18/1943–)
Poems, essays, short stories, novels

Among Southerland's published works are her novella *White Shadows* (1964), her poetry collection *The Magic Sun Spins* (1975), her first novel *Let the Lion Eat Straw* (1979, fictionalizing the story of her mother's life), and numerous poems and short stories published in various periodicals. *Let the Lion Eat Straw* was named the best book of 1979 by the American Library Association and an alternate selection of the Book-of-the-Month Club. Her poetry has won the Gwendolyn Brooks Poetry Award (1972). As of the mid-1990s, Southerland was working on a second novel, tentatively titled *A Feast of Fools,* and on a short-story collection tentatively titled *Before the Cock Crows Twice.* These and other works reflect her fondness for Africa, especially Nigeria and Egypt.

REFERENCES: Dandridge, Rita B., in *OCAAL*. Mitchell, Caroline, in *BWA:AHE*.

Southern, Eileen Stanza Johnson
(1920–)
Nonfiction—music criticism, historiography, biography; journal cofounder

Southern's publications include her historiographic books *The Music of Black Americans: A History* (1971; revised edition, 1983), *Source Readings in Black American Music* (1971), and *Biographical Dictionary of Afro-American and African Musicians*

(1982). In addition, she and her husband Joseph founded the journal *The Black Perspective in Music.*

REFERENCES: *BAAW.*

Spence, Eulalie (6/11/1894–3/7/1981)
Plays

Spence's 13 known plays include *Being Forty* (1920), *Brothers and Sisters of the Church Council* (1920), *Fool's Errand* (1927), *Her* (1927), *Hot Stuff* (c. 1927), *Episode* (1928), *La Divina Pastora* (1929), *Undertow* (1929), and *The Whipping* (1932). In addition, she wrote *Foreign Mail* (1926), which won second place in a *Crisis* magazine drama contest, as well as *The Hunch* (1926) and *The Starter* (1926), the second- and third-place winners of **Opportunity** magazine's 1927 competition. At least 8 of Spence's plays were published, 7 of them were produced, and 1 of them was sold to Paramount Pictures (but was never produced).

REFERENCES: Perkins, Kathy A., in *BWA:AHE*.

Spencer, "Anne" (née Annie Bethel Bannister) (2/6/1882–7/12/1975)
Poems; librarian

Annie's future did not look bright when she was born on a Virginia plantation to parents whose marriage was turbulent from the outset (her mother, Sarah Louise Scales, the mulatta daughter of a former slaveholder; and her father, Joel Cephus Bannister, a man of African, Native American, and European-American descent). When Annie Bethel Bannister was just 5 years old, she and Sarah left Joel in Virginia and moved to Bramwell, a mining town in West Virginia. There, Annie roomed with the Dixies, a foster family, while Sarah supported herself and her daughter by working as an itinerant cook. Although Annie loved to read and voraciously plowed through dime-store novels, newspapers, and whatever else was available, she didn't receive any formal education until she was 11 years old.

When Annie was 11, Joel threatened to take her with him unless Sarah enrolled Annie in school. As soon as she could, Sarah enrolled Annie at the Virginia Seminary in Lynchburg, under the name Annie Bethel Scales (Sarah's maiden name). Annie was the youngest student ever to attend the seminary, and she graduated as valedictorian when she was just 17 years old. She also started writing poetry, including her sonnet "The Skeptic" (1896). The road to the valedictory address was not untroubled, however. Although Annie excelled in all her humanities courses, she had difficulty with her science courses. In order to do well in these courses, she sought the help of a tutor, Edward Spencer.

Immediately after her 1899 graduation, Annie went back to Bramwell, where she taught school. Two years later, however, Annie returned to Lynchburg, where she married Edward on May 15, 1901, and the two of them subsequently raised three children: their daughters, Bethel Calloway (Stevenson) and Alroy Sarah (Rivers), and their son, Chauncey Edward (who later became a pioneer aviator). Annie was not devoted to homemaking and child-rearing, however. Her primary interests were poetry and lovingly tending to their backyard garden. She was so attentive to her garden that Edward built her a cottage (named "Edenkraal") looking onto it. Fortunately, Edward was able to pay for housekeepers and caregivers for the children, liberating Annie to work in her garden and to write poetry. These two passions often intersected, too, as she often used the garden as imagery for her poetic themes.

During these early decades of the twentieth century, Spencer also became increasingly interested in political activism. She stirred up a protest against the employment of all-white faculty at the segregated black-students-only high school in Lynchburg, and her actions led to the hiring of African-American teachers there. She boycotted Lynchburg's segregated public transportation and defiantly rode on the all-white trolley, refusing to leave when asked. She offered refuge to Ota Benfa, an African pygmy who had been exhibited in zoos, allegedly to show the presumed intrinsic inferiority of Africans (but instead showing the intrinsic inferiority of people who would treat fellow humans so inhumanely). In 1918, she worked with **James Weldon Johnson,** secretary of the National Association for the Advancement of Colored People (NAACP), to establish an NAACP chapter in Lynchburg. In 1923, she was instrumental in starting the only library in Lynchburg that was open to African Americans, and she served as its librarian until 1945. Spencer also did just plain outrageous things for her day, such as wearing pants in public, having interracial friendships, and writing stinging editorials denouncing any claims about the superiority of whites over blacks.

Spencer's contact with Johnson led to far more than her political activism, however. For one thing,

Johnson and Spencer formed a friendship that lasted the rest of his life. For another, while Johnson was visiting her home as they were working together to found the Lynchburg NAACP chapter, he happened to see some of her poetry. He liked what he read and urged her to publish some of her poems, using the name "Anne Spencer," rather than the informal-sounding "Annie." With his help, 38-year-old Anne Spencer published her first poem, "Before the Feast of Shushan" (February 1920) in the NAACP journal *Crisis*. Johnson also published five of her poems in his anthology *The Book of American Negro Poetry* (1922), and ten of her poems were published in **Countee Cullen**'s anthology, *Caroling Dusk* (1927).

Although Spencer treasured Johnson's friendship and his advice, she didn't always follow it. For instance, he introduced her to H. L. Mencken, well-regarded editor of the popular *American Mercury* magazine, advising her that Mencken had frequently launched the careers of African-American writers. When Mencken criticized Spencer's work, however, she refused to accept his suggestions, not because he was not African American, but because he was not a poet and therefore had no right to comment on her poetry. After Mencken helped her publish "Before the Feast of Shushan," she refused any further collaboration with him.

Spencer showed similar resistance to the editorial process with other editors, feeling that they misunderstood her meanings and intentions and that they tried to censor her either for being too assertive about the need for racial and sexual equality or for being too subtle in asserting those needs. These quarrels ended up limiting the degree to which her works were published. For instance, no collection of her poetry was ever published during her lifetime, and of her thousands of writings (including a novel as well as poems and cantos), only 50 remain, with fewer than 30 of those having ended up in print during her lifetime. Despite these difficulties, however, Spencer's work was favorably reviewed and highly esteemed during her day, and at least one of her poems appeared in virtually every poetry anthology published between the start of the 1920s and the end of the 1940s (e.g., those by Johnson, by Cullen, by **Alain Locke**, by **Sterling Brown**, and by **Langston Hughes** and **Arna Bontemps**).

Perhaps part of Spencer's appeal was her contradictions: While she embraced spiritual appreciation of the beauty of nature (e.g., in her poems "At the Carnival," 1922; "Lines to a Nasturtium," 1926; "Substitution," 1927; and "Requiem," 1931) and often used biblical and mythological imagery and allusions, she bluntly rejected religious dogma and prudery. For instance, her "Black Man O'Mine" revels in the erotic pleasures of lovemaking between an African-American man and woman. While her poems could never be categorized as "protest poems," she nonetheless addressed issues of racial oppression of blacks by whites (e.g., in "White Things," 1923) and feminist issues (e.g., in "The Wife-Woman," 1922; "Lady, Lady," 1925; and "Letter to My Sister," 1927). Her poetry reflected the more traditional themes of the earlier Romantic poets (e.g., nature's beauty, friendship, love), yet she wholeheartedly plunged into modern poetic forms, such as slant rhymes, haunting rhythms, and obscure symbolism. She has even been called the most modern, original, and unconventional poet of her time. Unsurprisingly, the adjective most often used to describe her poetry is "ironic."

Although Lynchburg, Virginia, certainly was a far cry from Harlem, Spencer's home was nonetheless a welcome hostel for numerous literary notables associated with the **Harlem Renaissance**, such as Sterling Brown, **W. E. B. Du Bois**, Langston Hughes, **Georgia Douglas Johnson**, **Claude McKay**, and **Paul Robeson**, as well as **Maya Angelou**, **Gwendolyn Brooks**, George Washington Carver, and others. To be sure, one of the reasons for her gracious hospitality and for their appreciative welcoming of it was because Jim Crow laws prohibited African Americans from staying in most hotels anywhere in the South. During those troublesome times, most African Americans expected to open their homes to visiting African Americans who were traveling through the South. Nonetheless, Spencer's home and its splendid garden at 1313 Pierce Street offered cordial, hospitable lodgings to her visitors. In addition to enjoying Spencer's agreeable accommodations, these visitors also exchanged ideas and literary critiques with their hostess.

In 1938, Spencer's mentor, James Weldon Johnson, died unexpectedly, and her tribute to him, "For Jim, Easter Eve," was the last of her poems to be published during her lifetime. After his death, she retreated from literary circles. After her husband died in 1964, she retreated further into seclusion, even allowing her garden to go to seed, but she never stopped writing. She wrote various historical pieces, and she began revising her poems by making notes on whatever slips of paper were handy. Unfortunately, when she died, her friends couldn't figure out what she intended with these scraps and tossed them away. Nonetheless, most of the completed poems that were found were gathered into *Time's Unfading Garden: Anne Spencer's Life and Poetry* (1977, edited by J. Lee Greene). In addition, Spencer's garden and the cottage, Edenkraal, have been restored and placed on the National Register of Historic Places.

REFERENCES: *BANP. NAAAL.* Aguiar, Marian, in *EA-99.* Barnes, Paula C., in *BWA:AHE.* Clark, Keith, in *OCWW.* McCaskill, Barbara, in *OCAAL.*

Spillers, Hortense J. (c. mid-1900s–)
Literary criticism, essays

Precious little has been written about Hortense Spillers, except to observe what she has written about other African-American women writers. An astute, outspoken literary critic and essayist, she is invariably mentioned whenever writers speak of African-American literary critics. Often invited to write the introductions to books identified with the Schomburg Library, Spillers has also edited works such as *Conjuring: Black Women, Fiction, and Literary Tradition* (1985, with Marjorie Pryse).

REFERENCES: Contributors' notes in *BWA:AHE, OCAAL,* and *OCWW.* Amazon.com, 7/1999.

Spingarn, Arthur B. (Barnett)
(1878–1971)
and Spingarn, Joel Elias (1875–1939)
Nonfiction, literary criticism; bibliophile, publisher, editor

Both Spingarn brothers (of European-American heritage) were heavily involved in the activities of the National Association for the Advancement of Colored People (NAACP): Arthur, an attorney, chaired the NAACP's legal committee for many years and served as the organization's president (1940–1965); Joel helped found the NAACP and was the board of directors chair (1913–1919), treasurer (1919–1930), and president (1930–1939). In 1914, he established the organization's prestigious Spingarn Medal, awarded to outstanding African Americans who have made significant contributions to their community in various fields of endeavor. Joel also encouraged many writers of the **Harlem Renaissance** and wrote such works of literary criticism as *A History of Literary*

Criticism in the Renaissance (1899) and *The New Criticism* (1911). Those volumes serve as bookends to his career teaching literature at Columbia University (i.e., 1899–1911). Another of Spingarn's books was *Creative Criticism and Other Essays on the Unity of Genius and Taste* (1917; reprinted 1979). Spingarn also worked closely with **Walter White**, whom he had met when White had consulted with Spingarn about his first novel (in 1922), when Spingarn was an editor at Harcourt and Brace, a publishing company he had helped to found. The two were instrumental in shaping the NAACP's financial and administrative policies during the 1930s.

In 1946, Arthur Spingarn, a noted collector of literature by (and about) people of African descent (especially rare editions of Cuban, Haitian, and Brazilian authors), made available his 5,000-plus books to Howard University. Howard's president at the time, Mordecai Wyatt Johnson, observed that it was "the most comprehensive and interesting group of books by Negroes ever collected in the world." Even after Howard acquired his collection, Arthur Spingarn continued to send to Howard a copy of every book he could find that was written by an author of African descent, including books on various academic topics written in African and European languages. In recognition of his contribution, in 1973 Howard named its world-renowned research center the Moorland-Spingarn Research Center.

REFERENCES: *MWBD*. Hornsby, Alton, "Spingarn, Joel Elias," in *WB-99*. Myers, Aaron, "Moorland-Spingarn Research Collection," in *EA-99*. Sekora, John, "Libraries and Research Centers," in *OCAAL*. Amazon.com, 8/1999. Moorland-Spingarn Research Center online card catalog, 5/1999 www. founders.howard.edu/moorland-spingarn/ HIST.HTM

Spirituals

African-American spirituals are overtly religious songs, which are believed to have been sung since the days when African Americans were brought to the New World as slaves. Although the word "spiritual" originally referred only to songs sung at religious congregations, as time progressed they were greatly influenced by African-American slave songs, and as such, the songs of slavery are included in the category of spirituals. Like **folktales**, spirituals were probably created to help slaves ad-

just to the conditions they found upon arriving in the New World from Africa. Spirituals also helped them come together as a single people despite the fact that they came from different areas of the African continent and thus had different traditions. Also, like folktales, when African Americans tried to get out from under the yoke of slavery, spirituals became instruments of underground rebellion.

The earliest spirituals remain mostly unknown to us because, also like folktales, these songs are part of the African-American **oral tradition**, arising from the interactions of people and thus composed by a group. No one composer, lyricist, or musician can be associated with any one song, nor do we have dates of composition because nothing was written down until 1801, when **Richard Allen** gathered some of them into a book. By then, however, many spirituals had been lost because they had fallen out of use or had been modified through the generations. Thus, even Allen's versions of the songs cannot be said to be authoritative, and when looking through the recorded texts and music of the spirituals, a researcher will find that the same song may be sung to a variety of tunes; additionally, a researcher might discover that the same phrases will appear in the lyrics of different songs.

Spirituals probably emerged out of the interplay between the traditions of the African slaves and those of Protestant Christianity in the South. At that time, many Christians were intent on spreading their religion to all races. Although African-American spirituals may have picked up the details of the Bible stories, evangelical sermons, and hymns from the Protestants, they are distinct from white religious songs because of the African influences that slaves incorporated into their spirituals. Protestant hymns were very European, traditional, and stately, stiffly sung. In contrast, African-American spirituals have long, repetitive choruses, employ call-and-response patterns of western and central Africa (in which the lead singer sings a line and the rest of the congregation sings the same line or a responding line), include percussion and syncopation (if not performed with instruments, singers would use their hands and feet to keep the beat), and encourage the congregation and singers to incorporate rhythmic body movements.

African-American spirituals differ from white spirituals not only in their melodic or performative elements but also in the layers of meanings beneath the words of the songs. Because African

Americans were slaves, when they were singing to God, they were singing not only of a spiritual redemption but also of a physical redemption. Slaves sang spirituals not only in congregations or at church time but also while they were working in the fields, while they were resting after a long day, and even during children's playtimes. In many ways, these songs were a way of mentally shielding themselves from the abuses of the slaveholders and the restrictions and cruelties of slavery. In imagining a kind God as father and heaven as a loving home where they would arrive after their work on Earth was through, the songs may have made the day easier to get through.

In many ways the songs were also more than shields—they were songs of protest and in some cases a call to arms. Spirituals were often linked with slave uprisings, and in those instances the songs brought together both religious and secular meanings. While songs such as "Swing Low, Sweet Chariot" and "Go Down Moses" call for a spiritual liberation that is overtly religious, they also hint at a yearning for actual freedom, which slaves were denied and were striving toward. Because these songs were sung by slaves, the fact that many of the spirituals seem to speak to three basic themes—the desire for justice, the desire for freedom, and the ways to survive unbearable hardship—becomes significant.

African Americans were transforming songs about the past into songs about the present as well, such as when the spirituals recalled and referred to the biblical tales of Daniel who was freed from the lion's den by a redeeming savior God, Jonah who was swallowed by a whale and also rescued by God, and the Israelites who were guided by Moses and aided by God in their escape from slavery in Egypt. So threatening were these double meanings that slaveholders forbade slaves to sing some songs such as "Go Down Moses" (which powerfully expresses the desire for human liberation in referring to the freeing of the Israelites) as they worked the plantations.

Although critics have disputed whether the slaves were really using the double meanings as they sang, conflating the yearning for spiritual release and actual release from bondage, testimonies of former slaves such as **Frederick Douglass** confirm that the spirituals were loaded with symbolic language. The song "Swing Low, Sweet Chariot," which refers to a chariot that will sweep down and "carry me home," seems to refer to a

chariot coming from heaven to take people back there. In actuality, it often signified the Underground Railroad or some means of escape and was sometimes sung to signal such opportunities for liberation. Other words with double meanings in the songs include Egypt or Babylon, which meant the oppressive South; the river Jordan, which represented any body of water that could be crossed to reach the North and thus freedom; and home, Canaan, or the Promised Land, which could mean anywhere slaves could be free, be it the North, Africa, free states, or even Canada.

Because African-American spirituals are based on experiences unique to slaves in the Americas, in many ways, they have been seen as the first indigenous music of the United States. In their mixture of sorrow and joy, spirituals paved the way for other genres of music such as blues and jazz. **Ralph Ellison** said that singing the blues "is an impulse to keep the painful details and episodes of a brutal experience alive in one's aching consciousness, to finger its jagged edge, and to transcend it . . . by squeezing from it near-tragic, near-comic lyricism." In many ways, spirituals are full of the sorrows of slaves and gave the oppressed people a way to finger the jagged edges of their sorrow while still affirming notions of what Richard Newman (1998) calls "divine redemption and human triumph."

Yet the influence of the spirituals is seen not only in modern music but also in the works of both African-American and European-American writers for more than a century. Some writers incorporated spirituals into their works to structure their stories. Others, such as **Zora Neale Hurston**, drew on the biblical parallels between African-American slaves and Moses's Israelites to develop her works. **James Baldwin**'s *Go Tell It on the Mountain* is informed by spirituals, and **Richard Wright** and Ralph Ellison both pay tribute to the formative effect spirituals had on their writing in various works, with Wright using a spiritual as an epigraph in one of his novels and Ellison's *Invisible Man* using spirituals as influences on the novel's characters, plot, and language. **Toni Morrison**'s *Song of Solomon* uses the spiritual's call-and-response patterns to advance the plot, repeating the theme in new ways at various points in the novel. Poets such as **James Weldon Johnson**, **Paul Laurence Dunbar**, and **Langston Hughes**, playwrights such as Eugene O'Neill, and novelists such as William Faulkner all incorporated spirituals into their work, using them as inspiration and models as they wrote.

The heart-piercing lyrics of the spirituals still hold as strong an impression for writers, readers, musicians, and listeners today as they did when they were first created. **Cornel West** sees in them a "depth of inarticulate anguish" and "a level of questioning about the nature of suffering previously unknown," which is made only more poignant by the fact that in these same songs, strength is found not by exacting murderous revenge but "in an all-embracing love and mercy." Thus, it is no wonder that one in particular, "Free at Last," became the cornerstone of **Martin Luther King, Jr.**'s "I Have a Dream" speech. Starting as songs that helped an uprooted people adjust to their new surroundings, continuing as songs of solace and eventually of rebellion against unjust oppressors, and finding their place in rallying cries for equality in the civil rights movement, spirituals truly seem to have the lasting power found only in great works of art.

—*Diane Masiello*

REFERENCES: *NAAAL.* Connor, Kimberly Rae, in *OCAAL.* Newman, Richard (1998), *Go Down, Moses: Celebrating the African-American Spiritual* (New York: Clarkson Potter). West, Cornel (1998), Foreword, in Newman, Richard, *Go Down, Moses: Celebrating the African-American Spiritual* (New York: Clarkson Potter).

Spivey, Victoria Regina
(10/6/1906–10/3/1976)
Songs

Hired as a songwriter for the St. Louis Publishing Company, Spivey both wrote and recorded songs (e.g., "TB Blues") during the late 1920s. During the 1960s, she wrote and recorded songs (e.g., "Murder in the First Degree") for her own Queen Vee (later named Spivey) Records and for the Bluesville and the Folkways labels.

REFERENCES: *EA-99.* Flandreau, Suzanne, in *BWA:AHE.*

Steptoe, John Lewis
(9/14/1950–8/28/1989)
Children's picture books

From an early age, John loved art, often preferring to draw and paint at home rather than play outside. In his teens, he attended the New York High School of Art and Design, and then during a summer art program in Vermont, he wrote and illustrated his first book, *Stevie.*

What motivated a 19-year-old to write *Stevie*? For one thing, he wanted to see more children's books featuring African-American children. In *Stevie,* Steptoe's characters use authentic urban African-American speech patterns. The main character's sentiments also ring true, as an older child candidly expresses his jealousy and resentment toward—and then reconciliation with and acceptance of—his younger brother Stevie. *Stevie* earned Steptoe numerous awards and national recognition.

After engendering his own readership—his children Bweela and Javaka—Steptoe wrote *My Special Best Words* (1974) and *Daddy Is a Monster . . . Sometimes* (1980), exploring the complexities of father-child relationships. Steptoe's *Marcia* (1976), a young adult novel, underscores the need for responsibility with sexual activity. This novel seems particularly poignant, given that Steptoe died young due to AIDS.

In the 1980s, Steptoe focused on **folktales.** In 1981, he illustrated **Rosa Guy's** *Mother Crocodile,* an adaptation of an African fable (first recorded by Birago Diop). He also wrote and illustrated the Caldecott Honor Book *The Story of Jumping Mouse: A Native American Legend* (1984). When he created his masterpiece, *Mufaro's Beautiful Daughters: An African Tale* (1987), Steptoe spent about two and a half years researching, writing, and illustrating it. He studied African zoology, anthropology, and archeology, unearthing the architectural and technological sophistication of ancient residents of what is now Zimbabwe. The story, similar to the European Cinderella tale, explores universal feelings of sibling rivalry. Steptoe's lush illustrations dazzle the eyes with vivid landscapes and beautiful Africans. His major effort paid off, as the book earned 1988 Caldecott Honors and a 1987 *Boston Globe–Horn Book* Honor Award for Illustration.

Steptoe's other books include *Uptown* (1970), *Train Ride* (1971), *Birthday* (1972), *Jeffrey Bear Cleans Up His Act* (1983), and *Baby Says* (1988). In addition, he illustrated several picture books written by Arnold Adoff (two books; see **Virginia Hamilton**), **Lucille Clifton**, and **Eloise Greenfield**. When accepting the 1982 Coretta Scott King Award for illustrating *Mother Crocodile,* Steptoe commented, "I'm gratified sometimes by the positive social effect my work may have had. But an effect comes after the aesthetic statement." In reviewing the body of his work, he clearly achieved both positive social effect and glorious aesthetics.

REFERENCES: *CBC. EBLG. IPOF.* Lowe, Barbara, in *OCAAL.*

Sterling (married surname), Dorothy
(1913–)
Juvenile books, nonfiction

Sterling's juvenile fiction includes *The Cub Scout Mystery* (1952) and *The Brownie Scout Mystery* (1955). Her biographical narratives for juveniles include *Freedom Train: The Story of Harriet Tubman* (1954), *Captain of the Planter: The Story of Robert Smalls* (1958), *Lucretia Mott* (1964), *The Making of an Afro-American: Martin Robison Delany, 1812–1885* (1971), and *Black Foremothers* (1979, about Ellen Craft [wife of **William Craft**], **Ida B. Wells**, and **Mary Eliza Church Terrell**). She has also written historical accounts such as *Forever Free: The Story of the Emancipation Proclamation* (1963) and *Tear Down the Walls! A Story of the American Civil Rights Movement* (1968). In addition, her nature study nonfiction for juveniles includes *Insects and the Homes They Build* (1954), *Creatures of the Night* (1960), and *Caterpillars* (1961). She also wrote *Tender Warriors* (1958), a book for adults resulting from her interviews of African-American children entering schools that were newly desegregated.

REFERENCES: B. B., in *CBC.*

Steward, Theophilus Gould
(4/17/1843–1/11/1924)
Novel, nonfiction—theology, history

Steward's history books include *The Haitian Revolution* (1914) and *The Colored Regulars* (c. 1899); his theology books include *Genesis Re-read* (1885) and *The End of the World* (1888); and his novel was titled *Charleston Love Story* (1899).

REFERENCES: Myers, Aaron, in *EA-99.*

Stewart, Maria W. (née Miller)
(?/1803–12/17/1879)
Essays, commentary, speeches

Born free but orphaned at age 5, Maria was indentured to a European-American cleric's family to earn her bed and board as a domestic servant. Released at age 15, she sought literacy and religious education while supporting herself through domestic service.

In 1826, she married James Stewart, a prosperous shipping agent. Sadly, after only three childless years of marriage, James died, and his estate's executors cheated Maria of her inheritance. Penniless, she returned to domestic service. Shaken, Maria awakened to her belief that opposition to the slavery and oppression of African Americans was God's will. In 1830, she began writing religious tracts, inspiring fellow African Americans to share her revelation.

In 1831, Stewart wrote *Religion and the Pure Principles of Morality, the Sure Foundation on Which We Must Build,* using both the Bible and the U.S. Constitution as authorities for asserting a universal right to freedom, equality, and justice. Stewart urged African Americans to organize resistance to slavery in the South and to oppose racist discrimination and restrictions in the North: "Sue for your rights and privileges. . . . You can but die if you make the attempt; and we shall certainly die if you do not."

William Lloyd Garrison, publisher of the *Liberator,* printed her manuscript as a pamphlet; thereafter, he published the texts of all her essays, speeches, and other writings. Stewart's second public speech made history: In 1832, she became the first American-born woman documented to have given a public lecture to a "promiscuous audience" (both men and women) on political topics. A year later, at her fourth public lecture, Stewart announced her retreat from public speaking, noting that both blacks and whites, women and men had reproached her for speaking to promiscuous public audiences. Not one to leave whimpering, however, she cited numerous powerful women of the Old Testament and in world history, asking, "What if such women . . . should rise among our sable race?"

Stewart's published works include her pamphlet *Meditations from the Pen of Mrs. Maria Stewart* (which she enlarged and published herself half a century later) and her 1835 *Productions of Mrs. Maria W. Stewart,* a collection of her speeches, some biographical facts, and several poems and essays on topics from abolition, human rights, and women's rights to economic equality, education, and moral uplift. Whenever she spoke or wrote, Stewart exhorted well-off white women to sympathize with the plight of their darker-skinned brothers and sisters, and she encouraged all women and African-

American men to gain education, citing it as a source of uplift. Further, she urged all women to participate fully and equally in the political and social life of their communities.

After retreating from lecturing, Stewart taught school, worked for abolition, and promoted literacy. A little over a century after Stewart's death, Marilyn Richardson edited the 1987 collection *Maria W. Stewart, America's First Black Woman Political Writer: Essays and Speeches.*

REFERENCES: *1TESK. BAAW. NAAAL. PBW.* Richardson, Marilyn, in *OCAAL.*

Still, William (?/1821–7/14/1902)
Nonfiction—history, abolition

From an early age, William Still knew that there were certain things he was never to mention: his parents' true names (Levin and Sidney Steele, not Levin and Charity Still), his mother's escape from slavery with his two older sisters, and his two older brothers, left behind in bondage so that the rest of the family might have a chance for escape. Sidney had at first tried to escape with all her children, but the slave hunters had found her and returned her to her owner—and cruel punishment for her attempt. After Sidney and her two daughters successfully escaped, the fugitive Still family grew quite large on a small farm in New Jersey, and William, the youngest, never revealed his secret. For more than 40 years, he knew that slave hunters might come to steal him, his siblings, and his mother back to slavery, so it was easy to keep quiet.

In the mid-1840s, William Still moved to Philadelphia and did odd jobs to earn his keep while learning to read and write. In 1847, the Pennsylvania Anti-Slavery Society hired him to do odd jobs for them, and gradually, his responsibilities expanded. He raised funds and disbursed them to conductors on the Underground Railroad, trained and coordinated the activities of the slave hunter lookouts, established safe houses, and found ways to provide forged free papers, food, clothing, medical care, jobs, money, and friends to fugitive slaves. He also provided contacts and resources for fugitives to escape farther north to the safety of Canada. He and his wife, Letitia George Still, also opened their homes to fugitives. In various ways, Still managed to help about 800 people find their way to freedom.

Still also started keeping a journal. At first, he just kept track of his expenses. Then something

happened to motivate him to keep more explicit records. In 1850, a former slave named Peter, somewhere in his forties, had reached Still's office, searching for some way to find his family. His grandmother had told him and his brother that their family was somewhere "up the Delaware River," just before the boys were sold down the river to Alabama. Peter also knew that his mother was named Sidney, and his father was Levin. After 40 years, Peter was reunited with a baby brother he never knew he had and with his mother, his older sisters, and his numerous younger siblings, nephews, and nieces, including William's four children. Sadly, Levin had died several years earlier, so he was never able to celebrate that reunion. William then worked with Peter for 3 years to have his wife and two children rescued from bondage and reunited with him, when at last they succeeded.

With this remarkable motivation, Still expanded his journal to include the names, aliases, and owners' names of everyone he served for the Anti-Slavery Society. He also recorded whatever details he could discover about their relatives, either still enslaved or in freedom. In 1872, long after Emancipation and the close of the Civil War, Still published the first edition of his most noteworthy book, including all the information he had been able to gather over the years: *The Underground Rail Road: a Record of Facts, Authentic Narratives, Letters, &C., Narrating the Hardships Hair-Breadth Escapes and Death Struggles of the Slaves in Their Efforts For Freedom, as Related by Themselves and Others, or Witnessed by the Author; Together with Sketches of Some of the Largest Stockholders, and Most Liberal Aiders and Advisers on the Road.*

After his years of service to the cause of abolition, following Emancipation, Still continued to serve, donating time and money to those in need. He also worked with various social and civic organizations, encouraging other people to donate whatever resources they had to their community, helping to found an old folks home, an orphanage, and a Young Men's Christian Association. In 1888, Still and his son-in-law Matthew Anderson started the Berean Building and Loan Association, which enabled many Philadelphia families to buy property, including their own homes. Anderson was the second husband of Still's daughter Caroline Virginia Still Wiley Anderson, one of the first African-American women to graduate from a medical school (in 1878) and to practice medicine.

EDITOR'S NOTE: Some have credited Still with

single-handedly helping 649 slaves escape. In additon to harboring fugitives, Still and his wife also raised four children and were active in the fight against racial discrimination—North and South. Still wrote about one such effort in *A Brief Narrative of the Struggle for the Rights of the Colored People of Philadelphia in the City Railway Cars* (1867/1970). (See *BDAA*.)

—*Tonya Bolden*

REFERENCES: *DANB. EAACH. SMKC.*

Stowe, Harriet (née) Beecher

(6/14/1811–7/1/1896)

Novels, biographical sketches, essays, short stories, poems

Stowe's novel *Uncle Tom's Cabin* (1852) was turned down by several publishers, and the publisher that finally accepted the work offered either to provide a 10 percent royalty or to share both the costs of the printing and the profits from the book's sales. European-American abolitionist Stowe unwisely chose the former option. The book sold 3,000 copies the first day out, its initial printing of 5,000 copies in two days, and half a million copies within five years. Later, on meeting her, Civil War President Abraham Lincoln said, "So you're the little woman who wrote the book that made this great war." She had based her novel on several **slave narratives**, such as those of **Frederick Douglass** and Josiah Henson. Henson subse-quently claimed the title "Uncle Tom" and wrote two more narratives after Stowe's book was published. Many other African-American authors (e.g., **Martin R. Delany**, **Frances Ellen Watkins Harper**, and **Paul Laurence Dunbar**) have written works directly or indirectly referring to Stowe and her antislavery novel.

REFERENCES: *SEW.* Wagner, Wendy, in *OCAAL*.

Sundiata, Sekou (c. 1945–)

Poems, script

Born in Harlem but with roots in South Carolina and in Florida, Sundiata grew up relishing the call-and-response patterns of African-American church services. He prefers to view himself as an oral poet, who records and performs his highly rhythmic, alliterative, sonorous poems. He usually gives his performances with jazz or other musical accompaniment. Sundiata has, nonetheless, written down many of his poems, such as in his collection *Free* (1977) and in an anthology he edited with Keith Gilyard and **Toi Derricotte**, *Spirit and Flame: An Anthology of Contemporary African American Poetry* (1997). He also wrote a script based on his performance piece, "The Circle Unbroken Is a Hard Bop," while a fellow at the Sundance Film Institute. He now teaches and is writer-in-residence (the first there) at the New School for Social Research in New York City.

REFERENCES: *LoL.*

Tanner, Benjamin Tucker

(12/25/1835–1/14/1923)

Nonfiction—theology and ethnology, editorials, poems; journal founder and editor

In addition to writing poems and journals, Tanner wrote several scholarly and theological books, including *Paul versus Pius Ninth* (1865), *An Apology for African Methodism* (1867), *The Negro's Origin, or Is He Cursed of God?* (1869), *The Outline of Our History and Government for African Methodist Churchmen* (1884), *Theological Lectures* (1894), *The Color Solomon: What?* (1896), *The Negro in Holy Writ* (1898), and *A Hint to Ministers, Especially Those of the African Methodist Episcopal Church* (1900). Tanner also edited publications of the African Methodist Episcopal (AME) Church and founded and edited the quarterly *A.M.E. Church Review*, the first African-American scholarly journal.

REFERENCES: *EA-99.* Connor, Kimberly Rae, in *OCAAL.*

Tarry, Ellen (9/26/1906–)

Editorials and columns, children's books, autobiography

Tarry's writing career started with editorials and an African-American heritage column ("Negroes of Note") for the *Birmingham Truth* (1927–1929). After she moved to New York City, she started writing children's literature and subsequently wrote *Janie Bell* (1940), *Herekiah Horton* (1942), *My Dog Rinty* (1946), and *The Runaway Elephant* (1950), which depicted nonstereotyped African Americans and interracial friendships among children. She also wrote her autobiography, *The Third Door: The Autobiography of an American Woman* (1955).

REFERENCES: Roberts, Janet M., in *OCAAL.*

Tate, Eleanora (1948–)

Children's and juvenile literature, poems, short fiction

Tate's books for juveniles include *Just an Overnight Guest* (1980, adapted to television and aired on Public Broadcasting System's *Wonderworks* series), *The Secret of Gumbo Grove* (1987), *Thank You, Dr. Martin Luther King, Jr.!* (1990), *Front Porch Stories at the One-Room School* (1992), *Retold African Myths* (1993), and *Blessing in Disguise* (1995).

REFERENCES: Johnson-Feelings, Dianne, in *OCAAL.*

Taylor, Mildred D. (Delois) (9/13/1943–)

Juvenile novels

When Mildred was just a few months old, her father had to flee from their home in Jackson, Mississippi, to avoid a violent confrontation with a white man. A few months later, his family joined him in Toledo, Ohio. Although her father left the South, he never left behind the rhythms and idioms of rural African-American Southern speech, the lifestyles and folkways of African-American Southern culture, and the Southern storytelling craft. Young Mildred sat at his knee and listened—and learned.

An excellent student (and editor of her high school newspaper), Mildred questioned the history taught in her textbooks, noting the distinct absence of African Americans. Perhaps, someday, she could write books that more accurately reflected U.S. history. After earning a bachelor's degree in education (1965) at the University of Toledo, she joined the Peace Corps, spending two years in Ethiopia teaching English and history. After her return, she earned her master's degree and spent several years teaching, but she eventually realized that if she was to write, she would have to get a less demanding job. In 1971, she resigned, moved to Los Angeles, and did proofreading and editing while spending her free time writing.

After a few unsuccessful publishing attempts, her novella *Song of the Trees* was published in 1975. This book introduces readers to the Logan family, which lived through slavery, Reconstruction, and the Jim Crow South. Her book's simple story, vividly appealing characters, and poetically authentic speech were critically acclaimed (named the *New York Times* Outstanding Book of the Year).

Taylor's protagonist, Cassie Logan, is less like Mildred (a quiet, bookish girl) and more like Mildred's sister and her aunt—spirited adventurers.

Taylor's second book about the Logans was *Roll of Thunder, Hear My Cry* (1976), winner of a Newbery Medal (the second book by an African American to do so), often cited as a contemporary classic of children's literature. Other books in the Logan saga include *Let the Circle Be Unbroken* (1981), *The Friendship* (1987), *Mississippi Bridge* (1990), and *The Well* (1995). Taylor has earned two *Boston Globe–Horn Book* Honor Book citations, a Buxtehude Bulle Award, a National Book Award nomination, two Coretta Scott King Awards, an American Book Award nomination, and selection as *New York Times* Outstanding Book of the Year. In all of these books, Taylor offers first-person narratives frankly addressing issues of racist segregation, race-based beatings and lynching, and racial injustice. Far from being grim stories, however, the family rises to confront these issues with dignity, strength, perseverance, determination, and hope. Also, any stories containing spunky Cassie's humor and warmth will leave readers feeling good.

Taylor also wrote the award-winning books *The Road to Memphis* (1990) and her semiautobiographical *The Gold Cadillac* (1987), primarily set in 1950s Toledo, Ohio. In these works, Taylor presents a view of U.S. history that complements the flawed, incomplete versions of history she was taught as a young girl. In 1988, the Children's Interracial Book Council honored Taylor "for a body of work that has examined significant social issues and presented them in outstanding books for young readers."

REFERENCES: *CBC. E-95. MAAL. MAI-1.* Harper, Mary Turner, in *OCWW.* Warren, Nagueyalti, in *OCAAL.*

Taylor, Susan L. (c. mid-1900s–)
Memoirs, editorials

The editor-in-chief of *Essence* magazine since 1980, Taylor has written two memoirs: *In the Spirit* and *Lessons in Living.*

REFERENCES: *PGAA.*

Taylor, Susie (née) Baker King
(8/6/1848–1912)
Memoir

In *A Black Woman's Civil War Memoirs: Reminiscences of My Life in Camp with the 33rd United States Colored Troops, Late 1st S. C. Volunteers* (1902, republished 1988, Eds. Patricia W. Romero and Willie Lee Rose), Taylor describes her experiences teaching illiterate freed slaves on Union Army–controlled St. Catherine Island, off the South Carolina coast, and then (after marrying Sergeant Edward King) working as a laundress and a nurse (with Clara Barton) for the Union Army. Her book is the only known personal account of the Civil War (and Reconstruction) written by an African-American woman.

REFERENCES: *EA-99. SEW.* Moody, Joycelyn, in *OCAAL.* Romero, Patricia W., in *BWA:AHE.*

Terrell, Mary Eliza (née) Church
(9/23/1863–7/24/1954)
Autobiography, articles, lectures

Mary's father, a former slave, was perhaps the first African-American millionaire in the South, so the Churches ensured that their daughter received an outstanding education by sending her to Northern schools. In 1884, she earned her baccalaureate at Oberlin College (in Ohio), one of the first three African-American women to do so. Despite Oberlin's liberal reputation, Church still felt the sting of racism. For instance, when Matthew Arnold observed her reciting verses in Greek, he showed surprise that she could do so: He had heard that African tongues were incapable of uttering Greek words.

After Mary graduated, despite her father's objections, she taught at Ohio's Wilberforce University and then in a segregated Washington, D.C., high school for African Americans. After a year of teaching, however, she agreed to a two-year tour of Europe, where she mastered French, Italian, and German. On returning to the United States, she became one of the first African-American women to receive a graduate degree, earning her master's degree (1888) from Oberlin. Three years later, she married Robert Terrell, a lawyer who later became the first African-American municipal court judge in the District of Columbia. The Terrells had four children, only one of whom survived to adulthood—their daughter Phyllis, named after **Phillis Wheatley**.

In 1890, Terrell embarked on a 30-year public-speaking career. In her lectures and her writings, she advocated for women's rights, women's suffrage, African-American voting rights, civil rights, racial and civil justice, world peace, educational reform, and even kindergartens and child care centers for the children of African-American working mothers. She also opposed lynching, racial segregation, racial discrimination in employment and schooling, unfair prosecution, and injustice and oppression in any form.

Although Terrell wrote numerous articles, her major literary contribution was her autobiography, *A Colored Woman in a White World* (1940/1980), which reflected on racial and social justice, African-American history and life experiences, and notable persons in whom she was interested (e.g., **Frederick Douglass**, Phillis Wheatley, and George Washington Carver). A lifelong learner, Terrell received doctor of letters degrees from Oberlin, Wilberforce, and Howard Universities during the 1940s. A well-respected scholar, she fought for three years to force the American Association of University Women (AAUW) to accept her and other nonwhite women as members; she was admitted in 1949, when she was in her mid-eighties.

Terrell also participated actively in various political, social, and cultural organizations, and she was the first African-American woman appointed to a school board. Terrell also reached out globally, representing numerous U.S. delegations at conventions in Germany, Switzerland, and England (addressing those gatherings in fluent German, French, and English). At ages 89 and 90, Terrell leaned on her cane as she led sit-ins, pickets, and boycotts to desegregate lunch counters and restaurants in our nation's capital. After a year of such actions, several department stores relented and desegregated their lunchrooms, but it took her lawsuit, culminating in a 1953 U.S. Supreme Court case, to desegregate the remaining eateries.

REFERENCES: *1TESK. BAAW. BDAA. BF:2000. EB-98. G-95. PGAA.* Eckard, Paula Gallant, in *OCAAL.*

Terry (married name: Prince), Lucy
(c. 1730–8/?/1821)
Poems, stories

Although Lucy was born free in West Africa, she was just an infant when she was captured—too young to remember a time before her enslavement. She spent her first few years in Rhode Island, and then at age 5 she was sold away to an "owner" in Massachusetts. In 1746, when she was about 16 years old, she wrote "Bars Fight," the first poem penned by a female African American. ("Bars Fight" wasn't actually published until 1855, so the

first published poetry by an African American was by **Jupiter Hammon**, and the first published poetry by an African-American woman was by **Phillis Wheatley**.) You might be thinking that Terry was writing about a tavern brawl, but actually, the "Bars" to which she referred was a patch of open meadow land by that name, and the "Fight" she described was an engagement resulting when some Native Americans (encouraged by French colonists) ambushed some English colonists.

With such an auspicious start in her mid-teens, Terry became renowned for her storytelling over the years. Fortunately for her, her life also provided quite a story to tell. In 1756, Justice of the Peace Ephraim Williams (later the founder of Williams College in Williamstown, Massachusetts) married her to Abijah Prince, from Curaçao, who was almost 25 years older than she. By the time they wedded, Prince was able to buy Lucy out of bondage and owned quite a bit of land. Their union proved fruitful—yielding six children, including one who later served in the Revolutionary War. Feisty to the end, even after her beloved Prince died, Lucy was always ready to take up a challenge and to fight for what she believed was right.

—*Tonya Bolden*

REFERENCES: *BAAW.*

Third World Press (TWP) (1967–)

Established in 1967, TWP is one of the oldest existing African-American publishing houses in the United States. It publishes fiction, history, essays, poetry, drama, and both young adult and children's literature. TWP's purpose statement is to "publish literature that contributes to the positive development of people of African descent." During the 1990s, TWP created a profitable niche for itself by publishing black authors who found it difficult to gain acceptance and publication by white publishers due to the controversial nature of their books. By publishing for this niche market, TWP has become financially stable and has remained black owned.

—*Lisa Bahlinger*

REFERENCES: *EAACH* (Vol. 5).

Thomas, Joyce Carol (5/25/1938–)
Poems, novels, plays, anthologies, juvenile books; editor

While raising her own four children and working as a telephone operator, Joyce Carol Thomas took college courses at night, earning her B.A. in Spanish (1966, San Jose State University, minoring in French) and her master's degree in education (1967, Stanford University). Then she really got busy. She has taught Spanish and French languages in California public schools and taught creative writing, African-American studies, and literature at several colleges in California (San Jose State University; Contra Costa College in San Pablo; St. Mary's College in Moraga; and the University of Santa Cruz) and across the nation (Purdue University and the University of Tennessee at Knoxville). She has lectured, offered seminars, and presented workshops on creative writing in the United States, Nigeria, and Haiti; and she has been a commissioner at Berkeley Civic Arts and a visiting scholar at Stanford's Center for Research on Women.

And then, of course, there is her writing. For starters, Thomas has contributed works to numerous periodicals such as the **Black Scholar** and *Calafia,* and she edited *Ambrosia,* an African-American feminist magazine published on the West Coast. In addition, her lyrical poems have been collected in *Bittersweet* (1973), *Crystal Breezes* (1974), *Blessing* (1975), *Inside the Rainbow* (1982, including both new and earlier poems), and *The Blacker the Berry* (1999).

Thomas has also written five plays (all of them produced in northern California), but she is best known for her work as a novelist. Her first novel, *Marked by Fire* (1982; reprinted 1999), won the Before Columbus Foundation American Book Award. Subsequent novels include *Bright Shadow* (1983, Coretta Scott King Honor Book), *Water Girl* (1986), *The Golden Pasture* (1986), *Journey* (1988), and *When the Nightingale Sings* (1992). Usually classified as novels for young adults, her books also address themes and issues of interest to other adults. Her anthology *A Gathering of Flowers: Stories about Being Young in America* (1992) is also tagged as being written for a young adult audience.

Thomas has also started writing books for younger readers, such as her poetry collections *Brown Honey in Broomwheat Tea* (1993, Coretta Scott King Honor Book; paperback 1996), *Gingerbread Days: Poems* (1997), and *Crowning Glory: Poems* (1999), intended for elementary school students. Her novel *I Have Heard of a Land,* about an African-American pioneer woman, is also written for elementary school students. For preschoolers, Thomas offers *Cherish Me* (1998) and *You Are My*

Perfect Baby (1999), lovingly written verse picture books. Throughout her works, she shows an appreciation of African-American culture and highlights the importance of children and their families within a community context.

REFERENCES: *MAI-2.* Harper, Mary Turner, in *OCWW.* Toombs, Charles P., in *OCAAL.* Amazon.com, 7/1999.

Thomas, Piri (né Juan Pedro Tomás)
(9/20/ or 9/30/1928–)
Autobiography, plays, young adult book, short stories, film documentary

Thomas's autobiographies include *Down These Mean Streets* (1967); *Saviour, Saviour, Hold My Hand* (1972); and *Seven Long Times* (1974), all of which reflect his Afro–Puerto Rican roots. Although he started writing his first autobiography in 1952 while in prison for attempted armed robbery (1950–1956), he has since done volunteer work in prisons and in drug rehabilitation programs. Thomas also wrote a play, *Las calles de oro* ([The Golden Streets], 1970); a collection of short stories for young adults, *Stories of El Barrio* (1978); and a film documentary, *Petey and Johnny* (1964, on youth gangs).

REFERENCES: *EA-99.* Dudley, David L., in *OCAAL.*

Thompson, Era Bell
(8/10/1906–12/29/1986)
Autobiography, criticism, articles, anthology; editor

Thompson wrote book reviews, feature articles, advertising copy, and news articles for various periodicals, including the *Bugle* (a weekly), the *Chicago Defender,* **Negro Digest** (of which she was an editor, 1947; later called *Black World*), and *Ebony* (associate editor, 1947–1951; co–managing editor, 1951–1964; international editor, 1964–1986). During this time, she still contributed essays to other journals, such as **Phylon.** She also wrote her autobiography, *American Daughter* (1946, funded by a fellowship from the Newberry Library), and a thoughtful pondering of her connection to Africa, *Africa, Land of My Fathers* (1954). She also edited *White on Black* (1963, with Herbert Nipson White), a collection of articles by European Americans about African Americans.

REFERENCES: Roberts, Janet M., in *OCAAL.* Thompson, Kathleen, in *BWA:AHE.*

Thurman, Howard

(11/18/1900–4/10/1981)
Nonfiction—religion, autobiography

The author of 20 books (e.g., his autobiography *With Head and Heart,* 1980) and many journal articles, Thurman lectured widely on the importance of Christian cooperation among the races and on the value of passive resistance as demonstrated by Mohandas Gandhi (whom he met personally on a trip to India). His writings helped shape the thinking and the philosophy of **Martin Luther King, Jr**. Some of his theological books include *Inward Journey* (1973), *Meditations of the Heart* (1976/1999), *Jesus and the Disinherited* (1996), *Temptations of Jesus* (1979), *Growing Edge* (1974), *Mysticism and the Experience of Love* (1961), *The Greatest of These* (1944), and *For the Inward Journey: The Writings of Howard Thurman* (1984, edited by Anne Spencer Thurman).

REFERENCES: *BDAA. EA-99. EBLG.* Amazon.com, 1/2000.

Thurman, Wallace (Henry)

(8/16/1902–12/22/1934)
Novels, poems, plays, articles, editorials, literary criticism; journal founder and editor

Wallace was born and raised in Utah and continued to live there after graduating from high school. After his first two years of studying medicine at the University of Utah, however, he suffered a nervous breakdown and withdrew from school. After he recovered, he transferred to the University of Southern California (USC), while he worked nights in a Los Angeles post office. At work, he often discussed literature and other topics with his coworker, **Arna Bontemps**. Thurman also wrote his column "Inklings" for a local African-American newspaper. As time went by, his interest in medicine diminished, and his interest in literature increased, fueled by news of the flourishing **Harlem Renaissance**.

In 1925, while Thurman worked at the post office by night and studied at USC by day, he founded *Outlet,* a literary magazine he had hoped would germinate a West Coast renaissance similar to that taking place in Harlem. Not! After just six months of operation, Thurman was forced to recognize that his best-laid plans weren't working, so in September of 1925, he packed his bags and left USC and Los Angeles for Harlem, as did his pal and coworker Bontemps.

Regarding his early years in Harlem, Thurman remarked, "Three years in Harlem have seen me become a New Negro (for no reason at all and without my consent), a poet (having had 2 poems published by generous editors), an editor (with a penchant for financially unsound publications), an exotic (see articles on Negro life and literature in *The Bookman, New Republic, Independent, World Tomorrow,* etc.), an actor (I was a denizen of Cat Fish Row in *Porgy*), a husband (having been married all of six months), a novelist (viz: *The Blacker the Berry,* Macaulay's, Feb. 1, 1929: $2.50), a playwright (being coauthor of *Black Belt*). Now—what more could one do?" Quite a bit, apparently.

The first of Thurman's "financially unsound publications" had been *Outlet,* but it was not to be his last. The most famous of these ventures was the literary journal *Fire!! A Quarterly Devoted to the Younger Negro Artists.* In the summer of 1926, **Langston Hughes** asked Thurman to cofound and edit a quarterly literary journal dedicated to publishing the works of the up-and-coming young writers of the Harlem Renaissance. Joining them in this venture were **Gwendolyn Bennett**, John P. Davis, Aaron Douglas, **Zora Neale Hurston**, and **Richard Bruce Nugent**, all of whom agreed that Thurman should edit the quarterly. This group of impoverished writers pooled all their resources—and came up with next to nothing—to finance the start of the journal. Thurman had to borrow a thousand dollars to get out the first issue, which included works not only by the coventurers but also by Arna Bontemps and others. With Thurman's guidance, the journal was an outstanding achievement, highlighting the avant-garde brilliance of these young, aspiring luminaries.

Without enough money to promote the journal and to ensure enough sales to pay back the loan, the journal was in trouble. When an actual fire ignited in a basement storing numerous issues of *Fire!!,* Thurman's (and his cofounders') hopes for continuing its publication went up in smoke. Thurman was left still owing $1,000 to creditors, which it took him four years to pay off. Since then, copies of the journal have become priceless rarities that collectors treasure. In 1985, the demand for these 60-year-old works was great enough that a paperback copy of the journal was reprinted and made available as a book.

Less well known—and less avant-garde—was Thurman's third attempt to launch a journal. In November of 1928, he published the first issue of *Harlem, a Forum of Negro Life,* which included contributions from Hughes and other young writers as well as from **Alain Locke**, **George Schuyler**, and **Walter White**. Despite the contributions of these established writers and scholars, this journal, too, failed after just one issue—again chiefly because it was underfinanced.

To finance his own livelihood, Thurman had sought work as an employee for various other publications. When he first arrived in New York, he started working as an editorial assistant and then a reporter for *Looking Glass* (a small magazine); next, he got work as the managing editor for about six months at the left-wing African-American periodical *The Messenger,* to which he contributed essays, reviews, and a short story ("Grist in the Mill"). Before the end of 1926, he took over as circulation manager for *The World Tomorrow,* a magazine intended for religious white readers, operated by whites. He also wrote numerous articles for other periodicals, including four essays that earned him particular praise: "Negro Artists and the Negro" (*The New Republic,* August 1927), "Nephews of Uncle Remus" (*The Independent,* September 1927), "Harlem Facets" (*The World Tomorrow,* November 1927), and "Negro Poets and Their Poetry" (*The Bookman,* July 1928). In his writings, he criticized **W. E. B. Du Bois**, **Alain Locke**, and other intellectuals of the day for tempering what they said in order to gain the approval of whites.

While Thurman was trying to recover from the financial disaster of *Fire!!* and perhaps germinating the idea for *Harlem,* he was hired at Macaulay's Publishing Company, a book-publishing house. There, he was the only African-American reader (low-level editor) and one of the first blacks to be hired as an editor by a major publishing house owned and operated by whites.

While continuing to earn a living at Macaulay's, Thurman also started writing novels and plays. He wrote his first play, *Harlem: A Melodrama of Negro Life in Harlem,* in collaboration with playwright William Jourdan Rapp, a European-American editor of *True Story* magazine, with whom he also produced the play. Originally titled *Black Mecca* and then *Black Belt,* the play grew out of "Cordelia the Crude, a Harlem Sketch," a short story he had contributed to *Fire!!* In the play, the Williams family of South Carolina struggles to make it in their new home in the heart of the Harlem ghetto. The play—which includes a provocatively erotic dance, a violent shootout, and various other sensational elements—earned mixed reviews but was a popular success, running for 93 performances after its opening at the Apollo Theater in February 1929. Despite its popularity, however, Thurman's ability to attract financial difficulties continued, and even though this play was his greatest financial success, it left him further in debt. His other three-act play, *Jeremiah, the Magnificent* (also written with Rapp), was never produced. He also started writing *Black Cinderella,* addressing color prejudice within the black community, but he never completed it. By the early 1930s, a California filmmaker had recruited Thurman to move back to California and write screenplays, reportedly paying him an exorbitantly high salary for doing so. After writing just two scripts, however, Thurman returned to New York in 1934.

The same year that *Harlem* was being produced on Broadway and driving Thurman into deeper debt, his first novel, *The Blacker the Berry: A Novel of Negro Life,* also appeared in print. Ever the iconoclast, Thurman addressed in this novel themes that continue to spark controversy as we begin a new millennium: abortion, homosexuality, ethnic conflict (between African Americans and Caribbean Americans), and intraracial prejudice (between light-skinned and dark-skinned blacks). An ebony-skinned man himself, Thurman was especially sensitive to intraracial color prejudice. Thurman's protagonist, Emma Lou Morgan, is similarly dark-skinned, and she suffers both self-criticism and criticism from her middle-class black family members and "friends" for her dark skin. Hoping to escape at least the persecution by others, she flees from her home in Boise, Idaho (suspiciously close to Salt Lake City, Utah), and runs first to Los Angeles and then to the black Mecca of Harlem. Nowhere does she find a safe haven from this prejudice, however, and she must decide whether to continue her self-loathing for her skin coloring or to reject European-American–based standards of physical beauty. This 1929 book was reprinted in hardcover in 1969 and 1972 and in paperback in 1996 and 1997, with large numbers of copies in each printing.

Thurman's next novel, *Infants of the Spring* (1932), bitingly satirizes the Harlem Renaissance and its participants. A critic said of the work, "Every serious student of the Harlem Renaissance must come to grips with this fictional critique by one of its most talented participants" (quoted in

BWA). Thurman centers the action in "Niggerati Manor," a mansion in Harlem where various writers and other artists congregate. In addition to thinly disguised cameo appearances by **Countee Cullen,** Hughes, Hurston, and Locke, Thurman includes an ensemble of characters meant to depict composite stereotypes of renaissance writers. Thurman takes sharp aim at the "New Negro" and other aspects of the renaissance, but he reserves his harshest critiques for Raymond Taylor, a self-aggrandizing young writer who most closely resembles Thurman himself. Thurman mocks Taylor's pretense and his presumed dedication to high art, and he ridicules Taylor's alcoholic proclivities and his cynical attitude. Through his novel, Thurman challenges readers to contemplate individual aspirations within the context of collective interests, the pursuit of art within a politically charged environment, and the conflicts between the goals of integration and of forging an independent cultural identity. This 1932 novel was reprinted in paperback in 1992 in two 1999 paperback editions, and as the first volume (1997) in the prestigious Modern Library's series about the Harlem Renaissance.

Thurman wrote his third and final novel, *The Interne* (1932), with Abraham Furman, a white writer. Their novel exposed the unethical behavior and social injustices perpetrated at City Hospital on Welfare Island (now Roosevelt Island). The novel does not really touch on racial issues but instead focuses on medical abuses of disadvantaged persons. Two years after the novel was published, Thurman was taken to that very hospital after he collapsed at a reunion party celebrating his return to New York. A few months later, he died in the charity ward of Bellevue Hospital due to tuberculosis exacerbated by chronic alcoholism.

His friends and acquaintances recalled that he aspired to be not just a good ("journalistic") writer, but a great writer (like Thomas Mann, Herman Melville, Marcel Proust, or Leo Tolstoy). He was a voracious reader and might have achieved greatness had he not been one of his own worst enemies. In fact, his frequent self-deprecation occasionally lapsed into threats of suicide, particularly when he had been drinking. His sexual (and bisexual) appetites and his thirst for alcohol also frequently diverted him from his literary pursuits. His perpetual financial difficulties also often led him to write (or ghostwrite) trashy stories for *True Story* magazine or other publications of questionable literary merit.

REFERENCES: *BWA. EA-99. EB-BH-CD. EBLG. NAAAL. WDAA.* Ferguson, Sally Ann H., in *OCAAL.* Amazon.com, 8/1999.

Tillman, Katherine Davis (née) Chapman (2/19/1870–?)

Poems, novels, plays, essays

Chapman's two novellas (*Beryl Weston's Ambition: The Story of an Afro-American Girl's Life,* 1893; and *Clancy Street,* 1898–1899) were serialized in the *A.M.E. Church Review,* which also published many of her poems and biographical essays (e.g., of Aleksandr Pushkin, Alexandre Dumas, and many famous African-American women). Her other works include a collection of verse (*Recitations,* 1902) and three dramas (*Aunt Betsy's Thanksgiving,* n.d.; *Thirty Years of Freedom,* 1902; *Fifty Years of Freedom, or From Cabin to Congress,* 1910), all of which were published by A.M.E. Book Concern. Her works have since been gathered in *The Works of Katherine Davis Chapman Tillman* (1991, introduced by Claudia Tate).

REFERENCES: Tate, Claudia, in *OCAAL.*

Tolson, Melvin (Beaunorus) ("Cap") (2/6/1898?–8/29/1966)

Poems, plays, columns, novels, libretto; journalist

When Reverend Tolson, an itinerant minister, moved from church to church through various midwestern towns, his four children moved from school to school. Tolson had only an eighth grade education, but he had a great thirst for knowledge, having taught himself more than one classical language. Although he was skeptical about the need for a college education, he taught his children the value of learning.

The Tolsons also encouraged their children to appreciate music, visual arts, and literature, as well as a broad range of cultural riches. Initially, Melvin seemed destined to become a painter, but when an unconventional artist invited Melvin to accompany him to Paris, Melvin's mother squelched that ambition. Fortunately for lovers of literature, Melvin merely turned his creative pursuits to poetry, and in 1912 his "The Wreck of the *Titanic*" was published in the Oskaloosa, Iowa, newspaper. In high school, he gave outstanding dramatic recitations of **Paul Laurence Dunbar** poems and other dramatic performances. In his last year of high school, he was elected senior class poet, and he had two of his poems and two of his short stories published in the school yearbook.

After high school, while earning his B.A. (with honors, 1923), Tolson met Ruth Southall, whom he married January 29, 1922. Shortly after they wedded, Ruth gave birth to the first of their four children. After graduating, Tolson started teaching English and speech (and coaching a team) at Wiley College in Marshall, Texas, where he remained until 1947. In addition to his academic duties, he was deeply involved in extracurricular organizations, organizing and cofounding various student clubs.

During the 1931–1932 school year, Tolson took a sabbatical to pursue his master's degree in comparative literature from Columbia University in New York City. Tolson and his family lived in Harlem during the last days of the **Harlem Renaissance**, and he wrote his thesis about "The Harlem Group of Negro Writers." While at Columbia, he also started writing *Harlem Gallery,* his much-celebrated poetry collection (not published until 1965). In 1940, Tolson earned his master's degree from Columbia.

In 1947 Tolson left Wiley and moved to Langston, Oklahoma, to become a professor of creative literature and the director of the Dust Bowl Theatre at Langston University. In addition to his professional, literary, and artistic pursuits, he served as the mayor of Langston for four terms. In the mid-1960s, he was invited to become the Avalon Professor of the Humanities at Tuskegee Institute as well as a writer-in-residence. According to former students at each of the institutions at which he taught, Tolson was an outstanding, enthusiastic teacher, deeply interested in the intellectual development of his students. He also encouraged his students to follow his lead in developing and using a broad, deep vocabulary in the pursuit of clarity.

Throughout Tolson's career, he wrote numerous novels and plays as well as stage adaptations of other authors' novels. Although these works went unpublished, his poems appeared regularly in various literary journals. In addition, Tolson wrote a weekly column, "Caviar and Cabbage," for the *Washington Tribune* (1937–1944). An idealistic Marxist, he addressed a wide range of social, political, and even religious topics in his columns, attacking racism and class-based oppression and promoting cultural pride and civil rights. (These columns were published posthumously in 1982 in *Caviar and Cabbage: Selected Columns by Melvin B. Tolson,* edited by Robert M. Farnsworth.)

The writings for which Tolson is best known, however, are his poems. "Dark Symphony," probably his best-known work, contrasts the historical contributions of African Americans with those of European Americans, addresses issues of class and race oppression, and then reaches a finale optimistically predicting great progress for African Americans through their unity with other oppressed peoples around the world. Tolson arranged the poem in six "movements," comparable to the musical movements of a symphony. Listen to the lyricality of the middle verse of his "Andante Sostenuto" movement: "They tell us to forget / Democracy is spurned. / They tell us to forget / The Bill of Rights is burned. / Three hundred years we slaved, / We slave and suffer yet: / Though flesh and bone rebel, / They tell us to forget!" "Dark Symphony" won the National Poetry Contest of the 1939 American Negro Exposition in Chicago, and then in 1941 *Atlantic Monthly* published it. Fortunately, his editor at *Atlantic Monthly* moved from the magazine to a book publisher. She so liked Tolson's poem that she asked him to produce his first published collection, *Rendezvous with America* (1944). Popularly and critically acclaimed, the book went through three editions.

In 1947, Liberia's president appointed Tolson to be the Liberian poet laureate. Tolson's only previous connection to Liberia was that a former student of his had once introduced him to the daughter of a Liberian consul. As poet laureate, he was commissioned to write a poem commemorating Liberia's first 100 years for the 1956 Liberian Centennial and International Exposition. Tolson completed his *The Libretto for the Republic of Liberia* in 1953. His complex, modernistic *Libretto* comprises eight sections, each one named for a sequentially ascending note on the diatonic musical scale, each section prefaced with the question, "Liberia?" Making extensive use of literary, classical, mythical, and cultural allusions, *Libretto* attacks colonial exploitation, embraces universal brotherhood, celebrates African history and achievements in science and the humanities, and looks forward to an African continent of free and independent nations. While many critics praised the work's complex splendorous language and subject matter, many others considered it to be modernism run amok—too unlyrical, too scholarly, and too allusive.

Tolson's next published collection of poems—*Harlem Gallery: Book I, The Curator,* was actually the collection he first started in the early 1930s—finally published in 1965. He originally planned this project to comprise five books, but only one was published during his lifetime. Each of the five books was to represent a distinct phase in the history of the African *diaspora* (the scattering of Africans throughout the American continents). The name "Gallery" suggests Tolson's strong orientation in the visual arts, and the poems in this first book are written from the point of view of the curator of a gallery illustrating the African-American experience.

Tolson's *Gallery* included a richly diverse wealth of scenes and portraits. In the *Gallery,* Tolson retained some of the modernism and metaphorical language of the *Libretto,* but he blended it with African-American oral storytelling and blues traditions, yielding lyrical vignettes, conversations, and folk philosophy. This blending makes the poetry compelling but also makes it difficult to classify. A devout nonconformist, he probably relished his resistance to categorization. Further enriching this blend, Tolson combined playfully humorous insights and investigations with serious study of the role of the artist in African-American culture.

Tolson died soon after the publication of his *Gallery,* and that might have been the end of his publications. Fortunately, Robert Farnsworth (who later published Tolson's posthumous essay collection) amplified the original *Gallery* with various free verse monologues by a culturally diverse cross-section of Tolson's characters to create *A Gallery of Harlem Portraits* (1979). This collection reflects Tolson's love of lyrics, his passion for plays, and his fondness for blues. As with his previous gallery, this gallery portrays a community of individuals who together illustrate the strengths of the culturally diverse Harlem community. Throughout this work, Tolson manages to highlight class and race oppression while maintaining an optimistic outlook for the future.

Tolson himself is also difficult to define. He came into his poetic voice after the **Harlem Renaissance** had waned and before the **Black Aesthetic** emerged. While embracing African-American folk traditions, he explored European-American modernism. While addressing issues of past and present class and racial oppression, he hopefully predicted a future in which such oppression would be thrown over by a culturally and nationally diverse union of oppressed peoples. An inveterate iconoclast, he never hesitated to express ideas that clashed starkly with those of his contemporaries. Yet he was no sourpuss, winning the

abiding affection of his students and of the citizens whom he served as mayor. This irreverent scholar received an honorary doctorate from Lincoln University in 1965 as well as numerous other awards, fellowships, and grants. He was also well respected by fellow poets, such as Robert Frost, Theodore Roethke, John Ciardi, and William Carlos Williams.

REFERENCES: *AA:PoP. BAL-1-P. BWA. EB-98. EBLG. G-95. MAAL. NAAAL.* Beaulieu, Elizabeth Ann, in *OCAAL.*

Toomer, Jean (né Nathan Pinchback Toomer) (3/29/1894–3/30/1967)

Novels, poems, essays, plays, nonfiction—philosophy

Jean Toomer's life was consumed by a search for spiritual wholeness. The search both preoccupied him throughout his life and has been blamed for ruining his promise as a brilliant writer. During his lifetime, Toomer produced only one great work—the novel *Cane* (1923)—but it was so brilliantly and artistically composed that it won Toomer great praise and renown as one of the most famous writers of the **Harlem Renaissance**. The fact that his first work exhibited such promise, however, led many to judge him to be, as Cynthia Kerman and Richard Eldridge say in their biography *The Lives of Jean Toomer,* "a comet that had one burst of glory before burning up." Yet Toomer did not die or stop living after the publication of *Cane* but led an extremely active life in pursuit of religion and spiritual identity.

Nathan Pinchback Toomer was born to his parents Nina Pinchback and Nathan Toomer. His father was a farmer and his mother the daughter of P. B. S. Pinchback, a prominent politician in Louisiana during the period of Reconstruction. Toomer's father and his maternal grandfather both claimed to have "black blood" but had very fair-skinned complexions, which Toomer inherited. After his mother and father divorced two years after he was born, Toomer's mother took him to live with her parents who, because of their wealth and fair skin, lived in a prominent white upper-middle-class neighborhood. A few years later, his mother married and moved to upstate New York with her (white) husband and her son.

Because the neighborhoods he lived in for the first 14 years of his life were predominantly white and upper class, and because his skin was so fair,

Jean Toomer with his bride, Marjery Latimer, 1932 (UPI/Corbis-Bettmann)

Toomer did not come into contact with real racial issues until his mother died in 1910. At that time, he moved from New York back to Washington, D.C., to live once again with his mother's parents. However, his grandparents' economic situation had taken a turn for the worse, and they had been forced to move out of their mansion in the upper-class white section of town and into a middle-class interracial community. Although for the most part he quickly adapted to his new environment and was almost invigorated by the change, it was at this point that he came into contact with issues of race and began to formulate his theories on the meaning of racial identity in a person's relationship with the world.

The fact that Toomer once described himself having a mixture of "Scotch, Welsh, German, English, French, Dutch, Spanish and some dark blood" might indicate his ideas about the importance he gave to racial identity. In essence, he tried to avoid labels and hated the idea of being classi-

fied; he once said, "I am of no particular race. I am of the human race, a man at large in the human world, preparing a new race." When pressed, he would reject the idea that he had to define himself as either black or white and insisted that he was a member of the "American" race—which he felt all Americans should claim to be.

However, as seems to be the case for many writers who eschew racial labels, Toomer is best known for the work that deals most clearly with racial themes—*Cane.* He decided to become a writer in 1919 after spending five years meandering through four different colleges and receiving no degrees. He found college disappointing because it failed to offer him "a sort of whole into which everything fits . . . a body of ideas which holds a consistent view of life." He thus turned to writing in an attempt to find that whole and moved to Greenwich Village in New York City, where he met a number of prominent writers and critics, including Waldo Frank, a writer who would later help him publish his novel. It was in New York that he changed his name from Nathan to Jean because he felt that the main character of Romain Rolland's *Jean Christophe* best embodied whom he would like to be as a writer.

Despite the time spent in New York, *Cane* was actually inspired by a trip Toomer took to Sparta, Georgia. He traveled there to take a position as an acting principal at the Sparta Agricultural and Industrial Institute. While there, he was struck by the landscape of Georgia and by its rich history of slavery and segregation. He was also amazed to hear folk songs and **spirituals** being sung by the residents of the area, and hearing that music made him realize that in that place, black folk culture seemed to have remained untouched by white cultural influences. In a sense, the segregation of the South had served to preserve an African-American folk culture that Toomer never knew existed. He noticed, however, that the culture was being lost, as many young black people in the area moved away from the Southern rural areas and into the large industrialized Northern cities where they were forgetting their rich cultural history and instead taking up the values of white society. On the way home from his two-month stay, he began penning the poem "Georgia Dusk" and many of the vignettes that would compose the first section of *Cane*.

The novel is divided into three sections. The first depicts the black experience in the rural South and tells, in vignettes interspersed with verse, the experiences of five Southern women. All the women are presented as beautiful, strong, and vulnerable, and they represent different parts of the black community throughout history. The second section depicts the lives of African Americans in the North and comprises vignettes interspersed with verse. This section attempts to illustrate the way that the natural tendencies of human nature are destroyed by the sterile, harsh, and mechanical elements of the modern city. It also focuses on the detrimental effects segregated society has on the human spirit and the way it prevents African Americans from achieving wholeness of mind or body, and it warns black Americans of the danger they face if they lose sight of the values of black folk life when they appropriate the sterile values of white society.

The third part of the novel attempts a kind of synthesis of Northern and Southern black experience and offers a resolution of the two; it is a drama called "Kabnis," which enacts the story of

an urban black writer who travels to the rural South. This section is written entirely in prose. The black writer in the story is having difficulty with his African-American identity, and that prevents him from succeeding as a writer. With some fear, he undertakes a spiritual quest for identity, and on the way, he ends up dealing with issues of racial inequality. The end of the novel is mostly optimistic, as the writer spends a night in a basement with a number of Southern blacks, all of whom talk about the damage that they have experienced because of racial conflict. He emerges from the basement determined to write of the struggles of blacks throughout history and thus finds a place for himself in African-American history.

Whether he intended it to be or not, the third section of *Cane* is highly autobiographical—for after his trip to the South, Toomer did write of the struggles of blacks in the North and the South and did make a place for himself in history with that one novel. After its publication, however, Toomer dropped out of literary circles and rejected all his friends. He had become a writer because he felt that his writings could help to stem the rapid flow of technology that was causing people to become increasingly isolated and materialistic; after publishing *Cane,* he came to believe that the literary arts were proving to be completely ineffective at helping resolve many of the world's problems. He also became very angry at the fact that in writing *Cane,* he began to be classified as a black writer and that it made people expect that he would continue to write about issues of race. He stated that "*Cane* was a song of end," which had helped him come to terms with his racial identity but which was really only a part of his search for a unifying principle in himself.

His quest for wholeness continued after he abandoned his literary community when, in 1924, he became involved with Georgei I. Gurdjieff, a spiritual philosopher who propounded theories of human development. Toomer hoped this spiritual program would help him to attain a higher consciousness, which would help him to locate where his self existed in relationship to the universal whole. During this time, he continued to write and tried to publish his writings, but no publishers were interested in his rather abstract, spiritual work. (EDITOR'S NOTE: Some of Toomer's philosophy may be found in his *Essentials* [1931].)

In the mid-1930s, Toomer formally disassociated himself from Gurdjieff, although the ideas of

Gurdjieff's teachings would appear in Toomer's writing for many more years. During that time Toomer was married twice—his first wife, Marjery Latimer, died in childbirth in 1931, and three years later, he married Marjorie Content. Continuing in his quest for spiritual wholeness, he and Marjorie became interested in the Society of Friends (known as the Quakers) in 1934 and became members in 1940.

His second and last literary milestone was achieved in 1936 when *New Caravan* agreed to publish his poem, "Blue Meridian." Although at the time it was published it received little attention, some contemporary critics have claimed that it is artistically equal to *Cane*. In this poem, Toomer writes about the fusion of black-, white-, and red-skinned people into a new creation, the blue man. This poem is extremely idealistic and still contains a great deal of Gurdjieff's philosophy, but it also makes some important social statements in a highly artistic way. The blue man represents a person who has shed all classifications—being of no sex, class, or color. This blue man lives in a new America, which has indeed become a melting pot. Everyone exists in harmony and oneness.

In many ways, "Blue Meridian" is yet another part of Toomer's quest to reconcile disparate parts —of the self, the nation, and the world. As in *Cane*, Toomer draws the readers' attention to the possibility of transformation and synthesis, for this is what Toomer had been searching for, unsuccessfully, throughout his life. His expectations for literature, religion, and the world were always unfulfilled, but in many ways that disappointment kept him always reaching—it kept him active as a thinking, living person but it stood in the way of fulfilling his promise as a brilliant writer. Gorham Munson, a friend of Toomer's for 45 years, wrote a review of Toomer's life after hearing of his death in 1967: "We must realize that there are many casualties on the road to self-development." The fact that Toomer was one of them makes him abundantly human, if nothing else.

—*Diane Masiello*

REFERENCES: *AAW. BW:SSCA. NAAAL. OCAAL.* Kerman, Cynthia Earl, and Richard Eldridge (1987), *The Lives of Jean Toomer: A Hunger for Wholeness* (Baton Rouge: Louisiana State University Press).

Torrence, Jackie (2/12/1944–)
Stories, folklore

A small portion of Torrence's rich treasure may be found in her collection of folklore and stories, *The Importance of Pot Liquor* (1994). Although her specialty is ghost stories (reputedly, she can tell 300 or so), Torrence can vividly recount a wealth of African and African-American stories as well as stories from other lands and other times.

—*Tonya Bolden*

REFERENCES: *BAAW.*

Touré, Askia M. (né Rolland Snellings) (10/13/1938–)
Poems, biography, sketches; journalist, editor

In addition to his illustrated biography (*Samory Touré*, 1963, with **Tom Feelings** and Matthew Meade), Touré wrote a book-length poem (*Juju: Magic Songs for the Black Nation*, 1970), a collection of poems and sketches (*Songhai!* 1973), and a poetry collection (*From the Pyramid to the Projects: Poems of Genocide and Resistance*, 1989 American Book Award winner). In addition, he has been a regular contributor to *Black Dialogue*, an editor-at-large for the *Journal of Black Poetry*, and a staff writer for *Liberator Magazine* and *Soulbook*.

REFERENCES: Richardson, James W., Jr., in *OCAAL*.

Trickster Tales

A *trickster tale* is a **folktale** in which the action of the story centers on a trickster character, and the fictional events in the story are intended to represent events in the real world. In most trickster tales, animal characters represent humans, and speak and behave like humans, but occasionally, tricksters are actually humans—or even superhumans with some godlike characteristics. In all cases, trickster characters are wily, charming, and mischievous, and they almost invariably come into conflict with characters who are physically larger and more powerful than they, so they must use their craftiness to trick these more powerful adversaries. Some tricksters may have supernatural powers, but most do not. The fundamental nature of the trickster may also vary across cultures. For instance, one culture's trickster may play a benevolent, creative role, whereas another culture's may play an evil, destructive role. The trickster may be a childlike, impulsive prankster; a wise, wily charmer; or a seemingly innocent fool whose actions coincidentally outwit a strong enemy.

Usually, the trickster encounters a difficult situation posed by an antagonist, to which the trickster responds with some clever trickery. In some variants, however, the trickster is simply mischievous, thereby creating her or his own problem. In most trickster tales, the prankster manages to get out of the difficulty through chicanery, but sometimes, the scamp is too clever for her or his own good and ends up being undone by the knavery. The undoing often results because the trickster has shown some human fallibility, such as pride or greed.

Another variant is the *escape story*, in which the trickster appears to be caught in a situation from which escape seems impossible. Occasionally, a powerful adversary presents the trickster with an impossible task, and the trickster must counter it by imposing an impossible condition on the adversary. In one tale, for instance, a wicked Dahomean king demanded that his subjects build him a castle, starting the building from the *top* and building *downward*. He warned them that their failure to do so would mean death for all. The terrified Dahomeans saw no way to avoid a seemingly certain death. A wise old trickster came up with a solution: He told the king that his people were ready to begin construction, and he asked the king to honor them by laying the foundation stone, as was customary.

What purposes do trickster tales serve? For one thing, whatever the outcome, the story usually teaches the reader a lesson (e.g., "Even if you're weaker than your adversary, you can succeed," or "Don't be greedy"). Often, trickster tales are told by folks without much power (physical, financial, political, and so on), and the trickster serves as a cultural hero, triumphing over more powerful foes. Such tales also allow the storytellers to poke fun at their nemeses, at human foibles shown by the story characters, or even at themselves (e.g., when the trickster is undone by greed or gluttony). Because trickster tales are allegorical, storytellers can parody more powerful members of a culture, signifying the failings of these adversaries without explicitly stating those faults—and risking the opponents' wrath. Around the world and across time, almost every culture offers amusing trickster tales, so that storytellers and listeners can project their hopes and fears onto these charming rascals. In addition, in some cultures, tricksters have supernatural powers and serve important roles in sacred rituals.

In Africa, tricksters may take on human forms, animal forms (e.g., hare, monkey, Ijapa the tortoise, or Anansi the spider), or divine forms (e.g., the trickster god Eshu). Both Anansi and Eshu may take on mythological characteristics. For instance, Eshu carries messages between gods and humans and influences luck. Tricksters often change as they travel from place to place, adapting to new environments and situations. For instance, in the United States, Eshu was transformed into the signifying monkey.

When differing cultures interact, interesting combinations sometimes emerge. For instance, when African slaves were brought to the American continent, African trickster tales and the hare trickster tales of Southeastern American Indians may have mated to give birth to the Brer Rabbit tales of the American South. Certainly, the need for trickster tales was magnified by the slaves' almost total powerlessness. The trickster could become an icon of survival and resistance in a savagely oppressive environment, where outright rebellion almost surely meant death.

As African slaves adapted to the American continent, they modified their tales to suit their new environs. They dropped animals native to Africa and incorporated animals of the American South. As Christianity became more widespread among African Americans, tricksters lost their mythical powers. Increasingly, tricksters used sly cunning rather than supernatural powers to succeed. Perhaps because of the slaves' grim circumstances, their trickster tales highlighted humorous characterizations, plots, and even wordings. Further, these slaves, forbidden from gaining any formal education or even learning to read in a land where education connotes success, tell of tricksters who have masterful verbal skills and cunning wit.

Prevented from open revolt, the African-American trickster uses artful subversion to undo the oppressor. Within the context of slavery, increasingly prominent characteristics of African-American tricksters are *masking*, in which tricksters conceal their true feelings, thoughts, intentions, and actions; and *signifying*, in which tricksters covertly communicate with their sympathizers without revealing their true meanings to their oppressors. When overt resistance was foolhardy, subversive tactics became ever more appealing. In most of these tales, the trickster uses wile and guile to trick the oppressor in some way.

Some stories, however, serve as cautionary tales,

showing how the trickster's greed, gluttony, pride, or selfishness ends up harming the trickster at least as much as the object of the trickery. Perhaps the best-known example is the traditional story of "Brer Rabbit and the Tar Baby": Brer Fox (a trickster in his own right) sets up a tar baby alongside the path he knows that Brer Rabbit takes. Brer Rabbit greets the tar baby, but the tar baby says nothing in response. Brer Rabbit, affronted that the tar baby doesn't politely greet him, chides the tar baby for such rudeness. When it continues to ignore him, Brer Rabbit swats it. When this effort not only fails but also gets Brer Rabbit's arm stuck in the tar baby, Brer Rabbit strikes the tar baby with his other fist, then kicks it with both legs, and finally thumps it with his tail. Once Brer Rabbit is thoroughly stuck, Brer Fox and his associates Brer Wolf and Brer Bear gleefully rejoice in having caught the prideful rabbit. (Don't worry too much, though; Brer Rabbit finds a way to be released before much harm comes to him. In this case, Brer Rabbit uses reverse psychology on his animal foes, begging them to *please* burn him, hang him, drown him, boil him, or inflict any other kind of torture they wish, as long as they *please* don't throw him in the briar patch—his native home.)

Many traditional African-American trickster tales were popularized by a white Southerner, **Joel Chandler Harris**. Harris had actually done extensive research into African-American folklore when he wrote his Brer Rabbit tales. Harris may have been drawn to the Brer Rabbit stories because he, too, identified with the underdog. Small, painfully shy, and raised by an unwed mother, he often used humor and practical jokes to win acceptance by others.

Harris's stories were pretty true to the original versions, and he tried his best to preserve the authentic dialect of the numerous storytellers whom he interviewed. What makes the tales inauthentic, however, is that he couches the stories within a peculiar framework: He has the storyteller, Uncle Remus, tell these stories to the blue-eyed, blond son of his master. In truth, slaves almost always told such stories *within* the slave community; they rarely tempted fate by telling these thinly disguised subversive tales to slaveowners. In addition, Harris couldn't help but perpetuate stereotypes of African Americans intrinsic to his worldview as a white Southerner. Thus, he portrayed Uncle Remus as a jovial old man delighted to have enjoyed the blessings of slavery. More contemporary writers, such as **Zora Neale Hurston** and **Julius Lester**, give more authentic versions of these tales—without the ludicrous Uncle Remus character.

After the Civil War, the trickster tale was modified to more specifically describe the situation of the slave. The small trickster animals were replaced by the servant John, and the oppressive larger animals were replaced by the master himself, usually called "Ol' Massa." In one particularly appealing John-and-Ol'-Massa tale, John manages to earn his freedom, and as he is walking down the road away from the plantation, the master, the mistress, and their children keep calling after him how much they love him and how well they will treat him in the future if he chooses to stay with them. John keeps walking down that road. The reader is left to imagine the puzzled expressions on the former slaveowners' faces. In other stories, John tricks the master by staging a contest in which John has rigged the outcome. For instance, John may use trickery to appear to have some special talent (such as fortune telling) and taunts the master to do what John has done. The master, not to be outdone by a mere slave, attempts to show similar talent but fails. By this means, John may win his freedom, earn money toward gaining his freedom, or at least get out of a particularly onerous task or punishment of some sort.

At the turn of the century, **Charles Waddell Chesnutt** took a different tack with his *The Conjure Woman* (1899), featuring former slave Uncle Julius McAdoo, who entertains white Northerners with stories that covertly reveal the tragedy of slavery. In Uncle McAdoo's stories, the trickster usually manages to turn the tables on the oppressor. During this era of Ku Klux Klan terrorism, lynchings, and Jim Crow laws, a new set of tales also emerged, which still might loosely be called "trickster tales." These tales center on self-identified "Bad Niggers" such as High John the Conqueror and Stagolee. Such protagonists are aggressive, cruel, and even bloodthirsty, lacking social conscience or moral constraints. Though not truly heroes, their bold fierceness held strong appeal to African Americans being brutalized around the turn of the twentieth century. Even legendary heroes such as John Hardy and Railroad Bill may be construed along these lines.

Another kind of trickster tale was the popular genre of stories about light-skinned African Americans who passed for white. A distinctive nonfiction version of this type of story was blue-eyed

Walter White's "I Investigate Lynchings" (1929), describing how he interviewed lynchers for the National Association for the Advancement of Colored People (NAACP) during the 1920s.

More contemporary trickster tales include **Toni Morrison**'s *Tar Baby* (1981); **Ishmael Reed**'s *The Last Days of Louisiana Red* (1974); **Ralph Ellison**'s *Invisible Man* (1952), featuring con artist, gambler, and petty criminal Bliss Proteus Rinehart; and **Kristin Hunter**'s *The Lakestown Rebellion* (1978), in which Bella Lake unites her community to slyly thwart the wishes of a huge corporation. A contemporary poem referring to tricksters is **Colleen McElroy**'s "The Griots Who Know Brer Fox" (1979). Contemporary children's books featuring African or African-American trickster tales include Gerald McDermott's *Anansi the Spider* (1972) and his West African *Zomo the Rabbit* (1992); **Ashley F. Bryan**'s *The Adventures of Aku* (1976) and *The Dancing Granny* (1977), featuring "Ananse"; Louise Bennett's books about "Brer Anancy"; Eric Kimmel's *Anansi and the Talking Melon* (1994); and **Julius Lester**'s *The Last Tales of Uncle Remus: As Told by Julius Lester* (1994).

REFERENCES: *CBC. E-98. EB-98. EBLG. G-96. MSE-CD. MSI-CD. MWEL. NAAAL. WB-98.* Harris, Trudier, "Passing," in *OCWW.* Newson, Adele S., "African American Oral Tradition," in *OCWW.* Smith, Jeanne R., "Trickster," in *OCAAL.*

Trotter, Geraldine ("Deenie") (Louise) (née) Pindell (10/3/1872–10/8/1918)
Editorials, columns, articles; newspaper copublisher

Deenie's childhood friend (and boyfriend, for a time) was **W. E. B. Du Bois**, who described her as both "fine" (because of her intellect, her cultured refinement, and her strength of purpose) and "fragile" (because of her precarious health). In 1899, after marrying her beloved Monroe (**William Monroe Trotter**), she started to settle into a life of relative comfort and ease in the upper-class Dorchester neighborhood of Boston.

A couple of years later, Monroe cofounded his *Boston Guardian,* in which he lambasted **Booker T. Washington** and other accommodationist African Americans, just as he opposed injustice, discrimination, and segregation wherever he saw it. In 1903, Monroe infuriated Washington when his cohorts interrupted Washington's address at a local meeting. Washington ensured that Monroe was arrested and jailed. For a month, Deenie

worked for his release and helped keep the *Guardian* running in his absence.

Washington continued to retaliate against the *Guardian* and its founders with the power and fierceness he was so capable of mustering. Pretty soon, Monroe's cofounder bailed out on him, leaving Deenie to fill in on a permanent basis. She was soon associate editor, business manager, bookkeeper, circulation manager, society column editor, and in charge of whatever other tasks were needed. Despite their joint efforts, Washington's all-out effort to crush them (through smear campaigns, dirty tricks, subterfuge, and full financing of rival papers) led to financial disaster, and Monroe had to sell his formerly prosperous real estate business—and even their lovely home. When Monroe was out of town, spreading his message or rallying support, Deenie was left to run the *Guardian* on her own.

Deenie had her own activist pursuits, as well. Raised in a family of activists, she wrote and gained signatures for petitions, organized committees, chaired societies, and raised funds for whatever causes she believed in—such as a shelter for women and children and the Boston Literary Society. She championed the cause of unjustly imprisoned African Americans, and she fought against lynching. Despite her fragile health and weak physical stamina, she believed that "those of us who have had the advantages of education, who have seen life in its broadest light, [should] be willing to sacrifice . . . to do for our own down-trodden people all in our power . . . to make their cause our cause, their suffering, our suffering" (from a 1905 speech on the 100th anniversary of abolitionist William Lloyd Garrison's birth).

—*Tonya Bolden*

REFERENCES: *BAAW.*

Trotter, James Monroe (2/7/1842–2/26/1892)
Nonfiction—musicology

Young James learned early about the complexities of race relations in a slavery-based society: His European-American father "owned" his African-American mother as well as James and his two siblings. In 1854, when James's father decided to marry, he sent his children and their mother to Cincinnati, Ohio, where slavery was outlawed. There, James had to work (e.g., as a hotel bellboy and a riverboat cabin boy), but he still managed to educate himself.

During the Civil War, Trotter's passion for equality and for civil rights became evident; among other things, he led black soldiers in the fight to be awarded equal pay for equal rank and work—comparable to white soldiers—and after the soldiers refused to accept inferior pay for more than a year, the federal government relented and gave them commensurate pay. After the war, he turned to civil service employment and continued to champion civil rights and equality.

In 1868, Trotter married Virginia Isaacs, with whom he had three children, including his son **William Monroe Trotter**. James Trotter's main claim to fame, however, was his book *Music and Some Highly Musical People* (1878), in which he asserted that slave **spirituals** are "our only distinctively *American* music" (emphasis in original). Although he touted the musical achievements of African Americans, he nonetheless was a man of his times, expressing the biases and worldview of those around him, which praised Eurocentric "classical" music traditions above Afrocentric and other non-European musical forms and traditions.

References: *BDAA. SMKC.*

Trotter, William Monroe
(4/7/1872–4/7/1934)
Editorials; newspaper cofounder, publisher, and editor

The son of **James Monroe Trotter**, a Civil War veteran, successful real estate broker, and author, young William attended mostly white schools, graduated magna cum laude from Harvard in 1895, and earned a master's degree a year later. In these early years, he had frequent near-misses with **W. E. B. Du Bois**, a year or two ahead of him at Harvard and a boyfriend of William's wife-to-be, **Geraldine (Louise) Pindell (Trotter)**.

Monroe (the name most folks called him) and "Deenie" wedded in 1899 and settled into a comfortable lifestyle among the Boston bourgeoisie. With his ample inheritance and his own prospering real estate business, they both could see much more comfort ahead. Naturally, the couple became involved in cultural and intellectual pursuits. He soon participated in founding the Boston Literary and Historical Association, which attracted the attention of some African Americans with decidedly uncomfortable views of things. In fact, his cohorts at the association tended toward rabble rousing. A frequent subject of conversation was their disap-

proval of the accommodationist policies and practices of **Booker T. Washington**, whom they considered a traitor to their race.

Over the course of a couple of years, Trotter had worked up quite a feverish opposition to Washington, and in 1901 he and George Forbes founded the *Boston Guardian,* in large part to speak out against accommodationism and its traitorous champion from the Tuskegee Institute (whose *Up from Slavery* came out in March of the same year). At first, Trotter intended the *Guardian* to be a sideline to his real estate business, but he made the mistake of giving the paper this motto—"For every right, with all thy might!"—and then trying to live up to it.

Late in July 1903, Trotter and the troops he had rallied attended a speech by Washington. Some of them (not Trotter in particular) loudly voiced their opposition to Washington's policies and practices. In the fracas that followed, Washington managed to have Trotter arrested and jailed for a month, and Washington—with many powerful friends and allies—launched an all-out campaign to destroy Trotter and his *Guardian*. Washington was able to finance rival papers, dig up—or make up—smears on Trotter and his wife, and pull any number of filthy tricks to demolish Trotter. In not too long, Forbes saw the futility of trying to oppose Washington, and he left Trotter in the lurch.

Well, Trotter's frail wife Geraldine filled in, working as business manager, associate editor, and whatever else was needed. So much for a comfy lifestyle. For a time, while waging war against lynching, Jim Crow, and foot-dragging-take-it-slow Washingtonians, Trotter joined forces with his former classmate and rival W. E. B. Du Bois, and they were united in founding the Niagara Movement in 1905 (progenitor of the National Association for the Advancement of Colored People, which emerged in 1909). Even Du Bois wasn't militant enough for Trotter, however, so Trotter split from W. E. B. to found the Negro Equal Rights League (NERL), with African Americans squarely (and solely) in positions of leadership. Through the nineteen-teens, Trotter continued to lead the way, opposing segregation in the federal government, protesting against D. W. Griffith's racist movie *Birth of a Nation,* and practicing in-your-face activism at every turn.

In the fall of 1918, Trotter lost his closest ally, his best friend, his beloved wife Deenie. Almost everything was slower and harder going after that.

Still, he never faltered or wavered from his course. Over the next 16 years, Trotter continued to fight racism, segregation, discrimination, and injustice wherever he saw it. He spent every last penny of his—of which there had once been quite a few—fighting "For every right." When at last, his might gave out, and he couldn't see how to continue the fight, he took his own life. Had he only known that he had made an important difference and that we would remember his efforts. His contemporary, W. E. B. Du Bois, later said of him that he "was a man of heroic proportions, and probably the most selfless of Negro leaders during all our American history"; one of Trotter's many successors, **Lerone Bennett, Jr.**, later wrote, "Trotter laid the first stone of the modern protest movement"; and Boston schools and libraries now honor Trotter by bearing his name.

—*Tonya Bolden*

REFERENCES: *BAAW. SMKC.* Fox, Stephen R. (1970/1971), *The Guardian of Boston: William Monroe Trotter* (New York: Scribner's).

Troupe, Quincy (Thomas) (Jr.)
(7/23/1943–)
Poems; journal editor and founder

Although Troupe loved reading from an early age, and his mother encouraged him to read widely, the kids in his neighborhood frowned on his love of books, and he never really thought he'd grow up to be a writer. Years later, while traveling the world with the U.S. Army basketball team, he started writing. In Europe, he was encouraged to write poetry by Jean-Paul Sartre and came under the influence of many other poets (e.g., **Sterling Brown**, Aimé Césaire, Pablo Neruda, **Jean Toomer**). After leaving the army, Troupe earned his bachelor's degree from Grambling College (now Grambling State University) in Louisiana. Next, he moved to Los Angeles, where he studied journalism and joined the Watts Writers' movement.

As Troupe started advancing his writing career, he also began lecturing and teaching creative writing at various colleges and universities, including Columbia University, the University of California at Berkeley, the University of Ghana, Lagos University (in Nigeria), the City University of New York, and a few others. By the mid-1990s, Troupe was a professor of creative writing and American and Caribbean literature at the University of California at San Diego.

When asked why he writes poetry, Troupe responded, "I write poetry because I *need* to write poetry. I need the music of language and the instant communication that I feel I get in writing poetry" (quoted in *LoL,* p. 413). That need is clear when viewing the abundance of poems he has produced. Troupe has had many of his poems published in such diverse periodicals as **Black Scholar**, *Black World* (see **Negro Digest**), **Callaloo**, *Umbra,* and *Village Voice;* and he served as associate editor for *Shrewd* magazine, was the founding editor of *Confrontation: A Journal of Third World Literature* and of *American Rag,* and is contributing editor of *Conjunctions* magazine and senior editor of *Styx* magazine.

Troupe's poems have also been widely anthologized, and he has edited two anthologies: *Watts Poets: A Book of New Poetry and Essays* (1968) and *Giant Talk: An Anthology of Third World Writings* (1970s, with Rainer Schulte). He also edited *James Baldwin: The Legacy* (1989). In addition, his poems have been gathered in his collections *Embryo Poems, 1967–1971* (1972), *Snake-Back Solos: Selected Poems, 1969–1977* (1979; 1980 American Book Award), *Skulls along the River* (1984), *Weather Reports: New and Selected Poems* (1978; reprints 1991, 1996), *Avalanche: Poems* (1996), and *Choruses: Poems* (1999).

Troupe's poems reflect his love for improvisational jazz and often have a spontaneous, go-with-the-flow feel to them. He observed, "I think every language has a musical core . . . the sounds of the American language come from *all* our different ethnic communities, and these sounds are beautiful to me. As a poet, I try to get the music that's underneath all that. . . . I grew up listening to blues and to the old African American people talking. . . . and I especially loved to listen to jazz musicians talk. So all that musical language that I grew up listening to is what I try to make *my* language" (quoted in *LoL,* p. 413, emphasis in original). In describing his own poetry (and that of other African Americans), Troupe sees the link between the rhythms and refrains of his poems and those of blues music, noting, "We tend to speak in circles—we come back and say things over and over again, just for emphasis—and there you have the whole repetition of lines coming back like refrains." He also feels that the improvisational aspects of jazz permeate and guide his own work: "Jazz provides the model for taking a text and improvising on it in a performance. That's why performance is part of the whole concept of poetry for me" (quoted in *LoL,* p. 417).

Troupe often reads his poems with a musical accompanist (e.g., George Lewis, Donal Fox) and has produced an audiocassette, *Shaman Man* (1990). As he noted, "In order to get into people's blood and into people's consciousness and into people's lives, poetry has to sing" (quoted in *LoL*, p. 417). Troupe also worked closely with Miles Davis to produce *Miles: The Autobiography* (1989, with Miles Davis), and he wrote and coproduced the *Miles Davis Radio Project* (1991–1992, PBS), for which he won a Peabody Award and the Ohio State Award. He has also been given two American Book Awards and was crowned the "World Heavyweight Poetry Champion" at the 1994 Taos Poetry Circus. "You have to make what you're coming from *live*. You have to find your central metaphor and your central meaning, and you have to make your language *live*—going back to the whole idea of language as being alive—so that when you read your poems you can become something else, a force" (quoted in *Lol*, p. 423, emphasis in original). "Great art . . . reveals our humanity and puts us in touch with it. That's what *all* great art is supposed to do" (quoted in *LoL*, p. 428, emphasis in original).

REFERENCES: *LoL. NAAAL. TtW.* Dillon, Kim Jenice, in *OCAAL*. Amazon.com, 7/1999.

Truth, Sojourner (legal name: Isabella Van Wagenen; slave name: Isabella Baumfree) (c.1797 or 1799–11/26/1883)
Speeches, sermons, slave narrative

Born into slavery in Hurley, Ulster County, New York, Isabella Baumfree (or Bomefree) was the second-youngest child of James and Elizabeth Baumfree's 10 or 12 children. The Baumfrees' primary language was Dutch, the language spoken by the family that "owned" them. While still a child, Isabella was sold again and again, ending up with John Dumont from 1810 until 1827, when the state of New York's Gradual Emancipation Act freed her.

When Isabella was about 14 years old, another of Dumont's slaves, Thomas, married her, and the twosome had five children: Diana, Sophia, Elizabeth, Peter, and Hannah (there is some question about her; perhaps she died in infancy). Even before Isabella's own emancipation, however, she boldly resisted the constraints of slavery. A year before New York's emancipation law was enacted, she chose to leave the Dumonts and went to work for Isaac Van Wagenen's family. Further, when Du-

mont illegally sold her son Peter into perpetual slavery in Alabama (just as New York state law was about to abolish slavery in New York), she solicited the aid of Ulster County Quakers and went to court to sue for his return—and won the suit!

About that time, she also underwent a religious conversion and pursued various unorthodox Christian faiths while supporting herself through domestic work. In 1843, she felt called to ramble around the country, preaching the gospel as she understood it, and on June 1 of that year, she renamed herself "Sojourner Truth," thereby acknowledging her calling as an itinerant preacher. By the end of that year, Truth moved to a utopian community in Massachusetts, where she became a feminist abolitionist (and where she met fellow abolitionists **Frederick Douglass**, **David Ruggles**, and William Lloyd Garrison). To add to her meager income and pay off her mortgage on a house she bought in Florence, Massachusetts, Truth dictated a **slave narrative** to Olive Gilbert, her neighbor in Massachusetts. (Like most slaves, Truth had never learned to read or write. By her own admission, "I cannot read a book, but I can read the people.") The Boston printer of Garrison's *Liberator* newspaper printed it as *The Narrative of Sojourner Truth: A Bondswoman of Olden Time* (1850; six or seven more editions by 1884; available from Oxford University Press, 1991), and Truth sold copies for 25 cents apiece to listeners at her sermons and speeches.

A powerful, insightful, and witty orator, in 1851 Truth gave perhaps one of the most famous speeches in U.S. history to the Ohio Women's Rights Convention: "And A'n't I a Woman?" (quoted either as "Ain't" or as "Ar'n't"). In that speech, she cited numerous ways in which she (and, by implication, other African-American and working-class women) had worked hard and had suffered much, thereby showing that many women are neither fragile nor protected from hardship. (In her speeches, she tended to take poetic license by exaggerating her authentic experiences in slavery to dramatic effect, such as stating that she had 13 children, rather than 5, and that she lived 40 years a slave, rather than about 30.) This speech (printed on June 21, 1851, in the *Anti-Slavery Bugle*) and a contact with **Harriet Beecher Stowe** (author of the 1852 book *Uncle Tom's Cabin*) helped publicize Truth and her book, thereby increasing her readership and her live audiences. In 1858, when a rude male listener challenged her femininity, asserting that no one as strong and smart and out-spoken as she could be a woman, she bared her breast, scorning his ridicule.

In 1856, Truth moved to Battle Creek, Michigan, and a neighbor there, Frances Titus, reprinted Truth's *Narrative* (1875, 1878), along with some additional material from Truth's "Book of Life" (a scrapbook with letters, clippings, and kudos from friends) and some articles by Stowe ("Sojourner Truth, the Libyan Sibyl," *Atlantic Monthly,* April 1863) and by another abolitionist feminist. In 1884, Titus came out with a final (posthumous) edition, which included eulogies for and obituaries about Truth.

During the Civil War, Truth helped supply food and clothing to African-American Union soldiers, and she fervently encouraged other African Americans to join that army. On October 29, 1864, President Abraham Lincoln received her at the White House. During the post–Civil War period, Truth worked tirelessly to aid former slaves and war refugees in gaining employment and job skills.

REFERENCES: *1TESK. ANAD. BAAW. BDAA. EB-BH-CD. EWHA. H. HWA. NAAAL. PGAA. SEW. WDAW. WW:CCC.* "Ain't I a Woman," in *EA-99.* Lewis, Ronald L., in *G-99.* Painter, Nell Irvin, in *BWA:AHE* and in *OCAAL.* Ross, Cheri Louise, in *OCWW.* Scruggs, Otey M., in *WB-99.* Sellman, James Clyde, in *EA-99.*

Tubman, Harriet (née Araminta Ross; renamed Harriet by her mother)

(c. 1820–3/10/1913)

Speeches, songs

Born a slave, Tubman escaped to freedom in 1849—but not with the help of her husband, John Tubman. A free man himself, he not only refused to leave Maryland with her but also threatened to reveal her plans for running away. After her successful escape, she did not seek safety and security for herself. Instead, for a decade or more, she led about 300 people out of bondage—including her parents and several other relatives of hers. In her 20 or so trips, she never lost a single Underground Railroad passenger, although she sometimes had to use some powerful motivation to get tired, worn-out, and just-plain-scared passengers to continue—sometimes even prodding with the point of a gun. By the time Civil War was declared, slave hunters and slaveholders had posted a $40,000 price tag on her head.

Although she never learned to read or write, she certainly knew how to turn a phrase to move people to action. Her speeches rallied support for abolition and motivated listeners to contribute time and money, and she even inspired some to put their own lives on the line just as she did, conducting and safe-housing fugitives on the Underground Railroad. "Wade in the Water" (her song for signaling escape) and several other Negro **spirituals** are attributed to her.

During the Civil War, she worked for the Union Army, spying, scouting, nursing, and even cooking as close to the action as she heard the call. She even led a Union raid, which freed 750 enslaved African Americans, and she served at the Battle of Fort Wagner, at which the 54th Massachusetts Colored Regiment fought so valiantly. Tubman's recollections of this battle and many others inspired many a writer who followed (e.g., **John Oliver Killens**'s *And Then We Heard the Thunder,* 1962).

After the war, in about 1868, Tubman married a Union Army veteran, Nelson Davis, who was about 20 years younger than she. About three decades later, in 1896, Tubman bought 25 acres of land adjacent to her house (a former way station on the Underground Railroad). There, she built the Harriet Tubman House for Aged and Indigent Colored People. She herself moved into that home in about 1911. On her death, she was given a burial with full military honors in recognition of her service to the Union Army. Both her funeral and her headstone were paid for by the National Association of Colored Women.

EDITOR'S NOTE: Tubman helped to author *Scenes in the Life of Harriet Tubman,* a short book about her life experiences. (See *BDAA.*)

—*Tonya Bolden*

REFERENCES: *ANAD. BAAW.*

Turner, Darwin T. (Theodore Troy)

(5/7/1931–2/11/1991)

Poems, criticism, anthologies

In addition to his poetry collection, *Katharsis* (1964), Turner contributed poetry to numerous anthologies and literary journals. His literary criticism also appeared in various journals, as well as in his books *Nathaniel Hawthorne's "The Scarlet Letter"* (1967) and *In a Minor Chord: Three Afro-American Writers and Their Search for Identity* (1971). The anthologies Turner edited include *Black American*

Literature: Essays, Poetry, Fiction, Drama (1970), *The Wayward and the Seeking: A Collection of Writings by Jean Toomer* (1980), and *Black Drama in America* (1993).

REFERENCES: *EBLG.*

Turner, Lorenzo Dow (1895–1969)
Nonfiction—linguistics, anthologies

Turner's *Africanisms in Gullah Dialect* (1949) was instrumental in revealing how much of African languages have been preserved in the speech of African Americans. For example, there's *danshiki* (Yoruba), from which we have the *dashiki* (a traditional African shirt); *dzug* (meaning "misbehave" in Wolof), which led to our *juke* joints; *mbanzo* (Kimdunu), our *banjo;* and *jaja* and *nyambi* (Bantu), which gave us our *jazz* and *yam*. Turner also turned out numerous articles and essays on linguistics as well as his doctoral dissertation (*Anti-Slavery Sentiment in American Literature Prior to 1865*), and he wrote two more books, based on his **proverb-** and **folktale**-gathering sojourn to West Africa: *An Anthology of Krio Folklore and Literature and Inter-linear Translations in English* (1963) and *Krio Texts: With Grammatical Notes and Translations in English* (1965).

—*Tonya Bolden*

REFERENCES: *SMKC.*

Turner, Nat (10/2/1800–11/11/1831)
Memoir

We know him chiefly through his "*Confessions.*" Although Turner had learned to read and write at an early age—unusual for a boy raised in slavery—he wasn't offered a means for writing his story in his own hand. Instead, he dictated it to his white confessor, Thomas Ruffin Gray, Turner's court-appointed attorney and unsympathetic scribe. Gray (who offered no defense of Turner in court) doubtless interpreted Turner's offerings through his own way of seeing things. For three days, Gray recorded Turner's story. In Gray's eyes, Turner was a mad fanatic whose religious fervor led him to insane acts of savage violence.

In Turner's eyes, God had specially chosen him to be his instrument of vengeance and of violent insurrection against white oppressors who were holding fellow blacks in bondage. Turner was a deeply religious child and youth. He believed that

God had revealed to him his mission through divine visions: The first, in 1825, showed him "white spirits and black spirits engaged in battle, and the sun darkened—the thunder rolled in the heavens, and blood flowed in streams." His second vision, May 12, 1828, gave him his messianic assignment to lead his slave rebellion: "I heard a loud noise in the heavens, and the Spirit instantly appeared to me and said . . . Christ had laid down the yoke he had borne for the sins of men, and that I should take it on and fight. . . . And by the signs in the heavens that it would make known to me when I should commence the great work, and until the first sign appeared I should conceal it from the knowledge of men."

When, in February of 1831, Turner saw a solar eclipse, he believed it to be the sign he awaited, and he started making his bold plan and sharing it with others. Though he had planned the strike for freedom to start on Independence Day, he ended up postponing his uprising until August 21. On that day, he and his followers (said to number 70 or 80 at the peak of the revolt) started on a 40-hour rampage, killing 57 white men, women (starting with the widow of his former owner), and children. Turner had expected not to have to murder every last white person. He had envisioned that once the whites were terrified into seeing the error of their cruel enslavement of blacks, the whites would surrender, and the bloodshed could stop.

This part of Turner's vision was definitely not to come to pass. A white militia had been called to arms, which killed many of the rebels outright, caught and hanged many others, and scattered the rest, and Turner went into hiding. On the eve of Hallow's Eve, Turner was captured and jailed. After his trial during the first few days of November, he was hanged on November 11. So furious were his executioners that his skin and his flesh were stripped away from his bones. Following the rebellion, blacks—enslaved or not—were targets for every malicious white brute in the South, and any Southern whites who might have been sympathetic to abolition were either turned around or silenced. The crime of teaching an African American to read drew much harsher penalties, African-American preachers had to go underground and avoid public notice, and the Bible was barred from being held by black hands. White Southerners intuitively knew that reading and writing could promote a little too much *free* thinking—and those passages about Moses in Egypt were downright dangerous.

—*Tonya Bolden*

REFERENCES: *DNPUS. EAACH. SMKC.*

Turpin, Waters (Edward)
(4/9/1910–11/19/1968)
Novels, plays, drama criticism, textbook

Turpin's plays include two he produced and directed: *And Let the Day Perish* (1950) and *St. Michael's Dawn* (1956, about **Frederick Doug-**lass). He also wrote a textbook (*Basic Skills for Better Writing,* 1959, with Aaron Ford), three novels that were published (*These Low Grounds,* 1937; *O Canaan!* 1939; *The Rootless,* 1957), and some other novels and numerous short stories and poems that were not published. Turpin was also the editor-in-chief of Morgan State College's *Morgan Newsletter* and coeditor of a reader (*Extending Horizons: Selected Readings for Cultural Enrichment,* 1969, with Aaron Ford).

REFERENCES: Reid, Margaret Ann, in *OCAAL.*

V

Van Dyke, Henry (1928–)
Novels, short fiction; journalist, editor

Van Dyke's novels include *Ladies of the Rachmaninoff Eyes* (1965), *Blood of Strawberries* (1968, dedicated to **Carl Van Vechten**), and *Dead Piano* (1971). In addition, he has contributed numerous short pieces to various literary journals. Van Dyke started his first novel while working as a journalist and completed it while on the editorial staff of Basic Books.

REFERENCES: Reid, Margaret Ann, in *OCAAL*.

Van Peebles, Melvin (8/21/1932–)
Plays, screenplays, novels, memoir, nonfiction—economics and finance

After graduating from Ohio Wesleyan's literature department, Van Peebles served for three and a half years in the U.S. Air Force and then found that civilian airlines weren't as willing as the government to employ an African American. After meeting and marrying his wife Maria in California, the couple moved to Mexico, where he worked for a time as a portrait artist and where their son Mario was born. When they returned to California, Melvin worked as a cable car operator and wrote a pictorial book about San Francisco cable cars, targeted to tourists: *The Big Heart* (1957). He then made a few shoestring-budget films, which Hollywood rejected.

At this point, Van Peebles decided to earn a Ph.D. in astronomy in Amsterdam, so he and his family (now also including his daughter Megan) left for Europe. While in Amsterdam, he was urged to go to France, having been told that the French film industry offered great opportunities. In France, those opportunities were rather ephemeral at first, so Van Peebles wrote crime reports, edited the French equivalent of *Mad* magazine, and wrote five novels in French (e.g., *Un Ours pour le F.B.I.,* 1964

[A Bear for the F.B.I., 1968]; *Un American en enfer,* 1965 [The True American, 1976]; *La Fete a Harlem,* 1967; and *La Permission* [The Story of the Three-Day Pass], 1967). With those works under his belt, he was then able to make his first feature film, the critically acclaimed *La Permission* (c. 1968).

Back in the United States, Van Peebles filmed his *Sweet Sweetback's Baadasssss Song* (1971), for which he wrote the script and the music; he also directed, produced, and starred in the film, which eventually earned $10 million, making it one of the highest-grossing independent films of that time. Van Peebles then turned to plays, writing three shows that were produced on Broadway: *Ain't Supposed to Die a Natural Death* (1971, for which he wrote the books, the music, the lyrics, and produced and directed the play), *Don't Play Us Cheap* (1972, adapted from his novel *Don't Play Us Cheap: A Harlem Party;* adapted for film in 1973), and *Waltz of the Stork* (1982, in which both he and his son Mario were actors). He also toured the nation with his one-man show *Out There by Your Lonesome* (1973). In the late 1970s, he wrote two screenplays produced as films by the NBC network (*Just an Old Sweet Song,* 1976; *Sophisticated Gents,* 1979).

Astonishingly, this rather socially aware, community-spirited entrepreneur became the only African-American trader on the American Stock Exchange in 1985, and he ended up writing two books about his experiences: *Bold Money: A New Way to Play the Options Market* (1986) and *Bold Money: How to Get Rich in the Options Market* (1987). In the 1990s, Van Peebles wrote another novel and returned to film work, acting in *Posse* (1993), a film written by his son Mario. Melvin and Mario then collaborated on the film *Panther* (mid-1990s), with Melvin writing the script and producing the film and Mario directing it (once again directing his father, who acted in the film).

REFERENCES: Robinson, Alonford James, Jr., in *EA-99*. Taft, Claire A., in *BH2C*.

Van Vechten, Carl
(6/17/1880–12/21/1964)
Novels, music and literary criticism, fashion commentary, articles, anthology, autobiography, photograph books

Of European-American ancestry, Van Vechten spent much of his life championing the literature and culture of African Americans. Among other things, he collected African-American literary works and founded the James Weldon Johnson Memorial Collection of Negro Arts and Letters (housed at Yale University), the Carl Van Vechten Collection at the New York City Public Library, and the George Gershwin Memorial Collection of Music and Musical Literature (music books) at Fisk University (in Nashville, Tennessee). He also hosted a literary salon during the **Harlem Renaissance** and advanced the writings of **Langston Hughes**, **Helene Johnson**, **James Weldon Johnson**, **Nella Larsen**, and other writers of that era. It could easily be said that he was the most prominent European American associated with the Renaissance in New York. In **Jessie Carney Smith**'s brief biographical essay on **Arna Bontemps** (in *BH2C*), she referred to Van Vechten as "the benefactor of the period and unofficial record-keeper of the 'New Negro' movement." His most acclaimed novel was written about these experiences and was intended to showcase the riches of African-American culture, but his choice of title, *Nigger Heaven* (1926), divided the African-American literary community. **Langston Hughes** provided songs for the book, and many other gay and bisexual participants in the Renaissance appreciated the work, but many others were outraged by the title—and by Van Vechten.

After Van Vechten graduated from the University of Chicago in 1903, he started working as a reporter, joining the *New York Times* in 1906 as an assistant music critic. In that role, he encouraged New Yorkers to enjoy jazz and ragtime music, introducing those forms to a wider audience. In 1907 Van Vechten went to Europe as the *Times*'s Paris correspondent. There, he met Mabel Dodge (Luhan), and she introduced him to a host of literary figures, including Gertrude Stein, who later named him as her literary executor. His popularly acclaimed novel *Peter Whiffle: His Life and Works* (1922) describes the experiences of a young man in Paris during that era.

While still in Europe, Van Vechten also married (1907) and divorced (1912) Anna Elizabeth Snyder. Snyder was awarded alimony, but by mutual consent he never paid it. In 1914, stateside, Van Vechten married again (to Fania Marinoff), prompting his first wife to decide that alimony would be nice indeed, and she pressed for back payments. Van Vechten refused to pay (at least in part because he simply didn't have the money), so

he ended up spending four months in jail—with a piano in his cell and a plethora of visitors passing through. Money problems continued to plague him through most of the 1920s, until his older brother died, leaving him $1 million in 1928—when being a millionaire was rare wealth indeed.

By 1928, Van Vechten had published five more novels (*The Blind Bow-Boy,* 1923, reprinted 1977; *The Tattooed Countess: A Romantic Novel with a Happy Ending,* 1924, reprinted 1987; *Firecrackers,* 1925; *Nigger Heaven,* 1926; and *Spider Boy: A Scenario for a Moving Picture,* 1928), and he had written several nonfiction works (*Music after the Great War,* 1915; *Music and Bad Manners,* 1916; *Interpreters and Interpretations,* 1917, 1920, a collection of music reviews; *The Merry-Go-Round,* 1918; *The Music of Spain,* 1918; *In the Garret,* 1920; *The Tiger in the House,* 1920, reprinted 1996; *Red,* 1925; and *Excavations: A Book of Advocacies,* 1926). He had also edited an anthology of cat stories, *Lords of the Housetops* (1921); and *My Musical Life* (1924, with composer Nikolay Andreyevich Rimsky-Korsakov). After receiving his inheritance, he produced two more novels (*Feathers,* 1930; and *Parties: Scenes from Contemporary New York Life,* 1930, reprinted 1993), a set of autobiographical essays (*Sacred and Profane Memories,* 1932), and *Fragments* (1955). He also edited Gertrude Stein's *Selected Writings of Gertrude Stein* (1946; reprinted 1990) and *Last Operas and Plays* (1949).

Although Van Vechten clearly had published works after 1932, some sources suggest that after publishing *Sacred and Profane Memories,* he vowed never to write again. He did turn his attention to photography and soon established his reputation as a preeminent portrait photographer of his time. Many of his photographs are considered crucial to the documentary collections at the New York Museum of Modern Art and other institutions. His photographs may be seen in *Dance Photography of Carl Van Vechten* (1981), *Passionate Observer: Photographs by Carl Van Vechten* (1993), and *Generations in Black and White: From the James Weldon Johnson Memorial Collection* (1997). Two other books are listed as being his on Amazon.com: *Ex-Libris* (1981) and *"Keep A-Inchin' Along"* (1979).

REFERENCES: *EB-98. G-97. OC20LE. RG20. WDAA.* French, Warren, in *G-97,* Amazon.com, 7/1999.

Vann, Robert Lee
(8/27/1879–10/24/1940)
Newspaper editor, journalist

Although Vann was a criminal defense attorney and participated in politics (as a Republican, then a Democrat, then a Republican again), he probably had the greatest influence on U.S. history through his work as editor of the *Pittsburgh Courier* (1910–1940), a preeminent black-owned and -operated newspaper with national readership. Educated at the Waters Training School (1901, a Baptist college in Winton, North Carolina), the Wayland Academy (1901–1903, Richmond, Virginia), Western University of Pennsylvania (starting in 1903, in Pittsburgh), and Wesleyan's law school, Vann was admitted to the Pennsylvania bar at the end of 1909 (cf. **George Vashon**, 1840). Within a few months, he was an attorney for the *Pittsburgh Courier,* and within another few months, he was the newspaper's editor, a position he continued to hold until his death. Through Vann's editorial policies, the *Courier* became known nationwide for its passionate stands against segregation and other forms of racial discrimination. Vann also challenged other newspapers of both the black press and the white press to address these issues. In fact, many credit the *Courier* with prompting coverage of these issues in the mainstream white-owned press. The *Courier* was also instrumental in motivating the Great Migration of blacks from the rural South to the urban North.

Vann was not without contradictions, however. For instance, although he opposed segregation in public institutions, he supported the efforts of **Booker T. Washington** and of **Marcus Garvey** to develop separate black businesses and vocations rather than attempting to integrate white businesses and professions. Vann also endorsed Garvey's plans for establishing a colony for African Americans in Africa, yet he urged African Americans to fight for Uncle Sam in World War I and World War II. He outspokenly opposed some union activity (e.g., strikes to have the workday limited to *just* 12 hours per day), yet he supported **A. Philip Randolph**'s attempt to unionize the Pullman porters—and then within a few years, he urged Randolph to resign from the leadership of that union because of Randolph's socialist views. Although many blacks and whites strongly disagreed with many of Vann's views, they always appreciated that his words could stimulate discussion and could prompt people to think deeply about the issues of his day.

REFERENCES: *BDAA.*

Vashon, George B. (Boyer) (1824–1878)
Poems, essays

In 1838, 14-year-old George was secretary of the first Junior Anti-Slavery Society in the United States, and in 1844 he made history as the first African American to graduate from Oberlin College. He then studied to become an attorney in Pittsburgh, Pennsylvania, but his race barred him from admission to the state bar (cf. **Robert Lee Vann**, 1909). Prior to a 30-month sojourn to Haiti, he was admitted to the New York bar in 1848, the first African American to do so in that state. In Haiti, he taught at College Faustin in Port-Au-Prince for a couple of years and then returned to New York, where he practiced law (1850–1854) and then taught college in McGrawville, New York, for three years. While back in New York, Vashon wrote "Vincent Oge" (1854), his 391-line epic poem about Haiti's slave revolt in the early 1790s.

In 1857, Vashon married Susan Paul Smith, with whom he had seven children, and for the next decade, he worked as a teacher and a school principal in Pittsburgh schools. After that, he held various governmental positions in Washington, D.C. Throughout his life, many of Vashon's essays, poems, and letters were published in various periodicals.

REFERENCES: Sherman, Joan R., in *OCAAL.*

Vroman, Mary Elizabeth (c. 1924?–1967)
Short stories, novels (adult and juvenile), screenplay, nonfiction

Vroman is most noted for her short story, "See How They Run" (1951), about an African-American teacher's enthusiastic efforts to educate impoverished rural African-American third graders; her story was later adapted to become the film *Bright Road* (starring Harry Belafonte and Dorothy Dandridge), for which she wrote the screenplay (1953). On writing the script, she became the first African-American woman to join the Screen Writers Guild. Vroman also wrote a novel for adults (*Esther,* 1963), a nonfiction book (*Shaped to Its Purpose,* 1965, about the history of Delta Sigma Theta sorority), and a novel for juveniles (*Harlem Summer,* 1967).

REFERENCES: *AAL.* Blicksilver, Edith, in *OCAAL.* Jordan, Shirley, in *BWA:AHE.*

W

Walker, A'Lelia (née Lelia McWilliams) (6/6/1885–8/16/1931)
Host of literary salon

Though her own writings were pretty much limited to correspondence and documents related to the business empire of her mother, Madame C. J. Walker, A'Lelia did quite a bit to promote African-American literature during the full blossom of the **Harlem Renaissance**. Although she was never at all as generous as her mother, she offered her house as a home for writers and other artists. Her townhouse, in particular, became the Dark Tower Tea Club (after **Countee Cullen**'s "Dark Tower" column in *Crisis* magazine), her formal and stylish literary salon. Among those whom she hosted were **Langston Hughes**, **Zora Neale Hurston**, **James Weldon Johnson**, **Richard Bruce Nugent**, and **Jean Toomer**, as well as **Carl Van Vechten** (among the many whites at Walker's gatherings).

—*Tonya Bolden*

REFERENCES: *BAAW.*

Walker, Alice (2/9/1944–)
Poems, essays, short stories, novels, anthology, biography for children; book publisher

Alice Walker's diverse writings are honest, direct, open writings about people who live the kinds of lives she has always known and has sometimes lived. Walker was born in rural Eatonton, Georgia, the eighth and last child of Willie Lee and Minnie Lou Grant Walker, who were sharecroppers. She was raised in a shack minutes from Flannery O'Connor's house, "Andalusia." (Perhaps because of this proximity, O'Connor's writing has also influenced Walker's own work.) At an early age, Walker was encouraged by her mother to read, study diligently, and appreciate doing so. She went on to become one of the best known and most respected writers in the United States.

Alice suffered a traumatic injury at the age of eight, when a brother accidentally blinded her right eye with an air rifle. From enjoying a self-confident, "womanish" little-girlhood, she sank into a period of adolescent depression and uncertainty. She secluded herself from the other children, and as she explains, "I no longer felt like the little girl I was. I felt old, and because I felt I was unpleasant to look at, filled with shame. I retreated into solitude, and read stories and began to write poems" (quoted in Christian, 1994, p. 56).

Nonetheless, the accident made Walker begin taking note of other people and their feelings. She arose from the despair to become a leader and valedictorian of her high school class. That achievement, coupled with a "rehabilitation scholarship" for disabled students, made it possible for her to go to Spelman, a college for black women in Atlanta, Georgia. There, her involvement in various civil rights demonstrations led to her dismissal. She then won another scholarship to the progressive Sarah Lawrence College. In 1964, she traveled to Uganda, Africa, where she studied as an exchange student. Upon her return in 1965, she received her bachelor of arts degree. One of Walker's teachers at Sarah Lawrence was Muriel Rukeyser, who saw Walker's poems and helped to publish her first poetry collection. Years later, in a commencement speech at Sarah Lawrence, Walker spoke out against the absence of African-American culture and history from that institution's curriculum. (EDITOR'S NOTE: Walker's poetry collections include *Once: Poems* [1968/1988], *Five Poems* [1972], *Revolutionary Petunias and Other Poems* [1973], *Goodnight, Willie Lee, I'll See You in the Morning* [1979], *Horses Make a Landcape Look More Beautiful* [1984], and *Her Blue Body Everything We Know, Earthling Poems, 1965–1990 Complete* [1993].

After college, Walker was awarded a writing fellowship and planned to spend it in Senegal, West Africa. However, after working as a case worker in the New York City welfare department, her plans changed. She decided to volunteer her time working for the voter registration drive in Mississippi in the summer of 1966. Walker later stated that her decision had been based on the realization that she could never live happily in Africa or anywhere else until she could live freely in Mississippi.

Alice Walker at a booksigning in New York, 1996 (Renato Rotolo/Corbis)

From the mid-1960s to the mid-1970s, she lived and worked in Tougaloo, Mississippi, and remained active in the civil rights movement. There she met and married a civil rights lawyer, Mel Leventhal. They had a daughter, Rebecca, in 1969. In her novel *Meridian* (1976), Walker used her own and others' experiences of this time as material for her searing examination of politics and black-white relations.

Walker came to greatly admire **Zora Neale Hurston**, whose works she later discovered and read. She also found Hurston's weed-covered gravesite and provided a marker for it, and she helped bring Hurston back to literary eminence. In 1979, Walker edited an anthology of Hurston's writing, *I Love Myself When I'm Laughing . . . and Then Again When I Am Looking Mean and Impressive: A Zora Neale Hurston Reader.*

In her first novel, *The Third Life of Grange Copeland* (1970), Walker told of how three generations of one family were affected by their move from the South to the North. She focused on a matrix that includes sexual and racial realities within black communities. For exposing this, she has been criticized by some African-American male critics and theorists. The book also highlights the unavoidable connections between family and society. For exploring this, she has been awarded numerous prizes while winning the hearts and minds of countless black and white readers.

Walker's writing career began to take off when she started teaching at Jackson State College, then Tougaloo College, and finally at Wellesley College. Walker was also a fellow at the Radcliffe Institute from 1971 to 1973. In her last year there, she published her first collection of stories, *In Love and Trouble* (1973).

Perhaps Walker's most famous work is *The Color Purple* (1982), for which she won the American Book Award and the Pulitzer Prize. She was the first African-American woman to win the Pulitzer Prize for a novel. *The Color Purple* captured the attention of mainstream America through the film adaptation by Steven Spielberg. In that novel of incest, lesbian love, and sibling devotion, Walker also introduces blues music as a unifying thread in the lives of many of the characters. *The Color Purple* also gained fierce criticism when Spielberg turned it into a movie. In her collection of essays, *The Same River Twice: Honoring the Difficult* (1996), Walker grapples with some of the issues raised in the making of the film.

Walker refuses to ignore the tangle of personal and political themes in her novels, which also include *The Temple of My Familiar* (1989) and *Possessing the Secret of Joy* (1992). She has also written a second collection of short stories titled *You Can't Keep a Good Woman Down* (1979), as well as numerous volumes of poetry and many books of essays. (EDITOR'S NOTE: Among Walker's essay collections are *Living by the Word: Selected Writings 1973–1987* [1988] and her acclaimed *In Search of Our Mothers' Gardens: Womanist Prose* [1983]; she also wrote a novel for children, *To Hell with Dying* [1988] and a biography of Langston Hughes for children [1974].)

Though she has attained fame and recognition in many countries, Walker has not lost her sense of rootedness in the South or her sense of indebtedness to her mother for showing her what the life of an artist entailed. Writing of this central experience in her famous essay, "In Search of Our Mothers' Gardens," she talks about watching her mother at the end of a day of back-breaking physical labor on someone else's farm return home, only to walk the long distance to their well to get water for her garden, planted each year at their doorstep. Walker observed her mother design that garden, putting tall plants at the back and planting so as to have something in bloom from early spring until the end of summer. As an adult, Walker names her mother an artist full of dedication, with a keen sense of design and balance and a tough conviction that life without beauty is unbearable.

Among Walker's numerous awards and honors are the Lillian Smith Award from the National Endowment for the Arts, the Rosenthal Award from the National Institute of Arts and Letters, the Townsend Prize, the Lyndhurst Prize, the Front Page Award for Best Magazine Criticism from the Newswoman's Club of New York, and a nomination for the National Book Award, as well as a Radcliffe Institute fellowship, a Merrill fellowship, and a Guggenheim fellowship.

Walker is still an involved activist. She has spoken for the women's movement, the antiapartheid movement, and the antinuclear movement, and she has cried out against female genital mutilation. Walker started her own publishing company, Wild Trees Press, in 1984.

—*Michael Strickland and Lisa Bahlinger*

REFERENCES: *2CAAWA*, pp. 291–293. *BW:SSCA*, pp. 571–573. *OCAAL*, pp. 163–164. Christian, Barbara T. (1994), *Everyday Use* (New Brunswick, NJ: Rutgers University Press). Jokinen, Anniina (1996), "Anniina's Alice Walker Page," http://www.alchemyweb.com/~alchemy/alicew/. McNaron, Toni (1996), "Voices from the Gaps: Women Writers of Color," University of Minnesota, Department of English and Program in American Studies. http://english.cla.umn.edu/lkd/vfg/Authors/AliceWalker. http://www.simonsays.com/279104371934306/0671521101/kidzone/teach/colorpurple/alicewalker.html. Simon & Schuster (1997), *Teacher's Guide to* The Color Purple (New York: Simon & Schuster). Walker, Alice (1982), *The Color Purple* (Orlando, FL: Harcourt Brace). Zinn, Howard (1996), "Lit Chat with Alice Walker," in *Salon: An Interactive Magazine of Books and Ideas,* http://www.salon1999.com/09/departments/litchat1.html. (See also *BDAA*.)

Walker, David (9/28/1785–6/28/1830)
Pamphlets

His pamphlet, *David Walker's Appeal in Four Articles; Together with a Preamble, to the Coloured Citizens of the World, but in Particular, and Very Expressly, to Those of the United States of America,* was certainly not the first abolitionist writing he did, but it was probably the cause of his own end. This outcome was no surprise to Walker himself: "I will stand my ground. *Somebody must die in this cause.* I may be doomed to the stake and the fire, or to the scaffold tree, but it is not in me to falter if I can promote the work of emancipation" (emphasis in original). His wife (Eliza) and his friends beseeched him to escape to Canada, on hearing that there was a reward being offered for his capture: $1,000 if caught dead, and $10,000 if captured alive.

What had Walker said that so enraged the white folks? He vociferously recited the atrocities of slavery, and he denounced all those who participated in perpetuating it—predicting that slave traders, slaveholders, and any others who dealt in the ownership of humans would suffer the wrath of God and the torment of hell. He also sought a more earthly retribution for these vile traders and owners of human beings, urging slaves to revolt and escape their enslavement.

Walker spared no one from his appeal, as he scathingly rebuked any blacks who were complicit in the bondage of their fellows, and he offered cold comfort to free blacks who didn't work hard to free their black sisters and brothers. He himself had been born the son of a free woman, yet he never hesitated to give every fiber of his being to the cause of abolition. He had little tolerance, too, for those of the American Colonization Society, whom he believed were falling prey to the wishes of slaveholders who wanted all free blacks out of earshot of their slaves, lest these free souls give their slaves any undesirable ideas. He even aroused the anger of fellow abolitionists who opposed violent insurrection as a means to that end. Walker was also a firm believer in the subversive power of education, holding that "for coloured people to acquire learning [in] this country, makes tyrants quake and tremble on their sandy foundations." (Apparently, many white Southerners agreed, for they tightened restrictions against letting slaves learn to read and write after Walker's pamphlet was published.)

A self-educated man, Walker self-published his 1829 *Appeal* (although an earlier, briefer version had appeared in *Freedom's Journal*, to which he was a frequent contributor). Among those who welcomed his *Appeal* with open arms was **Maria Stewart**, who may have had a hand in promoting its distribution in the South. Despite the banning of its circulation by several state legislatures (including Georgia's) and other energetic attempts to block its distribution, it slipped subversively into circulation. By early 1830, Walker had managed to release his third (revised) edition of his *Appeal*. By the end of that year, he was found dead, probably murdered by poisoning. His pregnant wife Eliza was left to raise their son Edward Garrison Walker alone.

For a time, it seemed that his *Appeal* might go out of print, but in 1848 **Henry Highland Garnet** reprinted it, along with his own provocative *Address to the Slaves of the United States.* As with all the great ideas of great people, they could slay the person, but not the idea.

—*Tonya Bolden*

REFERENCES: *EB-98. SMKC.* Eiselein, Gregory, in *OCAAL.*

Walker (married name: Alexander), Margaret (Abigail) (7/7/1915–12/1/1998)
Poems, novel, essays, biography, criticism, memoir

Margaret's parents, Methodist Episcopal minister Sigismund Walker and music teacher (and church musician) Marion Dozier, expected a great deal from their children. They instilled not only a love of church and of music but also a love of scholarship and of literature. Young Margaret grew

up listening to biblical verse, her father's sermons, her mother's readings of classical verse, and countless anecdotes, vignettes, and discussions. By the time Margaret was 11 years old, she was reading not only William Shakespeare and John Greenleaf Whittier but also **Countee Cullen** and **Langston Hughes**. As a youth, she met **James Weldon Johnson**, **W. E. B. Du Bois**, and other African-American celebrities. In many ways, her parents provided enriched cultural experiences that helped to shield their children from the personal sting of Southern racism, although they made their children well aware of racism's effects on other African Americans.

As a minister's daughter, Margaret was raised in various states across the Jim Crow South, attending numerous denominational schools in Alabama, Mississippi, and Louisiana. She earned her high school diploma from New Orleans's Gilbert Academy when she was just 14 years old. Despite her obvious talent and inclination, however, few of her teachers ever encouraged her to write. Later, in her "For My People," she wrote this about school: "For the cramped bewildered years we went to school to learn to know the reasons why and the answers to and the people who and the places where and the days when, in memory of the bitter hours when we discovered we were black and poor and small and different and nobody wondered and nobody understood."

After high school, Walker attended New Orleans University (later Dillard University), where her parents both taught (she was a third-generation college graduate). While there, in 1931, she met Langston Hughes, who read some of Margaret's poems and—at last—encouraged her to become a writer. Hughes also encouraged her to complete her education outside of the South—which she did, transferring to Northwestern University, from which she earned a B.A. in English in 1935 just before she turned 20 years old. While at Northwestern, she published her first poem ("Daydreaming") in *Crisis* magazine in 1934. She also started working for the Works Progress Administration (WPA) as a social worker for troubled youths. (She later wrote an unpublished novel, "Goose Island," about this experience.)

After graduating, Walker started working for the WPA's Federal Writers' Project. During this time, through **Margaret Burroughs**, Walker also became friends with **Gwendolyn Brooks**. While mastering the writing craft, she profited from friendships with novelists (e.g., **Frank Yerby**), poets (e.g., **Arna Bontemps**), and playwrights (e.g., **Theodore Ward**). Perhaps most importantly, she got to know **Richard Wright**, with whom she shared her political outlook, enjoyed a close friendship, and collaborated on literary works until he ended their friendship abruptly in 1939. That same year, Walker stopped working for the WPA and returned to graduate school to earn her M.A. in creative writing (1940) at the University of Iowa.

Walker's master's thesis was essentially her first volume of poems, *For My People* (published in 1942, only the second volume of poetry published by an African-American woman in more than two decades). In the 1941–1942 school year, she started teaching at Livingstone College in South Carolina. That summer, she won the Yale University Younger Poet's Award for her collection, thereby becoming the first African-American woman to win a prestigious national literary competition. In 1990, she recalled that she wrote most of the title poem (first published in 1937) within 15 minutes, after having been asked, "What would you want for your people?"

Walker's poem resonates with the rhythm, alliteration, and consonance; biblical phrasings; emotive tone; and cultural cadences of the sermons Walker heard throughout her youth. Her poem exults in the endurance and the triumphs of African Americans, mourns her people's suffering and losses, proudly points to their struggles, and demands freedom and fairness for her people ("Let another world be born . . . let a people loving freedom come to growth. . . . Let a race of men now rise and take control!"). Other poems in her *For My People* collection echo these themes as well as her interpretations of characters from African-American **folktales,** Southern settings, and African-American history.

In 1943, Margaret Walker married Firnist Alexander, and the following year, she gave birth to the first of their four children, after which her writing slowed considerably, and her teaching stopped altogether for a while (although she did continue to lecture occasionally). Her mentor Langston Hughes warned her, "All these babies you're having, every baby you have could have been a book." Years later, she observed, "I have four children, nine grandchildren, and eleven books."

In 1949 she returned to teaching to support her children (all of whom were less than six years old, including a nine-week-old) and her husband, who was "sick and disabled from the war." This started her 30-year tenure at Jackson State College in Mississippi. To boost her bread winning, Walker-Alexander spent several summers and a full academic year earning her Ph.D. in creative writing from the University of Iowa (1965). She used her Civil War novel (started many years earlier) as the basis for her doctoral dissertation (published as *Jubilee* in 1966). In 1968, she founded the Institute for the Study of the History, Life and Culture of Black People at Jackson State College, serving as its director until she retired 11 years later. The center has since been renamed in her honor.

Walker's subsequent poetry collections include *Ballad of the Free* (1966); *Prophets for a New Day* (1970), hailing abolitionist and civil rights leaders and comparing them with biblical prophets; and *October Journey* (1973), honoring Walker's personal heroes, such as **Harriet Tubman**, Gwendolyn Brooks, and her father. In 1989, she published *This Is My Century: New and Collected Poems,* which includes her poems from her earlier volumes *Prophets for a New Day* and *October Journey.* Her works have been widely anthologized by writers such as **Robert Hayden**, Bontemps, and Hughes.

Walker started writing her novel *Jubilee* in 1934, and she continued to work on it through her 1965 doctoral-dissertation version until her final version was published in 1966. She centered the well-researched novel on the true life experiences of her maternal great-grandmother, Margaret Duggans (named "Vyry Brown" in the novel), from slavery through the Civil War to the end of Reconstruction. Walker has observed that the long process of writing this novel was enriched by her own life experiences. Although Walker herself never knew the nightmares of slavery, Civil War, and Reconstruction terrorism, she nevertheless vividly recounted the stories she heard from her maternal grandmother (Elvira Ware Dozier), describing Walker's great-grandmother's firsthand accounts.

Walker's other prose includes *How I Wrote Jubilee* (1972), in which she tells just how she researched and wrote her novel; and *A Poetic Equation: Conversations between Nikki Giovanni and Margaret Walker* (2nd ed., 1983). Perhaps her most important prose work, however, is her biography of her former friend Richard Wright, entitled *Richard Wright, Daemonic Genius: A Portrait of the Man, a Critical Look at His Work* (1988). In reflecting on her biography, Walker noted, "Wright was just like somebody in my family. . . . I felt Wright wanted me to write his biography because nobody is going to be more sympathetic and understanding than I" (*BWWW,* pp. 194–195).

In addition to these books, Walker has written countless essays and scholarly articles on African-American literature and culture. Before she died, she was working on a sequel to *Jubilee,* focusing on the life experiences of Vyry's son and daughter-in-law; an autobiography; and her novel *Mother Broyer,* based on a folk story. As she noted, "I've got to write for the rest of my life, no matter how short or long it is. I've got to write. . . . Writing is the first thing on my list, and I can't live long enough to write all the books I have in me" (*BWWW,* p. 200). Sadly, she was right.

Walker's honors and awards include a 1944 Rosenwald Fellowship for Creative Writing, a 1954 Ford Fellowship at Yale University, a 1966 Houghton Mifflin literature fellowship, and a 1979 Ford grant for completing her biography. Also, the mayor of her hometown, Birmingham, Alabama, proclaimed June 17, 1976, as Margaret Walker Alexander Day.

REFERENCES: *AA:PoP. BAAW. BAL-1-P. BWA. BWW. BWWW. EB-98. EBLG. G-95. MWEL. NAAAL. NPR-ME*—12/1/1998. *OC20LE.* Campbell, Jane, in *OCWW.* Ward, Jerry W., Jr., in *OCAAL.*

Walker, Wyatt Tee (8/16/1929–)
Nonfiction—musicology

A minister instrumental in shaping the strategies of the Southern Christian Leadership Conference (SCLC), Walker wrote *Somebody's Calling My Name: Black Sacred Music and Social Change.*

REFERENCES: Fay, Robert, in *EA-99.*

Walrond, Eric (Derwent) (1898–1966)
Short stories; journalist, journal editor and publisher

A native of British Guiana (now Guyana), Walrond was educated at a boys' school in Barbados and in public schools in Panama. From 1916 to 1918, he reported for the Panama *Star-Herald* while working as a government clerk. In 1918, Walrond left Panama and came to the United States, where he lived for a decade before emigrating to Europe. During that decade, he continued his education at the College of the City of New York and at Columbia University, and he played an important role in the **Harlem Renaissance**.

When Walrond first arrived in New York, he felt assaulted by racism and was soon drawn both to **Marcus Garvey**'s Universal Negro Improvement Association (UNIA) and to the Urban League, the director of which, **Charles (Spurgeon) Johnson**, became Walrond's mentor. Soon, Walrond was contributing articles on Harlem and the Great Migration (from the rural South to the urban North) to newspapers, and in 1921 he started editing the *Brooklyn and Long Island Informer,* an African-American weekly, which he also co-owned. In 1923 he wrote "The New Negro Faces America," in which he analyzed and critiqued the philosophies of Marcus Garvey, **Booker T. Washington**, and **W. E. B. Du Bois**. That same year, he left the *Informer* to accept a job as associate editor of the UNIA organ, *Negro World,* where he continued to work until 1925, when he and Garvey had a falling-out. Afterward, Walrond took over as business manager of the Urban League's *Opportunity* magazine.

In the early and mid-1920s, Walrond started contributing short stories to various periodicals (e.g., the *New Republic, Opportunity, Smart Set*), and in 1926 he published his collection of eight short stories, *Tropic Death,* which addressed themes of race relations in the United States, migration, and the diaspora through which Africa's descendants scattered across the continents. In 1928 Walrond was awarded a Guggenheim fellowship and was named a Zona Gale scholar at the University of Wisconsin before moving to Europe. While in Europe, he and Garvey (then an exile) patched things up, and Walrond did some writing for Garvey. During the 1930s, Walrond's writing slowed to a trickle, and by 1940 he stopped writing entirely.

REFERENCES: *EA-99. EBLG. WDAA.* Barceló, Margarita, in *OCAAL.*

Walter, Mildred Pitts (1922–)
Children's picture books, novels, nonfiction for children and juveniles

Walter's fiction for children and youths includes her *Lillie of Watts: A Birthday Discovery* (1969) and its sequel *Lillie of Watts Takes a Giant Step* (1971), as well as *The Liquid Trap* (1975). She also wrote a pair of novels on school integration (*The Girl on the Outside,* 1982; *Because We Are,* 1983), *My Mama Needs Me* (1983), *Have a Happy . . .* (1984, about a family's celebration of Kwanzaa during a difficult time), *Trouble's Child* (1985), *Justin and the Best Biscuits in the World* (1986, Coretta Scott King Award–winner about an Exoduster family who settled in Missouri), *Mariah Loves Rock* (1988), *Mariah Keeps Cool* (1990), and *Two and Too Much* (1990). Her nonfiction book *The Mississippi Challenge* (1992, Coretta Scott King Award–winner) describes the historic struggle for the right to vote in Mississippi up through the mid-1960s. Her picture books include *Ty's One Man Band* (1980) and her original **folktale** *Brother to the Wind* (1985).

REFERENCES: Harris, Violet J., in *OCAAL*. M. F. S., in *CBC*.

Waniek, Marilyn (née) Nelson
(4/26/1946–)
Poems, criticism

Waniek's poetry collections include *The Cat Walked through the Casserole and Other Poems for Children* (1984, with Pamela Espeland), *For the Body* (1978, which uses free verse to explore childhood reminiscences), *Mama's Promises* (1985, using ballad stanzas), *The Homeplace* (1990, using multiple poetic forms—e.g., sonnet, villanelle, ballad, dramatic dialogue—and photos to tell family stories), *Magnificat: Poems* (1994), and *The Fields of Praise: New and Selected Poems* (1997). Waniek has also translated Danish author Phil Dahlerup's *Literary Sex Roles* (1975) and Danish poet Halfdan Rasmussen's humorous poetry in *Hundreds of Hens and Other Poems for Children* (1982).

REFERENCES: *VBAAP*. Boelcskevy, Mary Anne Stewart, in *OCAAL*. Amazon.com 3/2000.

Ward, Douglas Turner (5/5/1930–)
Plays

A native of Louisiana, Ward graduated from public school at age 15 and then left for Xenia, Ohio, to attend Wilberforce University. From there, he transferred to the University of Michigan, where he played junior varsity football. In 1948, his knee was injured, and at the end of the school year, he moved to New York, where he started writing articles and satirical sketches for the *Daily Worker,* a leftist newspaper. Soon, he was arrested, convicted, and shipped to Louisiana for draft evasion; he stayed there for two years until the U.S. Supreme Court reversed his conviction.

Ward returned to New York, eager to start a

Douglas Turner Ward dances in Ceremonies in Dark Old Men, *1969 (UPI/Corbis-Bettmann)*

career in theater writing plays. To better learn the craft, he studied acting and performed in several plays. Soon he was also writing his own plays, *Day of Absence* (1965), *Happy Ending* (1966), and *The Reckoning* (1969), while continuing to act. All three plays were reprinted in the 1990s. Probably his best-known play is *Day of Absence,* which was written after the historic (1955–1956) Montgomery bus boycott, and which showed the powerful influence of African Americans who are united in their aims. In the play, all the African Americans in a small Southern town go on strike, bringing the town to its knees.

In 1966 Ward wrote a *New York Times* article titled, "American Theatre: For Whites Only?" in which he assaulted the racist practices of the New York theater establishment and proposed the need for a permanent African-American theater to showcase the talents of African-American playwrights, actors, technicians, and managers. In 1967 Ward, Robert Hooks, and Gerald Crone cofounded the prestigious Negro Ensemble Company (NEC) of New York City, using a $434,000 grant from the Ford Foundation and naming Ward its artistic director. During the 1980s, the right-wing policies of the Reagan administration led to dramatic cuts in funding of arts programs in order to pay for bigger weapons programs. As a result, NEC struggled to stay afloat and in 1991 and 1992 it produced no plays. In 1993, NEC opened for business again, with Ward at the helm as company president.

REFERENCES: *BAL-1-P. G-97. WB-99.* Gaffney, Floyd, in *OCAAL.*

Ward, Samuel (1817–1864)
Essays, slave narrative, commentary

Born a slave, three-year-old Samuel escaped to freedom with his parents. In New York, he was deeply involved in the abolitionist movement and contributed to **Frederick Douglass**'s *North Star.* After passage of the fugitive slave law, he had to flee farther north to Canada, where he wrote *Autobiography of a Fugitive Slave* (1855).

REFERENCES: *AAW:AAPP.*

Ward, Theodore (9/15/1902–5/?/1983)
Plays

Ward's plays include his most critically acclaimed works *Big White Fog* (1938) and *Our Lan'* (1941), as well as *Sick and Tiahd* (c. 1936–1937), *Deliver the Goods* (1942), *John Brown* (1950), *Candle in the Wind* (1967), and *The Daubers* (1973).

REFERENCES: *NYPL-AADR.* Barthelemy, Anthony Gerard, in *OCAAL.*

Washington, Booker T. (né Booker Taliaferro) (4/5/1856–11/14/1915)
Essays, autobiography, nonfiction—self-help

Even as a young boy, Washington sensed that education was the key to success. As he put it himself, "I had the feeling that to get into a schoolhouse and study in this way would be about the same as getting into paradise." As soon as he gained his freedom, he started his own self-education, using an old copy of Noah Webster's *Elementary Spelling-Book* as his first text. In 1872, he heard about the Hampton Normal and Agricultural Institute some 500 miles away, and he stuffed everything he owned (which wasn't much) in a satchel, jammed all his money (less than $2) in his pocket, and journeyed to "Virginny." Once there, he cleaned his way into the classroom, janitored his way through school, and graduated with honors three years later. At that school, he learned not

only the knowledge he had sought but also a fundamental belief in self-reliance and industry as the sole route to success for African Americans. At Hampton, he also came to believe that civil rights activism was frivolous foolishness that would stand in the way of economic progress.

After a brief detour studying the law and then theology, Washington returned to Hampton to teach and, soon after, brought with him his longtime beloved Fannie Norton Smith. In 1881, he was recommended as the best person to start a new school in Tuskegee, Alabama. He was to use the $2,000 per year he received from the state of Alabama to convert "a broken down shanty and an old hen house" into the Tuskegee Normal and Industrial Institute. Tuskegee was to offer vocational training to artisans and tradespersons as well as schoolteachers. A hard worker himself, Washington instilled in his teachers and his students the importance of working hard.

In 1882, Washington married Fannie, and the couple had a daughter, Portia, in 1883. In 1885, Fannie died, and just a year later, widower Washington married Tuskegee teacher and Lady Principal Olivia America Davidson. Nine months and 18 days after their wedding, Olivia gave birth to Booker, Jr. (5/29/1887), and a little over a year-and-a-half later, Ernest Davidson was born (2/6/1889). Tragically, within a few months, Olivia too was dead (5/9/1889). Grief-stricken and broke (due to the expenses of trying to save Olivia's life), Washington tried to raise his sons and daughter alone. In 1892, however, he gave marriage another chance, choosing another Tuskegee Lady Principal (since 1890), Margaret Murray James.

Despite his personal and family tragedies, Washington managed to build his institute for African-American education in the hostile territory of the post-Reconstruction South. It was in this environment that Washington developed his philosophy of accommodation. He opposed the Northward emigration of Southern blacks and quietly complied with segregation. A hard worker but never a rabble rouser, he noted that "the wisest among my race understand that the agitation of questions of social equality is the extremest folly." Needless to say, many Northern blacks denounced him as a race traitor, but most Southern whites praised Washington as a leader of great insight, and many white Northerners liked what he had to say, too. More than one publisher encouraged him to write his life story. With the collaboration of African-American

Booker T. Washington, head of the Tuskegee Institute, 1906 (Culver Pictures)

journalist Edgar Webber, Washington wrote *The Story of My Life and Work* (1900), which was published by a small press. Despite the protests of black (and white) civil rights activists, Washington's *Story* sold well.

Washington realized that if he wrote an even better book, he could raise even more funds for his institute. Hence, he joined forces with Max Bennett Thrasher, a European-American journalist, and the two produced *Up from Slavery,* published by Doubleday, Page and Company. With Double-

day's backing, the book was published serially in *Outlook* magazine (November 3, 1900–February 23, 1901) before it was published as a book. When the book was released, it was an immediate bestseller. Not only did the book bring in bucks directly, but it also prompted many rich whites to open up their pocketbooks and to start writing checks to the Institute. Among the new benefactors was millionaire Andrew Carnegie (the industrialist), whose gifts included a Carnegie library and $600,000 in U.S. Steel bonds. Over the years,

Washington would commission or produce many more books promoting his philosophy, his school, and himself.

As wealthy whites (North and South) drew him close to their hearts, well-educated blacks drew away from him. The more praise whites heaped upon him, the more scorn blacks piled on. He soon had virulently outspoken opponents among civil rights activists such as **William Monroe Trotter** and **W. E. B. Du Bois**. Much to their chagrin, their cries of opposition in no way deterred Washington's supporters. In fact, Washington was ever more the darling of high society and people with power. He dined at the White House, was consulted by Presidents Theodore Roosevelt and William Howard Taft, and was respected as *the* African-American expert on race matters. If Washington smiled upon someone, that person was likely to receive healthy endowments and generous philanthropy for his or her causes. His good deeds to his supporters were numerous. He definitely had enough power to make it very rewarding to have him as a friend. Anyone on whom Washington didn't smile, however, was in for some *real* trouble. He could definitely make it painful to be his enemy, and he was not at all opposed to dirty tricks and manipulations to punish those whom he perceived as opposing him.

Washington was not completely averse to some quiet actions on behalf of civil rights, however. In the background, he managed to subvert a few Jim Crow laws. He also had some mixed messages about the value of education. For instance, he espoused the value of vocational training and denigrated scholarly pursuits as irrelevant, scorning the well-educated intellectuals who were criticizing him. On the other hand, he saw to it that his own children received a college education.

When Washington died, 34 years after he had opened the school (with 1 teacher, 2 ramshackle buildings, and 50 students), the Tuskegee Institute had a faculty of nearly 200 instructors, more than 100 well-equipped buildings, and an endowment of about $2 million.

EDITOR'S NOTE: Washington also wrote a biography of **Frederick Douglass**, some practical self-help books, and several other titles (see *OCAAL*).

—*Tonya Bolden*

REFERENCES: *SMKC*. Harlan, Louis R. (1972), *Booker T. Washington: The Making of a Black Leader, 1856–1901* (New York: Oxford University Press).

Harlan (1983), *Booker T. Washington: The Wizard of Tuskegee, 1901–1915* (New York: Oxford University Press).

Weatherly, Tom (11/3/1942–)
Poems

Weatherly's poetry volumes are *Maumau Cantos* (1970) and *Thumbprint* (1971), and he coedited *Natural Process: An Anthology of New Black Poetry* (1972), all of which reflect his involvement in the **Black Arts movement**.

REFERENCES: Toombs, Charles P., in *OCAAL*.

Weaver, Robert C. (Clifton) (12/29/1907–7/17/1997)
Nonfiction—economics, sociology

Weaver's explorations in the fields of sociology and economics include nearly 200 articles and 4 books: *Negro Labor: A National Problem* (1946/ 1969), *The Negro Ghetto* (1948/1967), *The Urban Complex* (1964), and *Dilemmas of Urban America* (1965). These works (and his involvement in several governmental positions) contributed to his becoming the first African American appointed to the U.S. cabinet, as the secretary of housing and urban development under President Lyndon Johnson (1966–1968).

REFERENCES: *BDAA. EB-BH-CD*. Fay, Robert, in *EA-99*. Thieme, Darius L., in *BH2C*.

Wells (married name: Wells–Barnett), Ida B. (Bell) (7/16/1862–3/25/1931)
Essays, pamphlets, editorials, diaries, autobiography, travel journal; journalist, newspaper co-owner

This daughter of slaves was freed by the Civil War, but she was not to live a carefree life. In 1878, her youngest brother and her parents (Lizzie Bell and James Wells) died of yellow fever, leaving teenage Ida to care for her six remaining younger siblings. Fortunately, she had received a good grammar school education at Rust College, where her father was a trustee after the Freedman's Aid Association set up the school in her hometown in Mississippi. With that education, she got a teaching job and supported her siblings on her $25 per month salary. After five years of struggling to support them, she decided to move to Memphis (in 1883) to get a better-paying teaching job and to attend Fisk University during summer breaks.

While at Fisk, Wells started writing for the student newspaper, and she soon started editing two church-related newspapers. In her subsequent reflections on this experience, Wells commented, "I wrote in a plain, common-sense way on the things which concerned our people." Wells soon started writing for numerous African-American newspapers on various topics (especially on issues relating to race and gender). (Wells also kept a diary of her experiences and of her observations of racism in the Jim Crow South, which she used later for writing her autobiography.)

Among Wells's many topics was an experience that heralded Rosa Parks's stand against segregated bus transportation in 1955. In 1884, Wells had paid for a first-class ladies coach ticket on a train, but she was physically removed from that car and dragged to the smoking car, where all "colored" people were ordered to ride. She sued the Chesapeake, Ohio, and Southwestern Railroad and won a $500 settlement in a Tennessee circuit court. (Unfortunately, she later lost when the railroad appealed to the Tennessee Supreme Court, which overturned the lower-court decision.)

Another of Wells's favorite topics was the inferiority of segregated schools for African-American children. As a teacher (and a former student of segregated schools), she knew her subject firsthand. Although she wrote all her newspaper articles under the pseudonym "Iola," the Memphis school board eventually realized she had authored these critical articles, and in 1891 the board refused to renew her teaching contract. Fortunately, two years earlier (1889), Wells had used her savings to buy a one-third interest in the *Memphis Free Speech and Headlight.* Now, with more time on her hands—and a greater need to earn money from her writing—Wells turned her attention to journalism full-time.

Did losing her teaching job make Wells's articles milder? Not at all. Then on March 9, 1892, three co-owners of a profitable grocery business were lynched, one of whom (Thomas Moss) was a close friend of hers. Did that violence quiet her voice? Nope. Instead, she wrote scathing editorials denouncing lynching as a brutal means of squelching economic competition from African Americans— not, as was often claimed, as an overly zealous defense of white women's virtue against black men's sexual aggression: "Nobody in this section of the country believes the old thread-bare lie that Negro men assault white women." She urged the

Ida B. Wells, undated (Archive Photos)

African Americans of Memphis to flee from lynching and Jim Crow racism and to go West to find genuine economic and social opportunity.

After publishing these editorial attacks on lynching, Wells took a trip up North to visit **Frances E. W. Harper** and to rally Northern support for her antilynching efforts. While she was away, an enraged mob of Memphis whites destroyed her newspaper's offices and loudly warned Wells never to return to Memphis—under penalty of death. That threat got her attention, and she stayed clear of Memphis, but she didn't stop speaking out against lynching and other aspects of racism.

Sarah Garnet (wife of **Henry Highland Garnet**) and other prominent African-American women helped raise funds for Wells to replace her ruined press equipment and offices. Once she realized she couldn't return to Memphis, she moved to New York and bought a partial interest in **T. Thomas Fortune**'s *New York Age,* and she was soon writing and editing for that paper. After conducting extensive research on incidents of lynching, she published her 1892 pamphlet, *Southern Horrors: Lynch Law in All Its Phases.* Her pamphlet cited numerous incidents, giving all the specifics of each case and clearly documenting her assertion that lynching related far more closely to economic competition by African Americans than to any alleged instances of rape.

Occasionally, Wells attacked problems of Northern racism. For instance, when African Americans were not included in the planning—and barely included in the exhibition—of the 1893 Chicago World's Fair, Wells asked **Frederick Douglass**, Chicago attorney and newspaper publisher Ferdinand Lee Barnett, and other prominent African Americans to join her in publishing 20,000 copies of her pamphlet *The Reason Why the Colored American Is Not in the World's Columbian Exposition*. Douglass wrote the foreword, and Barnett contributed an essay to the publication. During 1893 and 1894, Wells continued to denounce lynching and traveled throughout the North and in England to muster support for her antilynching campaign. (Years later, her travel journal was published in her autobiography.)

In 1895, she published *A Red Record: Tabulated Statistics and Alleged Causes of Lynching in the United States, 1892–1893–1894*. This publication provided extensive statistics and analyses of lynchings, which backed up her premise: Two out of three victims of lynching were never even accused of rape, and those who were accused of rape might have engaged in consensual relations with white women who were later forced to cry rape. In any case, most of the lynch victims had been economically competitive, educationally advanced, or politically assertive in relation to local whites. Among the statistics she cited were these: "During these years more than ten thousand Negroes have been killed in cold blood, without the formality of judicial trial and legal execution . . . the same record shows that during all these years, and for all these murders only three white men have been tried, convicted, and executed." Wells also pointed out how the transition from slavery to Reconstruction meant that whites no longer had an economic interest in the bodies of blacks, which had previously constrained whites from murdering or maiming blacks, so brutality against African Americans actually *increased* following emancipation.

On June 27, 1895, Wells married Barnett, the Chicagoan with whom she had collaborated previously. Barnett was a widower with two sons, and Wells later gave birth to four additional children: Charles Aked, Herman Kohlsaat, Ida B. Wells, Jr., and Alfreda (who later edited her mother's autobi-

ography, shortly after her mother's death). The Wells–Barnett merger also yielded journalistic fruit, as Wells purchased her husband's *Chicago Conservator* newspaper. Although her duties as the wife of an assistant state attorney (Illinois's first African American to have that job) and mother of six did slow down Wells's activism and her journalistic output, they certainly didn't stop her. She often took her babies with her to speaking engagements, expecting that local sponsors (usually women's clubs) would provide suitable child care arrangements.

Her postmarriage writings included her 1900 pamphlet on lynching, *Mob Rule in New Orleans,* and the essays "Lynching and the Excuse for It" (1901) and "Our Country's Lynching Record" (1913). She also wrote "Booker T. Washington and His Critics" (1904), one of the first articles questioning Washington's willingness to abandon the pursuit of civil rights in order to seek economic advancement—a surefire prescription for continuation of lynching, as far as Wells could see. In 1917, the *Chicago Tribune* published her letter warning that racial violence might erupt the following summer. The summer after that, she wrote a series of articles on the race riot that did indeed erupt. In 1922, she wrote and raised money to publish and distribute 1,000 copies of her pamphlet *The Arkansas Race Riot,* probing the unjust murder indictment of a dozen African-American farmers.

Wells continued to write diaries during many periods of her life, and between 1928 and 1934 she wrote her autobiography. Just as she was about to complete it, midsentence, uremic poisoning overtook her, and she died. Her daughter Alfreda M. Duster completed the work and oversaw its publication as *Crusade for Justice: The Autobiography of Ida B. Wells* (1970/1991).

Wells also joined with others in support of racial and gender equality. In addition to joining many organizations, she founded or cofounded the Ida B. Wells Club of Chicago (1893); the National Association of Colored Women (1896); the Niagara Movement (1905) and its successor, the National Association for the Advancement of Colored People (1910); the Negro Fellowship League (1910); and the Alpha Suffrage Club of Chicago (1913). In 1930, she rejected her Republican Party affiliation and ran as an independent candidate for the Illinois Senate but lost her bid. Sixty years later, however, she won a place on a U.S. postage stamp, the first African-American woman journalist to be so honored.

REFERENCES: *1TESK. AA:PoP. ANAD. BAAW. BaD. BDAA. BF:2000. EB-98. EBLG. G-95. H. NAAAL. PGAA. RLWWJ. WW:CCC.* DeCosta-Willis, Miriam, in *OCAAL.* Harris, Trudier, in *OCWW.*

Wesley, Charles Harris
(12/2/1891–8/16/1987)
Nonfiction—African-American history, biography

This AME minister and president of Wilberforce University wrote numerous articles on African-American history as well as several books, including *Negro Labor in the United States, 1850–1925* (1927), *Collapse of the Confederacy* (1937), *Richard Allen: Apostle of Freedom* (1969), and *The History of the National Association of Colored Women's Clubs: A Legacy of Service* (1984). In 1979, he wedded writer, historian, and archivist **Dorothy (Louise) Burnett Porter**.

REFERENCES: *EA-99.*

Wesley, Dorothy Burnett Porter
See **Porter Wesley, Dorothy (née) Burnett**

West, Cornel (6/2/1953–)
Nonfiction—sociology, commentary

Teacher? Philosopher? Writer? Theologian? Sociologist? Which of these disciplines best describes Cornel West and his large body of work? None of them—and all of them. Some say that West is the first leading African-American intellectual to rise to prominence since **W. E. B. Du Bois** in the late nineteenth and early twentieth centuries. Others assert that West says a lot without saying anything. West's admirers like his prophetic speech and his intellectual ability to cross and integrate disciplines, while his detractors say that West never fully completes his ideas and thoughts and has no plan to implement change. Regardless of one's opinion of West's writings, politics, or philosophies, it is apparent that West defies being placed into a simple category. He and his work are far too complex for that.

Cornel was born in Tulsa, Oklahoma. His mother was a schoolteacher and then a principal, and his father worked for the U.S. Air Force as a civilian. Cornel has one brother, Clifton. After several moves, the West family settled in Sacramento,

California, in a middle-class African-American neighborhood. After high school, Cornel graduated with a degree in Near Eastern languages and literature from Harvard University and later earned both his master's degree and his doctoral degree (in philosophy) from Princeton University. He then went to Union Theological Seminary.

In 1988, West led Princeton's Afro-American Studies program. In 1994, he went to Harvard University with dual teaching appointments (in the School of Divinity and in the Faculty of Arts and Sciences). West and his Harvard colleague **William Julius Wilson** simultaneously became full professors in 1995, the first African Americans to achieve the highest academic post possible at that university. Unlike associate professors, full professors can teach across academic disciplines, meaning that as a theologian, West can teach courses that encompass theological concerns within the law or history department, for example. This seems to be the perfect position for someone like West, who has a vision of the various academic disciplines akin to a spider's web, intricately linked and interdependent.

For West, scholarship is not done only in the ivory towers of colleges and universities. He believes that intellectuals must come down from those towers and help meet the needs of the society in which they live; their knowledge must be applicable on the streets. West adheres to what he calls "prophetic pragmatism." *Pragmatism* emphasizes the idea that "knowledge [is] derived from experience and experimentation"; it desires to "solve practical problems," and thus the philosophy's "truth is tested by its utility and consequences."

Additionally, West believes that there is a *prophetic* component to his philosophy. He sees a connection between prophecy and pragmatism. Although he does not seem to believe that he is speaking directly and literally for God, he does believe in the Christian idea of speaking the "truth in love," although he also says that prophetic insight is available "through a number of different traditions." For him, prophetic pragmatism means telling the truth about the human condition, the human struggle, and the chances for improvement. For West, practical problems in society are economic disparity, racism, cross-cultural relations, families and children, and homophobia.

West's lectures, speeches, interviews, essays, and books hold true to these beliefs. *Prophesy Deliverance! An Afro-American Revolutionary Christianity*

(1982), his first book, mixes several of his beliefs and ideas. These include Christian theology, the African-American experience, philosophy, and political ideologies. West's paternal grandfather was a Baptist preacher in Tulsa for 40 years and apparently influenced West profoundly, as West dedicated this book to his grandfather. He notes in that dedication that his grandfather is one "who through it all kept the faith." That, too, seems to be what West is trying to do. Ultimately, he sees Christianity as a liberating force for people to "have the opportunity to fulfill [their] potentialities," but he is not talking about eternal life; he is talking about the here and now. To many, this is a radical view of Christianity; to him, it is absolutely accurate and essential for the transformation of society, a transformation for which he hopes.

In the preface of *Prophesy Deliverance!* West describes himself and states his intellectual presuppositions: He is "committed to the prophetic Christian gospel," has an "affinity to a philosophical version of American pragmatism," and has an "abiding allegiance to progressive Marxist social analysis and political praxis." Additionally, West notes that he does not understand philosophy to be merely an intellectual exercise full of empty jargon and rhetoric but a discipline that affects and is affected by its cultural context, a context that is full of various problems and choices. West's other works follow this same pattern, mixing various intellectual ideas with an assortment of practical, real-life problems.

West's body of work includes the following titles: *Theology in the Americas: Detroit II* (1982, coeditor); *Post-Analytic Philosophy* (1985, coeditor); *Prophetic Fragments* (1988); *The American Evasion of Philosophy: A Genealogy of Pragmatism* (1989); *Out There: Marginalization and Contemporary Cultures* (1990, coeditor); *The Ethical Dimensions of Marxist Thought* (1991); *Breaking Bread: Insurgent Black Intellectual Life* (1991); *Beyond Eurocentrism and Multiculturalism:* Vol. 1, *Prophetic Thought in Postmodern Times* (1993), and Vol. 2, *Prophetic Reflections: Notes on Race and Power in America* (1993); *Race Matters* (1993); *Keeping Faith: Philosophy and Race in America* (1993); *Jews and Blacks: Let the Healing Begin* (1995, coauthor); *The Future of the Race* (1996, coauthor); and *The War against Parents: What We Can Do for America's Beleaguered Moms and Dads* (1998, coauthor).

Race Matters became a best-seller and is the book that earned West the most celebrity, leading him to accept numerous speaking engagements across the United States. It is also the book that is the most accessible to the general public, leading some to call him a "public intellectual." West says that current race problems within the United States are "an everyday matter of life and death." He further says that the current political atmosphere does not work, that neither liberals nor conservatives can effectively address or solve the problems of race. He also has strong beliefs on other current social issues, but none are a simple affirmation or condemnation of one perspective over another. West calls for individual responsibility and a political system structured for fairness and opportunity.

In *The War against Parents,* West and coauthor Sylvia Ann Hewlett call for both political and cultural changes, saying that parents are drowning in economic, social, and family demands, but that children must have this nurturing from their parents because the values taught serve as "the glue that holds society together." In a 1993 interview with *Black Collegian,* West seems to agree that both the Christian Bible and the Islamic Quran say that homosexuality is unacceptable behavior, yet he calls for a "different kind of dialogue" in which a "fundamental concern is to keep track of the humanity of folk."

Concerning relationships among Jews, non-Jewish whites, and non-Jewish blacks, West says that Jews do not fully understand the African-American identification with the plight of Palestinians living in Israel, nor do African Americans fully understand the importance of the state of Israel for Jews. He further states that African Americans should choose to put neither whites nor Jews "on a pedestal or in the gutter," that "the very ethical character of the black freedom struggle largely depends on the open condemnation by its spokespersons of any racist attitude or action." Like a prophet, West is calling for change, but like a pragmatist, he is calling for this change to be exhibited on the street corners in the United States. He maintains an "audacious hope," saying that it is essential for any transformation to a more humane and equal American society, claiming that "Either we learn a new language of empathy and compassion or the fire this time will consume us all."

—*Janet Hoover*

REFERENCES: Bolden, Tonya (1993), "Recovering Hope," *Black Enterprise* 23(12), online, EBSCO Host. Bowman, Jim (1994), "A Conference on

Racism," *Commonweal* 121(4), online, EBSCO Host. Cose, Ellis (1993), "A Prophet with Attitude," *Newsweek* 121(23), online, EBSCO Host. Donovan, Rickard (1991), "Cornel West's New Pragmatism," *Cross Currents* 41(1), online, EBSCO Host. Edwards, Audrey (December 1995–January 1996), "Cornel West: In Praise of the Combative Spirit," *Heart & Soul* 12, online, EBSCO Host. Engelhardt, Elizabeth Sanders Delwiche, "West, Cornel," in *OCAAL.* Gooding-Williams, R. (1991), "Evading Narrative Myth, Evading Prophetic Pragmatism: Cornel West's *The American Evasion of Philosophy,*" *Massachusetts Review* 32 (4), online, EBSCO Host. "Healing the Rift between Blacks and Jews" (1995), *Christian Century* 112(29), online, EBSCO Host. Iannone, Carol (1993), "Middle Man," *National Review* 65(14), online, EBSCO Host. Kazi, Kuumba Ferrouil (1993), "Cornel West: Talking about Race Matters," *Black Collegian* 24(1), online, EBSCO Host. Lewis, Judith A. (1995), "The Impact of Racism on American Family Life," *Family Journal* 3(2), online, EBSCO Host. McKim, Donald K. (1996), "Pragmatism," *Westminster Dictionary of Theological Terms* (Louisville, KY: Westminster John Knox Press). Pinsker, Sanford (1994), "What's Love, and Candor, Got to Do with it?" *Virginia Quarterly Review* 70(1), online, EBSCO Host. Sanoff, Alvin P. (1993), "A Theology for the Streets," *US News & World Report* 113(25), online EBSCO Host. Smith, Sande (Ed.) (1994), "West, Cornel," *Who's Who in African-American History* (New York: Smithmark). Van Leeuwen, Mary Stewart (1998), "Parenting and Politics: Giving New Shape to 'Family Values,'" *Christian Century* 115(21), online, EBSCO Host. West, Cornel (1982), *Prophesy Deliverance! An Afro-American Revolutionary Christianity* (Philadelphia: Westminster Press). "West, Wilson Named University Professor at Harvard" (1998), *Black Issues in Higher Education* 15(8), online, EBSCO Host. White, Jack E. (1993), "Philosopher with a Mission," *Time* 141(23), online EBSCO Host.

West, Dorothy (6/2/1907–8/16/1998)

Novels, short stories, essays, columns; publisher, journal founder and editor

Dorothy's father, Isaac West, had been born into slavery. After gaining his freedom, this blue-eyed middle-aged man built a profitable wholesale fruit business in Boston. When Dorothy's young mother, South Carolinian Rachel West, married Isaac, she began using her husband's wealth to support her large Southern family. Decades later, Dorothy wrote *The Living Is Easy* about a woman much like her mother.

Dorothy was provided with an excellent education, starting with tutoring at age 2, continuing through her 1923 graduation from the prestigious Girls' Latin High School, and ending with her studies at Boston University and the Columbia University School of Journalism. Clearly precocious, West started writing short stories when she was 7 years old. At age 15, her short story "Promise and Fulfillment" was published in the *Boston Post,* and thereafter she contributed regularly to the *Post,* also winning several literary prizes for her stories. As she once wrote, "I have no ability nor desire to be other than a writer, though the fact is I whistle beautifully."

In 1926, West and her cousin, poet **Helene Johnson**, attended the annual *Opportunity* magazine awards dinner, held in New York City. There, West's "The Typewriter" tied with **Zora Neale Hurston**'s "Spunk" for second place. With that recognition and encouragement, West stayed in New York. That year she started publishing her stories regularly in various literary journals. Most of these stories featured urban African Americans who felt constrained by their environment as well as by racism and sexism.

In the early 1930s West spent a year in the Soviet Union with about 20 other African-American intellectuals and artists. When she returned to New York, she founded *Challenge* magazine to promote the high-quality works of many **Harlem Renaissance** writers. Unfortunately, the Great Depression—and her own financial difficulties—forced her to stop publishing it. Many critics also charged that *Challenge* published only highly aesthetic, nonpolitical works by established writers, ignoring the works of many talented but unknown or highly political writers.

Although West was considered the youngest—and longest surviving—member of the Harlem Renaissance, most of her stories were published after the renaissance had peaked. In 1937, West scrounged together a little more money and launched *New Challenge,* with **Richard Wright** as associate editor, broadening the range of contributors. The sole issue of *New Challenge* included Wright's "Blueprint for Negro Writing" and the first piece to be published by then-unknown **Ralph Ellison**. Unhappily, editorial disagreements and financial problems sabotaged this journal, too.

To survive the Depression, West worked as a welfare investigator and then she worked for the Federal Writers' Project until it ended in the mid-

1940s. After that, West moved back to Massachusetts, settling permanently in Martha's Vineyard. There, she wrote *The Living Is Easy* (1948), an autobiographical novel satirizing the snobbery, shallowness, racism, sexism, and elitism of middle-class African-American New Englanders. Favorably reviewed when it was first published, the novel was even more widely acclaimed when reprinted in 1982 and it is now viewed as a central text in African-American women's literature.

West continued to write short stories until 1960, publishing more than two dozen stories before her death. In 1995, her stories were collected in *The Richer, the Poorer, Sketches and Reminiscences.* That same year, her second novel, *The Wedding,* was published. Set in Martha's Vineyard, the novel's dominant themes center around social class, financial status, and skin color variations among African Americans. In 1998, **Oprah Winfrey** produced a TV-movie adaptation of West's second novel. In addition, West continued to contribute weekly columns, essays, and other pieces to her local *Vineyard Gazette.*

REFERENCES: *About Books* TV show, 12/7/1997, 8/28/1998. *EBLG. NAAAL. NPR-ME-98. OC20LE. PBW.* Ferguson, Sally Ann H., in *OCWW.* Griffin, Farah Jasmine, in *OCAAL.*

Wheatley, Phillis (1753?–12/5/1784)
Poems

One of the earliest known African-American writers and the first to publish a book of poetry, former slave Phillis Wheatley has nevertheless been both revered and ignored by the African-American community. Wheatley was "purchased" by John and Susanna Wheatley in 1761 in Boston, and as was the custom, she was promptly given her master's surname. Although Wheatley is believed to have been born in West Africa, nothing is known about her life before her arrival in the United States. Her birth date is also unknown, though John Wheatley estimated her age to be seven or eight in 1761.

Susanna Wheatley is said to have taken pity on the frail black girl and begged her husband to purchase the child. John obliged his wife, and Phillis became Susanna's personal maid, an assignment that gave Phillis only light household responsibilities. This situation proved beneficial for Phillis, whom the Wheatleys recognized as being particularly bright. She was subsequently tutored by the Wheatleys' daughter and perhaps others and attained a level of education that most white females did not enjoy at that time. Her education was rooted in literary classics, including the Bible and the writings of Alexander Pope and John Milton. Thus she and her poetry made what was considered to be an odd combination—a black female slave with much education and low social status who wrote critically acclaimed poetry. (EDITOR'S NOTE: Phillis's intelligence may be illustrated by the observation that she spoke no English and couldn't read when she met the Wheatleys, and within 16 months she could read fluently even very difficult passages from the Bible.)

This combination of factors was so unusual that when Wheatley's book, *Poems on Various Subjects, Religious and Moral by Phillis Wheatley, Negro Servant to Mr. John Wheatley, of Boston, in New England,* was released in London in 1773, it included statements that testified to the authenticity of Wheatley and her 38 poems. One such statement, written by John Wheatley, retold the author's personal story, and another included the signatures of 18 well-respected Boston men, such as the governor of Massachusetts and John Hancock.

Wheatley sailed to England in the spring of 1773 to participate in the publication of her book. While in London, Wheatley toured the city as a free human being, giving readings of her poetry and meeting Benjamin Franklin and other noted personalities. Unfortunately, she had to return to Boston prematurely in the fall of 1773 when Susanna Wheatley became seriously ill. Susanna's death in March 1774 deeply affected Phillis, as she truly cared for her mistress. Around the time of her return to Boston, John Wheatley granted Phillis her freedom, although she stayed with the Wheatley family until John's death in March 1778.

Phillis married John Peters, a free black man, in April 1778. They had three children, two of whom preceded their mother in death. Peters often changed occupations, and the family struggled to survive financially. Eventually, Peters was sentenced to a Massachusetts debtors' prison, and Phillis worked in a boardinghouse, trying to support herself and her last surviving child. While still a young woman, Phillis died December 5, 1784. Her third child died soon after, and they are buried together at an unknown location.

Though *Poems on Various Subjects* gained Wheatley much recognition and respect, it was not her first or last important work. She was previously published in New England area newspapers, and she continued to write for several more years after the publication of her book. Her works include elegies written upon the deaths of either well-known citizens or her own children. She also wrote a letter and poem to George Washington in 1776, which so impressed him that Wheatley gained an audience with him during the Revolutionary War.

Some scholars have criticized Wheatley for placating white society and neglecting to include antislavery messages in her poetry. The first line of her poem, "On Being Brought from Africa to America," can be read to exhibit a certain emotional distance from Africa, which she calls "my Pagan land." The last two lines of the poem, however, call for equality and justice. Here Wheatley writes, "Remember, Christians, Negroes, black as Cain, / May be refined, and join the angelic train." These two lines serve as a reminder to Christians—a religion Phillis knew well, as she had been baptized in 1771—that the Christian God accepts everyone, regardless of race or ethnicity, with the same love and grace.

Wheatley has also been accused of being too imitative of Milton and Pope. Although it is true that Wheatley's poetry leans on the styles of Milton, Pope, and the neoclassic period of literature, readers must remember that Wheatley's education included these writings, and it follows that they would influence her work.

In recent years, Wheatley's work has enjoyed a revival. Readers are giving more consideration to her high command of both the English language and the art of poetry. Many scholars believe that her vulnerable social status led her to realize that she could not disrupt the status quo with too much vigor, but that she did indeed find a way to send antislavery messages.

As a Christian and an ardent supporter of the Revolutionary War, Wheatley initially decried slavery by promoting principles attested to by Christianity and the framers of the new republic. Her 1773 poem to the Earl of Dartmouth compares the oppression of the colonies by England with the oppression of the slaves by whites. Wheatley writes, "Can I then but pray / Others may never feel tyrannic sway?" A letter written to Samson Occom in 1774 shows sarcasm for those who "Cry for Liberty" when their "Words and Actions are so diametrically opposite" where slaves are concerned. In her later years, her protest became even more candid. By 1778, in Wheatley's poem, "On the Death

of General Wooster," she writes that Africa's people are a "blameless race," and that whites "disgrace [blacks] / And hold [blacks] in bondage."

Wheatley was indeed a remarkable woman and writer, one who lived in two worlds—the slave and the free. Yet while still a young woman, she managed to work within a political system and produce poetic works that reflect both an unusually high level of education and a growing social conscience.

—*Janet Hoover*

REFERENCES: *AAWW. BLC-3. NAAAL.* Abarry, Abu (1990), "The African American Legacy in American Literature," *Journal of Black Studies* 20, pp. 379–399, *Infotrac: Magazine Index Plus.* Flanzbaum, Hilene (1993), "Unprecedented Liberties: Re-reading Phillis Wheatley," *MELUS* 18, pp. 71–82, *Infotrac: Magazine Index Plus.* Hayden, Lucy K., "The Poetry of Phillis Wheatley," in *MAAL.* Shields, John C., in *OCAAL.* (See also *BDAA.*)

Whipper, Frances A. (née) Rollin
(11/19/1845–10/17/1901)
Biography, diaries

Young Frances Rollin certainly went out of her way to repay a favor. In 1865, **Martin R. Delany**, in his work for the Freedmen's Bureau in South Carolina, helped her press—and win—a lawsuit against a South Carolina steamer captain who had refused to let her travel in first class, despite her possession of a first-class ticket. During the course of that case, Rollin and Delany struck up a friendship, and Delany mentioned his interest in having a biography written about himself. Rollin was quite a skilled writer, and the pair soon agreed that he would pay her to write it.

Around the end of 1867, Rollin had finished gathering materials for her endeavor, and she was ready to start writing the book. She trudged off to Boston, bringing along her prodigious notes as well as Delany's own writings. Unfortunately, Delany ran out of funds for the project before he finished paying Rollin to complete it. At that point, Rollin was committed, and even though her own father was also undergoing financial difficulties, she managed to continue writing in the time she had left after doing clerical work and sewing to keep herself afloat financially. She also got a little financial help from some distinguished African-American Bostonians.

In 1868, *Life and Public Services of Martin R. Delany,* by Frank A. Rollin, was published. "Frank" was Rollin's nickname, and the reason she used it instead of "Francis" has been the source of much speculation. In any event, the book sold modestly well, and when the first print run ran out, the book was reissued again in 1883.

If that book had been Rollin's sole contribution to literature, it would merit her inclusion in this volume. It wasn't all she wrote, however. Perhaps an even greater treasure was her diary. The oldest surviving diary by a Southern African-American woman, it reveals her thoughts, her experiences, and her opinions. Rollin also offers glimmers about noteworthy African Americans of her day, such as **William C. Nell**, Richard Greener, the first African American to graduate from Harvard College, **William Wells Brown**, **Elizabeth Hobbs Keckley**, and **Charlotte Forten**. Rollin also makes comments about various Europeans and European Americans of her day—**Lydia Maria Child**, Frances A. Kemble, Charles Dickens, Ralph Waldo Emerson, and William Lloyd Garrison, among others.

On July 28, 1868, with her book published, Rollin returned to her home in South Carolina. There, she went to work for William J. Whipper, an attorney who was a partner in what was probably the first all–African-American law firm in the country. Soon after she started there, she married William and became Mrs. Whipper. Although their marriage ended in 1881, their union produced five children, three of whom survived to adulthood: Leigh (who became a noted actor of the 1940s and 1950s), Winifred (who became a schoolteacher), and Ionia (who became an obstetrician and founded the Whipper Home for Unwed Mothers).

Another of Frances A. Rollin Whipper's descendants, her great-granddaughter Ione, inherited her ancestor's interest in writing. Ione's 1991 book *Pride of Family: Four Generations of American Women of Color,* includes a recollection of her delight in discovering her great-grandmother's diary.

—*Tonya Bolden*

REFERENCES: *BAAW.*

Whipper, William (2/22/1804–3/9/1876)
Essays, commentary; journal editor, library cofounder

William's mother was an African-American servant in the household of his father, a European-American lumber merchant in Little Britain township, Pennsylvania. At his father's request, the same tutor who educated William's half-siblings also educated him. By the time Whipper was in his twenties, he had become well known in literary circles as a lecturer on moral reform, giving addresses at conventions, small meetings, and other gatherings. In 1828 Whipper published his landmark "Address on Non-Resistance to Offensive Aggression," which suggested moral suasion through nonviolence as a route to political change, more than a century ahead of the 1960s civil rights movement's nonviolent strategies of social protest. (The address was widely read when it appeared in the *Colored American* magazine in 1837.) (NOTE: An entirely different journal, *Colored American Magazine,* was published from 1900 to 1909.)

By 1830, Whipper had moved to Philadelphia, where he managed a grocery store that promoted temperance and advertised that its goods were made and sold using only free (i.e., not enslaved) labor; he also operated a business for cleaning clothes using a special steam-scouring process. In 1832, he joined **James Forten** and Forten's son-in-law **Robert Purvis** in sponsoring a petition opposing the enforcement of the Fugitive Slave Act in Pennsylvania. In 1833, this upright grocer joined eight other Philadelphians in cofounding the Philadelphia Library of Colored Persons. In 1835, he moved to Columbia, Pennsylvania, where he formed a business partnership that made him one of the richest African Americans of his day. He used his wealth to promote the causes in which he believed, which were chiefly moral reform and abolition.

In addition to contributing numerous essays and letters to abolitionist papers such as the *Liberator,* the *North Star,* and the *National Antislavery Standard,* Whipper edited the *National Reformer,* the journal of the American Moral Reform Society (AMRS), which he had helped found. Some sources say that he was therefore the first African American to edit a national magazine. Whipper also drafted the organizational documents and constitutions for the AMRS (which folded in 1841) and for the National Negro Convention, which he attended through the 1830s, 1840s, and 1850s. In Columbia, Whipper also offered his home as a safehouse for the Underground Railroad and spent nearly $1,000 each year helping runaway slaves. In 1853 Whipper bought property in Canada and considered emigration, but after the Civil War, he returned to live in Philadelphia.

REFERENCES: *1TESK*. Andrews, William L., in *OCAAL*. Myers, Aaron, in *EA-99*.

White, Paulette (née) Childress
(12/1/1948–)
Short stories, poems

White's poetry has been published in her collection *Love Poems to a Black Junkie* (1975) and her narrative poem *The Watermelon Dress: Portrait of a Woman* (1984). Her short stories have appeared in several periodicals and anthologies, including **Tonya Bolden**'s *Rites of Passage* (1994).

REFERENCES: *AAL. OCAAL.*

White, Walter F. (Francis)
(7/1/1893–3/21/1955)
Autobiography, historical fiction, novels, essays, articles, columns, nonfiction reportage, political analysis

George White had finished high school and his freshman year of college (at Atlanta University) when his parents died, forcing him to end his formal education. He got a job as a mail carrier and saved up his money to buy a lot. Soon, he had built a five-room house on the lot and married Madeline Harrison, a teacher. Eventually, George built an eight-room house on the lot, moved the smaller house to the back of the lot, and earned extra income by renting out the little house.

George's racial heritage was one-fourth black and three-fourths white; Madeline's was one-sixteenth black, one-sixteenth Native American, and seven-eighths white. George and Madeline had seven children: two boys (the eldest—George, Jr.—and Walter—the middle child) and five girls (Alice, Olive, Ruby, Helen, and Madeline). George looked so white that when he was injured and struck unconscious in a car accident in 1931, he was at first taken to the white part of the hospital; only when his brown-skinned son-in-law asked about him did the staff realize that George was black and take him to the black part of the hospital, where he died a little over two weeks later.

George and Madeline's son Walter was a blond-haired, light-skinned, blue-eyed boy, and in his racially mixed neighborhood—or anywhere—he could easily have "passed" as white. He chose not to, however—except when it was advantageous to

the civil rights cause for him to do so. Why was he so committed to his African-American heritage and to civil rights? Long before racism took the life of his father, he had another experience with his father that wakened him to the injustice of racial prejudice. In September 1906 Atlanta erupted in race riots. A marauding band of whites threatened to invade and burn down the White home when the marauders noticed guns protruding from the house and changed their plans. Walter decided then and there to do whatever he could to oppose racism and embrace his own African-American identity.

By the time of this incident, Walter had also developed a ravenous appetite for literature, having read his family's copies of books by Shakespeare, Dickens, Thackeray, and Trollope as well as countless books he borrowed from his church's library. (Public libraries were not available to young black children in Atlanta and other places in the South, and although White might have been able to check out books, unnoticed as being black, he chose not to do so.)

Walter attended high school at Atlanta University, as Atlanta had no public high schools for blacks at the time. After graduating from high school he went on to college, also at Atlanta University, and worked as a hotel bellhop. In 1915, the summer before he graduated from college, White started selling life insurance for Harry Pace's insurance company. (Pace later used his profits from his insurance business to establish a music-publishing company; see **W. C. Handy**.) Raised in the city, White learned a lot about country living conditions as he roamed the rural South, selling insurance.

In 1916 after White had graduated from Atlanta University, the Atlanta public school board moved to cut out education for black students beyond the sixth grade. Such cuts would leave the board more money to pay for superb education for Atlanta's white students, using the taxes paid by whites and blacks. Previously, the board had successfully cut out eighth-grade education for blacks for the same reason, so its members didn't anticipate any problems with cutting out the seventh grade. For White and his boss, Harry Pace, however, that action was all they needed to motivate them to form a branch of the National Association for the Advancement of Colored People (NAACP) involving the Atlanta African-American community. With Pace as the chapter president and White as the secretary, the NAACP and the local community forced the

Walter White, secretary of the NAACP, 1938 (Archive Photos)

school board to back down on its plans, and in 1920 Atlanta established its very first high school for African-American students.

By 1917, the NAACP national field secretary, **James Weldon Johnson**, noticed how fervently and effectively the newfound Atlanta chapter was fighting for civil rights. He was particularly impressed with the chapter secretary, and in 1918 Johnson helped White get a position in New York as assistant secretary for the national organization. White served as the NAACP's assistant secretary until 1929 and then as executive secretary from 1931 until his death in 1955.

On the last day in January of 1918, White started doing clerical and office duties in the New York office, but within two weeks he and Johnson had decided that he would best serve in a very different role. On February 12, Johnson and White had read about an atrocious lynching in Estill Springs, Tennessee. White proposed that he go to Estill Springs and investigate the lynching, using his European-American appearance to pose as a

white journalist uncovering exactly what had happened. Johnson agreed, and this turned out to be the first of many times White put his life at risk to investigate lynchings and other manifestations of racial hatred, such as segregation, restrictions on voting, and job and housing discrimination. On numerous occasions, White narrowly escaped being lynched, shot, and otherwise attacked during his investigations.

White sent his reports of 41 lynchings and 8 race riots not only to the NAACP but also to various periodicals, so that blacks and whites across the country would read about what was going on throughout the nation, particularly in the South. These reports were instrumental in getting the U.S. Congress to pass an antilynching law, as well as laws opposing discrimination, segregation, and voting restrictions. Also, during White's tenure at the NAACP, the organization grew in size and status, becoming the preeminent civil rights organization in the land. Among White's numerous achievements at the helm of the NAACP, he established the organization's Legal Defense and Education Fund, which made possible the 1954 *Brown v. Board of Education* Supreme Court decision. In 1937, White was awarded the NAACP's Spingarn Medal for his work in advancing the civil rights of African Americans.

In addition to his civil rights work, White was well respected as a writer. When **Alain Locke** was putting together his historic anthology *The New Negro* (1925), Locke invited White to contribute an essay to it. In addition to White's reports and articles on his NAACP-related activities, White wrote a great deal, including six books, two of which were novels. White's articles were printed in numerous major national magazines such as the *Saturday Evening Post* and *Reader's Digest* as well as in anthologies of his era. Two noteworthy essays of his are "Negro Literature" (printed in John A. Macy's *American Writers on American Literature,* 1931) and "Why I Remain a Negro" (*The Saturday Review of Literature,* October 11, 1947). White also wrote a regular column for the *Chicago Defender* and a syndicated column for the *New York Herald-Tribune,* and he even worked for a while as a correspondent for the *New York Post* (1943–1945), reporting on the living conditions among African-American troops serving in World War II. (His 1945 nonfiction book, *A Rising Wind,* was based on his reports for the *Post* during that war.) White also wrote a couple of small booklets, labeled as "Little Blue

Books," for a well-known series: *The American Negro and His Problems* (1927) and *The Negro's Contribution to American Culture* (1928).

In 1922, White disparaged a white author who had written a novel about blacks in the presence of the famous editor and writer H. L. Mencken. Mencken challenged White to write something better and more relevant. White had long been praised for his ability to tell a good—though true—story, so he took up Mencken's challenge. In the summer of 1922, White and his family vacationed in the Massachusetts cottage of Mary White Ovington, and after 12 days of intensive work, he had completed his first draft of his first novel. Within four years of Mencken's challenge, White had produced two novels: *The Fire in the Flint* (1924) and *Flight* (1926). Both books address the ways in which well-educated African Americans respond to racial injustice.

In *Fire in the Flint,* Kenneth Harper, an African-American native of a small town in Georgia, has just returned home after having completed his training (in Northern schools) to become a physician. Back home, he works hard to improve the health and the economic conditions of the blacks in his home town, but in doing so, he butts heads with the local whites. As White reported all too often in his real-life experiences, this conflict led to Harper's lynching death at the hands of the local whites. The novel was printed in hardcover by prestigious major publisher Knopf in 1924 and has since been reprinted (e.g., 1996, paperback, Brown Thrasher Books). A modest best-seller in the United States (particularly good for a first novel), the book did well in several European editions.

Flight (1926; reprint 1998) centers on Mimi Daquin, a light-skinned Creole woman from New Orleans who "passes" for white for a while. When Mimi finds herself unexpectedly pregnant—and unmarried—she flees North, first to Philadelphia and then to Harlem. Eventually, Mimi embraces her African heritage and abandons her attempts to "pass." As you might expect, this novel sparked a lot of controversy in 1926 (and might do so among some people today, as well).

In 1926 White was awarded a Guggenheim fellowship for his literary accomplishments. He used his fellowship money to move with his family to southern France for about a year (mid-1927–1928), where he intended to write his third novel. Despite his best intentions, he ended up writing *Rope and Faggot: A Biography of Judge Lynch*

(1929; hardcover reprint 1978), a sharp attack on lynching. In it, White analyzed the ways in which politics, economics, sexuality, religion, and social policies and conditions influenced lynching. White also wrote about 45,000 words of an expected 70,000-word novel, telling the story of three generations of his family, but he ran out of steam before he ever finished it.

After returning to the United States and taking on the executive secretary job at the NAACP, White found little time to write any book-length projects. As mentioned previously, however, he did pull together his writings on the experiences of African-American soldiers during World War II and produced the book *A Rising Wind: A Report on the Negro Soldier in the European Theater of War* (1945; hardcover reprint 1978). Just before he died, he completed another nonfiction work analyzing racial relations in America, *How Far the Promised Land?* (1955), published after his death. White also produced his critically acclaimed autobiography, *A Man Called White: The Autobiography of Walter White* (1948; paperback reprint 1995), documenting his own experiences, particularly those related to the NAACP, as an illustration of race relations in the United States during the first half of the twentieth century.

In addition to his civil rights work and his own writing, White encouraged the careers of other writers. For one thing, White introduced numerous other African-American writers of the **Harlem Renaissance** to **Carl Van Vechten**, a European American and an ardent patron of African-American literature. Van Vechten valued White's friendship, his writing, and his opinion of other people's writing. White also used other NAACP contacts to help young writers and other artists (e.g., **Countee Cullen, Claude McKay**, and even **Paul Robeson**) in their careers, and he helped start the Negro Fellowship Fund to support young writers directly.

White also enjoyed close relationships with friends (e.g., James Weldon Johnson) and family. On February 15, 1922, White married Leah Gladys Powell, a fellow NAACP staffer. The couple had two children: Jane (b. 1923) and Walter Carl Darrow (b. 1927). After 27 years of marriage, the couple divorced, and White married Poppy Cannon, a white woman, despite the objections of whites and blacks who opposed intermarriage. Cannon wrote a biography of him in 1956, *A Gentle Knight: My Husband, Walter White.* An obituary reported that he was survived by his widow and the two children from his first marriage.

REFERENCES: *AA:PoP. BDAA. BWA. EA-99. EB-BH-CD. EBLG. PGAA.* "African Americans Challenge the President," "NAACP's Legal Strategy in the 1930s," and "Walter Francis White (1893–1955)," in *1TESK.* Cady, Edwin H., in *WB-99.* Johns, Robert L., in *BH2C.* Wald, Gayle, in *OCAAL.* Zangrando, Robert L., in *G-99.* Amazon.com, 8/1999.

Whitfield, James Monroe (1822–1871)
Poems, essays

Before publishing his 400-line epic *Poem* (1867), Whitfield published his collection *America and Other Poems* (1853). Many more of his poems as well as his letters and essays were published in the *North Star* and other periodicals. (His great-grandniece was **Pauline Hopkins**.)

REFERENCES: *NYPL-AADR.* Sherman, Joan R., in *OCAAL.*

Whitman, Albery Allson (1851–1901)
Poems

Whitman's five poetry books include *Leelah Misled* (1873, 118-stanza poem); *Not a Man, and Yet a Man* (1877, 197-page narrative); and *The Rape of Florida* (1884, reprinted as *Twasinta's Seminoles,* 1885, comprising 251 Spenserian stanzas).

REFERENCES: *NYPL-AADR.* Sherman, Joan R., in *OCAAL.*

Wideman, John Edgar (6/14/1941–)
Plays, novels, short stories

As a novelist, John Edgar Wideman has been compared to William Faulkner. Such praise is not uncommon for this author, a two-time recipient of the PEN/Faulkner award, the only major award in the United States to be judged, administered, and largely funded by writers. He is best known for his writings about his childhood neighborhood Homewood, an African-American community on the eastern side of Pittsburgh. Wideman's characters, like Faulkner's, are often haunted by their pasts, and both authors have an ear for voices. Enthusiastic reviews have established Wideman as a major talent. He is one of America's premier writers of fiction.

John was the oldest of Edgar and Betty French Wideman's five children. The Widemans moved to Homewood shortly before John's first birthday, and there he spent the first ten years of his life. Sybela Owens, his great-great-great grandmother, had escaped slavery with the help of her "owner's" son (who later became her husband) and settled in Homewood. Much of Wideman's extended family still lived there when John was a boy. John's father worked as a paperhanger, waiter, and garbage collector. Even though the family was poor, they followed what Wideman called "the traditional middle-class pattern," moving to the predominantly white, upper-middle-class neighborhood of Shadyside in 1951.

In Shadyside, Wideman associated with his white friends in the classroom and gym and his black friends outside of school. He was senior class president, valedictorian, and a basketball star. Recruited by the University of Pennsylvania for its basketball team, Wideman's grades earned him a Benjamin Franklin scholarship.

In college, Wideman began to deal with the issues of race that he had compartmentalized in high school. He later described what he has called his collegiate theatrical performance in the autobiographical novel, *Brothers and Keepers* (1984): "Just two choices as far as I could tell: either/or. Rich or poor. White or black. Win or lose. . . . To succeed in the man's world you must become like the man and he sure didn't claim no bunch of nigger relatives in Pittsburgh." Wideman first majored in psychology, but he switched to English after he discovered that he would be spending time with lab rats, as opposed to exploring the mysteries of the human psyche.

Wideman played basketball well enough to be named to the Philadelphia Basketball Hall of Fame. When his lifelong dream to play in the National Basketball Association waned, however, he concentrated on a different achievement. In 1963, he became the second African American to earn a Rhodes Scholarship (see **Alain Locke**). At Oxford, Wideman began to concentrate on his writing. His first novel, *A Glance Away* (1967), was published shortly after he received his degree from Oxford. Wideman had written it while a Kent Fellow at the University of Iowa's Writer's Workshop. The story of a day in the life of a drug addict, *A Glance Away* reflects the harsh realities Wideman saw and experienced during his youth in Homewood. Although he later resided in other locales, including Wyoming, his novels have continued to depict black urban experiences. His critically acclaimed "Homewood Trilogy" comprises the short-story collection *Damballah*

(1981) and two novels, *Hiding Place* (1981) and *Sent for You Yesterday* (1983), which trace the lives of two Homewood families between the 1920s and the 1970s. Switching back and forth across the eras, Wideman celebrates the power of humanity to transcend adversity and restore bonds between people.

Literary devices that Wideman uses include stream of consciousness, first-person and third-person narrators, flashback, fast-forward, journals, identity exchange, interior monologue, epiphanies, dreams (historical and personal), letters, and puns. Wideman is much more than a storyteller, however. His characters represent aspects of the African-American mind, the elements that have been at the center of the recent African-American experience. His complex psychological approach uses language that ranges from ghetto slang and Ebonics to a style reminiscent of James Joyce, T. S. Eliot, and William Faulkner, often at the flip of a page.

After *A Glance Away,* Wideman chose to support himself through teaching while he continued to write, holding a faculty position at the University of Pennsylvania from 1967 to 1973. He published his second novel, *Hurry Home,* in 1970. Wideman directly faced the crisis of the African-American intellectual in his third novel, *The Lynchers* (1973). In it, Littleman is a crippled genius whose idea it is to lynch a white policeman as a way to save the spirit of the black community, and he is willing to sacrifice a few "insignificant" African-American lives to that "higher" purpose. He comes into conflict with Orin Wilkerson, the schoolteacher who finally destroys the bizarre, inhuman plot. Critic Philip Keith said, "The issue is also faced implicitly in the relation between *The Lynchers* and the other major works in the tradition of black novels, particularly Wright's *Native Son,* the novel that led black writers away from the minstrel novels into serious naturalistic fiction that spoke of and to the condition of the black masses."

In 1973, Wideman began teaching at the University of Wyoming at Laramie, where he studied the history and linguistics of African-American writers and searched for a new language to express the people, places, and experiences that he found important. Another event happened while Wideman was in Wyoming that also greatly influenced his work. His younger brother Robby was arrested, tried for murder, and sentenced to life in prison without parole.

Wideman ventured into autobiography for the first time with *Brothers and Keepers* (1984). In it, he continued to draw inspiration from the same source, Homewood. In that book, Wideman comes to terms with the fate of his brother Robby. Younger by ten years, Robby was influenced by the street, its drugs, and its crime. The book is Wideman's attempt to understand what happened. The author writes, "Even as I manufactured fiction from the events of my brother's life, from the history of the family that nurtured us both, I knew something different remained to be extricated." The book is a depiction of the inexorably widening chasm that divides middle-class African Americans from underclass ones.

Wideman often uses storytelling to deal with painful realities. *Reuben* (1987) is a harsh indictment of the judicial system through its portrayal of a lawyer for poor African Americans in Homewood. In *Philadelphia Fire* (1990), Wideman brings together two stories, combining fact and fiction. In the first, he describes the events in which Philadelphia police, under the direction of Mayor Wilson Goode, bombed the headquarters of the MOVE organization, which had received city eviction notices. The bombing killed 6 adults and 5 children and left 262 people homeless. The other story is the fact-based tale of Wideman's youngest son who, like Robby, is serving a life sentence for murder. The thoughts on these prose pages convey enormous pain, the author's feelings of confusion as a father.

In 1992 Wideman gathered two previous collections of short stories into *All Stories Are True,* and in 1995 he published *Fatheralong: A Meditation on Fathers and Sons, Race and Society.* His *The Cattle Killing* (1996) is a passionate and revealing novel about ancestors, family, and subjugation to the shackles of racial ideology. With fiercely poetic prose, the novel spans two centuries and three continents in haunting, powerful, and mythic fashion. In plague-infested eighteenth-century Philadelphia, a young itinerant black preacher searches for a mysterious, endangered African woman. Most blacks living there were free, but the freedom was precarious due to poverty and prejudice. The preacher's struggle to find her and to save them both plummets him into the nightmare of a society violently dividing itself into white over black. White demagogues blame the city's blacks for the killing fever. They irrationally accuse the blacks of being carriers of the pestilence, who are somehow immune to it. The blacks are nearly wiped out, but they nonetheless make great efforts to attend to the dying. In the novel, Wideman utilizes the core image of a cattle killing, the Xhosa people's ritual destruction of their herd in a vain attempt to resist European domination. Out from this metaphor spirals the narrator's search for meaning and love in the United States, Europe, and South Africa of yesterday and today. Wideman grapples with the nature of truth. He has spent his career challenging, testing, and pushing the boundaries of writing.

In 1992, Wideman was elected to the American Academy of Arts and Sciences. The following year, the MacArthur Foundation awarded him a $350,000 "genius" grant. He also won the American Book Award. Wideman has spoken extensively throughout Europe and the Near East. He teaches in the English department at the University of Massachusetts at Amherst.

—*Michael Strickland*

REFERENCES: *NAAAL.* Houghton Mifflin Company Web Page (1996), Fiction and Poetry Aisle: *The Cattle Killing,* by John Edgar Wideman, http://www.hminet.com/hmco/trade/fictionpoetry/catalog/Title0–395–78590–1.html. Keith, Philip (1974, Winter), "Philadelphia Story," *Shenandoah: The Washington and Lee University Review,* pp. 99–102. Nasso, Christine (Ed.) (1980), *Contemporary Authors* (Detroit: Gale Research). Strahinich, John (1995), "Oh Brother," *Globe Magazine* 12(3). Wideman, John Edgar (1996), *The Cattle Killing* (Boston: Houghton Mifflin).

Wilkinson, Brenda (1946–)
Juvenile novels

Wilkinson has written numerous books for middle school and juvenile readers, including her contemporary fiction (*Definitely Cool,* 1993) and her historical novels such as *Ludell* (1975), *Ludell and Willie* (1976), *Ludell's New York Time* (1980), and *Not Separate, Not Equal* (1987). Wilkinson's Ludell character is a high-spirited teenage girl, showing all the conflicting emotions and behavior characteristic of her age and stage in life (childish/mature, insensitive/thoughtful, and so on).

REFERENCES: Harris, Violet J., in *OCAAL.*

Williams, George Washington
(10/16/1849–8/2/1891)
Nonfiction—history

Generally recognized as the first major African-American historian, Williams wrote *History of the Negro Race in America from 1619 to 1880* (1883;

reprint 2 vols., 1968), considered the first fully encompassing history of African Americans up to that time. Williams started his historical writing with his 80-page *History of the Twelfth Street Baptist Church* (1875), of which he was pastor for a few months. A Union Army Civil War veteran, Williams later wrote the *History of the Negro Troops in the War of Rebellion* (1887), also considered an authoritative first in the field.

Williams received no formal education during his childhood, which he spent in an orphanage. As an adult, he attended Howard University and the Wayland Seminary and graduated from Massachusetts Newton Theological Seminary in 1874. That same year he married Sarah Sterrett, with whom he later had a son.

REFERENCES: *BDAA. EA-99. NYPL-AADR.* Hall, Stephen Gilroy, in *OCAAL.* See also John Hope Franklin's *George Washington Williams* (1985).

Williams, John A. (Alfred) (12/5/1925–)
Novels, biographies, essays, articles, travel account, poems, anthologies, play, libretto

A native of Mississippi, Williams grew up in Syracuse, New York. After a stint in the navy during World War II, he graduated from high school, went on to Syracuse University (B.A., English and journalism, 1950), and started graduate school. Lack of finances forced Williams to leave school and earn money in various jobs: foundry worker, grocery clerk, social worker, insurance company employee, television publicity coordinator, and publicity director for a vanity press. Meanwhile, Williams was contributing articles to such periodicals as *Ebony, Newsweek,* and *Jet.* Early in his career, *Holiday* magazine commissioned Williams to write a series of articles about his experiences and the people he met while traveling across the country in 1963, which he later printed in his book *This Is My Country Too* (1965). By the early 1970s, Williams was able to leave menial jobs behind and started teaching at various colleges in the Virgin Islands, New York, and California, and from 1973 to 1977 he was named a distinguished professor of English at the City University of New York; during most of his career, he was the Paul Robeson Distinguished Professor of English at Rutgers University at Newark, from which he retired in 1994.

By the late 1950s, Williams also started writing novels, and in 1960 he published his first novel, *The Angry Ones* (reprint 1996), followed by *One for*

New York (1960/1975), *Night Song* (1961), and *Sissie* (1963; reprint 1988). In all of these works, Williams's African-American protagonists successfully triumph over the racist oppression they confront in the United States. In 1962, the American Academy of Arts and Letters sent Williams a letter, informing him that he would be awarded the Prix de Rome for his *Night Song.* He was also asked to be interviewed as a mere formality before being awarded the prize. Apparently, the interview didn't go well, as the academy then withdrew the prize. In Williams's eyes, their action was an outrageous act of racism. Williams reported this experience in his essay "We Regret to Inform You That" (reprinted in his essay collection *Flashbacks,* 1973), and he then fictionalized this incident in his celebrated novel *The Man Who Cried I Am* (1967). This incident occurred around the time that the civil rights movement seemed to be losing ground, two great African-American leaders had been assassinated (**Malcolm X** in 1965, **Martin Luther King, Jr.** in 1968), black nationalist fervor was peaking, and the **Black Arts movement** was in full swing.

The next few novels Williams wrote were far more pessimistic about race relations in Williams's native land, including *Sons of Darkness, Sons of Light* (1969); *Novel of Some Probability* (1969); and *Captain Blackman* (1972). By the middle of the 1970s, both the mood of the country and Williams's next few novels seemed milder and more hopeful, including *Mothersill and the Foxes* (1975); *The Junior Bachelor Society* (1976), which was made into a television movie; *Sophisticated Gents* (1981); *!Click Song* (1982), which won the Before Columbus Foundation's American Book Award (1983); *The Berhama Account* (1985); *Jacob's Ladder* (1987); and *Clifford's Blues* (1999).

In addition to his articles and his travel account (*This Is My Country Too,* 1965), Williams has written numerous other nonfiction works, including *Africa: Her History, Lands, and People, Told with Pictures* (1962) and two essay collections (*Flashbacks: A Twenty-Year Diary of Article Writing,* 1973; and *Flashbacks 2: A Diary of Article Writing,* 1991). He has also written biographies of **Martin Luther King, Jr.**, *The King God Didn't Save: Reflections on the Life and Death of Martin Luther King, Jr.* (1970), indicting King's nonviolent methods of social and political change; of **Richard Wright**, *The Most Native of Sons: A Biography of Richard Wright* (1970); and of comedian Richard Pryor, *If I Stop I'll Die: The Com-*

edy and Tragedy of Richard Pryor (1991, with his son, Dennis A. Williams; reprint 1993). He also edited a few anthologies: *Beyond the Angry Black* (1966), *Amistad 1* (1970, with Charles F. Harris) and *Amistad 2* (1971, with Charles F. Harris), and *Bridges: Literature across Cultures* (1993, with Gilbert H. Muller). Muller and Williams also cowrote *Ways in: Approaches to Reading and Writing about Literature* (1994) and *The McGraw-Hill Introduction to Literature* (1995). In 1999 Williams published *Safari West,* a collection of his poetry, written from the mid-1950s through 1997; this collection won the 1998 Before Columbus Foundation's American Book Award. Not one to leave any avenue of literature untouched, Williams wrote a play and wrote the libretto for the opera *Vanqui.* Williams is married and has three sons (Gregory, a drug company executive; Dennis, a writer, former *Newsweek* journalist, and college administrator; and Adam, a musician).

REFERENCES: *1TESK. EBLG. G-97. NAAAL. OC20LE.* Mazique, Marc, in *EA-99.* Nash, William R., in *OCAAL.* Amazon.com, 7/1999. His papers are collected at the John A. Williams Archive, founded at the University of Rochester in New York in 1987.

Williams, Myrlie Evers–
See Evers–Williams, Myrlie (Louise) (née Beasley)

Williams, Peter, Jr. (?/1780–10/10/1840)
Newspaper founder

In 1827, Williams helped found *Freedom's Journal,* an ardently abolitionist newspaper. Williams, the first African-American Episcopalian priest, was active in the American Anti-Slavery Society until rumors that he had celebrated an interracial marriage abruptly ended his leadership role, although he continued to hold church services.

REFERENCES: *EA-99.*

Williams, Robert Franklin
(2/26/1925–10/15/1996)
Autobiography, commentary, nonfiction—politics

Williams's grandfather had edited the *People's Voice,* which crusaded valiantly for civil rights. Williams grew up listening to his grandmother tell stories of how his grandfather had challenged white supremacy during the virulently racist post–Civil War era. In the 1960s, Williams initially affiliated with the National Association for the Advancement of Colored People (NAACP), but when he decided against nonviolent tactics and organized a militia to fight off Ku Klux Klan terrorism, he was ousted from the organization. In response, he became more certain that armed struggle was the best route to civil rights for African Americans. During this time, because of legal trouble, Williams had exiled himself to Cuba and then to North Vietnam and China. In Cuba, he published his own newsletter, aptly titled *The Crusader,* which had a circulation of 40,000. Williams also published *Negroes with Guns* (1962), which had a profound effect on the future founders of the Black Panther Party for Self-Defense as well as many other militant African Americans during the 1960s (and 1970s). In 1969, while in China, he negotiated a deal with the Nixon administration for his return to the United States, where he became involved with the Center for Chinese Studies at the University of Michigan. Just before he died, Williams wrote his own account of his life, *While God Lay Sleeping* (1996).

REFERENCES: Tyson, Timothy, in *EA-99.*

Williams, Samm-Art (né Samuel Arthur) (1/20/1946–)

Plays

Williams's plays include *Welcome to Black River* (1975), *The Coming* (1976), *Do Unto Others* (1976), *A Love Play* (1976), *The Frost of Renaissance* (1978), *Brass Birds Don't Sing* (1978), *The Sixteenth Round* (1980), *Eve of the Trial* (c. 1980), *Eyes of the American* (1980), and *Cork* (1986), as well as his Tony Award–nominated and Outer Critics' Circle Award–winning play *Home* (1979–1980).

REFERENCES: Walker, Robbie Jean, in *OCAAL.*

Williams, Sherley Anne

(8/25/1944–7/7/1999)

Literary criticism, poems, novel, essays, children's book

Sherley and her three sisters labored alongside their parents in the fields of California. Tuberculosis killed her father when Sherley was eight years old, and eight years later, her mother died, leaving Sherley to the care of her older sister Ruise (Ruby Louise). Despite financial difficulties, Sherley earned her B.A. in history (1966) and her M.A. in

black studies (1972). After earning her M.A., Williams taught African-American literature at several universities and spent time in Ghana under a 1984 Fulbright grant, eventually settling at the University of California at San Diego.

Williams's first book of literary criticism, *Give Birth to Brightness: A Thematic Study of Neo-Black Literature* (1972), explored heroism in music, poetry, folklore, and drama. For instance, she examined the heroes depicted by several African-American male writers, contrasting the European-American traditions and African-American folk traditions evident in these works. She highlighted historical continuity, showing the connections between the **Black Aesthetic** of the 1960s and the ongoing toasts and boasts originating in the **oral tradition** of African-American males. In other works of literary criticism, Williams focused on other ways in which aspects of African-American culture interrelate, such as the relation between the blues tradition and contemporary African-American poetry.

Williams's own poetry resonates with the rhythms of the blues, and her poems frequently appear in anthologies and periodicals. Her poems were first collected in her National Book Award–nominated *The Peacock Poems* (1975), which included poems about her own childhood and the childhood of her son, John Malcolm. Her second collection, *Some One Sweet Angel Child* (1982), traces African-American women's history from the nineteenth century through the twentieth century. It particularly highlights the life experiences of jazzy blues singer Bessie Smith and Williams's own life experiences as a mother and an African-American woman.

Williams's novel *Dessa Rose* (1986) was inspired by historical events. The main event was an 1829 slave uprising in Kentucky led by a pregnant African-American woman, Dessa Rose. Historically, this event was paralleled by the actions of a white North Carolinian woman (Miss Rufel in Williams's narrative) who turned her isolated farm into a sanctuary for runaway slaves. Williams brought together these two women's stories, refuting the stereotypes of antebellum Southern white women and African-American slave women, highlighting instead the strength and determination of each woman.

Through *Dessa Rose,* Williams also provided insight into the **slave narrative** form: Readers can hear Dessa's story from her own viewpoint (as omniscient narrator), through the ears of a white male amanuensis (much as traditional slave narratives were recorded), and through Miss Rufel, who is sympathetic but who cannot truly see the world as Dessa does. Thus, readers gain insight into not only how Dessa views her experiences, but also how others interpret her experiences. *Dessa Rose* was both popularly acclaimed (in its third printing within months after publication) and critically acclaimed (being called "artistically brilliant, emotionally affecting and totally unforgettable" by a *New York Times* reviewer).

What genre did Williams, then a grandmother, try next? A children's picture book. *Working Cotton* (1992) gives her child's-eye-view of picking cotton with her family, starting before dawn and finally stopping long after sunset.

Although Williams's first book focused primarily on African-American males, her subsequent work has primarily illuminated the experiences and perspectives of African-American women. Williams observed, "I wanted specifically to write about lower-income black women. . . . We were missing these stories of black women's struggles and their real triumphs" (*BWWW*, p. 207).

REFERENCES: *BWWW. MAAL. NAAAL.* Mickle, Mildred R., in *OCAAL*. Schulz, Elizabeth, in *OCWW.* Personal communication, June 1999.

Williams, Spencer, Jr.
(?/1893–12/13/1969)
Screenplays

Williams started out in movies in the mid-1920s, writing the screen adaptations for the stories of Octavsus Roy Cohen for an affiliate of Paramount Pictures. Later on, Williams got into acting and wrote the screenplays for films that he directed and in which he starred, such as *Marching On* (about blacks in the military), *The Blood of Jesus* (1941, an allegory about a man who kills his wife), and *Juke Joint* (1947, a comedy). Nowadays, however, Williams is chiefly known as an actor who played the "Andy Brown" character on the much-derided popular television show, *Amos 'N' Andy* (1951–1954; syndicated reruns continued until 1966), which exaggerated African-American stereotypes in a situation comedy context.

REFERENCES: *EA-99. SMKC.*

Wilson, August (né Frederick August Kittel) (4/27/1945–)
Plays, poems

Young Frederick August Kittel grew up in a mixed-race neighborhood in Pittsburgh, Pennsylvania, the setting for many of his plays. His father (Frederick, Sr.), a baker, was a German immigrant, and his mother (Daisy Wilson Kittel), a cleaning woman, was an African-American native of North Carolina who had literally walked to Pittsburgh in search of better opportunities. Frederick, Sr., was rarely around, so Daisy struggled to support herself and her six children (Frederick was the fourth) in their two-room apartment behind a grocery store, with the income she could get from her cleaning jobs and from welfare subsidies. Eventually, his parents divorced, and Frederick Sr. disappeared altogether from his son's life. Despite these difficult economic circumstances, Frederick learned to read at age 4 and had started reading African-American writers such as **Arna Bontemps**, **Ralph Ellison**, **Langston Hughes**, and **Richard Wright** at age 12.

When Frederick was a teenager, his mother remarried. His stepfather, David Bedford, moved the family to a mostly white suburb, where the Bedford family confronted intense racism, including having bricks thrown through the window of their home. At the local school, his classmates refused to sit by him and left him notes saying, "Nigger go home." His teachers weren't helpful, either. When Frederick was 15 years old, a history teacher falsely accused him of plagiarizing a paper on Napoleon, suggesting that such a well-written paper could not have been written by an African-American student. That was the end of Frederick's school career, but it wasn't the end of his education.

In the Carnegie-funded public libraries of Pittsburgh, Frederick read voraciously, undertaking his own rigorous program of study. By his own account, "Basically the years from fifteen to twenty I spent in the library educating myself." He also worked at various odd jobs to help support himself and his family. Over time, however, he felt sure that he would become a writer. Daisy didn't want to see her son pursue such an unstable profession, in which the risk of remaining in poverty was great. Instead, she wanted him to become an attorney and forced him to leave the Bedford home if he was unwilling to return to school to make something of himself. Unable to support himself alone on his odd jobs, Frederick quickly enlisted in the

Playwright August Wilson won a Pulitzer Prize for The Piano Lesson, *1990 (Bettmann/Corbis)*

U.S. Army in 1963. A year later, however, he was sure that he had to find some other way to support himself and managed to get an early discharge.

Turned loose on the streets of Pittsburgh, Frederick was unsure of how he was going to make his way in the world. On those streets, however, he managed to find a rich source of literary material: He listened to a bunch of old retired railroad porters hanging out in a cigar store called "Pat's Place." These old guys would stand around and tell each other stories, anecdotes, sketches, and advice-laden parables. The cigar-store guys opened Frederick's ears to the sound of everyday black folks, and soon he started hearing their voices in barbershops, in cafés, and on street corners. About this time, he also heard, for the first time, Bessie Smith's "Nobody in Town Can Bake a Sweet Jellyroll Like Mine" and realized the value of his own cultural

heritage and of the tremendous contributions African Americans had made to American culture.

By piecing together an assortment of menial jobs (short-order cook, stock boy, mailroom clerk, gardener, dishwasher, porter, and so on), Frederick managed to get by. All the while, he continued to aspire to be a writer, with poetry as his first efforts. He scribbled many of his early poems on paper bags while sitting in restaurants. On April 1, 1965, while living in a Pittsburgh rooming house, Frederick bought his first typewriter. That year, he also started getting involved in theater, helping to form the Second Avenue Poets Theatre Workshop. Soon, he started writing short fiction, as well. As Wilson later recalled, the Second Avenue poets also produced their "own stapled-together magazines with names like *Connection* and *Signal*."

As the 1960s progressed, Frederick continually

perfected his writing skills and embedded himself ever more deeply in the community of African-American writers and theater artists. He helped his friend, playwright and teacher Rob Penny, found the Black Horizons Theatre Company in his old mixed-race neighborhood in Pittsburgh. The company, of which Frederick was the director, produced various plays by and about African Americans.

As Frederick immersed himself ever more deeply into the **Black Aesthetic**, he sought further ways in which to embrace and celebrate his African-American heritage. In the late 1960s, he rejected his surname of Kittel from his German-born father and adopted his mother's maiden name, Wilson, as his own surname, honoring her and his African-American heritage. In 1969, Wilson married Brenda Burton (a Black Muslim), and the couple had a daughter, Sakina Ansari (b. 1970). The marriage didn't last long, however, and when it dissolved in 1972, Wilson turned ever more attentively to his writing.

In the late 1960s, Wilson also started publishing his poetry. The first poem of his that was published was "For Malcolm X and Others" (*Negro Digest,* September 1969). Subsequent poems included "Bessie" (*Black Lines,* summer of 1971, for Bessie Smith), "Morning Song," "Muhammad Ali," and "Theme One: The Variations." Although his poems appeared in such popular journals as *Black World* (see **Negro Digest**) and in at least one anthology, he found himself turning more toward writing plays.

After completing his play *Rite of Passage,* his unpublished play *Recycle* was produced in 1973 by a Pittsburgh community theater. In 1976 he wrote *The Homecoming,* about Blind Lemon Jefferson, a legendary blues singer and guitarist who froze to death in Chicago in 1930. (The play wasn't produced until 1989, however.) In 1977, Wilson wrote *Black Bart and the Sacred Hills,* about a legendary Wild West outlaw. (That play was produced in 1981 in St. Paul, Minnesota.)

In 1978 Wilson moved to St. Paul, where he took a job writing plays for Claude Purdy and writing scripts for the Science Museum of Minnesota. His scripts included *An Evening with Margaret Mead, How Coyote Got His Special Power,* and *Eskimo Song Duel.* He also founded the Black Horizons Theatre Company and wrote his two-act play *Jitney,* set in 1971 in a Pittsburgh taxicab station, during that time. Wilson has claimed that he wrote *Jitney* in just ten days, "while sitting in a fish-and-chips restaurant." In 1980 he was awarded a

Jerome fellowship and was named associate playwright in Minneapolis's Playwrights' Center. He also wrote his play *Fullerton Street,* set in 1949, about blacks who have migrated to the urban North from the rural South. Both *Fullerton Street* and *Jitney* were rejected by the Eugene O'Neill Theatre Center's National Playwrights Conference, and *Fullerton Street* has never been produced, but *Jitney* was produced in regional theaters in Minneapolis (1980) and Pittsburgh (1980). Wilson also wrote a few other unpublished, unproduced plays.

In 1981, Wilson married a second time, wedding Judy Oliver, a social worker of European-American ancestry. Judy encouraged him to quit his museum job to dedicate more of his time to writing his own plays. With this encouragement, August wrote *Ma Rainey's Black Bottom* (1984), his first commercial success. (Sadly, his mother Daisy had died the previous year, never having seen his writing career pay off financially.) *Ma Rainey* is set in 1927 Chicago in a backstage room for a celebrated blues singer who verbally abuses the musicians who accompany her. The musicians talk about their experiences in the United States of the 1920s, including the exploitation of black musicians by white managers, promoters, and record producers. Their rage eventually explodes in a tragically misdirected violent outburst. Despite the gravity of the situation and the pain the speakers clearly feel, the dialogue shows great humor, and Wilson's writing shows deep compassion and sensitivity for his characters.

Ma Rainey was accepted for production at the O'Neill Theatre workshop, and this production launched both Wilson's playwriting career and his collaborative relationship with Lloyd Richards, the O'Neill's director. Richards is also the dean of the highly respected Yale Drama School and director of Yale's Repertory Theatre, where Wilson's subsequent plays have been produced before going on to Broadway. *Ma Rainey* went on to be produced on Broadway in 1984 and earned a New York Drama Critics Circle (NYDCC) Award for best new play, was nominated for several Tony Awards, and enjoyed commercial success (running for 275 performances). The play was also published as *Ma Rainey's Black Bottom: A Play in Two Acts* (paperback reissue 1988).

With *Ma Rainey,* Wilson clearly had "arrived" at success, and his subsequent plays have ensured that his success has continued. Wilson has announced that he plans a complete cycle of plays, with each play set in a different decade of the twentieth century, telling a distinctive aspect of the African-American experience. Thus far, he has completed plays for the 1910s: *Joe Turner's Come and Gone* (1988); the 1920s: *Ma Rainey's Black Bottom* (1984); the 1930s: *The Piano Lesson* (1990; Pulitzer Prize winner); the 1940s: *Seven Guitars* (1995); the 1950s: *Fences* (1987; Pulitzer Prize winner); the 1960s: *Two Trains Running* (1992); and the 1970s: *Jitney.*

After *Ma Rainey,* Wilson wrote *Fences,* about a father-son conflict set in 1957. The fences include a literal fence, which the father, Troy Maxson, is building around his yard, as well as metaphorical fences, which Troy is unwittingly building between himself and his loved ones, and which his wife Rose is trying to build around her family, between them and the surrounding world. Troy, a garbage collector and former Negro League baseball player, had been barred from playing Major League baseball. Based on his personal history, Troy tries to prevent his son from accepting a football scholarship, believing that he is helping his son to avoid the disappointment and heartbreak he experienced. *Fences* is the only one of Wilson's plays that centers entirely around one main character; the others involve an ensemble of characters (or a pair of characters, as in *The Piano Lesson*).

Fences was produced at the O'Neill Theatre in 1983, at Yale Repertory Theatre in 1985, and on Broadway in 1987. The Broadway production earned Wilson the 1987 Pulitzer Prize for drama, the John Gassner Outer Critics Circle Award for Best American Playwright, and the Drama Desk Award, as well as another NYDCC best play award and a Tony Award for best play, in addition to Tony Awards for best director, best actor, and best featured actress. Following *Fences,* the *Chicago Tribune* also named Wilson its Artist of the Year. In addition to achieving great critical success, the play grossed a record-breaking $11 million in one year, more than any other nonmusical play at that time. A paperback reissue of the play was published in 1995.

Joe Turner's Come and Gone (written in 1984), Wilson's next play, debuted on Broadway while *Fences* was still enjoying its successful run. Like *Fences, Joe Turner* was first produced at the O'Neill Theatre (1984), then at the Yale Repertory Theatre (1986), and finally on Broadway (1988). *Joe Turner* is set in 1911 in a Pittsburgh boarding house inhabited by former sharecroppers and other impoverished Southerners who migrated North in hopes of a better life. Wilson's story suggests that the characters must struggle to preserve their African-American roots and cultural identity after having left their Southern homeland. (Wilson's unpublished play *Fullerton Street* also highlights South-to-North migration, but during the later period of the 1940s.) In *Joe Turner,* the protagonist is a former slave and ex-convict whose wife had fled North while he was still enslaved, and he goes North hoping to find her again. The play earned Wilson another NYDCC Award (1988) and another Drama Desk Award, and it was nominated for multiple Tony Awards. Wilson was also added to the New York Public Library's list of Literary Lions in 1988. A paperback reissue of *Joe Turner's Come and Gone: A Play in Two Acts* was published in 1992.

In 1986, while *Joe Turner* was working its way to Broadway, Wilson was writing *The Piano Lesson,* set in 1936 in a family living room where the heirloom piano is the center of sibling conflict. To the brother, Boy Willie, the piano represents hope and possibilities for the future, if he can convince his sister to sell it so that he can buy some land on which his ancestors had been enslaved. To the sister, Berniece, the piano represents family, heritage, roots, and their link to the past. The siblings' grandfather had seen his "owners" sell his wife and son in exchange for the piano, and in his grief at losing them, he had carved their likenesses into the piano. Fantasy and mysticism figure into the resolution of the conflict.

Three years after its initial 1987 production at the Yale Repertory Theatre, the 1990 Broadway production of *The Piano Lesson* earned Wilson a second Pulitzer Prize for drama (1990), as well as an additional Tony Award for best play, another NYDCC best-play award, another Drama Desk Award, and the American Theatre Critics Outstanding Play Award. On February 5, 1995, Wilson's adaptation of the play was aired on CBS television, with its Broadway star (Charles Dutton) reprising his stage role. A paperback reprint of the script was published in 1990.

The year that *The Piano Lesson* debuted on Broadway, Wilson was writing his next play, *Two Trains Running,* set in 1969 in a Pittsburgh eatery frequented by some regular customers. The characters, a group of friends, discuss their experiences within the chaotic context of the Vietnam War (and opposition to it) and racial turbulence. Following its production at the Yale Repertory Theatre, *Two Trains'* 1992 Broadway production won another American Theatre Critics Association Award and another NYDCC Award, and it was nominated for another Tony. A paperback of the play was published in 1993.

In 1995 Wilson wrote *Seven Guitars,* set in Pittsburgh in 1948, purportedly following the death of Floyd "Schoolboy" Barton, a local blues guitarist. Schoolboy's friends, fellow musicians, gather round to celebrate his life and to affirm their own hopes for the future. Its 1995 Broadway production won rave reviews and yet another NY-DCC Award for best new play. In 1997, a paperback reprint was published.

In addition to the numerous awards already mentioned and his Jerome fellowship, Wilson has won Bush, McKnight, Rockefeller, and Guggenheim fellowships in playwriting. He has also been elected to the American Academy of Arts and Sciences (1991), and he was one of ten writers to win the generous Whiting Writer's Awards in recognition of his "exceptionally promising, emerging talent." Wilson also received an honorary degree from Yale University, the home of the repertory theater where most of his plays have been produced, in 1988. During the late 1980s, Wilson moved to Seattle, where he now lives with his third wife, Costanza Romero, a costume designer who designed the costumes for *Seven Guitars,* among other works.

REFERENCES: *AA:PoP. EA-99. EB-BH-CD. EBLG. G-99. NAAAL. OC20LE. WDAA.* Adler, Thomas P., in *WB-99.* Carter, Linda M., in *BH2C.* Elkins, Marilyn, in *OCAAL.* "*The Piano Lesson* (1990)," in *1TESK.* Amazon.com, 8/1999.

Wilson, Harriet E. (née Adams) (1827? or 1828?–1863? or 1870?)
Novel

Historians and other scholars have been able to find out very little about Harriet before 1850, when she was in her early twenties. What is known about her after that time is based on her autobiographical novel *Our Nig,* some of the facts of which have been confirmed or refuted by public records. According to the 1850 federal census of the state of New Hampshire, Harriet Adams was born in Milford, New Hampshire, in 1828 or 1827 (her age was given as 22 years old), the daughter of Charles Adams (a native of New Ipswich, New Hampshire). According to the 1860 federal census of Boston, where she was living at that time, how-

ever, she was born in Fredericksburg, Virginia, in 1807 or 1808. Other data about her life make the 1820s New Hampshire birth information seem more probable.

When Harriet published *Our Nig,* she included in it letters from three acquaintances who corroborated her account. According to one of these acquaintances, Margaret Thorn, when Harriet was just 6 years old, she had been hired out to the Hayward family, who made her work hard, "both in the house and in the field." Apparently, it was the female head of household who was the most abusive to Harriet. Thorn observed that the tortuous difficulty of the work ruined Harriet's health, so that by the time she was 18 years old, her poor health prevented her from doing hard labor, and she left the Hayward household. Another letter, written by "Allida," noted that Harriet then worked sewing straw in Massachusetts, where she lived in the home of a Mrs. Walker, probably in or near Worcester. Apparently, she was even impaired in performing this work, and Mrs. Walker kept her in a room adjoining her own, so that she could minister to Harriet as needed. (Another source suggests, however, that Harriet was Mrs. Walker's domestic servant.)

Other documentation about Harriet shows that she was living in the Samuel Boyles household, a white family, still in Milford. The 1850 federal census listed four adults who were not family members living with them, so historians have inferred that the Boyles were running a boarding house, possibly one for which the county subsidized them for providing shelter to aged or disabled adults. The year of the census, the federal Fugitive Slave Act had been passed, so all African Americans living in the North were endangered, particularly if they lived or worked alone.

While living with the Boyles, Harriet met Thomas Wilson, a beguiling abolitionist lecturer who passed himself off as a Virginia-born fugitive slave reporting the horrors of his slave experiences, but who was actually a freeman. Harriet married Thomas October 6, 1851. (According to one source, however, her marriage license was issued in 1852.) Soon after, the couple left Massachusetts and moved to New Hampshire. Around the time of their marriage, Harriet had become pregnant. Before she gave birth, Thomas abandoned her and went to sea, so she had to move to the "County House," a facility for paupers in Goffstown, New York. The facility comprised a big farmhouse, a barn, and several other small buildings, most of which housed paupers, all of whom suffered from malnutrition and many of whom were highly vulnerable to infectious disease. There, in late May or early June of 1852, Harriet gave birth to a son, George Mason Wilson, apparently the only child of the Wilsons.

After George's birth, Thomas returned from the sea and retrieved his wife and child. He moved them to yet another town and supported them fairly well for a while. After a bit, however, he left again, never to return, and Harriet had to place George in the care of kindly white foster parents in New Hampshire while she tried to improve her health and to make enough money to retrieve him. According to one source, Harriet was able to make money by using a sympathetic stranger's recipe for removing (or covering) gray hair in her clients; other sources suggest that she worked as a dressmaker (or even as a milliner, making women's hats); perhaps she did both, either simultaneously or consecutively. In any case, according to the Boston City Directory, by 1855 Harriet had moved to Boston, and she continued living there through 1863. Eventually, her health worsened again, confining her to bed, so she couldn't do any work outside her home. In this situation, she turned to writing, hoping to make enough to support herself and to retrieve George by writing a novel.

Wilson based her novel, *Our Nig; or, Sketches from the Life of a Free Black, in a Two-Story White House, North. Showing That Slavery's Shadows Fall Even There* (1859), on her own experiences, but she definitely freely fictionalized her account. For the most part, the plot of Wilson's *Our Nig* closely parallels the fluid, well-structured plotting found in the sentimental novels of her white female contemporaries, rather than the structure of the **slave narratives** of her era. Nonetheless, she freely borrowed the dramatic flourishes employed in slave narratives, and she frequently used many of the literary techniques employed in these narratives as well. Among other things, Wilson borrowed the technique of cataloging various abuses and the themes of self-empowerment through education and literacy, spiritual awakening, and independent-mindedness and even defiance in the face of oppression.

Hence, Wilson created her own unique literary contribution, drawing on the techniques of her white female contemporaries when it suited her tale and borrowing the techniques of slave narrators when it fit her purpose. In addition, Wilson was distinctive in speaking of the virulent racism of the North and the near-servitude of many Northern African Americans due to extreme economic deprivation, rather than the horrors of Southern slavery or the lifestyles of Northern whites. She further broke new ground by realistically examining the life experiences of an ordinary African-American woman. Even without these distinctions, Wilson would play a significant role in the history of African-American literature, as she is widely acclaimed as the first African American to publish a novel in the United States (**William Wells Brown**'s *Clotel* [1853] and Frank J. Webb's *The Garies and Their Friends* [1857] were both published in England), the first African-American woman to publish a book of any kind in English, the fifth African American to publish a book of fiction in English, and one of the first two African-American women to publish a novel written in any language.

Wilson's protagonist, Alfrado ("Frado"), is born out of wedlock and intentionally abandoned by her white mother and then unintentionally abandoned (through death) by her black father. From that point on, Wilson powerfully shows that "slavery's shadows fall" in the North. Like Wilson herself, Frado is physically beaten, emotionally assaulted, starved, overworked, and mistreated by the mother ("Mrs. Bellmont") and one of the daughters ("Mary") of a white family to whom she is an indentured servant from early childhood. The men of the family appear relatively benign, but they do little to protect her from the abuse she receives at the hands of the females. Similarly, Frado, like Wilson, marries and becomes pregnant and is soon deserted by her husband. At the end of the novel, Frado and her infant are homeless and desperately impoverished. Her novel's ending certainly deviates from the typical ending of sentimental novels, in which the heroine is happily wedded at the conclusion of the book. Wilson closes her book with a direct appeal to her readers to help her gain enough money to retrieve her son from foster care. (Her preface made a similar appeal to her "colored brethren" to purchase her book to provide her a means of supporting herself and her son.)

Wilson finished writing her novel in 1859, and on August 18, she registered its copyright in the clerk's office of the district court of Massachusetts. On September 5, she paid to have the book published by an obscure Boston printer, the George C. Rand & Avery Company, known as a "job printer," meaning that they didn't have a regular major customer (such as a newspaper) but instead took on miscellaneous odd jobs at a set rate per job.

Tragically, Wilson's son died before she could earn enough to retrieve him. Less than six months after her book was published, early in 1860, the *Farmer's Cabinet* of Amherst, New Hampshire, published the obituary of George Mason Wilson, seven years old, the only son of "H. E. Wilson." The boy's death certificate listed his "color" as "Black" and identified his cause of death as "fever," a commonly cited cause of death at that time. No public records document Wilson's presence after 1863, so many scholars presume that she died about that time, but her exact location and date of death are not now known.

For generations, Wilson's work had languished in obscurity. In 1984, however, **Henry Louis Gates, Jr.**, and David Curtis uncovered evidence of her work. Up until that time, any literary scholars who had come across *Our Nig* had believed that the author was white, perhaps even a male. That year, Gates affirmed that Wilson was a black woman (based largely on the evidence of George's death certificate), thereby revealing her to be the first African American to publish a novel in the United States.

Although there is wide acceptance of Gates's contention, not everyone agrees with him. Gates himself notes astonishment that such a groundbreaking work would have been published without one single notice or review of the book in any publications of the day: No report of this historical work can be found in any of the contemporary abolitionist newspapers or magazines, African-American–governed periodicals, Boston daily newspapers, or even the Amherst *Farmer's Cabinet,* which recorded George's death. If any periodical of that time did notice Wilson's remarkable achievement, no scholar has been able to find any such notices or reviews to date, despite extensive searches.

Skeptics find this total lack of any notice or review all too remarkable, given that Wilson's Boston was a hotbed of zealous abolitionist reform and the news that an African-American woman had published such an outstanding work would have greatly benefited their cause. They find it similarly implausible to think that the growing number of African-American–owned and operated presses, eager to celebrate any noteworthy African Americans, would have ignored Wilson's work if they believed that she were of African-American descent. Similarly, historians, librarians, and bibliographers also overlooked Wilson's contribution for more than a century. Apparently, the first bibliographer to take notice of Wilson was Howard Mott, who quietly asserted that Wilson's book was the first published novel written by an African-American woman in his 1980 catalogue of materials for antiquarians. Mott had reached this conclusion based on the three letters of recommendation appended to the novel.

Gates counters this criticism by noting that Wilson's contemporaries may have been reluctant to make much of a novel that attacks the racism of the North, particularly villifying Northern white women. Perhaps they feared alienating Northern whites who favored abolition, wishing to focus on the horrors of Southern slavery rather than divert their readers' attention to the abuses of Northern economic oppression. Perhaps they wished not to stir up trouble because of Wilson's candid mention of a sexual relationship between a black man and a white woman (Frado's father and mother). Another argument might be made that the male-dominated presses of the day were reluctant to acknowledge the literary achievement of any woman, particularly one who had so little good to say about men of any color. Whatever the reason, Wilson's novel didn't sell well enough to lift her out of poverty or to earn her much—if any—popular or critical attention in her day.

REFERENCES: *BF:2000. EB-BH-CD. EBLG. MWEL. NAAAL.* Blockson, Charles L. (1998), *"Damn Rare": The Memoirs of an African-American Bibliophile* (Tracy, CA: Quantum Leap Publisher). Fay, Robert, in *EA-99.* Foreman, P. Gabrielle, in *OCAAL.* Gates, Henry Louis, Jr., in *BWA:AHE.* Johnson, Claudia Durst, in *G-99.* "*Our Nig* (1859)," in *1TESK.* Woodard, Helena, in *OCWW.*

Wilson, William Julius (12/20/1935–)
Nonfiction—sociology

A highly influential sociologist, Wilson has written several books that highlight the importance of socioeconomic status but that have often been wrongly misinterpreted to suggest that racism has ceased to affect African Americans. These include *Power, Racism and Privilege: Race Relations in Theoretical and Sociohistorical Perspective* (1973), *The Declining Significance of Race: Blacks and Changing American Institutions* (1978), *The Truly Disadvantaged*

(1987), *When Work Disappears: The World of the New Urban Poor* (1996), and *The Bridge over the Racial Divide: Rising Inequality and Coalition Politics* (1999). Wilson's scholarship has been recognized by his peers (elected 1989 president of the American Sociological Association; elected to the American Academy of Arts and Letters) and by the wider community (awarded a MacArthur Foundation fellowship, nicknamed the "genius award").

REFERENCES: *BDAA. EB-BH-CD.* Taub, Richard, in *EA-99.* Amazon.com, 1/2000.

Winfrey, Oprah (Gail) (1/29/1954–)
Autobiography, memoir, book-club host, nonfiction—health; talk-show host

Young Oprah had an inauspicious beginning. To start with, her mother, Vernita Lee, had intended to name her "Orpah," after a biblical character in the book of Ruth, but somehow the name ended up being spelled "Oprah" when it was registered by the clerk at the courthouse in Kosciusko, Mississippi, and the misspelling stuck. Oprah's mother wasn't married to her father, 20-year-old Vernon Winfrey, who had been on leave from the service when Oprah was conceived. After his furlough, Vernon returned to duty, unaware that he had fathered a child until he received a card from Vernita announcing Oprah's arrival and asking him to send money for clothing.

While Oprah was still an infant, Vernita realized that she'd have to leave Kosciusko if she was to have any chance of earning a decent living, given that she had no specific skills and very little education. Vernita left Oprah in the South with Vernon's mother, and she went to Milwaukee to earn enough to send for Oprah. At her grandmother's farm, Oprah learned to read by the time she was three years old and was in the third grade at school by the time she was six (having asked her kindergarten teacher to place her in the first grade and having skipped second grade as well). Oprah also started performing at an early age, making her first speaking appearance in an Easter program at her grandmother's beloved church when she was just three years old.

Oprah's grandmother was desperately poor, however, and when Vernita sent for her daughter to join her in Milwaukee, Oprah went. Vernita was working long hours as a domestic servant, for $50 per week, and she and Oprah shared a room in another woman's house. Oprah hated having so little of her mother's time and so little in the way of material comforts or diversions—and she made her feelings known very clearly. Pretty soon, Vernita threw up her hands and sent Oprah to live with Vernon in Nashville, Tennessee.

Vernon had married and owned his barbershop, and he and his wife welcomed Oprah's arrival during the summer of 1962. Like his mother, Vernon was active in his church, and he encouraged Oprah to get involved in the church's numerous activities and presentations. Oprah thrived in school and in the church, participating in pageants, choral performances, and whatever other opportunities she had to shine in the limelight. The following summer, however, Vernita pleaded with Vernon and his wife to have Oprah return to her for a visit, noting how much she had missed Oprah. Just as they had feared, Oprah stayed on with Vernita at the end of summer. Vernita was planning to marry a man who already had a son and daughter through a previous relationship, and she felt sure she could provide Oprah with a more pleasant home life than she had offered her before.

For Oprah, this decision proved emotionally disastrous. For one thing, she felt physically unattractive, and her mother reinforced her negative feelings toward herself. Even more detrimental to her emotional well-being, starting when she was just 9 years old, her male cousin and other male family members and acquaintances repeatedly sexually abused her. Like so many other young victims of sexual abuse, she felt confused and frightened, unsure of what to do, and guilty, sensing that somehow she was to blame for the bad behavior of her abusers. Initially, she continued to do well in school, and one of her teachers at Lincoln Middle School, Gene Abrams, helped her get a scholarship to a high-status school in an affluent suburb of Milwaukee. By the time she reached her teen years, however, Oprah was both troubled and troublesome, running away from home, destroying her family members' possessions, and faking a burglary. When Oprah was 14 years old, she became pregnant (and later miscarried), and Vernita again threw up her hands. She told Oprah that she could either go to a school for wayward girls or go to live with Vernon and his wife in Nashville.

Oprah knew that Vernon would again impose strict discipline and close supervision, but she still chose him over her other option. After initial resistance, she again started excelling academically, and started performing and speaking in public, partici-

Oprah Winfrey at a benefit for women entering the workforce, 1987 (UPI/Corbis-Bettmann)

pating in speech and drama clubs, and serving on the student council. While she was a senior at East High School, she got a job reading the news on local African-American–owned radio station WVOL. She also earned a partial scholarship to attend Tennessee State University (TSU) after having won an oratorical contest sponsored by the Elks Club. Although she would rather have gone to college out of town, perhaps in New England, she followed her father's wishes and attended TSU in Nashville.

At TSU, Oprah majored in speech and drama. Her freshman year, she was named Miss Black Nashville and Miss Black Tennessee and was a Miss Black America contestant. Meanwhile, she had moved from WVOL to WLAC, a more mainstream radio station. After she appeared in the beauty contests, WLAC's CBS television affiliate (later WTVF) offered Oprah a job as Nashville's first woman coanchor (and reporter), with a five-figure salary (*very* unusual for a college student in the early 1970s). In her new job, she was not only the first African American to anchor a newscast in Nashville but also one of the youngest persons (at age 19) to do so.

Pretty soon, Oprah's career success made it difficult for her to continue to conform to Vernon's strict guidance, and she looked for a job outside of Nashville. In 1976, a few months before Oprah would have earned her bachelor's degree, WJZ-TV, an ABC affiliate station in Baltimore, Maryland, offered her a job as reporter and coanchor, and she jumped at the chance to leave. (In 1988, TSU invited her to give a commencement address, at which they awarded her an honorary degree. Oprah has since established a scholarship fund at TSU, which pays the expenses for ten students whom she chooses and gets to know each year.)

At WJZ-TV, Oprah—and the station management—quickly discovered that her lack of journalistic training made her ill prepared for objective reporting. She had signed a very favorable contract, however, so the management needed to find a way to use the talents she had. They soon discovered that the very characteristics that essentially disqualified her from journalism made her beautifully suited to a talk-show format: empathy, passion and compassion, and subjectivity. From 1977 to 1984, she cohosted *Baltimore Is Talking* (or *People*

Are Talking) with Richard Sher, helping to boost the popularity of that show.

In 1984 she went on to host a half-hour television talk show, *A.M. Chicago,* which aired against the highly popular national talk-show host Phil Donahue; no previous hosts had been able to touch Donahue in the ratings. Within a month, however, Winfrey's ratings were equaling Donahue's. In 1985, the expanded hour-long show was renamed *The Oprah Winfrey Show,* and Donahue moved his show from Chicago to New York. In 1986 Winfrey's show was syndicated (broadcast nationally), and over time, she topped Donahue's national ratings. A decade later, she was still number one in national syndication, when she decided to refocus her show toward positive themes and away from sensationalism. In a television market crowded with sensationalized talk shows, she was taking a big chance, but she has continued to make syndication history. In 1997 Winfrey was still reaching about 15–20 million U.S. TV viewers every day, in addition to numerous other viewers in more than 130 other countries.

The show has earned Winfrey 6 Emmy awards for best host as well as 19 other Emmys. Her other awards include having been named one of the 25 most influential people in the world by *Time* magazine (1996) and earning the Woman of Achievement Award from the National Organization for Women (1986), the highly esteemed Peabody Award (both for her talk show and for her charitable work), and the National Association for the Advancement of Colored People Image Award four years in a row (1989–1992).

Winfrey's show has also made her quite wealthy. She owns her own production company, Harpo ("Oprah" spelled backward) and has assets sometimes estimated at $250 million (one fourth of $1 billion); in one year in the mid-1990s, her income was estimated at $105 million. In addition to funding scholarships, Winfrey finances countless charitable and philanthropic endeavors, having donated millions to her alma mater, other colleges and universities (e.g., Morehouse), the United Negro College Fund, the Harold Washington Library, a program for economically disadvantaged Chicago-area young girls, a program for training people of color to get jobs in TV and film, and numerous other worthy projects and institutions. She has also been instrumental in lobbying for national laws aimed at protecting children from abuse.

Harpo Productions has also enabled Winfrey to produce television and film projects she believes in, such as the 1988 miniseries *The Women of Brewster Place* (based on **Gloria Naylor**'s novel; with Winfrey acting in it), the 1998 television movie *The Wedding* (based on **Dorothy West**'s novel), and the 1998 film *Beloved* (based on **Toni Morrison**'s novel; with Winfrey starring in it). In addition to her roles in *Brewster Place* and in *Beloved,* Winfrey gave an Oscar-nominated performance in **Alice Walker**'s *The Color Purple* (1985).

In addition to promoting the works of individual women writers, Winfrey has done much to promote reading through "Oprah's Book Club," launched in 1996, which has highlighted such books as the *Norton Anthology of African American Literature.* Through her club, she announces in advance particular books to read and then discusses these books with viewers on subsequent shows. A profile on Oprah's Book Club essentially ensures that a book will become a best-seller.

Winfrey has been also involved with several book projects of her own: *Oprah: An Autobiography* (Oprah Winfrey and Joan Barthel, 1997); *In the Kitchen with Rosie: Oprah's Favorite Recipes* (Rosie Daley, with an intro by Oprah Winfrey, 1994); *The Uncommon Wisdom of Oprah Winfrey: A Portrait in Her Own Words* (Bill Adler and Oprah Winfrey, 1996, 1999); *Oprah Winfrey Speaks: Insights from the World's Most Influential Voice* (Janet C. Lowe and Oprah Winfrey, 1998); *Make the Connection: 10 Steps to a Better Body—And a Better Life* (Bob Greene and Oprah Winfrey, 1996, hardcover/audio cassettes; paperback, 1999); and *Journey to Beloved* (Oprah Winfrey, with photographer Ken Regan and with Jonathan Demme, 1998), about her decade-long process of getting **Toni Morrison**'s novel *Beloved* onto the silver screen.

REFERENCES: *BDAA. BF:2000. EB-BH-CD. G-99. PGAA. RWTC. SEW. WDAW.* Angelou, Maya, in *L:WW.* Dunn, Lois L., and Michelle Banks, in *BH2C.* Fay, Robert, in *EA-99.* Feder, Robert, in *WB-99.* Joyce, Donald Franklin, in *AA:PoP.* Thompson, Kathleen, in *BWA:AHE.* Amazon.com, 7/1999.

Wonder, Stevie (né Steveland Morris)
(5/13/1950–)
Songs

Blind from birth and musically gifted from an early age, at age 10 "Little Stevie Wonder" signed a contract with Motown Records. Since then,

Wonder has written many of the popular songs he has recorded (e.g., "I Was Made to Love Her," "Yester-Me, Yester-You, Yesterday," and "I Just Called To Say I Love You"). Many of his songs are intended to communicate messages important to him (e.g., "Happy Birthday" [to lobby for celebrating Martin Luther King, Jr.'s, birthday as a national holiday], "Don't Drive Drunk," and "Ebony and Ivory" [seeking racial harmony]). Wonder has also donated much of his time, effort, and money to numerous worthy causes such as Wonderland, a facility for research and treatment of eye disease.

REFERENCES: *EB-98. EB-BH-CD.* Fay, Robert, in *EA-99.*

Woodson, Carter G. (Godwin)

(12/19/1875–4/3/1950)

Nonfiction—history; journal founder and editor

Dire poverty didn't stop young Carter from getting the education he sought. While working in the coal mines of West Virginia, he managed to gain some schooling, at least some of the time, and after finishing high school (c. 1895), he went on to get a bachelor's degree, then a master's degree, and finally—in that exalted Cambridge, Massachusetts, institution of higher learning—he earned his Ph.D. in history from Harvard (1912). In Cambridge, he also taught school to pay his way through graduate school. Throughout all his studies, one thing emerged more clearly than all the things he saw in his readings: what *wasn't* in the history books he read. Where were all the African Americans while the European Americans were fighting this or that battle, making this or that discovery, or inventing this or that new product? Where were they in the world of business and industry? What had they contributed to the world of literature, art, and music? (Ironically, perhaps, Woodson never noticed the distinct absence of women in history, and he rarely mentioned their contributions in his work.)

These were not idle musings for Carter G. Woodson. No, he made up his mind to do something about these lacks. He spent the next four or so decades of his life doing whatever he could to unearth the unspoken contributions of African Americans to their country of birth, to probe the hidden lives of African Americans, and to unveil the secrets of African-American culture and lift up the glories of the African past. In 1915 Woodson cofounded the Association for the Study of Negro (renamed Afro-American) Life and History (ASNLH) in Washington, D.C., with the aim of collecting "sociological and historical data on the Negro, the study of peoples of African blood, the publishing of books in the field, and the promoting of harmony between the races by acquainting the one with the other." Through the ASNLH, young scholars were encouraged to conduct research and to publish their findings. Natural outgrowths of this association were two journals: The *Journal of Negro History* (starting in 1916) was aimed at scholars, and the *Negro History Bulletin* (starting in 1937) was intended to aid schoolteachers from the primary grades through high school. Another vehicle for scholars in this field was the ASNLH's Associated Publishers, which was established (in 1920, 1921, or 1922) to put out publications (e.g., books and other materials) on African-American history that would otherwise never reach their increasingly numerous readers.

Woodson's own works in this field were probably enough to justify the establishment of Associated Publishers. His 20 or so books include many that he authored, such as *Education of the Negro Prior to 1861* (1915), *A Century of Negro Migration* (1918), *The History of the Negro Church* (1921), *Negro Makers of History* (1928), *The Rural Negro* (1930), *The African Background Outlined* (1936/1969), and *African Heroes and Heroines* (1939/1944/1969). Important collections that he edited include *Negro Orators and Orations* (1925); *Mind of the Negro as Reflected in Letters Written During the Crisis, 1800–1860* (1926); *African Myths, Together with Proverbs, a Supplementary Reader Composed of Folk Tales from Various Parts of Africa* (1928/1972); and *The Works of Francis J. Grimké* (1942, 4 vols.).

Two of the books he authored deserve special notice. First, for decades, his *The Negro in Our History* (1922; 10th ed., 1962) was the primary textbook on African-American history, used chiefly in colleges but also in high schools. Second, his *The Mis-Education of the Negro* (1933/1972) stimulated a lot of thought. The title itself offers an idea of where he was going with his book. He saw the miseducation of African Americans as a tragic waste of potential, and he urged readers to focus on developing the most precious resource of the African-American community: the minds of black people. He pointed out the absence of African Americans in textbooks and in the curricula, starting in the primary grades and continuing through college and even into graduate schools.

He repudiated the self-loathing that a flawed education can provoke.

One of the ways in which Woodson attempted to correct the educational failures he saw was by initiating Negro History Week (starting in 1926). Initially set for the second week in February, embracing the birthdays of **Frederick Douglass** and Abraham Lincoln, the celebration has since expanded to make all of February Black History Month. A lifelong bachelor, Woodson devoted his every waking moment and his every last dime to his noble purpose. In gratitude for all he gave, he is called the "Father of Black History."

—*Tonya Bolden*

REFERENCES: *BDAA. E-98. EB-98. SMKC.* Ashwill, Gary, in *OCAAL*. Bolden, Tonya (1997), *Through Loona's Door: A Tammy and Owen Adventure with Carter G. Woodson* (Oakland, CA: Corporation for Cultural Literacy). Myers, Aaron, in *EA-99*.

Wright, Jay (c. 1935–)
Poems

Wright's mother is of African and Native American descent, and his father is of Cherokee, African-American, and Irish-American descent. Jay himself spent most of his childhood living in foster homes in Albuquerque, New Mexico. When he reached his teens, he moved to San Pedro, California, to live with his father. There, he started playing the bass and playing Minor League baseball. After high school, he served in the army medical corps (1954–1957), spending most of his time in Germany, from which he traveled extensively throughout Europe whenever he could. After his military service ended, he used the G.I. Bill (government allotments to pay for veterans' education) to attend the University of California at Berkeley, from which he graduated (in comparative literature) within three years. From Berkeley, he went to the Union Theological Seminary in New York, after which he went to Rutgers University (in 1962) to continue his postgraduate study of literature. In 1964 Wright took a year out to teach English and medieval history in Guadalajara, Mexico (at the Butler Institute). After returning to Rutgers, he completed all his coursework for a doctorate in comparative literature.

While at Rutgers, Wright lived in Harlem and associated with writers of the **Black Arts movement**, such as **Henry Dumas**, LeRoi Jones (**Amiri Baraka**), and **Larry Neal**. Unlike these writers, Wright took more of a cross-cultural approach in his writing, embracing both African-American cultural traditions and European-American ones. His poems traverse Africa, Asia, the Caribbean, South America, Western Europe, and North American locales from New Hampshire (where he has lived since 1973) to Mexico to California. Wright wrote some book-length poems (*Dimensions of History,* 1976; *The Double Invention of Komo,* 1980; and *Explications/Interpretations,* 1984), as well as his poetry collections *The Homecoming Singer* (1971), *Soothsayers and Omens* (1976), *Selected Poems of Jay Wright* (1987, edited by Robert B. Stepto), and *Boleros* (1991). Wright has also been recognized as a musician, an educator, and a MacArthur fellow.

REFERENCES: Kutzinski, Vera M., in *OCAAL*.

Wright, Richard (Nathaniel)
(9/4/1908–11/28/1960)
Autobiography, novels, short stories, essays, nonfiction, travelogues, poems; journal editor

Richard was born on a sharecropper's farm (formerly a plantation) in Roxie, Mississippi, where he was immersed in the hateful hostility of the local white folks. His area of Mississippi, near Natchez, has been called one of the most racist regions in the most racist state in the land. Richard's grandparents had been slaves, and his alcoholic father fared little better as a sharecropper. When Richard was three or four years old, his father moved the family to Memphis, Tennessee, where he abandoned Richard and Richard's mother and younger brother (Leon Alan) two years later, running off with another woman.

Richard's mother, Ella Wilson Wright, had been a schoolteacher, but in Memphis, with two young sons to support, she had to get work right away in a series of low-paying, unskilled jobs. In a desperate attempt to eke out enough of a living to support her children, Ella moved them from town to town and from state to state, everywhere finding it impossible to keep her children from their perennial companion, hunger. (Anyone who flips through Wright's autobiography *Black Boy* will see the word *hunger* appearing frequently; in fact, Wright had originally called his full autobiography *American Hunger.*) Ella also suffered from health problems, including a stroke that partially paralyzed her, and at one point Richard and his brother were briefly placed in an orphanage.

Richard Wright at his desk before the publication of White Man, Listen!, *1957 (Archive Photos)*

When Ella recovered, she retrieved her sons, taking them first to Jackson, Mississippi, and then to Elaine, Arkansas. In Elaine, they stayed with Ella's sister and her husband, a successful property owner. Richard adored his uncle, and the Wright family enjoyed an all-too-brief period of respite from desperate poverty and deprivation. All too soon, his uncle was lynched and murdered by whites who seized his property. Terrified, Ella, her sister, and the boys left town and returned to drifting from place to place, with Ella's ill health increasingly limiting her ability to provide for the boys. After a while, young Leon was sent to live with relatives in the North, and Richard was sent back down to Mississippi to be passed around among his maternal grandparents and other relatives in Jackson and other places in the deep South. (Between his moves with his mother and his moves among relatives, Richard figured he had moved about 20 times.)

After a year of being passed around, Richard settled into the household dominated by his tyrannical grandmother, a fanatical Seventh-Day Adventist. She and he were at odds from the start, and she was soon openly—and lastingly—hostile toward him. Prior to the move to his grandmother's home, Richard's formal schooling had been a string of segregated—separate and definitely unequal—schools. His constant hunger, frequent illnesses, sporadic attendance, frequent moves, and other distractions from concentrating on his schoolwork made it unlikely that Richard would profit much from his formal education, although he enjoyed writing from an early age. While in ninth grade, his story "The Voodoo of Hell's Half-Acre" was published in the local black-owned Jackson, Mississippi, *Southern Register.*

Following his completion of the ninth grade, Richard's formal education ended. His informal education suffered too. When he was living with his grandmother and at last had a fairly consistent place to call home, her zealously held religious beliefs opposed nonreligious books of any kind—especially novels—and she barred them from her home. Fascinated with literature, Richard surreptitiously pored over whatever cheap fiction he could put his hands on, but he had to carefully guard it from discovery by his grandmother and his aunt.

Anyone who saw Richard in 1925, with this inauspicious beginning—desperate poverty, inadequate nutrition, poor health, a highly dysfunctional family life, utter lack of a decent education, oppressive racism including racial prejudice, hostility, and segregation—would surely have concluded that the chances of his being an acclaimed writer, gifted in his command of the language and of literature, were between zero and none. Richard himself concluded that if he were to have a chance for a decent life of any kind, he would have to escape the racism of the deep South and the anything-but-warm bosom of his family. To be sure, Richard's childhood gave him a bleak outlook that continued throughout his life, but the surprising observation is that he felt any hope at all for his own future based on his early experiences. In 1925, he left his family and Mississippi behind and proceeded North to Memphis, Tennessee, desperately hoping that life could hold some possibility for anything but hatred, hunger, and hopelessness.

In Memphis, Richard roomed with a warm, loving family and found work as an errand boy for an optical company. There, his hunger for literature was again whetted, and he voraciously devoured whatever literature he could put his hands on, starting with national magazines such as *Atlantic Monthly, Harper's,* and *American Mercury.* He was particularly interested in the writing by the editor of *American Mercury* magazine, H. L. Mencken. When he heard that Mencken had written books, he was interested in reading more. He couldn't afford to buy books on his errand-boy salary, and even if he could, a black person seen buying books would immediately become suspect and would call unwanted attention to himself. Lynchings were still quite common in the South at that time, and unwanted attention was *definitely* unwanted.

The library in Memphis was for whites only, so he knew that he would have to find a white person to help him get access to the library's books. His boss at the optical company was a Northerner, and he treated Richard well enough, so Richard

asked him if he could use his library card to check out some books. Although his boss was at first reluctant, he later agreed to give Richard his library card, saying he could use his wife's library card for checking out books of his own.

Even with the library card of a white man in hand, Richard knew he couldn't just walk in, present the card, and ask for books. He would need to convince the librarian that he was obtaining books for the white man to read. He forged a note to the librarian, saying, "Dear Madam: Will you please let this nigger boy have some books by H. L. Mencken?" The ploy worked. The librarian never suspected that a note referring to "this nigger boy" would have been forged by the young man presenting the note. She was a little annoyed that the requestor didn't specify which book by Mencken he wanted, but she still complied with the request. Richard was careful not to glance at the book until he got home.

In his autobiography *Black Boy,* Wright described his experience of reading Mencken's book in this way: "I opened [Mencken's] *A Book of Prefaces* and began to read. I was jarred and shocked by the style, the clear, clean, sweeping sentences. Why did he write like that? And how did one write like that? I stood up, trying to realize what reality lay behind the meaning of the words. Yes, this man was fighting, fighting with words. He was using words as a weapon, using them as one would use a club. Could words be weapons? Well, yes, for here they were. Then, maybe, perhaps, I would use them as a weapon?"

After that, Richard read other books by Mencken, as well as books by Sherwood Anderson, Fyodor Dostoyevsky, Theodore Dreiser, Alexandre Dumas (a French writer of African descent), Frank Harris, O. Henry, Sinclair Lewis, and Edgar Lee Masters, among others. After two years of Richard's self-education in Memphis, he moved North to Chicago (in 1927), where he continued his self-guided course of study, reading more modern, experimental authors such as Henry James, Marcel Proust, and Gertrude Stein. Wright later reflected that in Stein's *Three Lives,* her character Melanctha was among the few African-American characters portrayed by a white author, who was believably realistic. Wright later said of this awakened passion, "I had once tried to write, had once reveled in feeling, had let my crude imagination roam, but the impulse to dream had been slowly beaten out of me by experience. Now it surged up again and I hungered for books, new ways of looking and seeing."

In Chicago, Wright was joined by masses of other African Americans fleeing the harshness and hopelessness of the Jim Crow South. Once there, he worked in a series of menial jobs until he heard that jobs at the post office paid quite well, particularly for someone with as little formal education as Wright. Wright took the competitive civil-service exam and scored high on it. The federal government was barred from considering race in hiring decisions, so Wright was hired as a postal clerk. At the post office, Wright worked alongside blacks and whites as coequals. This was the first time in his life when he had interacted with whites on an equal footing. Many of his coworkers were left-wing intellectuals, and one of his white coworkers was Abraham Aaron, who invited him to find out about communism at a Chicago-area John Reed Club, a fellowship of writers with left-wing views.

As Wright attended meetings of the (mostly white) John Reed Club, he felt increasingly drawn to communism, as did many workers, writers, and other intellectuals during this time. As the Great Depression skulked across the landscape, many observers felt that capitalism was disproportionately impoverishing and oppressing workers at the bottom of the economic scale, compared with capitalist owners of companies at the top of the economic scale. Communists asserted the absolute right of all races to be given equal rights and equal opportunities and was dedicated to changing the political and economic system so that the kind of desperate poverty Wright had known as a youth would be eliminated.

By 1933, Wright had joined the Communist Party, despite his numerous disagreements with the party regarding Marxist doctrine, especially concerning the relationship of African Americans to the U.S. political, economic, and social system. Other than his first two published short stories ("Voodoo . . . ," published in the Jackson newspaper, and "Superstition," published in *Abbott's Monthly Magazine,* 1931 [see **Robert Abbott**]), most of his early short stories, essays, and poems were printed in various communist-affiliated or at least leftist periodicals (newspapers and journals). Wright continued to be associated with the Communist Party and leftist causes until 1944, but when the John Reed Club disbanded (in 1935), Wright turned his attention to writing longer fiction works, rather than the short, principally nonfiction

pieces he had written earlier. In 1937 Wright's focus on literature, rather than rigidly ideological polemics, led to strong disagreements with the party; in 1942 he officially resigned from the Communist Party, chiefly over artistic freedom but also because the party failed to speak out against racial discrimination in the military during World War II as well as other issues of civil rights for African Americans; and in 1944 his break with the party became public when "I Tried to Be a Communist," an excerpt from *American Hunger,* was published in the *Atlantic Monthly.* He later elaborated his rationale in an essay included in Richard Crossman's symposium anthology of essays by former communists, *The God That Failed* (1950).

In 1935 Wright got a job with the Illinois Federal Writers' Project (FWP) of the Works Progress Administration (WPA). This was the first job at which Wright was paid to write full-time—writing travel guides and doing historical research for the FWP. In 1936 Wright also became involved in the Chicago-area Negro Federal Theatre, working as its press agent and literary adviser, as well as being involved in various dramatic productions at the theater. During this time, he also joined Chicago's new South Side Writers' Group, where he met **Arna Bontemps**, a fellow writer and FWP employee (and also a former postal employee and a Seventh-Day Adventist, though Wright was definitely not a practicing Adventist after his youth). There, he also got to know sociologist **Horace Cayton, Jr.** (later a close friend), **Frank Marshall Davis**, **Fenton Johnson**, **Margaret Walker** (who was a close friend while he was in Chicago and remained his friend for a short time afterward), and **Theodore Ward**.

In May of 1937, Wright moved to Harlem, where he initially continued to work for the FWP while contributing articles and poems to such leftist magazines as the *Partisan Review, Left Front, New Masses,* and *International Literature* as well as the *Communist Daily Worker* (of which he became the Harlem editor and chief correspondent). By the time he reached New York, he had also written at least two of the four novellas in his collection *Uncle Tom's Children* and most of his manuscript for *Lawd Today!* the first novel he wrote (which wasn't published until after his death).

One of his earliest pieces published in New York, however, was "Blueprint for Negro Writing," Wright's outline of what African-American literature should be—as distinct from what it had been. In Wright's view, the black writers of the **Harlem Renaissance** (and earlier eras) had kow-towed to wealthy white patrons and bourgeois blacks. He urged fellow writers to turn away from European-American–centered writing and to embrace both Marxism and African-American–centered writing targeted to working-class African-American readers. "Blueprint" was printed in the first (and only) issue of *New Challenge* magazine, which he coedited with **Dorothy West** and Marian Minus.

The first of Wright's book-length projects to appear in print was his collection *Uncle Tom's Children: Four Novellas* (1938). Each of the novellas shows how the racial hatred of the Jim Crow South affected various African-American males and how they attempted to resist or escape those effects. Although the book sold well and was critically acclaimed, Wright had hoped his readers would come away with a greater awareness of how racism harms all Americans, not just its direct victims. The stories distinctively blend African-American literary traditions with then-contemporary Marxist thinking as well as Wright's personal take on his deplorably miserable experiences in the deep South. Also, he never hesitated to twist the plot as needed to convey the political and race-related statements he wished to make. Wright's opinion of the work differed from those of his critics: He called the stories too sentimental.

The original 1938 edition comprised these four novellas: "Big Boy Leaves Home" (a *Story* magazine prize winner when it was first published in 1936), "Fire and Cloud" (second-prize winner of an O. Henry award and first-prize winner of a 1938 *Story* magazine award), "Down by the Riverside" (written while Wright was still living in Chicago), and "Long Black Song." Although "Long Black Song" is purportedly written from the point of view of a woman (a rare stance in Wright's work), the protagonist's experiences are still described in terms of their effects on men (e.g., when she is raped, it is described as an affront to her husband's pride and masculinity rather than as a violation of her body and sense of humanity). One critic pointed out that the protagonists resist racism in three different ways: through individual escape ("Big Boy"), through protecting the family ("Down by the Riverside" and "Long Black Song"), and through banding together with others to take collective action ("Fire and Cloud"). Three of the four stories end with tragic deaths (e.g., at

the hands of lynch mobs, appallingly common in those times).

Wright's collection was awarded the 1938 *Story* magazine prize for the best book written by anyone involved in the WPA's FWP. It also won Wright a 1939 Guggenheim fellowship with enough money ($2,500) to stop writing for the *Daily Worker,* to quit his New York FWP job, and to focus on writing a novel full time. About this time, Wright married Rose Meadman, a Russian-Jewish dance teacher; the couple separated in 1940 and divorced soon after. The following March (1941), Wright married Ellen Poplar, the Polish-Jewish head of his cell in the Communist Party in New York. Later on, Ellen and Richard had two daughters: Julia (b. 4/14/1942) and Rachel (b. 1/17/1949).

In 1940 a second edition of the volume of novellas was expanded to include an introductory semiautobiographical essay, "The Ethics of Living Jim Crow," and a fifth story, "Bright and Morning Star," and the subtitle was changed to "Five Long Stories" (instead of "Four Novellas"). Many critics observed that these additions not only added little but even disrupted the integrity of the original work. Wright reworked much of "The Ethics of Living Jim Crow" to form the central core of his 1945 autobiography, *Black Boy.* A 1993 reissue paperback includes all the works from the 1940 edition as well as passages that were deleted by the publishers in the original and earlier expanded editions.

The novel Wright finished writing (while living on his Guggenheim fellowship money) was *Native Son,* published in 1940, the same year as his expanded version of *Uncle Tom's Children*. The novel was inspired by the actual case of Robert Nixon of Chicago. (Because Wright was living in Brooklyn while writing the book, he asked his old pal Margaret Walker to send him newspaper clippings about the case from Chicago, which she did. Around the time he finished writing the book, however, he abruptly ended their friendship.) The story revolves around Bigger Thomas, an African American from the South (Mississippi) who has moved to the urban North (Chicago) in the hope of finding greater opportunities for himself. He finds work as a chauffeur for a wealthy white family, in which the mother is blind and the daughter is involved with a young white communist man. The daughter and her boyfriend attempt to befriend Bigger and to treat him as an equal, but their behavior only confuses Bigger, as he doesn't know how to respond to their overtures. On one occasion, he drives the young woman home after she has had too much to drink, so he helps her to her bed. While he is beside her bed, her mother comes to the bedroom door, calling to her daughter to see whether the girl is home yet. Fearing the consequences of being in a drunk white girl's room, he puts a pillow over her head to keep her quiet until her mother leaves. Unfortunately, the girl suffocates to death before her mother has gone.

Up until this time, Bigger has not intentionally done anything wrong, but again fearing what will happen to him if he is found out, he burns the girl's body in the family's furnace. He then flees and meets up with his girlfriend, to whom he tells all. As his girlfriend sleeps, he suddenly realizes that she, too, is now a threat to him, and he intentionally kills her. When his link to the deaths is discovered, the white girl's boyfriend gets a Communist Party attorney to defend him (partly to use him as a cause célèbre for the party), but Bigger's conviction and death sentence are inevitable. Wright's story shows how the environment in which a person lives almost fatalistically determines what the person will do and what will befall the person. (This outlook reflects the dialectical materialism of communist philosophy, which Richard embraced.)

Wright purposely wrote Bigger's character to be unsympathetic, so that the intensity of his story would be, as he said, "so hard and deep that [readers] would have to face it without the consolation of tears." Indeed, Bigger's character inspires anger and fear, not sympathy. (Wright had titled the first of three parts of the book "Fear.") Even so, Wright's editors had toned down his original manuscript, and it wasn't until 1992 that the restored original text that Wright intended was published. Jack Miles, a *Los Angeles Times* reviewer (December 1997, quoted in Amazon.com), noted, "This new edition gives us a *Native Son* in which the key line in the key scene is restored, to the great good fortune of American letters. The scene as we now have it is central both to an ongoing conversation among African-American writers and critics and to the consciousness among all American readers of what it means to live in a multiracial society in which power splits along racial lines." In 1940, however, Wright's toned-down text stirred a maelstrom of heated response.

Native Son also gained critical acclaim and commercial success right away, virtually a first for an African-American writer at that time. To this day, literary scholars and critics credit it as a landmark in African-American literature, not just for its success, but also for its heralding of a new era of protest novels, which were to come into vogue following World War II. Within three weeks of its publication, 200,000 copies had been sold, breaking a 20-year sales record for its mainstream publisher, Harper & Brothers. It even outsold John Steinbeck's Pulitzer Prize–winning *Grapes of Wrath,* which appeared at about the same time. It was also a Book-of-the-Month Club selection—probably the surest sign of commercial success at the time, much like being chosen for Oprah's Book Club now—the first such selection of a book by an African-American author, and it was reviewed in every major periodical in the country.

Most literary reviewers enthusiastically raved about the work, whether they were American or foreign, black or white, communist or not. Critics particularly remarked on Wright's skill in forcing white American readers to see their own part in Bigger's crime, despite depicting Bigger unsympathetically. Nonetheless, many African Americans criticized Wright for depicting yet another African-American victim and for portraying him as little more than a stereotype; they criticized the unsympathetic characterization with which Wright was so pleased and of which many of his critics were so appreciative. Naturally, conservative whites refuted Wright's theme that Bigger's environment created who he was; in their view, he was just a bad man, doing bad things—no excuses!

Wright was invited to travel all over the country, giving lectures, talks, and readings, and the book thrust Wright not only to national prominence but also to international celebrity; it was translated into at least six languages and quickly sold more than 300,000 copies worldwide. (The money from the sales of *Native Son* enabled Wright to buy his mother a house in Chicago as well as to purchase a lot of freedom from want for himself.) Among other honors, it earned Wright a prestigious Spingarn Medal from the National Association for the Advancement of Colored People (NAACP). Perhaps one of the greatest honors Americans give to novels is to adapt them to stage and to film. Wright and a collaborator (at first, Paul Green, and then John Houseman) adapted the novel as a play (*Native Son: The Biography of a Young American: A Play in Eleven Scenes to Be Performed without Intermission*), which Orson Welles dramatized on Broadway; the play's Broadway run was followed by a national tour. A decade later, Wright participated in making the play into a film (*Sangre Negra*), produced in Argentina, with Wright playing the part of Bigger. (Critics noted that he didn't miss his calling by returning to writing instead of sticking to acting.)

Wright's next project was *Twelve Million Black Voices: A Folk History of the American Negro* (1941), a pictorial (photographic) history of Africa's descendants in the United States. Most of the photographs were culled from the federal government's Farm Security Administration files. Wright's underlying Marxist sentiments were evident throughout the text. In it, he analyzed how the Great Migration from the rural South to the urban North affected African Americans in both locations. In his view, lack of property ownership oppressed African Americans both North and South. The Southern blacks who were left behind were doomed to sharecropping and tenant farming, unable to reap the rich rewards of their own labor or of the crops they sowed. The Northern blacks were doomed to perpetually paying rent to live in kitchenette apartments they would never own and to working in lightless, airless factories, with their labor enriching the owners of the factories but doing little to lift them out of poverty. (The U.S. government didn't take kindly to Wright's commentary, believing it to be subversive and perhaps even seditious. In 1943, they started keeping a file on Wright's writings and activities.) In 1988, a paperback edition of the book was reissued by Thunder's Mouth Press.

Although Wright continued to write shorter works (e.g., his 1944 surrealistic novella *The Man Who Lived Underground*), his next major work was his powerful autobiography *Black Boy: A Record of Childhood and Youth* (1945). In it, Wright candidly and compellingly tells readers how he experienced life as a boy in the Jim Crow South, bereft of the basic sustenance of plentiful and nourishing food, a consistent place to call home, and a dependable and loving family. Avoiding sentimentality, he shows his readers exactly how his hellish upbringing affected him. He never tries to evoke sympathy, yet readers cannot help but wish to shield young Richard from the harsh brutalities of his early environment.

The book, another Book-of-the-Month Club selection, outsold even *Native Son,* having sold more than 400,000 copies within months of its publication. It was also translated into six languages and was critically acclaimed, both at the time and by literary scholars ever since. Many don't hesitate to call it Wright's finest work. Originally, Wright had written a more comprehensive autobiography, which he had titled *American Hunger.* His publishers cut out the second section on his adulthood, and this section was never published during Wright's lifetime, although it was published as a separate volume in 1977.

More recently, the prestigious Library of America reunited the two as the originally intended single work, which also restores much of Wright's original text (again, edited out by his publisher at the time). The Library of America volume, *Richard Wright, Later Works: Black Boy (American Hunger) / The Outsider / 2 Books in 1* (1991, edited by **Arnold Rampersad**), also includes a novel Wright wrote years later. (Another volume published by Library of America is *Richard Wright, Early Works: Lawd Today! / Uncle Tom's Children / Native Son* (1991, edited by Arnold Rampersad). In reviewing these volumes, Alfred Kazin, in the *New York Times Book Review* (quoted in Amazon.com) said, "Superb . . . The Library of America has insured that most of Wright's major texts are now available as he wanted them to be read. . . . Most important of all is the opportunity we now have to hear a great American writer speak with his own voice about matters that still resonate at the center of our lives." Andrew Delbanco, in *New Republic* (also quoted in Amazon.com), observed, "The publication of this new edition is not just an editorial innovation, it is a major event in American literary history." A paperback edition of the complete autobiography was published by Perennial Classics in 1998.

During this time, Wright also wrote a novella for juveniles: *Rite of Passage,* which wasn't published until 1993 (with an afterword by Rampersad; 1996, paperback). In it, 15-year-old Johnny Gibbs takes home his usual straight-A report, when he is greeted with shocking news: The people whom he believed to be his parents (since he was six months old) are actually his foster parents, and a heartless bureaucrat has decided that it is time for him to be switched to a new family. Confused, hurt, betrayed, he flees into the cold, damp night, feeling utterly alone, orphaned, lost, homeless, and hungry for the first time in his life. Soon, he hooks up with a brutal street gang, and after winning a challenge to the gang's leader (rather improbable, but it *is* fiction), he participates in a mugging and then becomes embroiled in a theft scheme with corrupt police officers who pay the gang members to steal.

Despite Wright's literary successes, he was not immune to racial prejudice. As an example, in 1940, Wright was returning to the United States from Mexico, and fellow writer John Steinbeck was at the train station saying good-bye to Wright. Before Wright got on the train, Steinbeck urged Wright to ship, rather than carry in his bags, some communist literature he had. Steinbeck warned that Wright would have trouble getting the materials through U.S. customs at the Texas border. Indeed, the customs official in Texas started to focus on the books, when he noticed Wright's typewriter as well. The official was so shocked to see an African American who identified himself as a writer that the official neglected to pursue his interest in the books.

Far more insulting and distressing incidents occurred every hour of every day, everywhere in the United States, and in 1946 Wright happily accepted an invitation from the French government to be hailed as a literary luminary. (Actually, noted existentialist Jean-Paul Sartre had invited him originally, but when the U.S. government refused to give him a passport, Gertrude Stein, Claude Levi-Strauss, and Dorothy Norman helped him get an official invitation, which smoothed the passport authorization process.) The contrast between his gracious reception in France and his hostile one at home in the United States was stark. Having abandoned all hope of eliminating—or even diminishing—racism in the United States, in August 1947 Wright and his family settled permanently in Paris.

In Paris, Wright became associated with existentialist writers such as Jean-Paul Sartre, Albert Camus, and Simone de Beauvoir, as well as fellow expatriates such as Gertrude Stein. Although their cultures and life experiences sharply differed, Wright shared their sense of alienation. His own outlook fit well with that of existentialism, a philosophy that highlighted each individual's isolation in an inhospitable and apathetic cosmos. To many literary scholars, the move to Paris may have given Wright his first opportunity to experience life without feeling the constant oppressive burden of racism every moment of every day, but it had deleterious effects on his writing. They suggest that it blunted the edge of his passionate opposition to racism, deprived him of hearing the lyrical nuances and cadences of African-American speech,

dimmed his memories of his tortured childhood and youth, and removed him from the changing political, economic, and social circumstances of African Americans (e.g., the emerging civil rights movement).

Back in the United States (in 1947), Wright was targeted by Senator Joseph McCarthy's red-baiting witch hunts, searching for "dirty commies" in every nook and cranny. Even though Wright had pointedly resigned from the Communist Party in the early 1940s, he was still subject to CIA and FBI surveillance. This scrutiny continued even after he returned to France, where he spent the rest of his life. For instance, he frequently had to report to the U.S. embassy in Paris to undergo lengthy interrogations about his activities and his writings. He had trouble getting a passport, and he was prevented from moving to England by both the U.S. and the British governments, even though his family had moved to London in anticipation that he would soon follow. The U.S. State Department may even have interfered with the publication and sales of his books, although that has not been confirmed, and his U.S. sales would probably have waned in any case.

Though Wright's U.S. sales declined (and therefore his income), his literary output did not. He became involved with poets and novelists of the Negritude movement, including Léopold (Sédar) Senghor and Aimé Césaire, with whom he founded *Présence Africaine*. This association and his travels throughout Europe and Africa during the 1950s gave Wright a broader global perspective on how economic and racial oppression affects persons around the world. Communism had offered him a philosophical framework for taking a global view, but his international experiences and associations put flesh on this skeleton.

During his Parisian exile, Wright wrote seven more books: three more novels, a collection of lectures, a conference report, and two other works of nonfiction. His novels include *The Outsider* (1953; reprinted in 1993, with lengthy editorial cuts restored), *Savage Holiday* (1954; reprinted 1965, 1995), and *The Long Dream* (1958). His conference report was *The Color Curtain: A Report of the Bandung Conference* (1956; reprinted in 1995), about the 1955 Conference of Asian and African nations held in Bandung, Indonesia; and his lecture collection was *White Man, Listen!* (1957), essays gathered from a European lecture series (1950–1956) on racial issues from a global perspective. His other two nonfiction works were *Black Power: A Record of Reactions in a Land of Pathos* (1954), about his observations of colonialism and independence movements in Africa, particularly the Gold Coast; and *Pagan Spain* (1957), a highly readable travelogue and political commentary on Spain.

Among the last Americans to see Wright was **Langston Hughes**, who visited Wright at Wright's home just before Wright entered a clinic. At the time, Wright was just 52 years old, but he was again impoverished, in ill health (with amoebic dysentery), separated from his family, constantly harassed with interrogations by federal agents, and estranged from many fellow expatriates and French existentialists for various reasons. (Wright's life was characterized by frequent instances of close associations terminated abruptly because of conflict or perceived betrayal, perhaps one of the consequences of his turbulent childhood and youth.) Two days after Hughes's visit, Wright died, with the cause of death listed as heart attack. Wright's chief biographer, Michel Fabre, has said that all of these factors combined to lead to Wright's premature death.

Others have suggested more sinister causes due to foul play, noting that he died in a hospital almost immediately following an injection; he was cremated right away, thereby making autopsy impossible; the cremation was performed without familial consent; and in fact, his family wasn't informed of his death until after the cremation. Some have even posited that he was killed by the CIA or other federal agents. Fabre disagrees, saying that their frequent harassment may have contributed to Wright's stress and his early demise, but Fabre doubts that they directly assaulted him.

In any case, when Wright died, he had been working on several literary projects, including a short-story collection, some radio plays, a novella, and an autobiographical essay. Following his death, several of his works have been published. In 1961 a collection of short stories he had written previously, *Eight Men,* was published (paperback reprint, 1996). Each of the stories in the collection presents a different slant on how black men struggle to survive in the racial hatred of the white-dominated United States.

In 1963 the novel he had written in the mid-1930s, *Lawd Today!* was published by Walker & Co. The novel humorously treats the events in the life of an angry, unhappy African-American postal worker in Chicago on one day: February 12, 1936.

Wright had originally titled the manuscript "Cesspool." The 1963 version, like so many of Wright's works, was expurgated, and in 1993 the Northeastern Library of Black Literature published an unexpurgated paperback edition two years after the Library of America published an uncut version in their *Early Works* volume (1991, hardcover).

In 1978 Wright's biographer (Michel Fabre) and his widow (Ellen Wright) collaborated to edit *A Richard Wright Reader.* Not intended to be a comprehensive tome, it omits some of his works and includes only excerpts from some of his novels and other book-length works. It also includes some of his short stories, his journalistic pieces, his memoirs, his poems, and even some of his correspondence. In addition, Fabre introduced the works, offering an overview of Wright's contribution and setting his work in historical context.

Early in his career, Wright had written poetry, and during his final illness, he again turned to writing poems. About two years before he died, Wright was introduced to an English translation of Japanese haiku. Wright was captivated by the form and proceeded to write more than 4,000 haiku poems, strictly following the traditional three-line format (with five syllables in the first line, seven in the second, and five in the last line), with some implicit or explicit reference to the season within the body of the poem. Before he died, Wright had chosen a few more than 800 of his haikus for publication. It took nearly 40 years for them to reach print, but in 1998 a hardcover collection was published, *Haiku: This Other World* (edited by Yoshinobu Hakatuni and Robert L. Tener). Two of the poems quoted in *Library Journal* (September 15, by Judy Clarence, quoted in Amazon.com) illustrate the gentle tenderness and even whimsy of Wright's final writings: "As my delegate / The spring wind has its fingers / In a young girl's hair"; "For seven seconds / The steam from the train whistle / Blew out the spring moon."

The breadth and variety of Wright's literary contribution cannot be doubted, and his contributions to each genre were significant. Probably most important, however, were his contributions to contemporary African-American novels and autobiographies. His novel *Native Son* and his autobiography *Black Boy* are often required reading in high schools and colleges throughout the land. Further, **James Baldwin** (whom he had befriended while living in Harlem), **Ralph Ellison** (who had been the best man at Wright's first wedding, during his Chicago days), and numerous other important writers have credited Wright with blazing the trail for fellow African-American novelists to follow. He pulled no punches in assaulting white America for its treatment of black compatriots, yet he never sentimentalized the victims of racism, and he frankly depicted the consequences of racism in terms of black rage and violence. In looking over his literary career, Wright could definitely answer "yes" to the questions he had asked himself in his youth, "Could words be weapons? . . . Then, maybe, perhaps, I would use them as a weapon?" Occasionally using them as a sledgehammer and at other times as a sharp-edged razor, he definitely mastered the ability to use words to disarm his readers and render them defenseless against his attacks on their beliefs about racism and their misconceptions about how many young black boys (and men) have been treated in white America.

REFERENCES: *AAL. BAL-1-P. BC. BDAA. BWA. EA-99. EB-BH-CD. EBLG. MWEL. NAAAL. NYTBC. OC20LE. PGAA. RG20. WDAA.* "Native Son (1940)" in *1TESK.* "Native Son," in *BF:2000.* Fisher, Vivian Njeri, in *BH2C.* Gayle, Addison, in *G-99.* Gibson, Donald B., in *OCAAL.* McKay, Nellie Y., in *WB-99.* Rampson, Nancy, in *AA:PoP.* Amazon.com, 7/1999.

Wright, Sarah E. (Elizabeth)

(12/9/1928–)

Novel, poems, essays, short stories, biography

In Wetipquin, Maryland, Sarah was born to Willis Charles and Mary Amelia Moore Wright. By the time she was in third grade, she was already starting to write, and her parents and teachers encouraged her to keep it up. At Howard University, she received further encouragement from renowned poet and literary critic **Sterling Allen Brown** and then from poet and novelist **Owen Dodson**. During her years at Howard (1945–1949), she also became active in various literary and journalistic organizations, and she was inspired by the writing of **Langston Hughes**, who became her lifelong friend.

After graduating from Howard, Wright first moved to New York City and then to Philadelphia, where she worked as a teacher and then in a publishing house. There, she also cofounded the Philadelphia Writers' Workshop, dedicated to promoting the work of African-American writers. In 1955, she and Lucy Smith coauthored their poetry collection *Give Me a Child* (1955), to which Wright contributed 7 of 17 poems about African Americans struggling to survive despite racist oppression. One such poem was her oft-anthologized "To Some Millions Who Survive Joseph Mander, Sr." Since its publication, she has contributed numerous short stories and essays to such publications as *Freedomways, American Pen,* the *Amsterdam News* (New York), **Black Scholar,** and *African American Review* (see **Black American Literature Forum**) as well as various anthologies.

In 1957 Wright returned to New York, where she was drawn to the Harlem Writers Guild (HWG). There, she associated with authors such as **Alice Childress**, **John Henrik Clarke**, **John Oliver Killens**, and **Paule Marshall**, who were quickly becoming well known, as well as such up-and-coming authors as **Maya Angelou**, **Ossie Davis**, **Lonne Elder III**, **Rosa Guy**, **Audre Lorde**, **Julian Mayfield**, and **Douglas Turner Ward**. Wright remained actively involved in the HWG until 1972, when she started turning her attention to teaching, offering workshops showing others how to write. Around that time, Wright also joined Guy and Angelou and dramatist Aminata Moseka (Abby Lincoln) in forming the Cultural Association for Women of African Heritage, dedicated to promoting racial pride and self-esteem.

Other organizations in which Wright has been involved include PEN, the Authors Guild, the International Women's Writing Guild, and Pen & Brush, Inc. (president, 1992–1993), said to be the oldest U.S. professional organization for women. She also helped organize the First (1959) and the Second National Conference of Black Writers as well as the Congress of American Writers (1971). In addition to these organizations and her workshops, she is certified as a poetry therapist and has presented readings, lectures, and television and radio talk shows at high schools, libraries, community centers, and various other locations.

Wright's main literary contribution is her novel *This Child's Gonna Live* (1969), about an impoverished African-American mother, her husband (Jacob), and their children, who are desperately struggling to survive in Tangierneck, a rural Maryland fishing town. The mother, Mariah Upshur, physically and verbally abuses her children, particularly her son Rabbit, who eventually dies, perhaps in part because of willful maternal neglect. Previously, her infant daughter had died due to an infection caused by an unsanitary bandage. Mariah constantly calls on Jesus and on God to help her, but apparently to no avail. She nonetheless remains hopeful that she can get herself and her children out of "the Neck" (Tangierneck), and when she finds herself pregnant again, she continually asserts her determination that "this [unborn] child's gonna live." When the novel was first published, the *New York Times* named it one of the most important books of the year, and the *Baltimore Sun* gave it the year's Readability Award. The Feminist Press reissued it in 1986, with an essay by HWG founder John Oliver Killens; in 1994 the press issued a silver anniversary edition, and the press and Pen & Brush, Inc., celebrated its 25 years of continuous sales. In the mid-1990s, Wright was reported to be working on a sequel to *This Child,* tentatively titled *Twelve Gates to the City, Halleluh, Halleluh!*

Wright also wrote an important nonfiction work, a biography of the activist, union organizer, and cofounder of *The Messenger* magazine, **A. Philip Randolph**. The resulting *A. Philip Randolph: Integration in the Workplace* (1990) was included in a history series on the civil rights movement. The New York Public Library chose it as one of the Best Books for Young Adults for that year (1990).

In addition to awards for her individual works, Wright has been given two MacDowell Colony fellowships for creative writing, the CAPS Award for Fiction (1975), the Howard University Novelist-Poet Award (1976), and the Zora Neale Hurston Award.

REFERENCES: *EBLG. TAWH.* Ferguson, Sally Ann H., in *OCWW.* Houston, Helen R., in *OCAAL.* Amazon.com, 9/1999.

X, Malcolm (né Malcolm Little; Islamic name: El-Hajj Malik El-Shabazz) (5/19/1925–2/21/1965)

Autobiography, commentary, speeches; newspaper founder

Itinerant Baptist minister Earl Little, a fierce follower of **Marcus Garvey**, was constantly switching from church to church, moving his wife and eight children from town to town across the Midwest and the Northeast. After Ku Klux Klan members burned down one of their homes, the friction between Earl and his wife Louise intensified, and he beat her more frequently and severely. Earl's seventh son, Malcolm, was six years old when irate Ku Klux Klan members finally murdered Reverend Earl. Louise was ill equipped to handle the financial, emotional, and physical burden of caring for her children. After doing her best to hold things together, in 1937 she ended up in a mental institution, her family fell apart, and Malcolm and his siblings were dispersed to various foster homes.

Academically, Malcolm showed great promise and was popular in his almost-all-white classroom (elected class president in the seventh grade). His optimistic outlook was squelched, however, when his teacher told him that his intelligence would in no way help him escape his certain destiny as a Negro: to become a laborer—at best, a skilled laborer. When he left school, he drifted through a series of jobs into a life as a drug dealer, burglar, and petty criminal. Following a few narrow escapes and some clever dodges, he was eventually busted for burglary.

At age 21, in 1946 convicted burglar Malcolm Little started serving six years of his ten-year prison sentence in the Charlestown State Prison in Massachusetts. In prison, he underwent a spiritual awakening and conversion to the Black Muslim faith, following the teachings of the "Honorable" Elijah Muhammad. Following his conversion, he became highly disciplined, educating himself in the prison library and beginning a daily correspondence with the Nation of Islam's spiritual leader. To expand his vocabulary and his knowledge, he copied every page of the dictionary, and he read African-American history so prodigiously that he needed glasses by the time he left prison.

On being released from prison in 1952, he immediately went to Detroit to work for the Black Muslims. He also rejected the surname given to his family by his ancestor's slaveowner and adopted the surname "X," signifying his lost and unknown African family name. Malcolm's oratory skills were soon recognized, and in 1954 Elijah Muhammad moved him to Harlem's prominent Temple (Mosque) Seven, where he gained prominence as the primary spokesperson for the Black Muslims across the nation.

A powerful and charismatic orator, Malcolm called for African Americans everywhere to work together, independently from European Americans, to form their own businesses, schools, and communities; to patronize businesses run by African Americans and avoid or even boycott businesses run by racists of other races; and to take pride in their own distinctive cultural heritage. He opposed the nonviolent struggle for civil rights as an ineffectual means of gaining equality and integration. Further, he held that the goals of racial equality and integration were unworthy goals in a racist nation. Though he never advocated violence as a form of aggression, he did say that African Americans should defend themselves and their communities "by any means necessary," including violent means. Although his speeches moved myriad listeners across the land, they weren't published in book form until after his death. Since his death, many of his key speeches have been published in such collections as *Malcolm X Speaks: Selected Speeches and Statements* (1965/1990) and *By Any Means Necessary: Speeches, Interviews, and a Letter* (1970), both edited by George Breitman; and *The Speeches of Malcolm X at Harvard* (1968), edited by Archie Epps. Two of the more recent collections of his work are *Malcolm X: The Last Speeches* (1989) and *Malcolm X on Afro-American History* (1990).

In 1956, Sister Betty (a nursing student) joined Temple Seven. After a respectable and courtly courtship, Malcolm married Betty January 14,

Malcolm X speaks at a fundraising rally of Black Muslims, 1960s (Archive Photos)

1958. Over the next seven years, they had four daughters: Attilah, Qubilah, Ilyasah, and Amilah; Betty was also pregnant when Malcolm was shot in February 1965.

Malcolm's oratory skills were matched by his leadership skills, and he directed the establishment of two universities of Islam to provide a Black Muslim education to school-age children in Detroit and Chicago. He also founded many new mosques and recruited countless new members, lecturing around the nation on college campuses and anywhere else he could gather listeners. In 1961, he founded the official publication of the Nation of Islam, *Muhammad Speaks.* He was soon considered second only to Elijah Muhammad in the Nation of Islam.

After a while, however, Muhammad started to envy his chief aide's fame—often in the press and on television news, Malcolm's face and name were far more widely recognized than Muhammad's. For his part, Malcolm was an extremely devoted follower until he became aware of Muhammad's sexual promiscuity and excessive use of Muslim resources for his own material gain. Meanwhile,

Muhammad's envy increased. Following the November 22, 1963, assassination of President John F. Kennedy, Malcolm remarked that this was a "case of chickens coming home to roost," meaning that the violence of powerful white men was being turned back against them. The nation—and the Nation—bristled at Malcolm's cavalier attitude. He was chastised by Muhammad and ordered to be silent for 90 days. Malcolm complied obediently, but his period of silence allowed him to reflect on his allegiance to a leader who so betrayed what he believed to be the core principles of Islam.

When Malcolm learned that Muhammad was also badmouthing him behind his back, he foresaw the next steps to come: He was suspended as a minister, then ostracized ("isolated"). Before he was expelled altogether, Malcolm split from the Nation of Islam and organized his own Muslim Mosque , Inc., in Harlem. He also decided to dedicate himself to traditional Islam as it is practiced throughout the world. One of the primary duties of each Muslim is to make a pilgrimage (known as the *hajj*) to Mecca, the holy city of all followers of Islam. In April 1964 Malcolm made his hajj.

His hajj offered him a second spiritual awakening. By sharing the spiritual rituals of the hajj with fellow Muslims from Asia, Africa, Europe, and the Americas, he realized that whites were not by nature evil, but that racism was the evil he righteously hated. Instead of advocating racial division and separatism, he wished to promote international solidarity to overcome the evils of racism. He changed his name from Malcolm X to the Arabic name El-Hajj Malik El-Shabazz.

On his return to the United States, El-Shabazz formed the secular Organization of Afro-American Unity (OAAU) in 1964, to promote African-American cultural pride through an internationalist framework of brotherhood, linking Africans, Asians, and Americans of all racial and cultural heritages. He was soon traveling throughout the Middle East, Africa, and Europe, giving speeches reflecting his new worldly attitude, urging others around the globe to help African Americans in the fight against racism and oppression. He also spoke to the United Nations in New York, charging the United States with denying human rights to African Americans.

Once he embraced orthodox Islam and renounced the Nation of Islam as inauthentic, the hostility between him and the Nation intensified. Threats of violence assaulted him and his family at an increasing rate. On February 21, 1965, when he was addressing an OAAU rally at the Audubon Ballroom in Harlem, he was assassinated. Three Black Muslims were later convicted of his murder. After his death, it became clear that Black Muslims' accusations that he hoarded huge caches of money while he worked for the Nation of Islam were false. In fact, he left his wife and 5 children almost destitute; he hadn't even bought life insurance to provide for them after his death. Just as he had always claimed, all of his earnings had gone to the Nation of Islam.

Months before Malcolm X broke with Elijah Muhammad, he had—with Elijah Muhammad's permission—begun working with **Alex Haley** to write his autobiography. Haley had interviewed Malcolm for a *Playboy* article, and he had found Malcolm reluctant to say much about himself, focusing instead on the worthiness of Elijah Muhammad, the Nation of Islam, and the black nationalist outlook they proposed.

In writing the autobiography, Malcolm still sought to promote the Nation of Islam, but he had no intention of producing a puff piece touting his own accomplishments. In the autobiography, Malcolm was surprisingly frank, candidly revealing his own past crimes and misdeeds. Just as he was brutally honest in addressing past and present U.S. atrocities, he was unhesitatingly open about his own unworthy actions, thoughts, and feelings. For instance, he frankly described his use of drugs, his mistreatment of women, his thefts and burglaries, and his neglect of his family. He even revealed the extent of his own limitations, such as when describing the first letter he wrote to Elijah Muhammad: "At least twenty-five times I must have written that first one-page letter to him, over and over. I was trying to make it both legible and understandable. I practically couldn't read my handwriting myself; it shames even to remember it. My spelling and my grammar were as bad, if not worse" (*Autobiography,* p. 11). Later on, he wrote that he regretted his lack of formal education more than he regretted any of the numerous mistakes he had made.

When establishing their relationship, Malcolm and Haley agreed that Haley would include everything that Malcolm had said, leaving nothing out, and that Haley would not add anything that Malcolm did not say. (After Malcolm died, Haley did add a lengthy epilogue, but this was in keeping with their agreement, as Haley clearly distinguished it from the text that Malcolm had authored.) Stylistically, the book retains much of the lively oratory flair of Malcolm's speaking voice. Haley's writing is transparent, so each reader can readily hear Malcolm's voice. We hear his passions, practical advice, and moral pronouncements; his changing political and religious philosophy; his impatience, frustration, and humor; his personal gibes and his feelings of hurt when duped or betrayed; and his loving appreciation of those who had shown him kindness and care.

Although the book clearly expresses Malcolm's political and religious philosophy, it does so through the narrative of his life experiences, without going into lengthy diatribes many might have suspected he would infuse into the work. When Malcolm underwent his radical transformation in 1964, Haley and he agreed not to revise the work to focus on attacking the Nation of Islam to which he had previously been so devoted. (He did, however, inject a few comments into the earlier portion of the book, reflecting his later hindsight on the events that transpired.)

Almost immediately after its posthumous publication (1965), the book became a national best-seller (selling more than 6 million copies), an internationally acclaimed work (translated into eight or more languages), the object of extensive scholarly interest, required reading for various college courses, and—over the next few decades—a modern classic. In 1992, **Spike Lee** translated the story into a popular movie. As a literary work, it has been compared to **slave narratives**, with its authentic autobiographical commentary, and to bildungsromans, in its revelation of Malcolm's personal development. Although he left his family without financial resources, he left the world much enriched by his words. Many of his contemporaries and his successors have written substantial works about him, such as **James Baldwin** (who wrote a screenplay about Malcolm's autobiography) and **John Henrik Clarke**, and new biographies of him are written every year.

REFERENCES: *1TESK. AA:PoP. BaD. BAL-1-P. BC. BDAA. BF:2000. BWA. DA. E-98. EB-98. EBLG.*

G-95. MAAL. NAAAL. PGAA. Scrimgeour, J. D., in *OCAAL.* X, Malcolm, with the assistance of Alex Haley (1965), *The Autobiography of Malcolm X* (New York: Grove Press). Amazon.com, 7/1999.

X, Marvin (né Marvin Ellis Jackmon) (5/29/1944–)

Poems, plays, essays; book press founder and owner

X's plays include *Flowers for the Trashman* (1965, one act), *The Black Bird* (1969, one act), *The Trial, Resurrection of the Dead,* and *In the Name of Love.* In addition to his writing, X founded his own press (El Kitab Sudan, 1967) and cofounded a theater (Black Arts/West Theatre, with **Ed Bullins**, 1966), and he works as a producer, director, lecturer, editor, and spokesperson on behalf of Islam. His publishing house has published several volumes of his poetry (e.g., *Fly to Allah, Black Man Listen,* 1969) and his **proverbs** (*The Son of Man,* 1969).

REFERENCES: Greene, Michael E., in *OCAAL.*

Y

Yarbrough, Camille (1938–)
Children's and young adult books

Yarbrough's fiction books (e.g., *Cornrows* [1979/1999]; Coretta Scott King Award–winner *The Shimmershine Queens,* [1989/1996]; and *Little Tree Growin' in the Shade,* [1996]) attempt to go to the core of social discord and hurtful interactions and to find ways to resolve these problems (usually with the guidance of elders in the community). Her books encourage young African-American girls to take pride in all aspects of their cultural heritage and all manifestations of their African inheritance.

REFERENCES: Harris, Violet J., in *OCAAL.*

Yerby, Frank G. (Garvin)
(9/5/1916–11/29/1991)
Novels, short stories, poems

In Augusta, Georgia, Frank was the second of four children of racially mixed parents, Rufus Garvin and Wilhelmina Yerby. The South's racial segregation and discrimination made a lifelong impression on young Frank, and even decades after he had fled North, he used the South as the setting—and the subject—of much of his fiction.

The South wasn't able to prevent Frank from getting a good education, however, as he was an outstanding student in the Haines Institute, the private black school he attended. In college, he started writing his own poetry, fiction, and drama while earning his bachelor's degree in English from Paine College (1937). While he was still at Paine, Frank's sister showed some of his poems to **James Weldon Johnson**, who taught at Fisk University (in Nashville, Tennessee). Johnson liked what he saw and urged Frank to do his postgraduate studies at Fisk University—which he did, earning an M.A. in English (1938) and continuing to write. After earning his master's degree, he moved to Chicago and started working toward a Ph.D. in English.

Nine months into Yerby's Ph.D. program, he ran into financial difficulties and left school to start working with the Federal Writers' Project (FWP) of the Works Progress Administration. While working with the FWP, he met other up-and-coming Chicago-area writers, such as **Arna Bontemps** and **Margaret Walker**. Within months, however, Yerby decided that he wanted to try working in academia, and in 1939 he went back South to teach at Florida A&M University and then at Louisiana's Southern University. In 1941, however, he decided he couldn't take Southern living any more, so he quit academia, and he and his first wife moved first to Dearborn, Michigan, where he worked as a technician in a defense plant for Ford Motor Company (1941–1944), and then to Jamaica, New York, where he worked for Ranger (Fairchild) Aircraft (1944–1945).

Throughout this time, Yerby was continuing to write short stories, and he wrote a protest novel about an African-American steelworker. He sent the novel to *Redbook* magazine, which sometimes published serialized versions of novels. The editor there, Muriel Fuller, rejected his novel as unsuitable for her almost-all-female audience, but she encouraged him to send her another piece. He sent her his short story "Health Card," about a racist encounter between a white congressman and a black GI's girlfriend. Fuller decided that the story didn't suit her audience, but she liked the writing and sent it on to an editor at *Harper's* magazine, a highly esteemed and popular general-interest magazine. As a result, in 1944 Yerby's writing first appeared in print: "Health Card" was published in *Harper's*. The story won the O. Henry Memorial Award for best first published short story (1944), and Yerby's career as a writer was launched. "Health Card" was followed in short order by various other short stories, including "White Magnolias," "Homecoming," and "My Brother Went to College."

While continuing to write (and to publish) short stories, Yerby continued to try to sell the manuscript for his protest novel—without success. Eventually, he gave up on it and turned his attention to writing historical fiction, quite a popular genre at that time. He also switched to featuring mostly white protagonists in his works. The switch in genre and in protagonists did the trick. His next novel, *The Foxes of Harrow* (1946), a historical romance set in New Orleans in the nineteenth century, was an immediate best-seller, selling millions of copies. It was also translated into at least 12 languages and was adapted to film (1947 or 1951). The book is still being read—and praised—by contemporary readers; numerous readers took the time to comment on it in 1998 and 1999 (on Amazon.com), identifying it as "very moving!" and "the best book I've ever read!!!" Some of those who commented had read the book 20, 30, or more years earlier, yet still recalled savoring it.

Yerby followed this success with more than 30 other novels, becoming the first African American to write a series of best-selling novels in his day, having sold more than 55 million copies of his works. Probably surprising to many of his critics, Yerby's books continue to be printed and sold to this day. Some of his books were also made into successful movies: In addition to *The Foxes of Harrow,* they made *The Golden Hawk* (1948) and *The Saracen Blade* (1952/1985) into movies. The first book after *Foxes* was *The Vixens* (1947), followed by a trilogy of novels beginning in the Civil War era, *Pride's Castle* (1949).

Yerby's next book, *The Devil's Laughter* (1953), centers around the French Revolution. It was at about this time that Yerby himself moved to Europe. After spending time in France, he eventually settled himself into self-imposed exile in Spain, where he married his second wife and continued to live until his death nearly four decades later.

Among the books Yerby wrote in Europe were *Fair Oaks* (1957), followed by a series that again returned to issues of race in the historical U.S. South, including *The Serpent and the Staff* (1958), *The Garfield Honor* (1961), and *Tents of Shem* (1963). He followed those with a novel set in medieval, Moor-dominated Spain, *An Odor of Sanctity* (1965). Next was *Judas, My Brother* (1968), followed by *Speak Now* (1969), about a contemporary (1968) Parisian romance between an African-American jazz musician and a European-American student from the South. Surprisingly, *Speak Now* was his first published novel with an African-American protagonist, though not the last. In *The Dahomean* (1971), Yerby directly addresses issues of race and America's shameful history with slavery. Readers follow the protagonist, Hwesu, from his home in the Dahomean empire in Africa through his capture by neighboring Africans, his sale to white slave merchants, and his subsequent life as "Wesley Parks" in America. Yerby wrote *The Voyage Unplanned* (1974) and *Tobias and the Angel* (1975) before returning to African-American characters and themes in *A Darkness at Ingraham's Crest* (1981). Other novels of his include *Captain Rebel* (1983), *Devilseed* (1984), *McKenzie's Hundred* (1985), and *Goat Song* (set in ancient Greece, in which a Spartan youth is enslaved by Athenians), as well as *Bride of Liberty, Floodtide, The Girl from Storyville: A Victorian Novel, Hail: The Conquering Hero, The Man from Dahomey: An Historical Novel, Mayo Fue el Fin del Mundo* [May Was the End of the World], *Old Gods Laugh, A Rose for Ana Maria: A Novel,* and *Western.*

Although no one can fault Yerby for his ability to tell an appealing story or for working hard to put out a large volume of literary works, he is not without his detractors. Many literary critics scorned him for using the very sensationalizing writing techniques that won him countless fans around the world. Also, fellow African-American writers continually pleaded with him to pay more attention to racial concerns in his works, and although he did so in some books, he was never able to please many writers and other prominent figures in the African-American community.

Even more irritating to fellow African Americans was his writing about European-American protagonists, which appealed to white readers but provoked black ones. Only rarely did Yerby tell stories with African-American protagonists. When he did, however, he shrewdly targeted Southern myths about U.S. history and stereotypes of African Americans, and he savagely attacked U.S. racism.

Even in his novels set in distant times and places (e.g., in the early days of Christianity or during the thirteenth-century Crusades) or featuring European Americans, Yerby relished debunking myths and setting the historical record straight through his fictional narratives. On the other hand, his action-packed novels with strong male heroes did manage to perpetuate gender stereotypes, past and present. In this regard, some of his critics have labeled him misogynistic and homophobic.

Yerby's proponents point to his intricate and intriguing story lines, colorful language, and inclusion of characters with diverse ethnic backgrounds. Most of all, they say that Yerby offers "a good read." Yerby himself managed to elude definition, and little is known about his life after he moved to Europe. Other than occasional business or personal trips to the United States, he never returned to live here. Even his death was mysterious, as he made his wife promise to keep his death a secret for five weeks—which she did. If only we had a good storyteller to give an account of why he made this request . . .

REFERENCES: *BF:2000. EB-BH-CD. EBLG. G-99. OC20LE. WDAA.* Hill, James L., in *OCAAL.* Amazon.com, 8/1999.

Young, Al (5/31/1939–)

Novels, poems, short stories, screenplays, essays; literary journal founder and editor

Young's screenplays include *Nigger, Sparkle* (1972) and *Bustin Loose* (1981, for Richard Pryor). His "musical memoirs" include *Bodies & Soul* (1966), *Kind of Blue* (1984), *Things Ain't What They Used to Be* (1987), and *Drowning in the Sea of Love* (1995). Music also pervades his novel *Snakes* (1970), his biography *Mingus/Mingus* (1989, with Janet Coleman, about jazz bassist, composer, and bandleader Charles Mingus), and his poetry collections *Dancing* (1969), *The Song Turning Back into Itself* (1971), *Geography of the Near Past* (1979), *The Blues Don't Change: New and Selected Poems* (1982), and *Heaven: Collected Poems 1958–1988* (1989). His other novels include *Sitting Pretty* (1976), *Seduction by Light* (1988), *Who Is Angelina?* (1975), and *Ask Me Now* (1980). Young has also edited, founded, or cofounded numerous literary journals, particularly multicultural ones.

REFERENCES: *NAAAL.* Chirico, Miriam M., in *OCAAL.*

Young, Whitney M. (Moore), Jr. (7/31/1921–3/11/1971)

Columns, commentary, nonfiction—politics and race

In 1958 Young coauthored *A Second Look: The Negro Citizen in Atlanta* (1958), published in connection with Atlanta's Committee for Cooperative Action, a civil rights organization he helped found. Six years later, Young's weekly political opinion columns ("To Be Equal," in Harlem's *Amsterdam News*) were collected into the book *To Be Equal* (1964). This book included what he called a "domestic Marshall Plan," developed while he was the executive director of the National Urban League and designed to expand both economic and educational opportunities for African Americans—much as the European Marshall Plan had done for Europeans following World War II. Many aspects of Young's plan were incorporated into President Lyndon Johnson's War on Poverty program (much of which ended up being siderailed by the Vietnam War). Young also wrote *Beyond Racism: Building an Open Society* (1970), which won a Christopher Book Award. Since Young's death (in 1971), his widow Margaret Buckner Young (whom he married in 1944 and with whom he had two daughters, Marcia Elaine and Lauren Lee) has written several children's books on history, focusing especially on the civil rights struggle.

REFERENCES: *EA-99. EB-BH-CD. EBLG. G-97. PGAA.* McDaniel, Karen Cotton, in *BH2C.*

Zu-Bolton, Ahmos, III
(10/21/1935–)
Poems; editor, bookstore owner

Zu-Bolton's free-verse poems reflective of the **Black Arts movement** have been collected in his *A Niggered Amen* (1975) and anthologized in several works. Zu-Bolton has also been deeply involved in the literary journals *HooDoo* and *Blackbox,* of which he was coeditor, and he has contributed articles to New Orleans's *Times-Picayune* and the *Louisiana Weekly.* For a decade (1982–1992), he also owned the Copasetic Bookstore and Gallery in New Orleans.

REFERENCES: Thomas, Lorenzo, in *OCAAL.*

APPENDIX: WRITERS BY GENRE

Autobiographies/Memoirs/Diaries/Letters

Allen, Richard
Angelou, Maya
Ashe, Arthur
Banneker, Benjamin
Bonner, Marita
Brooks, Gwendolyn
Brown, Claude
Brown, Elaine
Brown, William Wells
Bunche, Ralph
Campbell, Bebe Moore
Chisholm, Shirley
Clark, Septima Poinsette
Cleaver, Eldridge
Clifton, Lucille
Corrothers, James D.
Cosby, Bill
Davis, Angela Yvonne
Dee, Ruby
Delany, "Bessie"
Delany, "Sadie"
Delany, Samuel R.
Derricotte, Toi
Douglass, Frederick
Du Bois, W. E. B.
Dunbar Nelson, Alice Ruth
Dunham, Katherine
Edelman, Marian Wright
Evers-Williams, Myrlie
Forten (Grimké), Charlotte L.
Franklin, J. E.
Gayle, Addison, Jr.
Geddes, Norman Bel
Goldberg, Whoopi
Golden, Marita
Green, J. D.
Greenfield, Eloise
Gregory, "Dick"
Haley, Alex
Hammon, Briton
Handy, W. C.

Haskins, James S.
Henson, Matthew Alexander
Hill, Anita Faye
Himes, Chester
Holiday, Billie
hooks, bell
Hughes, Langston
Hunter, Latoya
Hunter-Gault, Charlayne
Hurston, Zora Neale
Iceberg Slim
Jackson, George Lester
Jackson, Jesse, Jr.
Jackson, Mahalia
Jackson, Mattie J.
Jackson, Rebecca Cox
Johnson, James Weldon
Johnson, John H.
Johnson, Kathryn Magnolia
Johnson, William
Jordan, Barbara
Keckley, Elizabeth
Kennedy, Adrienne
King, "B. B."
King, Coretta Scott
Latifah, Queen
Lee, Andrea
Lee, Spike
Lester, Julius
Lorde, Audre
Major, Clarence
Marrant, John
Moody, Anne
Motley, Willard
Murray, "Pauli"
Parks, Gordon, Sr.
Patterson, William
Payne, Daniel A.
Paynter, John H.
Pickens, William
Prince, Nancy Gardner
Randall, Dudley
Reagon, Bernice Johnson

Ringgold, Faith
Robeson, Eslanda Cardozo Goode
Robeson, Paul
Rowan, Carl T.
Schuyler, George Samuel
Schuyler, Philippa Duke
Shakur, Assata Olugbala
Smith, Amanda Berry
Tarry, Ellen
Taylor, Susan L.
Taylor, Susie Baker King
Terrell, Mary Eliza Church
Thomas, Piri
Thompson, Era Bell
Thurman, Howard
Tubman, Harriet
Turner, Nat
Van Peebles, Melvin
Van Vechten, Carl
Walker, Margaret
Washington, Booker T.
Wells, Ida B.
Whipper, Frances A. Rollin
White, Walter F.
Williams, Robert Franklin
Winfrey, Oprah
Wright, Richard
X, Malcolm

Biographies

Bolden, Tonya
Bontemps, Arna Wendell
Boyd, Melba
Brawley, Benjamin
Brown, Hallie Quinn
Deveaux, Alexis
Du Bois, Shirley Graham
Du Bois, W. E. B.
Fauset, Jessie Redmon
Franklin, John Hope
French, William P.
Garvey, Amy Jacques
Gayle, Addison, Jr.

Graham, Lorenz
Greenfield, Eloise
Griggs, Sutton E.
Grimké, Archibald Henry
Haley, Alex
Hare, Maud Cuney
Haskins, James S.
Haynes, Elizabeth Ross
Hine, Darlene Clark
Hopkins, Pauline
Jackson, Jesse
Killens, John Oliver
King, Coretta Scott
Logan, Rayford
Mathis, Sharon Bell
McKissack, Pat
Meriwether, Louise
Murray, Albert L.
Myers, Walter Dean
Park, Robert E.
Patterson, Lillie
Petry, Ann
Plato, Ann
Rampersad, Arnold
Robeson, Eslanda Cardozo Goode
Rollins, Charlemae Hill
Rowan, Carl T.
Shockley, Ann
Simmons, William J.
Smith, Jessie Carney
Southern, Eileen Stanza Johnson
Sterling, Dorothy
Stowe, Harriet Beecher
Touré, Askia M.
Walker, Alice
Walker, Margaret
Washington, Booker T.
Wesley, Charles Harris
Whipper, Frances A. Rollin
Williams, John A.
Wright, Sarah E.

**Children's and
Juvenile Literature**
Baldwin, James
Bolden, Tonya
Bontemps, Arna Wendell
Bryan, Ashley F.
Burroughs, Margaret Taylor
Child, Lydia Maria
Childress, Alice
Clifton, Lucille
Cosby, Bill
Crews, Donald
Cullen, Countee
Curtis, Christopher Paul
Dee, Ruby

Deveaux, Alexis
Evans, Mari
Fauset, Jessie Redmon
Feelings, Tom
Fields, Julia
Giovanni, Nikki
Graham, Lorenz
Greenfield, Eloise
Guy, Rosa Cuthbert
Hamilton, Virginia
Harris, Joel Chandler
Haskins, James S.
Herron, Carolivia
hooks, bell
Hughes, Langston
Hunter, Kristin Eggleston
Jackson, Jesse
Jordan, June
Killens, John Oliver
Lester, Julius
Mathis, Sharon Bell
Matthews, Victoria Earle
McKissack, Pat
Meriwether, Louise
Miller, May
Mossell, Gertrude Bustill
Myers, Walter Dean
Newsome, Effie Lee
Patterson, Lillie
Petry, Ann
Richardson, Willis
Ringgold, Faith
Rollins, Charlemae Hill
Steptoe, John Lewis
Sterling, Dorothy
Tarry, Ellen
Tate, Eleanora
Taylor, Mildred D.
Thomas, Joyce Carol
Thomas, Piri
Torrence, Jackie
Vroman, Mary Elizabeth
Walker, Alice
Walter, Mildred Pitts
Wilkinson, Brenda
Williams, Sherley Anne
Wright, Richard
Yarbrough, Camille

**Comic Strips/Cartoons/
Parody/Humor**
Brandon, Barbara
Cosby, Bill
Feelings, Tom
Goldberg, Whoopi
Gregory, "Dick"
Harrington, Oliver Wendell

Johnson, Charles (Richard)
Ormes, "Jackie"
Reed, Ishmael
Schuyler, George Samuel

**Criticism/Anthologies/
Bibliographies/
Translations**
Allen, Samuel W.
Amini, Johari
Baker, Augusta
Baker, Houston A.
Bambara, Toni Cade
Baraka, Amiri
Bennett, Gwendolyn B.
Bogle, Donald
Bontemps, Arna Wendell
Bradley, David, Jr.
Braithwaite, William Stanley
    Beaumont
Brawley, Benjamin
Braxton, Joanne M.
Brown, Sterling Allen
Clarke, John Henrik
Crouch, Stanley
Davis, Frank Marshall
Delaney, Sara Marie Johnson
Delany, Samuel R.
Dunbar Nelson, Alice Ruth
Ellison, Ralph
Evans, Mari
Fauset, Jessie Redmon
French, William P.
Fuller, Hoyt
Gates, Henry Louis, Jr.
Gayle, Addison, Jr.
Giddings, Paula
Golden, Marita
Guy, Rosa Cuthbert
Hansberry, Lorraine
Hare, Maud Cuney
Harper, Michael S.
Haskins, James S.
Hernton, Calvin C.
hooks, bell
Hughes, Langston
Hutson, Jean Blackwell
Johnson, Charles (Richard)
Johnson, James Weldon
Jones, Gayl
Jordan, June
Josey, E. J.
King, Woodie, Jr.
Knight, Etheridge
Latimer, Catherine A.
Locke, Alain
Madgett, Naomi Long

Major, Clarence
Matheus, John F.
Mayfield, Julian
McMillan, Terry
Miller, E. Ethelbert
Millican, Arthenia J. Bates
Milner, Ronald
Moore, Opal
Morrison, Toni
Murphy, Beatrice M.
Murray, Albert L.
Neal, "Larry"
Perkins, Eugene
Plumpp, Sterling
Porter Wesley, Dorothy Burnett
Rampersad, Arnold
Randall, Dudley
Redding, Jay Saunders
Redmond, Eugene
Richardson, Willis
Rodgers, Carolyn
Rollins, Charlemae Hill
Salaam, Kalamu ya
Scarborough, William Sanders
Schomburg, Arthur A.
Shockley, Ann
Smith, Barbara
Smith, Jessie Carney
Southern, Eileen Stanza Johnson
Spillers, Hortense J.
Spingarn, Joel Elias
Thompson, Era Bell
Thurman, Wallace
Turner, Darwin T.
Turner, Lorenzo Dow
Turpin, Waters
Van Vechten, Carl
Walker, Margaret
Waniek, Marilyn Nelson
Williams, Sherley Anne

**Nonfiction Essays,
Articles, and Books**
Abbott, Robert S.
Abu-Jamal, Mumia
Amini, Johari
Andrews, Raymond
Ashe, Arthur
Baker, Houston A.
Baldwin, James
Bambara, Toni Cade
Banneker, Benjamin
Baraka, Amiri
Barber, Jesse Max
Barnett, Claude Albert
Bass, Charlotta Spears
Beasley, Delilah

Bennett, Gwendolyn B.
Bennett, Lerone, Jr.
Berry, Mary Frances
Bibb, Henry
Bogle, Donald
Bonner, Marita
Bontemps, Arna Wendell
Boyd, Melba
Bradley, David, Jr.
Brandon, Barbara
Brawley, Benjamin
Brown, "Charlotte Eugenia"
Brown, Claude
Brown, Hallie Quinn
Brown, William Wells
Burroughs, Nannie Helen
Cabrera, Lydia
Carmichael, Stokely
Cary, Mary Ann Shadd
Childress, Alice
Clarke, John Henrik
Cleage, Pearl
Cleaver, Eldridge
Cliff, Michelle
Clifton, Lucille
Cobb, Charles E., Jr.
Cobb, William Montague
Colón, Jesús
Cooper, Anna Julia
Coston, Julia Ringwood
Cotter, Joseph Seamon, Jr.
Crosswaith, Frank Rudolph
Crouch, Stanley
Cruse, Harold Wright
Cullen, Countee
Damas, Léon-Gontran
Davis, Angela Yvonne
Davis, Frank Marshall
Davis, Thulani
Delany, Clarissa
Delany, Martin R.
Delany, Samuel R.
Dent, Tom
Deveaux, Alexis
Douglass, Frederick
Douglass, Sarah Mapps
Dove, Rita
Du Bois, W. E. B.
Dunbar, Paul Laurence
Dunbar Nelson, Alice Ruth
Dunham, Katherine
Ellison, Ralph
Evans, Mari
Fisher, Abby
Forten (Grimké), Charlotte L.
Fortune, T. Thomas
Franklin, John Hope

Frazier, Edward Franklin
Fuller, Charles H.
Fuller, Hoyt
Garvey, Amy Jacques
Garvey, Marcus
Gayle, Addison, Jr.
Geddes, Norman Bel
Giddings, Paula
Giovanni, Nikki
Gomez, Jewelle
Greenlee, Sam
Griggs, Sutton E.
Grimké, Angelina Weld
Grimké (Weld), Angelina (Emily)
Grimké, Archibald Henry
Grimké, Sarah (Moore)
Guinier, Lani
Haley, Alex
Hammon, Jupiter
Handy, W. C.
Hansberry, Lorraine
Hare, Maud Cuney
Hare, Nathan
Harper, Frances Ellen Watkins
Harrington, Oliver Wendell
Haskins, James S.
Haynes, Elizabeth Ross
Haynes, Lemuel
Heard, Nathan C.
Hernton, Calvin C.
Hine, Darlene Clark
hooks, bell
Hopkins, Pauline
Houston, Charles
Hunter, Kristin Eggleston
Hunter-Gault, Charlayne
Hurston, Zora Neale
Iceberg Slim
Johnson, Amelia E.
Johnson, Charles (Richard)
Johnson, Charles (Spurgeon)
Johnson, Fenton
Jordan, June
Kelley, William Melvin
Killens, John Oliver
Kincaid, Jamaica
King, Martin Luther, Jr.
King, Woodie, Jr.
Latimer, Lewis Howard
Lee, Spike
Lester, Julius
Lewis, Samella Sanders
Locke, Alain
Logan, Rayford
Lomax, Louis E.
Lorde, Audre
Madgett, Naomi Long

Major, Clarence
Malveaux, Julianne
Marshall, Paule
Matthews, Victoria Earle
Mayfield, Julian
McKissack, Pat
Meriwether, Louise
Merrick, Lyda Moore
Miller, E. Ethelbert
Millican, Arthenia J. Bates
Mitchell, Loften
Moody, Anne
Moore, Opal
Mossell, Gertrude Bustill
Motley, Willard
Moutoussamy-Ashe, Jeanne
Murray, Albert L.
Murray, "Pauli"
Myers, Walter Dean
Neal, "Larry"
Nell, William C.
Ormes, "Jackie"
Park, Robert E.
Parks, Gordon, Sr.
Parsons, Lucy Gonzalez
Patterson, Orlando
Payne, Daniel A.
Payne, Ethel L.
Paynter, John H.
Pennington, James W. C.
Perkins, Eugene
Petry, Ann
Pickens, William
Plato, Ann
Polite, Carlene Hatcher
Porter, James Amos
Poussaint, Alvin Francis
Powell, Adam Clayton, Jr.
Prince, Nancy Gardner
Quarles, Benjamin
Randolph, A. Philip
Reagon, Bernice Johnson
Reason, Charles L.
Redding, Jay Saunders
Reed, Ishmael
Rowan, Carl T.
Rustin, Bayard
Salaam, Kalamu ya
Schomburg, Arthur A.
Schuyler, Philippa Duke
Shange, Ntozake
Shockley, Ann
Smith, Barbara
Smith, Jessie Carney
Smith, Lillian Eugenia
Southerland, Ellease
Southern, Eileen Stanza Johnson

Spillers, Hortense J.
Sterling, Dorothy
Steward, Theophilus Gould
Stewart, Maria W.
Still, William
Stowe, Harriet Beecher
Tanner, Benjamin Tucker
Terrell, Mary Eliza Church
Thompson, Era Bell
Thurman, Wallace
Tillman, Katherine Davis Chapman
Toomer, Jean
Touré, Askia M.
Trotter, Geraldine Pindell
Trotter, James Monroe
Trotter, William Monroe
Turpin, Waters
Van Peebles, Melvin
Van Vechten, Carl
Vann, Robert Lee
Vashon, George B.
Vroman, Mary Elizabeth
Walker, Alice
Walker, Margaret
Walker, Wyatt Tee
Walrond, Eric
Walter, Mildred Pitts
Ward, Samuel
Washington, Booker T.
Weaver, Robert C.
Wells, Ida B.
Wesley, Charles Harris
West, Dorothy
Whipper, William
White, Walter F.
Whitfield, James Monroe
Williams, George Washington
Williams, John A.
Williams, Robert Franklin
Williams, Sherley Anne
Wilson, William Julius
Winfrey, Oprah
Woodson, Carter G.
Wright, Richard
Wright, Sarah E.
X, Marvin
Young, Al
Young, Whitney M., Jr.

Novels
Andrews, Raymond
Attaway, William
Baldwin, James
Bambara, Toni Cade
Baraka, Amiri
Beckham, Barry
Bennett, Hal

Bontemps, Arna Wendell
Bradley, David, Jr.
Brown, Cecil
Brown, Linda Beatrice
Brown, William Wells
Bullins, Ed
Butler, Octavia E.
Campbell, Bebe Moore
Chase-Riboud, Barbara
Chesnutt, Charles Waddell
Child, Lydia Maria
Childress, Alice
Cleage, Pearl
Cliff, Michelle
Clifton, Lucille
Conwell, Kathleen
Cooper, J. California
Danticat, Edwidge
Davis, Ossie
Davis, Thulani
Delany, Martin R.
Delany, Samuel R.
Demby, William
Deveaux, Alexis
Dodson, Owen
Dove, Rita
Du Bois, W. E. B.
Dunbar Nelson, Alice Ruth
Ellison, Ralph
Fauset, Jessie Redmon
Fisher, Rudolph
Forrest, Leon
Gaines, Ernest J.
Goines, Donald
Golden, Marita
Gomez, Jewelle
Graham, Lorenz
Greenlee, Sam
Griggs, Sutton E.
Guy, Rosa Cuthbert
Hamilton, Virginia
Hansen, Joyce
Harper, Frances Ellen Watkins
Harris, Joel Chandler
Heard, Nathan C.
Hernton, Calvin C.
Herron, Carolivia
Heyward, DuBose
Himes, Chester
Hopkins, Pauline
Hughes, Langston
Hunter, Kristin Eggleston
Hurston, Zora Neale
Iceberg Slim
Jeffers, Lance
Johnson, Amelia E.
Johnson, Charles (Richard)

Johnson, James Weldon
Jones, Gayl
Jordan, June
Kelley, Emma Dunham
Kelley, William Melvin
Killens, John Oliver
Kincaid, Jamaica
Larsen, Nella
Lee, Andrea
Lester, Julius
Major, Clarence
Marshall, Paule
Matthews, Victoria Earle
Mayfield, Julian
McKay, Claude
McMillan, Terry
Meriwether, Louise
Micheaux, Oscar
Milner, Ronald
Mitchell, Loften
Morrison, Toni
Mosley, Walter
Motley, Willard
Murray, Albert L.
Myers, Walter Dean
Naylor, Gloria
Neely, Barbara
Parks, Gordon, Sr.
Patterson, Orlando
Paynter, John H.
Petry, Ann
Polite, Carlene Hatcher
Reed, Ishmael
Rodgers, Carolyn
Schuyler, George Samuel
Shange, Ntozake
Shockley, Ann
Simmons, Herbert Alfred
Smith, Lillian Eugenia
Smith, William Gardner
Southerland, Ellease
Steward, Theophilus Gould
Stowe, Harriet Beecher
Taylor, Mildred
Thomas, Joyce Carol
Thurman, Wallace
Tillman, Katherine Davis Chapman
Tolson, Melvin
Toomer, Jean
Turpin, Waters
Van Dyke, Henry
Van Peebles, Melvin
Van Vechten, Carl
Vroman, Mary Elizabeth
Walker, Alice
Walker, Margaret
Walter, Mildred Pitts

West, Dorothy
White, Walter F.
Wideman, John Edgar
Wilkinson, Brenda
Williams, John A.
Williams, Sherley Anne
Wilson, Harriet E.
Wright, Richard
Wright, Sarah E.
Yerby, Frank G.
Young, Al

Opinion: Columns, Editorials, Political Commentaries

Abbott, Robert S.
Baldwin, James
Banneker, Benjamin
Baraka, Amiri
Beasley, Delilah
Bennett, Gwendolyn B.
Bibb, Henry
Briggs, Cyril Valentine
Bunche, Ralph
Burroughs, Nannie Helen
Carmichael, Stokely
Cary, Mary Ann Shadd
Cayton, Horace Roscoe, Jr.
Child, Lydia Maria
Childress, Alice
Cleaver, Eldridge
Colón, Jesús
Crouch, Stanley
Crummell, Alexander
Davis, Angela Yvonne
Davis, Frank Marshall
Delany, Martin R.
Douglass, Frederick
Douglass, Sarah Mapps
Du Bois, W. E. B.
Dunbar Nelson, Alice Ruth
Edelman, Marian Wright
Fortune, T. Thomas
Fuller, Hoyt
Garland, Hazel B.
Garnet, Henry Highland
Garvey, Amy Jacques
Garvey, Marcus
Gregory, "Dick"
Guinier, Lani
Hammon, Jupiter
Hansberry, Lorraine
Hare, Maud Cuney
Harper, Frances Ellen Watkins
Hernton, Calvin C.
Hoagland, Everett H., III
Hopkins, Pauline

Houston, Drusilla Dunjee
Hughes, Langston
Hunter, Kristin Eggleston
Ice-T
Jackson, Jesse, Jr.
Jackson, Joseph Harrison
Johnson, Georgia Douglas
Johnson, James Weldon
Jordan, Barbara
Jordan, June
Kincaid, Jamaica
King, Coretta Scott
King, Martin Luther, Jr.
Lester, Julius
Locke, Alain
Lomax, Louis E.
Malveaux, Julianne
Marshall, Thurgood
Mathis, Sharon Bell
McKay, Claude
Murphy, Beatrice M.
Murphy, Carl
Owen, Chandler
Park, Robert E.
Parsons, Lucy Gonzalez
Patterson, William
Payne, Ethel L.
Perkins, Eugene
Petry, Ann
Polite, Carlene Hatcher
Powell, Adam Clayton, Jr.
Randolph, A. Philip
Raspberry, William
Reed, Ishmael
Robeson, Eslanda Cardozo Goode
Ross-Barnett, Marguerite
Rowan, Carl T.
Ruggles, David
Russwurm, John Brown
Rustin, Bayard
Scarborough, William Sanders
Schuyler, George Samuel
Schuyler, Philippa Duke
Smith, Barbara
Smith, Lillian Eugenia
Stewart, Maria W.
Tanner, Benjamin Tucker
Tarry, Ellen
Taylor, Susan L.
Thurman, Wallace
Tolson, Melvin
Touré, Askia M.
Trotter, Geraldine Pindell
Trotter, William Monroe
Van Vechten, Carl
Walker, David
Ward, Samuel

Washington, Booker T.
Wells, Ida B.
West, Cornel
West, Dorothy
Whipper, William
White, Walter F.
Williams, Robert Franklin
Wright, Richard
X, Malcolm
Young, Whitney M., Jr.

Periodicals and Presses
Baltimore Afro-American
Black American Literature Forum
Black Scholar
Broadside Press
Brownies' Book
Callaloo
Colored American Magazine
Crisis
Fire!!
Freedom's Journal
Negro Digest
Negro World
Opportunity: A Journal of Negro Life
Phylon
Third World Press

**Plays/Screenplays/
Documentary Scripts**
Anderson, Regina M.
Angelou, Maya
Attaway, William
Aubert, Alvin
Baldwin, James
Bambara, Toni Cade
Baraka, Amiri
Bonner, Marita
Bourne, St. Claire
Brown, Cecil
Brown, William Wells
Bullins, Ed
Burroughs, Nannie Helen
Campbell, Bebe Moore
Carroll, Vinnette
Childress, Alice
Cleage, Pearl
Clifton, Lucille
Coleman, Wanda
Conwell, Kathleen
Cooper, J. California
Cotter, Joseph Seamon, Jr.
Cotter, Joseph Seamon, Sr.
Cullen, Countee
Dash, Julie
Davis, Ossie
Davis, Thulani

Dee, Ruby
Dent, Tom
Deveaux, Alexis
Dodson, Owen
Dove, Rita
Du Bois, Shirley Graham
Elder, Lonne, III
Evans, Mari
Fields, Julia
Fishburne, Laurence, III
Franklin, J. E.
Fuller, Charles H.
Gerima, Haile
Gibson, P. J.
Gordone, Charles
Greenlee, Sam
Grimké, Angelina Weld
Guy, Rosa Cuthbert
Hansberry, Lorraine
Hare, Maud Cuney
Heyward, DuBose
Hopkins, Pauline
Hughes, Langston
Hunter, Kristin Eggleston
Jackson, Angela
Jackson, Elaine
Johnson, Charles (Richard)
Johnson, Georgia Douglas
Jones, Gayl
Jones-Meadows, Karen
Jordan, June
Kennedy, Adrienne
Killens, John Oliver
King, Woodie, Jr.
Lee, Spike
Lewis, Samella Sanders
Matheus, John F.
Mayfield, Julian
McKissack, Pat
Micheaux, Oscar
Miller, May
Milner, Ronald
Mitchell, Loften
Naylor, Gloria
Neal, "Larry"
Nugent, Richard Bruce
Parks, Gordon, Sr.
Parks, Suzan-Lori
Perkins, Eugene
Peterson, Louis Stamford
Pietri, Pedro Juan
Rahman, Aishah
Redmond, Eugene
Reed, Ishmael
Richardson, Willis
Riggs, Marion Troy
Rivers, Conrad Kent

Rush, Gertrude E. Durden
Salaam, Kalamu ya
Shange, Ntozake
Simmons, Herbert Alfred
Smith, Anna Deveare
Spence, Eulalie
Thomas, Joyce Carol
Thomas, Piri
Thurman, Wallace
Tillman, Katherine Davis
   Chapman
Tolson, Melvin
Toomer, Jean
Turpin, Waters
Van Peebles, Melvin
Vroman, Mary Elizabeth
Ward, Douglas Turner
Ward, Theodore
Wideman, John Edgar
Williams, John A.
Williams, Samm-Art
Williams, Spencer, Jr.
Wilson, August
X, Marvin
Young, Al

Poems
Ai Ogawa, Florence
Allen, Samuel W.
Amini, Johari
Angelou, Maya
Aubert, Alvin
Baker, Houston A.
Baldwin, James
Banneker, Benjamin
Baraka, Amiri
Barrax, Gerald W.
Bell, James Madison
Bennett, Gwendolyn B.
Bontemps, Arna Wendell
Boyd, Melba
Braithwaite, William Stanley
   Beaumont
Braxton, Joanne M.
Brooks, Gwendolyn
Brown, Linda Beatrice
Brown, Sterling Allen
Bullins, Ed
Burroughs, Margaret Taylor
Campbell, James Edwin
Chase-Riboud, Barbara
Cleage, Pearl
Cliff, Michelle
Clifton, Lucille
Cobb, Charles E., Jr.
Coleman, Wanda
Corrothers, James D.

Cortez, Jayne
Cotter, Joseph Seamon, Jr.
Cotter, Joseph Seamon, Sr.
Crayton, Pearl
Cullen, Countee
Damas, Léon-Gontran
Danner, Margaret
Davis, Frank Marshall
Davis, Thulani
Dee, Ruby
Delany, Clarissa
Dent, Tom
Derricotte, Toi
Deveaux, Alexis
Dodson, Owen
Dove, Rita
Dumas, Henry L.
Dunbar, Paul Laurence
Dunbar Nelson, Alice Ruth
Equiano, Olaudah
Evans, Mari
Fabio, Sarah
Fields, Julia
Garvey, Marcus
Giovanni, Nikki
Golden, Marita
Gomez, Jewelle
Greenfield, Eloise
Greenlee, Sam
Grimké, Angelina Weld
Hammon, Jupiter
Hansberry, Lorraine
Harper, Frances Ellen Watkins
Harper, Michael S.
Hayden, Robert
Hernton, Calvin C.
Heyward, DuBose
Hoagland, Everett H., III
Horton, George Moses
Hughes, Langston
Iceberg Slim
Ice-T
Jackson, Angela
Jackson, Mae
Jeffers, Lance
Joans, Ted
Johnson, Amelia E.
Johnson, Fenton
Johnson, Georgia Douglas
Johnson, Helene
Johnson, James Weldon
Jones, Gayl
Jordan, June
Knight, Etheridge
Komunyakaa, Yusef
Lane, Pinkie
Latimer, Lewis Howard

Lester, Julius
Lorde, Audre
Madgett, Naomi Long
Madhubuti, Haki
Major, Clarence
Mathis, Sharon Bell
McElroy, Colleen
McKay, Claude
Miller, E. Ethelbert
Miller, May
Millican, Arthenia J. Bates
Moore, Opal
Mossell, Gertrude Bustill
Murphy, Beatrice M.
Murray, "Pauli"
Myers, Walter Dean
Neal, "Larry"
Newsome, Effie Lee
Nugent, Richard Bruce
Osbey, Brenda Marie
Payne, Daniel A.
Perkins, Eugene
Pietri, Pedro Juan
Plato, Ann
Plumpp, Sterling
Randall, Dudley
Ray, Henrietta Cordelia
Reason, Charles L.
Redmond, Eugene
Reed, Ishmael
Rivers, Conrad Kent
Rodgers, Carolyn
Salaam, Kalamu ya
Sanchez, Sonia
Shange, Ntozake
Simmons, Herbert Alfred
Smith, Effie Waller
Southerland, Ellease
Spencer, "Anne"
Stowe, Harriet Beecher
Sundiata, Sekou
Tanner, Benjamin Tucker
Tate, Eleanora
Terry, Lucy
Thomas, Joyce Carol
Thurman, Wallace
Tillman, Katherine Davis Chapman
Tolson, Melvin
Toomer, Jean
Touré, Askia M.
Troupe, Quincy
Turner, Darwin T.
Vashon, George B.
Walker, Alice
Walker, Margaret
Waniek, Marilyn Nelson
Weatherly, Tom

Wheatley, Phillis
White, Paulette Childress
Whitfield, James Monroe
Whitman, Albery Allson
Williams, John A.
Williams, Sherley Anne
Wilson, August
Wright, Jay
Wright, Richard
Wright, Sarah E.
X, Marvin
Yerby, Frank G.
Young, Al
Zu-Bolton, Ahmos, III

**Publishers/Editors/
Founders/Patrons**
Angelou, Maya
Barber, Jesse Max
Barnett, Claude Albert
Bass, Charlotta Spears
Beckham, Barry
Bibb, Henry
Braithwaite, William Stanley
  Beaumont
Briggs, Cyril Valentine
Bullins, Ed
Cary, Mary Ann Shadd
Child, Lydia Maria
Clarke, John Henrik
Cornish, Samuel E.
Cortez, Jayne
Coston, Julia Ringwood
Crosswaith, Frank Rudolph
Davis, Frank Marshall
Delaney, Sara Marie Johnson
Delany, Martin R.
Delany, Samuel R.
Dent, Tom
Deveaux, Alexis
Douglass, Frederick
Du Bois, Shirley Graham
Du Bois, W. E. B.
Dunbar, Paul Laurence
Dunbar Nelson, Alice Ruth
Ellison, Ralph
Fauset, Jessie Redmon
Fortune, Amos
Fortune, T. Thomas
Fuller, Hoyt
Garland, Hazel B.
Garnet, Henry Highland
Garvey, Amy Jacques
Garvey, Marcus
Giddings, Paula
Giovanni, Nikki
Griggs, Sutton E.

Grimké, Archibald Henry
Hansberry, Lorraine
Hare, Nathan
Harris, Joel Chandler
Hernton, Calvin C.
Herron, Carolivia
Hopkins, Pauline
Houston, Charles
Johnson, Charles (Spurgeon)
Johnson, Fenton
Johnson, Georgia Douglas
Johnson, James Weldon
Johnson, John H.
Johnson, Kathryn Magnolia
Knight, Etheridge
Lewis, Samella Sanders
Madgett, Naomi Long
Madhubuti, Haki
Mayfield, Julian
Merrick, Lyda Moore
Micheaux, Oscar
Miller, E. Ethelbert
Morgan, Garrett A.
Morrison, Toni
Motley, Willard
Murphy, Beatrice M.
Murphy, Carl
Neal, "Larry"
Nell, William C.
Newsome, Effie Lee
Nugent, Richard Bruce
Owen, Chandler
Park, Robert E.
Parsons, Lucy Gonzalez
Patterson, William
Powell, Adam Clayton, Jr.
Quarles, Benjamin
Randall, Dudley
Randolph, A. Philip
Redmond, Eugene
Reed, Ishmael
Robeson, Eslanda Cardozo Goode
Robeson, Paul
Rodgers, Carolyn
Ruggles, David
Russwurm, John Brown
Simmons, William J.
Smith, Barbara
Smith, Lillian Eugenia
Smith, William Gardner
Southern, Eileen Stanza Johnson
Spingarn, Arthur B.
Spingarn, Joel Elias
Tanner, Benjamin Tucker
Thomas, Joyce Carol
Thompson, Era Bell
Thurman, Wallace

Touré, Askia M.
Trotter, Geraldine Pindell
Trotter, William Monroe
Troupe, Quincy
Van Dyke, Henry
Vann, Robert Lee
Walker, A'Lelia
Walker, Alice
Walrond, Eric
Wells, Ida B.
West, Dorothy
Whipper, William
Williams, Peter, Jr.
Winfrey, Oprah
Woodson, Carter G.
Wright, Richard
X, Malcolm
X, Marvin
Young, Al
Zu-Bolton, Ahmos, III

Scholarly Writings
Asante, Molefi Kete
Baker, Augusta
Beasley, Delilah
Bennett, Lerone, Jr.
Berry, Mary Frances
Bogle, Donald
Bontemps, Arna Wendell
Brawley, Benjamin
Brown, William Wells
Cabrera, Lydia
Cayton, Horace Roscoe, Jr.
Clark, Kenneth B.
Clark, Mamie
Clarke, John Henrik
Cobb, Jewell Plummer
Cobb, William Montague
Delaney, Sara Marie Johnson
Delany, Martin R.
Dent, Tom
Drake, St. Clair
Driskell, David
Du Bois, W. E. B.
Dunham, Katherine
Franklin, John Hope
Frazier, Edward Franklin
French, William P.
Gates, Henry Louis, Jr.
Giddings, Paula
Granville, Evelyn Boyd
Grimké, Archibald Henry
Guinier, Lani
Hare, Maud Cuney
Hare, Nathan
Haynes, Elizabeth Ross
Haynes, Lemuel

Hernton, Calvin C.
Hine, Darlene Clark
hooks, bell
Houston, Drusilla Dunjee
Hurston, Zora Neale
Hutson, Jean Blackwell
Johnson, Charles (Spurgeon)
Josey, E. J.
Just, Ernest Everett
Ladner, Joyce A.
Latimer, Catherine A.
Latimer, Lewis Howard
Lewis, Samella Sanders
Locke, Alain
Logan, Rayford
Malveaux, Julianne
Millican, Arthenia J. Bates
Mitchell, Loften
Murray, "Pauli"
Nell, William C.
Park, Robert E.
Patterson, Orlando
Payne, Daniel A.
Porter, James Amos
Porter Wesley, Dorothy Burnett
Poussaint, Alvin Francis
Quarles, Benjamin
Rampersad, Arnold
Redding, Jay Saunders
Rollins, Charlemae Hill
Ross-Barnett, Marguerite
Scarborough, William Sanders
Schomburg, Arthur A.
Shockley, Ann
Smith, Barbara
Smith, Jessie Carney
Southern, Eileen Stanza Johnson
Steward, Theophilus Gould
Tanner, Benjamin Tucker
Thurman, Howard
Toomer, Jean
Turner, Lorenzo Dow
Weaver, Robert C.
Wesley, Charles Harris
West, Cornel
Williams, George Washington
Williams, Sherley Anne
Wilson, William Julius
Woodson, Carter G.

Short Stories and Sketches
Amini, Johari
Aubert, Alvin
Baker, Augusta
Baldwin, James
Bambara, Toni Cade
Banneker, Benjamin

Bennett, Gwendolyn B.
Bennett, Hal
Bonner, Marita
Bontemps, Arna Wendell
Brown, Cecil
Brown, "Charlotte Eugenia"
Burroughs, Margaret Taylor
Cabrera, Lydia
Campbell, Bebe Moore
Clarke, John Henrik
Cleage, Pearl
Cliff, Michelle
Clifton, Lucille
Coleman, Wanda
Cooper, J. California
Corrothers, James D.
Cotter, Joseph Seamon, Sr.
Crayton, Pearl
Danticat, Edwidge
Dee, Ruby
Delany, Samuel R.
Deveaux, Alexis
Dove, Rita
Dumas, Henry L.
Dunbar, Paul Laurence
Dunbar Nelson, Alice Ruth
Ellison, Ralph
Evans, Mari
Fields, Julia
Fisher, Rudolph
Gaines, Ernest J.
Gomez, Jewelle
Graham, Lorenz
Greenfield, Eloise
Grimké, Angelina Weld
Harper, Frances Ellen Watkins
Harris, Joel Chandler
Herron, Carolivia
Himes, Chester
Hopkins, Pauline
Hughes, Langston
Hunter, Kristin Eggleston
Hurston, Zora Neale
Jackson, Angela
Joans, Ted
Johnson, Amelia E.
Johnson, Charles (Richard)
Johnson, Fenton
Johnson, Georgia Douglas
Jones, Gayl
Jordan, June
Kelley, William Melvin
Kincaid, Jamaica
King, Woodie, Jr.
Larsen, Nella
Lester, Julius
Major, Clarence

Marshall, Paule
Matheus, John F.
McElroy, Colleen
McKissack, Pat
McPherson, James Alan
Meriwether, Louise
Millican, Arthenia J. Bates
Milner, Ronald
Moody, Anne
Moore, Opal
Neely, Barbara
Nugent, Richard Bruce
Oliver, Diane Alene
Petry, Ann
Rivers, Conrad Kent
Robeson, Paul
Salaam, Kalamu ya
Shockley, Ann
Smith, Effie Waller
Southerland, Ellease
Stowe, Harriet Beecher
Tate, Eleanora
Terry, Lucy
Thomas, Piri
Torrence, Jackie
Touré, Askia M.
Van Dyke, Henry
Vroman, Mary Elizabeth
Walker, Alice
Walrond, Eric
West, Dorothy
White, Paulette Childress
Wideman, John Edgar
Wright, Richard
Wright, Sarah E.
Yerby, Frank G.
Young, Al

Slave Narratives

Bayley, Solomon
Bibb, Henry
Brown, William Wells
Craft, William
Douglass, Frederick
Equiano, Olaudah
Green, J. D.
Hammon, Briton
Jackson, Mattie J.
Jacobs, Harriet Ann
Keckley, Elizabeth
Pennington, James W. C.
Prince, Mary
Roper, Moses
Smith, Venture
Truth, Sojourner
Ward, Samuel
Washington, Booker T.

Songs and Libretti

Allen, Richard
Brown, Elaine
Chapman, Tracy
Davis, Thulani
Diddley, "Bo"
Domino, "Fats"
Dorsey, Thomas
Edmonds, Kenneth
Handy, W. C.
Holiday, Billie
Hunter, Alberta
Ice-T
Johnson, James Weldon
Jordan, June
King, "B. B."
Latifah, Queen
Mayfield, Curtis
McGhee, "Brownie"
Pickett, Wilson
Rahman, Aishah
Rainey, "Ma"
Razaf, Andy
Reagon, Bernice Johnson
Redding, Otis
Reed, Ishmael
Rush, Gertrude E. Durden
Shakur, Tupac
Sissle, Noble
Spivey, Victoria Regina
Tolson, Melvin
Tubman, Harriet
Williams, John A.
Wonder, Stevie

Speeches/Sermons/
Lectures/Storytelling

Allen, Richard
Baker, Augusta
Bibb, Henry
Brown, Hallie Quinn
Carmichael, Stokely
Cooper, Anna Julia
Crummell, Alexander
Edelman, Marian Wright
Evans, Mari
Garnet, Henry Highland
Garvey, Marcus
Grimké (Weld), Angelina (Emily)
Grimké, Francis J.
Grimké, Sarah (Moore)
Harper, Frances Ellen Watkins
Jackson, Jesse, Jr.
Jordan, Barbara
King, Martin Luther, Jr.
Matthews, Victoria Earle

Murray, Albert L.
Owen, Chandler
Payne, Daniel A.
Pennington, James W. C.
Powell, Adam Clayton, Jr.
Powell, Adam Clayton, Sr.
Remond, Sarah Parker
Rodgers, Carolyn
Ruggles, David

Rustin, Bayard
Stewart, Maria W.
Terrell, Mary Eliza Church
Truth, Sojourner
Tubman, Harriet
X, Malcolm

Themes
Black Aesthetic

Black Arts Movement
Folktales
Harlem Renaissance
Oral Tradition
Proverbs
Slave Narratives
Spirituals
Trickster Tales

CHRONOLOGY OF WRITERS

Hammon, Briton (fl. 1700s)

Fortune, Amos (1710?–1801)

Hammon, Jupiter (1711–c. 1806)

Smith, Venture (c. 1729–1805)

Terry, Lucy (c. 1730–1821)

Banneker, Benjamin (1731–1806)

Equiano, Olaudah (c. 1745–1797)

Haynes, Lemuel (1753–1833)

Wheatley, Phillis (1753?–1784)

Marrant, John (1755–1791)

Allen, Richard (1760–1831)

Forten, James (1766–1842)

Williams, Peter, Jr. (1780–1840)

Forten, Charlotte Vandine
(1784–1884)

Walker, David (1785–1830)

Prince, Mary (c. 1788–after 1833)

Grimké, Sarah (1792–1873)

Cornish, Samuel E. (1795–1858)

Jackson, Rebecca Cox (1795–1871)

Horton, George Moses
(1797?–1883?)

Truth, Sojourner (c. 1797 or
1799–1883)

Prince, Nancy Gardner (1799–1856
or after)

Russwurm, John Brown
(1799–1851)

Bayley, Solomon (c. 1800s)

Plato, Ann (fl. 1800s)

Turner, Nat (1800–1831)

Child, Lydia Maria (1802–1880)

Stewart, Maria W. (1803–1879)

Whipper, William (1804–1876)

Grimké (Weld), Angelina
(1805–1879)

Douglass, Sarah Mapps (1806–1882)

Pennington, James W. C.
(1807–1870)

Johnson, William (1809–1851)

Purvis, Robert (1810–1898)

Ruggles, David (1810–1849)

Payne, Daniel A. (1811–1893)

Stowe, Harriet Beecher (1811–1896)

Delany, Martin R. (1812–1885)

Green, J. D. (1813–?)

Jacobs, Harriet Ann (c. 1813–1897)

Brown, William Wells (1814?–1884)

Forten, Sarah (1814–1883)

Bibb, Henry (1815–1854)

Garnet, Henry Highland
(1815–1882)

Nell, William C. (1816–1874)

Roper, Moses (1816–after 1856)

Douglass, Frederick (1818–1895)

Ward, Samuel (1817–1864)

Reason, Charles L. (1818–1893)

Crummell, Alexander (1819–1898)

Tubman, Harriet (c. 1820–1913)

Still, William (1821–1902)

Whitfield, James Monroe
(1822–1871)

Cary, Mary Ann Shadd
(1823–1893)

Keckley, Elizabeth (c. 1824–1907)

Vashon, George B. (1824–1878)

Harper, Frances Ellen Watkins
(1825–1911)

Bell, James Madison (1826–1902)

Craft, William (c. 1826–1900)

Remond, Sarah Parker (1826–1894)

Wilson, Harriet E. (1827 or
1828–1863? or 1870?)

Fisher, Abby (c. 1832–?)

Tanner, Benjamin Tucker
(1835–1923)

Grimké, Charlotte L. Forten
(1837?–1914)

Smith, Amanda Berry (1837–1915)

Trotter, James Monroe (1842–1892)

Jackson, Mattie J. (c. 1843–?)

Steward, Theophilus Gould
(1843–1924)

Brown, Hallie Quinn (1845–1949)

Whipper, Frances A. Rollin
(1845–1901)

Harris, Joel Chandler (1848–1908)

Latimer, Lewis Howard
(1848–1928)

Taylor, Susie Baker King
(1848–1912)

Grimké, Archibald Henry
(1849–1930)

Ray, Henrietta Cordelia
(c. 1849–1916)

Simmons, William J. (1849–1890)

Williams, George Washington
(1849–1891)

Grimké, Francis J. (1850–1937)

Whitman, Albery Allson
(1851–1901)

Scarborough, William Sanders
(1852–1926)

Parsons, Lucy Gonzalez
(1853–1942)

Mossell, Gertrude Bustill
(1855–1948)

Fortune, T. Thomas (1856–1928)

Washington, Booker T. (1856–1915)

Chesnutt, Charles Waddell
(1858–1932)

Johnson, Amelia E. (1858–1922)

Cooper, Anna Julia (1859–1964)

Hopkins, Pauline (1859–1930)

Cotter, Joseph Seamon, Sr.
(1861–1949)

Matthews, Victoria Earle
(1861–1907)

Paynter, John H. (1862–1947)

Wells, Ida B. (1862–1931)

Terrell, Mary Eliza Church
(1863–1954)

Park, Robert E. (1864–1944)

Powell, Adam Clayton, Sr.
(1865–1953)

Henson, Matthew Alexander
(1866–1955)

Campbell, James Edwin
(1867–1896)

Abbott, Robert S. (1868–1940)
Du Bois, W. E. B. (1868–1963)
Corrothers, James D. (1869–1917)
Coston, Julia Ringwood (fl. late 1800s)
Kelley, Emma Dunham (fl. late 1800s)
Tillman, Katherine Davis Chapman (1870–?)
Johnson, James Weldon (1871–1938)
Beasley, Delilah (1872–1934)
Dunbar, Paul Laurence (1872–1906)
Griggs, Sutton E. (1872–1933)
Trotter, Geraldine Pindell (1872–1918)
Trotter, William Monroe (1872–1934)
Handy, W. C. (1873–1958)
Hare, Maud Cuney (1874–1936)
Dunbar Nelson, Alice Ruth (1875–1935)
Morgan, Garrett A. (1875–1963)
Spingarn, Joel Elias (1875–1939)
Woodson, Carter G. (1875–1950)
Houston, Drusilla Dunjee (1876–1941)
Johnson, Georgia Douglas (1877–1966)
Barber, Jesse Max (1878–1949)
Braithwaite, William Stanley Beaumont (1878–1962)
Johnson, Kathryn Magnolia (1878–1955)
Spingarn, Arthur B. (1878–1971)
Burroughs, Nannie Helen (1879–1961)
Smith, Effie Waller (1879–1960)
Vann, Robert Lee (1879–1940)
Bass, Charlotta Spears (1880–1969)
Grimké, Angelina Weld (1880–1958)
Rush, Gertrude E. Durden (1880–1918)
Van Vechten, Carl (1880–1964)
Pickens, William (1881–1954)
Brawley, Benjamin (1882–1939)
Fauset, Jessie Redmon (1882–1961)
Spencer, "Anne" (1882–1975)
Brown, "Charlotte Eugenia" (1883–1961)
Haynes, Elizabeth Ross (1883–1953)
Just, Ernest Everett (1883–1941)
Micheaux, Oscar (1884–1951)
Heyward, DuBose (1885–1940)

Newsome, Effie Lee (1885–1979)
Walker, A'Lelia (1885–1931)
Locke, Alain (1886–1954)
Rainey, "Ma" (1886–1939)
Garvey, Marcus (1887–1940)
Matheus, John F. (1887–1983)
Briggs, Cyril Valentine (1888–1966)
Johnson, Fenton (1888–1958)
Barnett, Claude Albert (1889–1967)
Delaney, Sara Marie Johnson (1889–1958)
Delany, "Sadie" (1889–1999)
Murphy, Carl (1889–1967)
Owen, Chandler (1889–1967?)
Randolph, A. Philip (1889–1979)
Richardson, Willis (1889–1977)
Sissle, Noble (1889–1975)
McKay, Claude (1889 or 1890–1948)
Merrick, Lyda Moore (1890–1987)
Delany, "Bessie" (1891–1995)
Hurston, Zora Neale (1891?–1960)
Larsen, Nella (1891–1964)
Patterson, William (1891–1980)
Wesley, Charles Harris (1891–1987)
Crosswaith, Frank Rudolph (1892–1965)
Geddes, Norman Bel (1893–1958)
Johnson, Charles (Spurgeon) (1893–1956)
White, Walter F. (1893–1955)
Williams, Spencer, Jr. (1893–1969)
Frazier, Edward Franklin (1894–1962)
Spence, Eulalie (1894–1981)
Toomer, Jean (1894–1967)
Cotter, Joseph Seamon, Jr. (1895–1919)
Houston, Charles (1895–1950)
Hunter, Alberta (1895–1984)
Latimer, Catherine A. (c. 1895–1948)
Razaf, Andy (1895–1973)
Schuyler, George Samuel (1895–1977)
Turner, Lorenzo Dow (1895–1969)
Du Bois, Shirley Graham (1896?–1977)
Garvey, Amy Jacques (1896–1973)
Robeson, Eslanda Cardozo Goode (1896–1965)
Fisher, Rudolph (1897–1934)
Logan, Rayford (1897–1982)
Rollins, Charlemae Hill (1897–1979)
Smith, Lillian Eugenia (1897–1966)
Clark, Septima Poinsette (1898–1987)

Robeson, Paul (1898–1976)
Walrond, Eric (1898–1966)
Tolson, Melvin B. (1898?–1966)
Bonner, Marita (1899–1971)
Dorsey, Thomas (1899–1993)
Miller, May (1899–1995)
Cabrera, Lydia (1900–1991)
Jackson, Joseph Harrison (1900–1990)
Thurman, Howard (1900–1981)
Anderson, Regina M. (1901–)
Brown, Sterling Allen (1901–1989)
Colón, Jesús (1901–1974)
Delany, Clarissa (1901–1927)
Bennett, Gwendolyn B. (1902–1981)
Bontemps, Arna Wendell (1902–1973)
Graham, Lorenz (1902–1989)
Hughes, Langston (1902–1967)
Thurman, Wallace (1902–1934)
Ward, Theodore (1902–1983)
Cayton, Horace Roscoe, Jr. (1903–1970)
Cullen, Countee (1903–1946)
Bunche, Ralph (1904–1971)
Cobb, William Montague (1904–1990)
Quarles, Benjamin (1904–1996)
Davis, Frank Marshall (1905–1987)
Porter, James Amos (1905–1970)
Porter Wesley, Dorothy Burnett (1905–1995)
Johnson, Helene (1906–1995)
Nugent, Richard Bruce (1906–1987)
Redding, Jay Saunders (1906–1988)
Spivey, Victoria Regina (1906–1976)
Tarry, Ellen (1906–)
Thompson, Era Bell (1906–1986)
Weaver, Robert C. (1907–1997)
West, Dorothy (1907–1998)
Jackson, Jesse (1908–1983)
Marshall, Thurgood (1908–1993)
Murphy, Beatrice M. (1908–1992)
Petry, Ann (1908–1997)
Powell, Adam Clayton, Jr. (1908–1972)
Wright, Richard (1908–1960)
Himes, Chester (1909–1984)
Motley, Willard (1909–1965)
Dunham, Katherine (1909–)
Murray, "Pauli" (1910–1985)
Rustin, Bayard (1910–1987)
Turpin, Waters (1910–1968)
Attaway, William (1911–1986)

Baker, Augusta (1911–1998)
Drake, St. Clair (1911–1990)
Jackson, Mahalia (1911–1972)
Payne, Ethel L. (1911–1991)
Damas, Léon-Gontran (1912–1978)
Harrington, Oliver Wendell
    (1912–1995)
Parks, Gordon, Sr. (1912–)
Garland, Hazel B. (1913–1988)
Hayden, Robert (1913–1980)
Sterling, Dorothy (1913–)
Clark, Kenneth B. (1914–)
Dodson, Owen (1914–1983)
Ellison, Ralph (1914–1994)
Hutson, Jean Blackwell
    (1914–1998)
Randall, Dudley (1914–)
Clarke, John Henrik (1915–1998)
Danner, Margaret (1915–1984)
Franklin, John Hope (1915–)
Holiday, Billie (1915–1959)
McGhee, "Brownie" (1915–1996)
Walker, Margaret (1915–1998)
Childress, Alice (1916–1994)
Cruse, Harold Wright (1916–)
Killens, John Oliver (1916–1987)
Murray, Albert L. (1916–)
Yerby, Frank G. (1916–1991)
Allen, Samuel W. (1917–)
Brooks, Gwendolyn (1917–)
Burroughs, Margaret Taylor
    (1917–)
Clark, Mamie (1917–1983)
Davis, Ossie (1917–)
Ormes, "Jackie" (1917–1986)
Iceberg Slim (1918–1992)
Johnson, John H. (1918–)
Jeffers, Lance (1919–1985)
Mitchell, Loften (1919–)
Millican, Arthenia J. Bates (1920–)
Patterson, Lillie (1920–)
Southern, Eileen Stanza Johnson
    (1920–)
Haley, Alex (1921–1992)
Young, Whitney M. (1921–1971)
Carroll, Vinnette (1922–)
Demby, William (1922–)
Lomax, Louis E. (1922–1970)
Peterson, Louis (1922–)
Walter, Mildred Pitts (1922–)
Bryan, Ashley F. (1923–)
Evans, Mari (1923–)
Fuller, Hoyt (1923–1981)
Lane, Pinkie (1923–)
Madgett, Naomi Long (1923–)
Meriwether, Louise (1923–)
Baldwin, James (1924–1987)

Chisholm, Shirley (1924–)
Cobb, Jewell Plummer (1924–)
Dee, Ruby (1924–)
Granville, Evelyn Boyd (1924–)
Josey, E. J. (1924–)
Lewis, Samella Sanders (1924–)
Vroman, Mary Elizabeth
    (c. 1924–1967)
Gordone, Charles (1925–1995)
Guy, Rosa Cuthbert (1925 or
    1928–)
King, "B. B." (1925–)
Rowan, Carl T. (1925–)
Williams, John A. (1925–)
Williams, Robert Franklin
    (1925–1996)
X, Malcolm (1925–1965)
King, Coretta Scott (1927–)
Shockley, Ann (1927–)
Smith, William Gardner
    (1927–1974)
Angelou, Maya (1928–)
Bennett, Lerone, Jr. (1928–)
Diddley, "Bo" (1928–)
Domino, "Fats" (1928–)
Fabio, Sarah (1928–1979)
Joans, Ted (1928–)
Mayfield, Julian (1928–1985)
Thomas, Piri (1928–)
Van Dyke, Henry (1928–)
Wright, Sarah E. (1928–)
Greenfield, Eloise (1929–)
King, Martin Luther, Jr.
    (1929–1968)
Marshall, Paule (1929–)
Walker, Wyatt Tee (1929–)
Aubert, Alvin (1930–)
Bennett, Hal (1930–)
Crayton, Pearl (1930–)
Greenlee, Sam (1930–)
Hansberry, Lorraine (1930–1965)
Ringgold, Faith (1930–)
Simmons, Herbert Alfred (1930–)
Smith, Jessie Carney (1930–)
Ward, Douglas Turner (1930–)
Driskell, David (1931–)
Elder, Lonne, III (1931–1996)
Hunter, Kristin Eggleston (1931–)
Kennedy, Adrienne (1931–)
Knight, Etheridge (1931–1991)
Morrison, Toni (1931–)
Schuyler, Philippa Duke
    (1931–1967)
Turner, Darwin T. (1931–1991)
Dent, Tom (1932–)
Gayle, Addison, Jr. (1932–1991)
Gregory, "Dick" (1932–)

Perkins, Eugene (1932–)
Polite, Carlene Hatcher (1932–)
Van Peebles, Melvin (1932–)
Barrax, Gerald W. (1933–)
Evers-Williams, Myrlie (1933–)
Feelings, Tom (1933–
Gaines, Ernest J. (1933–)
Rivers, Conrad Kent (1933–1968)
Andrews, Raymond (1934–1991)
Baraka, Amiri (1934–)
Dumas, Henry L. (1934–1968)
Hare, Nathan (1934–)
Hernton, Calvin C. (1934–)
Lorde, Audre (1934–1992)
Poussaint, Alvin Francis (1934–)
Sanchez, Sonia (1934–)
Amini, Johari (1935–)
Bullins, Ed (1935–)
Cleaver, Eldridge (1935–1998)
McElroy, Colleen (1935–)
Raspberry, William (1935–)
Wilson, William Julius (1935–)
Wright, Jay (c. 1935–)
Zu-Bolton, III, Ahmos (1935–)
Clifton, Lucille (1936–)
Cortez, Jayne (1936–)
Hamilton, Virginia (1936–)
Heard, Nathan C. (1936–)
Jordan, Barbara (1936–1996)
Jordan, June (1936–)
Major, Clarence (1936–)
Rahman, Aishah (1936–)
Brown, Claude (1937–)
Cosby, Bill (1937–)
Forrest, Leon (1937–)
Franklin, J. E. (1937–)
Goines, Donald (1937–1974)
Kelley, William Melvin (1937–)
King, Woodie, Jr. (1937–)
Mathis, Sharon Bell (1937–)
Myers, Walter Dean (1937–)
Neal, "Larry" (1937–1981)
Redmond, Eugene (1937–)
Berry, Mary Frances (1938–)
Crews, Donald (1938–)
Fields, Julia (1938–)
Harper, Michael S. (1938–)
Milner, Ronald (1938–)
Reed, Ishmael (1938–)
Thomas, Joyce Carol (1938–)
Touré, Askia M. (1938–)
Yarbrough, Camille (1938–)
Bambara, Toni Cade (1939–1995)
Brown, Linda Beatrice (1939–)
Chase-Riboud, Barbara (1939–)
Edelman, Marian Wright (1939–)
Fuller, Charles H. (1939–)

Lester, Julius (1939–)
Young, Al (1939–)
Moody, Anne (1940–)
Patterson, Orlando (1940–)
Plumpp, Sterling (1940–)
Carmichael, Stokely (1941–1998)
Derricotte, Toi (1941–)
Haskins, James S. (1941–)
Jackson, George Lester (1941–1971)
Jackson, Jesse, Jr. (1941–)
Neely, Barbara (1941–)
Pickett, Wilson (1941–)
Rampersad, Arnold (1941–)
Redding, Otis (1941–1967)
Wideman, John Edgar (1941–)
Asante, Molefi Kete (1942–)
Conwell, Kathleen (1942–1988)
Delany, Samuel R. (1942–)
Hansen, Joyce (1942–)
Hoagland, Everett H., III (1942–)
Hunter-Gault, Charlayne (1942–)
Madhubuti, Haki (1942–)
Mayfield, Curtis (1942–1999)
Reagon, Bernice Johnson (1942–)
Ross-Barnett, Marguerite
    (1942–1992)
Weatherly, Tom (1942–)
Ashe, Arthur (1943–1993)
Baker, Houston A. (1943–)
Bourne, St. Claire (1943–)
Brown, Cecil (1943–)
Brown, Elaine (1943–)
Cobb, Charles E., Jr. (1943–)
French, William P. (1943–1997)
Giovanni, Nikki (1943–)
Jackson, Elaine (1943–)
Ladner, Joyce A. (1943–)
McPherson, James Alan (1943–)
Oliver, Diane Alene (1943–1966)
Pietri, Pedro Juan (1943–)
Southerland, Ellease (1943–)
Taylor, Mildred D. (1943–)
Troupe, Quincy (1943–)
Beckham, Barry (1944–)

Davis, Angela Yvonne (1944–)
McKissack, Pat (1944–)
Torrence, Jackie (1944–)
Walker, Alice (1944–)
Williams, Sherley Anne
    (1944–1999)
X, Marvin (1944–)
Crouch, Stanley (1945–)
Rodgers, Carolyn (1945–)
Sundiata, Sekou (c. 1945–)
Wilson, August (1945–)
Cliff, Michelle (1946–)
Coleman, Wanda (1946–)
Gerima, Haile (1946–)
Jackson, Mae (1946–)
Smith, Barbara (1946–)
Waniek, Marilyn Nelson (1946–)
Wilkinson, Brenda (1946–)
Williams, Samm-Art (1946–)
Ai Ogawa, Florence (1947–)
Butler, Octavia E. (1947–)
Herron, Carolivia (1947–)
Hine, Darlene Clark (1947–)
Komunyakaa, Yusef (1947–)
Salaam, Kalamu ya (1947–)
Shakur, Assata Olugbala (1947–)
Cleage, Pearl (1948–)
Deveaux, Alexis (1948–)
Giddings, Paula (1948–)
Gomez, Jewelle (1948–)
Johnson, Charles (Richard)
    (1948–)
Shange, Ntozake (1948–)
Tate, Eleanora (1948–)
White, Paulette Childress (1948–)
Goldberg, Whoopi (1949–)
Jones, Gayl (1949–)
Kincaid, Jamaica (1949–)
Cooper, J. California (mid-
    1900s?–)
Davis, Thulani (mid-1900s?–)
Gibson, P. J. (mid-1900s?–)
Spillers, Hortense J. (mid-1900s?–)
Taylor, Susan L. (mid-1900s?–)

Boyd, Melba (1950–)
Bradley, David, Jr. (1950–)
Braxton, Joanne M. (1950–)
Campbell, Bebe Moore (1950–)
Gates, Henry Louis, Jr. (1950–)
Golden, Marita (1950–)
Guinier, Lani (1950–)
Miller, E. Ethelbert (1950–)
Naylor, Gloria (1950–)
Smith, Anna Deveare (1950–)
Steptoe, John Lewis (1950–1989)
Wonder, Stevie (1950–)
Jackson, Angela (1951–)
McMillan, Terry (1951–)
Moutoussamy-Ashe, Jeanne
    (1951–)
Bogle, Donald (1952–)
Dash, Julie (1952–)
Dove, Rita (1952–)
hooks, bell (1952?–)
Mosley, Walter (1952–)
Curtis, Christopher Paul (1953–)
Jones-Meadows, Karen (1953–)
Lee, Andrea (1953–)
Malveaux, Julianne (1953–)
Moore, Opal (1953–)
West, Cornel (1953–)
Abu-Jamal, Mumia (1954–)
Winfrey, Oprah (1954–)
Hill, Anita Faye (1956–)
Lee, Spike (1957–)
Osbey, Brenda Marie (1957–)
Riggs, Marion Troy (1957–1994)
Brandon, Barbara (1958–)
Ice-T (1958–)
Bolden, Tonya (1959–)
Edmonds, Kenneth (1959–)
Fishburne, Laurence, III (1961–)
Parks, Suzan-Lori (1963–)
Chapman, Tracy (1964–)
Danticat, Edwidge (1969–)
Latifah, Queen (1970–)
Shakur, Tupac (1971–1996)
Hunter, Latoya (1978–)

CHRONOLOGY OF FIRSTS

Year	First	Details	Page(s)
	Autobiographical Firsts		
1760	Probably the first published narrative written by an African-American slave	*A Narrative of the Uncommon Sufferings, and Surprising Deliverance of Briton Hammon, A Negro Man—Servant to General Winslow* (14-page memoir allegedly authored by Briton Hammon, but Hammon's authorship has been questioned)	153
1789/ 1791	First African American to write and publish his own candid account of his life, without help or direction from white ghostwriters, amanuenses, or editors	Olaudah Equiano, *The Interesting Narrative of the Life of Olaudah Equiano, or Gustavus Vassa, the African* (1789, England; 1791, United States); *see* 1831	109
1825	One of the first to write his own spirituale slave narrative (without the aid of an amanuensis)	Solomon Bayley (*A Narrative of Some Remarkable Incidents in the Life of Solomon Bayley, Formerly a Slave in the State of Delaware, North America; Written by Himself, and Published for His Benefit* (2nd London ed.)	19
1831	First published slave narrative written by an African-American woman	*The History of Mary Prince, a West Indian Slave, Related by Herself* (published in London); *cf.* 1861	287
1833	One of the first African-American autobiographies (other than a slave narrative)	*The Life, Experience and Gospel Labors of the Right Reverend Richard Allen* (published posthumously)	3
1845	Most successful, best-selling slave narrative	*Narrative of the Life of Frederick Douglass, an American Slave, Written by Himself*	88
1861	First U.S.-published slave narrative by an African-American woman; also the first such narrative to describe the sexual exploitation and other physical abuse of African-American women slaves	*Incidents in the Life of a Slave Girl: Written by Herself* (Harriet Jacobs); *cf.* 1831	192, 327
	Book-Publishing Firsts		
1852	Probably the first published travel book by an African American	*Three Years in Europe* (by William Wells Brown)	39

Year	First	Details	Page(s)
		Book–Publishing Firsts, *continued*	
1980	First press to publish the writings of such notables as Houston A. Baker, Lance Jeffers, Gayl Jones, Pinkie Lane, and Paulette Childress White	Lotus Press (founded by Naomi Long Madgett, Jill W. Boyer, and Leonard Andrews)	235
1981	First U.S. publisher dedicated to publishing the writings of women of color (including Third World women)	Kitchen Table: Women of Color Press (cofounded by Barbara Smith, Myrna Bain, Cherríe Moraga, and Mariana Romo-Carmona)	328
by the 1990s	One of the largest African-American publishers in the United States and abroad	Third World press (founded by Don Lee [Haki Madhubuti], Carolyn Rogers, and Johari Amini)	237
		Drama Firsts	
1856	Perhaps the first play written by an African American	*Experience; or, How to Give a Northern Man a Backbone* (by William Wells Brown; written in 1856, never published, now lost)	40
1858	First published play written by an African American	*The Escape; or, A Leap for Freedom* (by William Wells Brown; actually the second play he wrote)	40
1916/ 1920	First successful full-length drama written by an African-American woman and performed by African-American actors, for a European-American audience	*Rachel* (first produced in 1916 and published in 1920, written by Angelina Weld Grimké)	123
1921	One of the first musicals to be written, directed, produced, and performed by African Americans; also the first all-black musical that didn't cater to white audience tastes	*Shuffle Along* (lyrics by Noble Sissle, music by Eubie Blake)	323
1923	First African American to have a nonmusical play produced on Broadway (in New York)	Willis Richardson (*The Chip Woman's Fortune*)	300
1899– 1995	Probably the most widely published and produced woman playwright of the Harlem Renaissance	May Miller	255
1927	First collection of African-American dramatic works	*Plays of Negro Life: A Source-book of Native American Drama* (edited by Alain Locke and T. Montgomery Gregory)	229
c. 1910	One of the first African-American movie companies	Lincoln Film Motion Picture Company	254
1931	First all-black-cast talkie (nonsilent movie)	*The Exile* (by Oscar Micheaux)	254
1932	First major opera written and produced by a woman, featuring an all-black cast	*Tom-Tom: An Epic of Music and the Negro* (written by Shirley Graham [Du Bois])	92

Year	First	Details	Page(s)
1935	Set records as the longest-running play on Broadway, written by an African American	*Mulatto* (Langston Hughes); kept this record until 1955; *see* 1955	178
1953	First·African-American woman to join the Screen Writers Guild	Mary Elizabeth Vroman (on writing the screenplay *Bright Road*)	363
1955	First African-American woman to have a play produced on Broadway; set records as the longest-running play on Broadway, written by an African American	Lorraine Hansberry (*A Raisin in the Sun*); *see also* Ntozake Shange (1970s), *for colored girls who have considered suicide when the rainbow is enuf;* Anna Deveare Smith (1003), *Twilight*	155; *see also* 321, 327–328
1968	First African American to produce, direct, and script a major Hollywood movie	Gordon Parks, Sr. (*The Learning Tree*); *see* 1989	280
1976	First American feature film that was filmed entirely in Africa, using only black professionals	*Countdown at Kusini* (coproduced by Ossie Davis and Ruby Dee)	76
1989	One of the top 25 most significant U.S. films, as identified by the National Film Registry of the Library of Congress	*The Learning Tree* (by Gordon Parks, Sr.); *see* 1968	280
1991	First full-length general-release film with a screenplay by an African-American woman	*Daughters of the Dust* (by Julie Dash)	74

Education Firsts

Year	First	Details	Page(s)
1826	One of the first African Americans to earn a bachelor's degree from a U.S. college	John Brown Russwurm (Bowdoin College in Brunswick, Maine)	310
1844	First African American to graduate from Oberlin College (in Ohio)	George B. Vashon	363
1863	First president of the first U.S. college governed by African Americans	Daniel A. Payne (Wilberforce University in Xenia, Ohio)	282
1884	One of the first three African-American women to earn her baccalaureate	Mary Eliza Church (Terrell) (Oberlin College, in Ohio)	340
1888	One of the first African-American women to receive a postgraduate degree	Mary Eliza Church (Terrell) (master's degree, from Oberlin College in Ohio)	340
1896	First African American to be awarded a Ph.D. from Harvard	W. E. B. Du Bois	93
1907	First African American to be awarded a Rhodes Scholarship	Alain Locke	227
1963	Second African American to be aswarded a Rhodes Scholarship	John Edgar Wideman	386
1987	First African-American woman writer to sit in an endowed chair at an Ivy League university	Toni Morrison (named the Robert F. Goheen Professor in the Council of Humanities at Princeton University	259

Year	First	Details	Page(s)
		Fiction Firsts	
1853	Probably the first published novel by an African American	*Clotel; or, the President's Daughter: A Narrative of Slave Life in the United States* (by William Wells Brown, published in England)	39, 50, 396
1859	Generally considered the first published short story by an African American	"The Two Offers" (by Frances Ellen Watkins [Harper])	162
1859	Probably the first African-American woman to publish a novel in English	Harriet Wilson (*Our Nig;* second: Emma Dunham Kelley, *Megda,* 1891; third: Frances Ellen Watkins Harper, *Iola Leroy,* 1892)	137, 163, 207, 396–397
1859	Probably the first U.S.-published novel by an African American	*Our Nig* (Harriet E. Wilson)	396–397
1859	Considered the first black nationalist novel	*Blake, or the Huts of America* (written by Martin R. Delany)	80
1887	First short story by an African-American writer to be published in the prestigious *Atlantic Monthly*	"The Goophered Grapevine" (written by Charles Waddell Chesnutt)	51
1900	First African-American novel published by a major (white-owned) American publishing company	*The House Behind the Cedars* (by Charles Waddell Chesnutt)	52
c. 1900	Often considered the first major African-American novelist; also one of the first American writers published by mainstream publishers to realistically portray African-American experiences	Charles Waddell Chesnutt	52
1912	First novel to describe the tension within the African-American community between light-skinned and dark-skinned blacks	*The Autobiography of an Ex-Coloured Man* (by James Weldon Johnson)	200
1926	Probably the first published short story written by an African American that explicitly depicts a homosexual encounter	"Smoke, Lilies and Jade" (by Richard Bruce Nugent)	272
1928	First best-selling, commercially successful novel written by an African American	*Home to Harlem* (by Claude McKay)	158, 246
1932	First African-American detective novel	*The Conjure-Man Dies: A Mystery Tale of Dark Harlem* (by Rudolph Fisher)	116
1940	One of the first novels by an African-American writer to gain both critical acclaim and commercial success immediately after publication	*Native Son* (by Richard Wright)	407
1940s	First African American to write a series of best-selling novels	Frank Yerby	418

Year	First	Details	Page(s)
1945	One of the first young-adult books to address racial prejudice as a central theme	*Call Me Charley* (Jesse Jackson)	189
1946	First African-American woman to write a book selling more than a million copies	Ann Petry, *The Street* (novel)	283
1927– 1935	First African American to collect (1927– 1931) and publish (1935) African-American folklore	Zora Neale Hurston	182
1972– 1974 to present	Perhaps the best-selling African-Americanr author	Donald Goines	141

Journalism Firsts

Year	First	Details	Page(s)
1827– 1829	First African-American weekly newspaper	*Freedom's Journal* (founding editors Samuel E. Cornish and John Brown Russwurm)	64, 125– 126, 310
1853	First African-American woman to own and operate a periodical of any kind	Mary Ann Shadd (Cary) (with Samuel Ringgold Ward, founded, published, edited, and contributed to the weekly newspaper *Provincial Freeman*)	49
c. 1880	First African-American newspaper in New England	*Boston Hub* (Archibald Grimké, founding editor)	121
1892	Second-oldest continuously published African-American newspaper	*Baltimore Afro-American* (published by John Henry Murphy, then by Carl Murphy)	262
before	Oldest African-American newspaper in the West	*Eagle* (later the *California Eagle*)	1910
1937	First comic strip to feature an African- American female	"Torchy Brown in Dixie to Harlem" (*Pittsburgh Courier,* by Jackie Ormes)	276
early 1940s	First African-American woman cartoonist to be nationally syndicated	Jackie Ormes ("Patty Jo 'n' Ginger," first appearing in the *Chicago Defender*); *cf.* 1990	277
1955	First African-American journalist to start a column critiquing television	Hazel B. Garland, *Pittsburgh Courier*	131
1955– 1988	One of the longest-running newspaper columns about television ever published	"Video Vignettes" (by Hazel B. Garland, *Pittsburgh Courier*)	131
1972	First woman to head a nationally circulated African-American newspaper chain	Hazel B. Garland (editor-in-chief, *Pittsburgh Courier*)	131
1990	First African-American woman to have her cartoons syndicated nationally in mainstream, white-owned newspapers	Barbara Brandon (for United Press Syndicate); *cf.* 1937; early 1940s	32, 277
1990	First African-American woman journalist to win placement on a U.S. postage stamp	Ida B. Wells (–Barnett)	376

Year	First	Details	Page(s)
		Journal/Magazine Firsts	
1838	Perhaps the first African-American weekly magazine in the United States	*Mirror of Liberty* (founded and published by David Ruggles)	310
1859	Probably the earliest African-American literary journal	*Anglo-African Magazine* (coedited by Frederick Douglass, Frances Ellen Watkins [Harper], and others)	162
1884– 1909	First African-American scholarly journal	*A.M.E. Church Review* (a quarterly founded [1884] and edited [1884–1888] by Benjamin Tucker Tanner)	339
1891	First fashion magazine for African-American women	*Ringwood's Afro-American Journal of Fashion* (published by Julia Ringwood Coston)	67
1893	First women's home magazine for African-American women	*Ringwood's Home Magazine* (published by Julia Ringwood Coston)	67
Early 1920s	First African-American editor of the *Harvard Law Review*	Charles Houston	176
1936	First journal published by a white Southerner that regularly printed literary and scholarly writings by blacks	*The North Georgia Review* (founded by Lillian Eugenia Smith)	329
1950	One of the first few African-American reporters to be employed by a major white-owned and -operated urban daily newspaper	Carl Rowan (for the *Minneapolis Tribune*)	308
c. 1957	First African-American member of the Gridiron Club (founded in 1885)	Carl Rowan	309
1964	First African-American director of the United States Information Agency (USIA)	Carl Rowan	309
1964	First African American to be named *Time* magazine's "Man of the Year"	Martin Luther King, Jr.	216
		Nonfiction firsts	
1833	Probably the first published nonautobiographical book denouncing slavery, segregation, and other mistreatment of African Americans	*An Appeal in Favor of That Class of Americans Called Africans* (by Lydia Maria Child and David Lee Child)	53
1837– 1838	Two of the first American writings calling for women's rights	Angelina Grimké's *Letters to Catherine Beecher in Reply to an Essay on Slavery and Abolitionism Addressed to A. E. Grimké* (1837) and Sarah Grimké's *Letters on the Equality of the Sexes, and the Condition of Woman* (1838); *cf.* 1892	121
1852	Probably the first published pamphlet written by an African-American woman, which based a persuasive message on a factual database	*Notes on Canada West* (written and published by Mary Ann Shadd [Cary])	49

Year	First	Details	Page(s)
1867	First military history of African Americans	*The Negro in the American Rebellion: His Heroism and Fidelity* (by William Wells Brown)	40
1849– 1891	Considered the first major African-American historian	George Washington Williams	388
1881	First published cookbook authored by an African-American woman	*What Mrs. Fisher Knows about Old Southern Cooking* (by Abby Fisher)	116
1883	Generally considered the first fully encompassing history of African Americans up to 1880	*History of the Negro Race in America from 1619 to 1880* (by George Washington Williams)	388
1892	Cited as the first book-length work of African-American feminism	*A Voice from the South by a Black Woman of the South* (written by Anna Julia Cooper); *cf.* 1837–1838	63
1899	Cited as the first published sociological study of African Americans	*The Philadelphia Negro* (by W. E. B. Du Bois)	93
1935	One of the earliest efforts to accurately record the oral tradition of African-American communities	*Mules and Men* (by Zora Neale Hurston)	118

Poetry and Song Firsts

Year	First	Details	Page(s)
1746/ 1855	First African American to have written poems that survive to this day	Lucy Terry (Prince) ("Bars Fight," written in 1746, but published in 1855)	154, 341
1761	First literary work written by an African American and published in the United States	"An Evening Thought. Salvation by Christ with Penitential Cries: Composed by Jupiter Hammon, a Negro belonging to Mr. Lloyd of Queen's Village, on Long Island, the 25th of December, 1760" (88-line poem, published as a broadside)	154, 341
1761	First African American to have his own writing published	Jupiter Hammon	154, 341
1773	First African-American writer to publish a book of any kind	Phillis Wheatley (*Poems on Various Subjects, Religious and Moral by Phillis Wheatley, Negro Servant to Mr. John Wheatley, of Boston, in New England*, published in London)	380
1773	First African-American woman to have her works published	Phillis Wheatley (*Poems on Various Subjects, Religious and Moral by Phillis Wheatley, Negro Servant to Mr. John Wheatley, of Boston, in New England*, published in London)	154, 341, 380
by 1801	First distinctive song form to emerge in the United States	Spirituals	334
1801	First black hymnal	*Collection of Spiritual Songs and Hymns, Selected from Various Authors* (included lyrics only; compiled by Richard Allen)	3

Year	First	Details	Page(s)
		Poetry and Song Firsts, *continued*	
1829	First book of any kind authored by an African American that was published in the South, and the third book of poetry by an African American published in the United States	*The Hope of Liberty, Containing a Number of Poetical Pieces* (George Moses Horton)	175
1797?– 1883?	Preeminent nineteenth-century African-American male poet	George Moses Horton	174–175
1825– 1911	Preeminent nineteenth-century African-American female poet	Frances Ellen Watkins Harper	161–163
1872– 1906	Generally recognized as the first major African-American poet	Paul Laurence Dunbar	95–98
1912	Reportedly the first blues song to be published as sheet music	"Memphis Blues" (W. C. Handy; written in 1909; in 1908, Handy and lyricist Harry Pace founded the Pace and Handy Music Company, which published songs; *cf.* 1931)	154
1889/ 1890– 1948	Considered the first major poet of the Harlem Renaissance	Claude McKay	244
1903– 1946	First African-American poet to receive wide acclaim in the United States	Countee Cullen	70
1928	First twentieth-century African-American woman to gain national attention for her poetry	Georgia Douglas Johnson (*An Autumn Love Cycle*)	198
1931	First gospel music publishing company	The Dorsey House of Music, founded by Thomas Dorsey; *cf.* 1912	86
1941	Probably the first anthology of African-American poetry for youths	*Golden Slippers, an Anthology of Negro Poetry for Young Readers* (compiled by Arna Bontemps)	30
1976	First African-American poet named consultant in poetry to the Library of Congress	Robert Hayden	166
1985	First African-American woman to serve as poetry advisor to the Library of Congress	Gwendolyn Brooks	35
1988	First poet laureate of Rhode Island	Michael S. Harper	165
1993– 1995	First African American, first woman, and youngest person to be named poet laureate of the United States	Rita Dove	91

EDITOR'S NOTE: According to *OCAAL* (p. 121), the very first anthology of poetry by Americans of color was *Les Cenelles,* published in 1845.

Year	First	Details	Page(s)
	Prize-Winning Firsts		
1826–1834	First U.S. periodical published for children	*Juvenile Miscellany* (founded and edited by Lydia Maria Child)	53
1912	First black writer to receive a medal from the Jamaican Institute of Arts and Sciences	Claude McKay	245
1915	First winner of the National Association for the Advancement of Colored People (NAACP) Spingarn Medal	Everett Just (for his scientific research and publications)	206
1925	First winner of *Crisis* magazine's drama contest (established by W. E. B. Du Bois)	Willis Richardson (*Broken Banjo, a Folk Tragedy*)	300
1930	First African-American woman to win a Guggenheim fellowship	Nella Larsen	222
1942	First African-American woman to win a prestigious mainstream national literary competition	Margaret Walker (Yale University Younger Poet's Award, for *For My People*)	369
1949	First African American to win the Pulitzer Prize for poetry	Gwendolyn Brooks (*Annie Allen*)	35
1950	First African American to win the Nobel Peace Prize	Ralph Bunche; *see 1964*	43
1953	First African American to win the National Book Award for fiction	Ralph Ellison (*The Invisible Man*, published in 1952); *see 1990*	106
1956	First woman of any race to receive an Obie for writing a play	Alice Childress (for her 1954–1955 *Trouble in Mind*)	54
1959	First African American, youngest person, and fifth woman to win the New York Drama Critics Circle Award for the Best Play	Lorraine Hansberry (*A Raisin in the Sun*)	156
1964	Second African American to win the Nobel PeacePrize	Martin Luther King, Jr.; *see 1950*	216
1967	First African-American writer to receive the John Newbery Award	Virginia Hamilton (for *Zeely*); *see 1976*	153
1969	First African American to win a Pulitzer Prize for photojournalism	Moneta Sleet, Jr., for *Ebony*	201
1970	First African American to win the Pulitzer Prize for drama	Charles Gordone (*No Place To Be Somebody*, produced in 1969); *see 1982*	142
1971	First book to win both the National Book Award and the John Newbery Award	*M. C. Higgins, the Great* (by Virginia Hamilton)	151
1976	Second book by an African American to win a Newbery Medal	*Roll of Thunder, Hear My Cry* (Mildred Taylor); *see 1967*	340

Year	First	Details	Page(s)

Prize-Winning Firsts, continued

Year	First	Details	Page(s)
1978	First novel to win the James Baldwin Prize for literature	*Appalachee Road* (by Raymond Andrews)	40
1982	Second African American to win the Pulitzer Prize for drama	Charles Fuller (*A Soldier's Pay*, 1981); *see* 1970	126
1983	First African-American woman to win a Pulitzer Prize for a novel	Alice Walker (American Book Award–winning *The Color Purple*, 1982)	366
1990	Second African American to win the National Book Award for fiction	Charles (Richard) Johnson, for *Middle Passage; see* 1953	194
1991	First author to receive two PEN/Faulkner awards	John Edgar Wideman (*Brothers and Keepers*, 1984; *Philadelphia Fire*, 1990)	386–387
1993	First African-American woman to receive the Nobel Prize for literature	Toni Morrison, also the eighth woman to receive the prize	257, 260
2000	First book to win both a Coretta Scott King Award and a Newbery Medal	*Bud, Not Buddy* (by Christopher Paul Curtis)	72
2000	First book to win a Michael L. Printz Award from the American Library Association	*Monster* (1999, by Walter Dean Myers)	267

Professional Firsts

Year	First	Details	Page(s)
c. 1830	First African American to edit a national magazine	William Whipper (*National Reformer*, journal of the American Moral Reform Society, which he cofounded and edited)	382
1832	First American-born woman documented to have given a public lecture to a "promiscuous audience" (both men and women) on political topics	Maria W. Stewart	336
1834	Cited as the first person to open a bookshop for works by or about African Americans	David Ruggles (in New York City)	310
1920	First African-American professional librarian hired by the New York Public Library	Catherine A. Latimer	222
1928	One of the first African Americans to be hired as an editor by a major (white-owned and -operated) book-publishing house	Wallace Thurman (Macaulay's Publishing Company)	344
1951–1957	First African-American assistant editor at *Poetry: The Magazine of Verse*	Margaret Danner	73

REFERENCES

Abbrev.	Bibliographical citation
1TESK	Stewart, Jeffrey C. (1996). *1001 Things Everyone Should Know about African American History.* New York: Doubleday.
2CAAWA	Hedgepeth, Chester M., Jr. (Ed.). (1971). *Twentieth-Century African American Writers and Artists.* Washington, DC: American Library Association.
33T	**Bolden, Tonya** (Ed.). (1998). *33 Things Every Girl Should Know: Stories, Songs, Poems, and Smart Talk by 33 Extraordinary Women.* New York: Crown.
AA:AJS	**Johnson, Charles [Spurgeon]**, Patricia Smith, and WGBH Series Research Team. (1998). *Africans in America: America's Journey through Slavery.* New York: Harcourt Brace.
AA:PoP	Estell, Kenneth. (1994). *African America: Portrait of a People.* New York: Visible Ink.
AAB	Editors at Globe Fearon. (1995). *African-American Biographies.* Paramus, NJ: Globe Fearon Educational Publisher.
AABL	Livingston, Michael E. (1997). *The African-American Book of Lists.* New York: Perigee Books, Berkley Publishing Group, Putnam.
AAL	Worley, Demetrice A., and Perry, Jesse Jr. (with foreword by **Nikki Giovanni**). (1993). *African American Literature: An Anthology of Nonfiction, Fiction, Poetry, and Drama.* Lincolnwood, IL: National Textbook Company, NTC Publishing Group.
AAP	Strickland, Michael R. (1996). *African-American Poets.* Springfield, NJ: Enslow Publishers.
AAW	Smith, Valerie (Consulting Ed.); Lea Baechler and A. Walton Litz (General Eds.). (1991). *African American Writers.* New York: Charles Scribner's Sons.
AAW: AAPP	Long, Richard A., and Eugenia W. Collier (Eds.). (1985). *Afro-American Writing: An Anthology of Prose and Poetry* (2nd, enlarged ed.). University Park: Pennsylvania State University Press.
AAWW	**Shockley, Ann Allen**. (1988/1989). *Afro-American Women Writers, 1746–1933: An Anthology and Critical Guide.* Boston: G. K. Hall (1988); New York: Meridian/NAL (1989).
ADD	Beeching, Cyril Leslie. (1997). *A Dictionary of Dates* (2nd ed.). New York: Oxford University Press.
AHL	Holman, C. Hugh, and William Harmon. (1936/1992). *A Handbook to Literature* (6th ed.). New York: Macmillan.
AL	Bradbury, Malcolm (Ed.). (1996). *The Atlas of Literature.* New York: De Agostini Editions.
ALA	Hendrickson, Robert. (1990). *American Literary Anecdotes.* New York: Penguin.
ANAD	**Bolden, Tonya** (Ed.). (1998). *And Not Afraid to Dare: The Stories of Ten African American Women.* New York: Scholastic Press.
AP	Leslau, Charlotte, and Wolf Leslau. (1985). *African Proverbs.* White Plains, NY: Peter Pauper Press, Inc.
AP&W	Stewart, Julia. (1997). *African Proverbs and Wisdom: A Collection for Every Day of the Year from More Than 40 African Nations.* Secaucus, NJ: Citadel Press, Carol Publishing Group.
AWA	Bernikow, Louise, and the National Women's History Project. (1997). *The American Women's Almanac: An Inspiring and Irreverent Women's History.* New York: Berkley Books.
AWAW . . .	Hull, Gloria T., Patricia Bell Scott, and **Barbara Smith** (Eds.). (1982). *All the Women Are White, All the Blacks Are Men, But Some of Us Are Brave: Black Women's Studies.* Old Westbury, NY: Feminist Press.
AWBD	Wettenstein, Beverley. (1994/1998). *A Woman's Book of Days.* New York: Barnes & Noble.
BA	**Quarles, Benjamin**. (1969). *Black Abolitionists.* New York: Oxford University Press.

BAAW   **Bolden, Tonya**. (1996). *The Book of African-American Women: 150 Crusaders, Creators, and Uplifters.* Holbrook, MA: Adams Media Corporation.

BaD   Currie, Stephen. (1996). *Birthday a Day: Grades 3 and Up.* Glenview, IL: GoodYearBooks.

BAL-1-P Miller, Ruth (Ed.). (1971). *Black American Literature, 1760–Present.* Beverly Hills, CA: Glencoe Press (Macmillan).

BANP   **Johnson, James Weldon** (Ed.). (1922/1959). *The Book of American Negro Poetry.* New York: Harcourt Brace Jovanovich.

BASS   **Clarke, John Henrik** (Ed.). (1966/1993). *Black American Short Stories: 100 Years of the Best.* New York: Hill and Wang; Farrar, Straus and Giroux.

BBG   Rand, Donna, Toni Trent Parker, and Sheila Foster. (1998). *Black Books Galore! Guide to Great African American Children's Books.* New York: John Wiley & Sons.

BC   Diefendorf, Elizabeth. (1996). *New York Public Library's Books of the Century.* New York: Oxford University Press.

BDAA   Kranz, Rachel, and Philip J. Koslow. (1999). *The Biographical Dictionary of African Americans.* New York: Checkmark Books, Facts on File.

BF:2000 **Smith, Jessie Carney** (Ed.), with Casper L. Jordan and Robert L. Johns. (1994). *Black Firsts: 2,000 Years of Extraordinary Achievement.* New York: Visible Ink.

BFC   Christian, Barbara. (1985). *Black Feminist Criticism: Perspectives on Black Women Writers* (Athene Series). New York: Pergamon Press.

BH2C   **Smith, Jessie Carney** (Ed.). (1998). *Black Heroes of the 20th Century.* New York: Visible Ink.

BI   **McMillan, Terry** (Ed.). (1990). *Breaking Ice: An Anthology of Contemporary African-American Fiction.* New York: Penguin.

BLC-1   Draper, James P. (Ed.). (1992). *Black Literature Criticism* (Vol. 1). Detroit: Gale Research.

BLC-2   Draper, James P. (Ed.). (1992). *Black Literature Criticism* (Vol. 2). Detroit: Gale Research.

BLC-3   Draper, James P. (Ed.). (1992). *Black Literature Criticism* (Vol. 3). Detroit: Gale Research.

BM: **Quarles, Benjamin**. (1988). *Black Mo-
EAAHH   saic: Essays in Afro-American History and Historiography.* Amherst: University of Massachusetts Press.

BPEAR   Kaplan, Sidney, and Emma Nogrady Ka-

plan. (1989). *The Black Presence in the Era of the American Revolution, 1770–1880* (rev. ed.; original 1975). Amherst: University of Massachusetts Press.

BPSI   Haber, Louis. (1970). *Black Pioneers of Science and Invention.* New York: Harcourt Brace.

BRE   Benét, William Rose. (1945/1987). *Benét's Reader's Encyclopedia* (3rd ed.). New York: Harper & Row.

BS:AAE Christian, Charles M. (1995). *Black Saga: The African American Experience.* Boston: Houghton Mifflin.

BV   Chapman, Abraham (Ed.). (1968). *Black Voices: An Anthology of Afro-American Literature.* New York: Mentor, New American Library.

BW   Furman, Laura, and Elinore Standard (Eds.). (1997). *Bookworms: Great Writers and Readers Celebrate Reading.* New York: Carroll & Graph Publishers.

BW:AA   **Cade [Bambara], Toni**. (1970). *The Black Woman: An Anthology.* New York: Mentor, New American Library.

BW:SSCA Metzger, Linda. (1989). *Black Writers: A Selection of Sketches from* Contemporary Authors. Detroit, Michigan: Gale Research, Book Tower.

BWA   Barksdale, Richard, and Keneth Kinnamon (Eds.). (1972). *Black Writers of America: A Comprehensive Anthology.* New York: Macmillan.

BWA:AHE **Hine, Darlene Clark**, Elsa Barkley Brown, and Rosalyn Terborg-Penn. (Eds.). (1993). *Black Women in America: An Historical Encyclopedia* (2 Vols.). Bloomington: University of Indiana Press.

BWW   **Evans, Mari** (Ed.). (1984). *Black Women Writers (1950–1980).* New York: Anchor, Doubleday.

BWWW   Tate, Claudia. (Ed.). (1983/1984). *Black Women Writers at Work.* New York: Continuum.

CBC   Silvey, Anita (Ed.). (1995). *Children's Books and Their Creators.* Boston: Houghton Mifflin.

CBD   Crystal, David (Ed.). (1990). *Cambridge Biographical Dictionary.* Cambridge, England: Cambridge University Press.

CBE   Crystal, David (Ed.). (1994). *The Cambridge Biographical Encyclopedia.* Cambridge, England: Cambridge University Press.

CdlF   Dalin, Anne Safran (Ed.). (1997). *Creme de la Femme: A Collection of the Best Contemporary Women Writers, Lyricists, Playwrights and Cartoonists.* New York: Random House.

CSN **Gates, Henry Louis, Jr.** (Ed.). (1987). *The Classic Slave Narratives.* New York: Penguin Books, Mentor.

CT Kremer, John. (1996). *Celebrate Today! More Than 4,000 Holidays, Celebrations, Origins, and Anniversaries.* Rocklin, CA: Prima Publishing.

CYI **McKissack, Patricia.** (1997). *Can You Imagine?* Katonah, NY: Richard C. Owen Publishers.

DA Weekly Reader. (1995). *Dear Author: Students Write about the Books that Changed Their Lives.* Berkeley, CA: Conari Press.

DANB **Logan, Rayford W.**, and Michael R. Winston (Eds.). (1982). *Dictionary of American Negro Biography.* New York: W. W. Norton.

DGR Boyd, Herb. (1995). *Down the Glory Road: Contributions of African Americans in United States History and Culture.* New York: Avon.

DMM Kothari, Geeta (Ed.). (1994). *Did My Mama Like to Dance? and Other Stories about Mothers and Daughters.* New York: Avon.

DNPUS Aptheker, Herbert (Ed.). (1951, 1973). *A Documentary of the Negro People in the United States* (3 vols.). Secaucus, NJ: Citadel Press.

E:NAH Katz, William Loren. (1974). *Eyewitness: The Negro in American History.* Belmont, CA: Pitman Learning.

E-98 Encarta. (1998). *Encarta 98 Encyclopedia: The Ultimate Learning Resource* (deluxe ed.). Seattle, WA: Microsoft.

E-99 Encarta. (1999). *Encarta 99 Encyclopedia: The Ultimate Learning Resource* (deluxe ed.). Seattle, WA: Microsoft.

EA-99 Appiah, Kwame Anthony, and **Henry Louis Gates, Jr.** (Eds.). (1999). *Encarta Africana CD-ROM Encyclopedia.* Seattle, WA: Microsoft.

EAACH Salzman, Jack, David Lionel Smith, and **Cornel West** (Eds.). (1996). *Encyclopedia of African-American Culture and History.* New York: Macmillan.

EB-98 Encyclopædia Britannica (1998). *Encyclopædia Britannica CD 98: Knowledge for the Information Age* (multimedia ed.). Springfield, MA: Merriam-Webster.

EB-99 Encyclopædia Britannica (1999). *Encyclopædia Britannica CD 98: Knowledge for the Information Age* (multimedia ed.). Springfield, MA: Merriam-Webster.

EB-BH-CD Encyclopædia Britannica (1997). *Encyclopædia Britannica Profiles: Black History CD.* Springfield, MA: Merriam-Webster.

EBLG Valade, Roger M., III. (1996). *The Essential Black Literature Guide.* Detroit, MI: Visible Ink Press.

EGW Payne, Tom. (1997). *Encyclopedia of Great Writers: The World's Leading Authors and Their Works.* New York: Barnes & Noble Books.

EL:CCR Fadiman, Anne. (1998). *Ex Libris: Confessions of a Common Reader.* New York: Farrar, Straus and Giroux.

ENW **Porter, Dorothy**. (1971/1995). *Early Negro Writing, 1760–1837.* Baltimore: Black Classic Press.

EWHA Cullen-DuPont, Kathryn (with Annelise Orleck, historical consultant). (1998). *The Encyclopedia of Women's History in America.* New York: Da Capo Press.

EWJ Price-Groff, Claire. (1997). *Extraordinary Women Journalists.* Chicago: Children's Press.

EWS Stille, Darlene R. (1995). *Extraordinary Women Scientists.* Chicago: Children's Press.

FSF **Franklin, John Hope**, and Alfred A. Moss, Jr. (1988). *From Slavery to Freedom: A History of Negro Americans* (6th ed.). New York: Knopf.

G-94 *1994 Grolier Multimedia Encyclopedia.* Danbury, CT: Grolier Interactive.

G-95 *1995 Grolier Multimedia Encyclopedia.* Danbury, CT: Grolier Interactive.

G-97 *1997 Grolier Multimedia Encyclopedia.* Danbury, CT: Grolier Interactive.

G-99 *1999 Grolier Multimedia Encyclopedia* (deluxe ed., 2 CDs). Danbury, CT: Grolier Interactive.

H Ashby, Ruth, and Deborah Gore Ohrn. (1995). *Herstory: Women Who Changed the World.* New York: Viking.

HR:AHD Kellner, Bruce (Ed.). (1987). *The Harlem Renaissance: A Historical Dictionary for the Era.* New York: Methuen.

HWA Hymowitz, Carol, and Michaele Weissman. (1978). *A History of Women in America.* New York: Bantam.

ICDWR Craughwell, Thomas. (1998). *I Can't Decide What to Read . . . Great Books for Every Book Lover: 2002 Great Reading Suggestions for the Discriminating Bibliophile.* New York: Black Dog and Leventhal Publishers, Workman.

IPOF Hudson, Wade, and Cheryl Willis Hudson. (1997). *In Praise of Our Fathers and Our Mothers: A Black Family Treasury by Outstanding Authors and Artists.* East Orange, NJ: Just Us Books.

ITF Chase, Henry (Ed.). (1994). *In Their Footsteps: The American Visions Guide to African-American Heritage Sites.* New York: Henry Holt.

L:WW Miller, John. (1998). *Legends: Women Who Have Changed the World, through the Eyes of Great Women Writers.* Novato, CA: New World Library.

LA *The Literary Almanac: The Best of the Printed Word, 1900 to the Present.* (1997). Kansas City, MO: A High Tide Press Book, Andrews McMeel Publishing.

LDW Goring, Rosemary (Ed.). (1994). *Larousse Dictionary of Writers.* New York: Larousse.

LLBL Strouf, Judie L. H. (1998). *Literature Lover's Book of Lists: Serious Trivia for the Bibliophile.* Paramus, NJ: Prentice Hall Press.

LoL Moyers, Bill. (1995). *Language of Life: A Festival of Poets.* New York: Doubleday.

MAAL Magill, Frank (Ed.). (1992). *Masterpieces of African-American Literature.* New York: HarperCollins.

MAI-1 Kovacs, Deborah, and James Preller. (1991). *Meet the Authors and Illustrators: Vol. 1. 60 Creators of Favorite Children's Books Talk about Their Works.* New York: Scholastic.

MAI-2 Kovacs, Deborah, and James Preller. (1994). *Meet the Authors and Illustrators: Vol. 2. 60 Creators of Favorite Children's Books Talk about Their Works.* New York: Scholastic.

MSA MicroSoft Reference Library, CD version: Almanac. (1998).

MSC MicroSoft Reference Library, CD version: Chronology. (1998).

MSD MicroSoft Reference Library, CD version: Dictionary. (1998).

MSE MicroSoft Reference Library, CD version: Encyclopedia. (1998).

MSI MicroSoft Reference Library, CD version: Internet. (1998).

MSQ MicroSoft Reference Library, CD version: Quotations. (1998).

MWEL Merriam-Webster. (1995). *Merriam-Webster Encyclopedia of Literature.* Springfield, MA: Merriam-Webster.

MW-10 Merriam-Webster. (1993). *Merriam-Webster's Collegiate Dictionary* (10th ed.). Springfield, MA: Merriam-Webster.

MWBD Merriam-Webster. (1988). *Webster's New Biographical Dictionary.* Springfield, MA: Merriam-Webster.

NAAAL **Gates, Henry Louis, Jr.**, and Nellie Y. McKay (Eds.). (1997). *The Norton Anthology of African American Literature.* New York: Norton.

NBAW **Smith, Jessie Carney** (Ed.). (1992). *Notable Black American Women.* Detroit: Gale Research.

NBH **Brawley, Benjamin**. (1937). *Negro Builders and Heroes.* Chapel Hill: University of North Carolina Press.

NPR-ME National Public Radio, *Morning Edition.* (See http://www.npr.org)

NYPL-AADR New York Public Library (Eds.). (1999). *New York Public Library African-American Desk Reference.* New York: Wiley.

NYTBC McGrath, Charles, and the staff of the *New York Times Book Review* (Eds.). (1998). *Books of the Century: A Hundred Years of Authors, Ideas, and Literature.* New York: Random House, Time Books.

OC20LE Stringer, Jenny (Ed.). (1996). *Oxford Companion to Twentieth Century Literature in English.* New York: Oxford University Press.

OCAAL Andrews, William L., Frances Smith Foster, and Trudier Harris (Eds.). (1997). *The Oxford Companion to African American Literature.* New York: Oxford University Press.

OCWW Davidson, Cathy N., and Linda Wagner-Martin (Eds.). (1995). *The Oxford Companion to Women's Writing in the United States.* New York: Oxford University Press.

ODHQ Sherrin, Ned (Ed.). (1995). *The Oxford Dictionary of Humorous Quotations.* New York: Oxford University Press.

OPL Halpern, Daniel (Ed.). (1988). *Our Private Lives: Journals, Notebooks, and Diaries.* Hopewell, NJ: Ecco Press.

OTD Helicon Publishing (1996). *On This Date.* New York: Random House (Reference & Information Publishing).

PBW **Smith, Jessie Carney** (Ed.). (1996). *Powerful Black Women.* New York: Visible Ink.

PC:PEL Hass, Robert (Ed.). (1998). *Poet's Choice: Poems for Everyday Life.* Hopewell, NJ: Ecco Press.

PDMHQ Metcalf, Fred (Ed.). (1986). *The Penguin Dictionary of Modern Humorous Quotations.* London: Penguin Books.

PGAA Smallwood, David, Stan West, and Allison Keyes. (1998). *Profiles of Great African Americans.* Lincolnwood, IL: Publications, International.

PiP **Bennett, Lerone, Jr.** (1968). *Pioneers in Protest.* Chicago: Johnson Publishing Co.

Q:P **Clifton, Lucille**. (1991). *Quilting: Poems, 1987–1990.* Brockport, NY: BOA Editions.

RG20   Parker, Peter (Ed.). (1995/1996). *A Reader's Guide to Twentieth-Century Writers.* New York: Oxford University Press.

RHWDS   *Random House Webster's Dictionary of Scientists.* (1996/1997). New York: Random House.

RLWHS   Bailey, Brooke. (1994). *The Remarkable Lives of 100 Women Healers and Scientists.* Holbrook, MA: Bob Adams.

RLWWJ   Bailey, Brooke. (1994). *The Remarkable Lives of 100 Women Writers and Journalists.* Holbrook, MA: Bob Adams.

RP   **Bolden, Tonya**. (1994). *Rites of Passage: Stories about Growing Up by Black Writers from around the World.* New York: Hyperion Books for Children.

RT   Mullen, Bill (Ed.). (1995). *Revolutionary Tales: African American Women's Short Stories, from the First Story to the Present.* New York: Dell.

RtW   Goldberg, Bonni. (1996). *Room to Write: Daily Invitations to a Writer's Life.* New York: Jeremy P. Tarcher / Putnam, Penguin.

RWTC   Golden, Kristen, and Barbara Findlen. (1998). *Remarkable Women of the Twentieth Century: 100 Portraits of Achievement.* New York: Friedman/Fairfax Publishers.

SBA   **Bennett, Lerone, Jr.** (1993). *The Shaping of Black America: The Struggles and Triumphs of African-Americans, 1619 to the 1990s* (2nd ed.). Chicago: Johnson Publishing.

SEW   Keenan, Sheila. (1996). *Scholastic Encyclopedia of Women in the United States.* New York: Scholastic Reference.

SMKC   **Bolden, Tonya**. (1999). *Strong Men Keep Coming: The Book of African-American Men.* New York: Wiley.

SofE   McCrum, Robert, William Cran, and Robert MacNeil. (1986). *The Story of English.* New York: Viking.

ST:2C   Blassingame, John W. (Ed.). (1977). *Slave Testimony: Two Centuries of Letters, Speeches, Interviews and Autobiographies.* Baton Rouge: Louisiana State University Press.

ST:LW   Parker, Tony. (1996). *Studs Terkel: A Life in Words.* New York: Henry Holt.

T&T   Smitherman, Geneva. (1977). *Talkin and Testifyin: The Language of Black America.* Boston: Houghton Mifflin.

TAWH   Heinemann, Sue. (1996). *Timelines of American Women's History.* New York: A Roundtable Press Book / Perigee Book, Berkley Publishing Group.

TTS   **Clifton, Lucille**. (1996). *The Terrible Stories.* Brockport, NY: BOA Editions, Ltd.

TtW   Ward, Jerry W., Jr. (Ed.). (1997). *Trouble the Waters: 250 Years of African-American Poetry.* New York: Penguin (Mentor Books).

TWL   Edgarian, Carol, and Tom Jenks. (1997). *The Writer's Life: Intimate Thoughts on Work, Love, Inspiration, and Fame from the Diaries of the World's Great Writers.* New York: Vintage Books, Random House.

TWT   Madison, D. Soyini (Ed.). (1994). *The Woman That I Am: The Literature and Culture of Contemporary Women of Color.* New York: St. Martin's Griffin.

VBA   Foner, Philip S. (Ed.). (1972). *The Voice of Black America: Major Speeches by Negroes in the United States, 1797–1971.* New York: Simon and Schuster.

VBAAP   Harper, Michael S. and Anthony Welton (Eds.). (2000). *The Vintage Book of African American Poetry: 200 Years of Vision, Struggle, Power, Beauty, and Triumph from 50 Outstanding Poets.* New York: Vintage Books.

VOO   Pearlman, Mickey, and Katherine Usher Henderson. (1990, 1992). *A Voice of One's Own: Conversations with America's Writing Women.* Boston: Houghton Mifflin.

VR   Kanigel, Robert. (1998). *Vintage Reading, from Plato to Bradbury: A Personal Tour of Some of the World's Best Books.* Baltimore: Bancroft Press.

WABD   *The Woman Artists Book of Days.* (1988). New York: Hugh Lauter Levin Associates, Macmillan.

WB-98   *World Book 1998 Multimedia Encyclopedia.* (CD-ROM)

WB-99   *World Book 1999 Multimedia Encyclopedia.* (CD-ROM)

WC   Plimpton, George. (1989). *The Writer's Chapbook: A Compendium of Fact, Opinion, Wit, and Advice from the 20th Century's Preeminent Writers [Edited from* The Paris Review *Interviews].* New York: Penguin Books.

WCE-CD   *Webster's Concise Encyclopedia* (in CD-ROM form). (1994).

WDAA   *Webster's Dictionary of American Authors, Created in Cooperation with the Editors of Merriam-Webster Inc.* (1996). New York: Smithmark Reference, US Media Holdings.

WDAW   *Webster's Dictionary of American Women, Created in Cooperation with the Editors of Merriam-Webster Inc.* (1996). New York: Smithmark Reference, US Media Holdings.

WI   Moyers, Bill D. (1990). *A World of Ideas: Conversations with Thoughtful Men and*

Women about American Life Today and the Ideas Shaping Our Future. New York: Doubleday.

WS   Dunaway, David King, and Sara L. Spurgeon. (1995). *Writing the Southwest.* New York: Plume, Penguin.

WW:CCC   Stephens, Autumn. (1992). *Wild Women: Crusaders, Curmudgeons and Completely Corsetless Ladies in the Otherwise Virtuous Victorian Era.* Berkeley, CA: Conari Press.

WWMGA   Safire, William, and Leonard Safir (Eds.). (1989). *Words of Wisdom: More Good Advice.* New York: Fireside, Simon & Schuster.

WYL2   Steinberg, Sybil. (1995). *Writing for Your Life #2: 50 Outstanding Authors Talk about the Art of Writing and the Job of Publishing.* Wainscott, NY: Pushcart Press, W. W. Norton.

INDEX

Shari Dorantes Hatch is a freelance writer specializing in history, biography, and social sciences.

Michael R. Strickland is an assistant professor of Literacy Education at New Jersey City University and a Paul Robeson Fellow at the Institute for Arts and Humanities Education. He is the author of several works, including *African-American Poets*.